Lecture Notes in Computer Science   **15888**

Founding Editors

Gerhard Goos
Juris Hartmanis

AF172592

Editorial Board Members

The series Lecture Notes in Computer Science (LNCS), including its subseries Lecture Notes in Artificial Intelligence (LNAI) and Lecture Notes in Bioinformatics (LNBI), has established itself as a medium for the publication of new developments in computer science and information technology research, teaching, and education.

LNCS enjoys close cooperation with the computer science R & D community, the series counts many renowned academics among its volume editors and paper authors, and collaborates with prestigious societies. Its mission is to serve this international community by providing an invaluable service, mainly focused on the publication of conference and workshop proceedings and postproceedings. LNCS commenced publication in 1973.

Osvaldo Gervasi · Beniamino Murgante ·
Chiara Garau · Yeliz Karaca ·
Maria Noelia Faginas Lago · Francesco Scorza ·
Ana Cristina Braga
Editors

Computational Science and Its Applications – ICCSA 2025 Workshops

Istanbul, Turkey, June 30 – July 3, 2025
Proceedings, Part III

 Springer

Editors
Osvaldo Gervasi
University of Perugia
Perugia, Italy

Beniamino Murgante
University of Basilicata
Potenza, Italy

Chiara Garau
University of Cagliari
Cagliari, Italy

Yeliz Karaca
University of Massachusetts
Worcester, MA, USA

Maria Noelia Faginas Lago
University of Perugia
Perugia, Italy

Francesco Scorza
University of Basilicata
Potenza, Italy

Ana Cristina Braga
University of Minho
Braga, Portugal

ISSN 0302-9743   ISSN 1611-3349 (electronic)
Lecture Notes in Computer Science
ISBN 978-3-031-97595-0   ISBN 978-3-031-97596-7 (eBook)
https://doi.org/10.1007/978-3-031-97596-7

Preface

The compiled 14 volumes (LNCS volumes 15886–15899) consist of the peer-reviewed papers from the 68 Workshops of the 2025 International Conference on Computational Science and Its Applications (ICCSA 2025), which was held between June 30 – July 3, 2025 in Istanbul (Türkiye). The peer-reviewed papers of the main conference tracks are published in a separate set made up of three volumes (LNCS 15648–15650).

The conference was held in a hybrid form, with the large majority of participants in presence, hosted by Galatasaray University, Istanbul, Türkiye. We enabled virtual participation for those who did not attend the event in person due to logistical, political and economic problems, by adopting a technological infrastructure via open-source software (jitsi + riot) and a commercial Cloud infrastructure.

With the 2025 edition, ICCSA celebrated its 25th anniversary, a quarter of a century as a memorable moment that is harmoniously aligned with Istanbul, an extraordinary city located at the crossroads and acting as a bridge connecting Asia and Europe, representing different cultures, beliefs as well as lifestyles, which highlights its intercultural fabric.

ICCSA 2025 marked another fruitful and thought-provoking academic event in the International Conferences on Computational Science and Its Applications (ICCSA) conference series, previously held in Hanoi, Vietnam (2024), Athens, Greece (2023), Málaga, Spain (2022), Cagliari, Italy (hybrid with a few participants in presence in 2021 and completely online in 2020), whilst earlier editions took place in Saint Petersburg, Russia (2019), Melbourne, Australia (2018), Trieste, Italy (2017), Beijing, China (2016), Banff, Canada (2015), Guimaraes, Portugal (2014), Ho Chi Minh City, Vietnam (2013), Salvador, Brazil (2012), Santander, Spain (2011), Fukuoka, Japan (2010), Suwon, South Korea (2009), Perugia, Italy (2008), Kuala Lumpur, Malaysia (2007), Glasgow, UK (2006), Singapore (2005), Assisi, Italy (2004), Montreal, Canada (2003), and (as ICCS) Amsterdam, the Netherlands (2002) and San Francisco, USA (2001).

Computational Science constitutes the main pillar of most present research, industrial and commercial applications, and plays a unique role in exploiting ICT innovative technologies, and the ICCSA conference series has, accordingly, provided ample opportunities to researchers and industry practitioners to discuss new ideas, to share complex problems and their solutions, and to shape new trends in Computational Science. As the conference mirrors society from a scientific point of view, this year's undoubtedly dominant theme was large language models, machine learning and Artificial Intelligence (AI) and their applications in the most diverse technological, economic and industrial fields, amongst the others.

The ICCSA 2025 conference was structured in six general tracks covering the fields of computational science and its applications: Computational Methods, Algorithms and Scientific Applications – High Performance Computing and Networks – Geometric Modeling, Graphics and Visualization – Advanced and Emerging Applications – Information Systems and Technologies – Urban and Regional Planning. In addition, the conference consisted of 68 workshops, focusing on topical issues of utmost importance to science, technology and society: from new computational approaches for earth science, to mathematical methods for image processing, new statistical and optimization methods, several Artificial Intelligence approaches, sustainability issues, smart cities and related technologies, to name some.

In the Workshops' proceedings, we accepted 362 full papers, 37 short papers and 2 Ph.D. Showcase papers from total of 1043 submissions (Acceptance rate 38.4%). In the Main Conference Proceedings, we accepted 71 full papers, 6 short papers and 1 Ph.D. Showcase paper from 269 submissions to the General Tracks of the Conference (with an acceptance rate of 29.9%). We would like to convey our sincere appreciation to the workshops' chairs and co-chairs and program committee members for their diligent work, commitment and dedication.

The success and consistent maintenance of the ICCSA conference series in general, and of ICCSA 2025 in particular, rely upon the support of many people: authors, presenters, participants, keynote speakers, workshop chairs, session chairs, organizing committee members, student volunteers, Program Committee members, Advisory Committee members, International Liaison chairs, reviewers and other individuals in various roles. Thus, we take this opportunity to wholehartedly thank each and everyone.

We additionally wish to thank publisher Springer for their agreement to publish the proceedings, besides sponsoring part of the best papers awards and for their kind assistance and cooperation during the editing process.

We would cordially like to invite you to refer to the ICCSA website https://iccsa.org, where you can find the relevant details regarding this academic endeavor and event of ours.

June 2025

Osvaldo Gervasi
Yeliz Karaca
Beniamino Murgante
Chiara Garau

A Welcome Message from the Organizers

The International Conference on Computational Science and Its Applications (ICCSA) reflects a culmination of meticulous and dedicated efforts and academic endeavors toward the progress of science and technology.

One of the most noteworthy aspects of ICCSA is its fostering of a collective spirit, bringing together a plethora of participants from all over the world. Correspondingly, this merging power manifests itself in the 25th anniversary of ICCSA, which is a quarter of a century, in Istanbul, Türkiye, which connects and acts as a bridge between two continents, namely Asia and Europe. This unique location in the world hosts the 25th year of ICCSA at Galatasaray University, located on Çırağan Avenue by Istanbul's Bosphorus, which is an established international university bestowed with a distinctive past of teaching tradition, research and education exceeding five centuries.

Istanbul, having served as the capital city of four empires, namely the Roman Empire (330–395), the Byzantine Empire (395–1204 and 1261–1453), the Latin Empire (1204–1261) and the Ottoman Empire (1453–1922), is an exceptional city of the Republic of Türkiye founded by Mustafa Kemal Atatürk.

Situated at a strategic location along the historic Silk Road, Istanbul is at the core of extending rail networks which span across Europe and West Asia along with the only sea route between the Black Sea and the Mediterranean.

The cultural, historical and economic pulses of the country are evident in Istanbul whose rooted origins have embraced varying beliefs, lifestyles and populace, which highlights the city's mosaic quality with blended fabric in a constant harmonious flow. This has enabled cultures to grow and be nurtured, which is profoundly rooted in its urban culture.

Computational Science constitutes the main pillar of most present research, industrial and commercial activities besides manifesting a unique role in exploiting and addressing innovative Information and Communication Technologies. Thus, the 25-year-old ICCSA conference series provides remarkable opportunities to get acquainted with leading researchers, scientists, scholars, practitioners and many more while exchanging innovative ideas and initiating new partnerships, associations and bonds.

With the hosting of Galatasaray University, I would personally and on behalf of the Local Organizing Committee, with the members Emre Alptekin, Gülfem Işıklar Alptekin, Cengiz Kahraman, Abdullah Çağrı Tolga and Ayberk Zeytin, like to convey our sincere gratitude and thanks to everyone who exerted their efforts in and contributed to the realization of ICCSA 2025. With these notes and remarks, welcome to Istanbul!

Cordially yours,

On behalf of the Local Organizing Committee.

June 2025   Yeliz Karaca

Organization

Honorary General Chairs

Bernady O. Apduhan	Kyushu Sangyo University, Japan
Kenneth C. J. Tan	Sardina Systems, UK

General Chairs

Yeliz Karaca	University of Massachusetts, USA
Osvaldo Gervasi	University of Perugia, Italy
David Taniar	Monash University, Australia

Program Committee Chairs

Beniamino Murgante	University of Basilicata, Italy
Chiara Garau	University of Cagliari, Italy
Ana Maria A. C. Rocha	University of Minho, Portugal
A. Çağrı Tolga	Galatasaray University, Turkey

International Advisory Committee

Jemal Abawajy	Deakin University, Australia
Dharma P. Agarwal	University of Cincinnati, USA
Rajkumar Buyya	Melbourne University, Australia
Claudia Bauzer Medeiros	University of Campinas, Brazil
Manfred M. Fisher	Vienna University of Economics and Business, Austria
Pierre Frankhauser	University of Franche-Comté/CNRS, France
Marina L. Gavrilova	University of Calgary, Canada
Sumi Helal	University of Florida, USA & Lancaster University, UK
Bin Jiang	University of Gävle, Sweden
Yee Leung	Chinese University of Hong Kong, China

International Liaison Chairs

Ivan Blečić	University of Cagliari, Italy
Giuseppe Borruso	University of Trieste, Italy
Elise De Donker	Western Michigan University, USA
Maria Noelia Faginas Lago	University of Perugia, Italy
Maria Irene Falcão	University of Minho, Portugal
Robert C. H. Hsu	Chung Hua University, Taiwan
Yeliz Karaca	University of Massachusetts Chan Medical School, USA
Tae-Hoon Kim	Zhejiang University of Science and Technology, China
Vladimir Korkhov	Saint Petersburg University, Russia
Takashi Naka	Kyushu Sangyo University, Japan
Rafael D. C. Santos	National Institute for Space Research, Brazil
Maribel Yasmina Santos	University of Minho, Portugal
Anastasia Stratigea	National Technical University of Athens, Greece

Workshop and Session Organizing Chairs

Beniamino Murgante	University of Basilicata, Italy
Chiara Garau	University of Cagliari, Italy

Award Chair

Wenny Rahayu	La Trobe University, Australia

Publicity Committee Chairs

Elmer Dadios	De La Salle University, Philippines
Nataliia Kulabukhova	Saint Petersburg University, Russia
Daisuke Takahashi	Tsukuba University, Japan
Shangwang Wang	Beijing University of Posts and Telecommunications, China

Local Organizing Committee Chairs

Emre Alptekin	Galatasaray University, Turkey
Gülfem Işıklar Alptekin	Galatasaray University, Turkey
Cengiz Kahraman	İstanbul Technical University, Turkey
A. Çağrı Tolga	Galatasaray University, Turkey
Ayberk Zeytin	Galatasaray University, Turkey

Technology Chair

Damiano Perri	University of Perugia, Italy

Program Committee

Vera Afreixo	University of Aveiro, Portugal
Vladimir Alarcon	Northern Gulf Institute, USA
Filipe Alvelos	University of Minho, Portugal
Debora Anelli	Polytechnic University of Bari, Italy
Hartmut Asche	Hasso-Plattner-Institut für Digital Engineering Ggmbh, Germany
Nizamettin Aydın	İstanbul Technical University, Turkey
Ginevra Balletto	University of Cagliari, Italy
Nadia Balucani	University of Perugia, Italy
Socrates Basbas	Aristotle University of Thessaloniki, Greece
David Berti	ART SpA, Italy
Michela Bertolotto	University College Dublin, Ireland
Sandro Bimonte	CEMAGREF, TSCF, France
Ana Cristina Braga	University of Minho, Portugal
Tiziana Campisi	Kore University of Enna, Italy
Yves Caniou	Université Claude Bernard Lyon 1, France
Alessandra Capolupo	Polytechnic University of Bari, Italy
José A. Cardoso e Cunha	Universidade Nova de Lisboa, Portugal
Rui Cardoso	University of Beira Interior, Portugal
Leocadio G. Casado	University of Almería, Spain
Mete Celik	Erciyes University, Turkey
Maria Cerreta	University of Naples Federico II, Italy
Ta Quang Chieu	Thuyloi University, Vietnam
Rachel Chien-Sing Lee	Sunway University, Malaysia
Birol Ciloglugil	Ege University, Turkey
Mauro Coni	University of Cagliari, Italy

Florbela Maria da Cruz
   Domingues Correia
Alessandro Costantini
Roberto De Lotto
Luiza De Macedo Mourelle
Marcelo De Paiva Guimaraes
Frank Devai
Joana Matos Dias
Aziz Dursun
Laila El Ghandour
Rafida M. Elobaid
Maria Irene Falcao
Florbela P. Fernandes
Paula Odete Fernandes
Adelaide de Fátima Baptista
   Valente Freitas
Valentina Franzoni
Andreas Fricke
Raffaele Garrisi

Ivan Gerace
Maria Giaoutzi
Salvatore Giuffrida
Teresa Guarda

Sevin Gümgüm
Malgorzata Hanzl
Maulana Adhinugraha Kiki
Clement Ho Cheung Leung
Andrea Lombardi
Marcos Mandado Alonso
Ernesto Marcheggiani
Antonino Marvuglia

Michele Mastroianni
Hideo Matsufuru

Fernando Miranda
Giuseppe Modica
Majaz Moonis
Nadia Nedjah
Paolo Nesi

Polytechnic Institute of Viana do Castelo,
   Portugal
INFN, Italy
University of Pavia, Italy
State University of Rio De Janeiro, Brazil
Federal University of Sao Paulo, Brazil
London South Bank University, UK
University of Coimbra, Portugal
Virginia Tech University, USA
Heriot-Watt University, UK
Canadian University Dubai, United Arab Emirates
University of Minho, Portugal
Polytechnic Institute of Bragança, Portugal
Polytechnic Institute of Bragança, Portugal
University of Aveiro, Portugal

University of Perugia, Italy
University of Potsdam, Germany
Centro Operativo per la Sicurezza Cibernetica,
   Italy
University of Perugia, Italy
National Technical University of Athens, Greece
University of Catania, Italy
Universidad Estatal Peninsula de Santa Elena,
   Ecuador
Izmir University of Economics, Turkey
Technical University of Lodz, Poland
Telkom University, Indonesia
Chinese University of Hong Kong, China
University of Perugia, Italy
University of Vigo, Spain
Katholieke Universiteit Leuven, Belgium
Luxembourg Institute of Science and Technology,
   Luxembourg
University of Salerno, Italy
High Energy Accelerator Research Organization,
   Japan
Universidade do Minho, Portugal
University of Reggio Calabria, Italy
University of Massachusetts, USA
State University of Rio de Janeiro, Brazil
University of Florence, Italy

Suzan Obaiys	University of Malaya, Malaysia
Marcin Paprzycki	Polish Academy of Sciences, Poland
Eric Pardede	La Trobe University, Australia
Ana Isabel Pereira	Polytechnic Institute of Bragança, Portugal
Damiano Perri	University of Perugia, Italy
Massimiliano Petri	University of Pisa, Italy
Telmo Pinto	University of Coimbra, Portugal
Alessandro Plaisant	University of Sassari, Italy
Maurizio Pollino	ENEA, Italy
Alenka Poplin	Iowa State University, USA
Marcos Quiles	Federal University of São Paulo, Brazil
Nguyen Huu Quynh	Thuyloi University, Vietnam
Albert Rimola	Universitat Autònoma de Barcelona, Spain
Humberto Rocha	University of Coimbra, Portugal
Marzio Rosi	University of Perugia, Italy
Lucia Saganeiti	University of L'Aquila, Italy
Francesco Scorza	University of Basilicata, Italy
Marco Paulo Seabra dos Reis	University of Coimbra, Portugal
Jie Shen	University of Michigan, USA
Francesco Tajani	Sapienza University of Rome, Italy
Rodrigo Tapia Mcclung	Centro de Investigación en Ciencias de Información Geoespacial, Mexico
Eufemia Tarantino	Polytechnic University of Bari, Italy
Sergio Tasso	University of Perugia, Italy
Ana Paula Teixeira	Universidade do Minho, Portugal
Yiota Theodora	National Technical University of Athens, Greece
Giuseppe A. Trunfio	University of Sassari, Italy
Toshihiro Uchibayashi	Kyushu University, Japan
Marco Vizzari	University of Perugia, Italy
Frank Westad	Norwegian University of Science and Technology, Norway
Fukuko Yuasa	High Energy Accelerator Research Organization, Japan
Ljiljana Zivkovic	Republic Geodetic Authority, Serbia

Workshops

Workshop on Advancements in Applied Machine-Learning and Data Analytics (AAMDA 2025)

Workshop Organizers

Alessandro Costantini	INFN, Italy
Daniele Cesini	INFN, Italy
Elisabetta Ronchieri	INFN, Italy
Barbara Martelli	INFN, Italy

Workshop Program Committee Members

Alessandro Costantini	Istituto Nazionale di Fisica Nucleare (INFN), Italy
Daniele Cesini	Istituto Nazionale di Fisica Nucleare (INFN), Italy
Elisabetta Ronchieri	Istituto Nazionale di Fisica Nucleare (INFN), Italy
Barbara Martelli	Istituto Nazionale di Fisica Nucleare (INFN), Italy
Luca Dell'Agnello	Istituto Nazionale di Fisica Nucleare (INFN), Italy

Advanced and Innovative Web Apps 2025 (AIWA 2025)

Workshop Organizers

Damiano Perri	University of Perugia, Italy
Osvaldo Gervasi	University of Perugia, Italy
Stelios Kouzeleas	International Hellenic University, Greece
Sergio Tasso	University of Perugia, Italy

Workshop Program Committee Members

David Berti	ART SpA, Italy
JungYoon Kim	Gachon University, South Korea
TaiHoon Kim	Zhejiang University of Science and Technology, China

Advanced Processes of Mathematics and Computing Models in Complex Data-Intensive Computational Systems (AMCM 2025)

Workshop Organizers

Yeliz Karaca	University of Massachusetts Chan Medical School and Massachusetts Institute of Technology, USA
Dumitru Baleanu	Lebanese American University, Lebanon
Osvaldo Gervasi	University of Perugia, Italy
Yudong Zhang	University of Leicester, UK
Majaz Moonis	University of Massachusetts Chan Medical School and Massachusetts Institute of Technology, USA

Workshop Program Committee Members

TaeHoon Kim	Zhejiang University of Science and Technology, China
Martin Bohner	Missouri University of Science and Technology, USA
Shuihua Wang	University of Leicester, UK
Khan Muhammad	Sungkyunkwan University, South Korea
Mahmoud Abdel-Aty	Sohag University, Egypt
Aziz Dursun	Virginia Polytechnic Institute and State University, USA
Kemal Güven Gülen	Namık Kemal University, Turkey
Akif Akgül	Hitit Üniversitesi, Turkey

Advanced Numerical Approaches for Assessment and Design of No-Tension Masonry Structures (ANAMS 2025)

Workshop Organizers

Antonino Iannuzzo	Universitá degli studi del Sannio, Italy
Carlo Olivieri	Universitá Telematica Pegaso, Italy
Andrea Montanino	CIMNE, Spain
Elham Mousavian	University of Edinburgh, UK

Workshop Program Committee Members

Pietro Meriggi	Roma Tre University, Italy
Francesca Perelli	University of Naples Federico II, Italy
Marialuigia Sangirardi	University of Oxford, UK
Sam Cocking	University of Cambridge, UK

Matteo Salvalaggio	University of Minho, Portugal
Vittorio Paris	University of Bergamo, Italy
Luigi Sibille	Norwegian University of Science and Technology, Norway
Natalia Pingaro	Politecnico di Milano, Italy
Martina Buzzetti	Politecnico di Milano, Italy
Generoso Vaiano	Pegaso Telematic University, Italy
Alessandra Capolupo	Politecnico di Bari, Italy
Amal Gerges	Università degli Studi di Cagliari, Italy
Fabian Orozco	National Autonomous University of Mexico, Mexico
Nathanael Savalle	Polytech Clermont and Université Clermont Auvergne, France
Luca Umberto Argiento	University of Naples Federico II, Italy
Bartolomeo Pantó	Durham University, UK

Unveiling the Synergies Between Air Quality and Climate PlAnning (AQCliPA 2025)

Workshop Organizers

Angela Pilogallo	University of L'Aquila, Italy
Luigi Santopietro	University of Basilicata, Italy
Filomena Pietrapertosa	IMAA CNR, Italy
Monica Salvia	IMAA CNR, Italy
Carlo Trozzi	IMAA CNR, Italy
Valeria Scapini	Central University of Chile, Chile

Workshop Program Committee Members

Lucia Saganeiti	IMAA-CNR, Italy
Lorena Fiorini	University of L'Aquila, Italy
Antonio Mazza	IMAA-CNR, Italy
Gabriele Nolè	IMAA-CNR, Italy
Carmen Guida	University of Naples "Federico II", Italy
Floriana Zucaro	University of Naples "Federico II", Italy
Sabrina Lai	University of Cagliari, Italy
Chiara Garau	University of Cagliari, Italy

Advancements in Spatial assessment of Socio-Ecological SystemS (ASSESS 2025)

Workshop Organizers

Daniele Cannatella	TU Delft, The Netherlands
Giuliano Poli	University of Naples Federico II, Italy
Eugenio Muccio	TU Delft, The Netherlands
Claudiu Forgaci	TU Delft, The Netherlands

Workshop Program Committee Members

Daniele Cannatella	TU Delft, The Netherlands
Giuliano Poli	University of Naples Federico II, Italy
Eugenio Muccio	University of Naples Federico II, Italy
Claudiu Forgaci	TU Delft, The Netherlands
Maria Cerreta	University of Naples Federico II, Italy
Maria Somma	University of Naples Federico II, Italy
Laura Di Tommaso	University of Naples Federico II, Italy
Sabrina Sacco	Politecnico di Milano, Italy
Piero Zizzania	University of Naples Federico II, Italy
Gaia Daldanise	CNR IRISS, Italy
Benedetta Grieco	University of Naples Federico II, Italy
Giuseppe Ciciriello	University of Naples Federico II, Italy
Marta Dell'Ovo	Politecnico di Milano, Italy
Francesco Piras	University of Cagliari, Italy
Diana Rolando	Politecnico di Torino, Italy
Stefano Cuntò	University of Naples Federico II, Italy
Ludovica La Rocca	University of Naples Federico II, Italy

Blockchain and Distributed Ledgers: Technologies and Applications (BDLTA 2025)

Workshop Organizers

Vladimir Korkhov	Saint Petersburg State University, Russia
Elena Stankova	Saint Petersburg State University, Russia
Nataliia Kulabukhova	Saint Petersburg State University, Russia

Workshop Program Committee Members

Adam Belloum	University of Amsterdam, the Netherlands
Dmitrii Vasiunin	Deutsche Telekom Cloud Services E.P.E., Greece
Serob Balyan	Osensus Arm LLC, Armenia
Suren Abrahamyan	Osensus Arm LLC, Armenia
Ashot Sergey Gevorkyan	NAS of Armenia, Armenia

Michal Hnatic	Univerzita Pavla Jozefa Šafárika v Košiciach, Slovakia
Michail Panteleyev	Saint Petersburg Electrotecnical University, Russia
Martin Vala	Univerzita Pavla Jozefa Šafárika v Košiciach, Slovakia
Nodir Zaynalov	Tashkent University of Information Technologies named after Muhammad al Khwarizmi, Uzbekistan
Michail Panteleyev	Saint Petersburg Electrotecnical University, Russia
Alexander Degtyarev	Saint Petersburg University, Russia
Alexander Bogdanov	St. Petersburg State University, Russia

Bio and Neuro Inspired Computing and Applications (BIONCA 2025)

Workshop Organizers

Nadia Nedjah	State University of Rio de Janeiro, Brazil
Luiza de Macedo Mourelle	State University of Rio de Janeiro, Brazil

Workshop Program Committee Members

Nadia Nedjha	State University of Rio de Janeiro, Brazil
Luiza de Macedo Mourelle	State University of Rio de Janeiro, Brazil
Luigi Maciel Ribeiro	State University of Rio de Janeiro, Brazil
Joelmir Ramos	Federal University of Rio de Janeiro, Brazil
Rogério Moraes	Brazilian Navy, Brazil
Marcos Santana Farias	Institute of Nuclear Energy, Brazil
Luneque Silva Jr.	Federal University of ABC, Brazil
Alan Oliveira	University of Lisboa, Portugal
Brij Bhooshan Gupta	Asia University, Taiwan

Computational and Applied Mathematics (CAM 2025)

Workshop Organizers

Maria Irene Falcão	University of Minho, Portugal
Fernando Miranda	University of Minho, Portugal

Workshop Program Committee Members

Fernando Miranda	University of Minho, Portugal
Graça Tomaz	Polytechnic of Guarda, Portugal
Helmuth Malonek	University of Aveiro, Portugal

Isabel Cacao	University of Aveiro, Portugal
João Morais	Autonomous Technological Institute of Mexico, Mexico
Lidia Aceto	University of Eastern Piedmont, Italy
Luís Ferrás	University of Porto, Portugal
M. Irene Falcão	University of Minho, Portugal
Patrícia Beites	University of Beira Interior, Portugal
Paulo Amorim	FGV EMAp, Brazil
Regina de Almeida	University of Trás-os-Montes e Alto Douro, Portugal
Ricardo Severino	University of Minho, Portugal

Computational and Applied Statistics (CAS 2025)

Workshop Organizer

| Ana Cristina Braga | ALGORITMI Research Centre, LASI, University of Minho, Portugal |

Workshop Program Committee Members

Adelaide Freitas	University of Aveiro, Portugal
Andreas Futschik	Johannes Kepler University Linz, Austria
Ana Cristina Braga	University of Minho, Portugal
Ângela Silva	University of Minho, Portugal
Arminda Manuela Gonçalves	University of Minho, Portugal
Carina Silva	Polytechnic Intitute of Lisbon, Portugal
Elisete Correia	University of Trás-os-Montes e Alto Douro, Portugal
Frank Westad	Norwegian University of Science and Technology, Norway
Isabel Natario	New University of Lisbon, Portugal
Irene Oliveira	University of Trás-os-Montes e Alto Douro, Portugal
Ivan Rodriguez Conde	University of Vigo, Spain
Joaquim Gonçalves	Instituto Politécnico do Cávado e do Ave, Portugal
Lino Costa	University of Minho, Portugal
Marco Reis	University of Coimbra, Portugal
Maria Filipa Mourão	Polytechnic Institute of Viana do Castelo, Portugal
Maria João Polidoro	Polytechnic Institute of Porto, Portugal
Martin Perez Perez	University of Vigo, Spain
Michal Abrahamowicz	McGill University, Canada
Vera Afreixo	University of Aveiro, Portugal

Werner G. Müller	Johannes Kepler University Linz, Austria
Bruna Silva Ramos	University Lusiada de Famalicão, Portugal
Inês Sousa	University of Minho, Portugal
Luís Miguel Rocha Matos	University of Minho, Portugal
Manuel Carlos Figueiredo	University of Minho, Portugal

Cyber Intelligence and Applications (CIA 2025)

Workshop Organizer

| Gianni D'Angelo | University of Salerno, Italy |

Workshop Program Committee Members

Gianni D'Angelo	University of Salerno, Italy
Francesco Palmieri	University of Salerno, Italy
Massimo Ficco	University of Salerno, Italy
Arcangelo Castiglione	University of Salerno, Italy

Computational Methods for Business Analytics (CMBA 2025)

Workshop Organizers

| Cláudio Alves | Universidade do Minho, Portugal |
| Telmo Pinto | Universidade do Minho, Portugal |

Workshop Program Committee Members

Abdulrahim Shamayleh	American University of Sharjah, United Arab Emirates
Ana Rocha	University of Minho, Portugal
Angelo Sifaleras	University of Macedonia, Greece
Cristóvão Silva	University of Coimbra, Portugal
José Valério de Carvalho	University of Minho, Portugal
Miguel Vieira	Universidade Lusófona, Portugal
Rita Macedo	Université de Lille, France
Ana Moura	Universidade de Aveiro, Portugal
Cristina Lopes	ISCAP, Portugal
Eliana Costa e Silva	Instituto Politécnico do Porto, Portugal

Computational Methods, Statistics and Industrial Mathematics (CMSIM 2025)

Workshop Organizers

Maria Filomena Teodoro	IST ID, Instituto Superior Técnico, Portugal
Marina Alexandra Pedro Andrade	ISCTE – Lisbon University Institute, Portugal
Paula Simões	University of Lisbon, Portugal
Teresa A. Oliveira	IST ID, Instituto Superior Técnico, Portugal

Workshop Program Committee Members

Amilcar Oliveira	Universidade Aberta and Universidade de Lisboa, Portugal
Victor Lobo	Escola Naval and NOVA IMS Almada, Portugal
António Pacheco	IST Universidade de Lisboa, Portugal
Eliana Costa	Escola Superior de Tecnologia e Gestão IPPorto, Portugal
Aldina Correia	Escola Superior de Tecnologia e Gestão IPPorto, Portugal
Fernando Carapau	University of Évora, Portugal
Ricardo Moura	Portuguese Naval Academy, Portugal
Ana Borges	Escola Superior de Tecnologia e Gestão IPPorto, Portugal
Cristina Lopes	ISCAP IPPorto, Portugal
Fernanda Costa	University of Minho, Portugal
Cabrita Carlos	IPBeja, Portugal
Maria Luísa Morgado	University of Trás os Montes e Alto Douro and University of Lisboa, Portugal
Rosário Ramos	Universidade Aberta, Portugal
Sofia Rézio	Iscal, Instituto Politécnico de Lisboa, Portugal
Matteo Sacchet	University of Turin, Italy
Marina Marchisio Conte	University of Turin, Italy
António Seijas-Macias	University of Coruña, Spain
Luís F. A. Teodoro	University of Glasgow, UK and University of Oslo, Norway
Christos Kitsos	University of West Attica, Greece
M. Filomena Teodoro	Universidade de Lisboa, Portugal
Marina A. P. Andrade	Instituto Universitário de Lisboa, Portugal
Paula Simões	Military Academy and Universidade Nova de Lisboa, Portugal
Teresa Oliveira	Universidade Aberta and Universidade de Lisboa, Portugal

Computational Optimization and Applications (COA 2025)

Workshop Organizers

Ana Rocha ALGORITMI Research Centre, LASI, University of Minho, Portugal, Portugal
Humberto Rocha ALGORITMI Research Centre, LASI, University of Minho, Portugal, Portugal

Workshop Program Committee Members

Florbela Fernandes Polytechnic Institute of Bragança, Portugal
Clara Vaz Polytechnic Institute of Bragança, Portugal
Ana Pereira Polytechnic Institute of Bragança, Portugal
Filipe Alvelos University of Minho, Portugal
Joana Dias University of Coimbra, Portugal
Eligius M. T. Hendrix University of Málaga, Spain
Emerson José de Paiva Federal University of Itajubá, Brazil
Ana Paula Teixeira University of Trás-os-Montes and Alto Douro, Portugal
Lino Costa Universidade do Minho, Portugal

Coastal Cities Versus Inland Areas. Hypotheses for Sustainable Regeneration Through Ecosystem Services of 'Hooking' and Rehabilitation of Brownfield Sites (CoastalCities_VS_InlandAreas 2025)

Workshop Organizers

Celestina Fazia Università di Enna Kore, Italy
Angrilli Massimo University of Chieti-Pescara, Italy
Valentina Ciuffreda University of Chieti-Pescara, Italy
Maurizio Oddo Università di Enna Kore, Italy
Marcello Sestito Università di Enna Kore, Italy
Clara Stella Vicari Aversa University of Reggio Calabria, Italy

Workshop Program Committee Members

Alessandro Camiz Università d'Annunzio, Italy
Thowayeb Hassan King Faisal University, Saudi Arabia
Alessandro Barracco Università Kore di Enna, Italy
Mario Morrica University of Urbino, Italy
Mariana Ratiu University of Oradea, Romania
Alanda Akamana Mohammed VI Polytechnic University, Morocco
Kaoutare Amini Alaoui Mohammed VI Polytechnic University, Morocco

Computational Astrochemistry 2025 (CompAstro 2025)

Workshop Organizers

Marzio Rosi	University of Perugia, Italy
Daniela Ascenzi	University of Trento, Italy
Nadia Balucani	University of Perugia, Italy
Stefano Falcinelli	University of Perugia, Italy

Workshop Program Committee Members

Dario Campisi	Università degli Studi di Perugia, Italy
Giacomo Giorgi	Università degli Studi di Perugia, Italy
Andrea Giustini	Università degli Studi di Perugia, Italy
Luca Mancini	Università degli Studi di Perugia, Italy
Albert Rimola	Universitat Autònoma de Barcelona, Spain
Gianmarco Vanuzzo	Università degli Studi di Perugia, Italy
Dimitrios Skouteris	Master-Tec, Italy
Piero Ugliengo	Università degli Studi di Torino, Italy
Franco Vecchiocattivi	Università degli Sudi di Perugia, Italy
Giacomo Pannacci	Università degli Studi di Perugia, Italy
Costanza Borghesi	Università degli Studi di Perugia, Italy
Marco Parriani	Università degli Studi di Perugia, Italy
Marta Loletti	Università degli Studi di Perugia, Italy
Fernando Pirani	Università degli Studi di Perugia, Italy
Andrea Lombardi	Università degli Studi di Perugia, Italy
Noelia Faginas Lago	Università degli Studi di Perugia, Italy
Paolo Tosi	Università di Trento, Italy
Cecilia Coletti	Università degli Studi Chieti-Pescara, Italy
Nazzareno Re	Università degli Studi Chieti-Pescara, Italy
Linda Podio	Osservatorio Astrofisico di Arcetri INAF, Italy
Claudio Codella	Osservatorio Astrofisico di Arcetri INAF, Italy
Gabriella Di Genova	Università degli Studi di Perugia, Italy

Computational Methods for Porous Geomaterials (CompPor 2025)

Workshop Organizers

Vadim Lisitsa	IPGG SB RAS, Russia
Evgeniy Romenski	IPGG SB RAS, Russia

Workshop Program Committee Members

Vadim Lisitsa	Institute of Petroleum Geology and Geophysics SB RAS, Russia
Evgeniy Romenski	Sobolev Institute of Mathematics SB RAS, Russia
Vladimir Cheverda	Sobolev Institute of Mathematics SB RAS, Russia
Tatyana Khachkova	IPGG SB RAS, Russia
Dmitry Prokhorov	IPGG SB RAS, Russia
Mikhail Novikov	Sobolev Institute of Mathematics SB RAS, Russia
Sergey Solovyev	Sobolev Institute of Mathematics SB RAS, Russia
Kirill Gadylshin	LLC RNBashNIPIneft, Russia
Olga Stoyanovskaya	Lavrentev Institute of Hydrodynamics SB RAS, Russia
Yerlan Amanbek	Nazarbaev University, Kazakstan

Workshop on Computational Science and HPC (CSHPC 2025)

Workshop Organizers

Elise de Doncker	Western Michigan University, USA
Hideo Matsufuru	High Energy Accelerator Research Organization, Japan

Workshop Program Committee Members

Elise de Doncker	Western Michigan University, USA
Hideo Matsufuru	High Energy Accelerator Research Organization (KEK), Japan
Fukuko Yuasa	KEK, Japan
Issaku Kanamori	RIKEN, Japan
Hiroshi Daisaka	Hitotsubashi University, Japan
Norikazu Yamada	KEK, Japan
Naohito Nakasato	University of Aizu, Japan
Robert Makin	Western Michigan University, USA

Cities, Technologies and Planning 2025 (CTP 2025)

Workshop Organizers

Giuseppe Borruso	University of Trieste, Italy
Beniamino Murgante	University of Basilicata, Italy
Malgorzata Hanzl	Lodz University of Technology, Poland
Anastasia Stratigea	National Technical University of Athens, Greece
Ljiljana Zivkovic	Republic Geodetic Authority, Serbia
Ginevra Balletto	University of Trieste, Italy

Workshop Program Committee Members

Giuseppe Borruso	University of Trieste, Italy
Beniamino Murgante	University of Basilicata, Italy
Malgorzata Hanzl	Lodz University of Technology, Poland
Anastasia Stratigea	National Technical University of Athens, Greece
Ljiljiana Zivkovic	Republic Geodetic Authority of Serbia, Serbia
Ginevra Balletto	University of Cagliari, Italy
Silvia Battino	University of Sassari, Italy
Mara Ladu	University of Cagliari, Italy
Maria del Mar Munoz Leonisio	University of Cádiz, Spain
Ahinoa Amaro Garcia	University of Las Palmas of Gran Canaria, Spain
Maria Attard	University of Malta, Malta
Enrico D'agostini	World Maritime University, Sweden
Francesca Krasna	University of Trieste, Italy
Brisol Garcia Garcia	Polytechnic University of Quintana Roo, Mexico
Tu Anh Trinh	UEH University, Vietnam
Giovanni Mauro	Università degli Studi della Campania, Italy
Maria Ronza	University of Naples Federico II, Italy
Massimiliano Bencardino	University of Salerno, Italy
Tomasz Bradecki	Silesian University of Technology, Poland
Dorota Kamrowska-Załuska	Gdańsk University of Technology, Poland
Iwona Jażdżewska	University of Lodz, Poland
Yiota Theodora	National Technical University of Athens, Greece
Apostolos Lagarias	University of Thessaly, Greece
George Tsilimigkas	University of the Aegean, Greece
Akrivi Leka	National Technical University of Athens, Greece
Maria Panagiotopoulou	National Technical University of Athens, Greece
Andrea Gallo	Ca' Foscari University of Venice, Italy
Francesca Sinatra	University of Trieste, Italy

Digital Transition: Effects on Housing Mobility, Market, Land Governance (DIGITRANS 2025)

Workshop Organizers

Fabrizio Battisti	University of Florence, Italy
Fabiana Forte	University of Campania, Italy
Orazio Campo	Sapienza University of Rome, Italy
Alessio Pino	Kore University of Enna, Italy
Carlo Pisano	University of Florence, Italy
Mariolina Grasso	Kore University of Enna, Italy

Workshop Program Committee Members

Fabrizio Battisti	University of Florence, Italy
Fabiana Forte	Università della Campania Luigi Vanvitelli, Italy
Orazio Campo	University of Rome "La Sapienza", Italy
Alessio Pino	Kore University of Enna, Italy
Carlo Pisano	University of Florence, Italy
Mariolina Grasso	Università Kore di Enna, Italy

Evaluating Inner Areas Potentials (EIAP 2025)

Workshop Organizers

Diana Rolando	Politecnico di Torino, Italy
Alice Barreca	Politecnico di Torino, Italy
Manuela Rebaudengo	Politecnico di Torino, Italy
Giorgia Malavasi	Politecnico di Torino, Italy

Workshop Program Committee Members

John Accordino	Virginia Commonwealth University, USA
Francesco Bruzzone	Università Iuav di Venezia, Italy
Maria Cerreta	Università degli Studi di Napoli Federico II, Italy
Maddalena Chimisso	Università degli Studi del Molise, Italy
Chiara Chioni	Università degli Studi di Trento, Italy
Annalisa Contato	Università degli Studi di Palermo, Italy
Cristina Coscia	Politecnico di Torino, Italy
Marta Dell'Ovo	Politecnico di Milano, Italy
Benedetta Di Leo	Università Politecnica delle Marche, Italy
Sara Favargiotti	Università degli Studi di Trento, Italy
Maddalena Ferretti	Università Politecnica delle Marche, Italy
Salvo Giuffrida	Università degli Studi di Palermo, Italy
Barbara Lino	Università degli Studi di Palermo, Italy
Umberto Mecca	Politecnico di Torino, Italy
Beatrice Mecca	Politecnico di Torino, Italy
Giuliano Poli	Università degli Studi di Napoli Federico II, Italy
Marco Rossitti	Politecnico di Milano, Italy
Alexandra Stankulova	Politecnico di Torino, Italy
Elena Todella	Politecnico di Torino, Italy
Asja Aulisio	Politecnico di Torino, Italy
Giulia Datola	Politecnico di Milano, Italy

Francesco Calabrò	Università degli Studi Mediterranea di Reggio Calabria, Italy
Valeria Saiu	Università degli Studi di Cagliari, Italy
Maria Rosa Trovato	Università di Catania, Italy

Econometric and Multidimensional Evaluation in Urban Environment (EMEUE 2025)

Workshop Organizers

Maria Cerreta	University of Naples Federico II, Italy
Carmelo Maria Torre	Polytechnic University of Bari, Italy
Pierluigi Morano	Polytechnic University of Bari, Italy
Simona Panaro	University of Naples Federico II, Italy
Felicia Di Liddo	University of Naples Federico II, Italy
Debora Anelli	University of Naples Federico II, Italy

Workshop Program Committee Members

Carmelo Maria Torre	Polytechnic University of Bari, Italy
Maria Cerreta	University of Naples Federico II, Italy
Pierluigi Morano	Polytechnic University of Bari, Italy
Francesco Tajani	Sapienza University of Rome, Italy
Simona Panaro	University of Naples Federico II, Italy
Felicia di Liddo	Polytechnic University of Bari, Italy
Debora Anelli	Sapienza University of Rome, Italy
Giuliano Poli	University of Naples Federico II, Italy
Maria Somma	University of Naples Federico II, Italy
Simona Panaro	University of Campania Luigi Vanvitelli, Italy
Laura Di Tommaso	University of Naples Federico II, Italy
Caterina Loffredo	University of Naples Federico II, Italy
Ludovica La Rocca	University of Naples Federico II, Italy
Sabrina Sacco	Politecnico di Milano, Italy
Piero Zizzania	University of Naples Federico II, Italy
Gaia Daldanise	CNR IRISS, Italy
Benedetta Grieco	University of Naples Federico II, Italy
Giuseppe Ciciriello	University of Naples Federico II, Italy
Marta Dell'Ovo	Politecnico di Milano, Italy
Daniele Cannatella	TU Delft University, The Netherlands
Eugenio Muccio	University of Naples Federico II, Italy
Sveva Ventre	University of Naples Federico II, Italy

Governance of Energy Transition: Environmental, Landscape, Social and Spatial Planning (ENERGY_PLANNING 2025)

Workshop Organizers

Mara Ladu	University of Cagliari, Italy
Ginevra Balletto	University of Cagliari, Italy
Emilio Ghiani	University of Cagliari, Italy
Alessandra Marra	University of Salerno, Italy
Roberto De Lotto	University of Pavia, Italy
Balázs Kulcsár	Chalmers University of Technology, Sweden

Workshop Program Committee Members

Riccardo Trevisan	University of Cagliari, Italy
Marco Naseddu	University of Cagliari, Italy
Giuseppe Borruso	University of Trieste, Italy
Andrea Gallo	University of Trieste, Italy
Francesca Sinatra	University of Trieste, Italy
Maria Attard	University of Malta, Malta
Tu Anh Trinh	UEH University Ho Chi Minh City, Vietnam
Marcello Tadini	University of Eastern Piedmont, Italy
Luigi Mundula	University for Foreigners of Perugia, Italy
Silvia Battino	University of Sassari, Italy
Maria del Mar Munoz Leonisio	University of Cádiz, Spain
Anna Richiedei	University of Brescia, Italy
Michele Pezzagno	University of Brescia, Italy
Federico Mertellozzo	University of Firenze, Italy
Marco Mazzarino	IUAV University Venice, Italy

Ecosystem Services in Spatial Planning for Climate Neutral Urban and Rural Areas (ESSP 2025)

Workshop Organizers

Sabrina Lai	University of Cagliari, Italy
Francesco Scorza	University of Basilicata, Italy
Corrado Zoppi	University of Cagliari, Italy
Beniamino Murgante	University of Basilicata, Italy
Carmela Gargiulo	University of Naples Federico II, Italy
Floriana Zucaro	University of Naples Federico II, Italy

Workshop Program Committee Members

Alfonso Annunziata	University of Basilicata, Italy
Ginevra Balletto	University of Cagliari, Italy
Ivan Blečić	University of Cagliari, Italy
Giuseppe Borruso	University of Trieste, Italy
Barbara Caselli	University of Parma, Italy
Maria Cerreta	University of Naples Federico II, Italy
Chiara Garau	University of Cagliari, Italy
Carmen Guida	University of Naples Federico II, Italy
Federica Isola	University of Cagliari, Italy
Francesca Leccis	University of Cagliari, Italy
Federica Leone	University of Cagliari, Italy
Silvia Rossetti	University of Parma, Italy
Luigi Santopietro	University of Basilicata, Italy
Carmelo Torre	Polytechnic of Bari, Italy

The 15th International Workshop on Future Information System Technologies and Applications (FiSTA 2025)

Workshop Organizers

Bernady O. Apduhan	Kyushu Sangyo University, Japan
Rafael Santos	Brazilian National Institute for Space Research, Brazil

Workshop Program Committee Members

Agustinus Borgy Waluyo	Monash University, Australia
Andre Ricardo Abed Grégio	Federal University of Paraná, Brazil
Eric Pardede	La Trobe University, Australia
Kai Cheng	Kyushu Sangyo University, Japan
Ching-Hsien Hsu	Asia University, Taiwan
Fenghui Yao	Tennessee State University, USA
Yusuke Gotoh	Okayama University, Japan
Alvaro Fazenda	Federal University of São Paulo, Brazil
Kazuaki Tanaka	Kyushu Institute of Technology, Japan
Tengku Adil	MARA Technological University, Malaysia
Toshihiro Yamauchi	Okayama University, Japan
Yasuaki Sumida	Kyushu Sangyo University, Japan
Earl Ryan Aleluya	MSU-Iligan Institute of Technology, Philippines
Cherry Mae G. Villame	MSU-Iligan Institute of Technology, Philippines
Anton Louise De Ocampo	Batangas State University, Philippines
Krishnamoorthy Ranganthan	Chennai Institute of Technology, India

Flow Management in Urban Contexts (FMUC 2025)

Workshop Organizers

Alessio Pino	Kore University of Enna, Italy
Giovanna Acampa	Kore University of Enna, Italy

Workshop Program Committee Members

Giovanna Acampa	University of Florence, Italy
Alessio Pino	Kore University of Enna, Italy
Mariolina Grasso	Università Kore di Enna, Italy
Fabrizio Battisti	University of Florence, Italy
Fabrizio Finucci	Roma Tre University, Italy
Antonella G. Masanotti	Roma Tre University, Italy
Daniele Mazzoni	Roma Tre University, Italy

Geographical Analysis, Urban Modeling, Spatial Statistics 2025 (Geog-And-Mod 2025)

Workshop Organizers

Beniamino Murgante	University of Basilicata, Italy
Giuseppe Borruso	University of Trieste, Italy
Hartmut Asche	University of Potsdam, Germany
Rodrigo Tapia McClung	CentroGeo, Mexico
Andreas Fricke	University of Potsdam, Germany

Workshop Program Committee Members

Giuseppe Borruso	University of Trieste, Italy
Beniamino Murgante	University of Basilicata, Italy
Hartmut Asche	University of Potsdam, Germany
Rodrigo Tapia-McClung	Centro de Investigación en Ciencias de Información Geoespacial (CentroGeo), Mexico
Andreas Fricke	University of Potsdam, Germany
Malgorzata Hanzl	Lodz University of Technology, Poland
Anastasia Stratigea	National Technical University of Athens, Greece
Ljiljiana Zivkovic	Republic Geodetic Authority of Serbia, Serbia
Ginevra Balletto	University of Cagliari, Italy
Silvia Battino	University of Sassari, Italy
Mara Ladu	University of Cagliari, Italy
Maria del Mar Munoz Leonisio	University of Cádiz, Spain
Ahinoa Amaro Garcia	University of Las Palmas of Gran Canaria, Spain
Maria Attard	University of Malta, Malta

Enrico D'agostini	World Maritime University, Sweden
Francesca Krasna	University of Trieste, Italy
Brisol García García	Polytechnic University of Quintana Roo, Mexico
Tu Anh Trinh	UEH University, Vietnam
Giovanni Mauro	Università degli Studi della Campania, Italy
Maria Ronza	University of Naples Federico II, Italy
Massimiliano Bencardino	University of Salerno, Italy
Andrea Gallo	Ca' Foscari University of Venice, Italy
Francesca Sinatra	University of Trieste, Italy
Salvatore Dore	University of Trieste, Italy

Geogames for Sustainable Development (Geogames 2025)

Workshop Organizer

Alenka Poplin	Iowa State University, USA

Workshop Program Committee Members

Alenka Poplin	Iowa State University, USA
Bruno Amaral de Andrade	Portucalense University, Portugal
Brian Tomaszewski	Rochester Institute of Technology, USA
Deepak Marhatta	Tribhuvan University, Nepal
Alessandro Plaisant	University of Sassari, Italy
David Schwartz	Rochester Institute of Technology, USA
Silvia Rossetti	University of Parma, Italy
Floriana Zucaro	University of Naples Federico II, Italy
Alfonso Annunziata	University of Basilicata, Italy
Reza Askarizad	University of Cagliari, Italy
Chiara Garau	University of Cagliari, Italy
Tanja Congiu	University of Sassari, Italy

Geomatics for Resource Monitoring and Management (GRMM 2025)

Workshop Organizers

Alberico Sonnessa	Politecnico di Bari, Italy
Eufemia Tarantino	Politecnico di Bari, Italy
Alessandra Capolupo	Politecnico di Bari, Italy

Workshop Program Committee Members

Umberto Fratino	Politecnico di Bari, Italy
Valeria Monno	Politecnico di Bari, Italy

Antonino Maltese	Università degli studi di Palermo, Italy
Athos Agapiou	Cyprus University of Technology, Cyprus
Michele Mangiameli	Università di Catania, Italy
Angela Gorgoglione	Universidad de la República de Uruguay, Uruguay
Roberta Ravanelli	University of Liège, Belgium
Ester Scotto di Perta	Università degli studi di Napoli Federico II, Italy
Giacomo Caporusso	CNR, Italy
Andrea Montanino	International Centre for Numerical Methods in Engineering of Barcelona, Spain
Antonino Iannuzzo	Università degli studi del Sannio, Italy
Alessandro Pagano	Politecnico di Bari, Italy
Francesco Di Capua	Università degli Studi della Basilicata, Italy
Albertini Cinzia	CNR-IREA, Italy
Alessandra Saponieri	Università degli studi del Salento, Italy
PierFrancesco Recchi	Università degli studi di Napoli Federico II, Italy
Vincenzo Totaro	Politecnico di Bari, Italy
Stefania Santoro	CNR Water Research Institute, Italy
Francesco Bimbo	University of Foggia, Italy
Cristina Proietti	Istituto Nazionale di Geofisica e Vulcanologia, Italy
Carla Cavallo	University of Salerno, Italy
Gaetano Falcone	Università degli Studi di Napoli Federico II, Italy
Valeria Belloni	Sapienza University of Rome, Italy
Alessandra Mascitelli	University of Chieti-Pescara, Italy

HERitage and CLIMAte neutrality. Resilient approach for nature centered/based sustainable cities (HERCLIMA 2025)

Workshop Organizers

Celestina Fazia	Università di Enna Kore, Italy
Angrilli Massimo	University of Chieti-Pescara, Italy
Clara Stella Vicari Aversa	University of Reggio Calabria, Italy
Dorina Camelia Ilies	University of Oradea, Romania
Mariana Ratiu	University of Oradea, Romania

Workshop Program Committee Members

Alessandro Camiz	Università d'Annunzio, Italy
Mario Morrica	University of Urbino, Italy
Thowayeb Hassan	King Faisal University, Saudi Arabia
Alessandro Barracco	Università Kore di Enna, Italy
Kaoutare Amini Alaoui	Mohammed VI Polytechnic University (UM6P), Morocco

Mariana Ratiu   University of Oradea, Romania
Valentina Ciuffreda   Università Chieti-Pescara, Italy

International Workshop on Information and Knowledge in the Internet of Things (IKIT 2025)

Workshop Organizers

Teresa Guarda   Universidad Estatal Península de Santa Elena, Ecuador

Luis Enrique Chuquimarca   Universidad Estatal Península de Santa Elena,
Jimenez   Ecuador
Gustavo Gatica   Universidad Andrés Bello, Chile
Filipe Mota Pinto   Polytechnic Institute of Leiria, Portugal
Arnulfo Alanis   Instituto Tecnológico de Tijuana, Mexico
Luis Mazon   Universidad Estatal Península de Santa Elena, Spain

Workshop Program Committee Members

Arnulfo Alanis   Instituto Tecnológico de Tijuana, Mexico
Bruno Sousa   University of Coimbra, Portugal
Carlos Balsa   Instituto Politécnico de Bragança, Portugal
Filipe Mota Pinto   Instituto Politécnico de Leiria, Portugal
Gustavo Gatica   Universidad Andrés Bello, Chile
Isabel Lopes   Instituto Politécnico de Bragança, Portugal
José-María Díaz-Nafría   Universidad a Distancia, Spain
Maria Fernanda Augusto   BiTrum Research Group, Spain
Maria Isabel Ribeiro   Instituto Politécnico Bragança, Portugal
Modestos Stavrakis   University of the Aegean, Greece
Simone Belli   Universidad Complutense de Madrid, Spain
Walter Lopes Neto   Instituto Federal de Educação, Brazil

International Workshop on territorial Planning to integrate Risk prevention and urban Ontologies (IWPRO 2025)

Workshop Organizers

Beniamino Murgante   University of Basilicata, Italy
Roberto De Lotto   University of Pavia, Italy
Elisabetta Maria Venco   University of Pavia, Italy
Caterina Pietra   University of Pavia, Italy

Workshop Program Committee Members

Stefano Borgo	Consiglio Nazionale delle Ricerche ISTC, Italy
Valentina Costa	Università di Genova, Italy
Hamid Danesh Pajouh	Middle East Technical University, Turkey
Ilaria Delponte	Università di Genova, Italy
Lorena Fiorini	Università de L'Aquila, Italy
Veronica Gazzola	Politecnico di Milano, Italy
Ghazaleh Goodarzi	Islamic Azad University, Iran
Michele Grimaldi	Università degli Studi di Salerno, Italy
Alessandra Marra	Università degli Studi di Salerno, Italy
Naghmeh Mohammadpourlima	Åbo Akademi University, Finland
Francesca Pirlone	Università di Genova, Italy
Silvia Rossetti	Università di Parma, Italy
Bahareh Shahsavari	University of Minnesota, USA
Ilenia Spadaro	Università di Genova, Italy
Maria Rosaria Stufano Melone	Politecnico di Bari, Italy

Regional Connectivity, Spatial Accessibility and MaaS for Social Inclusion (MaaS 2025)

Workshop Organizers

Mara Ladu	University of Cagliari, Italy
Ginevra Balletto	University of Cagliari, Italy
Gianfranco Fancello	University of Cagliari, Italy
Tanja Congiu	University of Sassari, Italy
Patrizia Serra	University of Cagliari, Italy
Francesco Piras	University of Cagliari, Italy

Workshop Program Committee Members

Marco Naseddu	University of Cagliari, Italy
Italo Meloni	University of Cagliari, Italy
Giuseppe Borruso	University of Trieste, Italy
Andrea Gallo	University of Trieste, Italy
Francesca Sinatra	University of Trieste, Italy
Maria Attard	University of Malta, Malta
Tu Anh Trinh	UEH University, Vietnam
Marcello Tadini	University of Eastern Piedmont, Italy
Luigi Mundula	University for Foreigners of Perugia, Italy
Silvia Battino	University of Sassari, Italy
Brunella Brundu	University of Sassari, Italy
Veronica Camerada	University of Sassari, Italy

Maria del Mar Munoz Leonisio	University of Cádiz, Spain
Anna Richiedei	University of Brescia, Italy
Michele Pezzagno	University of Brescia, Italy
Marco Mazzarino	IUAV University Venice, Italy

The Development of Urban Mobility Management, Road Safety and Risk Assessment (MANTAIN 2025)

Workshop Organizers

Antonio Russo	Università degli Studi di Enna, Italy
Corrado Rindone	University of Reggio Calabria, Italy
Antonio Polimeni	University of Messina, Italy
Florin Rusca	Politehnica University of Bucharest, Romania
Grigorios Fountas	Aristotle University of Thessaloniki, Greece
Antonio Comi	University of Rome Tor Vergata, Italy

Workshop Program Committee Members

Massimo Di Gangi	University of Messina, Italy
Orlando Marco Belcore	University of Messina, Italy
Antonio Polimeni	University of Messina, Italy
Socrates Basbas	Aristotle University of Thessaloniki, Greece
Claudia Caballini	Polytechnic of Torino, Italy
Efstathios Bouhouras	Aristotle University of Thessaloniki, Greece
Stefano Ricci	Sapienza University of Rome, Italy
Marina Zanne	University of Lubljana, Slovenia
Kh Md Nahiduzzaman	Mohammed VI Polytechnic University, Morocco
Alexsandra Deluka Tibljaš	University of Rijeka, Croatia
Guilhermina Torrao	Aston University, UK

Multidimensional Evolutionary Evaluations for Transformative Approaches (MEETA 2025)

Workshop Organizers

Maria Cerreta	University of Naples Federico II, Italy
Giuliano Poli	University of Naples Federico II, Italy
Maria Somma	University of Naples Federico II, Italy
Gaia Daldanise	CNR IRISS, Italy
Ludovica La Rocca	University of Naples Federico II, Italy

Workshop Program Committee Members

Maria Cerreta	University of Naples Federico II, Italy
Giuliano Poli	University of Naples Federico II, Italy
Maria Somma	University of Naples Federico II, Italy
Laura Di Tommaso	University of Naples Federico II, Italy
Sabrina Sacco	Politecnico di Milano, Italy
Piero Zizzania	University of Naples Federico II, Italy
Gaia Daldanise	CNR IRISS, Italy
Benedetta Grieco	University of Naples Federico II, Italy
Giuseppe Ciciriello	University of Naples Federico II, Italy
Marta Dell'Ovo	Politecnico di Milano, Italy
Daniele Cannatella	TU Delft, The Netherlands
Eugenio Muccio	University of Naples Federico II, Italy
Francesco Piras	University of Cagliari, Italy
Diana Rolando	Politecnico di Torino, Italy
Sveva Ventre	University of Naples Federico II, Italy
Caterina Loffredo	University of Naples Federico II, Italy
Ludovica La Rocca	University of Naples Federico II, Italy
Simona Panaro	University of Campania Luigi Vanvitelli, Italy

Building Multi-dimensional Models for Assessing Complex Environmental Systems (MES 2025)

Workshop Organizers

Vanessa Assumma	University of Bologna, Italy
Caterina Caprioli	Politecnico di Torino, Italy
Giulia Datola	Politecnico di Milano, Italy
Federico Dell'Anna	University of Bologna, Italy
Marta Dell'Ovo	Politecnico di Milano, Italy
Marco Rossitti	Politecnico di Milano, Italy

Workshop Program Committee Members

Vanessa Assumma	Università di Bologna, Bologna
Caterina Caprioli	Politecnico di Torino, Italy
Giulia Datola	DAStU Politecnico di Milano, Italy
Federico Dell'Anna	Politecnico di Torino, Italy
Marta Dell'Ovo	Politecnico di Milano, Italy
Marco Rossitti	Politecnico di Milano, Italy
Francesca Torrieri	Politecnico di Milano, Italy
Mariarosaria Angrisano	Università Telematica Pegaso, Italy
Maksims Feofilovs	Riga Technical University, Latvia

Danny Caprini	Politecnico di Milano, Italy
Giulio Cavana	Politecnico di Torino, Italy
Sebastiano Barbieri	Politecnico di Torino, Italy
Marta Bottero	Politecnico di Torino, Italy
Francesco Cosentino	Politecnico di Milano, Italy
Silvia Ronchi	Politecnico di Milano, Italy
Chiara Mazzarella	TU Delft, Netherlands
Marco Volpatti	Politecnico di Torino, Italy
Chiara D'Alpaos	Università degli Studi di Padova, Italy
Alessandra Oppio	Politecnico di Milano, Italy
Alessia Crisopulli	Politecnico di Milano, Italy
Domenico D'Uva	Politecnico di Milano, Italy
Giorgia Malavasi	Politecnico di Torino, Italy
Rubina Canesi	Università degli Studi di Padova, Italy
Elena Todella	Politecnico di Torino, Italy
Beatrice Mecca	Politecnico di Torino, Italy
Giulia Marzani	University of Bologna, Italy
Isabella Giovanetti	University of Bologna, Italy
Lucia Petronio	University of Bologna, Italy
Franco Corti	University of Padova, Italy
Salvatore De Pascalis	Politecnico di Milano, Italy
Valeria Vitulano	Politecnico di Torino, Italy
Lorenzo Diana	Università degli studi di Napoli Federico II, Italy
Maksims Feofilovs	Riga Technical University, Latvia
Marco De Luca	Politecnico di Torino, Italy
Ilaria Cazzola	Politecnico di Torino, Italy
Andrea De Toni	Politecnico di Milano, Italy
Eugenio Muccio	University of Naples Federico II, Italy
Giuliano Poli	University of Naples Federico II, Italy
Francesco Sica	University "La Sapienza" of Rome, Italy
Elena Di Pirro	Università degli Studi del Molise, Italy
Riccardo Alba	Università di Torino, Italy
Irene Regaiolo	Università di Torino, Italy
Francesca Cochis	Università di Torino, Italy

Modelling Liveable Cities: Techniques, Methods, Challenges, and Perspectives Behind the 'X-Minute' City (MLC 2025)

Workshop Organizers

Federico Mara	University of Pisa, Italy
Valerio Cutini	University of Pisa, Italy
Alessandro Araldi	Université Côte d'Azur, France

Flávia Lopes   Chalmers University of Technology, Sweden
Giovanni Fusco   Université Côte d'Azur, France

Workshop Program Committee Members

Simone Rusci   University of Pisa, Italy
Lorena Fiorini   University of L'Aquila, Italy
Chiara Di Dato   University of L'Aquila, Italy
Francesco Zullo   University of L'Aquila, Italy
Alfonso Annunziata   University of Basilicata, Italy
Beniamino Murgante   University of Basilicata, Italy
Alessandro Araldi   Universitè Côte d'Azur, France
Chiara Garau   University of Cagliari, Italy
Giampiero Lombardini   Università di Genova, Italy
Flavia Lopes   Chalmers University of Technology, Sweden
Giovanni Fusco   Universitè Côte d'Azur, France

Mathematical Methods for Image Processing and Understanding 2025 (MMIPU 2025)

Workshop Organizers

Ivan Gerace   Università degli Studi di Perugia, Italy
Gianluca Vinti   Università degli Studi di Perugia, Italy
Arianna Travaglini   Università degli Studi della Basilicata, Italy

Workshop Program Committee Members

Ivan Gerace   University of Perugia, Italy
Gianluca Vinti   University of Perugia, Italy
Arianna Travaglini   University of Basilicata, Italy
Marco Baioletti   University of Perugia, Italy
Marco Donatelli   University of Insubria, Italy
Anna Tonazzini   C.N.R. Pisa, Italy
Muhammad Hanif   Ghulam Ishaq Khan Institute of Engineering
                                Sciences and Technology, Pakistan
Francesco Marchetti   University of Padua, Italy
Wolfgang Erb   University of Padua, Italy
Danilo Costarelli   University of Perugia, Italy
Francesco Santini   University of Perugia, Italy
Valentina Giorgetti   University of Perugia, Italy

Mobility Opportunities Bridging Inequalities: Social Inclusion and Gender Equity Initiatives Strategies Against Fragmentation and Complexity of Mobility (MOBIL-EGI 2025)

Workshop Organizers

Tiziana Campisi	University of Enna Kore, Italy
Guilhermina Torrao	Aston University, UK
Socrates Basbas	Aristotle University of Thessaloniki, Greece
Tanja Congiu	University of Sassari, Italy
Stefanos Tsigdinos	National Technical University of Athens, Greece
Florin Nemtanu	Politehnica University of Bucharest, Romania

Workshop Program Committee Members

Massimo Di Gangi	University of Messina, Italy
Orlando Marco Belcore	University of Messina, Italy
Francesco Russo	Mediterranean University of Reggio Calabria, Italy
Alexandros Nikitas	University of Huddersfield, UK
Marilisa Nigro	Rome Tre University, Italy
Kh Md Nahiduzzaman	Mohammed VI Polytechnic University, Morocco
Efstathios Bouhouras	Aristotle University of Thessaloniki, Greece
Antonio Comi	University of Rome Tor Vergata, Italy
Edouard Ivanjko	University of Zagreb, Slovenia
Osvaldo Gervasi	University of Perugia, Italy
Beniamino Murgante	University of Basilicata, Italy
Chiara Garau	University of Cagliari, Italy

MOdels and indicators for assessing and measuring the urban settlement deVElopment in the view of NET ZERO by 2050 (MOVEto0 2025)

Workshop Organizers

Lorena Fiorini	University of L'Aquila, Italy
Lucia Saganeiti	CNR-IMAA, Italy
Angela Pilogallo	CNR-IMAA, Italy
Alessandro Marucci	University of L'Aquila, Italy
Francesco Zullo	University of L'Aquila, Italy

Workshop Program Committee Members

Ginevra Balletto	University of Cagliari, Italy
Giuseppe Borruso	University of Trieste, Italy
Chiara Garau	University of Cagliari, Italy

Beniamino Murgante	University of Basilicata, Italy
Giulia Desogus	University of Cagliari, Italy
Ljiljana Zivkovic	Republic Geodetic Authority, Serbia
Luigi Santopietro	University of Basilicata, Italy
Ilaria Delponte	University of Genoa, Italy
Carmen Guida	University of Naples Federico II, Italy
Chiara Di Dato	University of L'Aquila, Italy

5th Workshop on Privacy in the Cloud/Edge/IoT World (PCEIoT 2025)

Workshop Organizers

Lelio Campanile	Università degli Studi della Campania Luigi Vanvitelli, Italy
Mauro Iacono	Università degli Studi della Campania Luigi Vanvitelli, Italy
Michele Mastroianni	Università degli Studi di Foggia, Italy

Workshop Program Committee Members

Arcangelo Castiglione	Università degli Studi di Salerno, Italy
Maria Ganzha	Warsaw University of Technology, Poland
Daniel Grzonka	Cracow University of Technology, Poland
Antonio Iannuzzi	Università degli Studi Roma Tre, Italy
Armando Tacchella	Università degli Studi di Genova, Italy
Biagio Boi	University of Salerno, Italy
Marco De Santis	University of Salerno, Italy
Fiammetta Marulli	Università degli Studi della Campania "L. Vanvitelli", Italy
Christian Riccio	Università degli Studi della Campania "L. Vanvitelli", Italy
Luigi Piero Di Bonito	Università degli Studi di Napoli Federico II, Italy

Preserving Our Past: Spatial and Remote Sensing Technologies for Cultural Heritage in a Changing Climate (POP 2025)

Workshop Organizers

Maria Danese	CNR-ISPC, Italy
Nicola Masini	CNR-ISPC, Italy
Rosa Lasaponara	CNR-IMAA, Italy

Workshop Program Committee Members

Maria Danese	CNR-ISPC, Italy
Nicola Masini	CNR-ISPC, Italy
Rosa Lasaponara	CNR-IMAA, Italy
Dario Gioia	CNR-ISPC, Italy
Giuseppe Corrado	Università degli Studi della Basilicata, Italy
Canio Sabia	CNR-ISPC, Italy

Processes, methods and tools towards RESilient cities and cultural and historic sites prone to SOD and ROD disasters (RES 2025)

Workshop Organizers

Elena Cantatore	Polytechnic University of Bari, Italy
Dario Esposito	Polytechnic University of Bari, Italy
Alberico Sonnessa	Polytechnic University of Bari, Italy

Workshop Program Committee Members

Elena Cantatore	Politecnico di Bari, Italy
Dario Esposito	Politecnico di Bari, Italy
Alberico Sonnessa	Politecnico di Bari, Italy
Valeria Belloni	Sapienza University of Rome, Italy
Michela Ravanelli	Sapienza University of Rome, Italy
Silvano Dal Sasso	University of Basilicata, Italy
Francesco Chiaravalloti	CNR - IRPI, Italy
Roberta Ravanelli	University of Liège, Belgium
Alessandra Mascitelli	University of Chieti-Pescara, Italy
Francesco Di Capua	University of Basilicata, Italy
Gabriele Bernardini	Università Politecnica delle Marche, Italy
Vito Domenico Porcari	University of Basilicata, Italy
Carmen Rosa Fattore	University of Basilicata, Italy
Stefania Santoro	Water Research Institute, Italy

Scientific Computing Infrastructure (SCI 2025)

Workshop Organizers

Vladimir Korkhov	Saint Petersburg State University, Russia
Elena Stankova	Saint Petersburg State University, Russia
Nataliia Kulabukhova	Saint Petersburg State University, Russia

Workshop Program Committee Members

Adam Belloum	University of Amsterdam, the Netherlands
Dmitrii Vasiunin	Deutsche Telekom Cloud Services E.P.E., Greece
Serob Balyan	Osensus Arm LLC, Armenia
Suren Abrahamyan	Osensus Arm LLC, Armenia
Ashot Sergey Gevorkyan	NAS of Armenia, Armenia
Michal Hnatic	Univerzita Pavla Jozefa Šafárika v Košiciach, Slovakia
Michail Panteleyev	Saint Petersburg Electrotecnical University, Russia
Martin Vala	Univerzita Pavla Jozefa Šafárika v Košiciach, Slovakia
Nodir Zaynalov	Tashkent University of Information Technologies named after Muhammad al Khwarizmi, Uzbekistan
Michail Panteleyev	Saint Petersburg Electrotecnical University, Russia
Alexander Degtyarev	Saint Petersburg University, Russia
Alexander Bogdanov	St. Petersburg State University, Russia

Ports and Logistics of the Future - Smartness and Sustainability (SmartPorts 2025)

Workshop Organizers

Andrea Gallo	Università degli Studi di Trieste, Italy
Gianfranco Fancello	University of Cagliari, Italy
Giuseppe Borruso	Università degli Studi di Trieste, Italy
Enrico D'agostini	World Maritime University, Sweden
Silvia Battino	Università degli Studi di Sassari, Italy
Veronica Camerada	Università degli Studi di Sassari, Italy

Workshop Program Committee Members

Giuseppe Borruso	University of Trieste, Italy
Beniamino Murgante	University of Basilicata, Italy
Ginevra Balletto	University of Cagliari, Italy
Silvia Battino	University of Sassari, Italy
Mara Ladu	University of Cagliari, Italy
Maria del Mar Munoz Leonisio	University of Cádiz, Spain
Ahinoa Amaro Garcia	University of Las Palmas of Gran Canaria, Spain
Maria Attard	University of Malta, Malta
Enrico D'agostini	World Maritime University, Sweden
Francesca Krasna	University of Trieste, Italy

Tu Anh Trinh	UEH University - Ho Chi Minh City, Vietnam
Giovanni Mauro	Università degli Studi della Campania, Italy
Maria Ronza	University of Naples Federico II, Italy
Massimiliano Bencardino	University of Salerno, Italy
Andrea Gallo	Ca' Foscari University of Venice, Italy
Francesca Sinatra	University of Trieste, Italy
Salvatore Dore	University of Trieste, Italy
Veronica Camerada	University of Sassari, Italy
Brunella Brundu	University of Sassari, Italy
Gianfranco Fancello	University of Cagliari, Italy
Marcello Tadini	University of Eastern Piedmont, Italy
Marco Mazzarino	IUAV University Venice
José Ángel Hernández Luis	University of Las Palmas de Gran Canaria, Spain
Marco Naseddu	University of Cagliari, Italy
Maurizio Cociancich	Adriafer, Italy
Giovanni Longo	University of Trieste, Italy
Luca Toneatti	University of Trieste, Italy
Martina Sinatra	University of Cagliari, Italy
Enrico Vanino	University of Sheffield, UK
Patrizia Serra	University of Cagliari, Italy
Agostino Bruzzone	University of Genoa, Italy
Marco Petrelli	University of Roma 3, Italy

Smart Transport and Logistics - Smart Supply Chains (SmarTransLog 2025)

Workshop Organizers

Francesca Sinatra	University of Trieste, Italy
Maria del Mar Munoz	Universidad de Cádiz, Spain
Brunella Brundu	University of Sassari, Italy
Patrizia Serra	University of Cagliari, Italy
Salvatore Dore	University of Trieste, Italy
Marco Naseddu	University of Cagliari, Italy

Workshop Program Committee Members

Giuseppe Borruso	University of Trieste, Italy
Beniamino Murgante	University of Basilicata, Italy
Ginevra Balletto	University of Cagliari, Italy
Silvia Battino	University of Sassari, Italy
Mara Ladu	University of Cagliari, Italy
Maria del Mar Munoz Leonisio	University of Cádiz, Spain
Ahinoa Amaro Garcia	University of Las Palmas of Gran Canaria, Spain

Maria Attard	University of Malta, Malta
Enrico D'agostini	World Maritime University, Sweden
Francesca Krasna	University of Trieste, Italy
Tu Anh Trinh	UEH University, Vietnam
Giovanni Mauro	Università degli Studi della Campania, Italy
Maria Ronza	University of Naples Federico II, Italy
Massimiliano Bencardino	University of Salerno, Italy
Andrea Gallo	Ca' Foscari University of Venice, Italy
Francesca Sinatra	University of Trieste, Italy
Salvatore Dore	University of Trieste, Italy
Veronica Camerada	University of Sassari, Italy
Brunella Brundu	University of Sassari, Italy
Gianfranco Fancello	University of Cagliari, Italy
Marcello Tadini	University of Eastern Piedmont, Italy
Marco Mazzarino	IUAV University Venice
José Ángel Hernández Luis	University of Las Palmas de Gran Canaria, Spain
Marco Naseddu	University of Cagliari, Italy
Maurizio Cociancich	Adriafer, Italy
Giovanni Longo	University of Trieste, Italy
Luca Toneatti	University of Trieste, Italy
Martina Sinatra	University of Cagliari, Italy
Enrico Vanino	University of Sheffield, UK
Patrizia Serra	University of Cagliari, Italy
Agostino Bruzzone	University of Genoa, Italy
Marco Petrelli	University of Roma 3, Italy

Smart Tourism (SmartTourism 2025)

Workshop Organizers

Silvia Battino	University of Sassari, Italy
Francesca Krasna	University of Trieste, Italy
Ainhoa Amaro	University of Las Palmas de Gran Canaria, Spain
Maria del Mar Munoz	University of Cádiz, Spain
Brisol García García	Polytechnic University of Quintana Roo, Mexico
Marta Meleddu	University of Sassari, Italy

Workshop Program Committee Members

Giuseppe Borruso	University of Trieste, Italy
Beniamino Murgante	University of Basilicata, Italy
Gianfranco Fancello	University of Cagliari, Italy
Mara Ladu	University of Cagliari, Italy

Martina Sinatra	University of Cagliari, Italy
Salvatore Dore	University of Trieste, Italy
Marco Mazzarino	IUAV University Venice, Italy
Veronica Camerada	University of Sassari, Italy
Brunella Brundu	University of Sassari, Italy
Maria Attard	University of Malta, Malta
Ginevra Balletto	University of Cagliari, Italy
Giovanni Mauro	University degli Studi della Campania, Italy
Salvatore Lampreu	University of Sassari, Italy
Maria Ronza	University of Naples, Italy
Massimiliano Bencardino	University of Salerno, Italy

Sustainable evolution of long-Distance frEight and paSsenger Transport (SOLIDEST 2025)

Workshop Organizers

Francesco Russo	University of Reggio Calabria, Italy
Andreas Nikiforiadis	Democritus University of Thrace, Greece
Orlando Marco Belcore	University of Messina, Italy
Antonio Comi	University of Rome Tor Vergata, Italy
Tiziana Campisi	Kore University of Enna, Italy
Aura Rusca	Politehnica University of Bucharest, Romania

Workshop Program Committee Members

Massimo Di Gangi	University of Messina, Italy
Orlando Marco Belcore	University of Messina, Italy
Antonio Polimeni	University of Messina, Italy
Socrates Basbas	Aristotle University of Thessaloniki, Greece
Efstathios Bouhouras	Aristotle University of Thessaloniki, Greece
Marina Zanne	University of Lubljana, Slovenia
Marilisa Nigro	Rome Tre University, Italy
Edoardo Marcucci	Molde University College, Norway
Eugen Rosca	Polytechnic University of Bucharest, Romania
Kh Md Nahiduzzaman	Mohammed VI Polytechnic University, Morocco
Beniamino Murgante	University of Basilicata, Italy
Chiara Garau	University of Cagliari, Italy

Sustainability Performance Assessment: Models, Approaches, and Applications Toward Interdisciplinary and Integrated Solutions (SPA 2025)

Workshop Organizers

Francesco Scorza	University of Basilicata, Italy
Sabrina Lai	University of Cagliari, Italy
Francesco Rotondo	Università Politecnica delle Marche, Italy
Jolanta Dvarioniene	Kaunas University of Technology, Lithuania
Michele Campagna	University of Cagliari, Italy
Corrado Zoppi	University of Cagliari, Italy

Workshop Program Committee Members

Federico Amato	University of Lausanne, Switzerland
Ferdinando Di Carlo	University of Basilicata, Italy
Maddalena Floris	University of Cagliari, Italy
Federica Isola	University of Cagliari, Italy
Giuseppe Las Casas	University of Basilicata, Italy
Federica Leone	University of Cagliari, Italy
Giampiero Lombardini	University of Genoa, Italy
Federico Martellozzo	University of Florence, Italy
Alessandro Marucci	University of L'Aquila, Italy
Ana Clara Moura	Universidade Federal de Minas Gerais, Brazil
Beniamino Murgante	University of Basilicata, Italy
Silviu Nate	Lucian Blaga University of Sibiu, Romania
Anastasia Stratigea	National Technical University of Athens, Greece
Francesco Zullo	University of L'Aquila, Italy
Luigi Santopietro	University of Basilicata, Italy
Benedetto Manganelli	University of Basilicata, Italy

Specifics of Smart Cities Development in Europe (SPEED 2025)

Workshop Organizers

Chiara Garau	University of Cagliari, Italy
Katarína Vitálišová	Matej Bel University, Slovak Republic
Marco Fanfani	University of Florence, Italy
Anna Vaňová	Matej Bel University, Slovak Republic
Kamila Borsekova	Matej Bel University, Slovak Republic
Paola Zamperlin	University of Florence, Italy

Workshop Program Committee Members

Claudia Loggia	University of KwaZulu-Natal, South Africa
Francesca Maltinti	University of Cagliari, Italy
Alessandro Plaisant	University of Sassari, Italy
Alenka Poplin	Iowa State University, USA
Silvia Rossetti	University of Parma, Italy
Gerardo Carpentieri	University of Naples Federico II, Italy
Carmen Guida	University of Naples Federico II, Italy
Floriana Zucaro	University of Naples Federico II, Italy
Anastasia Stratigea	National Technical University of Athens, Greece
Yiota Theodora	National Technical University of Athens, Greece
Giovanna Concu	University of Cagliari, Italy
Paolo Nesi	University of Florence, Italy
Emanuele Bellini	University of Roma Tre, Italy
Mana Dastoum	Polytechnic University of Madrid, Spain
Barbara Caselli	University of Parma, Italy
Martina Carra	University of Brescia, Italy
Alfonso Annunziata	University of Basilicata, Italy
Elisabetta Venco	University of Pavia, Italy
Caterina Pietra	University of Pavia, Italy
Enrico Collini	University of Florence, Italy
Luciano Alessandro Ipsaro Palesi	University of Florence, Italy

Smart, Safe, and Healthy Cities (SSHC 2025)

Workshop Organizers

Chiara Garau	University of Cagliari, Italy
Gerardo Carpentieri	University of Naples Federico II, Italy
Carmen Guida	University of Naples Federico II, Italy
Tanja Congiu	University of Sassari, Italy
Martina Carra	University of Brescia, Italy
Alenka Poplin	Iowa State University, USA

Workshop Program Committee Members

Rosaria Battarra	Istituto di Studi sul Mediterraneo, Italy
Barbara Caselli	University of Parma, Italy
Francesca Maltinti	University of Cagliari, Italy
Romano Fistola	Università degli Studi di Napoli Federico II, Italy
Alessandro Plaisant	University of Sassari, Italy
Silvia Rossetti	University of Parma, Italy
Marco Fanfani	University of Florence, Italy
Reza Askarizad	University of Cagliari, Italy

Floriana Zucaro	University of Naples Federico II, Italy
Anastasia Stratigea	National Technical University of Athens, Greece
Yiota Theodora	National Technical University of Athens, Greece
Giovanna Concu	University of Cagliari, Italy
Francesco Zullo	University of L'Aquila, Italy
Paola Zamperlin	University of Florence, Italy
Vincenza Torrisi	University of Catania, Italy
Tiziana Campisi	University of Enna Kore, Italy
Katarína Vitálišová	Matej Bel University, Slovakia
Tazyeen Alam	University of Cagliari, Italy
Mana Dastoum	Polytechnic University of Madrid, Spain
Martina Carra	University of Brescia, Italy
Alfonso Annunziata	University of Basilicata, Italy
Elisabetta Venco	University of Pavia, Italy
Caterina Pietra	University of Pavia, Italy

Smart and Sustainable Island Communities (SSIC 2025)

Workshop Organizers

Chiara Garau	University of Cagliari, Italy
Anastasia Stratigea	National Technical University of Athens, Greece
Yiota Theodora	National Technical University of Athens, Greece
Giovanna Concu	University of Cagliari, Italy

Workshop Program Committee Members

Milena Metalkova-Markova	University of Portsmouth, UK
Tarek Teba	University of Portsmouth, UK
Alenka Poplin	Iowa State University, USA
Gerardo Carpentieri	University of Naples Federico II, Italy
Carmen Guida	University of Naples Federico II, Italy
Floriana Zucaro	University of Naples Federico II, Italy
Silvia Rossetti	University of Parma, Italy
Barbara Caselli	University of Parma, Italy
Martina Carra	University of Brescia, Italy
Alfonso Annunziata	University of Basilicata, Italy
Maria Panagiotopoulou	National Technical University of Athens, Greece
Apostolos Lagarias	University of Thessaly, Greece
Paola Zamperlin	University of Florence, Italy
Vincenza Torrisi	University of Catania, Italy
Giuseppina Vacca	University of Cagliari, Italy
Roberto Minunno	Curtin University, Australia
Marco Zucca	University of Cagliari, Italy

Elisabetta Venco   University of Pavia, Italy
Caterina Pietra   University of Pavia, Italy
Pietro Crespi   Politecnico di Milano, Italy

From STreet Experiments to Planned Solutions (STEPS 2025)

Workshop Organizers
Silvia Rossetti   Università degli Studi di Parma, Italy
Angela Ricciardello   Kore University of Enna, Italy
Francesco Pinna   Università degli Studi di Cagliari, Italy
Chiara Garau   Università degli Studi di Cagliari, Italy
Tiziana Campisi   Kore University of Enna, Italy
Vincenza Torrisi   University of Catania, Italy

Workshop Program Committee Members
Martina Carra   University of Brescia, Italy
Barbara Caselli   University of Parma, Italy
Tanja Congiu   University of Sassari, Italy
Gabriele D'Orso   University of Palermo, Italy
Matteo Ignaccolo   University of Catania, Italy
Md Kh Nahiduzzaman   Mohammed VI Polytechnic University, Morocco
Muhammad Ahmad Al-Rashid   University of Malaya, Malaysia
Alessandro Plaisant   University of Sassari, Italy
Marianna Ruggieri   University of Enna Kore, Italy
Michele Zazzi   University of Parma, Italy

Sustainable Tourism Evaluations: approaches, methods and indicators (STEva 2025)

Workshop Organizers
Mariolina Grasso   Università Kore di Enna, Italy
Fabrizio Finucci   Roma Tre University, Italy
Daniele Mazzoni   Roma Tre University, Italy
Antonella G. Masanotti   Roma Tre University, Italy
Giovanna Acampa   University of Florence, Italy

Workshop Program Committee Members
Giovanna Acampa   University of Florence, Italy
Fabrizio Finucci   Roma Tre University, Italy
Mariolina Grasso   "Kore" University of Enna, Italy

Alberto Marzo	Ministero della Cultura, Italy
Antonella G. Masanotti	Roma Tre University, Italy
Daniele Mazzoni	Roma Tre University, Italy
Rocco Murro	Sapienza University of Rome, Italy
Claudio Piferi	University of Florence, Italy
Alessio Pino	"Kore" University of Enna, Italy
Nicoletta Setola	University of Florence, Italy
Laura Calcagnini	Roma Tre University, Italy
Antonio Magarò	Roma Tre University, Italy
Janos Ghyerghyak	University of Pécs, Hungary
Ágnes Borsos	University of Pécs, Hungary
Fabrizio Battisti	University of Florence, Italy

Sustainable Development of Ports (SUSTAINABLEPORTS 2025)

Workshop Organizers

Tiziana Campisi	University of Enna KORE, Italy
Giuseppe Musolino	University of Reggio Calabria, Italy
Efstathios Bouhouras	Aristotle University of Thessaloniki, Greece
Elen Twrdy	University of Ljubljana, Slovenia
Elena Cocuzza	University of Catania, Italy
Aura Rusca	Politehnica University of Bucharest, Romania

Workshop Program Committee Members

Massimo Di Gangi	University of Messina, Italy
Orlando Marco Belcore	University of Messina, Italy
Antonio Polimeni	University of Messina, Italy
Claudia Caballini	Polytechnic of Torino, Italy
Gianfranco Fancello	University of Cagliari, Italy
Marina Zanne	University of Lubljana, Slovenia
Stefano Ricci	Sapienza University of Rome, Italy
Beniamino Murgante	University of Basilicata, Italy
Chiara Garau	University of Cagliari, Italy

Theoretical and Computational Chemistry and Its Applications (TCCMA 2025)

Workshop Organizers

Noelia Faginas Lago	Università di Perugia, Italy
Andrea Lombardi	Università di Perugia, Italy
Marcos Mandado Alonso	University of Vigo, Spain

Workshop Program Committee Members

Noelia Faginas-Lago	University of Perugia, Italy
Andrea Lombardi	University of Perugia, Italy
Marcos Mandado	University of Vigo, Spain
Angeles Peña	University of Vigo, Spain
Luca Mancini	Universiy of Perugia, Italy
Massimiliano Bartolomei	CSIC, Spain
Cecilia Coletti	University of Chieti-Pescara, Italy
Iñaki Tuñón	Universidad de Valencia, Spain
Albert Rimola Gilbert	Universitat Autònoma de Barcelona, Spain
Stefano Falcinelli	University of Perugia, Italy
Dario Campisi	University of Perugia, Italy
Ernesto García Para	University of the Basque Country, Spain
Giacomo Giorgi	University of Perugia, Italy
Tomás González Lezana	IFF CSIC, Spain
Enrique M. Cabaleiro Lago	Universidade de Santiago de Compostela, Spain
Aurora Costales	Universidad de Oviedo, Spain
Angel Martin	Universidad de Oviedo, Spain
Jose Manuel	University of Vigo, Spain
Annarita Laricchiuta	CNR ISTP Bari, Italy
Fernando Pirani	University of Perugia, Italy

Transport Infrastructures for Smart Cities (TISC 2025)

Workshop Organizers

Francesca Maltinti	University of Cagliari, Italy
Mauro Coni	University of Cagliari, Italy
Benedetto Barabino	University of Brescia, Italy
Nicoletta Rassu	University of Cagliari, Italy
James Rombi	University of Cagliari, Italy

Workshop Program Committee Members

Francesco Pinna	University of Cagliari, Italy
Chiara Garau	University of Cagliari, Italy
Mauro D'Apuzzo	University of Cassino, Italy
Roberto Minunno	Curtin University, Australia
Tiziana Campisi	University of Enna Kore, Italy
Roberto Ventura	University of Brescia, Italy
Alessandro Plaisant	University of Sassari, Italy
Massimo Di Francesco	University of Cagliari, Italy

| Vincenza Torrisi | University of Catania, Italy |
| Paola Zamperlin | University of Florence, Italy |

Transforming Urban Analytics: The Impact of Crowdsourced Mapping and Advanced AI Techniques on Future Cities (Tr-UrbAna 2025)

Workshop Organizers

Ayse Giz Gulnerman Gengec	Ankara Hacı Bayram Veli University, Turkey
Müslüm Hacar	Tildiz Technical University, Turkey
Himmet Karaman	Istanbul Technical University, Turkey

Workshop Program Committee Members

Beniamino Murgante	University of Basilicata, Italy
Abdulkadir Memduhoğlu	Harran University, Turkey
Zeynel Abidin Polat	İzmir Katip Çelebi University, Turkey
Güzide Miray Perihanoğlu	Van Yüzüncü Yıl University, Turkey
Tugba Memisoglu Baykal	Ankara Hacı Bayram Veli University, Turkey

From structural to TRAnsformative-change of City Environment: challenges and solutions and perspectives (TRACE 2025)

Workshop Organizers

Pierluigi Morano	Polytechnic University of Bari, Italy
Maria Rosaria Guarini	Sapienza University of Rome, Italy
Francesco Sica	Sapienza University of Rome, Italy
Francesco Tajani	Sapienza University of Rome, Italy
Marco Locurcio	Polytechnic University of Bari, Italy
Debora Anelli	Polytechnic University of Bari, Italy

Workshop Program Committee Members

Felicia di Liddo	Politecnico di Bari, Italia
Valeria Saiu	Università di Cagliari, Italia
Emma Sabatelli	Sapienza Università di Roma, Italia
Antonella Roma	Sapienza Università di Roma, Italia
Giuseppe Cerullo	Sapienza Università di Roma, Italia
Lucia della Spina	Università di Reggio Calabria, Italia
Alejandro Segura de la Cal	Politecnico di Madrid, Spain
Yilsy Nuñez	Politecnico di Madrid, Spain
Gabriella Maselli	Università di Salerno, Italy
Maria Rosa Trovato	Università di Catania, Italy

Manuela Rebaudengo   Politecnico di Torino, Italy
Pierfrancesco De Paola   Università di Napoli Federico II, Italy
Daniela Tavano   Università della Calabria, Italy
Maria Saez   University of Granada, Spain
Paola Amoruso   LUM "Giuseppe Degennaro" University, Italy

Temporary Real Estate management: Approaches and methods for Time-integrated impact assessments and evaluations (TREAT 2025)

Workshop Organizers
Chiara Mazzarella   TUDelft, The Netherlands
Hilde Remoy   TUDelft, The Netherlands
Maria Cerreta   University of Naples Federico II, Italy

Workshop Program Committee Members
Chiara Mazzarella   TU Delft, The Netherlands
Hilde Remoy   TU Delft, The Netherlands
Maria Cerreta   University of Naples Federico II, Italy
Maria Somma   University of Naples Federico II, Italy
Simona Panaro   University of Campania Luigi Vanvitelli, Italy
Laura Di Tommaso   University of Naples Federico II, Italy
Caterina Loffredo   University of Naples Federico II, Italy
Ludovica La Rocca   University of Naples Federico II, Italy
Sabrina Sacco   Politecnico di Milano, Italy
Piero Zizzania   University of Naples Federico II, Italy
Gaia Daldanise   CNR IRISS, Italy
Benedetta Grieco   University of Naples Federico II, Italy
Giuseppe Ciciriello   University of Naples Federico II, Italy
Marta Dell'Ovo   Politecnico di Milano, Italy
Daniele Cannatella   TU Delft, The Netherlands
Eugenio Muccio   University of Naples Federico II, Italy
Sveva Ventre   University of Naples Federico II, Italy

Supporting the Transition to Ecological Economy in Cities Regeneration: Circular Model Tools for Reusing Architecture and Infrastructures (TReE 2025)

Workshop Organizers
Mariarosaria Angrisano   Pegaso University, Italy
Giulio Cavana   Politecnico di Torino, Italy
Francesca Buglione   CNR-ISPC, Italy

Antonia Gravagnuolo   CNR-ISPC, Italy
Piera Della Morte   Pegaso University, Italy

Workshop Program Committee Members

Giulia Datola   Politecnico di Milano, Italy
Vanessa Assumma   University of Bologna, Italy
Marco Volpatti   Politecnico di Torino, Italy
Sebastiano Barbieri   Politecnico di Torino, Italy
Caterina Caprioli   Politecnico di Torino, Italy
Marta Dell'Ovo   Politecnico di Milano, Italy
Federico Dell'Anna   Politecnico di Torino, Italy
Elena Todella   Politecnico di Torino, Italy
Danny Casprini   Politecnico di Milano, Italy
Grazia Neglia   Università Telematica Pegaso, Italy
Francesca Nocca   Università degli Studi di Napoli Federico II, Italy
Giulio Cavana   Politecnico di Torino, Italy
Francesca Buglione   CNR-IPSC, Italy
Marco Rossitti   Politecnico di Milano, Italy
Jhon Escorcia   Politecnico di Torino, Italy
Beatrice Mecca   Politecnico di Torino, Italy
Sara Biancifiori   Politecnico di Torino, Italy

Urban Digital Twins and Data Spaces: Shaping the Future of Sustainable Cities (TwinAbleCities 2025)

Workshop Organizers

Dessislava Petrova Antonova   Sofia University, GATE Institute, Bulgaria
Beniamino Murgante   University of Basilicata, Italy
Senthil Rajendran   RMSI, Bahrain
Tiziana Campisi   Kore University of Enna, Italy
Mila Koeva   University of Twente, The Netherlands

Workshop Program Committee Members

Dessislava Petrova-Antonova   Sofia University, Bulgaria
Mila Koeva   The University of Twente, The Netherlands
Beniamino Murgante   University of Basilicata, Italy
Senthil Rajendran   RMSI, Bahrain
Tiziana Campisi   Kore University of Enna, Italy

Urban Regeneration: Innovative Tools and Evaluation Model (URITEM 2025)

Workshop Organizers

Fabrizio Battisti	University of Florence, Italy
Giovanna Acampa	University of Florence, Italy
Orazio Campo	Sapienza University of Rome, Italy
Melania Perdonò	University of Florence, Italy

Workshop Program Committee Members

Fabrizio Battisti	University of Florence, Italy
Giovanna Acampa	University of Florence, Italy
Orazio Campo	University of Rome "La Sapienza", Italy
Melania Perdonò	Università degli Studi di Firenze, Italy

Urban Space Accessibility and Mobilities (USAM 2025)

Workshop Organizers

Chiara Garau	DICAAR, University of Cagliari, Italy
Alessandro Plaisant	University of Sassari, Italy
Barbara Caselli	University of Parma, Italy
Mauro D'Apuzzo	University of Cassino and Southern Lazio, Italy
Gabriele D'Orso	University of Palermo, Italy
Matteo Ignaccolo	University of Catania, Italy

Workshop Program Committee Members

Mauro Coni	University of Cagliari, Italy
Martina Carra	University of Brescia, Italy
Tiziana Campisi	University of Enna Kore, Italy
Tanja Congiu	University of Sassari, Italy
Francesca Maltinti	University of Cagliari, Italy
Silvia Rossetti	University of Parma, Italy
Barbara Caselli	University of Parma, Italy
Angela Pilogallo	University of L'Aquila, Italy
Lorena Fiorini	University of L'Aquila, Italy
Reza Askarizad	University of Cagliari, Italy
Francesco Pinna	University of Cagliari, Italy
Aime Tsinda	University of Rwanda, Rwanda
Youssef El Ganadi	International University of Rabat, Morocco
Marco Migliore	University of Palermo, Italy
Alessio Salvatore	Italian National Research Council, Italy
Giuseppe Stecca	Italian National Research Council, Italy

Paola Zamperlin	University of Florence, Italy
Vincenza Torrisi	University of Catania, Italy
Gerardo Carpentieri	University of Naples Federico II, Italy
Carmen Guida	University of Naples Federico II, Italy
Floriana Zucaro	University of Naples Federico II, Italy
Alfonso Annunziata	University of Basilicata, Italy
Elisabetta Venco	University of Pavia, Italy
Caterina Pietra	University of Pavia, Italy
Tazyeen Alam	University of Cagliari, Italy
Valerio Cutini	University of Pisa, Italy

UX Mobility 2025: Placing User Experience at the Center of Urban Mobility: Methods and Frameworks (UXM 2025)

Workshop Organizers

Carmen Guida	Università degli Studi di Napoli Federico II, Italy
Gerardo Carpentieri	Università degli Studi di Napoli Federico II, Italy
Federico Messa	Systematica srl, Italy
Lamia Abdelfattah	Systematica srl, Italy

Workshop Program Committee Members

Rosaria Battarra	Istituto di Studi sul Mediterraneo CNR, Italy
Romano Fistola	Università degli Studi di Napoli Federico II, Italy
Lucia Saganeiti	IMAA-CNR, Italy

Virtual Reality and Augmented reality and applications (VRA 2025)

Workshop Organizers

Damiano Perri	University of Perugia, Italy
Osvaldo Gervasi	University of Perugia, Italy
Chau Ma Thi	University of Engineering and Technology, Vietnam National University, Hanoi, Vietnam
Paolo Nesi	University of Florence, Italy
Pierfrancesco Bellini	University of Florence, Italy

Workshop Program Committee Members

| David Berti | ART SpA, Italy |
| JungYoon Kim | Gachon University, South Korea |

TaiHoon Kim	Zhejiang University of Science and Technology, China
Marcelo de Paiva Guimares	Federal University of São Paulo, Brazil
Sergio Tasso	University of Perugia, Italy

Workshop on Advanced and Computational Methods for Earth Science Applications (WACM4ES 2025)

Workshop Organizers

Luca Piroddi	University of Cagliari, Italy
Patrizia Capizzi	University of Palermo, Italy
Marilena Cozzolino	University of Molise, Italy
Sebastiano D'Amico	University of Malta, Malta
Chiara Garau	University of Cagliari, Italy
Giuseppina Vacca	University of Cagliari, Italy

Workshop Program Committee Members

Andrea Angelini	CNR ISPC, Italy
Ilaria Barone	Università degli Studi di Padova, Italy
Patrizia Capizzi	University of Palermo, Italy
Luigi Capozzoli	CNR, Italy
Alberto Carletti	University of Cagliari, Italy
Emanuele Colica	University of Malta, Malta
Marilena Cozzolino	Università del Molise, Italy
Sebastiano D'Amico	University of Malta, Malta
Chiara Garau	University of Cagliari, Italy
Luciano Galone	University of Malta, Malta
Peter Iregbeyen	University of Malta, Malta
Mariano Lisi	Basilicata Aerospace Cluster CLAS, Italy
Raffaele Martorana	Università di Palermo, Italy
Paolo Mauriello	Università del Molise, Italy
Veronica Pazzi	University of Florence, Italy
Raffaele Persico	Università della Calabria, Italy
Luca Piroddi	University of Cagliari, Italy
Sina Saneiyan	Binghamton University, USA
Mercedes Solla	Universidade de Vigo, Spain
Deodato Tapete	ASI, Italy
Giuseppina Vacca	University of Cagliari, Italy
Enrica Vecchi	University of Cagliari, Italy

Sponsoring Organizations

ICCSA 2025 would not have been possible without the tremendous support of many organizations and institutions, for which all organizers and participants of ICCSA 2025 express their sincere gratitude:

Galatasaray University, Istanbul, Türkiye
(https://gsu.edu.tr/en)

African Mathematical Union
(https://www.africanmathunion.org/)

Springer Nature Switzerland AG, Switzerland
(https://www.springer.com)

The University of Massachusetts, USA
(https://www.umass.edu/)

University of Perugia, Italy
(https://www.unipg.it)

University of Basilicata, Italy
(http://www.unibas.it)

Monash University, Australia
(https://www.monash.edu/)

Kyushu Sangyo University, Japan
(https://www.kyusan-u.ac.jp/)

Universidade do Minho
Escola de Engenharia

University of Minho, Portugal
(https://www.uminho.pt/)
Venue
ICCSA 2025 took place in: **Galatasaray University, Istanbul, Türkiye**

Additional Reviewers

Reviewers
The review tasks for each workshop have been carried out by the workshop Organizers
and the members of the workshop Program Committee.

Plenary Lectures

Sky Safe with GAI and Post-quantum Computing

Elizabeth Chang

Professor of Cyber Security and Head of Discipline, University of the Sunshine Coast, Australia

Abstract. Professor Chang's talk in this presentation has two distinct parts. To start, she will introduce the landscape of cybersecurity development, attacks, threats, and vulnerabilities, as well as state-of-the-art cyber protection, cyber defence, and cyber incident prevention. This is followed by a discussion of the impact of Generative AI (GAI) and quantum-safe cryptographic computing, highlighting the major issues and challenges in research, education, and training. In conclusion, she will present a vision for Sky Safe solutions, aiming to achieve cyber resilience that supports business and economic stability, enhances human capabilities, and promotes environmental sustainability.

Disaster Preparedness and Risk Profiling in the Digital Era from Earth Observation Lens

Jagannath Aryal

Department of Infrastructure Engineering, University of Melbourne, Australia

Abstract. Natural hazards which turn into disasters result in severe losses of lives, infrastructure, and property. Disasters such as earthquakes and landslides and their impacts on transportation safety, infrastructure resilience, and displacement of people to new places are challenges. To address such challenges, earth observation data and intelligent methods can provide potential solutions in developing decision support systems. This talk will present the state of the art in Earth observation for disaster resilience using intelligent methods. In the Earth observation space, digitalisation has revolutionised the way we map, monitor, and develop decision support systems. Global case study examples covering earthquake-induced landslides from the Himalayan region will cover the digital capabilities. The digital capabilities will embrace object recognition, interpretation, and their accurate and precise capture to integrate into digital models. The developed digital models from representative case studies can be leveraged in other jurisdictions in profiling risks to protect lives and infrastructure and creating disaster preparedness in the era of digital age and digital economy.

Intelligent Image Enhancement for Real-World Applications in Adverse Atmospheric Conditions

Khan Muhammad

Department of Global Convergence, Sungkyunkwan University, South Korea

Abstract. The adverse impacts of atmospheric conditions such as haze, fog, and low-light environments pose significant challenges for real-world applications reliant on computer vision, including autonomous driving, surveillance, and remote sensing. This keynote explores cutting-edge advancements in intelligent image enhancement, drawing insights from two pivotal studies. The first introduces HazeSpace2M, a comprehensive dataset and novel classification-guided dehazing framework that improves image clarity across diverse atmospheric conditions, addressing the gap between synthetic and real-world dehazing performance. The second focuses on LoLI-Street, a benchmark for low-light image enhancement tailored to urban environments, extending beyond enhancement to enable robust object detection and scene understanding. Taken together, these contributions demonstrate how integrating domain-specific datasets, advanced algorithms, and performance benchmarks can significantly elevate the reliability of computer vision systems under challenging weather and lighting conditions. Attendees will gain valuable insights into the methodologies, datasets, and practical applications driving innovation in this field, with implications for research and industry alike.

In Memory of Carmelo Torre

Unfortunately, Professor Carmelo Torre, one of the cornerstones of the ICCSA Conference, passed away last December, leaving everyone stunned and deeply saddened. His loss has created a profound void within our academic community. Carmelo was not only a respected scholar and dedicated contributor to the success and growth of ICCSA, but also a generous colleague, mentor, and friend to many. His intellectual rigor, warm personality, and unwavering commitment to advancing research will be remembered with great admiration. As we continue the work he helped shape, we honor his legacy and the indelible mark he left on all of us. Carmelo Torre graduated in engineering at the Polytechnic of Bari with a thesis on urban planning under Dino Borri's guidance. He began his research career by collaborating with Franco Selicato. During his PhD at the University of Naples Federico II under Luigi Fusco Girard, he specialized in real estate market analysis and multi-criteria evaluation methods. He explored the social impacts of urban transformations with his lifelong friend Maria Cerreta. His first ICCSA participation was in Perugia in 2008, in the session Geographical Analysis, Urban Modeling, Spatial Statistics. Instantly captivated by the conference, his charisma enabled him to involve various Italian scientific communities, including those in real estate and statistics. ICCSA became a yearly commitment for him, where he valued the high editorial quality of the proceedings and the dynamic post-presentation discussions and debates he passionately and expertly enriched. In 2012, alongside Maria Cerreta and Paola Perchinunno, he organized the workshop Econometrics and Multidimensional Evaluation in the Urban Environment (EMEUE), fostering dialogue on critical topics. His influence steadily grew, drawing numerous research groups to ICCSA and establishing real estate and assessment as one of the conference's leading fields. A pillar of ICCSA, he was involved across all facets of the event. Torre's contributions to academic discourse were marked by intellectual rigor and innovative thinking. His conference interventions consistently challenged conventional wisdom, offering insights transcending disciplinary boundaries. Beyond the conference, he passionately advocated for equity and social justice. His left-leaning ideology, though firm, earned respect from those with differing views, thanks to his sincerity and loyalty. He was creative, generous, and always willing to help, even at a personal cost. Despite battling illness, he maintained his characteristic optimism, warmth, cheerfulness, and commitment, supported by his partner, Caterina Rinaldo. His legacy lives on in his ideas, dedication, and unmatched generosity.

Contents – Part III

Computational Optimization and Applications (COA 2025)

Computational Astrochemistry 2025 (CompAstro 2025)

Computational Methods for Porous Geomaterials (CompPor 2025)

Bio and Neuro Inspired Computing and Applications (BIONCA 2025)

Using Differential Evolution for Minimal Routing in Network-on-Chips with 2D and 3D Mesh Topology

Maamar Bougherara[1,2(✉)], Nadia Nedjah[3], Djamel Bennouar[1],
and Luiza de Macedo Mourelle[4]

[1] LIM Laboratory, Bouira University, Bouira, Algeria
bougherara.maamar@gmail.com
[2] Département d'Informatique, École Normale Supérieure Kouba, Algiers, Algeria
[3] Department of Electronics Engineering and Telecommunications, State University of Rio de Janeiro, Rio de Janeiro, Brazil
[4] Department of Systems Engineering and Computation, State University of Rio de Janeiro, Rio de Janeiro, Brazil

Abstract. Network-on-Chip (NoC) represents an innovative approach to interconnecting components in System-on-Chip (SoC) designs, enabling the integration of complex elements. However, being a relatively new technology, it requires substantial research efforts, particularly to streamline and accelerate the design process. NoCs can be organized in various topologies, including ring, mesh, and torus. Since multiple data packets can be transmitted simultaneously, an effective routing strategy is essential to prevent congestion and minimize delays. This paper investigates the performance of a Differential Evolution-based routing algorithm in 2D and 3D mesh NoC topologies. The proposed routing strategy aims to minimize total packet transmission latency between tasks. Simulation results demonstrate the effectiveness of this algorithm, highlighting its performance compared to other routing techniques.

Keywords: Network on Chip · Routing · Differential Evolution · Congestion

1 Introduction

Network-on-Chip (NoC) has emerged as a promising solution to address communication bottlenecks within chips, functioning like a general network but constrained by limited resources. A NoC is specifically tailored to support a particular application. These types of applications are often constrained by the number of tasks that are integrated into Intellectual Property (IP) blocks.

The process of designing a NoC-based system involves several key stages, including task assignment to IP blocks [1], the allocation of IP cores [2], and the implementation of static routing [3]. Task assignment is the phase in which each task (or group of tasks) is allocated to a suitable IP block, chosen from a pre-existing repository. Mapping, on the other hand, refers to the process of placing the assigned IP blocks onto the nodes of

O. Gervasi et al. (Eds.): ICCSA 2025 Workshops, LNCS 15888, pp. 3–18, 2026.
https://doi.org/10.1007/978-3-031-97596-7_1

the NoC's communication infrastructure. Finally, routing determines the switches to be used for establishing communication paths between the cores.

Each of these stages is optimized using computer-aided tools, commonly referred to as Electronic Design Automation (EDA). An ideal EDA tool takes the application specification as input and produces a complete system design. In practical scenarios, the EDA tool refines both hardware and software characteristics to arrive at a solution that satisfies the design requirements. This optimization process is carried out in an iterative manner. The main phases of NoC design are illustrated in Fig. 1.

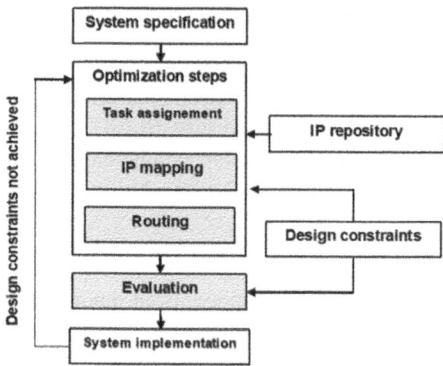

Fig. 1. Typical embedded system design flow for NoC platform.

In NoC architectures, communication delays can arise during congestion, when multiple packets attempt to pass through the same switch simultaneously. To mitigate this issue and enhance packet delivery speed, thereby improving overall system performance, this paper delves into route optimization. Specifically, it examines the static routing phase in NoC design, employing a genetic algorithm approach. The focus of this study is on routing within NoCs utilizing a 2D and 3D mesh topology.

The structure of the paper is as follows: Sect. 2 discusses 3D NoC topology and routing. Section 3 reviews prior research on routing algorithms. The routing approach is outlined in Sect. 4. In Sect. 5, we analyze the results of the simulation experiments. Finally, Sect. 6 presents the conclusion of the study and suggestions for future work.

2 Network Topology and Routing Problem

A Network-on-Chip (NoC) consists of four main components: resources (IPs), network interfaces (NIs), routers, and physical links. IPs include various components such as processors, memory, and controllers, which connect to routers via NIs.

The NI serves as a bridge between the NoC and IP protocols, separating computation from communication to enhance flexibility and IP reuse. Routers manage data transmission and arbitration between multiple port requests, while physical links establish logical connections between IPs, NIs, and routers. A tile in the NoC consists of an IP, an NI, and a router.

One of the simplest ways to connect tiles is through network topologies. Among them, the 2D mesh topology is the most widely adopted in NoCs due to its simplicity and scalability. Figure 2 illustrates the architecture of 2D Mesh Network on Chip.

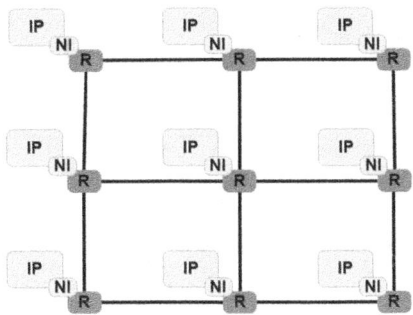

Fig. 2. 2D Mesh-based NoC.

However, two-dimensional NoCs often fail to meet the diverse requirements of System-on-Chip (SoC) designs. To address this, three-dimensional Network-on-Chip (3D NoC) architecture provides an effective solution to the interconnection complexities inherent in large-scale SoCs. By leveraging integrated circuit stacking technology, 3D NoC overcomes the performance and scalability limitations faced by traditional two-dimensional NoCs.

A three-dimensional (3D) mesh network is created by stacking multiple layers of 2D meshes and establishing vertical links for interlayer communication. One promising solution for these vertical interconnections is Through-Silicon Via (TSV) technology [5]. Each router in the network is responsible for buffering and routing messages between connected tiles. These routers can connect to up to six neighboring routers. This design allows one channel to transmit data while another channel buffers incoming data, enhancing overall efficiency. Figure 3 provides an illustration of the 3D mesh-based Network-on-Chip (NoC) architecture.

Routing algorithms play a vital role in determining the path a packet will follow from its source to its destination, and selecting the right algorithm is crucial when designing a 3D-NoC. Various challenges arise in NoC routing, such as congestion, deadlock, livelock, throughput, power consumption, delay, and more. The routing algorithm aims to optimize network performance by minimizing congestion and reducing communication delays between channels. Additionally, it considers factors like buffer size to select the best path, ensuring smooth traffic flow and preventing bottlenecks. Given the significance of these factors, routing algorithms have been the focus of extensive research since the introduction of NoCs. Below, we review some of the key studies on 3D routing.

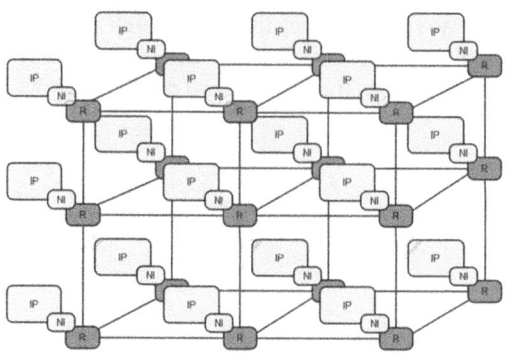

Fig. 3. 3D Mesh-based NoC with 27 resources.

3   Related Work

While numerous routing algorithms have been proposed for NoC systems, most focus primarily on 2D-NoC topologies. In the case of 3D-NoCs, relatively few studies have specifically addressed routing algorithms, which can be categorized into two main groups. The first group consists of well-established 2D-NoC routing schemes that have been adapted to the third dimension, such as Dimension Ordered Routing (DOR) [6], Valiant [7], O1TURN [8], and Odd-Even [9]. The second group is different from 2D NoCs, as only a few congestion-aware routing algorithms have been proposed for 3D NoCs, making it a less explored research area. DyXYZ [10] is an adaptive routing algorithm designed to address congestion issues in 3D NoCs. It uses congestion information from neighboring nodes to make handover decisions at the current node. The 3D-FAR algorithm, introduced in [11], is a regionally congestion-sensitive routing approach that organizes a clustering structure to gather and propagate congestion data. MAR, presented in [12], is an adaptive routing scheme that routes packets based on Hamiltonian paths, avoiding the need for virtual channels. In [13], the Global A (G-CARA) congestion-aware routing algorithm is introduced for traffic management in 3D NoCs. It effectively routes data packets to regions with lower traffic, preventing network congestion. FT-DyXYZ, discussed in [14], is an adaptive, fault-tolerant routing algorithm designed to handle permanent faulty links in 3D mesh NoCs. It uses proximity-based congestion information to balance the traffic load.

Metaheuristics have been employed as intelligent methods for creating efficient routing algorithms. One such approach is AntNet [15], a dynamic routing strategy for telecommunication networks. The routing problem is addressed in [16] for three different 3D NoC topology (mesh, torus and hypercube), based on the ant conlony metaheuristic. In [17, 18], a routing algorithm aimed at minimizing congestion is presented, utilizing Genetic Algorithm and Particle Swarm Optimization (PSO). The results show that PSO can achieve better performance, especially when the paths are deterministic, in both 2D and 3D NoCs.

4   Routing Algorithm Approach

The encoding of the routing problem relies on the definition and use of certain essential objects. Before presenting the routing algorithm, these objects must be defined, along with the key parameters, notably the concept of a solution:

1. Path: A path between a source (Src) and a destination (Dst) is a set of intermediate nodes that ensures the transport of packets from the source to the destination. There are two types of paths: minimal and non-minimal.
    - A path is said to be minimal if it connects a source with coordinates (x_i, y_i, z_i) to a destination with coordinates (x_j, y_j, z_j) with a length equal to the Manhattan distance.
    - A path is said to be non-minimal if its length is determined by Eq. 1:

$$\text{length}(r_i, r_j) = \text{nLinks}(r_i, r_j) + x, \tag{1}$$

   where x is a user-defined parameter that limits the number of additional hops required to construct a non-minimal path.
2. Set of paths: For optimal routing, the pair (Src, Dst) represents a communication between a source Src and a destination Dst, and it should not be based on a single path. It is necessary to create several different paths of the same pair, in order to be able to choose the efficient path. Despite the random aspect of our approach, we proposed to generate s different and random paths between each pair (Src, Dst). Among which, the best path will be kept in the final set of paths of the solution. The Table 1 shows 5 possible paths for the same pair (Src, Dst).

Table 1. Multiple paths of the same pair

Pair (Src, Dst)	Path ID	Path
(13, 8)	1	[13, 9, 5, 6, 7, 8]
	2	[13, 9, 10, 11, 12, 8]
	3	[13, 14, 15, 16, 12, 8]
	4	[13, 14, 10, 11, 7, 8]
	5	[13, 9, 10, 6, 7, 8]

3. Complete solution: A complete solution includes the set of paths connecting several pairs of nodes concerned by routing according to the type of application to implement in the NoC. In the first step, the choice of the best path among the s generated paths is done randomly. The algorithm then takes over to select the optimal solution based on the objective. Table 2 shows an example of a complete solution chosen among the paths that exist on each of the (Src, Dst) pairs.

The final solution obtained at this level consists of a set of paths connecting the different pairs, (Src, Dst), according to the type of application. These paths are saved in a file in the form of routing tables, used by the router.

Table 2. Complete routing solution

Pair (Src, Dst)	Chosen Path ID	Path Detail
(6, 16)	4	[6, 10, 11, 12, 16]
(1, 11)	1	[1, 2, 3, 7, 11]
(10, 4)	5	[10, 11, 12, 8, 4]
(9, 15)	2	[9, 10, 14, 15]
(13, 8)	3	[13, 14, 15, 16, 12, 8]

Routing optimization in NoCs aims to reduce communication latency, thereby shortening the execution time of embedded applications. For a set of simultaneous communications, two main objectives must be minimized: packet transmission delay and the number of nodes traversed between the source and destination.

Congestion occurs when incoming traffic exceeds the network's capacity, leading to queuing delays, packet loss, and communication blockages [19]. Increasing buffer size can help mitigate congestion but introduces area overhead, while limiting buffer size degrades Network-on-Chip (NoC) performance.

A congestion scenario arises when a single communication channel must handle multiple packets from different sources simultaneously, causing delays despite the use of minimal paths. To address this issue, adaptive routing algorithms consider both node positions and real-time network load, selecting less congested paths even if they are non-minimal.

Congestion is quantified as a cost reflecting network link usage. Initially set to zero, the cost increases as links are used. The congestion cost function for a path of length L is expressed as follows:

$$Congestion_p ath_i = \sum_{j=1}^{links(i)} C_{i,j}, \tag{2}$$

where $C_{i,j}$ represents the congestion cost of the jth link. The total network congestion is:

$$Congestion(S) = \sum_{i=1}^{l} Congestion_p ath_i. \tag{3}$$

4.1 Differential Evolution

Differential Evolution (DE), proposed by Price and Storn in 1997 [20], is an evolutionary algorithm related to genetic algorithms but uses different operators and mechanisms. It is an algorithm based on an initial population like genetic algorithms. In differential evolution, not only the operations are used with a different order, but the content of the operations also changes. The main distinction between DE and genetic algorithms resides in their exploration mechanisms. While genetic algorithms depend mainly on crossover to produce new solutions, DE is driven by mutation, which is based on the difference vectors computed from randomly selected solution pairs. The search process of the algorithm is driven by the mutation operator, whereas the selection mechanism directs the convergence towards optimal regions within the search space. The algorithm notation $(DE/x/y/z)$ is generally used to define a DE strategy [21] such that: The variable x identifies the target vector for mutation, which may correspond to a randomly selected population member or the best individual of the current generation. The parameter y specifies the number of differential vectors used to perturb the target vector, and z denotes the adopted crossover scheme, typically chosen between exponential and binomial variants.

4.2 DE Algorithm Steps

Differential Evolution (DE) is a population-based global optimization algorithm. It initializes a population composed of N individuals, each represented as a D-dimensional vector. Every individual corresponds to a potential solution, $X_{i,t} = \{x_{i,t}^1, .., x_{i,t}^D\}$, $i = 1, .., N$, where G indicates the generation to which the population belongs [22]. The initial population is randomly generated from the entire search space. The main steps of the DE algorithm are as follows [23]:

1. Mutation operation: The mutation operator is responsible for generating diversity within the population by producing a mutant vector $v_{i,t}$ for each individual $x_{i,t}$ at generation t. This operator is designed according to specific strategies, among which the most widely used are reported in Table 3 [24].

Table 3. Mutation strategies used

Mutation	Function
DE/rand/1	$v_{i,t} = x_{r_1,t} + F.(x_{r_2,t} - x_{r_3,t})$
DE/best/1	$v_{i,t} = x_{best,t} + F.(x_{r_1,t} - x_{r_2,t})$
DE/best/2	$v_{i,t} = x_{best,t} + F.(x_{r_1,t} - x_{r_2,t}) + F.(x_{r_3,t} - x_{r_4,t})$
DE/rand/2	$v_{i,t} = x_{r_1,t} + F.(x_{r_2,t} - x_{r_3,t}) + F.(x_{r_4,t} - x_{r_5,t})$
DE/current-to-best/2	$v_{i,t} = x_{i,t} + F.(x_{best,t} - x_{r_1,t}) + F.(x_{r_2,t} - x_{r_3,t})$
DE/current-to-rand/2	$v_{i,t} = x_{i,t} + F.(x_{r_1,t} - x_{r_2,t}) + F.(x_{r_3,t} - x_{r_4,t})$

The mutant vector $v_{i,t}$ is obtained through the mutation process. The integers r_1, r_2, r_3, r_4 and r_5 are randomly from $[1..N]$ and are distinct from the current index j. The vector $x_{best,t}$ represents the best solution identified at generation t. The scaling factor FF is a real constant, generally selected within the interval $[0..1]$, which adjusts the magnitude of the differential variation.

2. Crossover operation: This operation enhances the population diversity following the mutation phase. Subsequently, the crossover operator combines components of the mutant vector vi,tvi,t and the target vector xi,txi,t to generate the trial vector ui,tui,t. The crossover mechanism is mathematically defined in Eq. 4 [25]:

$$u_{i,t}^j = \begin{cases} v_{i,t}^j \text{ if} & (rand_j \leq CR) or (j = j_{rand}) \\ x_{i,t}^j \text{ otherwise,} \end{cases} \quad (4)$$

where $j = 1, 2, .., D$ and $rand_j$ denotes the j th evaluation from a uniform random number generator over the interval $[0..1]$ [26]. The crossover rate CR is a user-defined parameter within $[0..1]$, and j_{rand} represents a randomly chosen integer in the range $[1..D]$ [27].

3. Selection operation:

In order to preserve a constant population size throughout the evolutionary process, the selection phase is applied. Specifically, the trial vector is first evaluated according to the objective function and subsequently compared to its associated target vector from the current generation. In case the trial vector outperforms the target vector, it substitutes the target vector within the population, otherwise, the target vector is preserved. The selection operation is represented in Eq. 5 [28]:

$$x_{i,t+1} = \begin{cases} u_{i,t} \text{ if} & f(u_{i,t}) \leq f(x_{i,t}) \\ x_{i,t} \text{ otherwise,} \end{cases} \quad (5)$$

Each generation goes through the three steps of mutation, crossover, and selection until a stopping criterion is reached. The DE algorithm, which groups the steps presented above, is illustrated in Algorithm 1. The parameters used in the algorithm include the number of individuals (N), the maximum number of iterations (Max), the choice of mutation scheme, and the initialization of the scaling factor (F) and crossover rate (CR). The F parameter controls the mutation intensity and is applied during the mutation phase, while CR defines the probability of gene exchange and is used in the crossover phase. These parameters play a crucial role in balancing exploration and exploitation to enhance the algorithm's performance.

In [25, 28], the "rand" strategy was used for both assignment and mapping problems. Parameters such as the mutation factor (F), crossover rate (CR), and number of iterations were carefully calibrated, leading to better results compared to other strategies. These optimized parameters were adopted for the routing optimization phase to ensure consistent performance. We run the algorithm for 200 iterations with a swarm of 100 individuals. The cognitive scale factor is set to 0.5, and the crossover coefficient is 0.9. The mutation strategy used is based on the rand/1.

Algorithm 1. The main steps of DE
generate the individuals of the population

evaluate the individuals with the objective function
initialize the best global solution g
$t \leftarrow 0$
while $t <$ max of iteration **do**
    for each individual i **do**
        generate the mutant vector using the mutation operations described in Table 3
        generate the test vector using the crossover operation described by Equation 4
        select the individual using the selection operation described by Equation 5
        if individual is better than g **then**
            $g \leftarrow$ the individual
        end if
    end for
    $t \leftarrow t + 1$
end while
return best solution g

5   Simulations and Performance Results

In this section, we compare the results obtained using two deterministic routing algorithms: XY [31] and Odd-Even [9] for the 2D topology, and XYZ [32] and Odd-Even [9] for the 3D topology. The objective of this comparison is to evaluate the performance of these algorithms against a metaheuristic-based algorithm using Particle Swarm Optimization (PSO) [18], as well as our algorithms based on Differential Evolution (DE). We used the Access-Noxim simulator [29], an enhanced version of Noxim. Noxim is a Network-on-Chip (NoC) simulation tool [30], written in C++ and based on the SystemC library. Its flexibility allows for easy modification of the routing strategy by writing and testing code in C++.

In this study, we focus on latency, which is defined as the time elapsed between the injection of a packet at the local port and the consumption of the last data at the local port of the destination node.

We studied networks with the following topologies: 2D and 3D mesh with a size of 5×5 (a 2D mesh with 25 nodes) and 3×3×3 (a 3D mesh with 27 nodes). Four routing algorithms were tested in the simulator: DE, the algorithm we evaluated, along with DOR (XYZ), Odd-Even, and PSO. The parameters related to the complete system simulation configuration are detailed in Table 4.

The tests are performed by adjusting the Traffic Models and Packet Injection Rates (PIR). A source-destination pair is defined as the node that sends a packet and the node that receives it. These pairs are chosen randomly based on various distribution models, which fall into two primary categories: deterministic models and random models.

Under deterministic models, each node is assigned a specific destination based on its position. Examples of these models include Complement, Transpose Matrix 1, and

Table 4. Parameter setting

Parameter	Setting
Network	2D Mesh vs 3D Mesh
Network dimensions	5x5 vs 3x3x3
Packet size	8
Virtual channels	4
Warm-up time	1000
Simulation time	20,000 cycles
Routing algorithms	DE, PSO, XYZ and ODD-Even

Table 5. Destination nodes of deterministic patterns.

Network	Pattern	source node	Destination node
2D Mesh	Complement	(x,y)	(size - x - 1,size - y - 1)
	Transpose 1	(x,y)	(size - y - 1,size - x - 1)
	Transpose 2	(x,y)	(y,x)
3D Mesh	Complement	(x,y,z)	(size - x - 1, size - y - 1, size - z - 1)
	Transpose 1	(x,y,z)	(size - y - 1, size - z - 1, size - x - 1)
	Transpose 2	(x,y,z)	(y,z,x)

Transpose Matrix 2 [16]. The relationship between source nodes and their corresponding destinations is detailed in Table 5.

In random models, destinations are selected based on probability. In the Rand model, every node has an equal likelihood of being a source or a destination. The Hotspot model ensures that all nodes have the same probability of being sources, but certain nodes, known as Hot-spots, are more likely to be chosen as destinations [16]. In the Local model, any node can act as a source, but destinations are restricted to its immediate neighboring nodes, which are selected randomly.

For the routing schemes, the results of this analysis represent the latency obtained for different packet injection rates. These results allow us to observe how latency varies as the injection rate increases or decreases, providing a comprehensive overview of routing performance. Figure 4 corresponds to the Rand routing scheme, where packets are generated randomly across the network. Here, we present the results achieved by the four algorithms for both 2D and 3D routing. In the analysis of 2D routing, the PSO and DE algorithms achieved better results compared to the XY and Odd-Even algorithms. However, PSO performed better than DE. Nevertheless, when the packet injection rate (PIR) reached 0.06, DE outperformed PSO. On the other hand, in the case of 3D routing, the results highlight that the DE algorithm delivers better performance in terms of latency compared to PSO, XYZ, and Odd-Even for random patterns. It is also noted that PSO does not achieve better results than DE, while DE is superior to XYZ, and XYZ is superior to PSO. Figure 5 illustrates the latency results for both 2D and 3D

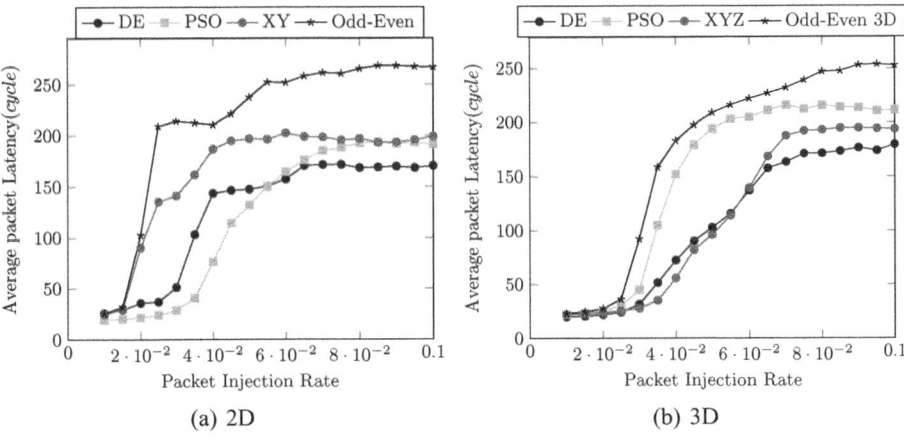

Fig. 4. Latency results obtained for the Rand routing scheme.

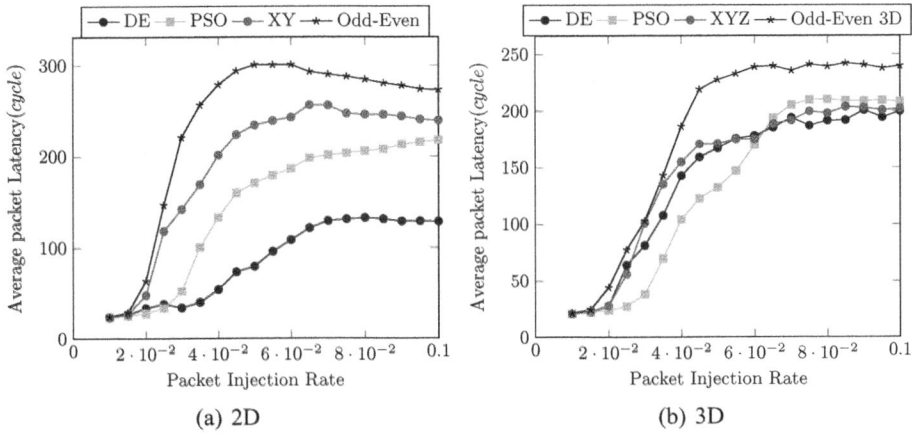

Fig. 5. Latency results obtained for the Hotspot routing scheme.

in the Hotspot routing scheme, where certain network nodes generate higher traffic than others.

In the case of the Hotspot traffic in a 2D NoC, the PSO and DE algorithms outperform the XY and Odd-Even algorithms, demonstrating their efficiency in handling high-intensity traffic. For the 3D NoC, PSO initially delivers strong latency performance until the PIR reaches 0.065. Beyond this point, DE surpasses both PSO and XYZ, while PSO continues to perform better than XYZ. Finally, Fig. 6 presents the latency curves for the Local routing scheme, where packets are generated locally by each node for both 2D and 3D routing. In 2D routing, all routing algorithms produce similar latency curves, indicating that their performance is comparable for this specific scenario, with no significant differences in latency. For 3D routing, XYZ, Odd-Even, and PSO exhibit almost identical latency curves, whereas DE outperforms the other

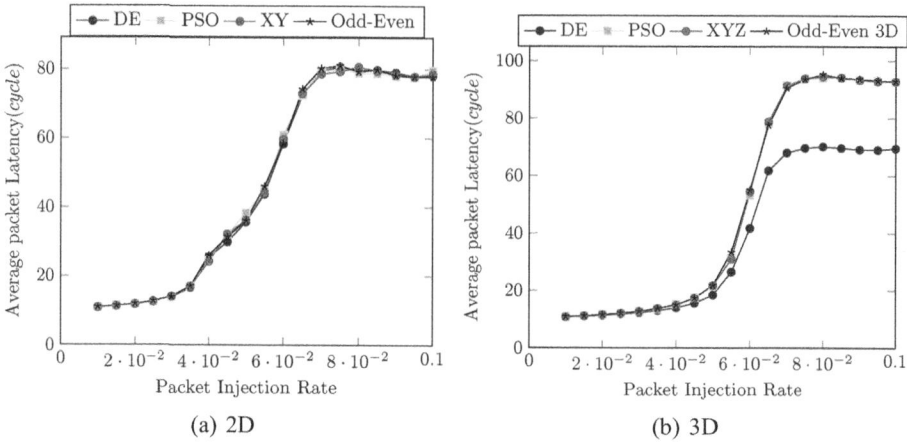

Fig. 6. Latency results obtained for the Local routing scheme.

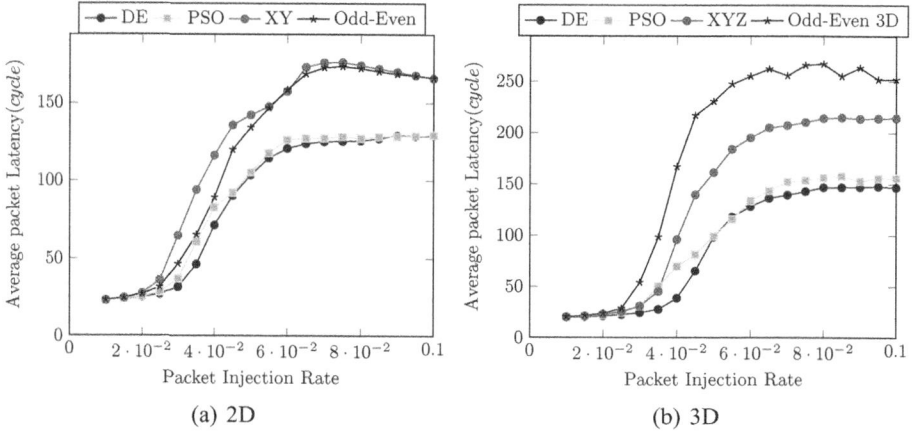

Fig. 7. Latency results obtained for the Transpose_1 routing scheme.

three algorithms. In deterministic routing schemes, Fig. 7 visually presents the latency curves for the Transpose_1 routing scheme in both 2D and 3D. In the analysis of 2D routing, we observe that the PSO and DE algorithms yield similar results and outperform the XY and Odd-Even algorithms. Regarding the 3D routing results, the latency curves of PSO and DE are nearly identical and surpass those of XYZ and Odd-Even. This indicates that PSO and DE achieve better performance in this scenario compared to XYZ and Odd-Even. Figure 8 visually represents the latency curves for the Transpose_2 routing scheme in both 2D and 3D. For the Transpose_2 scheme in a 2D NoC, DE demonstrates improved latency performance when the PIR exceeds 0.045. This suggests that DE is better suited for handling higher packet injection rates in this specific pattern. In contrast, in a 3D NoC, starting from a PIR of 0.04, both PSO and DE begin

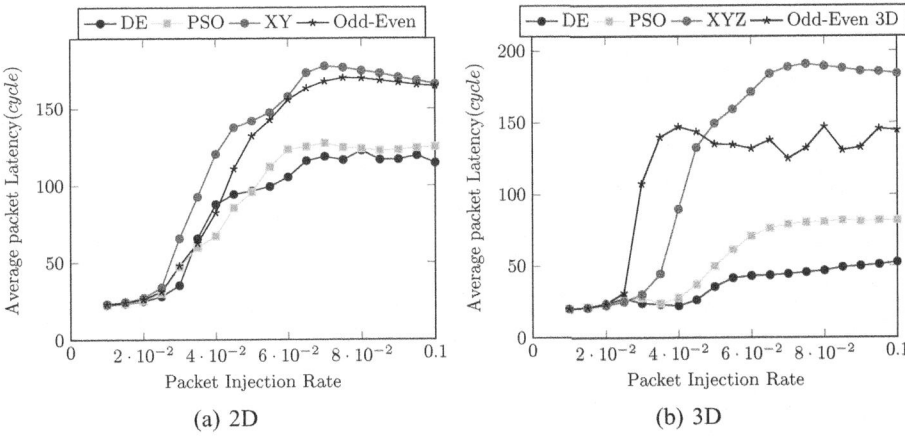

Fig. 8. Latency results obtained for the Transpose_2 routing scheme.

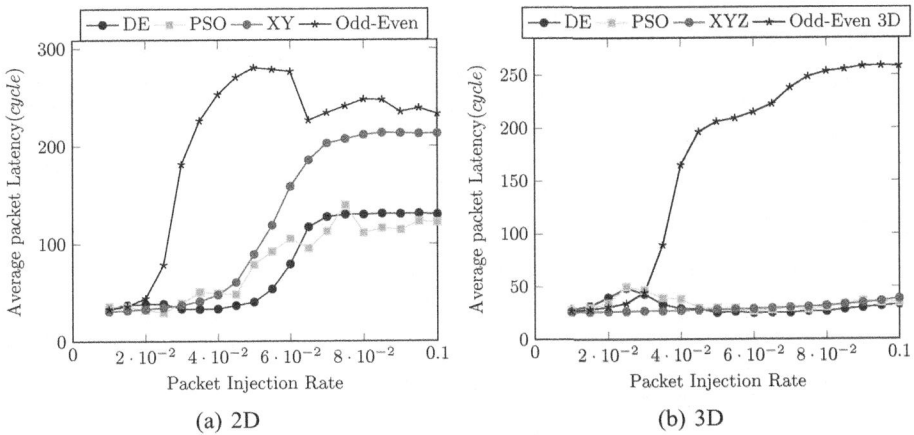

Fig. 9. Latency results obtained for the Complement routing scheme.

to show better latency results, with DE outperforming PSO. This indicates that DE is more effective than PSO in reducing latency for this particular traffic pattern. Finally, Fig. 9 visually depicts the latency curves for the Complement routing scheme in both 2D and 3D. In the Complement scheme for 2D NoC, PSO outperforms DE when the packet injection rate (PIR) exceeds 0.065, indicating that PSO adapts better to higher PIR values. For 3D routing, XYZ exhibits a flat latency curve, suggesting it does not significantly improve latency. Similarly, PSO follows a pattern close to XYZ, whereas DE delivers better results starting from a PIR of 0.045. This indicates that DE is more effective than both PSO and XYZ in reducing latency in the Complement scheme for 3D NoC.

6 Conclusion

This work introduces a routing algorithm based on Differential Evolution for Network-on-Chip (NoC) architectures in both 2D and 3D mesh topologies. Extensive testing was conducted using both deterministic and random traffic patterns, with comparisons against PSO, Odd-Even, and XYZ routing algorithms. The proposed approach consistently outperforms existing methods, achieving minimal latency compared to XY and Odd-Even in 2D, as well as XYZ and Odd-Even_3D in 3D. Despite these promising results, further improvements are necessary. Future work will explore additional meta-heuristic approaches and integrate real application task graphs while evaluating NoCs with larger dimensions.

References

1. Bougherara, M., Nedjah, N., Mourelle, L., Rahmoun, R., Sadok, A., Bennouar, D.: IP assignment for efficient NoC-based system design using multi-objective particle swarm optimisation. Inter. J. Bio-Inspired Comput. **12**(4), 203–213 (2018)
2. Bougherara, M., Nedjah, N., Bennouar, D., et al.: Core/task associations for efficient application implementation on Network-on-Chip. In: 2018 International Conference on Computer and Applications (ICCA), pp. 18-22. IEEE (2018)
3. Bougherara, M., Nedjah, N., Bennouar, D., Kemcha, R., de Macedo Mourelle, L.: Efficient application mapping onto three-dimensional network-on-chips using multi-objective particle swarm optimization. In: Misra, S., et al. (eds.) ICCSA 2019. LNCS, vol. 11620, pp. 654–670. Springer, Cham (2019). https://doi.org/10.1007/978-3-030-24296-1_53
4. Hu, J., Marculescu, R.: Energy-aware mapping for tile-based noc architectures under performance constraints. In: Proceedings of the 2003 Asia and South Pacific Design Automation Conference, pp. 233-239. ACM (2003)
5. Davis, W.R., et al.: Demystifying 3d ics: the pros and cons of going vertical. IEEE Design Test Comput. **22**(6), 498–510 (2005)
6. Sullivan, H., Bashkow, T.: A large scale, homogeneous, fully distributed parallel machine. ACM SIGARCH Comput. Architecture News **5**(7), 105–117 (1977)
7. Valiant, L., Brebner, G.: Universal schemes for parallel communication. In: Proceedings of the Thirteenth Annual ACM symposium on Theory of Computing, pp. 263–277. ACM (1981)
8. Seo, D., Ali, A., Lim, W., Rafique, N., Thottethodi, M.: Near-optimal worst-case throughput routing for two-dimensional mesh networks. In: ACM SIGARCH Computer Architecture News, vol. 33(2), pp. 432–443. IEEE Computer Society (2005)
9. Chiu, G.-M.: The odd-even turn model for adaptive routing. IEEE Trans. Parallel Distrib. Syst. **11**(7), 729–738 (2000)
10. Ebrahimi, M., Chang, X., Daneshtalab, M,, et al.: DyXYZ: fully adaptive routing algorithm for 3D NoCs. In: 2013 21st Euromicro International Conference on Parallel, Distributed, and Network-Based Processing, pp. 499-503. IEEE (2013)
11. Ebrahimi, M.: Fully adaptive routing algorithms and region based approaches for two-dimensional and three-dimensional networkson-chip. IET Comput. Digital Tech. **7**(6), 264–273 (2013)
12. Ebrahimi, M., Daneshtalab, M., Liljeberg, P., Plosila, J., Flich, J., Tenhunen, H.: "Path-based partitioning methods for 3D networks-on-chip with minimal adaptive routing. IEEE Trans. Comput. **63**(3), 718–733 (2014)

13. Nosrati, N., Shahhoseini, H.S.: G-cara: a global congestion-aware routing algorithm for traffic management in 3d networks-on-chip. In : 2017 Iranian Conference on Electrical Engineering (ICEE), pp. 2188-2193. IEEE (2017)
14. Jouybari, H.N., Mohammadi, K.: A low overhead, fault tolerant and congestion aware routing algorithm for 3D mesh-based Network-on-Chips. Microprocessors Microsyst. **38**(8), 991–999 (2014)
15. Silva, Jr., L., Nedjah, N., , De Macedo Mourelle, L.: ACO approach in static routing for Network-on-Chips with 3D mesh topology. In: 2013 IEEE 4th Latin American Symposium on Circuits and Systems (LASCAS), pp. 1-4. IEEE (2013)
16. Silva, Jr., L., Nedjah, N., De Macedo Mourelle, L.: Efficient routing in Network-on-Chip for 3D topologies. Inter. J. Electr. **102**(10), 1695–1712 (2015)
17. Bougherara, M., Amara, R.: Routing using genetic algorithm in network on chips with 3D mesh topology. In: 2023 International Conference on Computer and Applications (ICCA), pp. 1-5. IEEE (2023)
18. Bougherara, M., Nedjah, N., Bennouar, D., Mourelle, L.d.M.: Routing in 3D NoCs Using Genetic Algorithm and Particle Swarm Optimization. In: Gervasi, O., et al. (ed.) Computational Science and Its Applications – ICCSA 2023 Workshops. ICCSA 2023. LNCS, vol 14104. Springer, Cham (2023). https://doi.org/10.1007/978-3-031-37105-9_40
19. Alfaraj, N., Zhang, J., Xu,Y., Chao, H.J.: Hope: hotspot congestion control for clos network on chip. In: Proceedings of the Fifth ACM/IEEE International Symposium on Networks-on-Chip, pp. 17–24 (2011)
20. Fleetwood, K.: An introduction to differential evolution. In: Proceedings of Mathematics and Statistics of Complex Systems (MASCOS) One Day Symposium, 26th November, Brisbane, Australia, pp. 785–791 (2004)
21. Feoktistov, V.: Differential evolution. Springer (2006)
22. Robič, T., Filipič, B.: DEMO: differential evolution for multiobjective optimization. In: Coello Coello, C.A., Hernández Aguirre, A., Zitzler, E. (eds.) EMO 2005. LNCS, vol. 3410, pp. 520–533. Springer, Heidelberg (2005). https://doi.org/10.1007/978-3-540-31880-4_36
23. Bougherara, M., Amara, R., Kemcha R.: DEMAP: differential evolution mapping for network on chip optimization. Inter. J. Robot. Autom. (IJRA) **12**(4), 394-404
24. Das, S., Suganthan, P.N.: Differential evolution: a survey of the state-ofthe-art. IEEE Trans. Evolutionary Comput. **15**(1), 4–31 (2010)
25. Bougherara, M., Nedjah, N., Bennouar, D., Kemcha, R., de Macedo Mourelle, L.: Application mapping onto 3D NoCs using differential evolution. In: Gervasi, O., et al. (eds.) ICCSA 2020. LNCS, vol. 12251, pp. 89–102. Springer, Cham (2020). https://doi.org/10.1007/978-3-030-58808-3_8
26. Madavan, N.K.: Multiobjective optimization using a pareto differential evolution approach. In: Proceedings of the 2002 Congress on Evolutionary Computation. CEC 2002 (Cat. No. 02TH8600), vol. 2, p. 1145–1150. IEEE (2002)
27. Ahmad, M.F., Isa, N., Lim, W.H., et al.: Differential evolution: a recent review based on state-of-the-art works. Alexandria Eng. J. **61**(5), 3831–3872 (2022)
28. Bougherara, M., Kemcha, R., Nedjah, N., et al.: IP assignment optimization for an efficient noc-based system using multi-objective differential evolution. In: International Conference on Metaheuristics and Nature Inspired Computing (META), pp. 435-444 (2018)
29. Catania, V., et al.: Noxim: an open extensible and cycle-accurate network on chip simulator. In: IEEE 26th International Conference on Application-specific Systems Architectures and Processors (ASAP), pp. 162–163 (March 2015)
30. Access Noxim. http://access.ee.ntu.edu.tw/noxim/index.html

31. Alikhah-Asl, E., Reshadi, M.: XY-axis and distance based NoC mapping (XY-ADB). In: 2016 8th International Symposium on Telecommunications (IST), pp. 678–683. IEEE (2016)
32. Ahmed, A.B., Abdallah, A.B.: LA-XYZ: low latency, high throughput lookahead routing algorithm for 3D Network-on-Chip (3D-NoC) architecture. In: 2012 IEEE 6th International Symposium on Embedded Multicore SoCs, pp. 167–174. IEEE (2012)

MARS-SLAM: Marker-Assisted Region Scanning for Simultaneous Localization and Mapping

Luigi Maciel Ribeiro[1]([⊠]) [iD], Nadia Nedjah[1] [iD],
and Paulo Victor R. de Carvalho[2] [iD]

[1] State University of Rio de Janeiro (UERJ), Rio de Janeiro, Brazil
{luigi,nadia}@eng.uerj.br
[2] Federal University of Rio de Janeiro (UFRJ), Rio de Janeiro, Brazil
paulov@ien.gov.br

Abstract. This paper presents Marker-Assisted Region Scanning for Simultaneous Localization and Mapping (MARS-SLAM), a novel approach to optimizing the Simultaneous Localization and Mapping process in unknown environments. The method was specifically designed to address the challenges of autonomous exploration in extreme conditions, to enable efficient navigation and offer a systematic approach to determine the completion of mapping. The approach uses markers to indicate unexplored regions, ensuring an organized and complete exploration. During the process, the robot places markers in free areas identified by the LiDAR sensor, located at the sensor's range limit, building a list of regions yet to be explored. The mapping is considered complete when the marker list is empty, indicating that no unexplored regions remain. Target marker selection during navigation is based on age and distance. Age refers to the chronological order in which markers are created, while distance refers to the length of the route from the robot to the marker. The method is validated in two virtual environments of varying complexity. Experimental results demonstrate the effectiveness of MARS-SLAM in achieving complete mapping and accurately identifying mapping completion. Compared to alternative navigation methods, including predefined zigzag routes and routes generated by Ant Colony Optimization (ACO) algorithms, MARS-SLAM shows superior performance, particularly in reducing the number of poses required to complete the mapping, achieving a 64.39% reduction in poses compared to ACO and a 71.07% reduction compared to zigzag.

Keywords: SLAM · Robotic Navigation · Path Planning · Mapping optimization · 2D Mapping

1 Introduction

Simultaneous Localization and Mapping (SLAM) [1] is a cornerstone of mobile robotics [7], enabling autonomous navigation in unknown environments. SLAM

O. Gervasi et al. (Eds.): ICCSA 2025 Workshops, LNCS 15888, pp. 19–36, 2026.
https://doi.org/10.1007/978-3-031-97596-7_2

allows robots to build and update maps while tracking their position within them, a capability essential for applications ranging from autonomous vehicles [11] to space exploration robots [3]. However, ensuring the completeness of mapping in complex environments remains a critical challenge in SLAM research. Traditional SLAM approaches rely on random or exploratory navigation, which often result in gaps, shadow zones, and redundant paths due to unplanned trajectories [2,13]. These methods typically lack a deterministic process for verifying mapping completeness, leading to inefficient use of time, energy, and computational resources, particularly in scenarios requiring real-time mapping.

This research addresses the challenge of ensuring complete and efficient exploration during SLAM. Marker-Assisted Region Scanning for SLAM (MARS-SLAM) is proposed as a method that utilizes virtual markers derived from Light Detection and Ranging (LiDAR) data to identify and guide the exploration of unmapped regions. Markers are strategically placed in frontier areas and serve as navigation targets, optimizing trajectories based on their age and distance. Mapping is deemed complete when all markers have been visited and removed, ensuring no unexplored regions remain. By optimizing exploration, MARS-SLAM minimizes resource consumption while improving map accuracy and completeness, with applications ranging from industrial robotics to exploration missions in extreme environments. While MARS-SLAM offers significant improvements over traditional methods, it faces challenges in dynamic environments, where moving obstacles may interfere with marker placement. Additionally, its performance depends on the quality of LiDAR data and the computational cost of updating markers in cluttered spaces. Despite these challenges, the method provides a robust and objective solution for achieving mapping completeness.

This paper seeks to answer: How can marker-based exploration optimize the SLAM process to ensure complete and accurate mapping in unknown environments? To address this question, Sect. 2 reviews related works, identifying gaps in current methodologies. Section 3 details the proposed method, while Sect. 4 presents experimental results. Finally, Sect. 5 concludes with contributions, limitations, and future research directions.

2   Related Works

This section presents an overview of significant studies selected to showcase distinct approaches related to path planning and SLAM optimization, highlighting advances and limitations in each domain. Table 1 provides a comparative view of the characteristics each method addresses, facilitating a clear understanding of the innovation that MARS-SLAM brings to the field, particularly in terms of completion detection and uncertainty reduction.

Path planning approaches play a crucial role in enhancing SLAM performance by optimizing navigation and localization strategies. In [4], a method integrating inertial SLAM with trajectory planning for Unmanned Aerial Vehicles (UAVs) is proposed, leveraging entropy and observability to improve navigation accuracy in GPS-denied environments. This approach enhances map quality and localization by utilizing dynamic UAV maneuvers and real-time computational solutions, proving highly effective for applications in surveillance and exploration.

Table 1. Characteristics's comparison addressed in related works.

Feature	[4]	[5]	[9]	[12]	[14]	[8]	[10]	MARS-SLAM
Indoor Environment	✗	✓	✓	✓	✓	✓	✗	✓
Outdoor Environment	✓	✗	✗	✓	✓	✓	✓	✓
Path Planning	✓	✓	✓	✓	✓	✓	✓	✓
Dynamic Environments	✗	✗	✓	✗	✗	✗	✗	✗
Exploration Optimization	✓	✓	✗	✓	✗	✓	✓	✓
Real-Time Processing	✓	✓	✓	✓	✓	✓	✗	✓
Conclusion Detection	✗	✗	✗	✗	✗	✗	✗	✓
Map Building	✓	✓	✓	✓	✓	✓	✓	✓
Uncertainty Reduction	✓	✓	✓	✗	✓	✓	✗	✓

Similarly, in [9], an adaptation of the D* algorithm for active SLAM addresses the challenge of handling negative edge weights, a significant limitation in traditional path finding algorithms. This adaptation enables efficient path recalculation, improves loop closure, and reduces localization uncertainty, demonstrating robust performance in both simulations and real-world scenarios. Lastly, [14] evaluates the performance of SLAM algorithms (GMapping, Hector-SLAM, and Cartographer) when combined with the A* algorithm for global path planning and DWA for local planning in indoor rescue scenarios. The study highlights the specific strengths and limitations of these algorithmic combinations, offering valuable insights into selecting optimal solutions for rescue tasks.

SLAM optimization approaches, on the other hand, focus on improving the efficiency, accuracy, and overall applicability of SLAM in diverse environments. In [5], the P-SLAM algorithm predicts environmental structures in unexplored regions using a Rao-Blackwellized particle filter, which significantly reduces exploration time and accelerates the mapping process. This Bayesian formulation, combined with frontier cell strategies, proves effective for real-time applications, as validated through experimental results. In [12], an exploration EM algorithm, adapted for pose SLAM, is introduced, utilizing point cloud segmentation to construct maps and enhance place recognition. The method also predicts future uncertainty, achieving higher exploration rates and improved accuracy in real-time applications. Furthermore, [8] presents a boundary exploration method that integrates Double-Layer Rapid-Exploration Random Tree (DL-RRT), Affinity Propagation clustering, and Bayesian Optimization. This approach reduces execution time and path length while maintaining high stability, offering notable improvements over traditional RRT methods. Finally, [10] proposes FIT-SLAM, which combines Fisher information and navigability estimates for 3D exploration. By transforming 3D exploration spaces into 2D navigability maps, this method reduces computational costs, improves exploration efficiency, and enhances SLAM accuracy, as demonstrated through extensive simulations and experiments.

3   Marker-Assisted Region Scanning

To ensure the effective and accurate completion of mapping, we propose a methodology that uses markers to identify and track unexplored regions on the map. The primary goal of this method is to ensure that all areas of the environment are mapped, avoiding gaps that could compromise the navigability and usefulness of the generated map. Markers play a key role in this process, acting as indicators of regions that still need to be explored. As the robot progresses in building the map, it adds markers to unexplored areas based on sensor readings. These markers are stored in a list, which over time reflects the progress of the mapping. The process is considered complete when the list of markers is empty, indicating that no unexplored regions remain.

Initially, the robot performs a full 360° rotation, analyzing the surrounding environment and placing markers in locations corresponding to unexplored areas. Once the rotation is completed, the robot selects a marker as a target and moves toward it. The robot then chooses the next most relevant marker and repeats the process. This cycle of marker selection and navigation continues until all markers are removed, signaling the completion of the environment mapping. Algorithm 1 describes the process in detail.

Algorithm 1. Marker-Assisted Region Scanning

Ensure: Grid map of the environment (G)

  1: $G \leftarrow$ unknown map   ▷ Grid map with all cells as unknown (gray pixels)

  2: $P, M, L, \Psi \leftarrow$ empty list   ▷ Pose list, marker list, LiDAR measurements and path

  3: $\eta \leftarrow$ null   ▷ Target marker

  4: $k \leftarrow 0$

  5: $P_k \leftarrow$ initial position

  6: **while** full rotation not completed **do**

  7:      $P_{k+1}, L \rightarrow$ UpdateRobotState$(P_k, \eta, rotate, G, \Psi)$ ▷ Algorithm 2

  8:      $G \rightarrow$ UpdateGridMap(P_{k+1}, L)

  9:      $M \rightarrow$ MarkerAddition(G, L, M) ▷ Algorithm 3

10:      $k \leftarrow k + 1$

11: **end while**

12: **while** $M \neq$ empty list **do**

13:      **if** η is null **then**

14:          $\eta \rightarrow$ MarkerSelection(M) ▷ Algorithm 4

15:      **end if**

16:      $P_{k+1}, L \rightarrow$ UpdateRobotState$(P_k, \eta, towards, G, \Psi)$

17:      $G \rightarrow$ UpdateGridMap(P_{k+1}, L)

18:      **if** η is reached **then**

19:          $\eta \leftarrow$ null;

20:      **end if**

21:      $M \rightarrow$ MarkerRemoval(G, M) ▷ Algorithm 5

22:      $M \rightarrow$ MarkerAddition(G, L, M)

23:      $k \leftarrow k + 1$

24: **end while**

3.1   Update Robot State

This process continuously updates the robot's state during navigation, determining its new pose and LiDAR measurements based on its current action and the specified target. It plays a crucial role in ensuring that the robot remains aligned with its goal, dynamically adjusting its trajectory as needed while collecting essential data to support the ongoing mapping of the environment. The algorithm enables the robot to adapt its trajectory in real time, for effective decision-making that enhances its ability to navigate complex environments.

Algorithm 2 requires the following inputs: the robot's current pose (P_k), the target marker (η), the action to be executed (A), the grid map (G), and the path list (Ψ). It outputs the robot's updated pose (P_{k+1}) and the new LiDAR measurements (L). The process is divided into three main steps: First, the algorithm identifies the action assigned to the robot, which may involve either a rotation or movement toward the target. In the case of rotation, the algorithm updates the robot's pose and gathers new LiDAR measurements. If the action involves moving toward the marker, the algorithm checks for obstacles along the path. If the path is clear, the robot moves directly toward the target, updates the LiDAR measurements, and resets the path list to empty. If obstacles are detected, the algorithm employs a path-planning approach to determine an alternative route, stores the intermediate points in the list Ψ, and guides the robot along these points to bypass the obstacle and reach the target marker.

Algorithm 2. Update Robot State

Require: Current Pose (P_k), Target marker (η), Action (A), Grid Map (G), Path (Ψ)
Ensure: Updated Pose (P_{k+1}), Updated LiDAR Measurements (L)
1: **if** A is rotate **then**
2:      $P_{k+1} \leftarrow$ rotate robot
3:      $L \leftarrow$ LiDAR measurements
4: **else if** A is towards η **then**
5:      **if** way to η is free **then**
6:
7: $L \leftarrow$ LiDAR measurements
8:         $\Psi \leftarrow$ empty list
9:      **else**
10:          **if** Ψ is empty **then**
11:
12: $\Psi \leftarrow$ PathFinding(P, k, z))   ▷ Algorithm 6
13:          **end if**
14:
15: $L \leftarrow$ LiDAR measurements
16:          **if** $\Psi[0]$ has been reached **then**
17:              remove $\Psi[0]$ of the Ψ
18:          **end if**
19:      **end if**
20: **end if**

3.2   Marker Addition

Markers are created based on readings from the LiDAR, a sensor used by the robot to map the environment. Each measurement provides the distance to the first obstacle detected in the respective direction. The LiDAR has a maximum range, and measurements beyond this limit are not considered. During the robot's movement, at each registered pose, all LiDAR measurements are analyzed to identify potential obstacle-free areas. To ensure efficient distribution and avoid redundancies, the algorithm imposes a restriction: a new marker can only be added if no other marker exists within a predefined minimum distance. Figure 1 illustrates the process of identifying free areas and adding markers.

Algorithm 3 details the marker addition procedure. It takes as input the current grid map (G), the LiDAR measurements (L), and the list of existing markers (M), while also defining the minimum distance between markers, denoted as γ. For each LiDAR measurement, the algorithm checks whether it is within the sensor's maximum range. If the measurement exceeds this limit, the corresponding coordinates (x_l, y_l) are determined. Then, a loop checks whether a marker already exists within the minimum distance γ. If a marker is found too close, the creation of a new marker is avoided. Otherwise, if there are no nearby markers and the corresponding area on the map is unknown (represented by a gray pixel), the point (x_l, y_l) is added as a new marker. However, if the area already contains a marker, the algorithm checks the neighboring cells around the detected point. If any of these neighboring cells are also unknown, a new marker is added at that location.

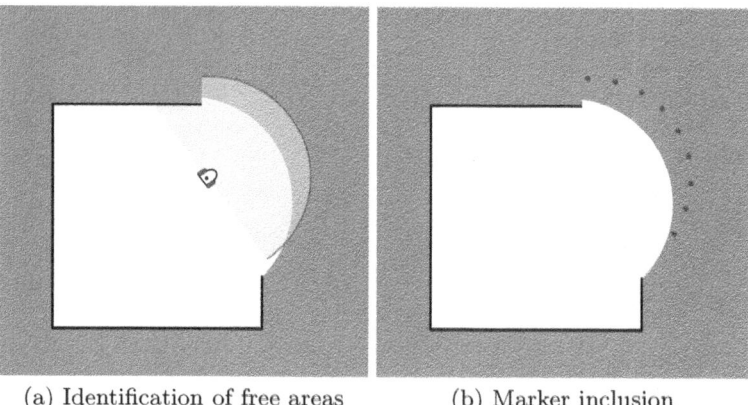

(a) Identification of free areas   (b) Marker inclusion

Fig. 1. Process of identifying free areas and adding markers during the robot's navigation. Figure (a) shows how free areas are identified based on LiDAR readings; figure (b) illustrates the addition of markers in these areas, ensuring a minimum distance between them.

Algorithm 3. Marker Addition

Require: Grid map (G), LiDAR measurements (L), Marker list (M)
Ensure: Updated Marker List (M)
 1: $\gamma \leftarrow$ minimum distance between markers
 2: **for** each l in L **do**
 3:      **if** l is outside LiDAR's maximum range **then**
 4:          $x_l, y_l \leftarrow$ coordinates of l
 5:          $\kappa \leftarrow$ true;
 6:          **while** κ **do**
 7:              **for** each m in M' **do**
 8:                  $x_m, y_m \leftarrow$ coordinates of m
 9:                  **if** $\sqrt{(x_l - x_m)^2 + (y_l - y_m)^2} < \gamma$ **then**
10:                      $\kappa \leftarrow$ false;
11:                  **end if**
12:              **end for**
13:          **end while**
14:          **if** κ **then**
15:              **if** $G[x_l, y_l]$ is unknown **then**
16:                  add (x_l, y_l) to M as a new marker;
17:              **else**
18:                  $\tau \leftarrow$ true;
19:                  $N \leftarrow \{(x_l + i, y_l + j) \mid i, j \in \{-1, 0, 1\}, (i, j) \neq (0, 0)\}$
20:                  **for** each n in N **do**
21:                      **if** $G[n]$ is unknown and τ **then**
22:                          add (x_l, y_l) to M as a new marker
23:                          $\tau \leftarrow$ false;
24:                      **end if**
25:                  **end for**
26:              **end if**
27:          **end if**
28:      **end if**
29: **end for**

3.3   Marker Selection

After the initial navigation period, the robot must choose a marker as a target to map an unexplored area. For this selection, the robot identifies markers with free access, meaning those for which a direct path can be traced from the robot's current position without encountering obstacles. Once the accessible markers are identified, the target marker is chosen based on two criteria: age and distance. Each marker is associated with a specific pose, recorded in a pose list that starts at pose 0 and progresses up to the robot's current pose. For example, a marker created at pose 10 is considered older than one created at pose 50. The robot then decides between the oldest marker and the closest marker. If the distance to the oldest marker exceeds μ times the distance to the closest marker, the closest marker is selected as the target (μ is a parameter adjustable according to the desired navigation behavior). Otherwise, the oldest marker is chosen. When there are no markers with free access, the robot uses the tournament selection method to determine the target.

Algorithm 4 describes this logic in a structured way, starting with the filtering of markers with free access (M_f) and, in their absence, applying the tournament selection method. After this filtering, the algorithm considers the distance (d_o) and the age of the oldest marker (η_o), comparing them with the distance to the closest marker (η_c). Based on this comparison and the parameter μ, the algorithm determines the target marker (η), which will guide the robot in the next exploration step. This efficient selection process allows the robot to balance the exploration of new areas while prioritizing older markers, while also optimizing the path by selecting closer markers when appropriate.

Algorithm 4. Marker Selection

Require: Marker list (M), Robot's current pose (P_k)
Ensure: Target marker (η)
 1: $M_f \leftarrow$ filter markers from M with free access
 2: $\mu \leftarrow$ navigation balance parameter
 3: **if** M_f is empty **then**
 4:     $M_t \leftarrow$ randomly select ρ markers from M
 5:     $\eta \leftarrow$ marker with the shortest distance in M_t
 6:     **return** η
 7: **end if**
 8: $\eta_o \leftarrow$ oldest marker in M_f
 9: $\eta_c \leftarrow$ closest marker in M_f
10: $x_{P_k}, y_{P_k} \leftarrow$ coordinates of P_k
11: $x_{\eta_o}, y_{\eta_o} \leftarrow$ coordinates of η_o
12: $x_{\eta_c}, y_{\eta_c} \leftarrow$ coordinates of η_c
13: $d_o \leftarrow \sqrt{(x_{P_k} - x_{\eta_o})^2 + (y_{P_k} - y_{\eta_o})^2}$
14: $d_c \leftarrow \sqrt{(x_{P_k} - x_{\eta_c})^2 + (y_{P_k} - y_{\eta_c})^2}$
15: **if** $d_o > \mu \times d_c$ **then**
16:     $\eta \leftarrow \eta_c$
17: **else**
18:     $\eta \leftarrow \eta_o$
19: **end if**

3.4   Marker Removal

Marker removal is an essential step to ensure that the map remains up to date, reflecting only the areas that still need to be explored. During the robot's navigation, at each step, it is checked whether any of the previously added markers are located in a region that has already been mapped. Specifically, a marker is removed when its cell, as well as its neighboring cells, are no longer unknown. Figure 2 illustrates the process of map updating and the subsequent removal of markers during the robot's navigation. Figure 2(a) shows the map being updated as the robot explores new areas. During these updates, previously unknown regions are converted into mapped areas, indicating that the robot has already explored these cells. Figure 2(b) demonstrates the marker removal process.

Algorithm 5 details the marker removal procedure. It takes as input the current grid map G and the list of markers M, aiming to return an updated marker list M' containing only those located in unexplored regions of the map. The process begins by creating an empty list M', where the markers that remain after evaluation will be stored. For each marker m in the original list M, the algorithm retrieves its coordinates (x_m, y_m), which indicate its position on the grid map. It then checks whether the corresponding cell in the map $G[x_m, y_m]$ is still unknown (represented by a gray value on the grid). If this cell remains unexplored, the marker m is kept in the updated list M'.

If the cell has already been explored, the algorithm proceeds to evaluate the neighboring cells around (x_m, y_m). These neighboring cells are represented by the set N, which includes the eight adjacent cells surrounding marker m. The algorithm then checks whether any of the cells in N are still unknown on the map G. If at least one of these neighboring cells remains unexplored, the marker m is retained in the updated list M'. Otherwise, if all neighboring cells have already been explored, the marker is removed, as it no longer points to an unexplored area. At the end of the procedure, the algorithm returns the updated marker list M', ensuring that only those markers located in or near unexplored regions are retained. This process guarantees the removal of markers in fully explored areas, optimizing both the marker distribution and the efficiency of the mapping process.

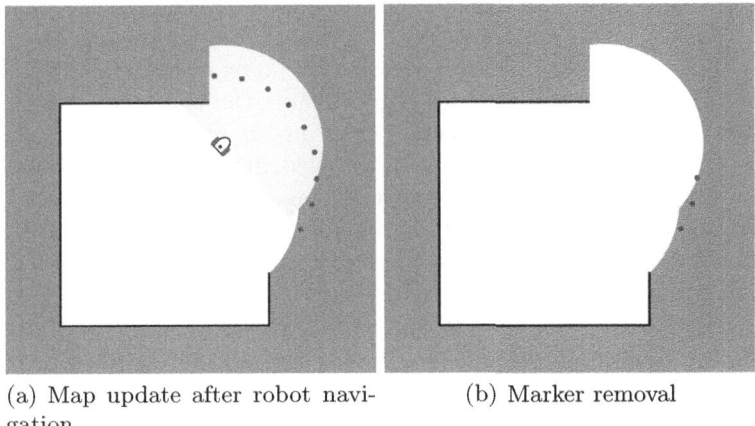

(a) Map update after robot navigation

(b) Marker removal

Fig. 2. Process of map updating and marker removal during navigation. Figure(a) illustrates the map update with new information obtained by the robot; figure(b) shows the removal of markers from areas that are no longer unknown, ensuring that only unexplored regions retain markers.

Algorithm 5. Marker Removal

Require: Grid map (G), Marker list (M)
Ensure: Updated marker list (M')
 1: $M' \leftarrow$ empty list
 2: **for** each m in M **do**
 3:    $x_m, y_m \leftarrow$ coordinates of m
 4:    **if** $G[x_m, y_m]$ is unknown **then**
 5:        add m to M'
 6:    **else**
 7:        $\alpha \leftarrow$ true
 8:        $N \leftarrow \{(x_m + i, y_m + j) \mid i, j \in \{-1, 0, 1\}, (i, j) \neq (0, 0)\}$
 9:        **for** each n in N **do**
10:            **if** $G[n]$ is unknown and α **then**
11:                add m to M'
12:                $\alpha \leftarrow$ false
13:            **end if**
14:        **end for**
15:    **end if**
16: **end for**

3.5 Path Finding

In situations where the target marker is not directly accessible, the robot must return to the pose where the marker was created to ensure a clear path. While backtracking through the pose list is an option, it can be inefficient. To optimize this, a method was developed to reduce the set of poses needed to reach the target. By leveraging the recorded path, the method identifies the smallest set of poses connecting the robot's current position to the target marker. Starting from the current position, the robot traverses poses at intervals defined by a constant until the target is reached. At each step, the closest pose with a clear path to the current position is selected, ensuring an efficient route.

The specifics of this procedure are detailed in Algorithm 6. Initially, the algorithm sets the path Ψ as an empty list and defines a search step size s. A loop continues until a valid path is found. In each iteration, the algorithm generates a set of candidate poses Ω by calculating the indices based on the target marker's pose index δ and the current pose index k, considering increments defined by the search step size. If there are no candidate poses available, the loop terminates. For each pose in the candidate set Ω, the algorithm checks for obstacles between the current pose and the candidate pose. If a clear path is identified (*i.e.*, no obstacles), the algorithm updates the path Ψ by adding the candidate pose and then updates the current pose index k to the candidate pose. This process repeats until a direct, obstacle-free route is established between the robot's current position and the target marker. Figure 3 visually illustrates this path optimization process, demonstrating the stages of checking and selecting intermediate poses until the final path is defined.

Algorithm 6. Path finding

Require: Pose list (P), Robot's pose index (k), Target marker's pose index (z)
Ensure: Path (Ψ)
  1: $\Psi \leftarrow$ empty list
  2: $s \leftarrow$ search step size
  3: $\Omega = \{i \mid i = z + ns,\, n \in \mathbb{Z}^+ \text{ e } i \leq k\}$
  4: **while** Ω is not empty **do**
  5:     $\tau \leftarrow$ true;
  6:     **for** each ω in Ω **do**
  7:         $obstacle \leftarrow$ check for obstacles between $P[\omega]$ and $P[k]$;
  8:         **if** without $obstacle$ and τ **then**
  9:             add $P[\omega]$ to Ψ;
 10:             $k \leftarrow \omega$;
 11:             $\tau \leftarrow$ false;
 12:         **end if**
 13:     **end for**
 14:     $\Omega = \{i \mid i = z + ns,\, n \in \mathbb{Z}^+ \text{ e } i \leq k\}$
 15: **end while**

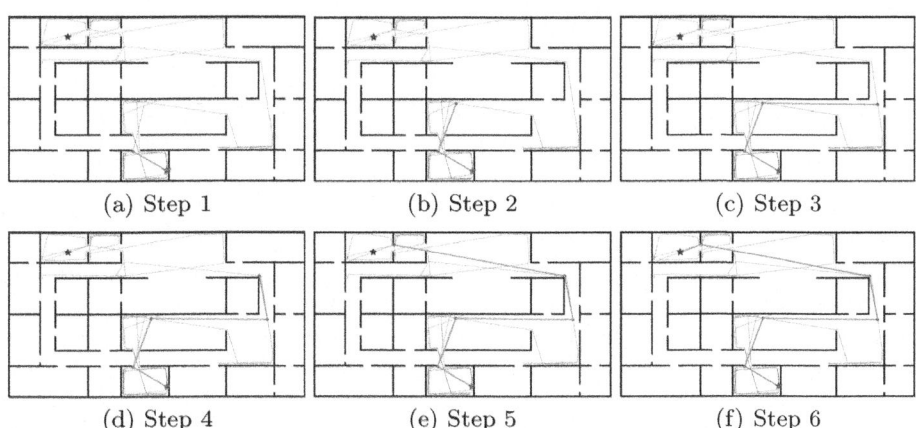

(a) Step 1   (b) Step 2   (c) Step 3

(d) Step 4   (e) Step 5   (f) Step 6

Fig. 3. The set of images shows the process of locating the optimized path using the list of poses. The goal is to identify a path from the red star (starting point) to the blue star (target point). The red points represent the list of posed already traversed by the robot. The green path represents the so-far constructed route. (Color figure online)

4   Results

In this section, the results of the experiments, conducted to evaluate the efficiency and stability of the proposed MARS-SLAM method, are presented. The experiments were performed in two distinct virtual environments to analyze the performance of the approach under different conditions. The maps used in the simulations are shown in Fig. 4, with increasing levels of complexity: Map 1 is the least complex, followed by the more challenging Map 2. These maps are designed to thoroughly test the adaptability of the MARS-SLAM method. The simulations were carried out on a computer with the following specifications: Intel(R) Core(TM) i7-10750H CPU @ 2.59GHz, 24 GB of RAM, and Microsoft Windows 11 Home operating system (version 10.0.22631). The development environment and tools used for the implementation and simulations included Python 3.7.7 and the necessary libraries for calculations and visualization of the results.

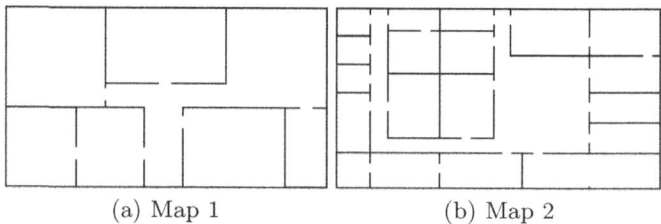

        (a) Map 1   (b) Map 2

Fig. 4. Maps of the virtual environments used in the simulations, designed with different levels of complexity to test the adaptability of the MARS-SLAM method. Map 1 presents a simple layout, while Map 2 has intermediate complexity.

To compare the performance of MARS-SLAM, two alternative routes are created, serving as benchmarks to establish a solid basis for evaluation. The goal of these simulations is to provide a comparative analysis of MARS-SLAM's efficiency in mapping environments with no prior knowledge. A pragmatic approach is adopted, assuming prior knowledge of the map, which allows for the distribution of markers in a grid format. The spacing between the markers is proportional to the LiDAR scan limit, ensuring that, by visiting all markers, the mapping process is completed. These routes will provide a reference for evaluating MARS-SLAM's efficiency. By comparing the performance of MARS-SLAM with these routes, we aim to determine if the method can map the entire environment with a similar number of poses, even without prior knowledge. If MARS-SLAM achieves comparable results to the alternative routes, it would indicate that the method is efficient and capable of producing similar results despite lacking map knowledge.

Two alternative routes are developed for comparison with MARS-SLAM, using markers distributed in a grid:

1. Standard Zigzag Route: In this route, the robot starts at the first marker in the first row and navigates left to right on even-numbered rows and right to left on odd-numbered rows, creating a zigzag pattern.
2. ACO-Optimized Route: In this route, a heuristic based on the Ant Colony Optimization (ACO) algorithm [6] is applied to construct a route that closely approximates the optimal path.

These routes are generated for the three virtual scenarios shown in Fig. 4. Figure 5 illustrates the mapping progress on Map 1, showing how each method

(Zigzag, ACO, and MARS-SLAM) covers the environment at three different stages: 0%, 50%, and 100%. Similarly, Fig. 6 presents the same stages for Map 2, demonstrating how each method performs in a more complex layout. In each of these three figures, the areas already mapped are shaded in pink, red dots represent the markers added by the robot, and the small pink dots indicate the robot's recorded poses throughout the mapping process.

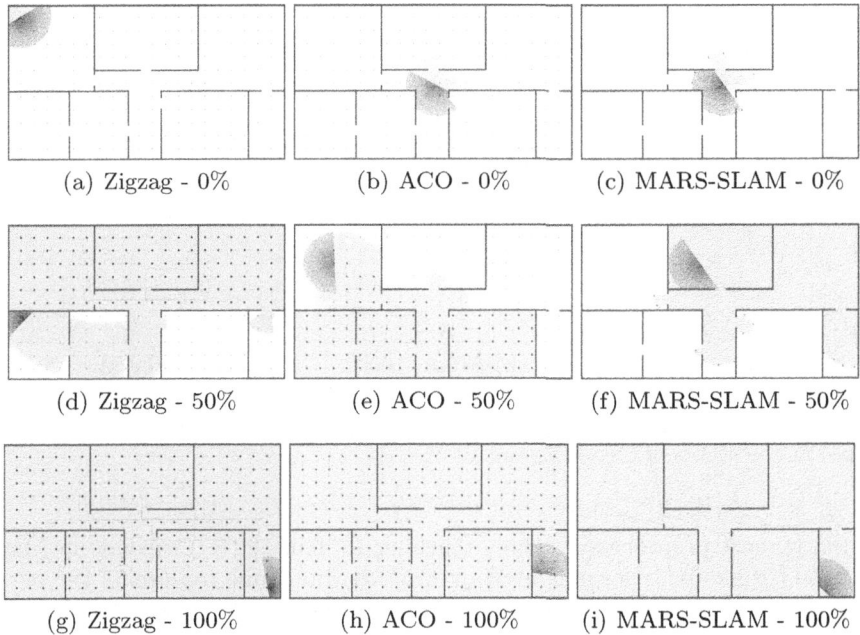

(a) Zigzag - 0%   (b) ACO - 0%   (c) MARS-SLAM - 0%

(d) Zigzag - 50%   (e) ACO - 50%   (f) MARS-SLAM - 50%

(g) Zigzag - 100%   (h) ACO - 100%   (i) MARS-SLAM - 100%

Fig. 5. Mapping progress on Map 1 using the three methods (Zigzag, ACO, and MARS-SLAM) at the stages of 0%, 50%, and 100%.

The simulations demonstrate that MARS-SLAM successfully achieves its main objective, which is to perform a complete mapping of the environment, utilizing an efficient stopping criterion to identify the conclusion of the navigation task. Each simulation is repeated 10 times to ensure the robustness of the results. Table 2 presents the averages and standard deviations for the number of poses required for complete mapping by each method, as well as the mapping completeness. MARS-SLAM achieves the lowest number of poses in both maps, with $4404.00(\pm280.85)$ poses in Map 1 and $7618.30(\pm1277.47)$ poses in Map 2, significantly outperforming Zigzag and ACO. Table 3 presents the average times and standard deviations related to three time categories: preprocessing, navigation, and total simulation time. The preprocessing time refers to the initial phase before navigation, which includes setting up specific parameters for each method. MARS-SLAM eliminates preprocessing time, unlike ACO, which

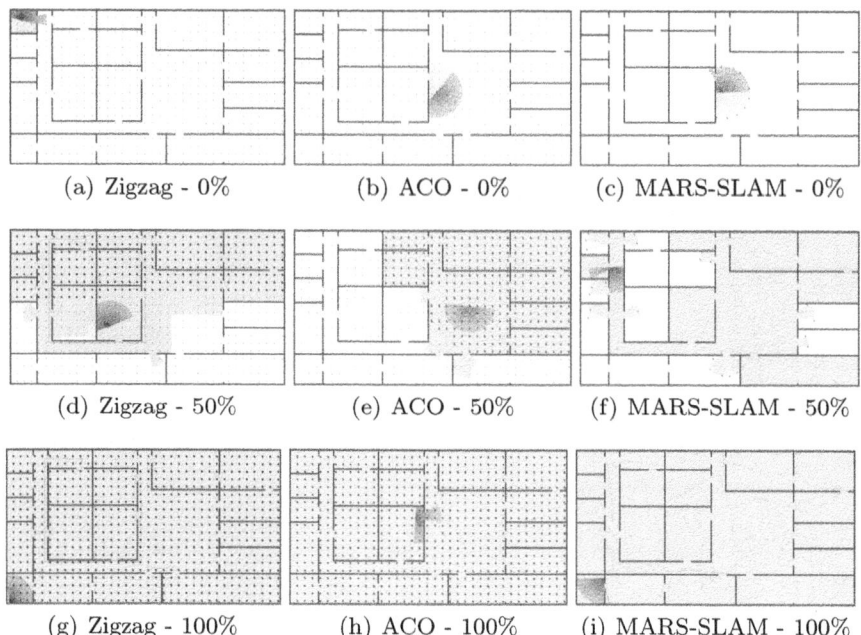

(a) Zigzag - 0%   (b) ACO - 0%   (c) MARS-SLAM - 0%

(d) Zigzag - 50%   (e) ACO - 50%   (f) MARS-SLAM - 50%

(g) Zigzag - 100%   (h) ACO - 100%   (i) MARS-SLAM - 100%

Fig. 6. Mapping progress on Map 2 using the three methods (Zigzag, ACO, and MARS-SLAM) at the stages of 0%, 50%, and 100%.

has the highest preprocessing time, reaching 1750.5($\pm$227.7) seconds in Map 1 and 12503.2($\pm$2501.3) seconds in Map 2. Navigation time represents the period in which the robot actively explores the environment. MARS-SLAM completes navigation in 5725.2($\pm$364.1) seconds for Map 1 and 13331.0($\pm$2554.9) seconds for Map 2, achieving a reduction compared to Zigzag, 10764.6($\pm$23.0) seconds and 28676.6($\pm$400.5) seconds, respectively, and ACO 6381.2($\pm$48.6) seconds and 18730.5($\pm$353.3) seconds, respectively.

Table 2. Data showing the number of poses (NP) and mapping completeness (MC) used by each method in the two maps: Zigzag, ACO, and MARS-SLAM.

	Map	Zigzag	ACO	MARS-SLAM
NP	M1	8970.50 $\pm$ 19.16	5317.70 $\pm$ 40.49	**4404.00 $\pm$ 280.85**
	M2	23897.20 $\pm$ 333.76	15608.73 $\pm$ 294.43	**7618.30 $\pm$ 1277.47**
MC %	M1	100.0 $\pm$ 0.0	100.0 $\pm$ 0.0	100.0 $\pm$ 0.0
	M2	100.0 $\pm$ 0.0	100.0 $\pm$ 0.0	99.7 $\pm$ 0.3

Figure 7 illustrates the comparison between the evaluated methods based on two criteria: the number of poses and the total simulation time. Figure 7(a)

Table 3. Data showing the preprocessing time (PT), navigation time (NT), and total simulation time (TT) used by each method in the two maps: Zigzag, ACO, and MARS-SLAM.

	Map	Zigzag	ACO	MARS-SLAM
PT (s)	M1	6.2 ± 1.1	1750.5 ± 227.7	$\mathbf{0.0 \pm 0.0}$
	M2	35.3 ± 5.2	12503.2 ± 2501.3	$\mathbf{0.0 \pm 0.0}$
NT (s)	M1	10764.6 ± 23.0	6381.2 ± 48.6	$\mathbf{5725.2 \pm 364.1}$
	M2	28676.6 ± 400.5	18730.5 ± 353.3	$\mathbf{13331.0 \pm 2554.9}$
TT (s)	M1	10770.8 ± 24.1	8131.7 ± 276.3	$\mathbf{5725.2 \pm 364.1}$
	M2	28711.9 ± 405.7	31233.7 ± 2854.6	$\mathbf{13331.0 \pm 2554.9}$

compares the number of poses used by each method across the three maps; Fig. 7(b) compares the required simulation time. It is observed that for Maps 1 and 2, MARS-SLAM demonstrates consistency, showing a significantly lower number of poses compared to the other methods.

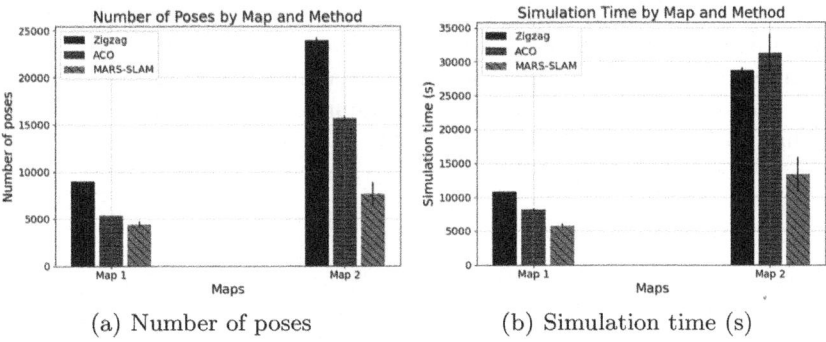

(a) Number of poses   (b) Simulation time (s)

Fig. 7. Comparison between the methods for the number of poses (a) and total simulation time (b) across three different maps.

Simulation time impacts resource costs during SLAM, but the number of poses is a more critical indicator of mapping quality. A lower number of poses reflects higher efficiency, avoiding redundancies while producing accurate and compact maps suitable for reuse. Table 4 shows the percentage variations in the number of poses across methods and scenarios, highlighting MARS-SLAM's superior performance. In Map 1, MARS-SLAM achieves a 50.9% reduction compared to Zigzag and 17.1% compared to ACO, while in Map 2, the reductions reach 68.1% and 48.8%, respectively. Unlike ACO and Zigzag, which require prior map knowledge for marker grid distribution, MARS-SLAM autonomously explores unknown environments, adapting in real time. This adaptability makes MARS-SLAM a robust solution for unpredictable scenarios, where pre-mapped data is unavailable.

Table 4. The number of poses variation in Maps 1 and 2, comparing Zigzag, ACO, and MARS-SLAM methods.

		The Number of Poses Variation (%) Compare To		
		Zigzag	ACO	MARS-SLAM
Map 1	Zigzag	0	+68.7	+103.7
	ACO	−40.7	0	+20.8
	MARS-SLAM	**−50.9**	−17.1	0
Map 2	Zigzag	0	+53.1	+213.6
	ACO	−34.7	0	+105.0
	MARS-SLAM	**−68.1**	−48.8	0

In terms of completeness, as presented in Table 2, all methods fully map the environment in Map 1, achieving 100.0% completeness. In Map 2, MARS-SLAM attains 99.7% completeness, with a slight variation due to the shadow effect, illustrated in Fig. 8. This phenomenon occurs when the LiDAR's limited reading angle ($-90°$ to $90°$) and marker placement strategy fail to detect narrow regions, such as doorways or dense structures. For example, when the robot passes perpendicularly through a narrow doorway, it may only detect the doorframe, missing inner spaces and leaving areas unmapped. This issue intensifies in dense environments, where marker dispersion is insufficient, creating shadow zones that falsely appear as mapped.

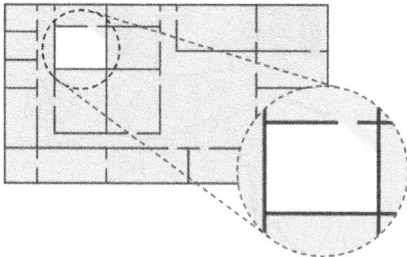

Fig. 8. Example of the shadow effect caused by the robot navigating through narrow areas. In such cases, the LiDAR may fail to accurately detect unmapped regions, leading to shadow zones where the robot incorrectly assumes the area has been fully mapped.

Overall, MARS-SLAM yields superior results, significantly reducing the number of poses while maintaining mapping completeness. This efficiency translates into more effective navigation and higher-quality mapping, making MARS-SLAM a valuable tool for real-world applications. A crucial distinction is that MARS-SLAM is designed to operate in completely unknown environments, unlike ACO and Zigzag, which require prior knowledge of the map for marker placement. This autonomy enables MARS-SLAM to adapt dynamically to the environment, making it a more robust and versatile solution for scenarios where no pre-mapped data is available.

5   Conclusion

This paper introduces MARS-SLAM, a novel method leveraging markers to optimize SLAM in unknown environments. MARS-SLAM ensures efficient and accurate mapping by identifying and tracking unexplored regions while minimizing resource usage, such as the number of poses. Experiments in two virtual scenarios demonstrated its superior performance compared to methods like Zigzag and ACO, achieving high mapping completeness while significantly reducing the number of poses and total simulation time. In Map 1, MARS-SLAM reduced the number of poses by 50.9% compared to Zigzag and 17.2% compared to ACO. In Map 2, the reduction was even more pronounced, with MARS-SLAM using 68.1% fewer poses than Zigzag and 51.2% fewer than ACO. This efficiency translates into lower computational cost and improved mapping quality, making MARS-SLAM particularly valuable for autonomous mobile robotics.

The use of markers provides a robust mechanism for optimizing the mapping process and verifying completeness, though challenges such as the shadow effect in narrow areas, caused by LiDAR limitations, led to slight reductions in mapping accuracy. In Map 2, MARS-SLAM achieved 99.7% mapping completeness, with minor errors due to undetected regions. Future improvements in sensor configuration, such as increasing measurement density or refining marker placement strategies, could mitigate these limitations.

While MARS-SLAM excelled in virtual environments, its performance in real-world settings remains to be validated. Factors like dynamic obstacles, varying obstacle density, and alternative sensor types (e.g., RGB-D cameras or radars) may impact results. Adapting MARS-SLAM to dynamic environments and integrating it with real-time autonomous navigation systems could broaden its applicability, including challenging missions like search and rescue. Additionally, optimizing preprocessing time and further refining the marker selection algorithm could enhance computational efficiency. These adaptations could strengthen MARS-SLAM's robustness and utility across diverse scenarios, solidifying its role as a powerful tool for autonomous exploration.

References

1. Aulinas, J., Petillot, Y., Salvi, J., Lladó, X.: The slam problem: a survey. Artifi. Intell. Res. Developm., 363–371 (2008)
2. Blochliger, F., Fehr, M., Dymczyk, M., Schneider, T., Siegwart, R.: Topomap: topological mapping and navigation based on visual slam maps. In: 2018 IEEE International Conference on Robotics and Automation (ICRA), pp. 3818–3825. IEEE (2018)
3. Bogue, R.: Robots for space exploration. Indust. Robot: Inter. J. **39**(4), 323–328 (2012)

4. Bryson, M., Sukkarieh, S.: Active airborne localisation and exploration in unknown environments using inertial slam. In: 2006 IEEE Aerospace Conference, pp. 13–pp. IEEE (2006)
5. Chang, H.J., Lee, C.G., Lu, Y.H., Hu, Y.C.: P-slam: Simultaneous localization and mapping with environmental-structure prediction. IEEE Trans. Rob. **23**(2), 281–293 (2007)
6. Dorigo, M., Birattari, M., Stutzle, T.: Ant colony optimization. IEEE Comput. Intell. Mag. **1**(4), 28–39 (2006)
7. Garcia, E., Jimenez, M.A., De Santos, P.G., Armada, M.: The evolution of robotics research. IEEE Robot. Autom. Mag. **14**(1), 90–103 (2007)
8. Liu, Y., Zhou, Z., Sang, H., Yu, S., Yan, Y., Er, M.J.: Efficient exploration of mobile robot based on dl-rrt and ap-bo. IEEE Trans. Instrument. Measure. (2024)
9. Maurović, I., Seder, M., Lenac, K., Petrović, I.: Path planning for active slam based on the d* algorithm with negative edge weights. IEEE Trans. Syst. Man Cybernet. Syst. **48**(8), 1321–1331 (2017)
10. Saravanan, S., Chauffaut, C., Chanel, C., Vivet, D.: Fit-slam–fisher information and traversability estimation-based active slam for exploration in 3d environments. arXiv preprint arXiv:2401.09322 (2024)
11. Takleh, T., Bakar, N.A., Rahman, S.A., Hamzah, R., Aziz, Z.: A brief survey on slam methods in autonomous vehicle. Int. J. Eng. Technol **7**(4), 38–43 (2018)
12. Wang, J., Shan, T., Englot, B.: Virtual maps for autonomous exploration with pose slam. In: 2019 IEEE/RSJ International Conference on Intelligent Robots and Systems (IROS), pp. 4899–4906. IEEE (2019)
13. Zhan, Z., Jian, W., Li, Y., Yue, Y.: A slam map restoration algorithm based on submaps and an undirected connected graph. IEEE Access **9**, 12657–12674 (2021)
14. Zhang, X., Lai, J., Xu, D., Li, H., Fu, M.: 2d lidar-based slam and path planning for indoor rescue using mobile robots. J. Adv. Transp. **2020**(1), 8867937 (2020)

Pollutant Spill Containment via Flocking

Luan Rodrigues[1,2], Nadia Nedjah[1,2(✉)],
and Luiza de Macedo Mourelle[1,2(✉)]

[1] Department of Electronics Engineering and Telecommunications,
State University of Rio de Janeiro, Rio de Janeiro, Brazil
{nadia,ldmm}@eng.uerj.br
[2] Department of Systems Engineering and Computation, State University of Rio de
Janeiro, Rio de Janeiro, Brazil

Abstract. The increasing contamination of water bodies by low-density
pollutants, such as oil and its derivatives, represents a significant environmental challenge, affecting aquatic ecosystems and coastal economies.
Conventional response relies on floating booms that teams must position
and maintain, present limitations due to adverse environmental factors
like winds and ocean currents. This study proposes an innovative approach based on swarm intelligence that automates the assembly, positioning, and dynamic stabilization of the same type of physical boom,
each autonomous surface vehicle is equipped with a short boom segment.
Inspired by collective behaviors in nature, the method combines the
Flocking algorithm and Particle Swarm Optimization, enabling mobile
agents to detect and surround the contaminated area in a distributed
and efficient manner. Simulations were conducted to evaluate the effectiveness of the technique in different scenarios, considering pollutant
patches with both geometric and abstract shapes. The results demonstrated that the method can form stable barriers, adapting to variations
in the shape and initial positions of the agents. Additionally, the approach proved robust against environmental challenges, ensuring effective
pollutant containment without the need for direct human intervention.

Keywords: Swarm Intelligence · Pollutant Containment ·
Multi-Agent Systems · Flocking · PSO · Oil Spill

1 Introduction

Among the various pollutants, oil spills stand out as one of the greatest threats
to ecosystems, as fish exposed to oil and its toxic compounds (for example, Polycyclic Aromatic Hydrocarbons, or PAHs) suffer from mutations in eggs, deformi-
ties in embryos and larvae, and damage to gills, impairing respiration, mobility,
and making these animals unsuitable for consumption [1]. Species with limited
mobility, such as crustaceans and benthic mollusks, are even more vulnerable,
often accumulating toxins that disrupt their natural growth and reproductive
cycles [2].

O. Gervasi et al. (Eds.): ICCSA 2025 Workshops, LNCS 15888, pp. 37–55, 2026.
https://doi.org/10.1007/978-3-031-97596-7_3

The most commonly used solution for pollutant spills involve the deployment of containment barriers to prevent the substance from spreading in the aquatic environment, as once dispersed, removal becomes nearly unfeasible. However, these measures heavily rely on human intervention and are subject to environmental adversities, such as winds, currents, and tides. These conditions can compromise the efficiency of the barriers, especially when wave heights exceed 1.5 m or when the current speed surpasses 0.5 m/s, leading to failures such as pollutants passing underneath or overflowing the barriers [3]. Additionally, the time required to position these barriers can be significant due to complex logistics and the need for specialized labor, particularly in large-scale spills or hard-to-reach areas. Under unfavorable weather conditions, the pollutant can spread rapidly, exacerbating the problem. Thus, although essential in the initial containment stage, the effectiveness of barriers is closely linked to environmental factors and the speed of their deployment [4].

In this work, the design and simulation of an approach based on swarm intelligence is proposed to enable the automatic containment of these low-density pollutants on the water [5]. Inspired by collective behaviors in nature, such as those observed in fish schools, swarm intelligence offers a scalable, flexible, and resilient solution in which each agent in the swarm collaborates to identify and isolate the contaminant, increasing efficiency compared to traditional methods, while also reducing operational costs and minimizing environmental impacts [6].

The primary objective is to propose a scalable, stable, and computationally low-cost method that efficiently identifies the boundary between areas of high and low pollutant concentration. This method is mainly based on the flocking behavior and should ensure a reduced convergence time. Furthermore, once the boundary is detected, the agents would be distributed to form a uniform and evenly spaced barrier to encapsulate the pollutant. It is intended that this barrier remains stable and in position, regardless of environmental conditions.

This paper is structured into five main sections. Section 2 describes related works addressing the problem of boundary identification and barrier formation using swarm intelligence. Section 3 details the methods required for the development of the control approach. The derivation of the proposed method is presented in Sect. 4. Simulation results and experiments are discussed in Sect. 5. Finally, Sect. 6 presents concluding remarks and potential extensions of this work for future research.

2   Related Work

This section presents a review of studies that served as inspiration and reference for the development of the present study, focusing primarily on the control and maintenance of formations of multiple distributed agents aiming to surround a target without prior knowledge of its position or speed. For example, the work presented in [7] addresses the control of circular formation of multiple agents around a moving target with unknown and variable speed. The agents use local sensors to capture information related to the target and their neighbors, considering connectivity constraints, collision avoidance, and uniformly spaced formation. The proposed controller employs the universal Lyapunov barrier function to ensure connectivity stability, formation maintenance, collision prevention, and operation under sensor limitations.

The study presented in [8] proposes a distributed algorithm for the formation of barriers by mobile agents around hazardous areas, using only local information and without prior knowledge of the boundaries of the risk region. The algorithm takes into account the detection and communication limitations of the agents, which operate within a specific radius, guiding the robots to form initial barriers at the edge of the hazardous area, followed by additional barriers at predefined distances. The process is divided into two main stages: border search and barrier formation. During the border search stage, agents adapt their movement based on their initial position: outside the area, near the edge, or inside it. Strategies such as spiral movement, direct movement, or straight-line paths are used to efficiently locate the border. In the barrier formation stage, agents adjust their positions based on the number of neighbors detected within the communication radius. Collision avoidance forces are applied to ensure proper spacing between agents, forming a uniform and functional barrier.

The work by [9] presents a decentralized control algorithm for swarms of minimalist robots aimed at encapsulating multiple targets while avoiding collisions with obstacles, whether static, dynamic, or with other swarm robots. The algorithm is based on three main components. In the initial phase, robots perform a random walk, autonomously exploring the environment and avoiding obstacles when no target is detected. In the second phase, upon detecting a signal below the safety threshold, robots approach the target, adjusting their positions in a coordinated manner to encapsulate it while continuing to avoid collisions. The use of the Lyapunov theorem in defining control parameters ensures stability during the approach. In the third phase, robots monitor signals above the safety threshold to prevent imminent collisions, adjusting their trajectories to maintain a minimum safe distance. The algorithm also addresses challenges such as sensor noise, asynchronous execution, and variations in control parameters, demonstrating robustness and scalability in simulations.

The study presented in [10] addresses formation control in distributed robotic swarms, focusing on multiple formations where robots must maintain appropriate distances from each other while navigating the environment and avoiding collisions with obstacles and other groups of agents. A distributed algorithm combining quadratic programming and control barrier functions was developed for this purpose. The barrier functions meet system requirements such as formation maintenance, collision prevention, and unified navigation. Formation maintenance is ensured by a rigid graph that defines the desired distances between pairs of robots, while obstacle collision avoidance is achieved by modeling obstacles as circles, ensuring that robots maintain a safe distance from their boundaries. To prevent collisions between groups, each formation is represented by an ellipse, enabling specific strategies to maintain safe distances. Additionally, the algorithm optimizes communication by using only one robot per formation to exchange information. Quadratic programming is employed to determine control parameters that comply with all imposed constraints.

3   Methodological Background

The method proposed in this study is inspired by algorithms that simulate the collective behavior of animals moving in groups in nature, such as fish schools and bee swarms. The algorithms that underpin the developed approach are *Flocking* [11] and *Particle Swarm Optimization* (PSO) [12]. These models serve as the foundation for creating a methodology aimed at containing pollutants in aquatic environments.

3.1   Flocking

The *Flocking* algorithm was developed to realistically simulate the behavior and movements of bird flocks in flight. In the context of the algorithm, birds are represented by agents called *boids* [11]. Through the application of three simple rules, collective behavior emerges, allowing the swarm members to remain separated (avoiding collisions), aligned (moving in the same direction), and cohesive (staying close to one another). Applying these rules to *boid* i results in a total force, which is the weighted combination of the three forces generated by each rule. The basic rules are called separation, alignment, and cohesion.

Separation. The separation rule aims to prevent collisions between *boids*, ensuring that each one maintains a minimum distance from its closest neighbors. This is achieved by calculating a repulsion force proportional to the inverse square of the distance between *boid* i and its neighbors in the neighborhood $\mathcal{N}_i$. Mathematically, this rule can be expressed by Eq. 1:

$$\mathbf{f}_{\text{sep}}^{(t)} = k_{\text{sep}} \sum_{j \in \mathcal{N}_i^{(t)}} \frac{\mathbf{p}_i^{(t)} - \mathbf{p}_j^{(t)}}{\|\mathbf{p}_i^{(t)} - \mathbf{p}_j^{(t)}\|^2}, \tag{1}$$

where k_{sep} controls the intensity of the tendency for each agent to move away from its neighbors, $\mathcal{N}_i^{(t)}$ represents the set of neighbors near *boid* i at iteration t, defined by a perception radius, $\mathbf{p}_i^{(t)}$ is the position of *boid* i, and $\mathbf{p}_j$ is the position of a neighbor $j \in \mathcal{N}_i^{(t)}$ at iteration t.

Alignment. The alignment rule adjusts the movement direction of *boid* i to match the average direction of its neighbors, promoting uniformity in the group's behavior. The alignment force is calculated as the difference between the average velocity of the neighbors and the velocity of *boid* i, as shown in Eq. 2:

$$\mathbf{f}_{\mathrm{ali}}^{(t)} = \frac{k_{\mathrm{ali}}}{|\mathcal{N}_i^{(t)}|} \sum_{j \in \mathcal{N}_i^{(t)}} \mathbf{v}_j^{(t)} - \mathbf{v}_i^{(t)}, \tag{2}$$

where k_{ali} represents the tendency of each *boid* to align its velocity (direction and magnitude) with its neighbors, $|\mathcal{N}_i^{(t)}|$ is the number of neighbors of *boid* i, $\mathbf{v}_j^{(t)}$ is the velocity of a neighbor j, and $\mathbf{v}_i^{(t)}$ is the current velocity of *boid* i at iteration t.

Cohesion. The cohesion rule encourages each *boid* to move towards the center of mass of its neighbors, promoting group aggregation. This rule is described by Eq. 3:

$$\mathbf{f}_{\mathrm{coh}}^{(t)} = \frac{k_{\mathrm{coh}}}{|\mathcal{N}_i^{(t)}|} \sum_{j \in \mathcal{N}_i^{(t)}} \mathbf{p}_j^{(t)} - \mathbf{p}_i^{(t)}, \tag{3}$$

where k_{coh} defines the attraction force that each *boid* exerts to approach the group's center of mass. The term $\mathbf{p}_j^{(t)} - \mathbf{p}_i^{(t)}$ represents the vector pointing from *boid* i to the position of a neighbor j, and the average over all neighbors provides the direction to the local center of mass at iteration t.

Model Extensions. In addition to the basic rules, the *Flocking* model can be extended to incorporate new behaviors into the group. For example, it is possible to implement a rule that guides the group to chase a specific target or reach a predetermined position [13].

Chase. The chase behavior directs the *boid* to move directly toward a target point, **a**. This is achieved by applying a desired force toward the target and adjusting the *boid*'s velocity for consistent movement. This behavior can be mathematically described by Eq. 4:

$$\mathbf{f}_{\mathrm{prsg}}^{(t)} = k_{\mathrm{prsg}} \left(\frac{\mathbf{p}_a^{(t)} - \mathbf{p}_i^{(t)}}{\|\mathbf{p}_a^{(t)} - \mathbf{p}_i^{(t)}\|} \cdot \mathbf{v}_{max} - \mathbf{v}_i^{(t)} \right), \tag{4}$$

where k_{prsg} controls the intensity of the force generated during the chase, $\mathbf{p}_a^{(t)}$ and $\mathbf{p}_i^{(t)}$ are the positions of the target point and *boid* i at iteration t, respectively. The maximum velocity of the swarm's *boids* is denoted by $\mathbf{v}_{max}$, and $\mathbf{v}_i^{(t)}$ is the velocity of *boid* i at iteration t. Equation 4 models the force guiding the *boid* toward the target point. However, it does not account for deceleration as the *boid* approaches the target, which may lead to abrupt movements.

Approach. The approach behavior is an extension of the chase behavior. It introduces gradual deceleration as the *boid* nears the target point, $\mathbf{p}_a^t$. This approach prevents the *boid* from overshooting the target or arriving abruptly. The force calculation logic for *boid* i is detailed in Eq. 5.

$$
f_{\mathrm{aprx}}^{(t)} = \begin{cases} k_{\mathrm{aprx}} \dfrac{\mathbf{p}_a^{(t)} - \mathbf{p}_i^{(t)}}{\|\mathbf{p}_a^{(t)} - \mathbf{p}_i^{(t)}\|} \cdot \mathbf{v}_{\max} \cdot \dfrac{\|\mathbf{p}_a^{(t)} - \mathbf{p}_i^{(t)}\|}{r}, & \text{if } \|\mathbf{p}_a^{(t)} - \mathbf{p}_i^{(t)}\| < r \\[4mm] k_{\mathrm{aprx}} \dfrac{\mathbf{p}_a^{(t)} - \mathbf{p}_i^{(t)}}{\|\mathbf{p}_a^{(t)} - \mathbf{p}_i^{(t)}\|} \cdot \mathbf{v}_{\max}, & \text{if } \|\mathbf{p}_a^{(t)} - \mathbf{p}_i^{(t)}\| \geq r \end{cases} \tag{5}
$$

where k_{aprx} defines how smoothly the progressive deceleration occurs, and the parameter r sets the deceleration radius. When the *boid* is at a distance $\|\mathbf{p}_a^{(t)} - \mathbf{p}_i^{(t)}\|$ less than r, it decelerates proportionally to the remaining distance, ensuring it reaches the target in a controlled manner without overshooting.

3.2   Particle Swarm Optimization

Particle Swarm Optimization is a metaheuristic inspired by the behavior of bird flocks, enabling the search for optimal values of a continuous objective function across the entire real domain. This search considers a d-dimensional space, where each variable has minimum and maximum limits. In PSO, a set of particles exchanges information among themselves, combining each particle's individual experience with the collective knowledge of the swarm to find the best global solution to the objective function [12]. The update dynamics of the particles, considering a limited field of view for the swarm members, is mathematically described by Eq. 6:

$$
\mathbf{v}_i^{(t+1)} = k_{\mathrm{pso}} \left(w \cdot \mathbf{v}_i^{(t)} + c_1 \cdot r_1^{(t)} \cdot \left(\mathbf{b}_i^{(t)} - \mathbf{p}_i^{(t)} \right) + c_2 \cdot r_2^{(t)} \cdot \left(\mathbf{g}_\alpha^{(t)} - \mathbf{p}_i^{(t)} \right) \right), \tag{6}
$$

where k_{pso} is a constant used to enhance the result of the PSO algorithm, $\mathbf{p}_i^{(t)}$ and $\mathbf{v}_i^{(t)}$ are, respectively, the position and velocity vectors of particle i at iteration t, $\mathbf{b}_i^{(t)}$ represents the best position found by particle i in its trajectory, and $\mathbf{g}_\alpha^{(t)}$ corresponds to the best position discovered by its neighborhood. The term w is the inertia weight, while c_1 and c_2 are the cognitive and social coefficients, responsible for balancing local exploration and global exploitation. Finally, $r_1^{(t)}$ and $r_2^{(t)}$ are random numbers uniformly distributed in $[0, 1]$.

At each iteration, $\mathbf{g}_\alpha^{(t)}$ is updated if $f(\mathbf{p}_i^{(t)}) > f(\mathbf{g}_\alpha^{(t)})$, meaning that if particle i finds a solution better than the global best solution, the global best is updated. Similarly, the personal best position $\mathbf{b}_i^{(t)}$ is updated if $f(\mathbf{p}_i^{(t)}) > f(\mathbf{b}_i^{(t)})$.

4   Proposed Method

The method proposed in this work is based on the combined application of the separation, alignment, and cohesion rules, along with the behaviors of chasing and approaching a target point. Additionally, new rules were developed to enable the emergence of behaviors within the swarm for detecting and containing pollutants.

To understand how the developed rules operate, it is essential first to formalize the conceptual model of a *boid*, the fundamental element of the swarm. All members of the swarm share identical characteristics with the standard *boid*, serving as the starting point for defining and implementing the proposed rules. Figure 1 presents the conceptual representation of a *boid*.

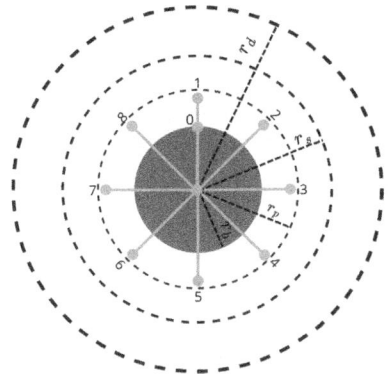

Fig. 1. Conceptual representation of a *boid*.

As shown in Fig. 1, the *boid* features four distinct radius: r_d, which defines the perception radius; r_s, corresponding to the safety radius to avoid collisions; r_p, representing the length of the arms equipped with probes at their ends; and r_b, referring to the size of the *boid*'s body.

The *boid* model includes nine probes to measure pollutant concentrations within its operating region. Eight of these probes are arranged around the body, as illustrated in Fig. 1, and are numbered from 1 to 8. There is also a central probe, identified as 0, capable of determining whether the *boid* is positioned over a contaminated area. The *boid* possesses a limited internal memory but is capable of storing relevant information from its local experience. This memory records the detected border position, denoted by $p_i^{(e)}$, and the time when the *boid* encountered the pollutant's edge, as well as attributes required for PSO, such as the local optimum and its neighborhood's best.

With the conceptual model of the *boids* properly established, the algorithm for pollutant detection and containment was developed. This operation involves deploying a swarm of identical agents into the water, with prior knowledge of the pollutant's source. If the pollutant is merely floating in the ocean, for instance, this information consists of an approximate position of its center, indicated by $p^{(S)}$. However, the agents have no knowledge of the shape or dimensions of the pollutant patch's borders, which are less dense than water. The agents' objective is to locate the boundary of this patch and encapsulate it, preventing its dispersion. Algorithm 1 details the procedure used to achieve this goal.

The algorithm begins by defining the fundamental parameters essential for the operation's effectiveness. The number of *boids* required to contain the pollu-

---

Algorithm 1. Detection and Containment of a Pollutant in Water.

Require: N_b, η, r_d, r_s, $p^{(S)}$, ξ, δ
Require: k_{sep}, k_{ali}, k_{coh}, k_{pso}, k_{prsg}, k_a, w, c_1, c_2
Ensure: $\Omega = 1$
1: $B \leftarrow$ initialize swarm with N_b; $f \leftarrow 0$; $\Omega \leftarrow 0$
2: **while** $\Omega = 0$ **do**
3:     **for all** $i \in B$ **do**
4:         $\boldsymbol{f} \leftarrow \boldsymbol{0}$
5:         **if** $\boldsymbol{p}_i^{(e)} \neq \emptyset$ **then**
6:             Check if *boid* i is in a dense region
7:             $\boldsymbol{p}_i^{(e)} \leftarrow$ Adjust position $\boldsymbol{p}_i^{(e)}$ of *boid* i using r_s, r_d and δ
8:             $\boldsymbol{f} \leftarrow$ Compute Eq. 5 for *boid* i using $\boldsymbol{p}_i^{(e)}$ as $\boldsymbol{p}_a$ and weight k_{aprx}
9:         **else**
10:            $\mathcal{N} \leftarrow$ Get neighborhood of i inside radius r_s
11:            $\mathcal{N}' \leftarrow \mathcal{N}' \cup \{p_k^{(e)} \mid p_k^{(e)} \neq \emptyset, k \in \mathcal{N}\}$
12:            **if** $|\mathcal{N}'| = 0$ **then**
13:                $\boldsymbol{f} \leftarrow \boldsymbol{f}+$ Compute Eq. 4 for *boid* i using $p^{(S)}$ as $\boldsymbol{p}_a$ and weight k_{prsg}
14:            **end if**
15:            $\beta \leftarrow$ Detect border using *boid* i with threshold η and radius r_s
16:            **if** $\beta = 1$ **then**
17:                $\boldsymbol{p}_i^{(e)} \leftarrow \boldsymbol{p}_i$
18:            **end if**
19:            $\boldsymbol{f} \leftarrow \boldsymbol{f}+$ Compute Flocking forces for *boid* i using k_{sep}, k_{ali}, k_{coh}
20:            $\boldsymbol{f} \leftarrow \boldsymbol{f}+$ Compute PSO force for *boid* i using w, c_1, c_2 and weight k_{pso}
21:            $\boldsymbol{f} \leftarrow \boldsymbol{f}+$ Compute polluted area avoidance force for *boid* i with η, r_s, k_a
22:        **end if**
23:        Move *boid* i using computed force $\boldsymbol{f}$
24:    **end for**
25: **end while**

---

tant is represented by N_b, while r_s corresponds to the safety radius, determining the minimum distance each *boid* must maintain from its immediate neighbor when positioning itself at the edge of the polluted region to avoid collisions. The parameter r_d refers to the perception radius of each *boid*, which defines the maximum distance for sending and receiving messages. The concentration threshold required to classify a region as highly polluted is indicated by η.

The collective behavior of the *boids* is regulated by a set of constants that influence their movement dynamics. The constants k_{sep}, k_{ali}, and k_{coh} determine the weights of the separation, alignment, and cohesion forces, respectively.

The term k_{pso} regulates the influence of the PSO Algorithm, while k_{prsg} controls the pursuit of the pollutant source, and k_a modulates the evasion of highly contaminated areas. Additionally, the parameters w, c_1, and c_2 represent the inertia coefficient and the weights associated with local and global knowledge in the PSO, respectively. The algorithm also employs a factor β, used to indicate whether the *boid* has already identified the position of the pollutant's edge, allowing efficient coordination of the collective formation.

After defining the initial parameters, the swarm is deployed, and the boolean variable Ω is introduced to indicate the complete formation of the barrier around the pollutant. The barrier is considered stabilized when the standard deviation and variance among the agents within its structure are less than or equal to ξ. While the pollutant is not fully contained, the algorithm remains in execution.

Each *boid* checks its internal memory to see if the position of the pollutant's edge has already been recorded. This verification is essential to prevent the agent from altering its previously identified position due to environmental influences. Next, it analyzes the validity of its position at the edge. If this edge has already been determined, the *boid* evaluates the number of agents within the radius r_s. If there is only one neighbor, it requests information from that neighbor regarding the total number of agents within r_s. If more than two agents are identified, *boid* i moves away from the edge, as its presence would compromise the uniformity of the pollutant containment barrier.

If this condition is not met, *boid* i recalculates its position to maintain an equidistant spacing from the nearest neighbor that has also identified the edge. This adjustment is performed according to the procedures described in Algorithm 2, ensuring the homogeneous distribution of agents and the stability of the barrier.

Algorithm 2. Adjust Position of *boid* i on the edge.

Require: r_d, $p_i^{(e)}$, r_s, δ

Ensure: $p_i^{(e)'}$

1: $\alpha \leftarrow 0.98r_s$; $\beta \leftarrow 1.02r_s$; $\mathcal{B} \leftarrow \emptyset$
2: $\mathcal{N} \leftarrow$ Get neighborhood of *boid* i inside radius r_d;
3: $\mathcal{N}' \leftarrow \mathcal{N} \cup \{p_k^{(e)} \mid p_k^{(e)} \neq \emptyset, k \in \mathcal{N}\}$; $\mathcal{N}' \leftarrow$ Sort $\mathcal{N}'$ by distance to *boid* i
4: $\mathcal{B} \leftarrow \mathcal{B} \cup \{\boldsymbol{p}_k^{(e)} \mid \alpha \leq \|\boldsymbol{p}_k^{(e)} - \boldsymbol{p}_i^{(e)}\| \leq \beta, k \in \mathcal{N}'\}$
5: **if** $|\mathcal{N}'| = 0$ **then**
6: $\quad p_i^{(e)'} \leftarrow p_i^{(e)}$
7: **else**
8: $\quad j \leftarrow \mathcal{N}'[0]$
9: $\quad$ **if** $|\mathcal{B}| = 1 \wedge t_i \geq \delta$ **then**
10: $\quad\quad k \leftarrow \mathcal{N}'[1]$
11: $\quad\quad$ **if** $\|p_k^{(e)} - p_j^{(e)}\| < \|p_k^{(e)} - p_i^{(e)}\|$ **then**
12: $\quad\quad\quad \boldsymbol{p} = \boldsymbol{p}_k^{(e)}$
13: $\quad\quad$ **else**
14: $\quad\quad\quad \boldsymbol{p} = \boldsymbol{p}_j^{(e)}$
15: $\quad\quad$ **end if**
16: $\quad$ **else**
17: $\quad\quad \boldsymbol{p} \leftarrow \boldsymbol{p}_j^{(e)}$
18: $\quad$ **end if**
19: **end if**
20: $\boldsymbol{p}_i^{(e)'} \leftarrow \boldsymbol{p} + r_s \cdot \frac{p_i^{(e)} - p}{\|p_i^{(e)} - p\|}$

Algorithm 2 performs a progressive adjustment of the edge position detected by *boid* i, ensuring a uniform distribution among the agents that have already identified this region of the pollutant. This adjustment is based on a vector operation that normalizes and scales the direction vector between the initial position of the edge detected by *boid* i and the position previously identified by its nearest neighbor. If *boid* i has a neighbor within a closed interval around r_s and has identified the edge for a time δ, it will adjust its position based on its second closest neighbor, *boid* k, located on the opposite side from i's nearest neighbor. To maintain the formation in Algorithm 1, each *boid* must remain at the position where it initially identified the edge. If this position is adjusted by Algorithm 2, the agent will consider the new position as its reference. For this purpose, Eq. 5 is applied, promoting the agent's gradual return to the recorded position whenever there is a deviation, ensuring the stability and cohesion of the containment barrier throughout the process.

During the execution of Algorithm 1, if the *boid* has not yet identified the edge position, the search phase begins. The first step is to guide the *boids* to move towards the pollutant source, represented by $p^{(S)}$. This behavior aims to provide an initial indication of the direction to be followed so that the agents can reach their objective. However, once more than one *boid* in the neighborhood detects the edge, this tendency is deactivated. Next, the set of probes embedded in the *boid*'s body is read, and the data is stored in the variable S_i. With this information, it is verified whether the agent is at the pollutant's edge. The verification process follows the procedures defined in Algorithm 3, ensuring correct edge identification and allowing the containment strategy to proceed.

Algorithm 3. Detect the edge for *boid* i

Require: η, r_s
Ensure: β
1: $N_S^P \leftarrow$ Count *boid* i probes above η; $S_i^b \leftarrow$ Check if body probe values are below η
2: $\mathcal{N} \leftarrow$ Get neighborhood of *boid* i within r_s
3: **if** $N_S^P \geq 1 \wedge S_i^b = 0 \wedge |\mathcal{N}| < 2$ **then**
4:     $\beta \leftarrow 1$
5: **else**
6:     $\beta \leftarrow 0$
7: **end if**

Algorithm 3 is designed to identify whether the *boid* is at the boundary between regions of high and low pollutant concentration. Using the provided parameters, it verifies the values measured by the probes, counting the number of probes that register values above η, represented by N_S^P. It then checks if the probe located on the *boid*'s body, S_i^b, indicates a high concentration of pollutants. The set of neighbors within the safety radius r_s is also obtained.

The determination of whether the *boid* is at the edge is evaluated based on three criteria, with the result indicated by the variable β, which takes the value 1 if the *boid* is at the edge. First, N_S^P must be greater than or equal to one, indicating that at least one of the probes detects a high concentration of pollutants. Second, S_i^b must not register a high concentration, ensuring that the body of the *boid* is not within the polluted region. Finally, the number of neighbors within the safety radius must be less than two, ensuring that the *boid* is not occupying a position already taken in the formation of the barrier.

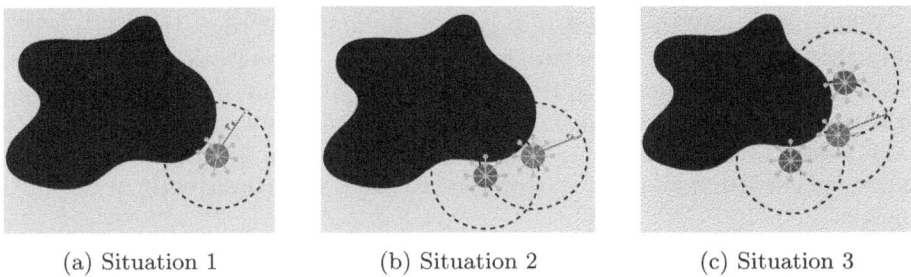

(a) Situation 1   (b) Situation 2   (c) Situation 3

Fig. 2. Illustration of the application of the edge detection rule.

The *boid* detects the edge when at least one of its probes enters the pollutant region while its body probe remains outside. An additional condition is required to validate the position where the *boid* identifies the edge. Figure 2 illustrates how this condition functions. In the first scenario, illustrated in Fig. 2a, the *boid* detects the edge without any neighboring *boids* within radius r_s, making the position valid. In the second scenario, as shown in Fig. 2b, the *boid* detects the edge with one neighbor within radius r_s, which is still considered valid. However, in the third scenario, presented in Fig. 2c, the *boid* detects the edge but has two neighbors within radius r_s, rendering the position invalid as it is already occupied in the formed barrier.

In Algorithm 1, if the *boid* determines the edge position during the iteration (i.e., if $\beta = 1$), it records this position in its memory as its current location. Then, the rules associated with *Flocking* [11] are applied, starting a verification to determine whether the *boid* is in a region with other agents that have already identified the edge. If so, the *boid* considers only the edge agents in the calculation of alignment and cohesion rules, directing itself towards those that have already detected the edge, thus increasing its chances of identification. However, all agents, regardless of their position, are included in the calculation of the separation rule.

If the *boid* is in a region with a low concentration of agents that have identified the edge, all neighbors within r_d are considered in the calculation of the alignment and cohesion rules. After these verifications, the sum of the separation, alignment, and cohesion forces is applied, ensuring the maintenance of the swarm's collective behavior and the stability of the formation over time.

After applying the *Flocking* rules [11] in Algorithm 1, the PSO Algorithm [12], described in Eq. 6, is employed to guide the *boids* towards the edge of the pollutant. In this process, the highest concentration value detected in the neighborhood is considered the global optimum. This information is obtained by querying the neighbors within radius r_d, and only these agents are considered in the evaluation. Moreover, *boids* that have already identified the edge position are automatically considered to hold the best global position in the neighborhood. Thus, the swarm tends to move toward the edge, ensuring that the containment of the pollutant is progressively reinforced by the collective dynamics of the agents.

While navigating the region in search of the pollutant edge, there is a possibility that the *boid* may enter an area with a high concentration of pollutants, potentially compromising both its operation and efficiency. To prevent this, the algorithm implements mechanisms that block the *boid*'s advancement under such conditions. These mechanisms are detailed in Algorithm 4, ensuring the *boid*'s safety and efficiency, allowing it to operate robustly and consistently in the environment.

Algorithm 4. Prevent *boid i* from entering the polluted region

---

Require: k_a, η, r_s
Ensure: f
1: $f \leftarrow 0$; $S_i \leftarrow$ Read probe values of *boid i*
2: $N_S^P \leftarrow$ Count *boid i* probes above η; $S_i^b \leftarrow$ check if body probe values are below η
3: **if** $N_S^P > 2 \vee S_i^b = 1$ **then**
4:     $p_i^{(s)} \leftarrow$ {Position of $s \mid s \in S_i \wedge s \leq \eta$}
5:     $f \leftarrow$ Compute Eq. 5 for *boid i* using $p_i^{(s)}$ as p_a and weight k_a
6: **end if**

The rule presented in Algorithm 4 performs an initial check of the probes of *boid i*, obtaining the values of N_S^P and S_i^b, as described in Algorithm 3. It then checks if the number of probes with values above η is greater than two, indicating that due to inertia, the *boid* will enter the polluted zone, or if the probe located on the *boid*'s body, S_i^b, is detecting pollutants. If neither condition is met, no action is taken. If at least one condition is true, the algorithm identifies the probe that is not detecting a concentration above η, as illustrated in Fig. 3. Based on this information, the *boid* calculates an approach to the position associated with this probe using Eq. 5. The force resulting from the approach equation is then used as the output of Algorithm 4.

Continuing with Algorithm 1, *boid i* is moved according to the direction of the resulting vector from the applied forces. With the complete update of the swarm, the stopping condition is evaluated based on the agents that have already determined the edge position.

Each *boid* on the edge transmits the distance to its closest neighbors to its adjacent neighbor, propagating this information throughout the formation until all agents on the edge are aware of these distances. After this step, the standard deviation and variance of these measurements are calculated. If the values of these metrics are less than or equal to ξ, it is considered that the algorithm

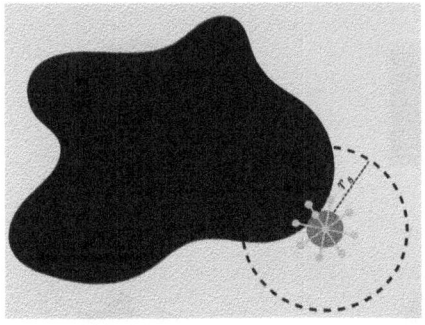 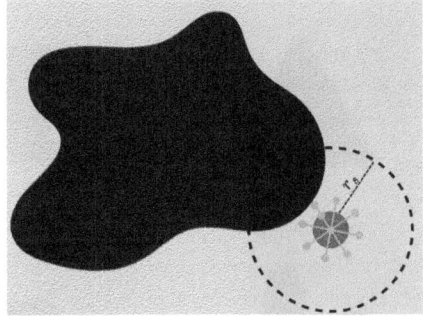

(a) *Boid* enters polluted zone.   (b) *Boid* backs out of the polluted zone.

Fig. 3. Illustration of the rule that prevents the *boid* entry into polluted zone.

has reached convergence, ensuring the stabilization of the barrier around the pollutant.

5   Results

In this section, we present the results obtained from the execution of the proposed approach. The experiments were conducted using the CPU of a computer equipped with an Intel Core i5-10400F processor, 2.9 GHz, and 16 GB of RAM.

To simulate the shape of the pollutant patch on the water surface, different shapes are generated. Initially, simple geometric shapes such as triangles, squares, and circles are used. Subsequently, additional tests are conducted using abstract shapes to showcase the applicability of the proposed approach to real-world scenarios. Figure 4 illustrates the synthetic shapes used in the experiments.

In Fig. 4, the pollutant patch is represented by the color black, while its surrounding blue area symbolizes the ocean. The sensing performed by the *boids* is based on extracting the RGB values from the region where their probes are positioned, with the color readings normalized on a scale from 0 to 1.

The shapes presented in Fig. 4 exhibit a slight gradient in the color tone representing the patch, allowing the agents to detect the edge through a threshold defined in Algorithm 1 as η. This approach is essential because, in the physical model, agents use sensors capable of measuring continuous pollutant concentrations. Without the color gradient, detection would occur in a binary manner, which would not accurately reflect the reality of the system. Therefore, the method employed enables a gradual transition in edge perception, making detection closer to the expected behavior in a physical environment.

Once the shapes to be used in the experiments were defined, the parameters for Algorithm 1 were set to ensure the best behavior for the swarm and the fastest convergence, allowing the algorithm to be evaluated under different conditions. The parameters used in the simulations are presented in Table 1.

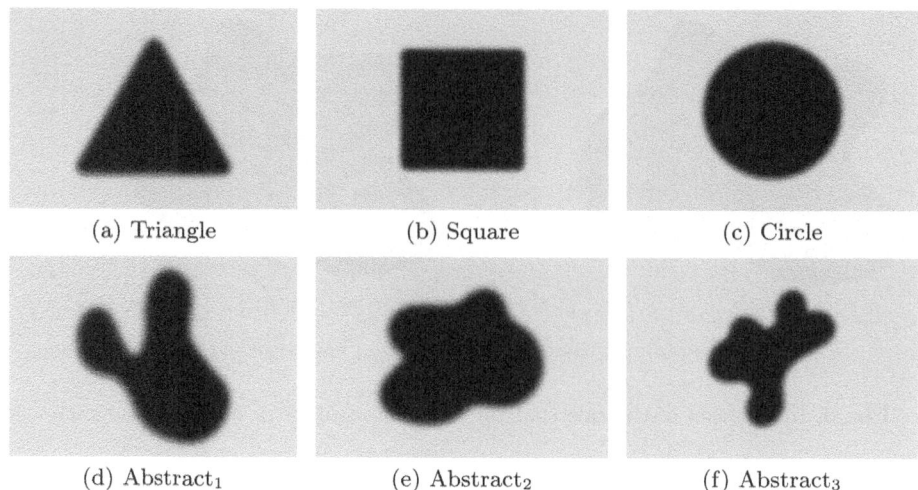

(a) Triangle	(b) Square	(c) Circle
(d) Abstract$_1$	(e) Abstract$_2$	(f) Abstract$_3$

Fig. 4. Set of synthetic forms created for experimental validation.

Table 1. Parameters setting.

Swarm setup		Boids parameters		PSO parameters		Flocking parameters	
N_b	96	r_b	10	w	2.9	k_{sep}	7.5
$v_{\max}$	2	r_d	80	c_1	1.8	k_{ali}	1.7
η	0.22	r_s	$0.35 r_d$	c_2	4	k_{coh}	1.7
$p^{(S)}$	(600,500)	r_p	$0.2 r_d$	k_{pso}	1.5	k_{prsg}	0.4
ξ	1.5	δ	5	-	-	k_{aprx}	3.0
-	-	-	-	-	-	k_{a}	12.5

In the experiments, the performance of the algorithm was evaluated based on the number of iterations required for convergence and the execution time. To ensure the reproducibility of the results, each experiment was executed 150 times, enabling the extraction and analysis of descriptive statistics for these metrics through tables and graphs.

Additionally, different initial configurations were tested by varying the launch positions of the agents, which could be distributed from any of the four corners of the figure. This strategy allowed for a more comprehensive evaluation of the algorithm's dynamics, assessing its ability to efficiently and distributively coordinate the identification and containment of the pollutant among the agents.

In the figures and tables used for the results analysis, the synthetic shapes considered are represented by *Shape*, while the number of distinct launch sites is indicated by #*LS*. When two launch sites are used, the notation 2′ denotes a variation in launch site location. The total number of iterations executed by the algorithm is indicated by #*IT*, and the execution time is represented by *ET*.

The first experiment conducted to evaluate the effectiveness of the developed method involved applying the algorithm to known geometric shapes previously presented in Fig. 4. This approach allowed testing the agents ability to detect and contain well-defined edges, providing a controlled environment for performance analysis.

Table 2 presents the mean, standard deviation, minimum, and maximum values for the total number of iterations and execution time across different geometric shapes and launch sites. The table analysis corroborates the hypothesis that the initial positions of the agents and the shape of the edge directly influence the algorithm's performance, resulting in significant variations in execution time and the number of iterations. The analysis highlights that the square is the most challenging shape to be contained, exhibiting the highest average execution time (94.84 ± 9.39 s) and the largest average number of iterations (5690.31 ± 563.48).

Table 2. Iterations and execution time for different geometric shapes across launch sites.

Shape	#LS	#IT				ET (s)			
		Mean	Std	Min	Max	Mean	Std	Min	Max
Triangle	1	4610.68	396.33	3977	6055	76.84	6.61	66.28	100.92
	2	2765.45	76.66	2591	2956	46.09	1.28	43.18	49.27
	2'	3015.39	730.52	1828	4955	50.26	12.18	30.47	82.58
	3	2811.23	525.8	2262	4845	46.85	8.76	37.7	80.75
	4	3762.57	1508.03	1695	10344	62.71	25.13	28.25	172.4
Square	1	5690.31	563.48	4451	7238	94.84	9.39	74.18	120.63
	2	5100.58	1560.09	2540	10696	85.01	26.0	42.33	178.27
	2'	4633.79	484.75	2987	5906	77.23	8.08	49.78	98.43
	3	5023.41	1559.17	2332	8918	83.72	25.99	38.87	148.63
	4	3003.37	450.48	2080	4401	50.06	7.51	34.67	73.35
Circle	1	3693.31	546.45	2406	5714	61.56	9.11	40.1	95.23
	2	4540.86	1315.5	2146	11388	75.68	21.93	35.77	189.8
	2'	4879.49	1198.71	2162	6986	81.32	19.98	36.03	116.43
	3	3035.83	803.54	1853	5929	50.6	13.39	30.88	98.82
	4	2944.4	814.09	1751	8490	49.07	13.57	29.18	141.5

This complexity arises from the difficulty of evenly dispersing agents around its sharp corners, leading to longer stabilization periods. In contrast, the triangle demonstrated the shortest average execution time (46.85 ± 8.76 s) and a reduced number of iterations (2811.23 ± 525.8), indicating a more efficient containment process. The circle, while presenting intermediate performance, displayed good uniformity in agent distribution, with execution times varying from 49.07 ± 13.57 s to 81.32 ± 19.98 s, depending on the launch site.

To further illustrate these findings, Fig. 5 presents boxplots of execution times for the different geometric shapes across various launch sites. The boxplots visually depict the distribution and variability of execution times, highlighting the impact of shape complexity and initial agent positions. Notably, the triangle consistently shows the shortest execution times, while the square reveals the largest spread, reinforcing its higher computational demand.

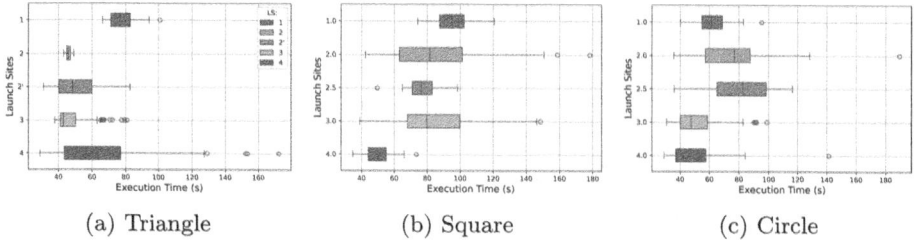

(a) Triangle   (b) Square   (c) Circle

Fig. 5. Boxplot of execution time for different geometric shapes across launch sites.

The presence of outliers in the boxplots suggests that the swarm's dynamics, influenced by the *Flocking* rules [11], occasionally led to random walks, impacting performance. Additionally, the initial distribution of agents played a crucial role in determining execution time, with varying launch points leading to notable differences in containment efficiency. This behavior is further visualized in the video available at: https://youtu.be/RFz8T2-FrYA, where the swarm dynamics and the algorithm's adaptation to distinct geometries are demonstrated.

Following the experiments with geometric shapes, the algorithm's ability to detect and contain a patch without a predefined shape was evaluated. For this purpose, the same parameters from the previous experiments were maintained, with only the shape configurations being altered. The new shapes used are represented in Fig. 4d–4f.

Table 3 presents the statistical data for the number of iterations and execution times across the tested abstract shapes and launch sites. The data confirm the hypothesis that the structural complexity of the shape and the variation in launch locations significantly affect the algorithm's performance. The containment of shape Abstract$_1$ shows the highest average execution times (104.63 s to 129.76 s) and iteration counts, while Abstract$_3$ demonstrates greater computational efficiency, with execution times ranging from 56.91 s to 88.55 s and fewer required iterations.

The data from Table 3 emphasize the influence of structural complexity and launch strategies on the containment process. The abstract shape Abstract$_1$ consistently required higher computational effort, while Abstract$_3$ exhibited a significant reduction in both execution time and iterations needed to stabilize the containment barrier. Additionally, the variation in launch sites directly impacted performance, with LS 4 consistently producing the best results across all shapes, significantly optimizing the algorithm's efficiency.

Table 3. Iterations and execution time for different abstract shapes across launch sites.

Shape	#LS	#IT				ET (s)			
		Mean	Std	Min	Max	Mean	Std	Min	Max
Abstract$_1$	1	7685.52	2732.61	2886	13585	128.09	45.54	48.1	226.42
	2	7785.65	3037.78	2972	13491	129.76	50.63	49.53	224.85
	2'	6853.44	2938.06	2405	13179	114.22	48.97	40.08	219.65
	3	7046.65	2844.43	2963	13317	117.44	47.41	49.38	221.95
	4	6277.76	2757.76	2031	12968	104.63	45.96	33.85	216.13
Abstract$_2$	1	6333.29	2694.35	2652	13677	105.55	44.91	44.2	227.95
	2	5942.18	2477.97	2411	12184	99.04	41.3	40.18	203.07
	2'	4464.37	2144.65	2031	12754	74.41	35.74	33.85	212.57
	3	4439.11	2183.51	1794	11011	73.99	36.39	29.9	183.52
	4	3831.38	2122.95	1738	13114	63.86	35.38	28.97	218.57
Abstract$_3$	1	5312.95	2353.21	2588	13880	88.55	39.22	43.13	231.33
	2	4145.83	1861.49	2001	11334	69.1	31.02	33.35	188.9
	2'	3921.22	2043.59	1920	11894	65.35	34.06	32.0	198.23
	3	4063.69	2132.92	1851	11583	67.73	35.55	30.85	193.05
	4	3414.47	1927.68	1775	12533	56.91	32.13	29.58	208.88

To further visualize these findings, Fig. 6 presents boxplots illustrating the distribution of execution times across different abstract shapes and launch sites. The figure highlights the spread and variability in execution times, reinforcing the observations derived from the statistical analysis. In particular, Abstract$_1$ displays a wider dispersion due to hard-to-reach regions, while Abstract$_3$ achieves a more consistent performance.

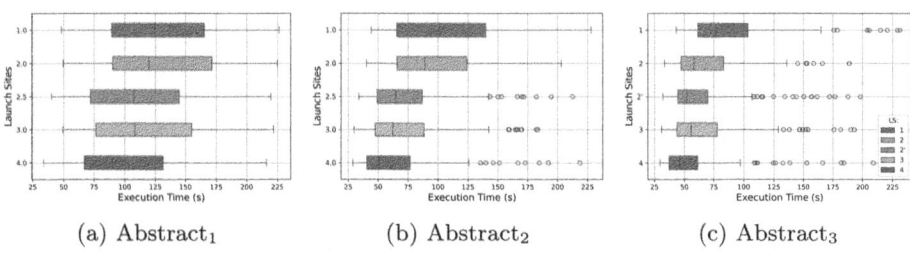

(a) Abstract$_1$ (b) Abstract$_2$ (c) Abstract$_3$

Fig. 6. Boxplot of execution time for different abstract shapes across launch sites.

The boxplots also reveal that in all scenarios, launching agents from four distinct points (LS 4) yielded the best containment results, evidenced by lower median execution times and reduced variability. This behavior is further validated in the video available at https://youtu.be/jLiOLX1hfOM, where the dynamics of agent distribution and the impact of varying launch strategies on containment efficiency are clearly demonstrated.

6 Conclusions

This study presented a swarm intelligence-based approach for the containment of low-density water pollutants, inspired by collective behaviors observed in nature, such as schools of fish and swarms of bees. The proposed methodology integrates the concepts of *Flocking* and Particle Swarm Optimization, combined with specific rules for detecting and dynamically forming barriers, providing a distributed, scalable, and efficient solution. The simulation results demonstrated that the developed method is capable of detecting and containing pollutant patches with varying geometries and levels of complexity, influenced by the initial distribution of agents and the shape of the patch. More regular shapes favored reduced containment times, while irregular geometries required a higher number of iterations. Among the main contributions, the application of swarm intelligence in mitigating environmental impacts stands out, offering an efficient alternative to traditional physical barriers.

For future work, we intend to reduce the algorithm's execution time, validate the method in robotic simulations, and implement parallel execution, allowing each *boid* to operate independently and in a decentralized manner. Furthermore, the incorporation of physical variables such as wind, tides, and currents will be essential to evaluate the algorithm's performance under dynamic environmental conditions, ensuring greater robustness and applicability in real-world scenarios. Although the current work outlines these objectives, the analysis of the simulation results could be enhanced through the inclusion of quantitative performance metrics, such as containment time, covered area, the workload distributed among agents, or comparative evaluations with existing approaches. This would allow a more rigorous assessment of the method's effectiveness and support its validation in future studies.

References

1. Silva, D.C.P., dos Santos Melo, C., de Oliveira, A.B., dos Santos, N.M.M., Pinto, L.C.: Oil spill in the sea and toxic implications of exposure to petroleum chemical. *Revista Contexto Saúde* **21**(44), 332–344 (2022)
2. Soares, M.O., Rabelo, E.F.: Severe ecological impacts caused by one of the worst orphan oil spills worldwide. Mar. Environ. Res. **187**, 105936 (2023)
3. Dhaka, A., Chattopadhyay, P.: A review on physical remediation techniques for treatment of marine oil spills. J. Environ. Manage. **288**, 112428 (2021)
4. Muttin, F.: Structural analysis of oil-spill containment booms in coastal and estuary waters. Appl. Ocean Res. **30**(2), 107–112 (2008)
5. Zahugi, E.M.H., Shanta, M.M., Prasad, T.V.: Oil spill cleaning up using swarm of robots. In: Meghanathan, N., Nagamalai, D., Chaki, N. (eds.) Advances in Computing and Information Technology. Advances in Intelligent Systems and Computing, vol. 178. Springer, Berlin (2013). https://doi.org/10.1007/978-3-642-31600-5_22

6. Kounte, M.R., Raghavendra Kashyap, T.M., Rahul, P., Ramyashree, M.K., Riya, J.K.: Oil spill detection and confrontation using instance segmentation and swarm intelligence. In: Mallick, P.K., Bhoi, A.K., Marques, G., Hugo C. de Albuquerque, V. (eds.) Cognitive Informatics and Soft Computing. AISC, vol. 1317, pp. 247–259. Springer, Singapore (2021). https://doi.org/10.1007/978-981-16-1056-1_20
7. Xiong, Y., Lu, K., Dai, S.-L.: Cooperative circular formation control design for enclosing a moving target with collision avoidance. In: 2022 41st Chinese Control Conference (CCC), pp. 4551–4556 (2022)
8. Shao, Y., et al.: Autobar: automatic barrier coverage formation for danger keep out applications in smart city. Sensors **23**(18) (2023)
9. Sinhmar, H., Gazit, H.K.: Decentralized control of minimalistic robotic swarms for guaranteed target encapsulation. In: 2022 IEEE/RSJ International Conference on Intelligent Robots and Systems (IROS). IEEE (October 2022)
10. Aynala, A., Atman, M.W.S., Gusrialdi, A.: Communication-efficient formation maintenance for multi-robot system with a safety certificate. In: 2022 IEEE Conference on Control Technology and Applications (CCTA), pp. 608–613 (2022)
11. Reynolds, C.W.: Flocks, herds, and schools: a distributed behavioral model, pp. 273–282. Association for Computing Machinery, New York, USA (1998)
12. Kennedy, J., Eberhart, R.: Particle swarm optimization. In: Proceedings of ICNN 1995 - International Conference on Neural Networks, vol. 4, pp. 1942–1948 (1995)
13. Reynolds, C.W., et al.: Steering behaviors for autonomous characters. In: Game Developers Conference, vol. 1999, pp. 763–782. Citeseer (1999)

Computational Methods for Business Analytics (CMBA 2025)

A Fast Savings Algorithm for Solving Large-Scale Euclidean CVRPs

Kenji Kanazawa[(⊠)]

University of Tsukuba, 1-1-1 Tennodai, Tsukuba, Japan
kanazawa@cs.tsukuba.ac.jp

Abstract. Clarke and Wright's savings algorithm (CW algorithm) is one of the most widely used heuristic methods for solving the capacitated vehicle routing problem (CVRP). Given a scenario with n customers and a depot, the CW algorithm initially generates n distinct delivery routes, each connecting a single customer to the depot. It then iteratively merges the two routes based on their saving values under the constraint that the total load of items delivered on the new route does not exceed the vehicle capacity. Herein, the saving value represents the distance reduction achieved merging two routes in to one by linking two customers from different routes. This involves generating $n \times (n-1)/2$ saving values and sorting them in descending order in order to merge the routes with larger saving values preferentially. However, it leads to the overall time complexity of $\mathcal{O}(n^2 \log n)$ when comparison-based sorting algorithms such as the merge sort are employed. In this paper, we propose a variant of the CW algorithm for solving large-scale Euclidean CVRPs achieving a best-case time complexity of $\mathcal{O}(n^2)$. Our proposed approach calculates the saving values using approximate Euclidean distances derived from only integer arithmetic, then sorts the obtained saving values by distribution-based sorting algorithms that can arrange integer values in linear time. Experimental results show that our proposed approach handles large-scale problems involving $3,000$ to $30,000$ customer nodes in 2.88 s on average while preserving the solution quality, which corresponds to 6.0× speedup over the original CW algorithm.

Keywords: capacitated vehicle routing problem · savings algorithm · approximate norm · distribution-based sorting algorithms

1 Introduction

The Capacitated Vehicle Routing Problem (CVRP) is a well-known NP-hard combinatorial optimization problem, which searches for a set of delivery routes starting and ending at a depot that cover all customers with multiple capacity-constrained vehicles. Its goal is to minimize the total distance of the vehicles traveled while ensuring that the total load of delivery items along each route does not exceed the capacity of vehicles.

CVRP instances are typically represented as undirected complete graphs, where nodes represent customers and a depot, and edge weights correspond to the distances between nodes.

O. Gervasi et al. (Eds.): ICCSA 2025 Workshops, LNCS 15888, pp. 59–74, 2026.
https://doi.org/10.1007/978-3-031-97596-7_4

Clarke and Wright's savings algorithm (CW algorithm) [1] is one of the most representative heuristic algorithms for solving CVRP owing to its simplicity and practicality. Given n customer nodes, the CW algorithm initially generates n distinct delivery routes, each linking the depot to a single customer. It then iteratively selects two distinct delivery routes to merge to a single route, guided by *saving* value, i.e., the distance reduction obtained by merging the two routes into one by linking two customer nodes that belong to different routes to each other, without violating the vehicle's capacity restriction.

The CW algorithm involves deriving the saving values for all possible pairs of the initial n routes and sorting the saving values in descending order so that the algorithm preferentially selects route pairs with greater distance reductions for merging. The sorting process introduces a computational bottleneck because it is forced to sort $\mathcal{O}(n^2)$ saving values. Consequently, the overall time complexity is $\mathcal{O}(n^2 \log n)$ when using standard comparison-based sorting algorithms such as merge sort and quick sort. Although the CW algorithm is relatively efficient among approaches for solving CVRP, its execution time rapidly grows as n increases.

In this paper, we propose a variant of the CW algorithm for efficient solving Euclidean CVRP where the distances adhere to the Euclidean metric. Our proposed approach calculates the saving values from an approximate Euclidean distance introduced by Chaudhuri et al. [2] using only integer arithmetic. It then sorts the saving values using distribution-based sorting algorithms such as counting sort [3] or pigeonhole sort [4], which efficiently sort elements with integer key values in linear time. By doing so, our proposed approach achieves a best-case time complexity of $\mathcal{O}(n^2)$. Experimental results show that our proposed approach obtains feasible solutions for large-scale problem instances involving $3,000$ to $30,000$ customers in 2.88 s on average while preserving the solution quality, which corresponds to $6.0\times$ speedup over the original CW algorithm.

2   Clarke and Wright's Savings Algorithm

Algorithm 1 illustrates the CW algorithm. Given a CVRP instance consisting of a triple (V, D, and q), where V represents a set of nodes comprising n customers and a depot, D denotes the demand set, indicating the load of items to deliver for each customer, and q describes the capacity of each vehicle, the algorithm proceeds as follows:

1. It generates an empty set S and an initial route set R_{init} composed of n separate routes, each linking a single customer to the depot, and sets R to R_{init} (Line 6 in Algorithm 1).
2. It then calculates the saving values s_{ij} (Lines 9–17). Herein, s_{ij} denotes the reduction in Euclidean distance achieved by merging two distinct routes linking customers i and j. In R_{init}, Euclidean distance to each customer i and j is calculated as $2 \cdot c_{0i}$ and $2 \cdot c_{0j}$, respectively, where c_{0i} represents the Euclidean distance between the depot (denoted as 0) and customer i. This is because each vehicle must travel back and forth the between the depot

and a customer. For a newly formed route generated by linking i and j, the total Euclidean distance is calculated as $c_{0i} + c_{ij} + c_{0j}$, yielding $s_{ij} = 2 \cdot c_{0i} + 2 \cdot c_{0j} - (c_{0i} + c_{0j} + c_{ij}) = c_{0i} + c_{0j} - c_{ij}$. Note that $s_{ij} > 0$ indicates a reduction in the distance. s_{ij} along with (i, j) is stored to a set S.

3. It sorts (s_{ij}, i, j) in S in descending order of s_{ij} (Line 18).
4. It iteratively executes the following steps over the elements in S from the head to the tail (Line 20):
   (a) For s_{ij} under consideration, two separate routes in R are merged by linking i and j subject to the following conditions:
       – Total load of delivery items along the two routes does not exceed q.
       – Neither i nor j is *interior* to its current route (i.e., at least one of them must be adjacent to the depot in the traversal order).
   (b) If S has not been exhausted, then it goes back to Step 4a to process the next element in S. Otherwise, it returns R at that time and terminates.

Algorithm 1. Procedure of CW algorithm

```
 1: function CW(V, D, q)
 2:    // V: node set of a depot (denoted as 0) and n customers (denoted as 1, ..., n)
 3:    // D: demand set
 4:    // q: capacity of each vehicle
 5:
 6:    R = R_init = GenInitialRouteSet(V);
 7:
 8:    S = ∅; /* S: set of the saving values along with the corresponding node indices */
 9:    for all (i, j) do /* i, j ∈ V, i ≠ j. */
10:        c_ij = EuclideanDistance(i, j);
11:        c_0i = EuclideanDistance(0, i);
12:        c_0j = EuclideanDistance(0, j);
13:        s_ij = c_0i + c_0j − c_ij;
14:        S = S ∪ {(s_ij, i, j)};
15:        //c_ij: distance between i and j.
16:        //s_ij: saving value when two distinct routes are merged by linking customers i and j.
17:    end for
18:    S = Sort_inDescendingOrder(S);
19:
20:    R = ConstructRoute(R, S, D, q);
21:    return R;
22: end function
```

In terms of time complexity, Step 1 takes $\mathcal{O}(n)$, while Steps 2 and 4 handle $O(n^2)$ saving values, leading to the time complexity of $\mathcal{O}(n^2)$ for both. Sorting $\mathcal{O}(n^2)$ saving values in Step 3 consumes $\mathcal{O}(n^2 \log n)$. Hence, the overall time complexity is $\mathcal{O}(n^2 \log n)$.

3   Literature Review

Many approaches for improving CW algorithm have been proposed till date [5–7,10,12,13]. Among them, literatures [5,6], and [7] mainly intended to improve the accuracy of the original CW algorithm but they did not evaluate their approach using large-scale CVRP instances (with at least 3,000 customer nodes). On the other hand, literatures [10,12,13] mainly aimed at reducing the time complexity to treat large-scale CVRP instances. Hereinafter, we focus on the latter ones.

In [10], a modified version of CW algorithm named CW^{100} was described. This approach reduced memory consumption and execution time of the original CW algorithm by constructing a solution only considering saving values between each customer and its 100 nearest nodes. Implemented in JAVA on an AMD Ryzen-3 1300X running at 3.5 GHz with 4 GB of main memory, CW^{100} reportedly required 3 to 34 s to solve instances ranging from 3,000 to 12,000 customer nodes, including post-optimization via the Lin-Kernighan (LK) heuristic.

Authors in [12,13] first presented a GPU-accelerated CW algorithm exploiting CUDA cores in [12], and then proposed more sophisticated approach in [13] to optimize the distance and saving value calculations by parallel processing on RTX-4090 GPU. In [13], they also introduced a "tabu list" of the saving values to exclude the saving values that became superfluous for solution construction. As a result, they achieved an average and peak speedups of 9.7× and 48×, respectively, compared with a Python-based sequential implementation running on a Core-i9 14900HX CPU operating at 2.2 GHz with 64 GB main memory [13]. However, their approach did not address the inefficiencies in sorting the saving values. This limitation left the method inefficient for large-scale instances, as solving a problem with 30,000 customer nodes still required 183 s [13].

4   Our Approach

As discussed previously, the most computationally intensive step is sorting the saving values, which requires $\mathcal{O}(n^2 \log n)$ time when using standard comparison-based sorting algorithms. To further enhance efficiency, our approach employs the approximate Euclidean distance proposed by Chaudhuri et al. [2] so that it can calculate the saving values via only integer arithmetic. This enables the sorting of the saving values through distribution-based sorting algorithms, specifically counting sort [3] and pigeonhole sort [4], which can operate in linear time for integer sorting. Given m elements with integer key values ranging from 0 to $k-1$, both counting sort and pigeonhole sort exhibit a worst case time complexity of $\mathcal{O}(m+k)$ [3] [4]. Consequently, by employing these sorting methods for sorting the saving values, the overall time complexity of the CW algorithm can be reduced to $\mathcal{O}(n^2)$ when the range of the saving values is sufficiently smaller than n^2, as discussed in Sect. 5.

The following subsections will first outline the principles of counting sort and pigeonhole sort for integer key sorting. Following that, we detail how to apply the approximate Euclidean distance by Chaudhuri et al. [2] to the CW algorithm to adopt these sorting techniques, and finally describe our modified CW algorithm.

4.1   Distribution-Based Sorting Algorithm

Counting Sort. Counting sort [3] is a sorting algorithm that sorts integers by counting their occurrences.

Algorithm 2 demonstrates the process of counting sort for sorting integers ranging from 0 to $k-1$ in *descending* order. Here, 'A' represents an array of given integers ranging from 0 to $k-1$. Algorithm 2 initially sets $cnt[i]$ to 0 ($i = 0$ to k), then increments $cnt[i]$ whenever $A[j] = i$ ($j = 0$ to $|A|-1$) to count the occurrences of $i \in A$ (Lines 6–8). Next, it takes the running sum of $cnt[\ ]$ from the tail to head (Lines 9–11). At this point, $cnt[A[j]]$ indicates the last position of $A[j]$ in the sorted array. Then, it iteratively places $A[j]$ to $B[cnt[A[j]]$ decrementing $c[A[j]]$ (Lines 12–15). This process ensures that elements with the equivalent value are placed in the array B in series without missing or exceeding. Finally it returns B.

Algorithm 2. Counting sort for sorting in descending order

```
 1: function COUNTINGSORT(A, k)
 2:   // A: array of integer key values.
 3:     for i = 0 to k do
 4:         cnt[i] = 0; /* cnt[i]: occurrences of values equal to or greater than i. */
 5:     end for
 6:     for j = 0 to |A| − 1 do
 7:         cnt[A[j]]++;
 8:     end for
 9:     for i = k − 1 to 0 do
10:         cnt[i] += cnt[i + 1];
11:     end for
12:     for j = |A| − 1 to 0 do
13:         B[cnt[A[j]]] = A[j];
14:         cnt[A[j]]−−;
15:     end for
16:     return B;
17: end function
```

Pigeonhole Sort. Pigeonhole sort [4] is a sorting algorithm that prepares for an array of "pigeonholes" and arranges the order of given integers by placing each integer into the pigeonhole whose order corresponds to the placed integer value.

Algorithm 3 demonstrates the process of pigeonhole sort for sorting integers ranging from 0 to $k-1$ in descending order. The definitions of A and k are the same as in Algorithm 2, while $occ[i]$ represents the number of occurrences of $i \in A$. The algorithm starts by initializing $occ[i]$ to 0 (Lines 3–5). It then places each element $A[j]$ into the pigeonhole at position $[A[j]][occ[A[j]]]$ (denoted as $pigeonhole[A[j]][occ[A[j]]]$) and increments $occ[A[j]]$ (Lines 6–9). Hence, $pigeonhole[i][\ ]$ gathers all integers in A that have the value i. Finally, the algorithm retrieves the integers from the pigeonholes by scanning from the tail to the top. It stores them to output array B from the first position to the last (Lines 11–17), and returns B.

Algorithm 3. Pigeonhole sort for sorting in descending order

```
 1: function PIGEONHOLESORT(A,k)
 2: // A: array of integer key values.
 3:     for i = 0 to k − 1 do
 4:         occ[i] = 0;
 5:     end for
 6:     for j = 0 to |A| − 1 do
 7:         pigeonhole[A[j]][occ[A[j]]] = A[j];
 8:         occ[A[j]]++;
 9:     end for
10:
11:     i_B = 0;
12:     for i = k − 1 to 0 do
13:         for j = 0 to occ[i] do
14:             B[i_B] = pigeonhole[i][j];
15:             i_B++;
16:         end for
17:     end for
18:     return B;
19: end function
```

4.2   Calculating the Saving Values in Integer Arithmetic Based on Approximate Euclidean Distance by Chaudhuri et al [2]

Both Algorithms 2 and 3, are designed to work with non-negative integer key values. However, in Euclidean CVRP, the saving values could be real numbers and might include negative values. Additionally, these methods require prior knowledge of the key value range. To address these constraints, the saving values are converted into integers by calculating and rounding them while simultaneously determining their maximum and minimum values. Once the minimum is identified, all the saving values can be offset by this minimum.

There are several possible options for rounding:

(1) Round coordinates of the customer and the depot nodes immediately on reading the CVRP instance. All subsequent process are then performed using integer operations.
(2) Input the CVRP node coordinates as floating-point values, calculate the Euclidean distances and round them to integers, and subsequently derive the saving values from these integer distances.
(3) Perform all calculations to derive the saving values in floating-point starting from reading the instance and ending with obtaining the saving values, and then round the saving values to integers.

Although the method (1) is potentially the least computationally intensive, it requires an alternative way to calculate Euclidean distances using only integer arithmetic. For this purpose, our approach adopts the approximate norm proposed by Chaudhuri et al. [2].

Chaudhuri et al. [2] introduced a method to approximate the L_n norm by combining L_∞ and L_1 norms. Formula (1) presents this approximation for two

n-dimensional vectors, X and Y.

$$L_n = |x_{i_{max}} - y_{i_{max}}| + \frac{1}{n - \lceil \frac{n-2}{2} \rceil} \cdot \sum_{i=0, i \neq i_{max}}^{n-1} |x_i - y_i|$$

$$= |x_{i_{max}} - y_{i_{max}}| + \frac{1}{n - \lceil \frac{n-2}{2} \rceil} \cdot (\sum_{i=0}^{n-1} |x_i - y_i| - |x_{i_{max}} - y_{i_{max}}|) \quad (1)$$

Herein, x_i and y_i denote the i-th elements of X and Y, respectively, while i_{max} represents the index of the largest component of $|x_i - y_i|$, i.e., $i_{max} = \operatorname{argmax}_{0 \leq i \leq n-1}(|x_i - y_i|)$. Recognizing that $|x_{i_{max}} - y_{i_{max}}|$ and $\sum_{k=i}^{n-1} |x_i - y_i|$ correspond to L_∞ and L_1 norms of X and Y, respectively, Formula (1) can be rewritten as follows:

$$L_n = L_\infty + \frac{1}{n - \lceil \frac{n-2}{2} \rceil} \cdot (L_1 - L_\infty) \quad (2)$$

Substituting $n = 2$ in Formula (2), we obtain L_2, i.e., the approximate Euclidean distance as follows:

$$L_2 = \frac{1}{2}(L_\infty + L_1) \quad (3)$$

Given X and Y as integers, Formula (3) can be calculated with only integer operations. Specifically, L_∞ is derived through two subtractions and absolute value calculations in integers, followed by a single multiplexing that selects the element with larger value from $|x_i - y_i|$ ($i = 0, 1$), while L_1 is computed through two integer subtractions and absolute calculations, and a single integer addition. $(L_\infty + L_1)/2$ is then acquired by addition of two integers L_∞ and L_1 and applying a right shift operation, which is equivalent to the division by 2. In this way, we can directly derive approximate Euclidean distance between two distinct nodes in a given CVRP instance using only integer arithmetic.

4.3 Procedure of Our Modified CW Algorithm

Algorithm 4 presents our modified version of the CW algorithm. Its procedure is basically same as Algorithm 1, except that the saving values are treated as integers as already mentioned. In Algorithm 4, s_{min} and s_{max} denote the minimum and maximum values of s_{ij}, respectively. **GenInitialRouteSet()** and **ConstructRoute()** are the same functions as those in Algorithm 1. The remaining functions work as follows:

- **Round()**: Rounds the coordinate data to the nearest integers.
- **ApproximateEuclideanDistance()**: Calculates approximate Euclidean distances based on the above-mentioned description.
- **Sort_inDescendingOrder()**: Sorts the saving values along with their corresponding customer indices in descending order of the saving values (using counting sort or pigeonhole sort). Unlike Algorithm 1, this function accepts s_{min} and s_{max} as inputs to determine the valid range of the saving values and also offsets them based on s_{min}.

Algorithm 4. Procedure of modified CW algorithm

```
1: function CW(V, D, q)
2:     s_min = inf;
3:     s_max = − inf;
4:     V = Round(V);
5:     R = R_init = GenInitialRouteSet(V);
6:
7:     S = ∅; /* S: set of the saving values along with the corresponding node indices */
8:     for all (i, j) do /* i, j ∈ V, i ≠ j. */
9:         c_ij = ApproximateEuclideanDistance(i, j);
10:        c_0i = ApproximateEuclideanDistance(0, i);
11:        c_0j = ApproximateEuclideanDistance(0, j);
12:        s_ij = c_ij − c_0i − c_0j;
13:        S = S ∪ {(s_ij, i, j)};
14:        if (s_max < s_ij) then
15:            s_max = s_ij;
16:        end if
17:        if (s_min > s_ij) then
18:            s_min = s_ij;
19:        end if
20:    end for
21:    S = Sort_inDescendingOrder(S, s_max, s_min); /* Counting sort or Pigeonhole sort */
22:
23:    R = ConstructRoute(R, S, D, q);
24:    return R;
25: end function
```

5   Evaluation

To assess our proposed approach, we evaluate the following four different variants of CW algorithm based on without/with discretizing the saving values and the sorting algorithms:

1. The original CW algorithm, in which the saving values are not discretized (denoted as CW_0).
2. A variant in which the saving values are discretized, and sorted by merge sort (CW_1).
3. A variant in which the saving values are discretized and sorted by counting sort ($OURS_c$).
4. A variant in which the saving values are discretized and sorted by pigeonhole sort ($OURS_p$).

Discretizing the savings values are performed based on the approximate Euclidean distance by Chaudhuri et al. [2] as described in Sect. 4. All tested codes are written in C language, compiled by gcc with -O3 optimization option, and executed on a single thread of AMD Threadripper 3970X operating at 3.7 GHz with 64 GB of main memory.

We evaluate above-mentioned four implementations using Euclidean CVRP instances ranging from 500 to 1,000 and 3,000 to 30,000 customer nodes drawn from two distinct benchmark sets in CVRPLIB [8], i.e., Uchoa et al. [9] and Arnold et al. [10] benchmark sets. Hereinafter, we denote the former as *Set_X* and latter as *Set_XXL*.

Table 1. Range and total count of the saving values (Set_X)

Instance	number of customers	m (number of saving values)	$s_{min} \sim s_{max}$	$(s_{max} - s_{min} + 1)/m$
X-n502-k39	501	125,250	$0 \sim 2365$	1.89×10^{-2}
X-n513-k21	512	130,816	$-2 \sim 1375$	1.05×10^{-2}
X-n524-k153	523	136,503	$-2 \sim 2061$	1.51×10^{-2}
X-n536-k96	535	142,845	$-2 \sim 1428$	1.00×10^{-2}
X-n548-k50	547	149,331	$0 \sim 2928$	1.96×10^{-2}
X-n561-k42	560	156,520	$-2 \sim 1449$	9.26×10^{-3}
X-n573-k30	572	163,306	$0 \sim 2356$	1.44×10^{-2}
X-n586-k159	585	170,820	$-1 \sim 2528$	1.48×10^{-2}
X-n599-k92	598	178,503	$-2 \sim 2206$	1.24×10^{-2}
X-n613-k62	612	186,966	$-2 \sim 1462$	7.82×10^{-3}
X-n627-k43	626	195,625	$0 \sim 2973$	1.52×10^{-2}
X-n641-k35	640	204,480	$0 \sim 2800$	1.37×10^{-2}
X-n655-k131	654	213,531	$-1 \sim 1333$	6.24×10^{-3}
X-n670-k130	669	223,446	$-2 \sim 2047$	9.16×10^{-3}
X-n685-k75	684	233,586	$-2 \sim 1425$	6.10×10^{-3}
X-n701-k44	700	244,650	$0 \sim 2903$	1.19×10^{-2}
X-n716-k35	715	255,255	$-2 \sim 2096$	8.21×10^{-3}
X-n733-k159	732	267,546	$-2 \sim 1450$	5.42×10^{-3}
X-n749-k98	748	279,378	$-2 \sim 1346$	4.82×10^{-3}
X-n766-k71	765	292,230	$0 \sim 2942$	1.01×10^{-2}
X-n783-k48	782	305,371	$-2 \sim 2645$	8.66×10^{-3}
X-n801-k40	800	319,600	$0 \sim 2931$	9.17×10^{-3}
X-n819-k171	818	334,153	$-2 \sim 1452$	4.35×10^{-3}
X-n837-k142	836	349,030	$-2 \sim 2506$	7.18×10^{-3}
X-n856-k95	855	365,085	$-2 \sim 1465$	4.01×10^{-3}
X-n876-k59	875	382,375	$0 \sim 2523$	6.60×10^{-3}
X-n895-k37	894	399,171	$-2 \sim 2342$	5.87×10^{-3}
X-n916-k207	915	418,155	$0 \sim 2906$	6.95×10^{-3}
X-n936-k151	935	436,645	$-2 \sim 1442$	3.30×10^{-3}
X-n957-k87	956	456,490	$-2 \sim 1871$	4.10×10^{-3}
X-n979-k58	978	477,753	$0 \sim 2965$	6.21×10^{-3}
X-n1001-k43	1,000	499,500	$-1 \sim 2678$	5.36×10^{-3}

Table 2. Range and total count of the saving values (Set_XXL)

Instance	number of customers	m (number of saving values)	$s_{min} \sim s_{max}$	$(s_{max} - s_{min} + 1)/m$
Leuven1	3,000	4,498,500	$-2 \sim 2295$	5.10×10^{-4}
Leuven2	4,000	7,998,000	$-2 \sim 3555$	4.44×10^{-4}
Antwerp1	6,000	17,997,000	$-2 \sim 2844$	1.58×10^{-4}
Antwerp2	7,000	24,496,500	$-2 \sim 4637$	1.89×10^{-4}
Ghent1	10,000	49,995,000	$-2 \sim 2817$	5.63×10^{-5}
Ghent2	11,000	60,494,500	$-2 \sim 3354$	5.54×10^{-5}
Brussels1	15,000	112,492,500	$-2 \sim 2488$	2.21×10^{-5}
Brussels2	16,000	127,992,000	$-2 \sim 3858$	3.01×10^{-5}
Flanders1	20,000	199,990,000	$-2 \sim 31141$	1.56×10^{-4}
Flanders2	30,000	499,985,000	$-2 \sim 42082$	8.42×10^{-5}

5.1   Suitability of Counting and Pigeonhole Sorts

First, we examine the range and the total count of the saving values to determine whether counting sort or pigeonhole sort is suitable for using in the CW algorithm. As mentioned in Sect. 4, the range of the key values must be less than the total count of the key values to enable efficient sorting by counting sort and pigeonhole sort. In this assessment, the saving values are discretized by the approximate distances by Chaudhuri et al. [2] as described in Sect. 4.2.

Tables 1 and 2 present the corresponding evaluation results. In each table, the first column lists the name of the instances, while the second to fifth columns indicate the number of customer nodes, the total count of the saving values, the minimum and maximum saving values, and the range of the saving values over the total count of the saving values. As shown in Tables 1 and 2, the range of the saving values is substantially smaller than the total count of the saving values, thereby making it possible for the CW algorithm to achieve a best-case time complexity of $\mathcal{O}(n^2)$ using counting sort or pigeonhole sort.

5.2   Solution Quality

Next, we compare the solution quality achieved by each implementation. To assess the influence of the approximation of saving values, we compare the solution quality obtained by CW_0 with that by the other three implementations (CW_1, $OURS_c$, and $OURS_p$). The metric of this evaluation is the total Euclidean distance of the resulting routes, which is computed in accordance with the method described in [11] for calculating 2D Euclidean distance.

Tables 3 and 4 present the comparison of the solution quality. In each table, the second column displays quality for the best known solutions reported in [8], while the third and fourth columns show the solution quality obtained by CW_0 and the other three implementations. The values in parentheses indicate the relative gap between the best known solution quality and the solution quality obtained by each approach, calculated as $(c - c_{bks})/c_{bks} \times 100$. Herein, c_{bks} and c denote the best known solution quality and the solution quality obtained by each approach. Values on the last row in each table shows the average relative gap for each benchmark set. Since CW_1, $OURS_c$, and $OURS_p$ attained the same solution quality in every test case, we present the results collectively in Tables 3 and 4. This arose because all these three implementations yielded the identical orderings of the discretized saving values regardless of sorting algorithms. As shown in Tables 3 and 4, deterioration of solution quality with approximating the saving values is very little across all the test cases.

5.3   Execution Time

Finally, we compare the execution time of each implementation. In this evaluation, we executed each approach 10 times, respectively, and then compared the average time of the 10 trials because we noticed that the variations of execution time were non-negligible especially for small instances. We are now finding

Table 3. Comparison of solution quality (*Set_X*)

Instance	Best [8]	CW_0		$CW_1,$ $\overline{OURS_c, OURS_p}$	
X-n502-k39	69,226	71,784	(3.70 %)	71,253	(2.93 %)
X-n513-k21	24,201	27,088	(11.93 %)	26,768	(10.61 %)
X-n524-k153	154,593	164,488	(6.40 %)	166,726	(7.85 %)
X-n536-k96	94,846	99,959	(5.39 %)	99,778	(5.20 %)
X-n548-k50	86,700	89,792	(3.57 %)	89,611	(3.36 %)
X-n561-k42	42,717	45,628	(6.81 %)	45,976	(7.63 %)
X-n573-k30	50,673	53,287	(5.16 %)	53,303	(5.19 %)
X-n586-k159	190,316	199,690	(4.93 %)	200,431	(5.31 %)
X-n599-k92	108,451	113,065	(4.25 %)	114,271	(5.37 %)
X-n613-k62	59,535	62,758	(5.41 %)	62,727	(5.36 %)
X-n627-k43	62,164	65,548	(5.44 %)	65,841	(5.91 %)
X-n641-k35	63,682	68,220	(7.13 %)	67,747	(6.38 %)
X-n655-k131	106,780	108,226	(1.35 %)	108,302	(1.43 %)
X-n670-k130	146,332	158,692	(8.45 %)	159,616	(9.08 %)
X-n685-k75	68,205	71,503	(4.84 %)	71,817	(5.30 %)
X-n701-k44	81,923	85,427	(4.28 %)	85,919	(4.88 %)
X-n716-k35	43,373	45,831	(5.67 %)	46,073	(6.23 %)
X-n733-k159	136,187	139,446	(2.39 %)	140,459	(3.14 %)
X-n749-k98	77,269	79,573	(2.98 %)	80,025	(3.57 %)
X-n766-k71	114,417	120,402	(5.23 %)	120,253	(5.10 %)
X-n783-k48	72,386	76,496	(5.68 %)	77,360	(6.87 %)
X-n801-k40	73,305	77,218	(5.34 %)	77,908	(6.28 %)
X-n819-k171	158,121	166,547	(5.33 %)	166,195	(5.11 %)
X-n837-k142	193,737	202,048	(4.29 %)	202,590	(4.57 %)
X-n856-k95	88,965	92,740	(4.24 %)	92,805	(4.32 %)
X-n876-k59	99,299	102,182	(2.90 %)	103,068	(3.80 %)
X-n895-k37	53,860	59,071	(9.68 %)	58,522	(8.66 %)
X-n916-k207	329,179	342,876	(4.16 %)	343,448	(4.33 %)
X-n936-k151	132,715	145,897	(9.93 %)	148,830	(12.14 %)
X-n957-k87	85,465	89,442	(4.65 %)	89,646	(4.89 %)
X-n979-k58	118,976	123,857	(4.10 %)	123,823	(4.07 %)
X-n1001-k43	72,355	77,700	(7.39 %)	77,947	(7.73 %)
			(5.41 %)		(5.71 %)

Table 4. Comparison of solution quality (*Set_XXL*)

Instance	Best [8]	CW_0		$CW_1,$ $\overline{OURS_c, OURS_p}$	
Leuven1	192,848	200,829	(4.14 %)	200,978	(4.22 %)
Leuven2	111,391	125,063	(12.27 %)	126,089	(13.19 %)
Antwerp1	477,277	498,916	(4.53 %)	498,870	(4.52 %)
Antwerp2	291,350	322,575	(10.72 %)	322,199	(10.59 %)
Ghent1	469,531	490,230	(4.41 %)	490,544	(4.48 %)
Ghent2	257,748	286,542	(11.17 %)	288,815	(12.05 %)
Brussels1	501,719	531,589	(5.95 %)	533,372	(6.31 %)
Brussels2	345,468	385,108	(11.47 %)	385,980	(11.73 %)
Flanders1	7,240,118	7,525,070	(3.94 %)	7,535,722	(4.08 %)
Flanders2	4,373,244	4,804,764	(9.87 %)	4,813,413	(10.07 %)
			(7.85 %)		(8.12 %)

the reasons, but the execution time for small instances might be affected by the task scheduling of the operating system on our evaluation platform.

Tables 5 and 6 present the execution time of CW_0 and Tables 7 and 8 display the execution time of CW_1, $OURS_c$, and $OURS_p$. The instance names are abbreviated in the first column, while T_{total}, $T_{calc.sv}$, and T_{sort} indicate the total execution time, time to compute the saving values, and time to sort the saving values. Columns labeled as X_0 and X_1 in Tables 7 and 8 display the speedup of T_{total} in each implementation over CW_0 and CW_1, respectively. Note that T_{total} includes solution construction and additional overhead such as reading the instance files and dynamic memory allocation. Overall, CW_1, $OURS_c$, and $OURS_p$ outperform CW_0 as can be seen in Tables 5, 6, 7 and 8.

Table 5. Execution time of CW_0 for Set_X (in seconds)

Instance	T_{total}	$T_{calc.sv}$	T_{sort}
n502	0.019	0.00191	0.0134
n513	0.022	0.00240	0.0159
n524	0.028	0.00258	0.0166
n536	0.025	0.00265	0.0162
n548	0.024	0.00262	0.0167
n561	0.026	0.00288	0.0186
n573	0.023	0.00242	0.0169
n586	0.031	0.00309	0.0185
n599	0.030	0.00330	0.0199
n613	0.030	0.00344	0.0214
n627	0.029	0.00364	0.0203
n641	0.031	0.00391	0.0222
n655	0.036	0.00392	0.0238
n670	0.036	0.00353	0.0231
n685	0.036	0.00430	0.0249
n701	0.034	0.00404	0.0245
n716	0.034	0.00391	0.0249
n733	0.042	0.00389	0.0276
n749	0.043	0.00514	0.0293
n766	0.042	0.00520	0.0298
n783	0.043	0.00545	0.0311
n801	0.045	0.00599	0.0327
n819	0.053	0.00630	0.0349
n837	0.051	0.00595	0.0346
n856	0.053	0.00643	0.0376
n876	0.053	0.00671	0.0383
n895	0.056	0.00740	0.0404
n916	0.065	0.00765	0.0413
n936	0.069	0.00787	0.0452
n957	0.067	0.00796	0.0456
n979	0.070	0.00930	0.0468
n1001	0.072	0.00808	0.0501
average	0.041	0.00481	0.0282

Time to calculate the saving values in CW_1, $OURS_c$, and $OURS_p$ is overall faster than that in CW_0, except for some cases like n573 in $OURS_c$ and n502

Table 6. Comparison of execution time for *Set_XXL* (in seconds)

Instance	T_{total}	$T_{calc.sv}$	T_{sort}
L1	0.63	0.0530	0.531
L2	1.11	0.0904	0.957
A1	2.68	0.193	2.376
A2	3.59	0.264	3.170
G1	7.74	0.535	6.896
G2	9.30	0.647	8.286
B1	18.29	1.180	16.453
B2	20.38	1.339	18.314
F1	32.88	2.049	29.717
F2	74.96	4.501	68.118
average	17.16	1.085	15.482

Table 7. Execution time of CW_1, $OURS_c$, and $OURS_p$ for *Set_X* (in seconds)

Instance	CW_1				$OURS_c$					$OURS_p$				
	T_{total}	$T_{calc.sv}$	T_{sort}	X_0	T_{total}	$T_{calc.sv}$	T_{sort}	X_0	X_1	T_{total}	$T_{calc.sv}$	T_{sort}	X_0	X_1
n502	0.018	0.00184	0.0124	1.1	0.0083	0.00163	0.00177	2.3	2.2	0.029	0.00192	0.0231	0.7	0.6
n513	0.017	0.00181	0.0116	1.3	0.0073	0.00160	0.00175	2.9	2.3	0.018	0.00177	0.0137	1.2	0.9
n524	0.023	0.00191	0.0124	1.2	0.014	0.00180	0.00195	2.0	1.7	0.031	0.00191	0.0197	0.9	0.8
n536	0.020	0.00211	0.0118	1.3	0.013	0.00222	0.00236	2.0	1.6	0.024	0.00231	0.0154	1.1	0.9
n548	0.020	0.00199	0.0132	1.2	0.011	0.00228	0.00241	2.2	1.8	0.034	0.00227	0.0273	0.7	0.6
n561	0.020	0.00229	0.0133	1.3	0.010	0.00223	0.00243	2.6	2.0	0.021	0.00230	0.0147	1.2	0.9
n573	0.019	0.00213	0.0134	1.2	0.010	0.00251	0.00269	2.2	1.9	0.028	0.00235	0.0222	0.8	0.7
n586	0.027	0.00257	0.0144	1.2	0.015	0.00223	0.00253	2.1	1.8	0.037	0.00282	0.0252	0.8	0.7
n599	0.025	0.00285	0.0157	1.2	0.013	0.00242	0.00254	2.4	2.0	0.031	0.00271	0.0218	1.0	0.8
n613	0.022	0.00236	0.0140	1.4	0.011	0.00258	0.00274	2.7	1.9	0.024	0.00290	0.0159	1.3	0.9
n627	0.024	0.00279	0.0158	1.2	0.012	0.00279	0.00302	2.4	2.0	0.036	0.00279	0.0281	0.8	0.7
n641	0.024	0.00289	0.0169	1.3	0.011	0.00265	0.00290	2.8	2.2	0.035	0.00325	0.0273	0.9	0.7
n655	0.029	0.00299	0.0171	1.3	0.016	0.00317	0.00318	2.3	1.8	0.025	0.00295	0.0140	1.5	1.1
n670	0.030	0.00303	0.0174	1.2	0.016	0.00299	0.00320	2.3	1.9	0.031	0.00274	0.0196	1.2	1.0
n685	0.028	0.00350	0.0180	1.3	0.014	0.00333	0.00359	2.5	2.0	0.025	0.00338	0.0156	1.4	1.1
n701	0.029	0.00371	0.0196	1.2	0.013	0.00321	0.00355	2.6	2.2	0.036	0.00324	0.0271	1.0	0.8
n716	0.027	0.00349	0.0188	1.2	0.013	0.00354	0.00377	2.6	2.1	0.029	0.00368	0.0205	1.2	0.9
n733	0.032	0.00322	0.0189	1.3	0.018	0.00332	0.00358	2.4	1.8	0.030	0.00386	0.0163	1.4	1.1
n749	0.033	0.00418	0.0208	1.3	0.017	0.00423	0.00452	2.5	1.9	0.028	0.00435	0.0161	1.5	1.2
n766	0.034	0.00461	0.0222	1.2	0.017	0.00448	0.00470	2.5	2.0	0.040	0.00427	0.0286	1.1	0.9
n783	0.032	0.00375	0.0225	1.3	0.016	0.00422	0.00447	2.7	2.1	0.038	0.00480	0.0269	1.1	0.9
n801	0.036	0.00480	0.0247	1.3	0.015	0.00453	0.00462	3.0	2.4	0.037	0.00386	0.0271	1.2	1.0
n819	0.041	0.00514	0.0242	1.3	0.020	0.00437	0.00429	2.7	2.1	0.034	0.00540	0.0174	1.6	1.2
n837	0.040	0.00425	0.0251	1.3	0.022	0.00540	0.00549	2.4	1.9	0.040	0.00480	0.0252	1.3	1.0
n856	0.038	0.00444	0.0249	1.4	0.019	0.00534	0.00551	2.7	2.0	0.030	0.00532	0.0164	1.8	1.3
n876	0.041	0.00521	0.0279	1.3	0.018	0.00544	0.00547	3.0	2.3	0.037	0.00463	0.0246	1.4	1.1
n895	0.043	0.00604	0.0296	1.3	0.017	0.00530	0.00551	3.3	2.5	0.038	0.00602	0.0249	1.5	1.1
n916	0.052	0.00644	0.0310	1.2	0.024	0.00539	0.00561	2.7	2.2	0.050	0.00635	0.0303	1.3	1.0
n936	0.050	0.00646	0.0302	1.4	0.025	0.00634	0.00622	2.8	2.0	0.037	0.00693	0.0176	1.9	1.4
n957	0.048	0.00616	0.0320	1.4	0.022	0.00704	0.00646	3.1	2.2	0.035	0.00585	0.0206	1.9	1.4
n979	0.050	0.00705	0.0338	1.4	0.022	0.00719	0.00675	3.2	2.3	0.045	0.00702	0.0295	1.6	1.1
n1001	0.051	0.00719	0.0357	1.4	0.022	0.00803	0.00670	3.2	2.3	0.043	0.00713	0.0279	1.7	1.2
average	0.032	0.00385	0.0206	1.3	0.016	0.00387	0.00395	2.6	2.0	0.033	0.00393	0.0219	1.3	1.0

Table 8. Comparison of execution time for *Set_XXL* (in seconds)

Instance	CW_1				$OURS_c$					$OURS_p$				
	T_{total}	$T_{calc.sv}$	T_{sort}	X_0	T_{total}	$T_{calc.sv}$	T_{sort}	X_0	X_1	T_{total}	$T_{calc.sv}$	T_{sort}	X_0	X_1
L1	0.41	0.0432	0.321	1.5	0.14	0.0434	0.0522	4.5	2.9	0.16	0.0438	0.0689	4.0	2.6
L2	0.76	0.0753	0.617	1.5	0.24	0.0749	0.102	4.7	3.2	0.27	0.0746	0.134	4.1	2.8
A1	1.65	0.157	1.390	1.6	0.48	0.158	0.215	5.6	3.5	0.50	0.158	0.239	5.4	3.3
A2	2.35	0.214	1.986	1.5	0.69	0.216	0.327	5.2	3.4	0.76	0.214	0.395	4.7	3.1
G1	4.68	0.433	3.971	1.7	1.28	0.435	0.566	6.1	3.7	1.28	0.433	0.572	6.1	3.7
G2	5.90	0.524	5.046	1.6	1.61	0.525	0.759	5.8	3.7	1.66	0.520	0.819	5.6	3.5
B1	10.50	0.959	9.001	1.7	2.74	0.955	1.252	6.7	3.8	2.68	0.951	1.197	6.8	3.9
B2	12.65	1.093	10.933	1.6	3.30	1.084	1.592	6.2	3.8	3.37	1.082	1.668	6.0	3.8
F1	20.01	1.687	17.419	1.6	5.50	1.678	2.917	6.0	3.6	6.56	1.676	3.990	5.0	3.0
F2	47.12	3.700	41.452	1.6	12.84	3.690	7.168	5.8	3.7	15.54	3.676	9.894	4.8	3.0
average	10.60	0.888	9.214	1.6	2.88	0.886	1.495	6.0	3.7	3.28	0.883	1.898	5.2	3.2

in $OURS_p$. This suggests that discretizing the saving values with Euclidean distance approximation by Chaudhuri et al. [2] makes more sense than just rounding Euclidean distance calculated by *sqrt()* function.

The fact that CW_1 outperforms CW_0 indicates that discretizing the saving values itself contributes speeding up CW algorithm. This is because comparing the saving values in merge sort as well as calculating the saving values can be carried out by only integer operation. However, CW_1 still requires the time complexity of $\mathcal{O}(n^2 \log n)$ owing to merge sort for sorting the saving values, thereby leading to the limited speedup.

$OURS_c$ outperforms CW_0 and CW_1 in all the tested cases. It elapses 0.016 s for *Set_X*, and 2.88 s for *Set_XXL* on average, corresponding to 2.6× and 6.0× performance gain over CW_0, respectively. In particular, it solves Flanders2 comprising 30,000 customer nodes in 12.8 s, yielding 5.8× and 3.7× speedup over CW_0 and CW_1, respectively. $T_{calc.sv}$ and T_{sort} under $OURS_c$ remain lower than those under CW_0 in all the tested cases. Notably, T_{sort} is approximately 1/10 on average in *Set_XXL* compared with CW_0 and CW_1, accounting for a substantial portion of the performance advantage. Considering that counting sort can be applicable for only integer sort key values, discretizing the saving values based on approximate Euclidean distance has an essential role for such that performance gain.

As for $OURS_p$, it shows smaller performance gains overall and even underperforms CW_0 in some instances of *Set_X* while it achieves the comparable performance to $OURS_c$ in *Set_XXL*. To simplify the implementation, $OURS_p$ allocates sufficient memory with the same size for each pigeonhole to deal with any distribution of the saving values. This may cause considerable overhead and lead to the performance degradation for *Set_X*.

5.4   Comparison to Related Work

Herein, we compare our approach with two previous work aiming at reducing the time complexity mentioned in Sect. 3, i.e., CW^{100} [10] and GPU acceleration [13].

As mentioned in Sect. 3, CW^{100} in [10] required 3 to 34 s to solve instances ranging from 3,000 to 12,000 customer nodes on AMD Ryzen-3 1300X running at 3.5 GHz with 4 GB RAM, including post-optimization via the Lin-Kernighan (LK) heuristic. As detailed in Sect. 5, $OURS_c$ solved comparably sized instances (Leuven1, Leuven2, Antwerp1, Antwerp2, Ghent1, and Ghent2) in 1.61 s. In addition, we have confirmed that our approach did not exceed 2.17 s for these benchmarks even with the post-optimization via LK. Although a direct comparison is difficult due to the different evaluation environments, it is noteworthy that our approach presented an order-of-magnitude speedup over CW^{100}.

As mentioned in Sect. 3, the GPU acceleration in [13] did not address the inefficiencies in sorting the saving values. thereby leading to left the method inefficient for large-scale instances. As a result, it was about one-fifth and one-tenth the speed of our approach on average in *Set_X* and *Set_XXL*, respectively.

6   Conclusion

In this paper, we have proposed a fast savings algorithm that efficiently solves large-scale Euclidean CVRPs. Our proposed approach derives the saving values through the approximate Euclidean distance proposed by Chaudhuri et al. [2] using only integer arithmetic, thereby enabling the use of linear-time sorting algorithms for integer value sorting and attaining a best-case time complexity of $\mathcal{O}(n^2)$ for CVRP instances with n customer nodes. Experimental results demonstrate that our approach processes large-scale CVRP instances with 3,000 to 30,000 customer nodes in 2.88 s on average while preserving the solution quality, corresponding to 6.0× speedup over the original CW algorithm.

References

1. Clarke, G., Wright, J.W.: Scheduling of vehicles from a central depot to a number of delivery points. Oper. Res. **12**(4), 568–581 (1964)
2. Chaudhuri, D., Murthy, C.A., Chaudhuri, B.B.: A modified metric to compute distance. Pattern Recogn. **25**(7), 667–677 (1992)
3. Cormen, T.H., Leiserson, C. E., Rivest, R.L., Stein, C.: Introduction to Algorithms (Third Edition). MIT-Press (2022)
4. Stephens, R.: Essential Algorithms: A Practical Approach to Computer Algorithms Using Python and C#. John Wiley & Sons, Inc (2019)
5. Altinel, İ., K., Öncan, T.: A new enhancement of the Clarke and Wright savings heuristics for the capacitated vehicle routing problem. J. Operat. Res. Soc. **56**(8), 954–961 (2005)
6. Doruyan, T., Çatay, B.: A robust enhancement to the Clarke-Wright savings algorithm. J. Operat. Res. Soc. **62**(1), 223–231 (2011)

7. Stanjoević, M., Stanjoević, B., Vujošević, M.: Enhanced savings calculation and its applications for solving capacitated vehicle routing problem. Appl. Math. Comput. **219**, 10302–10312 (2013)
8. CVRPLIB. http://vrp.galgos.inf.puc-rio.br/index.php/en/, Accessed 25th Mar 2025
9. Uchoa, E., Pecin, D., Pessoa, A., Poggi, M., Vidal, T.: New benchmark instances for the capacitated vehicle routing problem. Eur. J. Oper. Res. **257**, 845–858 (2017)
10. Arnold, F., Gendreau, M., Sörensen, K.: Efficiently solving very large-scale routing problems. Comput. Oper. Res. **107**, 32–42 (2019)
11. Reinelt, G.: TSPLIB-a traveling salesman problem library. ORSA J. Comput. **3**(4), 376–384 (1991)
12. Guerriero, F., Saccomanno, F.P.: Accelerating the Clarke-Wright algorithm using GPUs. Control Cybernet. **53**(2), 371–383 (2024)
13. Guerriero, F., Saccomanno, F.P.: A parallel implementation of the clarke-wright algorithm on GPUs. ICORES-2025, pp. 100–111 (2025)

Analyze and Predict Potential Customers Based on Customer Clustering

Ta Cong Binh, Ngo Chi Trung, Hoang Anh Tu, and Phan Duy Hung$^{(\boxtimes)}$ 🄳

FPT University, Hanoi, Vietnam
{binhtche186122,trungnche180620,tuhahe182038}@fpt.edu.vn,
hungpd2@fe.edu.vn

Abstract. Customer segmentation plays a vital role in designing effective marketing campaigns to drive business growth and maximize revenue. In this study, we apply Principal Component Analysis and Autoencoder to extract meaningful features, reducing data complexity while preserving essential information. To enhance clustering accuracy, we first utilize DBSCAN to detect and remove noise before employing the K-Means algorithm for customer segmentation. This approach helps identify distinct customer groups, providing valuable insights into consumer behavior. Furthermore, we analyze potential customers who have the possibility of being upgraded from loyal customers to VIP status. Finally, we implement a Random Forest Classification model to predict potential new customers based on fundamental customer information, enabling businesses to develop proactive strategies for customer acquisition and retention.

Keywords: Customer Clustering · Predicting Potential Customers · PCA · Autoencoder · K-Means Clustering · DBSCAN · Random Forest

1 Introduction

In the era of increasingly strong digital transformation, online shopping has greatly changed the shopping behavior of consumers. Businesses are increasingly focusing on consumer purchasing behavior to meet the growing trend of online shopping to improve service provision, enhance customer satisfaction, encourage customers to return to purchase and ultimately increase profits. Therefore, customer segmentation and prediction of potential customers are extremely important and to address the limitations in data mining on consumers' online shopping behavior, this paper aims to cluster and predict consumer behavior using machine learning techniques, thereby supporting companies in resource allocation and decision making.

Customer segmentation and predictive modeling have been extensively studied in data-driven marketing and customer management. Traditional segmentation methods have used techniques such as RFM (Recency, Frequency, Monetary) analysis [1] to segment customers based on their purchasing behavior. While the RFM has the advantage of simplicity and easy cheesiness, it does not offer the flexibility to accommodate complex behavioral patterns in high-dimensional datasets. K-Means clustering [2, 3]

O. Gervasi et al. (Eds.): ICCSA 2025 Workshops, LNCS 15888, pp. 75–87, 2026.
https://doi.org/10.1007/978-3-031-97596-7_5

has been used to cluster customers according to their behavior characteristics. K-Means does however not always fit the distribution of data in the real world, as it is presuming spherical clusters and a fixed number of clusters. To overcome the limitations of K-Means, consumer segmentation works found global optimality by using hierarchical clustering [4, 5] and density-based clustering (DBSCAN) [6]. DBSCAN is good for noise filtering and allows us to find clusters of arbitrary shape. Hierarchical clustering allows us a more flexible cluster architecture. However, due to their computational complexity, these approaches often struggle when applied to large-scale consumer databases. Predictive analytics is also useful in identifying potential customers who are likely to do repeat purchases in the future. Initial works used a combination of Bayesian and logistic regression models to estimate the probability of customer conversion [7], such models are, however, still limited when attempting to account for consumer data exhibiting non-linear correlations. To get over this limitation, machine learning methods like Random Forest, Gradient Boosting Machines (GBM), and Neural Networks have been extensively employed and have produced classification results that are more accurate [7, 8]. A significant quantity of both organized and unstructured data may be processed by these models, which also make it possible to identify special characteristics in consumer behavior. For example, XGBoost has been deployed to predict Customer Lifetime Value (CLV) which helps to improve the effectiveness of marketing strategies [9]. Customer segmentation and predictive modeling are important aspects of data-driven marketing. The use of RFM, K-means, DBSCAN models are traditional methods but they are quite simple and ineffective for complex and non-linear data or very large scale. Models like Random Forest, Boosted Gradient Machine (GBM) and Artificial Neural Networks perform better than traditional methods in handling large, complex data in terms of speed and accuracy.

The objective of this paper is to present a robust and suitable approach for customer segmentation and lead prediction by combining powerful algorithms into a common framework. This approach helps to provide a performance evaluation of the model which helps to optimize the algorithm selection process and improve computational efficiency. Before segmenting and predicting the leads, we use Principal Component Analysis (PCA) techniques and if the data is non-linear, dimensionality reduction using Autoencoder will help to reduce dimensionality more effectively than PCA. DBSCAN is used to detect customers with unusual behavior. Finally, K-means algorithm is applied to identify customer segments in the dataset and analyzed for each customer group to identify the behavioral characteristics of each group to come up with a good solution. Integrating this approach not only provides deeper insights into customer segmentation but also optimizes future predictions. For potential customer prediction, the Random Forest model is implemented to identify customers who are likely to become loyal or high-value customers for the business. By leveraging customer data, we can recommend solutions, helping businesses optimize strategies and allocate resources more effectively.

2 Methodology

2.1 Dataset

The data for the research paper was taken from Kaggle [10], which includes 2240 customers and 29 different characteristics collected from a shopping center. This database includes essential information about customers, and the main features of the data include: Personal information, Financial data, Family information, Purchase history, Shopping channels, Interaction with marketing campaigns, Web access behavior, feedback and complaints.

The statistical data includes the following information:

- The average income of 2216 people is 52,247.25 with a standard deviation of 25,173.08, ranging from 1,730 to 666,666.
- The average number of children and teenagers per household is 0.44 and 0.51, respectively.
- The average recent time is 49.11 days with a standard deviation of 28.96 days.
- The average amount spent on wine, fruit, meat products, fish products, sweet products, and gold products is 303.94, 26.30, 166.95, 37.53, 27.06, and 44.02, respectively.
- The average number of online, catalog, and in-store purchases is 4.08, 2.66, and 5.79, respectively.
- The average number of website visits per month is 5.32 with a standard deviation of 2.43.

2.2 Data Preprocessing

Before performing data analysis, preprocessing is a crucial step to ensure the accuracy and stability of the model. This process begins with data cleaning, which includes handling missing values by removing them or imputing them using mean or median values. After cleaning, data needs to be normalized to ensure that features are on the same scale, improving model performance. What makes this dataset difficult to apply customer clustering techniques to is that it is quite noisy (Table 1) and we cannot completely remove it, so RobustScaler is applied to this noisy dataset to reduce the impact of outliers. Additionally, Feature Engineering plays a vital role in creating and selecting useful features to reduce redundant variables and prevent overfitting. To reduce dimensionality while retaining essential information, methods such as Principal Component Analysis (PCA) and Autoencoder are used. PCA identifies principal components that carry the most information, whereas Autoencoder, with its ability to learn nonlinear representations, reduces dimensionality while allowing data to be reconstructed as accurately as possible (Fig. 1).

2.3 Model Selection

To perform customer segmentation, the DBSCAN and K-Means models are applied to group customers based on similar characteristics. First, DBSCAN (Density-Based Spatial Clustering of Applications with Noise) is used to remove customers with unusual purchasing behaviors, cleaning the dataset by filtering out noise (outliers). The cleaned

Table 1: Number of exceptions detected by feature (1285 outliers / 2240 values)

Feature	Outlier Count	Feature	Outlier Count
Marital_Status	0	NumWebPurchases	3
Income	8	NumCatalogPurchases	23
Kidhome	0	NumStorePurchases	0
Teenhome	0	NumWebVisitsMonth	8
Recency	0	Family_Size	31
MntWines	35	MntFishProducts	222
MntFruits	246	MntSweetProducts	246
MntMeatProducts	174	MntGoldProds	205
NumDealsPurchases	84		

dataset is then clustered using the K-Means approach, where the optimal number of clusters is determined using methods like the Silhouette Score and the Elbow method. In addition to improving consumer segmentation efficacy, the combination of the two models helps in precisely identifying unusual behaviors.

The next step after clustering is to create a predictive model that helps identify potential customers. Based on the distance measurements, we conduct an analysis and set a threshold to evaluate loyal consumers and promote them to potential VIP status when they are close to qualifying. This not only helps to evaluate customers better but also helps businesses to develop strategies to promote them to become VIP in the future. To accurately and reliably classify new potential customers based on their purchasing characteristics, we finally deploy the Random Forest algorithm.

2.4 Evaluation

The Elbow method will look at the proportion of variance explained as a function of the number of clusters (k) to find the ideal number of clusters. The best number of clusters can be determined from WCSS (within-cluster sums of squares), the point at which the WCSS slows down significantly, forming an "elbow". This point is the optimal number of clusters. Silhouette Score measures how well data points are clustered based on its cohesion inside the assigned cluster and separation from other clusters. The Silhouette Score, which ranges from -1 to 1, where near 1 means points were clustered well, near 0 that points are on the line between two natural clusters, and negative value means the points were clustered incorrectly.

To assess the quality of predictive models, several key metrics are used to measure accuracy. Precision calculates the percentage of predicted positive samples that are truly positive, while Recall measures the percentage of actual positive samples correctly identified by the model. Additionally, ROC-AUC provides an overall evaluation of classification performance. The ROC Curve visualizes the relationship between the True Positive Rate (TPR) and the False Positive Rate (FPR), while AUC (Area Under Curve)

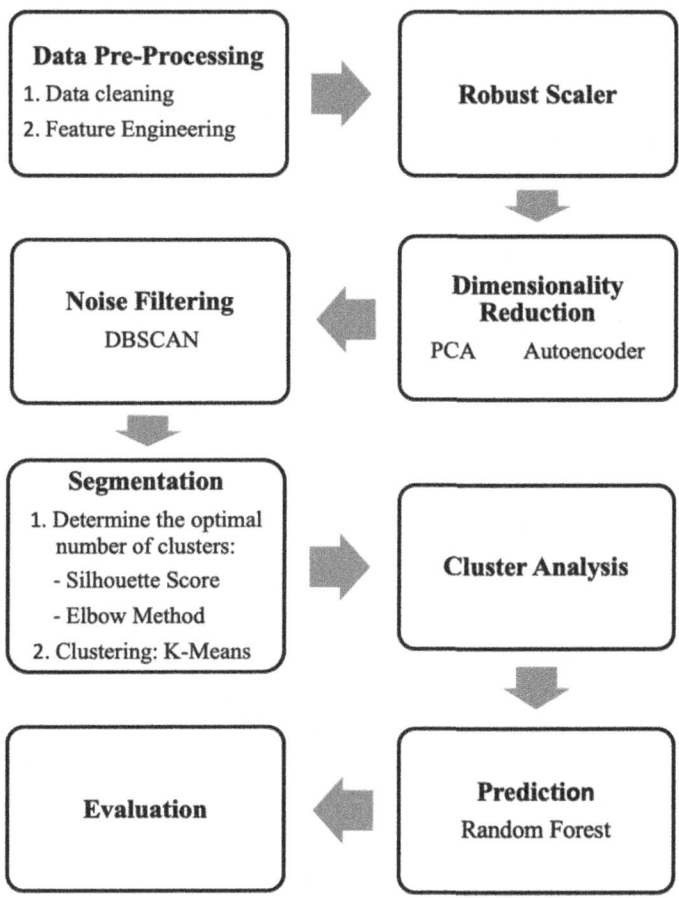

Fig. 1. Flow diagram of the study

quantifies the area under the ROC curve, ranging from 0 to 1. A higher AUC indicates a more effective classification model.

3 Implementation and Results Analysis

3.1 Dimensionality Reduction and Clustering

Before proceeding with customer clustering and classification, two dimensionality reduction techniques, PCA and Autoencoder, are applied to determine which method yields the most optimal results. One of the key issues to address is identifying the appropriate number of dimensions for these algorithms to function effectively before performing clustering. To achieve this, we evaluate the optimal number of components for PCA using the explained variance ratio (Fig. 2) and determine the appropriate latent space dimension for the Autoencoder based on reconstruction error minimization (Fig. 3). We decided to select 7 dimensions for both techniques. As shown in Fig. 2, retaining 7 principal components in PCA preserves approximately 83.5% of the original data variance, which is an acceptable level in practical applications where reducing complexity is necessary while maintaining essential information. For the Autoencoder, as illustrated in Fig. 3, encoding the data into 7 dimensions results in a relatively low reconstruction loss (approximately 0.51), reflecting the model's ability to effectively learn meaningful representations.

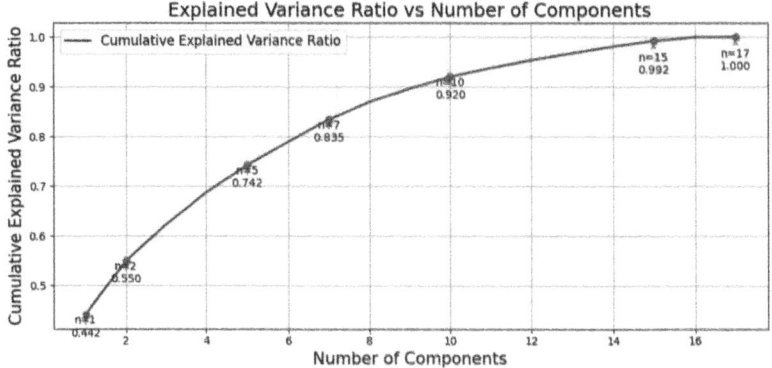

Fig. 2. Explained variance ratio of PCA

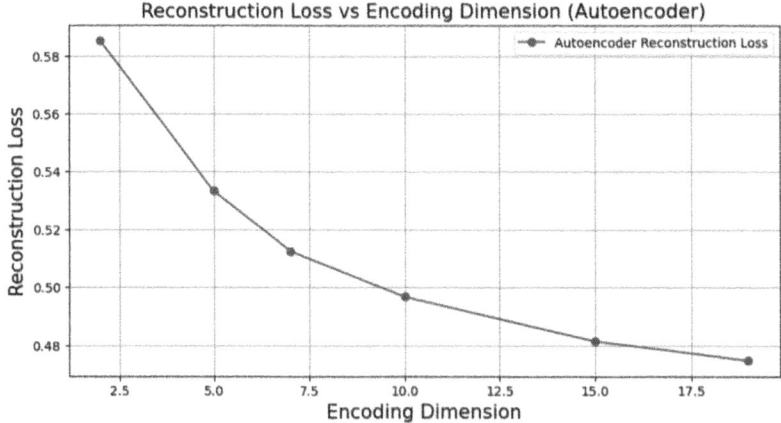

Fig. 3. Reconstruction Loss vs Encoding Dimension (Autoencoder)

Next, to enhance the performance of the K-Means algorithm, DBSCAN is applied to identify and remove unwanted outliers from the dataset. The effectiveness of DBSCAN relies heavily on two key parameters: the neighborhood radius (ε) and the minimum number of points (MinPts). Proper selection of these parameters significantly improves the accuracy of noise filtering, ensuring that the remaining data is well-suited for clustering. To optimize ε, the Silhouette Score can be used as a guiding metric. The optimal ε value is determined when the Silhouette Score reaches its peak, indicating that the clustering structure is well-defined, with clear separation between clusters and minimal noise. This approach ensures that DBSCAN effectively refines the dataset before applying K-Means clustering. Figure 4 shows the variation of Silhouette Score with ε values ranging from 0.5 to 6.0, applied on two different data representations: data after dimensionality reduction by PCA and data encoded by autoencoder. On PCA data, Silhouette Score gradually increases and peaks in the ε range from 4.0 to 5.5 (maximum value is approximately 0.55), then decreases sharply. Therefore, ε = 4.5 is chosen as the optimal value for this case. For encoded data, Silhouette Score improves significantly after ε = 3.0 and stabilizes around the highest level (~0.38) at ε = 5.5–6.0, so ε = 5 is chosen.

Additionally, to assess whether DBSCAN effectively filters out outliers, the k-distance plot can be utilized to observe the difference in distance between the outlier group and the main cluster, helping to establish an appropriate threshold for noise removal (Fig. 5).

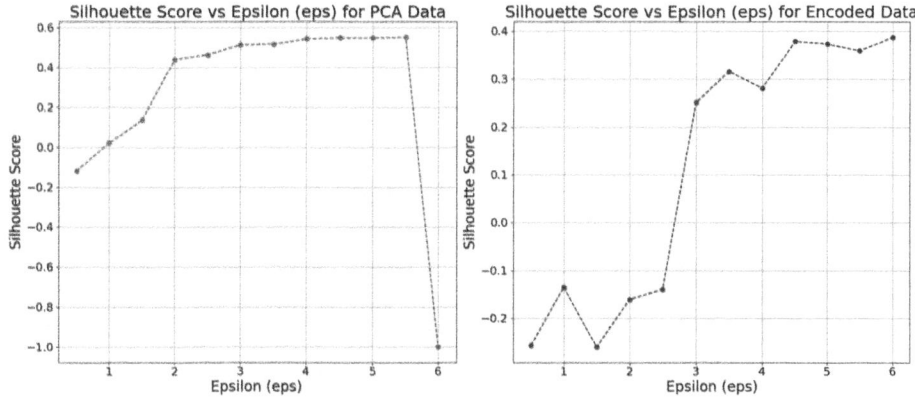

Fig. 4. Silhouette Score vs Epsilon (eps)

The K-Means algorithm is employed to cluster the data corresponding to each reduction method (Fig. 6) and evaluate the results based on features such as salary, total purchase amount, and total number of products purchased (Fig. 7, 8, 9). Finally, the obtained clusters are used in the customer classification task to identify VIP customers, potential customers, or those at risk of churning.

3.2 Clusters Analysis

When comparing two dimensionality reduction methods before applying K-Means, Autoencoder outperforms PCA based on three evaluation criteria: Silhouette Score, Inertia (WCSS), and Davies-Bouldin Index (DBI).

For the Silhouette Score, the chart shows that Autoencoder achieves a higher score than PCA when the number of clusters is 3. This indicates that Autoencoder enables K-Means to cluster more effectively, with greater separation between clusters and less overlap. Both methods show a decreasing trend in the Silhouette Score as the number of

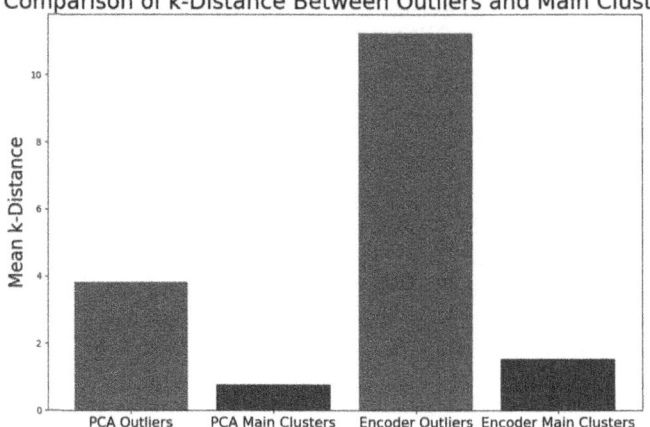

Fig. 5. Comparison of k-Distance Between Outliers and Main Clusters

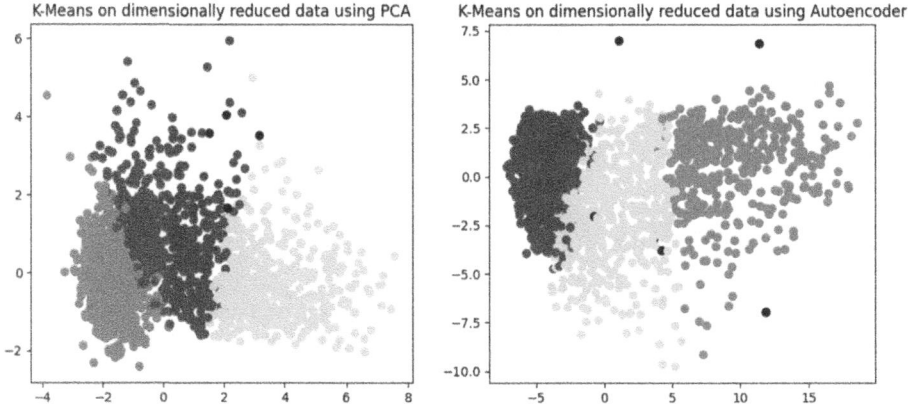

Fig. 6. Visualization of Customer Clusters

clusters increases, but Autoencoder consistently maintains a higher score in most cases, demonstrating its ability to enhance cluster separation.

Regarding Inertia (WCSS), the value for Autoencoder (42,740.07) is significantly higher than that for PCA (11,422.85). Inertia measures the total squared distance from each data point to its nearest cluster center, and the higher value obtained with Autoencoder suggests that the reduced-dimensional data retains better cluster separation, leading to larger distances between points and their cluster centers. This implies that Autoencoder preserves more important features for K-Means rather than simply compressing the data linearly, as PCA does.

Evaluated with the Davies-Bouldin Index (DBI), Autoencoder again demonstrates superiority with a lower value (1.2372) compared to PCA (1.4087). A lower DBI indicates more clearly separated clusters, meaning that Autoencoder enhances K-Means clustering efficiency by preserving the nonlinear structure of the data.

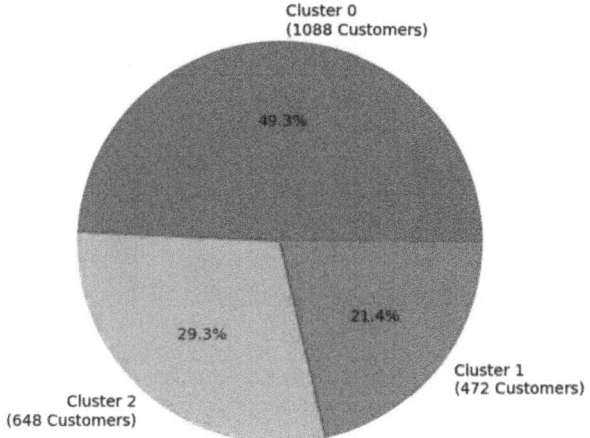

Fig. 7. Number of customers per cluster

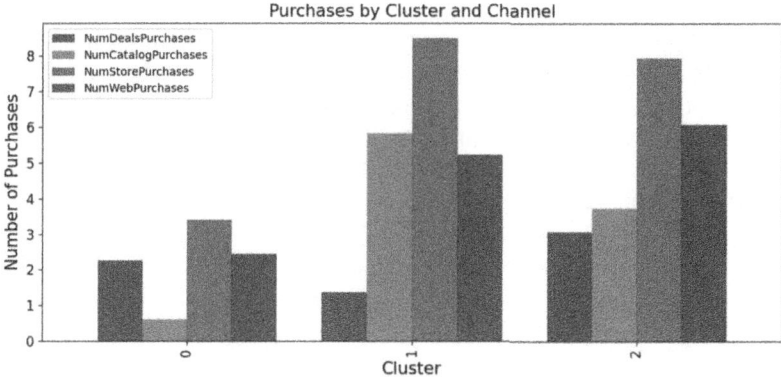

Fig. 8. Number of purchases per cluster

In conclusion, Autoencoder is a better dimensionality reduction method than PCA before applying K-Means. While PCA relies only on linear transformations, which may lose important information in complex data, Autoencoder can learn nonlinear features, maintaining cluster separability. Therefore, if the data has a nonlinear structure, Autoencoder is the preferred choice for improving K-Means clustering quality.

3.3 Potential Customers

In this study, we propose a method to identify potential VIP customers based on important characteristics that are similar between two groups of VIP and loyal customers by dynamic distance analysis. Specifically, the Loyal customer group is defined as those whose purchasing behavior closely resembles VIP customers but has not yet reached that

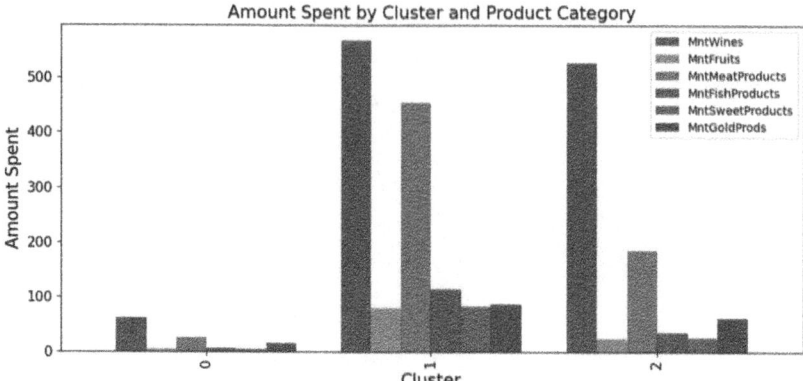

Fig. 9. Amount spent per cluster

level. To identify customers with the potential for status upgrade, we apply Min-Max Scaling to normalize customer features to a common range from 0 to 1, ensuring fairness and accuracy in comparisons. Next, we use Euclidean distance to measure the similarity between customers in the Loyal cluster and the centroid of the VIP cluster. This distance helps us determine which customer's behavior level is closest to the VIP group and from there we can determine the dynamic threshold to help classify the group of customers with the most potential to become VIP compared to the majority of customers in the loyalty group, then we need to calculate the average value (μ) and standard deviation (σ) of the distance from the loyal customer to the VIP center to determine this dynamic threshold. The dynamic threshold is defined as:

Threshold = mean (μ) − k. std (σ).

where k is an adjustment factor that helps us determine the number of corresponding customers we are interested in. Customers in the loyal group whose distance to the center of the VIP group is smaller than the distance to this threshold are identified as potential VIP customers.

The special feature of this method is that it can automatically adjust to new changes in data in the future and provides high flexibility. These results help businesses identify customers who need care, thereby optimizing customer care strategies and increasing VIP conversion rates.

Analyze the components of the chart (Fig. 10):

- X-Axis (Composite Behavior): Some customer behaviors after collection and dimension reduction for visualization purposes ('Income', 'Recency', 'Total Amounts', 'Total Purchase', 'Family_Size').
- Y-Axis (Distance to VIP): The distance of customers from the VIP group, which may be calculated based on a clustering model or a similar metric.
- Blue Dots (Cluster 2 Customers): Customers belonging to the second cluster (possibly loyal or regular customers).
- Red Dots (Potential VIP Customers): Customers with the potential to become VIP, meaning their distance to the VIP threshold is small.

- Green Dotted Line (Vip potential threshold): The distance threshold, below which customers have the potential to become VIP
- Black Dotted Line (Vip Threshold): This is the real VIP threshold when there are customers who reach this levels or higher then the customer has the ability to become a VIP in the future.

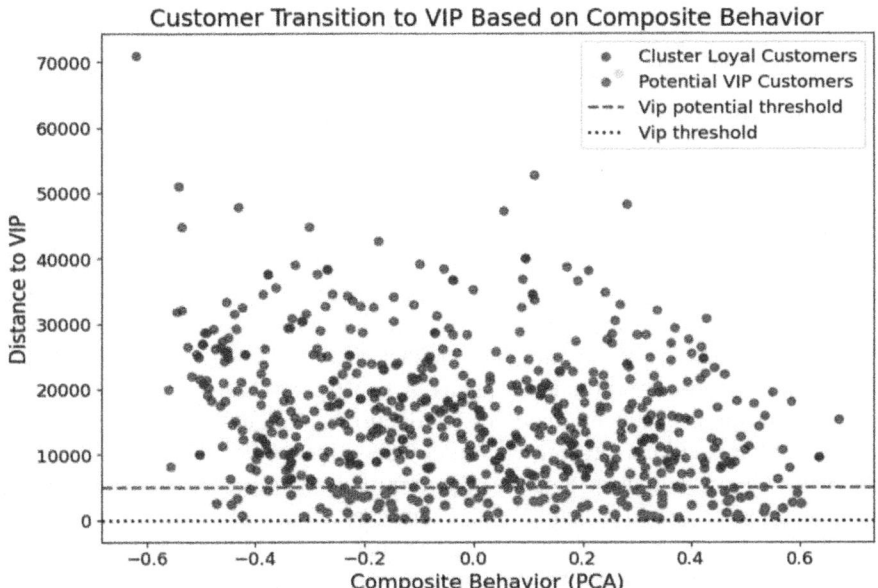

Fig. 10. Conversion rate among loyal customers with the potential to become

VIPAfter analyzing the data and identifying the group of customers with the potential to become VIPs, we calculated that the proportion of loyal customers with the potential to be upgraded to VIP status is 16.69%. This result indicates that a significant portion of loyal customers has the potential to be upgraded to VIP if approached and nurtured appropriately. Optimizing customer retention strategies based on this insight can help businesses enhance their customer engagement and increase Customer Lifetime Value (CLV).

Finally, we apply the Random Forest Classification model to predict which new customers have the potential to become loyal customers or VIP customers. New customers have identifiable input information such as income (Income), number of children in the household (Kidhome), family size (Family_Size), marital status (Marital_Status), and the amount spent on a single purchase (Amount_1_Time). First-time shoppers will be classified into the normally customer group based on their total spending and total quantity of items purchased. Then, we compare their spending characteristics with those of existing customer groups to determine which group they resemble most closely. If their spending behavior aligns with that of the VIP or loyal customer groups, they will be labeled as potential new customers. This approach allows us to early identify high-value customers, enabling the deployment of tailored marketing and customer care strategies to maximize their lifetime value (Fig. 11).

```
Customer Data:
    Income  Kidhome  Family_Size Marital_Status  Amount_1_Time
0  69245.0        2            3       Married           40.0
Model predictions: Potential
```

Fig. 11. Example of predicting new customers as potential

4 Conclusion and Future Works

This paper presents an optimized approach for analyzing and predicting customer segmentation behavior using machine learning techniques and analytical methods. By applying these techniques, we can help businesses better understand customer behavior based on shopping characteristics, helping them predict customer segments that are likely to convert and have more appropriate strategies. A key aspect of this study is the comparison of dimensionality reduction and noise reduction techniques to enhance clustering model performance. In this project, we found that Autoencoder performed more effectively than PCA on nonlinear datasets. By improving data preprocessing, we aim to achieve more accurate and meaningful segmentation results. The use of DBSCAN for noise filtering also enhances the clustering performance of PCA. Furthermore, this study explores customer cluster analysis to identify potential customers within the loyal customer who may be upgraded to VIP customer. Finally, we built a predictive model that helps predict which future new customers are potential customers that businesses should pay attention to and from there suggest more specific strategies for their businesses. The work can be applied when dealing with time-series data [11, 12], market segmentation [13, 14], etc.

References

1. Hosseini, M., Shabxani, M.: New approach to customer segmentation based on changes in customer value. J. Market. Anal. 3(3), 110–121 (2015). https://doi.org/10.1057/jma.2015.10
2. Khan, R.H., Dofadar, D.F., Alam, M.G.R.: Explainable customer segmentation using K-means clustering. In: Proceedings of the IEEE International Conference on Data Science and Business Analytics (2021). https://doi.org/10.1109/UEMCON53757.2021.9666609
3. Aslantaş, G., Gençgül, M., Rumelli, M., Özsaraç, M., Bakırlı, G.: Customer segmentation using K-Means clustering algorithm and RFM model. In: Proceedings of the International Conference on Artificial Intelligence and Data Science, 2023, vol. 25, no. 74, pp. 491–503 (2023). https://doi.org/10.21205/deufmd.2023257418
4. Afzal, A., et al.: Customer segmentation using hierarchical clustering. In: Proceedings of the International Conference on Machine Learning and Data Analytics (2024). https://doi.org/10.1109/I2CT61223.2024.10543349

5. Abdulhafedh, A.: Incorporating K-means, hierarchical clustering and PCA in customer seg-mentation. In: Proceedings of the IEEE International Conference on Big Data and Analytics (2021). https://doi.org/10.12691/jcd-3-1-3
6. John, J.M., Shobayo, O., Ogunleye, B.: An Exploration of clustering algorithms for customer segmentation in the UK retail market. Analytics. **2**(4), 809–823 (2023). https://doi.org/10.3390/analytics2040042
7. Balaji, S., Srivatsa, S.K.: Customer segmentation for decision support using clustering and association rule-based approaches. In: Proceedings of the International Conference on Computer Science and Information Technology (2012). https://www.ijcset.com/docs/IJCSET12-03-11-019.pdf
8. Tanhaei, H.G., Boozary, P., Sheykhan, S., Rabiee, M., Rahmani, F., Hosseini, I.: Predictive analytics in customer behavior: anticipating trends and preferences. In: Proceedings of the IEEE Conference on Business Intelligence and Data Analytics (2024). https://doi.org/10.1016/j.rico.2024.100462
9. Abidar, L., Zaidouni, D., El Asri, I., Ennouaary, A.: Predicting customer segment changes to enhance customer retention: a case study for online retail using machine learning. In: Proceedings of the IEEE International Conference on Machine Learning and Applications (2023). https://doi.org/10.14569/IJACSA.2023.0140799
10. https://www.kaggle.com/datasets/imakash3011/customer-personality-analysis
11. Dat, D.Q., Hung, P.D.: Clustering of time-series balance history data streams using apache spark. In: Luo, Y. (eds) Cooperative Design, Visualization, and Engineering. CDVE 2020. LNCS, vol 12341. Springer, Cham (2020)
12. Dat, D.Q., Hung, P.D.: Improvement for time series clustering with the deep learning approach. In: Luo, Y. (eds) Cooperative Design, Visualization, and Engineering. CDVE 2021. LNCS, vol 12983. Springer, Cham (2021)
13. Phan, D.H., Do, Q.D.: Analysing effects of customer clustering for customer's account balance forecasting. In: Nguyen, N.T., Hoang, B.H., Huynh, C.P., Hwang, D., Trawiński, B., Vossen, G. (eds) Computational Collective Intelligence. ICCCI 2020. LNCS, vol 12496. Springer, Cham. (2020). https://doi.org/10.1007/978-3-030-63007-2_20
14. Phan Duy Hung, Nguyen Duc Ngoc, and Tran Duc Hanh.: K-means clustering using R a case study of market segmentation. In Proceedings of the 2019 5th International Conference on E-Business and Applications (ICEBA 2019). Association for Computing Machinery, New York, NY, USA, 100–104 (2019)

Mixed-Integer Multi-objective Programming for Intermodal Supply Chain Design

Marco Marto[1]([✉])(iD), Valentina Chkoniya[1,2](iD), Eduardo B. Couto[3](iD),
Telmo Pinto[4](iD), Marco S. Reis[5](iD), and Agostinho Agra[6](iD)

[1] Aveiro Institute of Accounting and Administration, University of Aveiro,
3810-500 Aveiro, Portugal
{marcovmarto,valentina.chkoniya}@ua.pt

[2] GOVCOPP - Research Unit in Governance, Competitiveness and Public Policies,
University of Aveiro, 3810-193 Aveiro, Portugal

[3] Department of Economics, Management, Industrial Engineering and Tourism,
University of Aveiro, 3810-193 Aveiro, Portugal
belmiro@ua.pt

[4] Centre for Mechanical Engineering, Materials and Processes, ARISE, University of
Coimbra, 3004-531 Coimbra, Portugal
telmo.pinto@dem.uc.pt

[5] CERES, Department of Chemical Engineering, University of Coimbra, 3030-790
Coimbra, Portugal
marco@eq.uc.pt

[6] Department of Mathematics and CIDMA - Center for Research and Development
in Mathematics and Applications, University of Aveiro, 3810-193 Aveiro, Portugal
aagra@ua.pt

Abstract. In recent years, the occurrence of some political events
around the world, some diseases (e.g. Covid-19) and severe weather
events have led decision-makers to consider more about the uncertainty
and disruption of the routes available for the distribution of some important agricultural products such as soybeans and corn. This work aims to
study some advantageous Supply Chain Networks Design (SCND) for the
distribution of soybeans and corn considering the uncertainty in supply,
demand and transportation costs on intermodal routes for the distribution of soybeans and corn in Europe and North Africa. The objectives
considered are to minimize the costs associated with transportation and
distribution, and to consider environmentally friendly solutions as soon
as possible, taking into account the carbon footprint (green solutions).
Starting from a deterministic model, uncertainty is introduced by considering a set of scenarios, and then the multi-objective version of the
model is considered, taking into account the economic and environmental objective functions. The solutions emphasize the strategic positions of
the ports of Itaqui, and New Orleans as supply ports, and Sines, Lisbon,
Gijon, Tarragona, Casablanca, and Antwerp as distribution (transshipment) ports in the design of the networks according to the objectives.
The advantageous position of Port of Sines is analyzed and discussed
according to the aims of this work of building intermodal Supply Chain
Networks.

O. Gervasi et al. (Eds.): ICCSA 2025 Workshops, LNCS 15888, pp. 88–102, 2026.
https://doi.org/10.1007/978-3-031-97596-7_6

Keywords: Supply Chain Network Design · Mixed Integer Programming · Multi-Objective Programming · Intermodal

1   Introduction

This study focuses on the supply chain for soybeans and corn, mainly to be distributed to meet demand from Europe and North Africa.

Soybeans and corn are essential commodities in the food chain of Europe and North Africa not only to produce final consumer products, but also to raise livestock for human consumption [1–3]. European and North African countries are increasingly dependent on the cheaper and more productive land of South America to provide sufficient quantities of these products.

Demand for both commodities is seasonal (12 months) and prices (per ton) are strongly correlated. The price (per ton) of soybeans is more than 2 times higher than the price (per ton) of corn [4,5].

Since the beginning of the current century, soybean supply chains have been shifting towards South American countries (e.g. Brazil, Argentina) as the main suppliers, instead of North American suppliers (e.g. U.S.A, Canada). Corn supply chains are shifting in the same direction, but more slowly, so that South America will soon be the continent's main supplier [6].

Supply chains do not just change for economic reasons, they can also change for political reasons, environmental and social reasons and, possibly, natural disasters. They need to be flexible, easily adaptable and intermodal (using the sea, roads and railways, for example) to deal with any disruptions that may occur (e.g. political reasons; [7]). Intramodality is also important due to concerns about global warming and to reduce gas emissions [8]. Increasingly, government bodies are more concerned and have targets to meet with regard to gas emissions.

We must therefore add environmental objectives when we think about the food supply chain. Supply chains that take environmental objectives into account are sometimes referred to as green supply chains [9].

Considering the trend of the main suppliers moving from North to South America and the economic and environmental concerns in the design of supply chains, Port of Sines is seen as one of the main candidates for the supply of soy and corn, mainly to the Mediterranean countries and, eventually, as a transshipment port for the traditional North Sea ports [10].

The strategic advantages of Port of Sines [11] are illustrated in this study with an intermodal supply chain network design (SCND) deterministic model, which is run on some realistic scenarios to deal with route uncertainty and to better propose alternatives in case of route disruptions.

Previous studies have considered SCND models to supply commodities in countries or regions. Jia et al. [12], reviewed articles on soy supply chain management and sustainability. The term sustainability is often associated with economic, social and environmental objectives or goals. They mainly analyzed four themes: land use policies; value chain governance; CO_2 emissions reduction and barriers, for example, related to demand. A conceptual model was proposed.

Nadery et al. [13] developed a Benders decomposition approach in an SCND optimization to model wheat distribution in Iran. Previously, Bidhandi et al. [14] proposed a mathematical programming formulation and algorithms dedicated to deterministic, multi-commodity and single-period SCND models, where a modified version of the Benders decomposition is proposed. Wang et al. [9] introduced a multi-objective green SCND model interested in the trade-off between total cost and environmental influence for strategic company planning. The term "green" in supply chain models is often associated with environmental concerns, objectives or targets.

To design this type of supply chain, it is sometimes important to take into account uncertainties, for example in supply, demand and transportation costs. In these cases, sometimes stochastic programming techniques are used to model uncertainty, usually after constructing a set of realistic scenarios [15].

The main objective of this study is to build an economically and environmentally optimized supply chain network to distribute soy and corn enough to satisfy the demand in Europe and North Africa under eight realistic scenarios, considering the South American continent as the main source of these commodities. As expected, the results show the possible relevant role of Port of Sines as one of the main distribution centers (transshipment ports) in this SCND. This study may help to justify the opening of a grain terminal in Port of Sines.

The present study is divided into four main sections: Introduction, Materials and Methods, Results, and Discussion and Conclusion. After the presentation, context and objective of the study in the Introduction, the Materials and Methods section presents the scenarios used and their sources, the parameters and indices used in the modeling task, the decision variables used, the two objective functions and the constraints. It follows the Results section that presents and analyzes the main results that are last discussed and help us to emphasize the relevant position of port of Sines in this study in the Discussion and Conclusion section.

2   Materials and Methods

The SCND model was developed with two objectives: to minimize routing related costs and to minimize CO_2 equivalent emissions in transportation (Green Biobjective Mixed Integer Linear Programming Model).

Based on the historical demands for soybeans and corn in Europe and North Africa available in the FAOSTAT 2024 [16] databases and using Holt's additive forecasting model, the demands for the year 2024 were estimated according to the proportion of individual demands for the last known year. The averages of the monthly prices of soybeans and corn [4,5] were used to estimate the countries' demands for all twelve months of 2024. As well as being a multi-period model, it does not accumulate commodity stocks for future periods due to the perishability of commodities.

First, we present the scenarios. Then we present the deterministic model, its parameters, its decision variables, its objective functions and its constraints.

It is assumed that all demand is satisfied, although depending on the scenario, the proportion of supply required is limited to a specific port of origin in North or South America, depending on the proportion of commodity production. The tons of soybeans and corn that arrive at the distribution centers are processed (cleaned, dried, fumigated) and, in the case of soybeans, a portion is converted to meal at the transshipment ports. This results in a loss of production and a resulting transformed product, along with a portion of the remaining untransformed commodity.

2.1 Scenarios

The set of eight scenarios in Table 1 was used to adjust the parameters of the model according to some types of uncertainty in the supply chain market, supply and demand for soybeans and corn, as well as possibilities of (extreme) price changes for some modes of transportation.

Table 1. Scenarios used to change some parameters and run the model.

Scen. Nr.	Supply Prop. from North America - Soya	Supply Prop. from South America - Soya	Supply Prop. from North America - Corn	Supply Prop. from South America - Corn	Perc. Variation for Demand of Soya	Perc. Variation for Demand of Corn	Perc. Variation for Transp. Costs in Roads	Perc. Variation for Transp. Costs in Rails	Perc. Variation for Transp. Costs in Sea
1	41.00%	59.00%	77.29%	22.71%	3.87%	5.49%	4.11%	2.10%	17.50%
2	41.00%	59.00%	77.29%	22.71%	3.87%	5.49%	4.11%	2.10%	0.00%
3	34.98%	65.02%	69.11%	30.89%	0.00%	0.00%	0.00%	0.00%	0.00%
4	34.98%	65.02%	69.11%	30.89%	0.00%	0.00%	0.00%	bigM	0.00%
5	34.98%	65.02%	69.11%	30.89%	0.00%	0.00%	bigM	bigM	0.00%
6	47.40%	52.60%	85.64%	14.36%	0.00%	0.00%	0.00%	0.00%	0.00%
7	47.40%	52.60%	85.64%	14.36%	0.00%	0.00%	0.00%	bigM	0.00%
8	47.40%	52.60%	85.64%	14.36%	0.00%	0.00%	bigM	bigM	0.00%

The first column is the number of scenarios. The second through fifth columns represent the maximum share of total commodity demand that can be met by North or South American ports based on the historical variation of production proportions [17] in North (e.g., USA, Canada, Mexico) and South America (e.g., Brazil, Argentina, Paraguay) from 2004/2005 to 2023/2024. The scenarios change according to the minimum, average, and maximum proportions of production of these commodities in North and South America [17] over this historical period of twenty years. The sixth and seventh columns represent the percentage changes in commodity demand based on Mordor Intelligence reports [18–20] or no change, which means 0.00%. The eighth to tenth columns represent the percentage change in transportation costs (sea, road and rail) based on Mordor Intelligence reports and the ERSE (Portuguese Energy Services Agency) proposal to increase electricity prices or no change meaning 0.00%. Note that when the value bigM appears, represents an extremely high percentage increase to avoid that mode of transportation.

2.2 Parameters and Indices

The following parameters and indices are used in the bi-objective deterministic model:

- n is the number of suppliers (ports of origin) $i = \{1, 2, .., n\}$;
- b is the number of distribution centers (transshipment/intermodal points) $k = \{1, 2, ..., b\}$;
- m is the number of countries of destination $j = \{1, 2, ..., m\}$;
- ht is the number of months, $t = \{1, 2, ..., ht\}$;
- v_{jk} is the number of combinations of transportation modes for distribution center k and destination j (e.g. (sea, roads),(sea, rails),(sea, rails, roads)) $l_{jk} = \{1, 2, ..., v_{jk}\}$;
- np is the number of products $p = \{1, ..., np\}$;
- d_{jp}^t is the destination country j demand (Ktons) of product p to month t;
- f_{kp} is the fixed cost of distribution center k for product p;
- $st_{jkl_{jk}p}$ is the fixed cost of transport mode combination l_{jk} for product p from distribution center k to destination j;
- g_{ip}^t is the supplier i capacity of product p for month t in Ktons;
- e_{kp}^t is the distribution center (transshipment port) k capacity (Ktons) for product p for month t;
- c_{ikp} is the unit cost (EUR/Ktons) of transportation between supplier i and distribution center k for product p;
- $r_{jkpl_{jk}}$ is the unit cost (EUR/Ktons) of combination of transportation mode l_{jk} between distribution center k and destination j for product p;
- fc_k is the cost (EUR/Ktons) for using a distribution center k;
- fsc_i is the fixed cost (EUR) for using a supply port i;
- α_{ip} is the proportion of product p from supplier i to be transformed;
- β_{ip} is the useful transformed proportion of product p from supplier i;
- ex_{ik} is the CO_2 equivalent emissions in tons/Ktons for transportation from origin i to distribution center k;
- $ey_{jkl_{jk}}$ is the CO_2 equivalent emissions in tons/Ktons for transportation from distribution center k to destination j using transport mode combination l_{jk};

The objective is to meet the demand of destination countries (j) from origin ports (i) (suppliers in North and South America) while respecting the capacity constraints of the origin ports (i). Terminals in European or North African ports have distribution centers (transshipment ports) that can receive goods by sea from origin ports. If necessary, these centers can also process, fumigate, and dry perishable goods. Then, commodities (corn and soybeans) are delivered to the destination countries via the shortest route using combinations of transportation modes l_{jk}, taking into account various alternative intermodal routes by sea, road, or rail.

2.3 Decision Variables

The mixed integer programming model includes the following decision variables:

$$X_{ikp}^t = \begin{cases} 1, & \text{if supplier } i \text{ is serving distribution center } k \text{ for product } p \text{ and month } t \\ 0, & \text{otherwise} \end{cases},$$

$Y_{jkl_{jk}p}^t$ — continuous variable for the proportion of the destination country j
demand distributed with transport mode combination l_{jk} by distribution center k
for product p and month t,

$$Z_{kp}^t = \begin{cases} 1, & \text{if distribution center } k \text{ is opened for product } p \text{ and month } t \\ 0, & \text{otherwise} \end{cases},$$

$$W_{jkl_{jk}p}^t = \begin{cases} 1, & \text{if transport mode combination } l_{jk} \text{ is used to distribute product } p \\ & \text{from distribution center } k \text{ to destination } j \text{ in month } t \\ 0, & \text{otherwise} \end{cases},$$

H_{ikp}^t — continuous variable for the flow from supplier i to distribution center
k for product p and month t (in Ktons)

2.4 Objective Functions

This work uses multi-objective lexicographic optimization [20]. A higher priority
is given to minimizing the routing cost function and a lower priority to minimizing CO_2 equivalent emissions when routing supply sources to demand points in
Europe and North Africa. The following objective function minimizes the costs
in the supply chain network.

$$
\begin{aligned}
\text{Min} \quad & \sum_{t=1}^{ht}\sum_{p=1}^{np}\sum_{k=1}^{b} f_{kp}Z_{kp}^t + \sum_{t=1}^{ht}\sum_{p=1}^{np}\sum_{i=1}^{n}\sum_{k=1}^{b} c_{ikp}H_{ikp}^t \\
+ & \sum_{t=1}^{ht}\sum_{p=1}^{np}\sum_{k=1}^{b}\sum_{j=1}^{m}\sum_{l_{jk}=1}^{v_{jk}} r_{jkpl_{jk}}d_{jp}^t Y_{jkl_{jk}p}^t + \sum_{t=1}^{ht}\sum_{p=1}^{np}\sum_{k=1}^{b}\sum_{j=1}^{m}\sum_{l_{jk}=1}^{v_{jk}} st_{jkl_{jk}p}d_{jp}^t W_{jkl_{jk}p}^t \\
+ & \sum_{t=1}^{ht}\sum_{p=1}^{np}\sum_{i=1}^{n}\sum_{k=1}^{b} fc_k H_{ikp}^t + fsc_i X_{ikp}^t
\end{aligned}
\tag{1}
$$

The objective function below minimizes the CO_2 equivalent emissions in the
supply chain network.

$$
\text{Min} \quad \sum_{t=1}^{ht}\sum_{p=1}^{np}\sum_{i=1}^{n}\sum_{k=1}^{b} ex_{ik}H_{ikp}^t + \sum_{t=1}^{ht}\sum_{p=1}^{np}\sum_{k=1}^{b}\sum_{j=1}^{m}\sum_{l_{jk}=1}^{v_{jk}} ey_{jkl_{jk}}d_{jp}^t Y_{jkl_{jk}p}^t
\tag{2}
$$

2.5   Constraints

In this section, the constraints of the deterministic model are introduced.

$$\sum_{k=1}^{b} \sum_{l_{jk}=1}^{v_{jk}} Y_{jkl_{jk}p}^{t} = 1 \ , \forall j, p, t \tag{3}$$

$$\sum_{j=1}^{m} \sum_{l_{jk}=1}^{v_{jk}} d_{jp}^{t} Y_{jkl_{jk}p}^{t} \leq e_{kp}^{t} Z_{kp}^{t} \ , \forall k, p, t \tag{4}$$

$$\sum_{j=1}^{m} \sum_{l_{jk}=1}^{v_{jk}} d_{jp}^{t} Y_{jkl_{jk}p}^{t} \leq \sum_{i=1}^{n} \{(1 - \alpha_{ip}) + \alpha_{ip} \beta_{ip}\} H_{ikp}^{t} \ , \forall k, p, t \tag{5}$$

$$H_{ikp}^{t} \leq g_{ip}^{t} X_{ikp}^{t} \ , \forall i, k, p, t \tag{6}$$

$$Y_{jkl_{jk}p}^{t} \leq W_{jkl_{jk}p}^{t} \ , \forall j, k, l_{jk}, p, t \tag{7}$$

$$W_{jkl_{jk}p}^{t} \leq Z_{kp}^{t} \ , \forall j, k, l_{jk}, p, t \tag{8}$$

$$X_{ikp}^{t} \in \{0,1\} \ , \forall i, k, p, t; Y_{jkl_{jk}p}^{t} \in [0,1] \ , \forall j, k, l_{jk}, p, t; Z_{kp}^{t} \in \{0,1\} \ , \forall k, p, t;$$

$$W_{jkl_{jk}p}^{t} \in \{0,1\} \ , \forall j, k, l_{jk}, p, t; H_{ikp}^{t} \geq 0 \ , \forall i, k, p, t \tag{9}$$

Constraints (Eq. 3) ensure that the destination country's demand is fully satisfied by distribution centers and mode combinations for all products and months. Each country's demand for each product and month is satisfied by one or more distribution centers (transshipment ports). The constraints (Eq. 4), (Eq. 5) and (Eq. 6) guarantee that the capacities of the distribution centers and suppliers are not exceeded and that the demand in the countries is satisfied. (Eq. 4) means that the sum of demand from all countries coming from each distribution center for each product and for each period does not exceed its capacity. (Eq. 5) means that the sum of the demand from all countries, for all products and months, does not exceed the flow of the product that arrives at the distribution center from the supplier's port after the transformation process in the case of soybeans. (Eq. 6) means that the capacity of the supplier ports is not exceeded for all products and months. An origin can serve one or more distribution centers for each product and month. Constraints (Eq. 7) and (Eq. 8) assign a mode combination for each route from distribution center and destination country, if the route is used and if the distribution center is open, for all products and months. (Eq. 9) represent the supports of the decision variables.

3   Results

The scenarios constructed for the SCND problem of soybean and corn distribution in Europe and North Africa were run for the bi-objective deterministic model in the gurobi optimizer (version 11.0.3) in Python and resulted in eight solutions (one per scenario, with the same routes across all months), but some of them represent similar routes (Figs. 1, 2, 3, 4, 5, 6 and Fig. 7). A PC with 16 GB of RAM and a 3.20 GHz processor was used. All code was written in Python using the following libraries: networkx, geopandas, gurobipy, searoute and routingpy.

Most of them are based on the supply port of Itaqui with the transshipment or distribution ports of Sines and Lisbon, but also the ports of Gijon, Le Havre, Casablanca, Tarragona, Hamburg, Antwerp and Rotterdam (scenarios 1, 2, 3, 4, 5, 6 and 7). In these scenarios, the distribution of the two commodities is distributed among the different transshipment ports and always has the advantageous origin position of the port of Itaqui. On the other hand, if the use of rail and road is considered too expensive and the capacities of the South American ports are the lowest of all the scenarios (Scenario 8), the model selects the Port of Itaqui and the Port of New Orleans as supply ports and more or less the same set of distribution ports. Scenario 8 is slightly more favorable for distribution ports in Northern Europe to supply corn.

Both commodities flow from origin ports in the Americas to transshipment distribution ports in Europe and North Africa. In the case of soybeans, with the exception of soybeans from the port of Buenos Aires (which arrive already transformed), there is a process of transformation of a portion into meal at the transshipment ports (distribution centers). In the transshipment ports, there are some costs associated with cleaning, drying and fumigation operations, if necessary. The most common (and important) distribution centers in all scenarios are

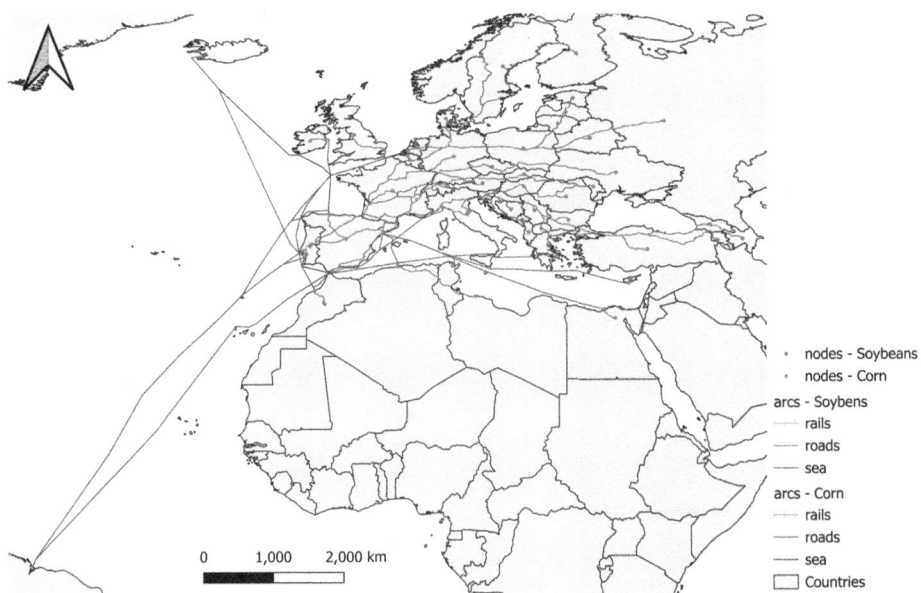

Fig. 1. Scenario 1 and scenario 2 (routes are very similar) from month 1 (January) to month 12 (December). Deterministic model routing solutions for scenarios 1 to 8.

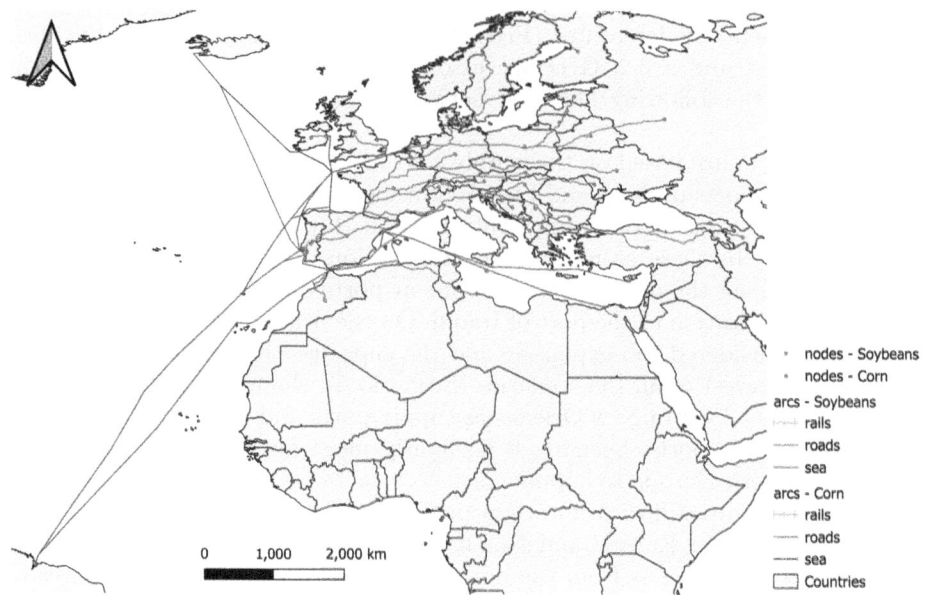

Fig. 2. Scenario 3 from month 1 (January) to month 12 (December). Deterministic model routing solutions for scenarios 1 to 8.

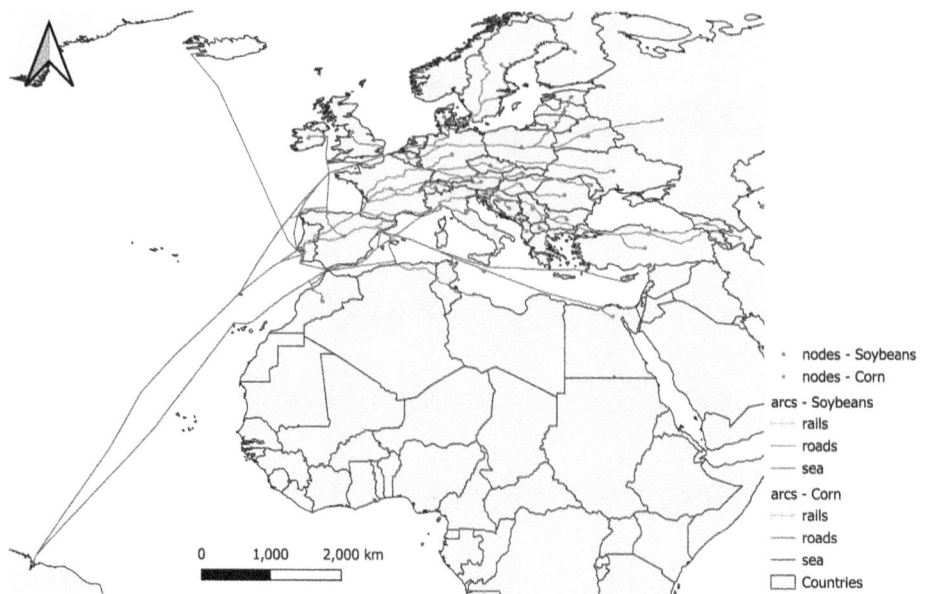

Fig. 3. Scenario 4 from month 1 (January) to month 12 (December). Deterministic model routing solutions for scenarios 1 to 8.

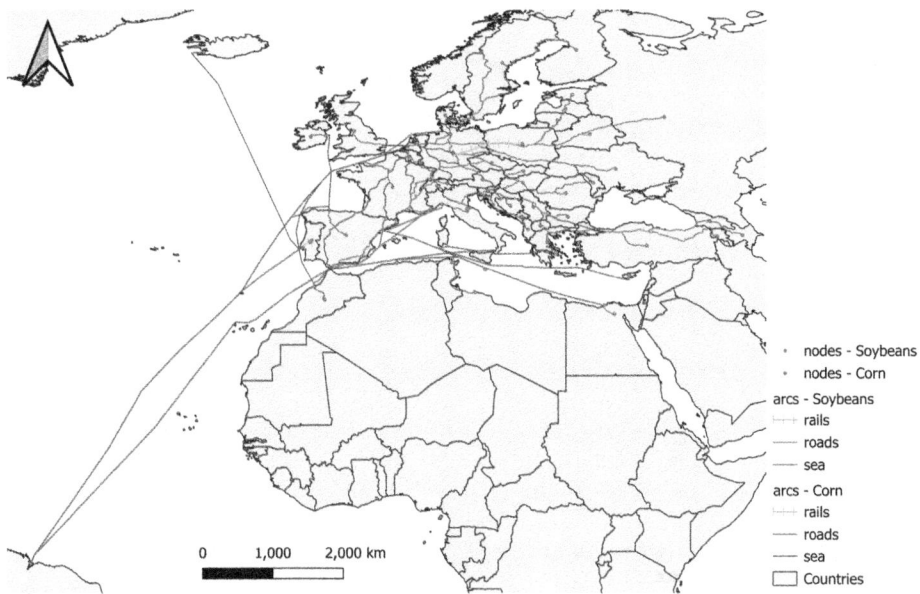

Fig. 4. Scenario 5 from month 1 (January) to month 12 (December). Deterministic model routing solutions for scenarios 1 to 8.

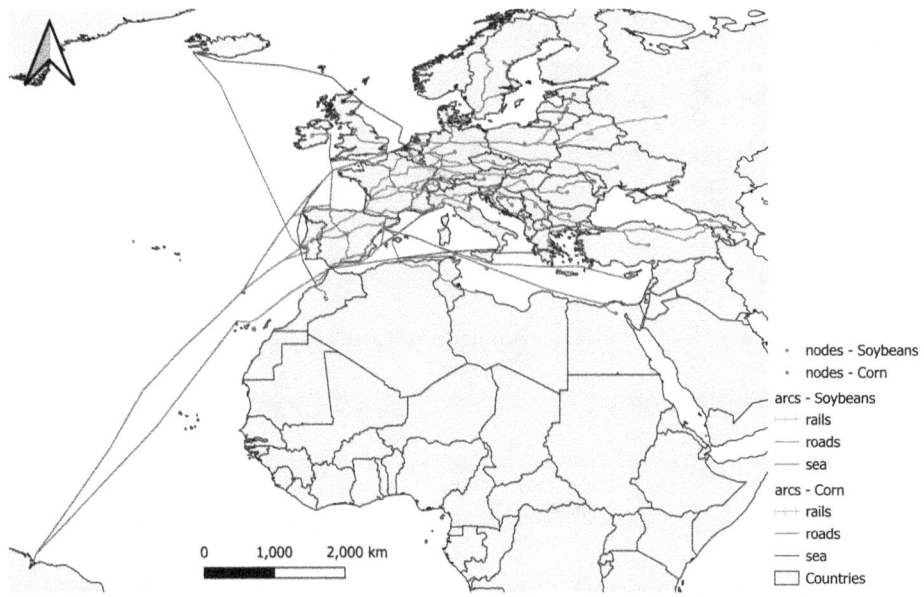

Fig. 5. Scenario 6 from month 1 (January) to month 12 (December). Deterministic model routing solutions for scenarios 1 to 8.

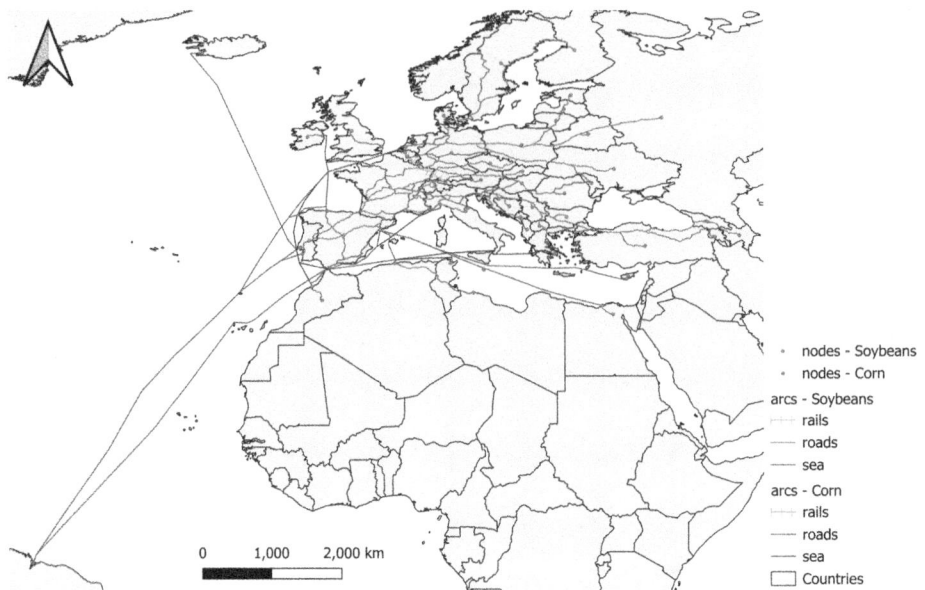

Fig. 6. Scenario 7 from month 1 (January) to month 12 (December). Deterministic model routing solutions for scenarios 1 to 8.

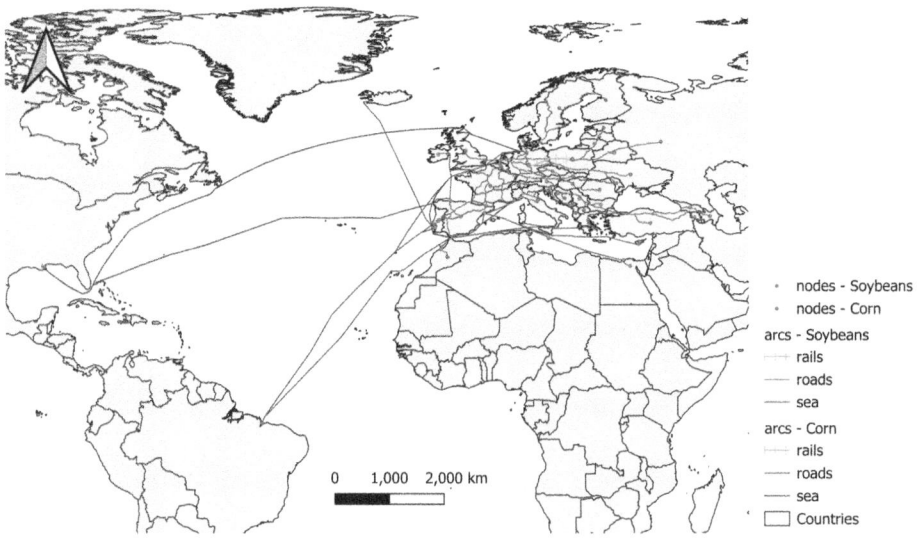

Fig. 7. Scenario 8 from month 1 (January) to month 12 (December). Deterministic model routing solutions for scenarios 1 to 8.

Port of Sines, Port of Lisbon, Port of Antwerp, Port of Gijon, Port of Tarragona, and Port of Casablanca.

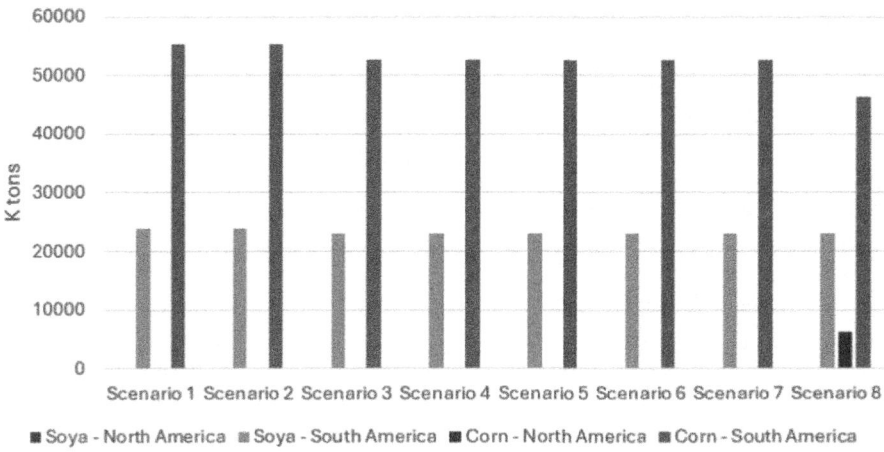

Fig. 8. Annual flow of commodities (soya and corn) from America to Europe and North of Africa for each scenario.

Figure 8 summarize the annual (sum of all months) commodity flows from the Americas to Europe and North Africa. The flows of both commodities from ports in America are the same in scenarios 1 and 2 (about 24,000 Ktons soy and 55,000 Ktons corn), slightly higher than the values for the other scenarios (about 23,000 Ktons soy and 52,500 Ktons corn), because scenarios 1 and 2 take into account the percentage increase in demand for both commodities.

The distribution of soybeans for all scenarios flows through the port of Itaqui (South America), which mainly reflects the effect of the cheapest origin of the commodities. The distribution of corn flows is more sensitive to the higher costs of both land transport modes (rail and road), partly due to the higher volumes that need to be transported compared to the volumes of soybeans. In Scenario 8, some flow of corn from North America is obtained to meet the required demand due to the lowest proportion of supply imposed on the South American port by this scenario (14%) and the comparatively favorable cost of transporting commodities by sea. Scenario 8 shows a higher flow of corn from North America compared to the other scenarios (with favorable ocean transportation costs), in part because the proportion of corn supply from the North American port is about 86% (the highest proportion of all scenarios).

In general, the main (and cheapest) shipping ports for soy and corn are in South America (namely the port of Itaqui), but it is useful to have several scenarios in case of route disruptions in the usual SCND.

4   Discussion and Conclusion

This work may justify the need for a strategic port in Southern Europe or North Africa to serve the demand for soy and corn in Europe and North Africa as a better alternative to the traditional North Sea ports in Northern Europe.

Soybean and corn production is shifting from North America to South America in this century.

Agricultural land in South America (e.g. Brazil, Argentina) is cheap and very productive, making it attractive for agro-industries related to the production of soy and corn. In this exercise, this trend can be seen in the soy supply chain and in the corn supply chain (Fig. 8), although the main corn producing region is still North America (USA).

Therefore, the main supply port for soy and corn is the port of Itaqui (South America, and in some cases the port of New Orleans), and the lower costs and CO_2 equivalent emissions associated with the transportation of commodities indicate that the main distribution center ports for Europe and North Africa are mainly port of Sines, but also the port of Lisbon, the port of Le Havre, the port of Casablanca, the port of Tarragona, the port of Gijon, the port of Hamburg, the port of Antwerp and the port of Rotterdam, depending on the scenario used.

Most scenarios show port of Sines as one of the main ports for supplying soy and corn to all of Europe and North Africa. The port of Sines has more favorable natural and strategic characteristics (e.g. deep water terminals, more functional) compared to the other candidates. Analyzing and comparing the routes from the transshipment port of Lisbon with the transshipment port of Sines to the destination countries, it can be observed that the main difference is the use of a segment of transportation by rail between Lisbon and the distribution point in Portugal.

The rail network used in this work allows intermodal transportation, but at the time of this work it was not the most recent and of poor quality. Fortunately, the more recent version of RNE would select port of Sines as the transshipment port more often in most scenarios, which would directly impact the available combinations of transportation modes and associated costs. The RNE rail network is being integrated into the intermodal network of this study at the time of writing.

Moreover, considering the commodity flows (more than 23,000 Ktons of soybean and 52,500 Ktons of corn), it is easy to justify the advantageous strategic (Moreira, 2015) position of port of Sines in the SCND of grains in Europe and North Africa.

This model can be used as a logistics optimization tool. It helps determine the optimal path based on logistics destinations and known constraints. The goal is to optimize overall costs and emissions, which includes time to market, vessel allocation, and capital implicitly.

It provides decision-makers with information on selecting logistics routes and transportation methods. It helps model transportation networks with various paths, identify the most efficient route, and ensure the effective transportation of goods using various combinations of transportation modes and vehicles that serve multiple hubs, ports, and destinations.

Future work will focus on stochastic and robust versions of the model, which are advantageous approaches for this study because they can take into account different sources of uncertainty (e.g. demand, supply, costs).

Acknowledgments. This study was funded by the PRR - Plano de Recuperação e Resiliência and by the NextGenerationEU funds at University of Aveiro, through the scope of the Agenda for Business Innovation "NEXUS: Pacto de Inovação - Transição Verde e Digital para Transportes, Logística e Mobilidade" (Project nº 53 with the application C645112083-00000059). This research was sponsored by national funds through FCT - Fundação para a Ciência e a Tecnologia, under projects UIDB/00285/2020, LA/P/0112/2020. Marco S. Reis acknowledges support from the Fundação para a Ciência e Tecnologia, I.P., through the projects with DOI:10.54499/UIDB/00102/2020 and DOI:10.54499/UIDP/00102/2020. This work is supported by CIDMA under the FCT (Portuguese Foundation for Science and Technology) Multi-Annual Financing Program for R&D Units. This research is sponsored by national funds through FCT - Fundação para a Ciência e a Tecnologia, under projects UID/00285 - Centre for Mechanical Engineering, Materials and Processes and LA/P/0112/2020.

Disclosure of Interests. The authors have no competing interests to declare that are relevant to the content of this article.

References

1. Goldsmith, P.D.: Economics of soybean production, marketing, and utilization. In: Soybeans, pp. 117-150. AOCS Press (2008). https://doi.org/10.1016/B978-1-893997-64-6.50008-1
2. Baraibar Norberg, M., Baraibar Norberg, M.: Agrofood Globalization: The Global Soybean and Beef Commodity Chains. The Political Economy of Agrarian Change in Latin America: Argentina, Paraguay and Uruguay, pp. 117-163 (2020). https://doi.org/10.1007/978-3-030-24586-3_3
3. Erenstein, O., et al.: Global maize production, consumption and trade: trends and R&D implications. Food Sec. **14**(5), 1295–1319 (2022). https://doi.org/10.1007/s12571-022-01288-7
4. Index Mundi - soybean. https://www.indexmundi.com/commodities/?commodity=soybeans&months=300&currency=eur, Accessed 01 March 2025
5. Index Mundi - corn. https://www.indexmundi.com/commodities/?commodity=corn&months=300&currency=eur, Accessed 01 March 2025
6. United States Department of Agriculture (USDA), Foreign Agricultural Service. https://apps.fas.usda.gov/psdonline/app/index.html#/app/advQuery, Accessed 01 March 2025
7. Ertem, M.A., İşbilir, M., Şahin Arslan, A.: Review of intermodal freight transportation in humanitarian logistics. Eur. Transp. Res. Rev. **9**(1), 1–11 (2017). https://doi.org/10.1007/s12544-017-0226-z
8. de Miranda Pinto, J.T., et al.: Road-rail intermodal freight transport as a strategy for climate change mitigation. Environ. Developm. **25**, 100–110 (2018). https://doi.org/10.1016/j.envdev.2017.07.005
9. Wang, F., Lai, X., Shi, N.: A multi-objective optimization for green supply chain network design. Dec. Support Syst. **51**(2), 262–269 (2011). https://doi.org/10.1016/j.dss.2010.11.020

10. Grossmann, H., et al.: Growth potential for maritime trade and ports in Europe. Intereconomics **42**(4), 226–232 (2007). https://doi.org/10.1007/s10272-007-0223-x

11. MOREIRA, P.P.: The Role of Seaports for Portuguese Economic Recovery: Port of Sines (2015)

12. Jia, F., et al.: soybean supply chain management and sustainability: a systematic literature review. J. Cleaner Product. **255**, 120254 (2020). https://doi.org/10.1016/j.jclepro.2020.120254

13. Naderi, B., Govindan, K., Soleimani, H.: A Benders decomposition approach for a real case supply chain network design with capacity acquisition and transporter planning: wheat distribution network. Annals Operat. Res. **291**, 685–705 (2020). https://doi.org/10.1007/s10479-019-03137-x

14. Bidhandi, H.M., et al.: Development of a new approach for deterministic supply chain network design. Euro. J. Operat. Res. **198**(1), 121–128 (2009). https://doi.org/10.1016/j.ejor.2008.07.034

15. Govindan, K., Fattahi, M., Keyvanshokooh, E.: Supply chain network design under uncertainty: a comprehensive review and future research directions. Euro. J. Operat. Res. **263**(1), 108–141 (2017). https://doi.org/10.1016/j.ejor.2017.04.009

16. FAOSTAT (2024). https://www.fao.org/faostat/en/#data/TCL, Accessed 03 Jan 2025

17. USDA (United States Department of Agriculture) (2025). https://apps.fas.usda.gov/psdonline/app/index.html#/app/advQuery, Accessed 03 Jan 2025

18. Mordor Intelligence (2025a). https://www.mordorintelligence.com/pt/industry-reports/europe-soy-protein-market, Accessed 03 Jan 2025

19. Mordor Intelligence (2025b). https://www.mordorintelligence.com/pt/industry-reports/maize-corn-seed-market, Accessed 03 Jan 2025

20. Mordor Intelligence (2025c). https://www.mordorintelligence.com/pt/industry-reports/european-freight-logistics-market, Accessed 03 Jan 2025

21. Isermann, H.: Linear lexicographic optimization. Operat. Res. Spektrum 4(4), 223–228 (1982). https://doi.org/10.1007/BF01782758

22. RNE 2025, Costumer Information Platform da RailNetEurope. https://cip.rne.eu/topology/interactive-map?welcome=true, Accessed 03 Jan 2025

23. Birge, J.R., Louveaux, F.: Introduction to stochastic programming. Springer Science & Business Media (2011)

24. Bertsimas, D., Hertog, D.d.: Robust and adaptive optimization. Dynamic Ideas LLC 958 (2022)

Computational Methods, Statistics and Industrial Mathematics (CM- SIM 2025)

Physiological Impact of Personal Protective Equipment in Distinct Thermal Environments

Rui Lucena[1] , Nuno Almeida[1], and Paula Simões[2]($\boxtimes$)

[1] Military Academy Research Center - Military University Institute (CINAMIL) and MRLab-Military Readiness Lab-Portugal and CIPER – Faculdade de Motricidade Humana, Universidade de Lisboa, Lisbon, Portugal
lucena.rjp@exercito.pt, almeida.nrc@academiamilitar.pt
[2] Military Academy Research Center - Military University Institute (CINAMIL) and MRLab-Military Readiness Lab-Portugal and NOVA MATH - Center for Mathematics and Applications, NOVA University of Lisbon, Lisbon, Portugal
paula.simoes@academiamilitar.pt

Abstract. Chemical, biological, radiological, and nuclear (CBRN) military teams face extreme conditions due to the hazardous nature of their work and the characteristics of personal protective equipment, which can cause a rapid and dangerous increase in vital physiological parameters in hot climates. This study investigated the physiological impact of personal protective equipment in distinct thermal environments (high vs ambient). A sample of Military Academy students, with characteristics similar to members of CBRN teams, performed a 30 min physical protocol while wearing personal protective equipment. The primary aim was to analyse the variation of physiological parameters (core temperature, skin temperature, and heart rate) and subjective perceptions of thermal stress (thermal sensation, thermal comfort, perception of skin moisture, and rate of perceived exertion) in military personnel. The data was analysed using various descriptive statistical methods, combined with adequate statistical inference techniques considering non-parametric statistical methods for hypothesis testing development. The results demonstrated that personal protective equipment use exacerbates thermal strain, particularly in hot environments, leading to increased core and skin temperatures, as well as heart rate. The perception of thermal discomfort and skin moisture also increased in warmer conditions. Particularly, male participants tended to report feeling warmer, less comfortable, and experiencing more skin moisture at ambient temperature compared to females. It is concluded that understanding the impact of personal protective equipment under varying thermal conditions is crucial for preventing adverse clinical situations and optimizing the safety and performance of military personnel in risk scenarios. The implemented protocol may also be valuable in assessing the adaptability to different environments in admission tests for CBRN teams.

Keywords: CBRN · physiological impact · thermal perception · non-parametric analysis

O. Gervasi et al. (Eds.): ICCSA 2025 Workshops, LNCS 15888, pp. 105–121, 2026.
https://doi.org/10.1007/978-3-031-97596-7_7

1 Introduction

Environmental conditions can be predictably extreme and severe, such as deserts, polar, alpine regions and deep oceans. However, even under normal habitat conditions, individuals may be exposed to transient, life-threatening extreme conditions due to daily work activities. Exercising/working in the heat has been shown to impair the ability to effectively regulate body temperature and may lead to decreased performance but also lead to possible injury or death [1].

Indeed, chemical, biological, radiological and nuclear (CBRN) military personnel are exposed to these types of extreme working conditions, due not only to the dangerous nature of the work (permissive, uncertain and hostile), but also to the characteristic of protective clothing, which causes a rapid and dangerous rise in vital physiological parameters in hot climates up to 45 °C [2].

Thus, CBRN threats are extremely dangerous to human life and rapid remediation actions are crucial to save lives, after an incident occurs. Mitigation responses are usually made by deploying military personnel to scenarios of extreme risk to human life, which require high-safety procedures. The response process usually includes: reconnaissance of the affected area, initial detection of the agent, sample collection, decontamination, first aid, medical evacuation, among others. One of the common aspects to all stages of the response process is the use of personal protective equipment (PPE), which may disturb the proper functioning of the human physiological systems.

1.1 Physiological Impact of Personal Protective Equipment

Whether in CBRN war scenarios or CBRN incidents of an accidental or deliberate nature, the military personnel in these teams present an additional risk associated with the use of PPE. The specificity of this equipment causes challenges in the regulation of body temperature through the increase of the energy cost of exercise as well as the reduction of movement efficiency.

Furthermore, the thickness of the PPE limits evaporation which does not allow correct heat loss and can lead to fast and unpredictable fatigue states. The prevention of extreme clinical situations such as: heat stroke, hyperthermia are fundamental in these cases thus ensuring the efficiency of the mission and health of the soldiers.

1.2 Thermoregulation and Thermal Perception

Heat balance can be affected by a number of external factors such as ambient environment, protective equipment and clothing, intensity and duration of the work, but also by internal factors as body composition, and degree of acclimation [2, 3].

Humans' thermal regulation system and the thermal perceptions depend on the proper functioning of the thermal receptors and the transmission of that information to the brain. These thermoreceptors are found along the surface of the skin and send inputs from cutaneous temperature to the brain [4].

The assessment of thermal perception is based on a subjective assessment, but do not always convey a direct relationship with the environmental conditions [5]. In this sense, in order to have a more complete assessment of the thermal perception one of the options is to apply scales that measure different thermal perceptions. These perceptions regarding thermal sensation and thermal comfort should be analysed at the same moment during the protocols [4, 6].

2 Objectives and Methods

2.1 Objectives

The primary aim was to analyse the variation of physiological parameters (core temperature, skin temperature, and heart rate) and subjective perceptions of thermal stress (thermal sensation, thermal comfort, perception of skin moisture, and rate of perceived exertion) in military personnel.

2.2 Description of the Protocol

All participants were instructed to hydrate with 45 ml of water per kg of body weight during the 24 h prior to the protocol. The experimental protocol consisted of 3 consecutive exercise cycles with a total of 30 min, conducted in two environmental conditions of 18,28 ± 0,7 °C (ambient temperature) and 26,92 ± 0,7 °C (high temperature). The test begins with the participant standing facing a 5 kg sandbag placed on the floor adjacent to a wall. Upon the "start" command, the individual must: Lift the sandbag and touch a pre-marked wall target at 1 m height, carry the sandbag while walking 5.7 m in a straight line to the opposite wall, repeat the touch maneuver with an identical 5 kg sandbag and wall marker. This sequence constitutes one complete repetition, performed continuously for 4 min (Exercise 1) following a metronome-paced rhythm of 6 beats per minute (primary movement cues) 13 sub-beats between main beats (providing intermediate timing reference), followed by 1 min rest for subjective assessments. Each metronome beat requires the participant to complete one wall touch with the sandbag, maintaining strict synchronization throughout the testing period.

After, participants performed step exercise for 4 min (Exercise 2), at 15 cycles/min, completing full step ascents and descents with each auditory cue, and an additional 1 min of rest, followed by a final 4 min recovery period after the 3 consecutive exercise cycles (Fig. 1). Exercises were performed with personal protective equipment (PPE) and followed metronome-controlled rhythms.

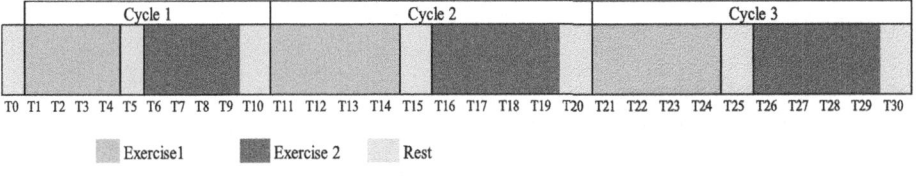

Fig. 1. Description of the protocol

2.3 Physiological Responses to Heat Stress

Core Temperature
The temperature in the abdominal area is representative of the Core Temperature (CT) of the trunk [7]. This measurement RPE is done using a reduced size sensor, which after ingestion, travels throughout the digestive system. During its course, the temperature varies depending on its location, which is higher in the areas near blood vessels and organs with higher metabolism and lower in the areas of abdominal walls [8]. The interpretation of the values is contingent on the time elapsed since the ingestion and the speed of the subject's gastrointestinal transit, reflecting different thermal patterns in different parts of the digestive system [8]. CT was assessed by the E-Celsius performance capsule, consisting in a telemetric system for continuous gastrointestinal temperature monitoring.

Skin Temperature
Skin Temperature (ST) can vary in a much wider range than that of the deep tissues of the body. While in hot environments the ST tends to be uniform throughout the body, in cold environments the extremities of the body tend to have a lower temperature than the torso and head [9].

ST is influenced by thermal exchanges as conduction, convection, radiation and evaporation on the surface, the variation in blood flow and temperature of arterial blood arriving at a particular area of the body [10].

During actual exercises, the military will be continuously monitored using the PLUX Biosignalsplux Integrated System. The collected signals will include 2 sensors for ST which were developed for research applications where it can be used to measure corporal or ambient temperatures. The sensor produces an accurate analog output signal with short response times to temperature alterations.

Heart Rate
Heart Rate (HR) is influenced by both branches of the autonomic nervous system however, it also depends on the endocrine system, whereas specific hormones contribute to the reabsorption of water for the regulation of blood pressure [11].

The relationship between the increase in HR and the increase in internal temperature is known as the cardiac response to temperature, measured in beats.min^{-1} °C^{-1} [12]. Furthermore, the individual variations play a crucial role, as they are influenced by the exercise mode, as well as by the origin of the heat stress, in this case exogenous (climatic conditions) or endogenous (metabolic) factors [13]. HR was monitored throughout the test (Polar H10; Kempele, Finland).

Rate of Perceived Exertion
The rate of perceived exertion (RPE) is an indicator that is measured using the RPE scale. This indicator works as a self-assessment instrument of fatigue, difficulty and physical exertion. This scale ranges from 6–20, where 6 refers to "Very Easy" and 20 to "Exhaustive" [14] and has been considered adequate to assess physical exertion in the military context [15].

2.4   Thermal Perception Analysis

Thermal Sensation

Although thermal sensation is a subjective variable that differs according to individual perceptions from individual to individual, it tends to increase with the increase in ambient temperature [5].

The most used scale to assess thermal sensation is the scale developed by ASHRAE, which consists of assessing the perception of thermal sensation and is graded between "Very Cold", "Cold", "Cool", "Slightly Cool", "Neutral", "Slightly Warm", "Warm", "Hot" and "Very Hot". This scale is often used to establish a relationship between variation of physiological factors monitored through specific devices with the thermal sensation perceived by individuals [16].

Thermal Comfort

The perception of thermal comfort is a subjective assessment that varies from individual to individual and is related to the variation in ambient temperature, ST, thermoregulation capacity and the thermal sensation inherent to each individual [6].

Thermal comfort has been shown to depend on the perception of moisture in the skin, since in warmer environments, temperatures considered less comfortable are associated with higher perceptions of moisture in the skin [4]. The scale that was utilized allows the perception of Thermal Comfort to be assessed, which is graded between "Very Uncomfortable", "Uncomfortable", "Slightly Uncomfortable", "Slightly Comfortable", "Comfortable" and "Very Comfortable" [4].

Perception of Moisture in the Skin

When performing physical activity in warmer environments, the perception of comfort and thermal sensation is more dependent on the perception of moisture in the skin and the sweating rate than on the temperature in the skin itself, because the ST values are constantly oscillating in order to adapt to the ambient temperature and facilitate the heat dissipation process. Thus, the perception of moisture in the skin is considered a good indicator to assess thermal comfort, especially in warmer environments [17].

According to Garson (2016), when more waterproof equipment is used, since this material restricts the heat dissipation capacity, the moisture in the skin tends to increase. In this study, we used a graduated scale of "Very Dry", "Dry", "Slightly Wet", "Wet", "Very Wet", "Wet" and "Very Wet" [4].

2.5   Statistical Methodology

In order to validate whether the Physical Protocol makes it possible to assess and draw conclusions about the heat tolerance of military personnel wearing PPE, analysing the variation in physiological variables and thermal perceptions throughout the performance of the protocol at different temperatures, a sample of 2nd and 5th year students from the Military Academy was selected, male and female. The protocol implementation was scheduled according to the students' availability between 11 March and 2 May of 2024. This is a quantitative study as it uses information collected in the field, based on a previously defined sample of soldiers, considering standardised information collection instruments as sources of analysis. The data collected on the physiological parameters monitored in the participants, who were exposed to exercises with different intensities of physical stress, with and without equipment and in different temperature environments, were structured and statistically analysed using IBM SPSS Statistics 28 and Microsoft Excel software, exploring the relevant variables, from those that correspond to physiological indicators (CT, ST and HR) to those associated with thermal perception indicators (RPE, thermal sensation, thermal comfort and perception of moisture in the skin). The data was analysed using various descriptive statistical methods, combined with adequate statistical inference techniques and probability models. Point estimation, interval estimation and implementation of various hypothesis tests for the parameters of interest (median value) are considered, taking into account the enunciated problem, with a significance level of 10% [18]. Considering non-parametric statistical methods for hypothesis testing development, considering the Wilcoxon test and also using the Kruskal-Wallis test, with multiple pairwise comparisons, the study is performed [18].

3   Results Analysis and Discussion

In this research, the population to be analysed was the military personnel who make up the CBRN teams. Thus, the necessary conditions have been created for this purpose so that the study can be validated by means of a quantitative method. This assessment was carried out using protocols in a controlled laboratory in order to measure, using both invasive and non-invasive methods, the chosen variables of military personnel while wearing PPE.

The active-duty military personnel have been chosen among the Military Academy students who have been considered as members of a possible CBRN team in order to constitute a representative sample. The participants were between 21 and 31 years old with an average of 23,22 years and a standard deviation (sd) of 2,5 years. Weight was between 53,25 kg and 82,15 kg, with an average of 68,07 kg and a SD of 11,93 kg; The height of the subjects ranged from 161 cm and 183 cm with an average of 170,2 cm and a SD of 7,31 cm. In terms of body mass index (BMI), lies between 20,3 kg/m^2 and 26,5 kg/m^2 with an average of 23,29 kg/m^2 and a SD of 2,34 kg/m^2. The male subjects have an average age of 24,4 ± 2,4 years (considering that the second value is the standard deviation), a height of 175,2 ± 5,3 cm and an average weight of 76,9 ± 7,1 kg, a BMI of 25,0 ± 1,4 kg/m^2. With regard to the female members, they have an average age of 21,8 ± 2,1 years, a height of 164,0 ± 3,5 cm and an average weight of 57,1 ± 4,5 kg, a BMI of 21,2 ± 1,1 kg/m^2. Table 1 summarizes the mentioned main statistics.

In addition, resting blood pressure and HR were measured as a safety protocol to check for any untimely medical conditions before carrying out the protocols at different temperatures. All the sample members were physically active, healthy, non-smokers, did not have any type of heart or respiratory disease or any injury that could influence their physical performance in this study.

3.1   Physiological Indicators Variation - Ambient vs High Temperature

The Physical Protocol was carried out at Ambient Temperature (18,28 °C ± 0,7 °C) and at the High Temperature (26,92 °C ± 0,7 °C). The data collected during these two

Table 1. Characteristics of the participants (values are mean ± sd)

Statistics	Age (years)	Weight (Kg)	Heigh (cm)	Body mass index
Mean Male	24,40 ± 2,41	76,88 ± 7,14	175,20 ± 5,31	24,97 ± 1,41
Mean Female	21,75 ± 2,06	57,05 ± 4,48	164,00 ± 3,46	21,19 ± 1,14
Mean	23,22 ± 2,54	68,07 ± 11,93	170,22 ± 7,31	23,29 ± 2,34

environments, with controlled temperatures of 18,28 °C ± 0,7 °C and 26,92 °C ± 0,7 °C were analysed in order to obtain the results in relation to the variation in physiological parameters, CT, ST and HR, throughout the physical protocol.

3.1.1 Core Temperature Throughout the Protocol at Different Environments

When analysing this physiological parameter, the average of the values within each minute was taken into account. It is evident that there was a slight increase in the CT of all the individuals during the 29 min of work at both temperatures. For ambient temperature, the values for the average variation in CT of the entire sample over the 29 min did not very much, with the average value being 37,41 °C ± 0,27 °C, the minimum value being 36,57 °C and the maximum 37,97 °C. With regard to the variation in the average for the entire sample during the 29 min protocol at the high temperature, although there was no great variation in the results, this variation was higher in all the individuals when compared to the variation obtained in the Ambient Temperature, as can be seen from the range of results obtained between the minimum and maximum values measured in both environments (see Fig. 2). The general average in this environment was 37,40 ± 0,32 °C, the minimum value collected was 36,66 °C and the maximum 38,19 °C.

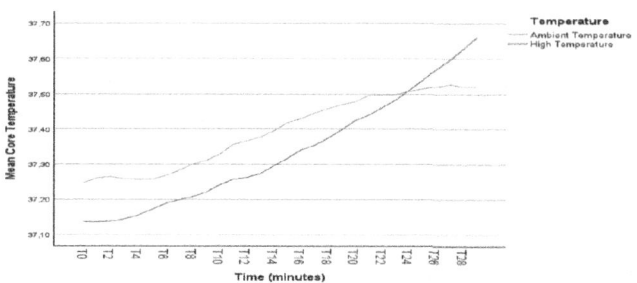

Fig. 2. CT Variation Throughout the Protocol at Different Temperatures.

For the null hypotheses H0: The median value of the CT is the same across times for Exercise 1, when going through the non-parametric statistical test, the hypothesis is not rejected in Ambient Temperature (p-value = 0,145), as well as for High Temperature (p-value = 0,552) (Fig. 3). Across times for Exercise 2, the same conclusion is reached, in Ambient Temperature (*p*-value = 0,128), as well as for High Temperature (*p*-value = 0,206) (Fig. 4).

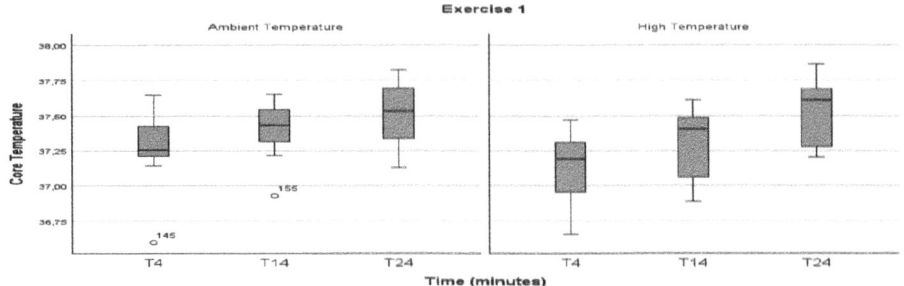

Fig. 3. Boxplot relative to CT across times (Exercise 1) in Ambient Temperature (left) and High Temperature (right).

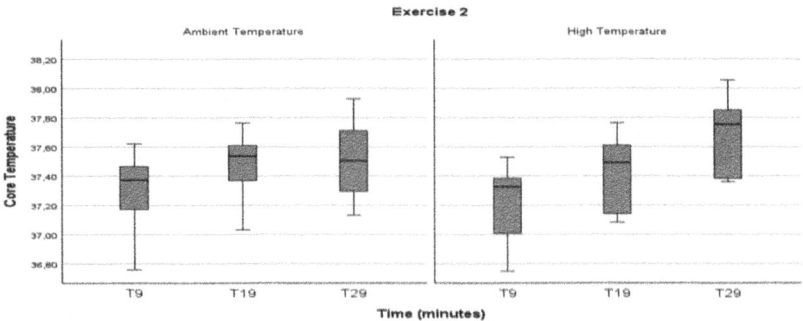

Fig. 4. Boxplot relative to CT across times (Exercise 2) in Ambient Temperature (left) and High Temperature (right).

In the present study, this protocol was used to analyse the differences between the CT medians for the different sexes during exercise 1 (in the moments T4, T14 and T24) and during exercise 2 (in the moments T9, T19 and T29) in both environments with different temperatures. The Wilcoxon non-parametric statistical test applied between categories of sexes in Ambient Temperature, for the null hypotheses H0: The median value of the CT is the same across categories of sex, is rejected (*p*-value = 0,021), in Exercise 1 (Fig. 5). For High Temperature they are not significantly different (*p*-value = 0,125), obtaining this same conclusion when analysing Exercise 2 for both temperatures (0,122 < *p*-value < 0,128) (Fig. 6).

3.1.2 Skin Temperature Throughout the Protocol at Different Environments

Taking into account the values within each minute over the 29 min of work in the carried-out protocol, at both ambient temperatures, the variation in ST was analysed. The average value during the 29 min of the protocol carried out at ambient temperature was 35,56 °C ± 1,21 °C, with a minimum of 32,22 °C and a maximum of 36,85 °C. With regard to the

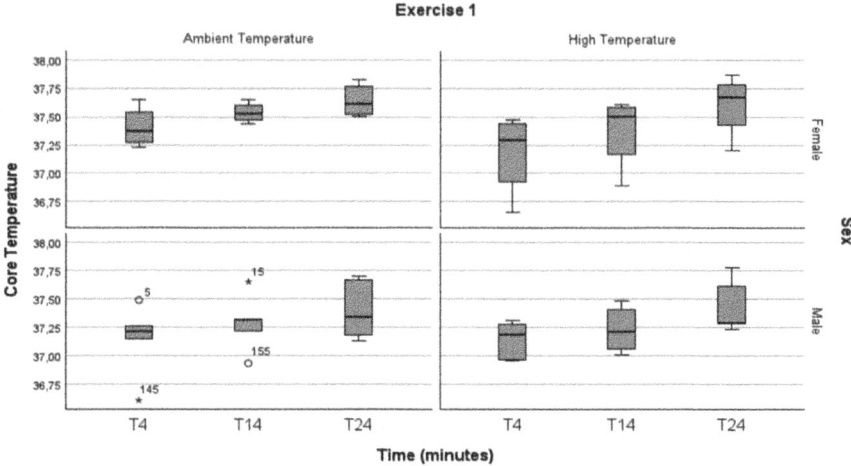

Fig. 5. Boxplot relative to CT (Exercise 1) across sex categories in Ambient Temperature (left) and High Temperature (right)

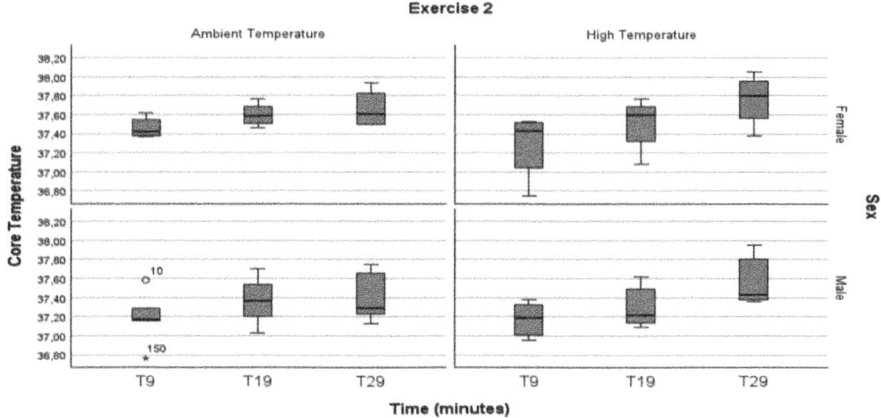

Fig. 6. Boxplot relative to CT (Exercise 2) across sex categories in Ambient Temperature (left) and High Temperature (right).

data collected in the environment with the highest temperature, similarly to what was observed at ambient temperature, there was a slight increase in the average variation of the sample in relation to the protocol, obtaining an average value at 29 min of 36,79 °C ± 0,53 °C, with a minimum temperature of 35,24 °C and a maximum of 37,89 °C. Thus, a slight increase in the sample average over the 29 min of the protocol in both environments is observed.

From the perspective of the ST variable, given the null hypothesis, H0: The medians are the same across times of the graded Exercise 1, for Ambient temperature as well as for High temperature, through the Wilcoxon test, H0 are rejected. So significant differences emerged between T4 and T14 ($0,018 < p$-value $< 0,046$) and between T4 e T24 ($0,018$

< *p*-value < 0,072) for in Ambient Temperature and also for high temperature (Fig. 7). In terms of Exercise 2 protocol, this shows only significant differences in Ambient temperature between T9 and T19 (*p*-value = 0,046) and between T9 e T29 (*p*-value = 0,005), and no significant differences between times at high temperature emerge (Fig. 8).

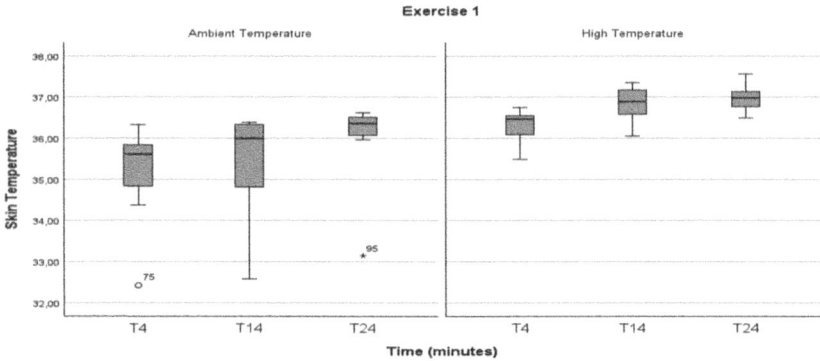

Fig. 7. Boxplot relative to ST across times (Exercise 1) in Ambient Temperature (left) and High Temperature (right).

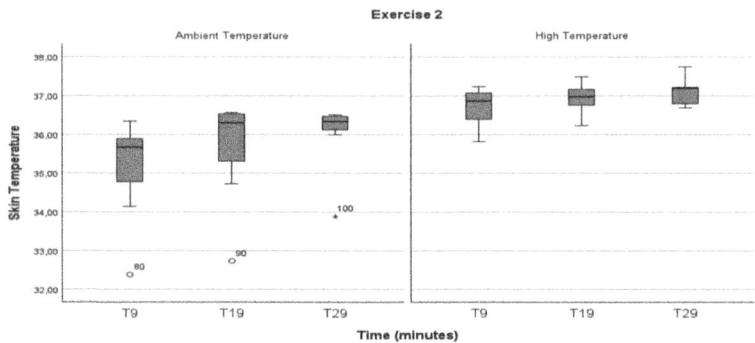

Fig. 8. Boxplot relative to ST across times (Exercise 2) in Ambient Temperature (left) and High Temperature (right).

The differences between the ST medians for the different sexes during exercise 1 (in the moments T4, T14 and T24) and during exercise 2 (in the moments T9, T19 and T29) in both environments with different temperatures are considered (Figs. 9 and 10).

Going through analysis between categories of sexes in ST, by applying the non-parametric statistical test, for the null hypotheses H0: The median value of the ST is the same across categories of sex, is rejected in Exercise 2 for high temperature (0,128 < *p*-value < 0,414) (Fig. 10). In Exercise 1 for Ambient temperature as well for High Temperature differences are not detected (0,122 < *p*-value < 0,128) (Fig. 9).

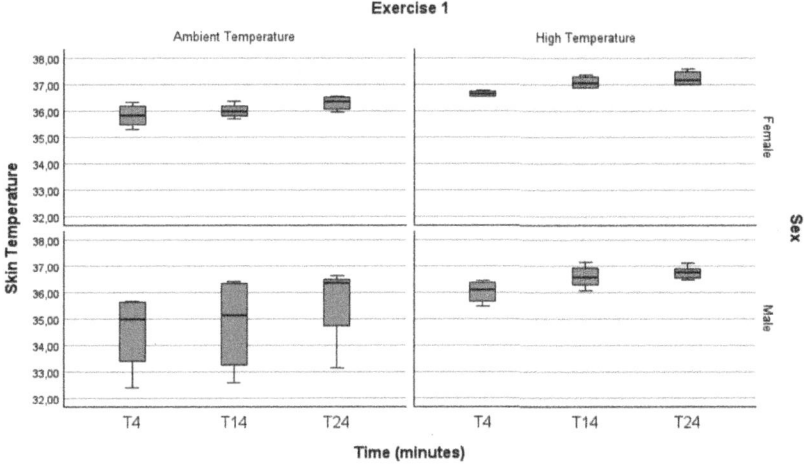

Fig. 9. Boxplot relative to ST (Exercise 1) across sex categories in Ambient Temperature (left) and High Temperature (right).

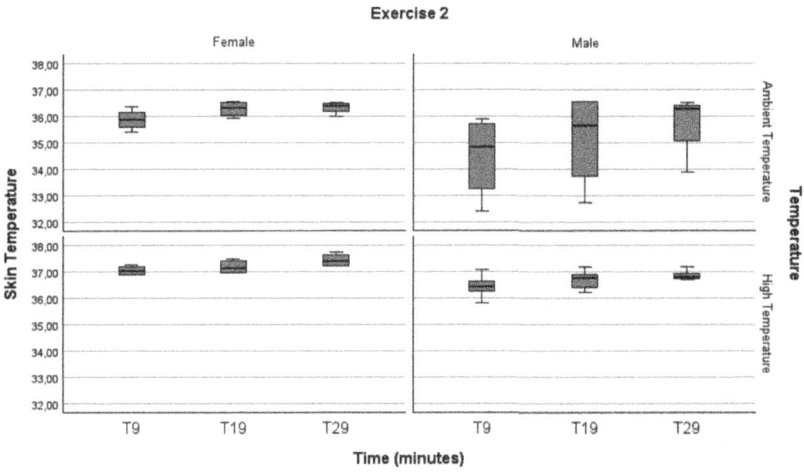

Fig. 10. Boxplot relative to ST (Exercise 2) across sex categories in Ambient Temperature (left) and Warmest Temperature (right).

3.1.3   Heart Rate Throughout the Protocol at Different Environments

Regarding the variation in HR values over the 29 min of implemented protocol, the average of the HR values for each minute was considered. Since HR values are influenced by the physical demands that the participants are subjected to, a slight decrease in HR during the resting minutes (between T4 and T5, T9 and T10, T14 and T15, T19 and T20, T24 and T25), is noted. At ambient temperature, the sample's average HR over the 29 min of the protocol was 101,16 bpm ± 12,23 bpm, with a minimum HR of 56 bpm and a maximum HR of 125 bpm. On the other hand, at a higher temperature, the average

HR over the 29 min of the protocol was 115,16 ± 16,00 bpm, with a minimum HR of 68 bpm and a maximum HR of 150 bpm.

It was therefore observed that, at both temperatures, there was an increase in HR during the course of the physical protocol, with greater variation in the protocol carried out at a higher temperature (Fig. 11).

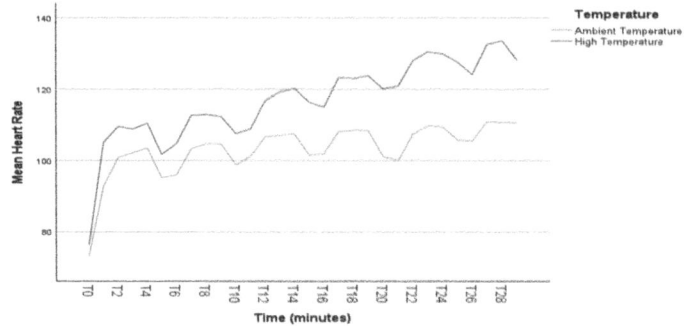

Fig. 11. HR Temperature Variation Throughout the Protocol at Different Temperatures.

For the null hypotheses H0: The median value of the HR is the same across times in Ambient Temperature, through the non-parametric statistical test, the hypothesis is rejected ($0,127 < p$-value $< 0,552$), for both Exercises, however, at high temperature, both exercises show significant differences ($0,003 < p$-value $< 0,060$), and when we go through the pairwise comparisons between times stands out that, for Exercise 1, T4 and T14 are significantly different (p-value $= 0,018$), and for Exercise 2, we conclude that between T9 and T29 (p-value $= 0,0016$) (Fig. 12). The differences between the HR medians for different sexes during exercise 1 (in the moments T4, T14 and T24) and during exercise 2 (in the moments T9, T19 and T29) are analysed for in both environments with different temperatures (Fig. 13).

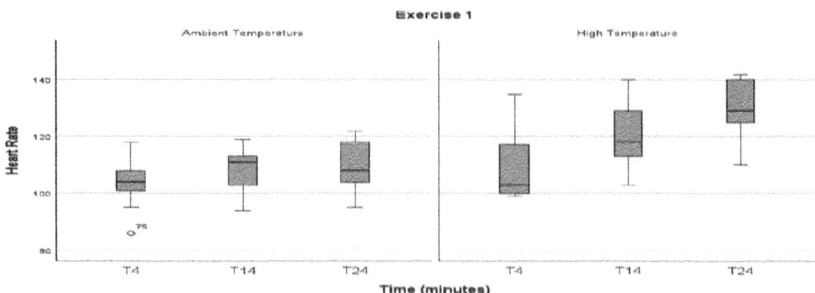

Fig. 12. Boxplot relative to HR across times (Exercise 1) in Ambient Temperature (left) and High Temperature (right).

Following the aim of the investigation for the third physiological indicator under analysis, and taking into account the null hypothesis, H0: The medians are the same

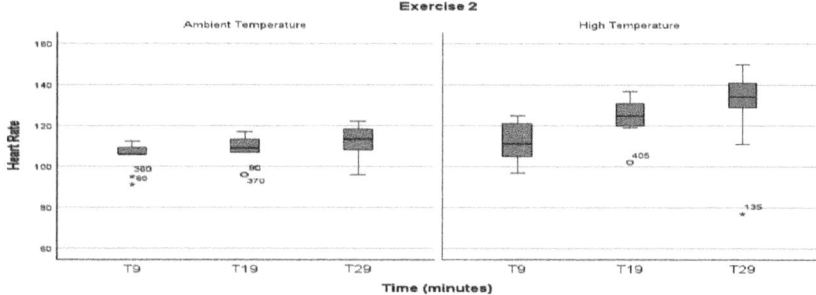

Fig. 13. Boxplot relative to HR across times (Exercise 2) in Ambient Temperature (left) and High Temperature (right).

across categories of Sex, the ambient temperature and high temperature, are compared in terms of HR, in each exercise of the protocol. When the non-parametric test is applied, the null is not rejected for both exercises (p-value ≈ 0.999), therefore from this level no significant differences are provided depending on the sex category (Figs. 14 and 15).

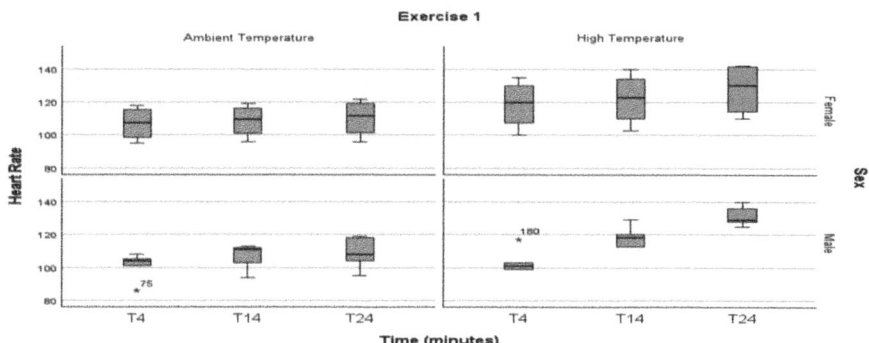

Fig. 14. Boxplot relative to HR (Exercise 1) across sex categories in Ambient Temperature (left) and High Temperature (right).

3.2 Thermal Perception Variables - Variation Throughout the Protocol at Different Temperatures

It seems that the physical protocol applied in environments with different temperatures does not require intense physical efforts, as variation of the RPE was not apparently different neither during the performance of the protocol at each of the temperatures, nor when comparing the values referring to the same exercise at the two temperatures (Fig. 16).

Regarding Thermal Comfort, Thermal Sensation and Moisture of the skin, we can verify that there is a relationship both in the isolated analysis of the protocols at the two temperatures, and it is also possible to verify a relationship between the variation of these

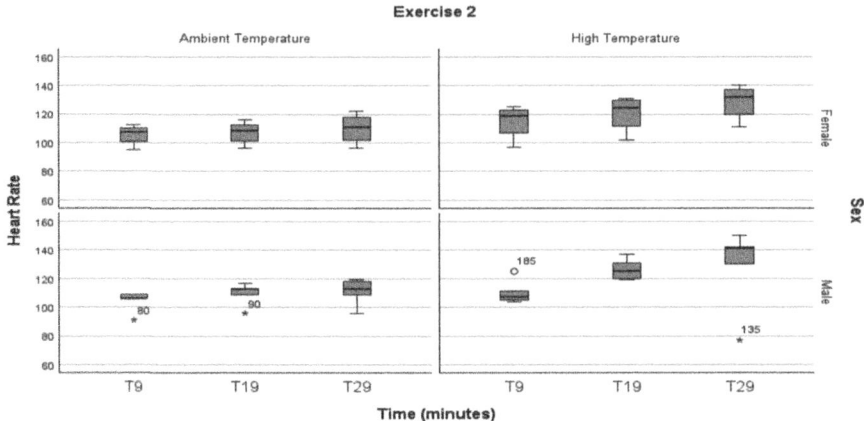

Fig. 15. Boxplot relative to HR (Exercise 2) across sex categories in Ambient Temperature (left) and High Temperature (right).

indicators for the same exercises of the physical protocol, but at different temperatures. The analysis carried out regarding the variation of Thermal Comfort, Thermal Sensation and Humidity in the Skin in the protocols at different temperatures in isolation is in accordance with the results obtained by other authors [6, 19].This increase in internal temperature, both in the protocol carried out at a temperature of 18,28 °C ± 0,7 °C and in the protocol carried out at 26,92 °C ± 0,7 °C was found that the perception of Moisture in the Skin and Thermal Sensation tend to increase and Thermal Comfort tends to decrease. When analysing the data regarding the perception of Thermal Sensation, Moisture of the skin and RPE in the same exercises, but performed at different temperatures, it was found an increase in ambient temperature and consequent increase in internal temperature, temperature in the skin, while Thermal Comfort tends to decrease [4, 5].

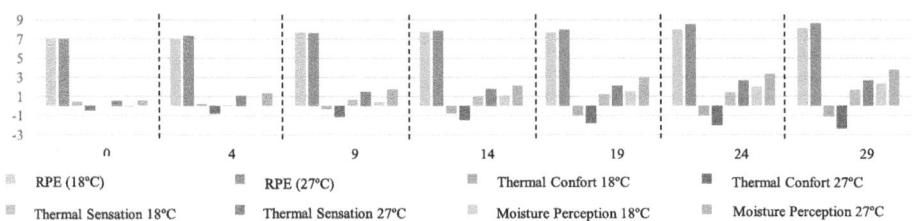

Fig. 16. Variation of thermal perception throughout the protocol at different temperatures

3.3 Thermal Perception Variables – Differences Between Sexes Throughout the Protocol at Different Temperatures

The analysis of the variation of heat stress indicators between sexes during the performance of the physical protocol at 18,28 °C ± 0,7 °C with the PPE shown in Fig. 17, shows that, although there are no differences, male elements tend to consider this temperature warmer and less comfortable when compared to female elements. Also in this environment, the biggest differences found between the two sexes were in relation to the perception of Moisture in the skin, and the male elements felt a considerably higher humidity in the skin.

The analysis of the variation of heat stress indicators between sexes during the performance of the physical protocol at 26,92 °C ± 0,7 °C with the PPE shown in Fig. 18, similarly to what happens in the protocol performed at Ambient Temperature, although there is a slight tendency in male elements to consider the temperature of the environment warmer and less comfortable when compared to female elements. In this case, there was a smaller discrepancy both in the perceptions of sensation and thermal comfort and in the perception of moisture in the skin.

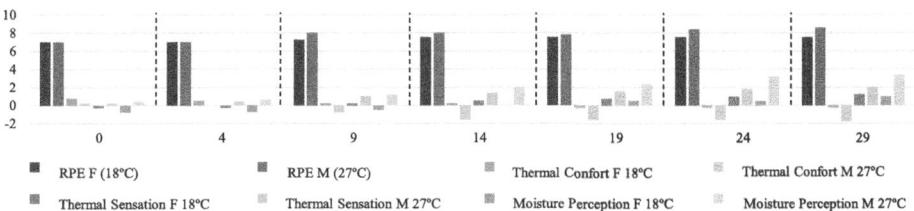

Fig. 17. Differences between sexes at Ambient temperature of thermal perception

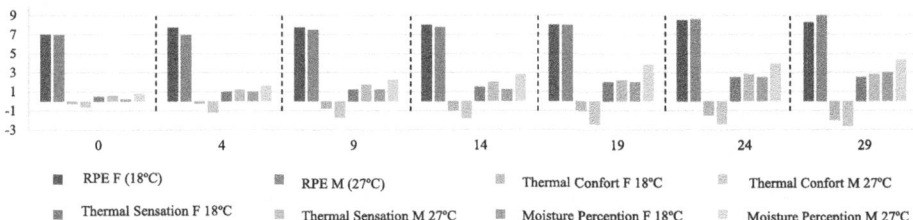

Fig. 18. Differences between sexes at High temperature of thermal perception

4 Conclusions and Final Remarks

The present research work analyses the variation of physiological factors and heat tolerance of a representative sample of members belonging to the CBRN teams, during the performance of a physical protocol with personal protective equipment, in environments with controlled temperatures of 18,28 °C ± 0,7 °C and 26,92 °C ± 0,7 °C.

The analysis carried out on the variation of physiological factors such as CT, ST and HR and the subjective perceptions of thermal *stress* such as Thermal Sensation and Thermal Comfort during the use of PPE, is based on the fact that there are several military contexts in environments with high temperatures and where there is the possibility of using the elements from the CBRN team. In this sense, it is important to understand the impact that the ambient temperature can have on the body during the performance of various tasks that require physical effort with PPE and thus be able to prevent undesirable clinical situations related to the use of these soldiers in the heat.

On the other hand, the variation of these physiological factors and heat tolerance also depends on the ability of individuals to acclimatize to environmental conditions. In this way, this protocol can also be used in the admission tests for CBRN teams in order to verify the ability of individuals to adapt to environments with different characteristics in the face of the practice of physical activity with the use of PPE.

Physiological indicators showed notable variations under different thermal conditions. Core temperature experienced a slight increase during the protocol at both ambient and high temperatures, with a slightly larger variation at the higher temperature; interestingly, a significant difference between sexes was observed during Exercise 1 at ambient temperature only. Skin temperature also increased slightly in both environments, with significant changes over time noted for Exercise 1 at both temperatures and for Exercise 2 at ambient temperature; a significant sex difference in ST emerged during Exercise 2 at the high temperature. Heart rate demonstrated a clear increase throughout the exercise protocol at both temperatures, with a more pronounced rise in the warmer environment; however, no significant differences in HR were found between male and female participants under either temperature condition.

Thermal perception variables were significantly influenced by the ambient temperature. The rate of perceived exertion did not show substantial differences across temperatures or exercises, suggesting the protocol did not induce extreme physical strain. However, thermal comfort decreased, while thermal sensation and the perception of moisture in the skin increased with rising ambient temperatures and the physiological strain induced by the PPE.

Nonetheless, the present investigation encountered certain inherent limitations. Firstly, the sample universe proved restricted, given that the time-consuming nature of the applied protocols precluded the participation of a larger number of individuals. Additionally, the protocol as devised and implemented did not generate the anticipated impact, with only a slight alteration observed in the physiological parameters even under elevated temperature conditions. These constraints affect the capacity for generalizing the obtained results and, particularly, the robustness of the analysis, especially concerning a precise prediction of internal temperature.

Considering the results achieved and the identified limitations, future lines of research should seek to bridge these gaps. Among the future projects outlined, is the remodeling of the study protocol, adjusting it based on the data gathered from the various physiological parameters analysed, with the expectation of provoking more pronounced effects. It is equally crucial to significantly increase the sample size in order to consolidate the algorithm intended for predicting internal temperature. In parallel, the creation of specific tables for assessing heat tolerance directed at CBRN teams is imperative, these tools being crucial for selection processes (access), evaluation of operational readiness, and supporting decisions on return to duty after absence due to illness. The realization of these steps is fundamental for deepening understanding, improving the predictive capacity, and effectively mitigating the physiological challenges faced by CBRN personnel in demanding environments, thus preventing undesirable clinical situations associated with their deployment in conditions of extreme heat.

References

1. Tipton, M.J.: Environmental extremes: origins, consequences and amelioration in humans. Exp. Physiol. **101**, 1–14 (2016)
2. McLellan, T.M., Daanen, H.A.M., Cheung, S.S.: Encapsulated environment. Compr. Physiol. **3**, 1363–1391 (2013)
3. McLellan, T.M., Boscarino, C., Duncan, E.J.S.: Physiological strain of next generation combat uniforms with chemical and biological protection: importance of clothing vents. Ergonomics **56**, 327–337 (2013)
4. Garson, C.N.: Thermoregulation in the Encapsulated Environment
5. Sharifi, S., Saman, W., Alemu, A., et al.: A proposed long-term thermal comfort scale. Build. Res. Inf. **49**, 661–678 (2021)
6. Li, Y.: Perceptions of temperature, moisture and comfort in clothing during environmental transients. Ergonomics **48**, 234–248 (2005)
7. Parsons, K.: Human Thermal Environments - The Effects OS Hot, Moderate and Cold Environments on Human Health, Comfort and Performance, 2nd edn. Taylor & Francis, London (2003)
8. Oliveira, A.: Estudo de ambientes térmicos frios: desenvolvimentos experimentais e avaliação de condições de trabalho (2007). https://hdl.handle.net/10316/1691
9. Olesen, B.W.: Thermal Comfort. Bruel & Kjaer (1982)
10. Smith, D.L., Fernhall, B.: Advanced Cardiovascular Exercise Physiology. Human Kinetics (2023)
11. Gordan, R., Gwathmey, J.K., Xie, L.-H.: Autonomic and endocrine control of cardiovascular function. World J. Cardiol. **7**, 204 (2015)
12. Carvalhais, C.: Contribuição para o Estudo da Tolerância Humana a Ambientes Térmicos Extremos: Ensaios de Validação de Câmara Climática
13. Kim, S.: Prediction of Heat Strain by Heart Rate for Firefighters in Protective Clothing. Seoul National University (2018)
14. Canino, M.C., Foulis, S.A., Cohen, B.S., et al.: Quantifying training load during physically demanding tasks in U.S. army soldiers: a comparison of physiological and psychological measurements. Mil Med **185**: e847–e852 (2020)
15. Canino, M.C., Cohen, B.S., Redmond, J.E., et al.: The relationship between soldier performance on the two-mile run and the 20-m shuttle run test. Mil. Med. **183**, e182–e187 (2018)
16. Schweiker, M., André, M., Al-Atrash, F., et al.: Evaluating assumptions of scales for subjective assessment of thermal environments–do laypersons perceive them the way, we researchers believe? Energy Build **211**, 109761 (2020)
17. Fukazawa, T., Havenith, G.: Differences in comfort perception in relation to local and whole-body skin wettedness. Eur. J. Appl. Physiol. **106**, 15–24 (2009)
18. Berger, R.L., Casella, G.: Statistical Inference. Duxbury (2001)
19. Han, T., Huang, L.: A model for relating a thermal comfort scale to EHT comfort index. SAE Technical Paper (2004)

Application of the DeepXDE Library for Solving Mathematical Models with PINNs

Gabriel Barboza$^{(\boxtimes)}$ (iD) and Isaac P. dos Santos (iD)

Federal University of Espírito Santo, Vitória, ES, Brazil
gabriel.i.barboza@edu.ufes.br, isaac.santos@ufes.br

Abstract. In this work, we investigate the capabilities of the DeepXDE library to solve mathematical models based on ordinary and partial differential equations using Physics-Informed Neural Networks (PINNs). PINNs are an important machine learning tool for solving complex problems modeled by differential equations, by incorporating physical laws into the neural network structure. We assess the versatility and effectiveness of DeepXDE by applying the PINNs methodology to several initial and boundary value problems, including the Verhulst logistic model, the 1D Gray-Scott reaction-diffusion system, the SIR epidemiological model, the incompressible Navier-Stokes equations, and an inverse problem derived from epidemiological data. The DeepXDE library facilitates the implementation of PINNs by providing an efficient and easy-to-use tool both for educational purposes (classroom use) and for solving direct and inverse problems in engineering and computational science.

Keywords: DeepXDE · Physics-Informed Neural Networks (PINNs) · Neural Networks

1 Introduction

Many complex problems in fields such as engineering, biology, epidemiology, economy, physics, etc. are described by mathematical formulations based on partial differential equations (PDEs) or ordinary differential equations (ODEs). Solving such equations often require specialized numerical methods for their solution, especially when the problems involve complex domains, high dimensions, or intricate physical processes. Among the various numerical methods, we highlight Finite Differences, Finite Element Method (FEM), and Finite Volume Method.

Recently, due to the rapid progress of artificial intelligence and data science, Physics-Informed Neural Networks (PINNs) have emerged as an important tool for solving such complex problems modeled by differential equations. The concept of PINNs can be traced back to the 1990s with early developments by Psichogios and Ungar (1992), Meade and Fernandez (1994), and Lagaris et al. (1998) [13,15,18,22]. Psichogios and Ungar (1992) introduced a hybrid learning approach that integrated physical laws, such as mass and energy balance,

O. Gervasi et al. (Eds.): ICCSA 2025 Workshops, LNCS 15888, pp. 122–139, 2026.
https://doi.org/10.1007/978-3-031-97596-7_8

into the network structure. This integration led to improved generalization and extrapolation capabilities compared to traditional machine learning methods. Lagaris et al. (1998) used a feedforward neural network to solve both ODEs and PDEs in rectangular domains, with a cost function that minimized the residuals of the equations at sampled points over the domain. This approach utilized a Quasi-Newton method for training the network.

In [23], Raissi et al. (2019) expanded the PINNs framework to solve PDEs directly, incorporating residuals from both the PDEs and the initial/boundary conditions into the loss function. The key feature of PINNs lies in their ability to integrate prior knowledge, such as physical laws and differential equations, directly into the neural network structure, ensuring that the network's outputs are consistent with the laws of physics. A considerable number of publications have emerged in recent times, focusing on the utilization of PINNs or deep learning models to solve differential equations [3, 5, 8, 10, 26].

One of the important properties of PINNs is their ability to solve high-dimensional problems in complex geometries without the need for meshing, which is a requirement in traditional numerical methods such as finite element or finite difference methods. Furthermore, PINNs provide a flexible framework for solving coupled systems of equations, making them an important tool in interdisciplinary applications that arise especially in engineering.

To facilitate the implementation of PINNs, several libraries and frameworks have been developed, each with distinct features and capabilities. TensorFlow [1] and PyTorch [21] are well known deep learning libraries that can be adapted for implementing PINN-based numerical methodology. Other more specialized libraries, such as DeepXDE [17] and SciANN [9], were created specifically to provide high-level abstractions and tools for solving differential equations using PINNs. These libraries are designed to simplify the process of defining the neural network architecture, integrating physical constraints, and training the network. SciANN, for example, uses TensorFlow and Keras [2] to implement PINNs. As emphasized in [17], DeepXDE is designed to be used both as a teaching tool in educational settings and as a research tool for solving problems in computational science and engineering. Specifically, DeepXDE enables the solution of forward problems, based on initial and boundary conditions, and inverse problems, based on additional measurements. DeepXDE supports domains with complex geometry and allows the creation of compact codes, similar to mathematical formulations.

In this paper, we explore the DeepXDE library for solving boundary and initial value problems with Physics-Informed Neural Networks. We begin by introducing the fundamental framework for solving ODEs and PDEs using PINNs. We then apply this methodology to a series of problems, evaluating the performance and effectiveness of the approach within the context of the DeepXDE library. The remainder of this paper is organized as follows. Section 2 presents the definition and formulation of PINNs. The DeepXDE library is briefly discussed in Sect. 3, while numerical experiments are presented in Sect. 4. Finally, Sect. 5 presents conclusions and concluding remarks.

2   The Fundamentals of PINNs Networks

The core idea of PINNs lies in embedding the governing equations directly into the loss function of the neural network (see Fig. 1). During training, the network aims to minimize a composite loss that accounts for the residuals of the differential equations, along with the initial and boundary conditions. These terms are evaluated at specific points in the spatiotemporal domain, known as collocation points. These points are typically sampled randomly and serve as locations where the model enforces the physical constraints of the problem [23].

In problems where observational data are available, PINNs offer a flexible framework that combines physical knowledge with data-driven learning. The loss function can incorporate both the equation residuals at collocation points and discrepancies between model predictions and known measurements. This unified approach enables the solution of a wide range of tasks, including inverse problems, where unknown parameters must be identified from data, and forward problems, where the objective is to predict the system's evolution from given initial and boundary conditions. When no data are provided, the network relies solely on the physical laws, effectively functioning as a mesh-free solver guided entirely by the underlying differential equations [10].

PINNs are capable of solving differential equations that can be represented in their most general form as:

$$\mathcal{L}(u(\boldsymbol{x},t);\boldsymbol{\lambda}) = f(u,\boldsymbol{x},t), \quad \boldsymbol{x} \in \Omega, \, t \in I, \tag{1}$$

$$\mathcal{B}(u(\boldsymbol{x},t)) = g(\boldsymbol{x},t), \quad \boldsymbol{x} \in \Gamma, \, t \in I, \tag{2}$$

$$\mathcal{I}(u(\boldsymbol{x},t_0)) = q(\boldsymbol{x}), \quad \boldsymbol{x} \in \Omega, \tag{3}$$

where $\Omega \subset \mathbb{R}^d$ is the spatial domain with boundary Γ; d is the dimension of the space; $I = [t_0, t_F]$ is the time interval, with $t_0 < t_F$; $\boldsymbol{x} = (x_1, x_2, \ldots, x_d)$ is the spatial coordinate vector; t denotes time; $u = u(\boldsymbol{x},t)$ denotes the unknown solution of the problem; $\boldsymbol{\lambda}$ is the vector of physical parameters; $\mathcal{L}$ is the differential operator associated with the equation; f is a given source term; $\mathcal{B}$ and $\mathcal{I}$ are operators representing boundary and initial conditions, respectively; and g and q are known functions defining those conditions.

In the PINNs approach, the function $u(\boldsymbol{x},t)$ is approximated computationally by a neural network parameterized by a vector $\boldsymbol{\theta} = (\boldsymbol{w}, \boldsymbol{b}) \in \mathbb{R}^{n_\theta}$, where $\boldsymbol{w}$ and $\boldsymbol{b}$ represent the weights and biases of the network, respectively, and n_θ denotes the total number of parameters. This yields an approximate solution $\hat{u}(\boldsymbol{x},t;\boldsymbol{\theta})$ for $u(\boldsymbol{x},t)$.

The loss function in PINNs typically includes the residual of the equation, initial/boundary conditions and measured data (if available). Thus, we define the loss function associated with problem (1)–(3) as

$$J(\boldsymbol{\theta}) = \omega_{\mathcal{L}} J_{\mathcal{L}}(\boldsymbol{x},t,\boldsymbol{\theta}) + \omega_{\mathcal{B}} J_{\mathcal{B}}(\boldsymbol{x},t,\boldsymbol{\theta}) + \omega_{\mathcal{I}} J_{\mathcal{I}}(\boldsymbol{x},t_0,\boldsymbol{\theta}) + \omega_{data} J_{data}(\boldsymbol{x},t,\boldsymbol{\theta}) \tag{4}$$

where

$$J_{\mathcal{L}}(\boldsymbol{x},t,\boldsymbol{\theta}) = \|\mathcal{L}(\widehat{u}(\boldsymbol{x},t,\boldsymbol{\theta});\boldsymbol{\lambda}) - f(\widehat{u}(\boldsymbol{x},t,\boldsymbol{\theta}),\boldsymbol{x},t)\|^2_{\Omega \times I},$$
$$J_{\mathcal{B}}(\boldsymbol{x},t,\boldsymbol{\theta}) = \|\mathcal{B}(\widehat{u}(\boldsymbol{x},t,\boldsymbol{\theta})) - g(\boldsymbol{x},t)\|^2_{\Gamma \times I},$$
$$J_{\mathcal{I}}(\boldsymbol{x},t_0,\boldsymbol{\theta}) = \|\mathcal{I}(\widehat{u}(\boldsymbol{x},t_0,\boldsymbol{\theta})) - q(\boldsymbol{x})\|^2_{\Omega}$$

represent the squared residuals of the equation (PDE/ODE), the boundary conditions, and the initial condition, respectively, evaluated at the collocation points and measured using the Euclidean norms $\|\cdot\|_{\Omega \times I}$, $\|\cdot\|_{\Gamma \times I}$, and $\|\cdot\|_{\Omega}$. When measured data are available, the operator J_{data} is defined as

$$J_{\text{data}}(\boldsymbol{x},t,\boldsymbol{\theta}) = \|\widehat{u}(\boldsymbol{x},t,\boldsymbol{\theta}) - u(\boldsymbol{x},t)\|^2_{\Omega \times I}.$$

The parameters $\omega_{\mathcal{L}}, \omega_{\mathcal{B}}, \omega_{\mathcal{I}}$, and ω_{data} are weighting coefficients that can be used to mitigate imbalance among the different loss terms.

Accordingly, solving problem (1)–(3) is equivalent to determining the parameter vector $\boldsymbol{\theta}$ such that the neural network approximation $\widehat{u}(\boldsymbol{x},t,\boldsymbol{\theta})$ closely matches the true solution $u(\boldsymbol{x},t)$ within a prescribed accuracy over the spatio-temporal domain. To this end, a set of N_c collocation points, $\{(\boldsymbol{x}_i,t_i)\}_{i=1}^{N_c}$, distributed across the spatio-temporal domain and its boundary, is used to evaluate the loss function defined in (4).

The optimization problem that must be solved consists of finding

$$\boldsymbol{\theta}^* = \arg\min_{\boldsymbol{\theta} \in \mathbb{R}^{n_\theta}} J(\boldsymbol{\theta}), \tag{5}$$

so that $\widehat{u}(\boldsymbol{x},t,\boldsymbol{\theta}^*)$ is the PINNs solution of (1)–(3).

Most methods for solving (5) rely on gradient-based optimization combined with the backpropagation algorithm. These methods minimize the discrepancy between predicted and expected outputs by adjusting the weights and biases in the direction of the steepest gradient descent. However, some studies have shown that this approach may exhibit undesirable behavior when training PINNs to solve complex problems, particularly when the solutions of the underlying PDEs involve high-frequency or multiscale features [28, 29]. In this work, we employ the Adam method (short for Adaptive Moment Estimation) [12] and BFGS-L, a quasi-Newton method that refines the solution by incorporating second-order information [16]. Both optimizers are available in the DeepXDE library.

3 The DeepXDE Library

Presented in [17] as an educational and research tool, DeepXDE is a deep learning library focused on solving differential equations (ODEs/PDEs) using neural networks. This open-source Python tool provides an intuitive and advanced interface for training neural networks to approximate mathematical models based on differential equations.

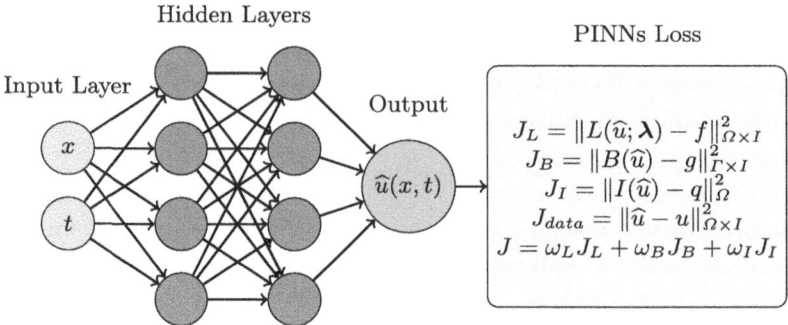

Fig. 1. PINNs graphical representation. Source: elaborated by the authors.

As mentioned in the Introduction, DeepXDE keeps the code concise and elegant, similar to the mathematical formulation. Solving differential equations with DeepXDE involves simply defining the problem using built-in modules, which include the computational domain (geometry and time), the equations (ODE/PDE), boundary/initial conditions, constraints, collocation points, neural network architecture, and training hyperparameters. It is also compatible with the most common back-end engines to perform the heavy computations.

3.1 Workflow for Solving Problems

The resolution of problems with DeepXDE can be easily accomplished by following a sequence of well-defined steps. To illustrate the use of DeepXDE, we consider the Burgers equation as formulated in [20]:

$$\frac{\partial u}{\partial t} + u\frac{\partial u}{\partial x} - c\frac{\partial^2 u}{\partial x^2} = 0, \quad x \in (-1, 1), \quad t \in (0, 5], \tag{6}$$

with the initial condition $u(x, 0) = -\sin(\pi x)$ for $x \in [-1, 1]$, and homogeneous Dirichlet boundary conditions $u(\pm 1, t) = 0$ for $t \in [0, 5]$. In Eq. (6), $c > 0$ denotes the viscosity coefficient.

First, import the back-end library and set the virtual environment variable. Then, import DeepXDE. You can choose between TensorFlow, PyTorch, JAX, and Paddle. This step is shown in Listing 1.1.

```
1 import os
2 import torch
3 os.environ['DDE_BACKEND'] = 'pytorch'
4 import deepxde as dde
```

Listing 1.1. Importing libraries

Any problem involving the solution of PDEs or ODEs requires the definition of a domain of interest. DeepXDE provides functions for representing spatial and temporal intervals, allowing the problem geometry to be easily specified as a combination of these components. The code shown in Listing 1.2 defines the spatial domain $[x_0, x_f] = [-1, 1]$ and the temporal domain $[t_0, t_f] = [0, 5]$.

```
x0, xf = -1, 1
t0, tf = 0, 5
geomx = dde.geometry.Interval(x0, xf)
tinterval = dde.geometry.TimeDomain(t0, tf)
geom = dde.geometry.GeometryXTime(geomx, tinterval)
```

Listing 1.2. Defining the domain

In the next step, the equation or system of equations is defined as a residual to be minimized, as shown in Listing 1.3. The first parameter represents the input features, while the second corresponds to the network output. Use both, along with the tools provided by DeepXDE, to compute the necessary derivatives and formulate the residuals.

```
def pde(training_data, network_output):

    # Compute the Jacobian of u w.r.t. x
    # First-order partial derivative of u w.r.t. x
    du_dx = dde.grad.jacobian(y, x, i=0, j=0)

    # Compute the time Jacobian
    # First-order partial derivative of u w.r.t. t
    du_dt = dde.grad.jacobian(y, x, i=0, j=1)

    # Compute the Hessian (second-order derivatives)
    # Second-order partial derivative of u w.r.t. x
    d2u_d2x = dde.grad.hessian(y, x, component=0, i
        =0, j=0)

    return [
        # Residual of Burgers' equation
        du_dt + u * du_dx - c * d2u_d2x
    ]
```

Listing 1.3. Defining the model

The specification of boundary and/or initial conditions is illustrated in Listing 1.4.

```
1 # Define the boundary conditions
2 bc = dde.icbc.DirichletBC(geom, lambda x: 0, lambda _
    , on_boundary: on_boundary)
3
4 # Define the initial conditions
5 ic = dde.icbc.IC(geom, lambda x: -np.sin(np.pi * x[:,
    0:1]), lambda _, on_initial: on_initial)
```

Listing 1.4. Defining the initial and boundary conditions

Neural networks require a dataset for training, and PINNs are no exception. In this case, the collocation points consist of points distributed throughout the domain, including the interior, the boundaries, and the initial time. The configuration of this dataset depends on the specific equations, domain, and conditions of the problem. DeepXDE allows you to define the number of such points, as detailed in Listing 1.5.

```
1 # Create the collocation points
2 data = dde.data.TimePDE(geom, pde, [bc, ic],
    num_domain=1024, num_boundary=40, num_initial=50)
```

Listing 1.5. Creating the data set

Then you need to define the neural network architecture. The number of input and output nodes depends on the specific model being solved, while the number of hidden layers and the number of neurons per layer are typically chosen empirically. The choice of activation function also varies with the problem, but the hyperbolic tangent (tanh) is generally recommended for this type of application. You must also configure the optimizer, the algorithm used to solve the optimization problem (5), and specify the learning rate, which controls the size of each update step during training. This configuration is illustrated in Listing 1.6, where the Adam optimizer [12] and a learning rate of 0.001 are used.

```
1 # 2 inputs node X 2 hidden layers of 5 nodes each X 1
    output node
2 layer_size = [2] + [5] * 2 + [1]
3
4 # Define the architecture and activation function
5 net = dde.nn.FNN(layer_size, "tanh")
6 model = dde.Model(data, net)
7 # Define the optimizer, learning rate
8 model.compile("adam", lr=1e-3)
```

Listing 1.6. Configuring the neural network

Finally, you can train your model. It is a common practice to train first with a faster, but not quite efficient, optimizer like Adam, then fine-tune your results with a more robust optimizer. The number of iterations and which optimizer to choose also depend on the problem that is being solved. Listing 1.7 illustrates a two-phase training strategy: first using Adam for fast initial convergence, then switching to BFGS-L, a quasi-Newton method that refines the solution by incorporating second-order information [16].

```
# Train the model for n iterations
losshistory , train_state = model.train(iterations
    =500)
model.compile("BFGS-L", lr=1e-3)
losshistory , train_state = model.train(iterations
    =500)
```

Listing 1.7. Training model

Save your results. DeepXDE offers built-in functionality to visualize the learned solution and the convergence history. Additionally, it allows you to export the generated data and model output for further analysis, as demonstrated in Listing 1.8.

```
model.train(iterations=500, model_save_path="path/to/
    model")
dde.saveplot(losshistory , train_state , issave=True,
    isplot=True)
```

Listing 1.8. Displaying the model

3.2   Inverse Problems

The previous example illustrates how DeepXDE can be applied to solve a forward problem. However, in many cases, we are interested in solving inverse problems, which consist of determining unknown parameters in a model given a known solution, whether analytical or numerical. These parameters often represent physical coefficients. As described by [24], PINNs are capable of solving such problems by treating the unknown parameters as learnable variables during training.

This can be accomplished in DeepXDE by defining the variable of interest with an initial guess, incorporating it into the PDE/ODE residual, and specifying it as a trainable parameter in the model. The learned values can be easily accessed after training, as shown in Listing 1.9.

```
v = dde.Variable(0.5)
model.compile("adam", lr=1e-3,
    external_trainable_variables=[v])
print(f"diffusion coefficient = {v.detach().cpu().
    numpy()}")
```

Listing 1.9. Inverse problems with DeepXDE

4   Applications

In this section, we address a series of initial and/or boundary value problems using DeepXDE. To quantitatively evaluate the quality of the PINNs solutions, we compute the errors using the infinity norm. In the first two examples, the solutions obtained with PINNs are compared to exact solutions. In the third case, the PINNs solution is compared with the explicit fourth-order Runge-Kutta method. The subsequent problem involves the simulation of incompressible fluid flow, where the PINNs results are compared with a reference numerical solution. Finally, we solve an inverse problem aimed at identifying the parameters of the SIR epidemiological model. The implementation of all these cases is available in the GitHub repository, where readers can access and explore the full source code and results.

4.1   The Verhulst Logistic Model

The Verhulst logistic model [19, 27], given by the initial value problem

$$\frac{dp(t)}{dt} = (a - bp(t)) p(t), \quad t > t_0, \tag{7}$$

$$p(t_0) = p_0, \tag{8}$$

describes the growth of a population, denoted by $p(t)$, over time t, considering both reproduction and limited resources. In the ODE (7) a is the growth rate, b is a constant that controls the strength of the limiting effect, whereas Eq. (8) describes the initial solution. This model is widely used in biology and ecology to study population dynamics, providing insights into how populations evolve when resources are finite. The solution of the equation exhibits logistic growth, where the population increases rapidly at first but slows down as it approaches the carrying capacity $K = \frac{a}{b}$ [19]. The carrying capacity represents the maximum population size that the environment can sustainably support, beyond which the population growth stabilizes. The Verhulst model helps understand how a population interacts with its environment and the limitations imposed by finite resources.

The exact solution of the problem (7)–(8) is given by

$$p(t) = \frac{ap_0}{bp_0 + (a - bp_0)e^{-(t-t_0)}}.$$

We solve this problem in the time interval $[0, 5]$, with $a = 1.0$, $b = 0.1$, $p_0 \in \{12, 8\}$, and $t_0 = 0$. Thus, the carrying capacity is $K = 10$. We used a network with three hidden layers, each containing 50 nodes, with the hyperbolic tangent activation function and the Adam optimizer, initialized with a learning rate of 10^{-3}. The network was trained for 20,000 iterations. Figure 2 shows both the PINNs and exact solutions, with virtually no visual difference, demonstrating good agreement between them. To quantify the quality of the PINN solution, we compute the error between the exact and predicted solutions in the infinity norm. We obtain $\|u - \widehat{u}\|_\infty = 2.336 \times 10^{-4}$ for $p_0 = 12$, and 2.743×10^{-4} for $p_0 = 8$, corroborating the satisfactory accuracy observed in the figures.

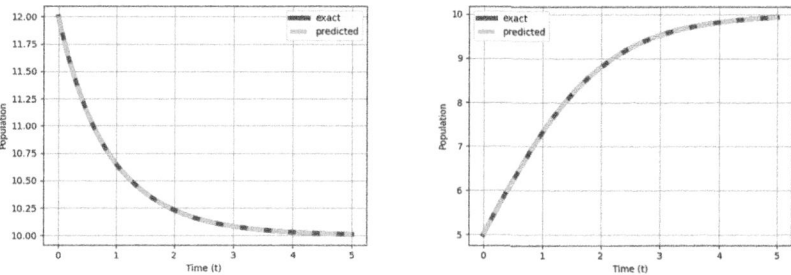

Fig. 2. Verhulst model with initial conditions: $p_0 = 12$ (left) and $p_0 = 8$ (right).

4.2   Grey-Scott Model for Pattern Formation

The Grey-Scott model [7] is a reaction-diffusion system that describes how two interacting chemical species, U and V, evolve over time, leading to complex pattern formation. It is widely studied in mathematical biology, physics, and nonlinear dynamics due to its ability to generate intricate spatial structures. The governing equations are:

$$\frac{\partial u}{\partial t} = D_u \nabla^2 u - uv^2 + F(1 - u), \tag{9}$$

$$\frac{\partial v}{\partial t} = D_v \nabla^2 v + uv^2 - (F + k)v. \tag{10}$$

Here, D_u and D_v are diffusion coefficients, F is the feed rate controlling u's introduction, and k is the removal rate of v. The reaction term uv^2 represents an autocatalytic process where v catalyzes the transformation of u into more v.

By tuning D_u, D_v, F, and k, the model produces diverse patterns, such as Turing structures, waves, and self-replicating spots, making it relevant in studying self-organization in nature. It has applications in chemical reactions, biological morphogenesis (e.g., animal coat patterns), and material science, offering insights into emergent complexity in dynamical systems.

We solve the system (9)–(10) in the one-dimensional case, with $D_u = D_v = 1$, and compare the PINNs solutions with the exact ones. Using the transformation $z = x - \theta t$, the analytical solution, as presented in [25], is given by

$$u(z) = \frac{3 - \sqrt{\eta}}{4} - \frac{\sqrt{2\xi}}{4} \tanh\left(\frac{\sqrt{\xi}}{4} z\right), \qquad v(z) = \frac{1 + \sqrt{\eta}}{4} + \frac{\sqrt{2\xi}}{4} \tanh\left(\frac{\sqrt{\xi}}{4} z\right),$$

where $\eta = 1-4F$, $\xi = 1+\sqrt{\eta}-2F$, and $\theta = \frac{\sqrt{2}}{4}(1-3\sqrt{\eta})$. We used a network with four hidden layers, 20 nodes each, sigmoid activation function, Adam optimizer with learning rate of 10^{-3}, and trained for 25,000 iterations. Figure 3 shows the PINNs and exact solutions. The predicted curves are very close to the reference solutions, with only slight visible deviations, indicating that the PINN model captures the spatiotemporal dynamics of the system with good accuracy. We have obtained the following errors in the infinity norm: $\|u-\widehat{u}\|_\infty = 2.625 \times 10^{-2}$ and $\|v-\widehat{v}\|_\infty = 2.467 \times 10^{-2}$, which quantitatively reflect the quality of the approximation.

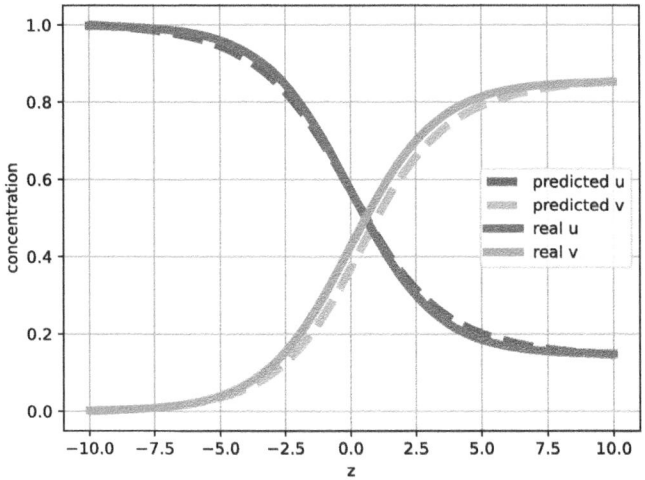

Fig. 3. 1D Grey-Scott model

4.3   The SIR Epidemiological Model

The SIR epidemiological model [11] describes the spread of infectious diseases in a population by dividing individuals into three compartments: Susceptible (S), Infected (I), and Recovered (R). It is a fundamental model in mathematical epidemiology and provides insights into disease transmission dynamics. The governing equations are:

$$\frac{dS}{dt} = -\beta SI, \tag{11}$$

$$\frac{dI}{dt} = \beta SI - \gamma I, \tag{12}$$

$$\frac{dR}{dt} = \gamma I. \tag{13}$$

Here, $S(t)$, $I(t)$, and $R(t)$ represent the number of susceptible, infected, and recovered individuals at time t. The parameter β is the infection rate, controlling how quickly the disease spreads, and γ is the recovery rate, determining how fast infected individuals recover and move into the recovered compartment.

We solve model (11)–(13) using synthetic data with parameters $\beta = 1.4$, $\mu = 0.9$, and initial conditions $S(0) = 0.99$, $I(0) = 0.01$, and $R(0) = 0$ (values given as percentages of the total population). The time domain is defined as $[0, 50]$. Figure 4 presents the PINNs solution (left) and the explicit fourth-order Runge–Kutta solution (right). The PINNs result is very similar to the one obtained with the Runge–Kutta method. The number of infected individuals increases rapidly at first, reaching a peak around days 7–8, and then decreases as more people recover and become immune. This behavior illustrates how the interaction between susceptible, infected, and recovered individuals affects the spread of the disease. For this problem, the network consisted of three layers with 50 nodes each. It was trained for 20,000 iterations using the hyperbolic tangent activation function and the Adam optimizer with a learning rate of 10^{-3}. To quantify the quality of the PINN solution, we compute the error between the Runge-Kutta and predicted solutions in the infinity norm, obtaining the following erros: 7.760×10^{-3}, 6.828×10^{-3} and 1.034×10^{-2} for the functions S, I and R, respectively, corroborating the satisfactory accuracy observed in the plots.

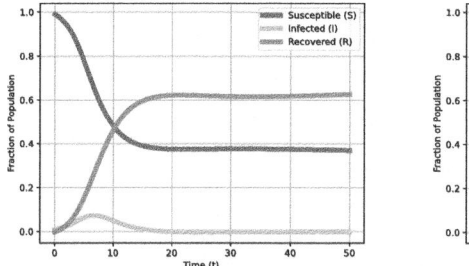 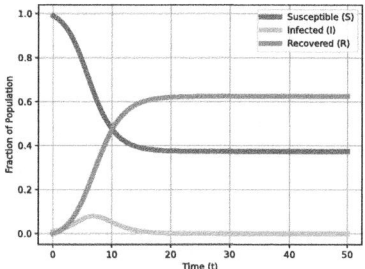

Fig. 4. PINNs (left) and fourth-order Runge-Kutta (right) solutions for the SIR model.

4.4   The Incompressible Navier-Stokes Equations

The incompressible Navier-Stokes equations [14], given by

$$\frac{\partial \mathbf{u}}{\partial t} + (\mathbf{u} \cdot \nabla)\mathbf{u} = -\frac{1}{\rho}\nabla p + \nu \nabla^2 \mathbf{u} + \mathbf{f}, \tag{14}$$

$$\nabla \cdot \mathbf{u} = 0, \tag{15}$$

describe the motion of a fluid under the influence of internal and external forces, where $\mathbf{u} = (u, v, w)$ is the velocity field, p is the pressure, ρ is the fluid density, ν is the kinematic viscosity, and $\mathbf{f}$ represents external forces such as gravity. The first equation expresses the conservation of momentum, balancing inertial, pressure, viscous, and external forces. The second equation enforces the incompressibility condition, ensuring mass conservation. To complete the mathematical model, initial and appropriate boundary conditions must be specified for equations (14)–(15).

The incompressible Navier-Stokes equations are essential for describing fluid flows in areas like aerodynamics, ocean currents, and turbulence. Because they are nonlinear, finding exact solutions is very difficult. As a result, numerical methods like the finite element method (FEM) and computational fluid dynamics (CFD) are widely used to solve them.

A well-known example of the model (14)–(15) is the two-dimensional lid-driven cavity flow. It describes the movement of an incompressible fluid inside a square cavity, where the fluid is set in motion by the top boundary (the lid) sliding at a constant speed. Thus, we consider the stationary and dimensionless form of equations (14)–(15) on the unit square, with $Re = 100$ and subject to the following Dirichlet boundary conditions (see Fig. 5):

$$u(0, y) = u(x, 0) = u(1, y) = v(0, y) = v(x, 0) = v(1, y) = v(x, 1) = 0,$$

$$u(x, 1) = 1, \quad p(0, 0) = 0.$$

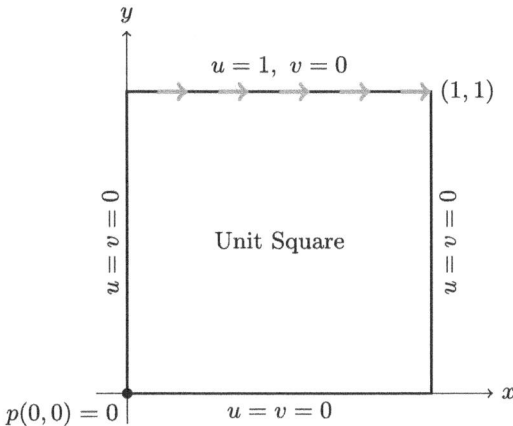

Fig. 5. Lid-driven cavity flow with boundary conditions. Source: elaborated by the authors.

For this problem, we employed a neural network with four hidden layers, each comprising 125 nodes, using the hyperbolic tangent activation function.

The network was initially trained for 30,000 iterations using the Adam optimizer, followed by an additional 15,000 iterations using the L-BFGS optimizer.

Figure 6 shows the heatmaps of velocity and pressure, where the typical laminar flow pattern is clearly visible. Figure 7 compares the model's results with the reference values from [4]. Compared to these reference values, we obtained an infinity norm of 8.327×10^{-1} for the velocity vector.

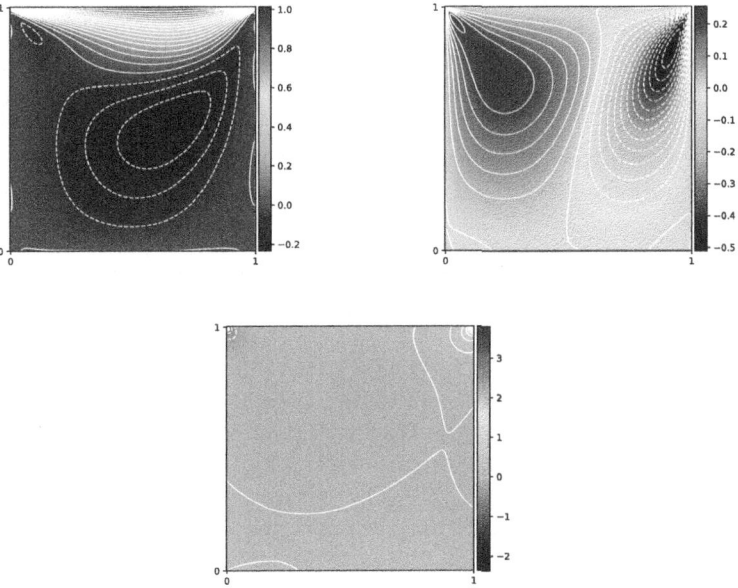

Fig. 6. Horizontal velocity (left), vertical velocity (right), pressure (bottom).

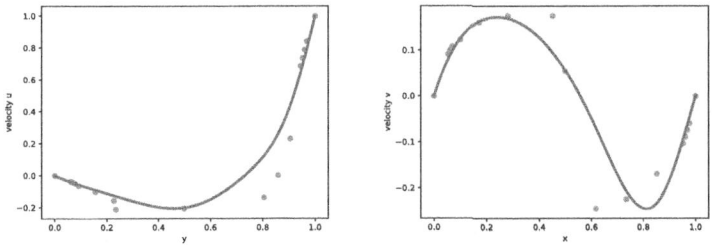

Fig. 7. Horizontal velocity (left) and vertical velocity (right) model solutions compared to reference values.

4.5   Inverse Problems

The four previous examples discussed focus on solving the mathematical models in a forward manner, that is, by determining the behavior of the system based on known initial and boundary conditions, as well as parameters. An inverse problem seeks to determine unknown parameters or inputs of a system based on observed data. These problems arise in various scientific fields, including medical imaging (such as medical tomography, where internal body structures are reconstructed from X-ray measurements), geophysics (in seismic imaging, where Earth's subsurface properties are inferred from wave propagation data), machine learning, and more. Unlike direct problems, where the system's response is computed from known parameters, inverse problems aim to reconstruct causes from effects.

We address an inverse problem associated with the SIR epidemiological model defined by equations (11)–(12). In this case, we are given the following data:

$$S_{observed} = (S(t_1), S(t_2), \cdots, S(t_n)),$$
$$I_{observed} = (I(t_1), I(t_2), \cdots, I(t_n)),$$
$$R_{observed} = (R(t_1), R(t_2), \cdots, R(t_n)),$$

over the time dataset $t_1, t_2, \cdots, t_n$. The goal is to determine the optimal parameters, β and γ, in the system (11)–(12) that best fit the sampled data.

The observed data refer to the Covid-19 pandemic in the state of Espírito Santo, Brazil, from January 2020 to January 2021. The data was collected from the official monitoring platform [6]. The network architecture employed here has the same configuration as that used for the direct problem in Sect. 4.3. The estimated values for the model parameters are $\beta = 0.0350$ and $\gamma = 0.0333$. Figure 8 displays the normalized real data and the predicted values obtained from the model. It is worth noting that, visually, the values are in good agreement.

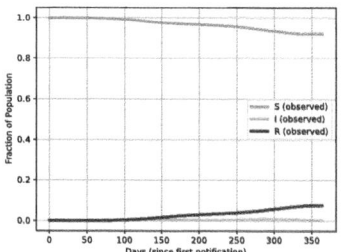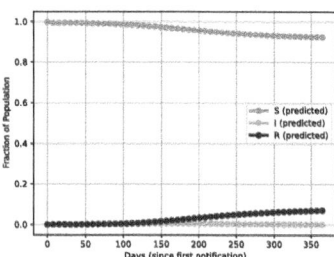

Fig. 8. Observed data and PINNs prediction for the SIR model.

5   Conclusions

Physics-Informed Neural Networks have emerged as a promising alternative to traditional methods for solving differential equations. Our intent with this paper was to provide a comprehensive and accessible introduction to PINNs, targeting readers who may not be familiar with neural networks or machine learning techniques. Through a series of illustrative examples, ranging from simple ordinary differential equations to complex partial differential equation systems, we demonstrated the versatility and effectiveness of PINNs in solving problems from fields such as epidemiology and fluid dynamics.

One of the greatest advantages of PINNs is their ease of implementation, requiring only the definition of a residual function to be incorporated into the network loss function. Python libraries like DeepXDE facilitate that process even more, by providing an easy-to-use interface to define the loss function, boundary and initial conditions, and the domain of interest. Nevertheless, as discussed in [28], a significant limitation is that the accuracy of PINNs solutions tends to be inferior compared to traditional methods, such as the finite element method, particularly in the case of highly stiff or multiscale problems.

Despite these challenges, the PINNs methodology remains in its infancy, with many open research gaps to be explored. Improving neural network architectures, discovering more effective activation functions, developing adaptive optimization strategies, and integrating techniques from broader machine learning domains, such as convolutional networks, recurrent structures, and attention mechanisms, constitute promising directions for future research. Advancements in these areas are expected to significantly enhance the performance, robustness, and applicability of PINNs across a broader range of scientific and engineering problems.

As future work, we plan to explore examples using alternative network topologies and architectures and to solve problems involving irregular boundaries, as well as three-dimensional unsteady transport phenomena, including both compressible and incompressible flows.

Disclosure of Interests. The authors declare that they have no known competing financial interests or personal relationships that could have appeared to influence the work reported in this paper.

References

1. Abadi, M., et al.: TensorFlow: a system for large-scale machine learning. In: 12th USENIX Symposium On Operating Systems Design and Implementation (OSDI 2016), pp. 265–283 (2016)
2. Chollet, F.: Keras. In: Proceedings of the 2015 Conference on Machine Learning and Systems (MLSys), pp. 1–6 (2015)
3. Duarte, D., de Lima, P., de Araújo, J.M.: Outlier-resistant physics-informed neural network. Phys. Rev. E **111**, L023302 (2025). https://doi.org/10.1103/PhysRevE.111.L023302. https://link.aps.org/doi/10.1103/PhysRevE.111.L023302
4. Ghia, U., Ghia, K., Shin, C.: High-resolutions for incompressible flow using the Navier-Stokes equations and a multigrid method. J. Comput. Phys. **48**(3), 387–411 (1982). https://doi.org/10.1016/0021-9991(82)90058-4. https://www.sciencedirect.com/science/article/pii/0021999182900584
5. Goswami, S., Anitescu, C., Rabczuk, T.: Deep learning for computational mechanics. Comput. Methods Appl. Mech. Eng. **404**, 115783 (2023)

6. Governo do Estado do Espírito Santo, Brasil: Painel covid-19 - espírito santo (2024). https://coronavirus.es.gov.br/painel-covid-19-es. Accessed 03 Apr 2025

7. Gray, P., Scott, S.K.: Autocatalytic reactions in the isothermal CSTR: oscillations and chaos. Chem. Eng. Sci. **49**(1), 1–7 (1994). https://doi.org/10.1016/0009-2509(94)80044-4

8. Guasti Junior, W., Santos, I.P.: Solving differential equations using feedforward neural networks. In: Gervasi, O., et al. (eds.) Computational Science and Its Applications - ICCSA 2021, pp. 385–399. Springer, Cham (2021)

9. Haghighat, E., Juanes, R.: SciANN: a Keras/TensorFlow wrapper for scientific computations and physics-informed deep learning using artificial neural networks. Comput. Methods Appl. Mech. Eng. **373**, 113552 (2021). https://doi.org/10.1016/j.cma.2020.113552

10. Karniadakis, G.E., Kevrekidis, I.G., Lu, L., Perdikaris, P., Wang, S., Yang, L.: Physics-informed neural networks: a survey. arXiv preprint arXiv:2103.15024 (2021)

11. Kermack, W.O., McKendrick, A.G.: A contribution to the mathematical theory of epidemics. Proc. Royal Soc. Lond. Ser. A Contain. Papers Math. Phys. Character **115**(772), 700–721 (1927). https://doi.org/10.1098/rspa.1927.0118

12. Kingma, D.P., Ba, J.: Adam: a method for stochastic optimization. arXiv preprint arXiv:1412.6980 (2014)

13. Lagaris, I.E., Likas, A., Fotiadis, D.I.: Artificial neural networks for solving ordinary and partial differential equations. IEEE Trans. Neural Networks **9**(5), 987–1000 (1998). https://doi.org/10.1109/72.712178

14. Landau, L.D., Lifshitz, E.M.: Fluid Mechanics, 2nd edn. Pergamon Press (1987)

15. Lee, H., Kand, I.S.: Neural algorithm for solving differential equations. J. Comput. Phys. **91**(1), 110–131 (1990). https://doi.org/10.1016/0021-9991(90)90007-N

16. Liu, D.C., Nocedal, J.: On the limited memory BFGS method for large scale optimization (1989). https://doi.org/10.1007/BF01589116

17. Lu, L., Meng, X., Mao, Z., Karniadakis, G.E.: DeepXDE: a deep learning library for solving differential equations. SIAM Rev. **63**(1), 208–228 (2021). https://doi.org/10.1137/19m1274067. http://dx.doi.org/10.1137/19M1274067

18. Meade, A.J., Fernandez, A.A.: The numerical solution of linear ordinary differential equations by feedforward neural networks. Math. Comput. Model. **19**(12), 1–25 (1994). https://doi.org/10.1016/0895-7177(94)90095-7

19. Murray, J.D.: Mathematical Biology: I. An Introduction, 3 edn. Springer (2002)

20. Nikolopoulos, S., Kalogeris, I., Papadopoulos, V.: Non-intrusive surrogate modeling for parametrized time-dependent PDES using convolutional autoencoders (2021). https://arxiv.org/abs/2101.05555

21. Paszke, A., et al.: PyTorch: an imperative style, high-performance deep learning library. In: Advances in Neural Information Processing Systems, pp. 8024–8035 (2019)

22. Psichogios, D.C., Ungar, L.H.: A hybrid neural network-first principles approach to process modeling. AIChE J. **38**(10), 1499–1511 (1992). https://doi.org/10.1002/aic.690381003

23. Raissi, M., Perdikaris, P., Karniadakis, G.E.: Physics-informed neural networks: a deep learning framework for solving forward and inverse problems involving nonlinear partial differential equations. J. Comput. Phys. **378**, 686–707 (2019). https://doi.org/10.1016/j.jcp.2018.10.045

24. Raissi, M., Perdikaris, P., Karniadakis, G.E.: Physics informed deep learning (part II): Data-driven discovery of nonlinear partial differential equations (2017). https://arxiv.org/abs/1711.10566

25. Rodrigo, M.R., Mimura, M.: Exact solutions of reaction-diffusion systems and non-linear wave equations. Jpn. J. Ind. Appl. Math. **18**(3), 593–619 (2001). https://doi.org/10.1007/BF03167410
26. Toscano, J., Oommen, V., Varghese, A., Karniadakis, G.: From PINNs to PIKANs: recent advances in physics-informed machine learning. Mach. Learn. Comput. Sci. Eng. **1**(15) (2025). https://doi.org/10.1007/s44379-025-00015-1
27. Verhulst, P.F.: Notice sur la loi que la population poursuit dans son accroissement. Correspondance Mathématique et Physique **10**, 113–121 (1838)
28. Wang, S., Teng, Y., Perdikaris, P.: Understanding and mitigating gradient flow pathologies in physics-informed neural networks. SIAM J. Sci. Comput. **43**(5), A3055–A3081 (2021). https://doi.org/10.1137/20M1318043
29. Wang, S., Yu, X., Perdikaris, P.: When and why PINNs fail to train: a neural tangent kernel perspective. J. Comput. Phys. **449**, 110768 (2022). https://doi.org/10.1016/j.jcp.2021.110768

Features of Designing Control Systems of Tested Aviation Moving Platforms

Olha Sushchenko[1] (ID), Yurii Bezkorovainyi[1](✉) (ID), Oleksandr Solomentsev[1] (ID),
Maksym Zaliskyi[1] (ID), Oleksii Holubnychyi[1] (ID), Ivan Ostroumov[1] (ID),
Yuliya Averyanova[1] (ID), Viktoriia Ivannikova[1] (ID), Borys Kuznetsov[2] (ID),
Ihor Bovdui[2] (ID), Tatyana Nikitina[3] (ID), Roman Voliansky[4] (ID),
Kostiantyn Cherednichenko[1] (ID), and Olena Sokolova[1] (ID)

[1] State University "Kyiv Aviation Institute", Liubomyra Huzara Avenue, 1, Kyiv 03058, Ukraine
yurii.bezkor@gmail.com
[2] Anatolii Pidhornyi Institute of Mechanical Engineering Problems of the National Academy of
Sciences of Ukraine, Pozhars′koho Street, 2/10, Kharkiv 61046, Ukraine
[3] Educational Scientific Professional Pedagogical Institute Ukrainian Engineering Pedagogical
Academy, University Street 16, Kharkiv 61003, Ukraine
[4] National Technical University of Ukraine "Igor Sikorsky Kyiv Polytechnic Institute",
Beresteiskyi Avenue, 37, Kyiv 03056, Ukraine

Abstract. This paper describes the features of designing control systems for moving platforms with equipment of different types including optical sensors, antennas, video cameras, and observation equipment. The features of linearization of the mathematical description are described. Such features include the influence of the hysteresis in the gyroscopic device and the backlash in the controlling drive of the platform. The recommendations for linearization of the non-linearities as mentioned earlier are given. The features of introducing disturbances in the mathematical description of moving platforms are represented. The technique of creating forming filters for the simulation of disturbances caused by irregularities of relief of road and terrain is described. Such an approach is relevant for moving platforms operated on land vehicles. The procedure for creating a robust controller resistant to internal and external disturbances is given. The synthesis of the control system for the moving platform has been realized. The simulation results are represented. The obtained results can be useful for the control systems of the different moving vehicles.

Keywords: Land Vehicle · Motion Control · Stabilization System · Linearization · Forming Filters · Disturbances · Simulation

1 Introduction

Currently, the relevance of improving existing and creating high-precision control systems for payloads intended for use on aviation-tested moving platforms is increasing. The solution to this problem requires using inertial stabilized platforms that, in turn, leads to the need to create systems for their control [1–3].

O. Gervasi et al. (Eds.): ICCSA 2025 Workshops, LNCS 15888, pp. 140–151, 2026.
https://doi.org/10.1007/978-3-031-97596-7_9

The typical tasks of control of payloads operated on aviation-tested moving platforms include the following items.

1. Stabilization of the payload in the vertical and horizontal planes during angular movement of the object.
2. Guidance of the payload sighting axis to fixed and moving reference points.
3. Combination of the first two modes, i.e. stabilized guidance of the payload sighting axis to the reference point.

It is worth mentioning that two-axis stabilization is generally relevant for payloads installed on ground-based mobile objects. In most cases, horizontal and vertical stabilization can be considered separately [4–6].

The purpose of this research is to study features of designing systems for the control of moving platforms assigned for the operation of vehicles. The moving platforms are used for stabilization of different payloads including optical sensors, antennas, and different equipment.

In the paper, such important features of designing motion control systems as linearization and introducing stochastic disturbances are considered. The efficiency of system synthesis is proved by modelling. It is worth mentioning that problems of the developing models of the considered class of systems were studied in detail in the paper [7]. The represented results and mathematical models described in [7] allow us to carry out the synthesis of the control system with good efficiency.

The paper's structure looks in the following way. Section 2 deals with features of the linearization of the theoretical representation of the considered system. The features of introducing stochastic disturbances mathematically are given in Sect. 3. The numerical demonstration of the results of the synthesized system is shown in Sect. 4.

2 Features of Linearization

The significance of developing improved perspective systems for controlling aviation-tested mobile platforms has recently been growing. The development of the mentioned systems requires the research of techniques for synthesis and analysis, which could ensure the successful production of improved researched system specimens. A well-known software tool of this type is the Control Toolbox containing a significant set of procedures for designing perspective control systems. However, the features of such a toolbox include its operation only with linear time-invariant models. At the same time, real stabilization systems are usually non-linear, so there is a need to analyze typical non-linearities and the possibilities of transition to a linearized model [8–10].

A mathematical model of a stabilization system for a land-based object is a set of mathematical models of devices included in this system. Before the main devices, there are a gyro device, electronic devices, and motors.

The change in the absolute velocity of a tested aviation moving platform can be measured using an additional gyro device. The mathematical description of the gyro device in terms of the output rotation angle and voltage becomes [11]:

$$
\begin{aligned}
J_g \ddot{\alpha} + 2v\sqrt{J_g c_t}\dot{\alpha} + M_\alpha - M_{gt}^1 + M_{gt}^2 - M_{fr} &= M_{im} - \dot{\omega}_\eta J_g; \\
\ddot{U} &= k_{adt}\alpha + U_0,
\end{aligned}
\tag{1}
$$

here J_g is the torque of inertia of gyro device gimbals; v is the damping coefficient; c_t is torsion rigidity; M_α is the moment taking into account the torsion's hysteresis; $M_{gt}^1 = S\omega_\xi \cos \alpha$ is the gyroscopic moment caused by the influence of measured angular rate ω_ξ, here S is the kinetic moment of the gyroscopic device; $M_{gt}^2 = S\omega_\zeta \sin \alpha$ is the gyroscopic moment due to the action of the angle rate ω_ζ perpendicular to the measured one; $M_{fr} = -M_f \text{sign}\dot\alpha$ is the friction torque in gimbals bearings; $M_{im} = \delta W$ is the moment of imbalance, here δ is the displacement due to imbalance; W is acceleration, which leads to imbalance; $\dot\omega_\eta$ is the angle acceleration along to the longitudinal axis of the gyro device; k_{adt} is the transfer factor of the angle data transmitter; U_0 is the zero shift of the angle sensor.

The main nonlinearity in the model of the gyro device arises due to the necessity to regulate the influx of torsion bar hysteresis. This method is used to formulate a moment consistent with such an algorithm.

As soon as the condition $\dot\alpha \le 0$ is finalized, then the moment M_α, depending on the range of vibrations, is formed in this way:

$$\left\{ \begin{array}{l} M_\alpha = c_t\alpha_0, \text{ if } \alpha_0 - k_{gis}\alpha_0 \le \alpha \le \alpha_0; \\ M_\alpha = c_t\alpha, \quad \text{if } \alpha \le \alpha_0(1 - k_{gis}), \end{array} \right. \tag{2}$$

where k_{gis} is the transfer coefficient, which characterizes the hysteresis value.

As soon as the condition $\dot\alpha > 0$ comes to an end, the moment M_α lies within the range of extinction and is designated as follows:

$$\left\{ \begin{array}{l} M_\alpha = c_t\alpha_0, \text{ if } \alpha_0 \le \alpha \le \alpha_0 + k_{gis}\alpha_0; \\ M_\alpha = c_t\alpha, \quad \text{if } \alpha < \alpha_0(1 + k_{gis}). \end{array} \right. \tag{3}$$

The expressions (1) – (3) allow us to use the mathematical description of the gyro device with the non-linearity due to the hysteresis providing the qualitative synthesis of the system for control of the moving platform.

The next essential non-linearity of the stabilization system is caused by the backlash of the drive.

Manner is that the system of the considered type is assigned for stabilization of the equipment of large mass. In this case, the drive consists of a motor with great rotational speed and the reducer. Therefore, the effect of the backlash of the united system consisting of the stabilization object (platform with payload) and drive with the reducer has arisen [12–14].

The mathematical description of the stabilization object can be described in the form of a second-order differential equation [15]:

$$J_a\ddot\varphi_a + M_{fr}\text{sign}\dot\varphi_a - M_{im}\sin\varphi_a + k_s\varphi_a + c_r\varphi_a = k_sA + \frac{c_r\varphi_b}{n_r} - M_{im}, \tag{4}$$

where M_{fr} is the torque moment; M_{im} is the imbalance torque; k_s is the spring rigidity; A is an angle of the spring's deviation; J_a is the inertia torque; φ_a is the angle of rotation of the stabilization object.

The main non-linearities in the expression (4) are related to the moments of rubbing. They can be approximated by linear expressions represented in [16].

In this case, for the designated moment of rubbing $M = M_{fr}\text{sign}\dot{\varphi}_a$, it is replaced with linear constituent $M = f_a\dot{\varphi}_a$. At this rate, the coefficients f_a will appear as $f_a = 4M_{fr}/(\pi\Omega_a)$.

The flow chart of the modelling process for motor rotation due to non-linearity, resulting in engine backlash, is shown in Fig. 1.

Results of the simulation of the non-linearity due to backlash are described in Figs. 2 and 3.

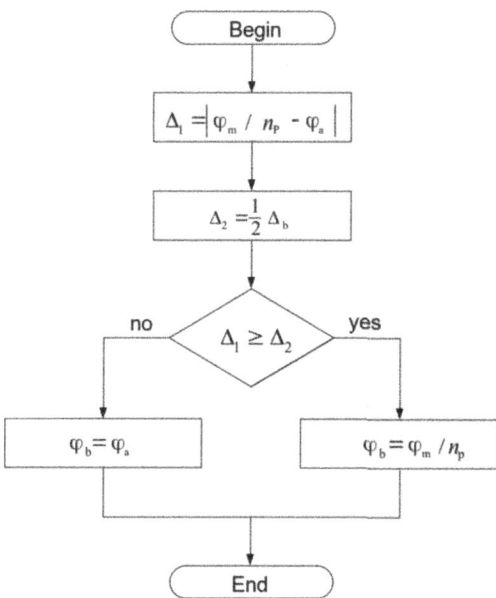

Fig. 1. Flow chart of the molding of the rotation of the motor taking into account the motor backlash due to inherent non-linearities (Δ_b. – backlash zone).

To confirm the obtained results, the horizontal channel of the system of stabilization of an aviation-tested moving platform was modeled. The presented results allow us to conclude the possibility of linearizing the model of the studied stabilization system [17–19].

Figures 2 and 3 illustrate the influence of the engine backlash (0.006 rad) on the transient processes of the angular velocity of an aviation-tested moving platform in the guidance mode. Typical nonlinearities of the studied model should also include the need to limit signals, which is easily implemented by Simulink tools. When dealing with such nonlinearities, it is recommended to work with relatively small values when using a linearized model. The most typical nonlinearities include the presence of insensitivity zones in real equipment, which cannot be taken into account in state space models. The corresponding modeling showed the appropriate transient processes. The simulation results also showed that neglecting such typical nonlinearities does not lead to a significant deterioration of the quality indices by the nonlinear component of the unbalanced moment for angles of rotation of the payload within 5–10 degrees.

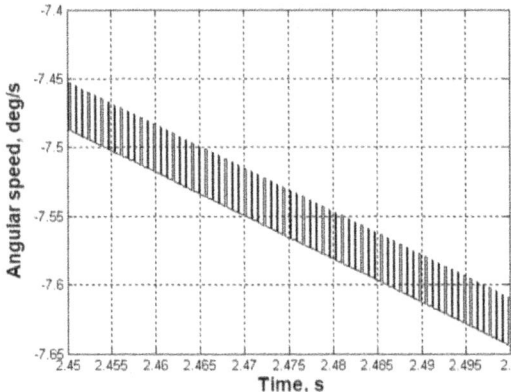

Fig. 2. The non-linearity due to backlash 0.006 rad.

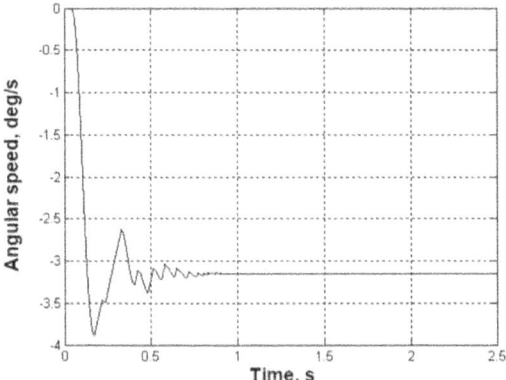

Fig. 3. Influence of the backlash on the transient process of the angular rate.

3   Features of Introducing External Disturbances

It is essential to perform the design procedure for the researched system using operating perturbations. For aviation-tested moving platforms, the disturbed action depends on the action roughnesses caused by the relief profile. For its part, the influence of relief roughnesses depends on terrain topographic features. Therefore, the simulation technique is based on the usage of roughnesses profile. This characteristic is defined by a section of the relief by the vehicle's motion direction [20–22].

For example, such specified relief as terrain with bumps can be expressed in random variables depending on bump altitudes. These random variables are connected also with length, i.e. the distance traveled, or the time. Random variables of this kind could be applied in studying the disturbed motion.

It is worth mentioning that in scientific and technical literature, distance functions are given. Nevertheless, this approach does not disagree with the earlier mentioned proposal as random variables can be expressed in distances using definite relationships.

In frequent situations, we could change the profile by the microprofile when determining random external movements. The specific feature of the microprofile is connected with the absence of constituents with low frequency.

The basic excellence of such a representation can be explained by the possibility of representing microprofile in the form of a random time-invariant process. Namely, such representation can be efficiently applied in procedures of analysis and synthesis of systems for controlling mobile platforms. The transformation of the profile $h(t)$ into microprofile $q(t)$ can be implemented by the fractional-rational transfer function H_q [23, 24].

As both profile and microprofile can be described by random processes, it is appropriate to apply them in procedures of the analysis and synthesis of spectral densities of these processes. These characteristics in dependencies of distance and time $q(l)$, $h(l)$ can be represented by the relations [24].

$$K_l(\lambda) = v K_l(\lambda v); K_l(\omega) = \frac{1}{v} K_l \frac{\omega}{v}. \tag{5}$$

The spectral density of the microprofile looks like

$$K_q(\omega) = |H_q(\omega)|^2 K_h(\omega), \tag{6}$$

where $H_q(\omega)$ is the transfer function of microprofile conversion

$$H_q(\omega) = \frac{(j\omega)^2}{(j\omega)^2 + \sqrt{2}\omega_n j\omega + \omega_n^2}. \tag{7}$$

In the simplified form, the expression (7) becomes

$$H_q(\omega) = \frac{j\omega}{j\omega + \omega_n}. \tag{8}$$

The classification of the spectral densities of the profile of roads and terrain is performed depending on the short roughnesses heights of the microprofile (6). At the same time, based on (5), (6), (8) and considering the length of the wave, we can divide relief roughnesses into three groups, which can be represented by the relationships [24]:

$$K(\lambda) = \frac{D_m}{\lambda^2}; K(\lambda) = \frac{D_c}{\lambda^n}; 0 \leq n \leq 4; K(\lambda) = \frac{D_n}{\lambda^2}. \tag{9}$$

The relationships (9) include factors D_m, D_c, D_n that describe the type and characteristics of the terrain relief. Every group of roughnesses is divided into some subgroups. These subgroups differ in various values of earlier mentioned factors:

- $D_m = 10^{-1}$ defines very rugged terrain with rolling hills;
- $D_c = 10^{-2}$, n = 2 corresponds to a field or meadowland characterizing high roughnesses and nearly equal influence of long and short waves;
- $D_n = 3 \bullet 10^{-3}$ corresponds to the terrain with inhomogeneous land, arable land, and stony ground.

Another way of roughnesses classification foresees four subgroups including prevalence of long unevennesses, bottom land, bulges, and uniform roughnesses. The spectral density for every subgroup is described by the following relationships.

- $K(\lambda) = \frac{D_2(3.1^2+\lambda^2)}{\lambda^2(\lambda_2^2+\lambda^2)}$ (five groups, the fifth group corresponds to very cross terrain $D_2 = 10^{-2}, \lambda_2 = 1$);
- $K(\lambda) = \frac{D_2(10+\lambda^2)(\lambda_1^2+\lambda^2)}{\lambda^2(1+\lambda^2)}$ (five groups, for the fourth group corresponds to large shafts $D_2 = 3.16 \bullet 10^{-3}, \lambda_1 = 0.178$);
- $K(\lambda) = \frac{D_2(\lambda_1^2+\lambda^2)}{\lambda^2(10^2+\lambda^2)}$ (six groups, the fifth group corresponds to large ramparts $D_2 = 10^{-1} \lambda_1 = 1$;
- $(\lambda) = \frac{D_2}{\lambda^2}$ (five groups, the fourth group corresponds to the spectral density of a the high level $D_2 = 10^{-2}$).

Both the first and second classifications could be applied to the simulation of mobile platform motion accompanied by terrain roughnesses. It is worth mentioning that namely the second classification is the most suitable for simulating motion of considered mobile platforms. As the relief microprofile can be described by a normal random process. To imitate this process, we must set the white noise $\delta(t)$ at the input of forming filter with the transfer function H_m.

To design the forming filter, we must take into account the condition [24]

$$H_m(j\omega)H_m^*(j\omega) = K_\delta^{-1}K_q(\omega). \tag{10}$$

According to the second classification, the creation of forming filters has been implemented in the following way:

- $K_h(j\omega) = \frac{\sqrt{D_2 v}}{j\omega} \frac{(3.1v+j\omega)}{(v\lambda_2+j\omega)}$;
- $K_h(j\omega) = \frac{\sqrt{D_2 v}}{j\omega} \frac{(10v+j\omega)(v\lambda_1+j\omega)}{(v+j\omega)(v+j\omega)}$;
- $K_h(j\omega) = \frac{\sqrt{D_2 v}}{j\omega} \frac{(v\lambda_1+j\omega)}{(10v+j\omega)}$;
- $K_h(j\omega) = \frac{\sqrt{D_2 v}}{j\omega}$.

Finally, the expression for the representation of forming filters looks like

$$K_q(\omega) = K_h(j\omega)H_q(j\omega), \tag{11}$$

where $H_q(j\omega)$ is the transfer function of the microprofile conversion.

To synthesize the stabilization system of considered mobile platforms, it is desired to accept some definite kind of contact between the terrain and tires. This assumption must be supplemented by requirements for the kind of profile. The considered problem requires using a smoothed profile for simulation of the disturbed motion. It is characterized by averaging in the contact area. The transfer response of the averaged contact area corresponds to wheel smoothing possibility. Nearly, it can be given in the following representation [24]

$$H_k(\omega) = \frac{\omega_b^2}{(j\omega)^2 + \sqrt{2}\omega_d j\omega + \omega_b^2}, \tag{12}$$

The expression (12) can be represented in the simplified form

$$H_k(\omega) \approx \frac{\omega_b}{j\omega + \omega_b}, \qquad (13)$$

where $\omega_b(0.9 - 1.3)v/a$; v is the velocity of the mobile platform, a is the width of a contacting area.

In order to take into account the disturbances acting on the system, it is necessary to consider the serial connection of the system model and the forming filter based on expressions (10), (11), and (13).

The process of stabilizing the spatial position of a moving platform under the condition of the test signal and under the condition of the disturbance is shown in Figs. 4 and 5, where the stabilized spatial location of the platform in conditions of the tested signal and simulated disturbances are represented.

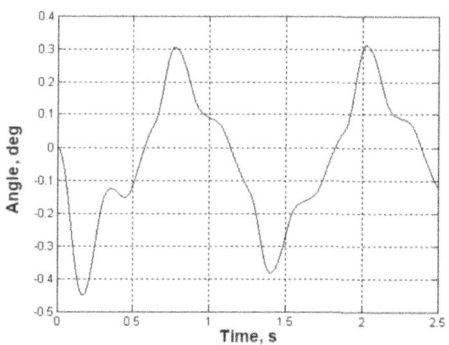

Fig. 4. Stabilization of the platform in conditions of the tested signal.

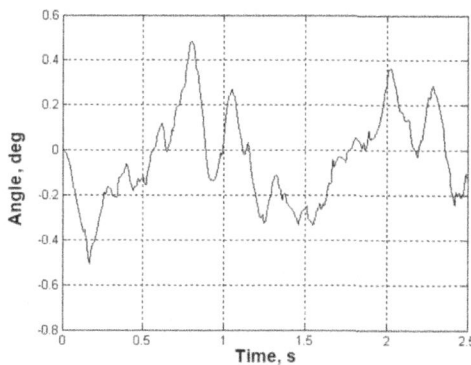

Fig. 5. Stabilization of the platform in conditions of the disturbed signal.

4   Design of the System for Motion Control and Modelling Results

The block diagram of the algorithm for the stabilization system synthesis is presented in Fig. 6.

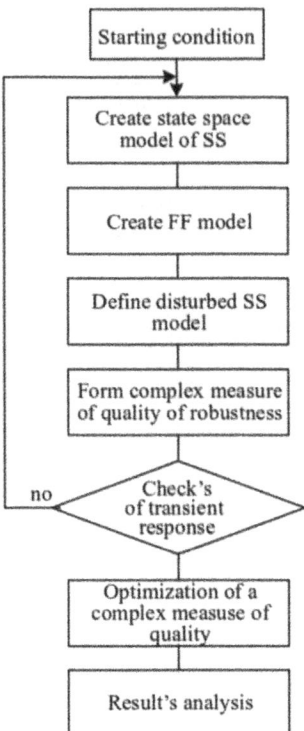

Fig. 6. Flow chart of the procedure for the synthesis of the control system for moving platform: SS is the stabilization system, FF is the forming filter.

The synthesis procedure is grounded on an objective function that considers the most important feature of the designed system. For the considered systems, the most preferred is applying the combined optimization function taking into account the quality and robustness. Such an approach ensures both the accuracy of the system and its resistance to internal and external disturbances. Namely, these properties are of great importance for control systems of mobile platforms. Separate constituents of the objective function have been created using H_2, H_∞ – norms [25]. The H_2-norm represents the square root of the averaging impulse response. This constituent could be expressed as the output signal power in the system's stable state under the influence of the white noise with the unit intensity. The H_∞– norm represents the maximum of the system's frequency response. The influence of every constituent in the combined objective function is defined by weight coefficients. These coefficients are defined by requirements to the system [26]. Modelling results are represented in Figs. 7 and 8.

The synthesized system is characterized by amplitude stability margins of 53.3 dB and phase 91.2 degrees, values of accuracy and robustness $H_2 = 0.3736$ and $H_\infty = 0.1177$, and angular stiffness of 175 Nm/arcmin. Given this, the proposed procedure of the synthesis of considered systems simultaneously takes into account the quality and robustness [27–29]. The proposed synthesis procedure has been implemented with the help of Nelder-Mead method. The controller of the system has been created on the basis

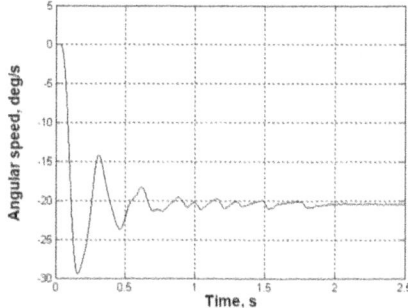

Fig. 7. The transient process on the angular rate for the terrain with middle roughnesses.

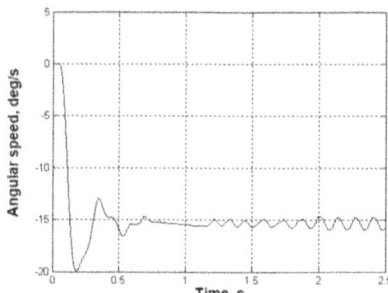

Fig. 8. The transient process on the angular rate for the terrain with bumps.

of the robust structural synthesis. The designed controller is grounded on the feedback by an angular rate of the platform [30]. The structure of the robust controller is automatically obtained as a result of the procedure of the robust structural synthesis. It is represented in the form of a quadruple of state-space matrices of the sixth order and is not given here for simplicity. On the whole, it represents PID controller with additional components caused by specific features of the mobile platform.

5 Conclusions

Approaches to linearization of the mathematical description and simulation disturbances arising due to terrain relief roughnesses using forming filters are considered. The flow chart of the procedure for the synthesis of a control system for the mobile platform is presented. The features of linearization for the control system of mobile platforms are explained.

The procedure of the synthesis of the considered system is represented. The proposed procedure is grounded on the combined objective function including accuracy and robustness of the system.

The obtained simulation results prove the efficiency of the proposed synthesis procedure. This is shown by the transient processes of the mobile platform motion in normal and disturbed conditions.

It is planned during future research to carry out similar research relative to unmanned aerial vehicles. The approach to introducing disturbances in the mathematical description of the moving platforms for equipment operated on unmanned aerial vehicles is planned.

References

1. Hilkert, J.M.: Inertially stabilized platform technology. IEEE Control. Syst. Mag. **1**, 26–46 (2008)
2. Masten, M.K.: Inertially stabilized platforms for optical imaging systems. IEEE Control. Syst. Mag. **1**, 47–64 (2008)
3. Ostroumov, I., Kuzmenko, N., Bezkorovainyi, Y., Averyanova, Y., Larin, V., et al.: Relative navigation for vehicle formation movement. In: 3rd KhPI Week on Advanced Technology, pp. 1–4. IEEE, Kharkiv, Ukraine (2022). https://doi.org/10.1109/KhPIWeek57572.2022.9916414
4. Zoppoli, R., Sanguineti, M., Gnecco, G., Parisini, T.: Neural Approximations for Optimal Control and Decision. Springer, Cham (2020)
5. Osadchy, S.I., Zozulya, V.A., Bereziuk, I.A., Melnichenko, M.M.: Stabilization of the angular position of hexapod platform on board of a ship in the conditions of motions. Autom. Control. Comput. Sci. **56**(3), 221–229 (2022)
6. Bittanti, S.: Model Identification and Data Analysis. John Wiley & Sons, New Jersey (2019)
7. Sushchenko, O., Bezkorovainyi, Y., Salyuk, O., Yehorov, S.: Mathematical description of system for stabilization of aviation equipment in problems of synthesis and simulation. In: Ostroumov, I., Zaliskyi, M. (eds.) Proceedings of the 2nd International Workshop on Advances in Civil Aviation Systems Development. ACASD 2024, Lecture Notes in Networks and Systems, vol. 992, pp. 73–85. Springer, Cham (2024). https://doi.org/10.1007/978-3-031-60196-5_7
8. Sushchenko, O.A., Shyrokyi, O.V.: H2/H∞ optimization of system for stabilization and control by line-of-sight orientation of devices operated at UAV. In: IEEE 3rd International Conference Actual Problems of Unmanned Aerial Vehicles Developments (APUAVD), pp. 235–238. IEEE, Kyiv, Ukraine (2015). https://doi.org/10.1109/APUAVD.2015.7346608
9. Fu, J., Ma, R.: Stabilization and Hinf Control of Switched Dynamic Systems. Springer, Berlin (2020)
10. Kuznetsov, B.I., Nikitina, T.B., Bovdui, I.V.: Structural-parametric synthesis of rolling mills multi-motor electric drives. Electr. Eng. Electromechanics **5**, 25–30 (2020). https://doi.org/10.20998/2074-272X.2020.5.04
11. Zhuang, X., Li, P., Li, D., Sui, W.: Gyroscopes – Principles and Applications. IntechOpen, London (2020)
12. Hernandez-Gurman, V.M., Silva-Ortigoza, R.: Automatic Control with Experiments. Springer, Berlin (2019)
13. Zerrik, El. H., Castillo O.: Stabilization of Infinite Dimensional Systems. Springer, Cham (2021)
14. Kuznetsov, B.I., Nikitina, T.B., Bovdui, I.V.: Multiobjective synthesis of two degree of freedom nonlinear robust control by discrete continuous plant. Tech. Electrodynamics **5**, 10–14 (2020). https://doi.org/10.15407/techned2020.05.010
15. Niu, S.S., Xiao, D.: Process Control: Engineering Analysis and Best Practices. Springer, New York (2022)
16. Sanfelice, R.G.: Hybrid Feedback Control. Princeton University Press, Princeton (2021)
17. Wang, L.: PID Control System Design and Automatic Tuning using MATLAB/Simulink. Wiley, Hoboken (2020)

18. Le, A.T.: Adaptive Robust Control Systems. Intech Open, Vienna (2018)
19. Osadchyi S., Zozulia, V.: Synthesis of optimal multivariable robust systems of stochastic stabilization of moving objects. In: 5th International Conference Actual Problems of Unmanned Aerial Vehicles Developments (APUAVD), pp. 106–111. IEEE, Kyiv, Ukraine (2019). https://doi.org/10.1109/APUAVD47061.2019.8943861
20. Wright, S.J., Recht, B.: Optimization for Data Analysis. Cambridge University Press, Cambridge (2022)
21. Lia, Y., Huang, N.Z., Jiang, T.: Selective Maintenance Modelling and Optimization. Springer, Cham (2023)
22. Khachaturov, A.A.: Dynamics of system road-tyre–car–driver. https://h.twirpx.link/file/570103/
23. Popp, K., Schiehlen, W.: Ground Vehicle Dynamics. Springer, Berlin (2010)
24. Scogestad, S., Postlathwaite, I.: Multivariable Feedback Control. Analysis and Design. John Wiley & Sons, London (2005)
25. Asadi, F.: State-Space Control Systems: The MATLAB/Simulink Approach. Morgan & Claypool, Sun Rafael (2021)
26. Zhiteckii, L.S., Azarskov, V.N., Solovchuk, K.Y., Sushchenko, O.A.: Discrete-time robust steady-state control of nonlinear multivariable systems: a unified approach. IFAC Proc. Volumes **47**(3), 8140–8145 (2014). https://doi.org/10.3182/20140824-6-ZA-1003.01985
27. Voliansky, R., Sadovoi, A., Volianska, N.: Interval model of the piezoelectric drive. In: 14th International Conference on Advanced Trends in Radioelecrtronics, Telecommunications and Computer Engineering (TCSET), pp. 1–6, IEEE, Lviv-Slavske, Ukraine (2018). https://doi.org/10.1109/TCSET.2018.8336211
28. Niu, S.S., Xiao, D.: Process Control. Springer, Berlin (2022)
29. Sushchenko, O.A., Bezkorovainyi, Y.N., Novytska, N.D.: Dynamic analysis of nonorthogonal redundant inertial measuring units based on MEMS-sensors. In: 38th International Conference on Electronics and Nanotechnology, ELNANO-2018, pp. 464–469. IEEE, Kyiv, Ukraine (2018). https://doi.org/10.1109/ELNANO.2018.8477553
30. Chikovani, V., Sushchenko, O., Tsiruk, H.: Redundant information processing techniques comparison for differential vibratory gyroscope. Eastern Eur. J. Enterp. Technol. **4**(7), 45–52 (2016). https://doi.org/10.15587/1729-4061.2016.75206

Modeling the Service Quality Indicators TIEPI and END Using Quantile Regression

Marina A. Andrade[1,2]($\boxtimes$) (ID) and M. Filomena Teodoro[3,4] (ID)

[1] ISCTE, University Institute of Lisbon, Av. das Forças Armadas,
1649-026 Lisbon, Portugal
[2] ISTAR-ISCTE - Information Sciences, Technologies and Architecture Research
Center, Lisbon, Portugal
marina.andrade@iscte-iul.pt
[3] CINAV, Center of Naval Research, Portuguese Naval Academy Military
Universitary Institute, 2810-001 Almada, Portugal
[4] CEMAT - Center for Computational and Stochastic Mathematics, Instituto
Superior Técnico, Lisbon University, 1048-001 Lisbon, Portugal

Abstract. This study investigates the continuity of electricity distribution service in mainland Portugal using quantile regression models applied to two key technical indicators: TIEPI (Time of Interruption Equivalent to Installed Power) and END (Energy Not Delivered). Based on data from E-REDES (2014–2022), the analysis evaluates how interruption frequency and duration, measured by SAIFI (System Interruption Average Frequency Index) and SAIDI (System Interruption Average Duration Index), affect energy supply resilience across different service quality zones and municipalities. Results show that SAIDI has a consistently positive and increasing effect on both END and TIEPI across quantiles, especially at the uppermost, indicating higher exposure to supply loss in the Municipality Codes with poor performance. Fixed effects highlight considerable municipal level heterogeneity, while QSR zone classifications alone do not significantly explain performance after accounting for local variation. These findings support the need for geographically target investment and regulation, and demonstrate the value of distribution sensitive modeling in infrastructure performance assessment.

Keywords: Service continuity indicators · Electricity distribution · Quantile regression

1 Introduction

The global demand for electrical energy has grown substantially in recent decades, driven by technological innovation, demographic expansion, industrialization, and increasing reliance on electronic devices. The widespread adoption of smartphones, computers, and electrified transport technologies has further intensified energy consumption, imposing considerable pressure on electricity generation and distribution systems. This presents environmental, economic, and infrastructure challenges that underscore the urgent need for sustainable energy

O. Gervasi et al. (Eds.): ICCSA 2025 Workshops, LNCS 15888, pp. 152–163, 2026.
https://doi.org/10.1007/978-3-031-97596-7_10

solutions. Ensuring a reliable and continuous electricity supply is essential for public safety and quality of life, economic productivity, and social stability.

Whether brief or prolonged, power supply interruptions can have significant implications for individuals, businesses, and critical infrastructures, these outages result from various causes, including equipment failures (e.g., transformers, circuit breakers), adverse weather conditions, planned maintenance, network overloading, and generation issues. The impacts are widespread, ranging from financial losses and disruptions to industrial processes to risks in healthcare settings and decreased public safety due to communication and lighting systems failures.

In Portugal, the Quality of Service Regulation (QSR), administered by the Energy Services Regulatory Authority (ERSE), regulates electricity distribution service quality. This framework sets performance standards for distribution network operators, incorporating national and European guidelines tailored to the specific characteristics of the Portuguese electricity sector, [1–4]. ERSE is central in establishing annual quality targets and monitoring compliance through operators' periodic reporting. Penalties are imposed for failure to meet the defined standards, ensuring accountability and service improvement.

The QSR encourages investments in network modernization, preventive maintenance, and the adoption of advanced grid technologies to enhance resilience and consumer satisfaction. Regulatory measures address service continuity (e.g., frequency and duration of interruptions), commercial quality, and customer service standards. Outages are categorized as short (1 s to 3 min) or long (over 3 minutes), and either planned or accidental. Legal provisions such as Decree-Law No. 215-B/2012 further defines the conditions under which supply interruptions are permissible, including public interest, safety, or contractual agreement cases.

This paper uses Quantile Regression Models to present a quantitative analysis of service continuity in the Portuguese electricity distribution network, [5–7]. The objective is to identify structural differences across service quality zones and determine which factors significantly influence performance, particularly in the distribution's tails, where conventional mean-based models fall short.

The paper is structured as follows: Sect. 1 introduces the paper; Sect. 2 presents the dataset and outlines the quantile regression methodology; Sect. 3 discusses the model results for END and TIEPI, followed by a comprehensive discussion in Sect. 4; and Sect. 5 outlines conclusions and future research directions.

2 Quantile Regression Approach to Service Continuity Indicators

This study applies quantile regression analysis to investigate the determinants of service continuity performance in the Portuguese electricity distribution network, focusing on the indicators TIEPI (Time of Interruption Equivalent to Installed

Power) and END (Energy Not Delivered). These indicators are critical to evaluating the efficiency and resilience of the medium-voltage distribution system, as they directly reflect the impact of interruptions on installed capacity and energy availability. Their outcome is particularly dependent on the interruptions, both in duration (SAIDI) and number (SAIFI) and location (Municipal Code and QSR zone).

2.1 Data and Scope

The analysis is based on data provided by E-REDES, mainland Portugal's leading electricity distribution system operator, through its Open Data Portal. The dataset spans 2014 to 2022 and includes detailed records on service interruptions across all Portuguese municipalities. Indicators are disaggregated by Municipality Codes and classified according to the Quality of Service Regulation (QSR) zones:

▷ Zone A: District capitals or municipalities with over $25,000$ customers;

▷ Zone B: Municipalities with $2,500$ to $25,000$ customers;

▷ Zone C: Remaining municipalities with fewer than $2,500$ customers.

The Municipality Codes are 278 which spread into the 3 QSR Zones referred.

Service continuity is assessed through the standard reliability indicators:

- SAIDI (System Average Interruption Duration Index);
- SAIFI (System Average Interruption Frequency Index).

In this study, we treat TIEPI and END as dependent variables, hypothesizing that they are functions of both interruption patterns (SAIDI and SAIFI) and contextual variables, including geographic classification, as Municipality Codes, and also considering different zones of Quality of Service Regulation (QSR).

2.2 Methodology

To analyze the determinants of these service continuity indicators, we implement quantile regression models, [8,9] which allow for the estimation of covariate effects across different points of the conditional distribution of the response variable. Unlike ordinary least squares (OLS), which models the mean of the dependent variable, quantile regression is robust to outliers and reveals heterogeneity in predictor effects across quantiles. These seem more appropriate for analyzing performance in both high and low reliability municipalities exhibiting non-homogeneous variability.

The quantile regression model is formally specified as:

$$Q_{Y_i}(\tau \mid X_i) = \sum_{j=1}^{k} \beta_j(\tau) X_{ij}, \tag{1}$$

where $Q_{Y_i}(\tau \mid X_i)$ is the τ-th quantile of the response variable (TIEPI or END) conditional on the covariates X_i, and $\beta_j(\tau)$ are the quantile-specific regression coefficients. The presented model excludes the constant to be in accordance with the interest variables in study.

2.3   Model Specification

The models for TIEPI and END include the following predictors:

- SAIDI and SAIFI: Continuous variables measuring the average duration and frequency per customer;
- QSR Zone: Categorical variable (zone A, zone B, and zone C) representing the regulatory zone classification;
- Municipality Code: Fixed effects to control for unobserved heterogeneity at the local level.

The models were estimated for multiple quantiles (e.g. $\tau = 0.25$, 0.50, 0.75) to capture differences between municipalities with low, median, and high levels of interruption severity.

2.4   Analytical Objectives

This study applies the proposed quantile regression framework to assess the heterogeneity in the continuity of the electricity service in municipalities on mainland Portugal. We are interested in analyzing the influence of interruption indicators such as the System Average Interruption Duration Index (SAIDI) and SAIFI (System Average Interruption Frequency Index) on the distribution of TIEPI and END. The goal is to determine whether and which Municipality Codes experience frequent or more extended outages and are disproportionately more vulnerable regarding installed capacity and not delivered energy. In addition, to evaluate whether the classification of Municipality Codes under the Quality of Service Regulation (QSR) Zones remain significant predictor of performance.

3   Results

This section presents the results of the quantile regression analysis, which TEIPI and END variables as functions of average interruption duration (SAIDI), QSR Zone classification, and Municipality Codes. The model was estimated at three quantiles: the 25th, 50th (median), and 75th percentiles, to capture variation across the distribution of TEIPI and END values and better understand performance drivers under different service continuity levels.

3.1 Descriptives

The descriptive statistics are presented below only for TIEPI, END and SAIDI medium voltage (mv) in Table 1, [10,11]. It turned out that the number of interruptions, despite being an important indicator, did not have a significant impact on the TEIPI and END variables.

Table 1. TIEPI, END and SAIDI medium voltage (mv) – QSR Zone—descriptive statistics.

	QSRZone	N	Mean	Median	SD	Min.	Max.
TEIPI	Zone A	2502	4.01	0.0	16.96	0	423.18
	Zone B	2502	24.67	0.41	42.69	0	493.53
	Zone C	2502	83.71	67.18	72.31	0	885.27
END	Zone A	2502	1.61	0.0	8.39	0	136.87
	Zone B	2502	3.29	0.01	8.42	0	95.56
	Zone C	2502	8.15	5.33	8.83	0	104.22
SAIDI	Zone A	2502	4.52	0.0	819.33	0	423.18
	Zone B	2502	27.86	0.68	46.17	0	602.26
	Zone C	2502	96.11	76.61	81.41	0	748.40

In the descriptive analysis, it was pointed out that the effect of QSR Zones is not significant in TEIPI and END results. Although the same variables result reveals key differences concerning the Municipality Codes, as can be observed in the graphical representations, Fig. 1, in which the line regression of the variables across the Municipality Codes is plotted.

3.2 Model Fit

Results for TEIPI. Variable TIEPI (Time of Interruption Equivalent to Installed Power) was modeled as a dependent variable using quantile regression. The explanatory variables included SAIDI, QSR Zones classification, and Municipality Codes. The model was estimated at the 25th, 50th, and 75th percentiles to capture variation in system vulnerability.

The pseudo R-squared values for the TIEPI model were:

- 0.737 at the 25th percentile,
- 0.834 at the 50th percentile,
- 0.875 at the 75th percentile.

These results suggest improved model performance at higher quantiles, indicating that greater variability in TIEPI can be explained among Municipality Codes with poorer continuity results. The Mean Absolute Error (MAE) are 7.62 (25th), 6.16 (50th), and 7.38 (75th), similar for the considered quantiles.

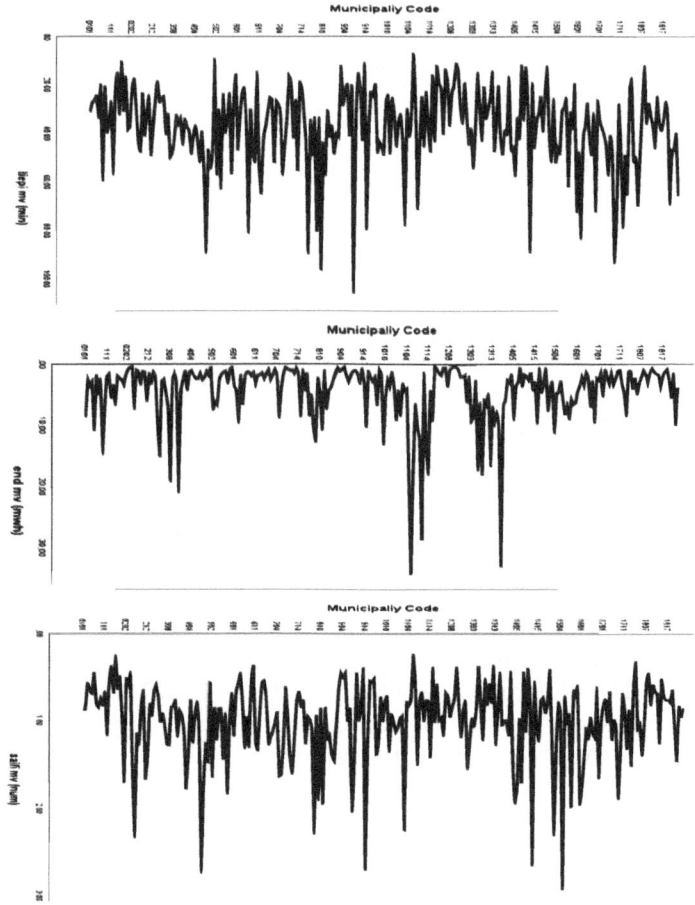

Fig. 1. Three vertically aligned X-Y charts display data trends across different munici-pality codes. Each chart has a horizontal axis labeled "Municipality Code". The vertical axes represent different measurements: the top chart shows "TEIPI mv (mm)," the mid-dle chart "END mv (mwh)," and the bottom chart "SAIDI mv (num)." The data lines fluctuate significantly across all charts, indicating variability in measurements across municipalities.

Effect of SAIDI

The variable SAIDI (System Average Interruption Duration Index) had a positive and statistically significant effect on TIEPI across all quantiles, increasing as the quantiles increase:

- $\beta = 0.767$ at the 25th percentile,
- $\beta = 0.879$ at the 50th percentile,
- $\beta = 0.984$ at the 75th percentile.

This finding indicates that longer average interruption durations lead to higher capacity weighted exposure, which is more pronounced among the worst-performing Municipality Codes.

Municipality Codes Effects

Municipality Codes fixed effects revealed considerable variation in TIEPI outcomes. It was observed that several Municipality Codes show high coefficients, particularly for 75th quantile, $(q = 0.75)$:

- Municipality Code 107: coefficient = 3.907 $(q = 0.75)$,
- Municipality Code 314: coefficient = 3.146 $(q = 0.75)$,
- Municipality Code 1301: coefficient = 3.905 $(q = 0.75)$,
- Municipality Code 1503: coefficient = 4.485 $(q = 0.75)$,

With respect quantiles $q = 0.25$ and $q = 0.5$ the coefficients present low values, thus no referring critical locations.

These findings point to localized structural deficiencies, operational stress, or environmental vulnerabilities affecting system reliability. Figure 2, below, presents Time of Interruption Equivalent to Installed Power (TEIPI) values across municipalities for the 25th, 50th, and 75th quantiles are presented. The vertical axis represents TEIPI, and the horizontal axis denotes the Municipality Codes. Prediction lines correspond to estimated conditional quantiles from the regression model

QSR Zone Effects

The QSR Zone effects were constrained due to colinearity with Municipality Codes specific effects. This outcome suggests that localized characteristics explain most of the variance in TIEPI, and that QSR zones classification alone is insufficient to differentiate performance.

Results for END: Model diagnostics indicate an increasing explanatory power across quantiles. The pseudo R-squared values were:

- 0.219 at the 25th percentile,
- 0.376 at the 50th percentile,
- 0.534 at the 75th percentile.

These results suggest that the model performs better at higher quantiles, capturing more variation in END among Municipality Codes with poorer service continuity. The mean absolute error (MAE) are 3.19 (25th), 2.71 (50th), and 3.79 (75th), similar for the considered quantiles.

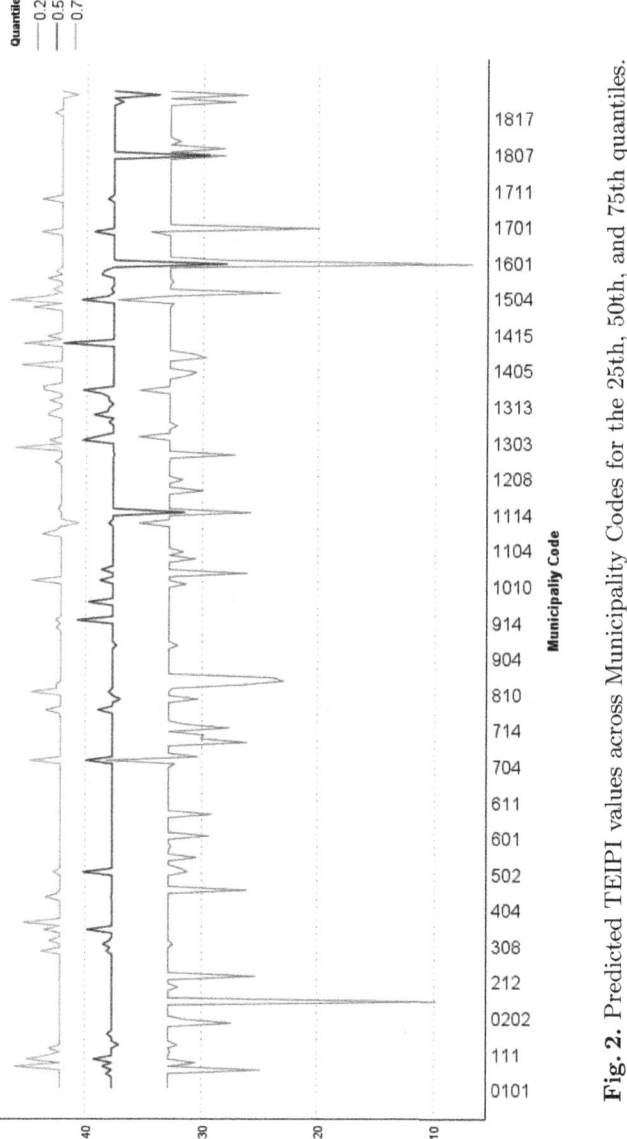

Fig. 2. Predicted TEIPI values across Municipality Codes for the 25th, 50th, and 75th quantiles.

Effect of SAIDI

The variable SAIDI (minutes) had a consistently positive and statistically significant effect across all quantiles, with increasing magnitude:

- $\beta = 0.029$ at the 25th percentile,
- $\beta = 0.046$ at the 50th percentile,
- $\beta = 0.068$ at the 75th percentile.

These results confirm that longer average outage durations are associated with higher volumes of non supplied energy, and this relationship becomes more pronounced in municipalities already experiencing greater service disruption.

Municipality Codes Effects

The fixed effects of Municipality Codes show considerable variation in their contribution to the END. Several municipalities exhibit markedly higher coefficients in the 75th percentile, suggesting structural vulnerabilities or repeated exposure to extreme outages. Several municipalities exhibited particularly high coefficients at the 75th percentile, suggesting chronic network stress or environmental vulnerability:

- Municipality Code 1306: coefficient $= 36.173$ $(q = 0.75)$,
- Municipality Code 1312: coefficient $= 40.486$ $(q = 0.75)$,
- Municipality Code 1106: coefficient $= 83.230$ $(q = 0.75)$.

Figure 3, below, presents the non-supplied energy (END) values across Municipality Codes for the 25th, 50th, and 75th quantiles are presented. The vertical axis represents END, and the horizontal axis denotes the Municipality Codes. Prediction lines correspond to estimated conditional quantiles from the regression model. Municipality Codes show considerable variation in predicted END values, particularly at the 75th percentile, where peaks are significantly higher. This indicates that a small number of Municipality Codes experience disproportionately large energy losses, confirming the presence of local performance asymmetries. The 25th and 50th percentile lines remain relatively stable across most Municipality Codes.

QSR Zone Effects

The effects of QSR Zone classifications were set to zero in the model due to collinearity, likely resulting from including detailed municipality-level fixed effects. This suggests that QSR zone membership does not independently explain variation in END once local heterogeneity is accounted for.

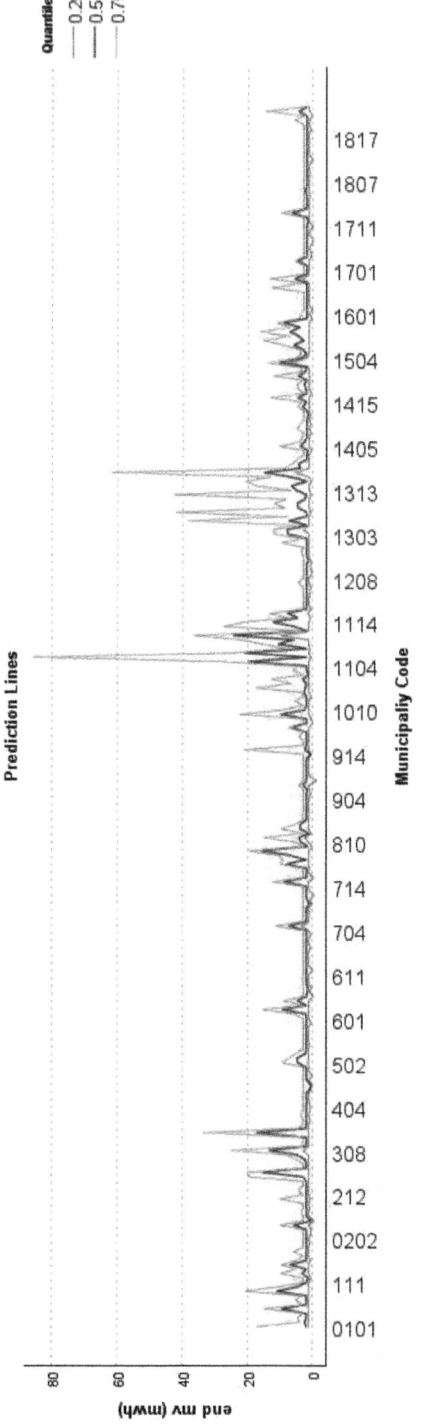

Fig. 3. Predicted END values across Municipality Codes for the 25th, 50th, and 75th quantiles.

4   Discussion

Including TIEPI in the quantile regression analysis offers complementary insight into system resilience under conditions of service interruption. TIEPI, representing the duration of supply loss relative to installed power, reflects the capacity weighted exposure of the network and its users. The strong positive association between SAIDI and TIEPI–especially at the upper quantiles–further confirms that duration of outages is a key driver of systemic vulnerability.

As with END, the variation in municipality-level effects across quantiles suggests that a few locations bear a disproportionate burden of service unreliability. This finding calls for geographically granular regulation, potentially informed by cluster analysis or machine learning-based risk profiling.

Moreover, the parallel behavior of END and TIEPI indicates that the same underlying drivers (network age, design, maintenance regime, or environmental exposure) may jointly affect both energy loss and system-level outage duration. Cross-validating the two indicators across municipalities could strengthen infrastructure prioritization frameworks.

5   Conclusion

Following the work presented in [12–14] in this study, the authors applied quantile regression to model service continuity indicators, focusing on two critical performance indicators: TIEPI (Time of Interruption Equivalent to Installed Power) and END (Energy Not Delivered), in the Portuguese electricity distribution system, similarly to [8,9]. Using data over a decade, the dataset disaggregated by Municipality Codes and QSR Zone, the results demonstrate that the duration of interruptions (SAIDI) significantly and increasingly impacts TIEPI and END as we move to higher quantiles. This implies that Municipality Codes experiencing poor service continuity are more vulnerable to additional disruptions.

The analysis also reveals that Municipality Codes effects explain most of the variability, while QSR zone classifications lose explanatory power once local heterogeneity is included. These findings suggest that infrastructure investments and regulatory oversight should be geographically targeted to address systemic vulnerability.

These findings carry significant implications for regulatory policy and investment prioritization. National distribution strategies should adopt a more geographically robust approach, identifying and targeting municipalities with persistent underperformance. Regulatory frameworks may also benefit from integrating quantile regression to evaluate performance targets that recognize and address extremes.

Future research could extend this model by incorporating dynamic factors such as environmental risk, climate exposure, and population density to provide deeper insights into the systemic drivers of energy resilience and inform infrastructure planning. In addition, a possible approach may be to develop faster algorithms based on [15] to contribute to better performance.

Acknowledgments. The first author was supported by Fundação para a Ciência e a Tecnologia, I.P. (FCT) [ISTAR Projects: UIDB/04466/2020 and UIDP/04466/2020]. The second was supported by Portuguese funds through the Center of Naval Research (CINAV), Naval Academy, Portugal and The Portuguese Foundation for Science and Technology (FCT), through the Center for Computational and Stochastic Mathematics (CEMAT), University of Lisbon, Portugal, project UIDB/Multi/04621/2020, DOI: (https://doi.org/10.54499/UIDB/04621/2020

References

1. Regulação da Energia — Legislação Essencial. Entidade Reguladora dos Serviços Energéticos (2024)
2. 4th Benchmarking Report on Quality of Electricity Supply 2008. Council of European Energy Regulators ASBL (2008)
3. 7th Benchmarking Report on the Quality of Electricity and Gas Supply. Council of European Energy regulators (CEER) and the Energy Community Regulatory Board (ECRB) (2022)
4. Towards Voltage Quality Regulation in Europe – an ERGER conclusions paper. European Regulators' Group for Electricity and Gas (2007)
5. Uche, E., Das, N., Cifuentes-Faura, J., et al.: Globalization, remittances, and income inequality: a novel multivariate quantile-on-quantile regression (M-QQR) perspective for top receiving countries. J. Knowl. Econ. (2025). https://doi.org/10.1007/s13132-025-02738-1
6. Čížek, P.: Quantile Regression. In: XploRe – Application Guide. Springer, Heidelberg (2000). https://doi.org/10.1007/978-3-642-57292-0_1
7. Xiao, Z.: Time series quantile regressions. In: Rao, T.S., Rao, S.S., Rao, C.R. (eds.) Handbook of Statistics, vol. 30, pp. 213–257 (2012). https://doi.org/10.1016/B978-0-444-53858-1.00009-0
8. Hammoudeh, S., Khoung, D., Sousa, R.M.: Energy prices and CO2 emission allowance prices: a quantile regression approach. Energy Policy **70**, 201–206 (2014)
9. Xu, M.: Quantile regression model and its application research. Acad. J. Sci. Technol. **8**(3) (2023). https://doi.org/10.54097/vt1qpm59
10. Morgado, L., Teodoro, M.F., Perdocoulis, T.: Manual de Métodos Estatísticos em Ciências. Universidade de Trás os Montes e Alto Douro (UTAD, Vila Real). Série Didáctica Ciências Aplicadas, 400 (2010). ISBN 978-972-669-018-2
11. Seltman, H.J.: Experimental Design and Analysis. https://www.stat.cmu.edu/~hseltman/309/Book/Book.pdf. Accessed 05 May 2025
12. Andrade, M.A.P., Teodoro, M.F.: Portuguese service electricity continuity indicators: municipality code and quality service zones evaluation – 2014 to 2022. In: Gervasi, O., Murgante, B., Garau, C., Taniar, D., Rocha, A.M.A.C., Faginas Lago, M.N. (eds.) Computational Science and Its Applications – ICCSA 2024 Workshops. ICCSA 2024. LNCS, vol. 14816. Springer, Cham (2024). https://doi.org/10.1007/978-3-031-65223-3_11
13. Andrade, M.A., Teodoro, M.F.: Portuguese service electricity continuity indicators: quality of service evaluation. In: Golubitsky, M., Lacarbonara, W., Pinto, C.M.A. (eds.) To appear in: Mathematical Analysis and Applications in Science and Engineering: ICMASC 2024, Porto, Portugal
14. Andrade, M.A., Teodoro, M.F.: Service Electricity Quality Evaluation – a cluster approach. To appear in AIP Proceedings
15. Chernozhukov, V., Fernández-Val, I., Melly, B.: Fast algorithms for the quantile regression process. Empir. Econ. **62**, 7–33 (2022). https://doi.org/10.1007/s00181-020-01898-0

Computational Optimization and Applications (COA 2025)

On Augmented Lagrangian for LP Feasibility

Pablo Guerrero-García[1][iD], Eligius M. T. Hendrix[2][iD],
and Ana Maria A. C. Rocha[3(✉)][iD]

[1] Applied Mathematics, Universidad de Málaga, 29071 Málaga, Spain
pablito@ctima.uma.es
[2] Computer Architecture, Universidad de Málaga, 29071 Málaga, Spain
eligius@uma.es
[3] ALGORITMI Research Centre/LASI, University of Minho, Campus de Gualtar,
4710-057 Braga, Portugal
arocha@dps.uminho.pt

Abstract. Finding an initial feasible point which is both accurate and sparse for a linear programming (LP) problem has been known as the Phase I problem. Literature provides various ideas based on Lagrange relaxation that imply solving a sequence of convex quadratic subproblems with nonnegativity constraints. This paper provides a small elaboration of several ideas and adds a novel approach to generate a feasible point or certify that it does not exist. Moreover, we perform a comparative computational study on the smallest Netlib sparse LP problems to generate the performance profiles on five metrics where subproblems are solved to optimality with FMINCON from MATLAB® Optimization Toolbox.

Keywords: linear programming · Phase I · quadratic optimization · augmented Lagrangian

1 Introduction

The concept of linking constraints to an objective in optimization problems was found due to Lagrange in the 19th century. The so-called Lagrange multipliers were related to duality theory in the 20th century. At the same time, ideas from penalty methods were linked with ideas from Lagrange multipliers, resulting in the so-called Augmented Lagrangian (AL) methods. The concepts have been applied to nonlinear programming (NLP), global optimization and to linear programming (LP) [3].

Our focus is on an algorithm from late 90 s (cf. [6,7] and references therein) based on a specific active-set strategy to solve a generic sparse LP problem

$$(P) \quad \begin{array}{ll} \min & c^T x \\ \text{s.t.} & A^T x \geq b \end{array} , x \in \mathbb{R}^n \quad \substack{< \\ >} \quad (D) \quad \begin{array}{ll} \max & b^T y \\ \text{s.t.} & Ay = c , y \geq 0 \end{array} , y \in \mathbb{R}^m , \quad (1)$$

This work has been supported by FCT - Fundação para a Ciência e Tecnologia within the R&D Unit Project of ALGORITMI Centre.

where $A \in \mathbb{R}^{n \times m}$ with $m \geq n$ and $\text{rank}(A) = n$. The vectors c and b denote the gradient of the objective function of the primal and dual respectively. The data a_j and b_j represent the coefficient vector and right-hand side value j of primal constraint $a_j^T x - b_j \geq 0$. Experiments have been reported in [7] on a specific active set LP algorithm. It requires an initial feasible point of the dual (D). Our research question is whether an augmented Lagrangian methodology can be applied to generate such a dual feasible point. Specifically, we are interested in a procedure that finds either a dual feasible point y or a direction d of the primal feasible region to certify that the dual (D) does not have a feasible point (i.e., that (P) has an unbounded objective function).

To investigate the question, we introduce the notation in Sect. 2 and discuss several algorithms in Sect. 3. We sketch the behaviour of the algorithms and compare them computationally in Sect. 4 and Sect. 5 summarizes our findings.

2   Mathematical Description and Literature Embedding

2.1   Nonlinear Optimization View on Augmented Lagrangians

The handbook [9] provides an introduction to the concepts of nonlinear optimization including concept of Lagrangian relaxation and penalty terms up to what is called Augmented Lagrangians (AL). First of all, consider a NLP description with objective function $g(y)$ and set of equalities written as $s(y) = 0$. These are similar to the constraints of the dual (D):

$$
\begin{aligned}
\min \quad & g(y) && , y \in \mathbb{R}^m \\
\text{s.t.} \quad & s_i(y) = 0, i = 1, \ldots, n \,, y \geq 0.
\end{aligned}
\tag{2}
$$

Let x be an estimate of the dual solution of (2) (so a solution of the primal) and ρ a penalty parameter. A quadratic penalty based AL taking the equality constraints into account and leaving out the nonnegativity constraints is

$$
\mathcal{L}_D(y; x, \rho) := g(y) - x^T s(y) + \frac{\rho}{2} s(y)^T s(y).
\tag{3}
$$

Notice that to be consistent with the format of the problems, we write the Lagrangian term with a minus sign. A general AL algorithm can be based on minimizing $\min_{y \geq 0} \mathcal{L}_D(y; x_k, \rho_k)$ slowly increasing the penalty parameter ρ_k and updating the dual estimate according to $x_{k+1} = x_k - \rho_k s(y_k)$.

As outlined in [9], the hard part from a point of view of smooth optimization is not the equality constraints, but the inequality constraints; in fact, the problem is related to $\min_{y \geq 0} \mathcal{L}_D(y; x_k, \rho_k)$. This could be promoted by adding to (3) a nonsmooth term

$$
\frac{\rho}{2} \sum_j (y_j^-)^2,
\tag{4}
$$

where the expression $z^- := \max\{-z, 0\}$. There exist several variants of penalty functions like using the $1-$norm rather than the 2-norm and exponential terms.

2.2   Derived Augmented Lagrangian Steps for Linear Programming

It may be clear that the generic NLP expressions can be translated directly for problems (P) and (D) to derive algorithms, which will be outlined in Sect. 3 in the shape of pseudocodes. First of all, the objective function of the dual is $g(y) = -b^T y$ and the slack is $s(y) = c - Ay$.

To find an initial feasible point of the dual (D), our research question is whether an augmented Lagrangian methodology can be applied for that. Specifically, we can set the objective vector $b = 0$ and investigate whether algorithms from the literature reach either a dual feasible point y or a direction d of the primal feasible region which certifies that the dual feasible region is empty. The question is whether and how to use the theory to derive a dual feasible point solving several nonnegativity bound constrained sub-problems.

One of the algorithms we investigate for generating an initial point y of problem (D) has been an application of the concept for LP in the software Clp in the open source COIN-OR software. The corresponding so-called "idiot crash" algorithm has been outlined in [3]. The basic iterate direction d_k in the primal space relates to the AL (3) of the dual:

$$y_{k+1} = \mathrm{argmin}_{y \geq 0} \left(-b^T y - d_k^T (c - Ay) + \frac{\rho_k}{2} (c - Ay)^T (c - Ay) \right), \qquad (5)$$

where looking for a feasible point of (D), we put $b = 0$ and iteratively solve the quadratic problem under nonnegativity constraints

$$y_{k+1} = \mathrm{argmin}_{y \geq 0} \left(-d_k^T (c - Ay) + \frac{\rho_k}{2} (c - Ay)^T (c - Ay) \right). \qquad (6)$$

We will see that such ideas have already been implemented in algorithms in 1972 due to [10].

3   Algorithms

One of the investigations on providing an initial point is due to the so-called "idiot crash" algorithm. The motivation of the research is due to its use in the LP implementation Clp by Forrest in the open source COIN-OR software. We use the description of Galabova and Hall in [3] (see Algorithm1). Therefore, in the experiments we will refer to it as the FoGaHa algorithm. The idea is to force a basic solution "idiot crash" by having the objective $-b^T y$ in the further quadratic objective function. A surprising aspect is that the penalty parameter $\rho_k \to \infty$ is used in division mode to determine the Lagrange multipliers d_k in line 9, such that the primal direction is getting smaller during the iterations. Notice that in our description, we keep a minus sign to be consistent with having a direction d of the primal feasible region.

A second question in the investigation of Clp by [3] deals with the criterion used in line 4 to decide on the update of ρ_k. For the criterion we follow the description in [3] and update ρ_k every three iterations.

Algorithm 1. Idiot crash algorithm (A, c, b, ω)

Require: A: matrix
    c and b: vectors
    $\omega > 1$: multiplication parameter
1: Initialize $k = 0, d_0 = 0, y_0 = 0, \rho_0 > 0$
2: **repeat**
3:    $y_{k+1} \in \mathrm{argmin}_{y \geq 0} \left(-b^T y - d_k^T(c - Ay) + \frac{\rho_k}{2}(c - Ay)^T(c - Ay)\right)$
4:    **if** a criterion is satisfied **then**
5:        $d_{k+1} = d_k$
6:        $\rho_{k+1} = \omega \rho_k$ ▶ update ρ
7:    **else**
8:        $\rho_{k+1} = \rho_k$
9:        $d_{k+1} = -\frac{1}{\rho_k}(c - Ay_{k+1})$
10:    $k = k + 1$
11: **until** stopping criterion
12: **return** y_k or d_k with $A^T d_k \geq 0$ and $c^T d_k < 0$

We are having a challenge for cases where no feasible point exists and consequently the primal problem (P) is unbounded. A certificate is a direction d of the primal feasible region with $A^T d \geq 0$ and $c^T d < 0$. This is not directly provided by the algorithm. Therefore, in the sequel, we will provide a first stage which first focuses on the feasibility question, before looking for a basic (vertex) solution. It should be noticed again that actually the algorithm does not guarantee to generate a basic solution and requires a post-processing with a crossover procedure. This question goes beyond the investigation of this paper.

Notice that in fact the minimizer of the augmented Lagrangian in line 3 is not necessarily unique. The Hessian $\rho A^T A$ is positive semi-definite. This is why in contrast to other papers, we see argmin as a set of minimum points. Actually, we realized this after running several optimization routines and comparing results.

Algorithm 2. Polyak-Tretiakov (A, c, b, ω)

Require: A: matrix
    c and b: vectors
    $\omega > 1$: multiplication parameter
1: Initialize $k = 0, d_0 = 0, y_0 = 0, \rho_0 > 0$
2: **repeat**
3:    $y_{k+1} \in \mathrm{argmin}_{y \geq 0} \left(-b^T y - d_k^T(c - Ay) + \frac{\rho_k}{2}(c - Ay)^T(c - Ay)\right)$
4:    $d_{k+1} = d_k - \rho_k(c - Ay_{k+1})$
5:    $\rho_{k+1} = \omega \rho_k$ ▶ update ρ
6:    $k = k + 1$
7: **until** stopping criterion
8: **return** y_k or d_k with $A^T d_k \geq 0$ and $c^T d_k < 0$

A second algorithm is due to [10] published already in 1972. We studied the description and implemented the interpretation described in [8] similar to Algorithm 2. It has been shown that if an optimal primal and dual solution exists, the procedure converges in a finite number of steps. The penalty parameter is updated in each iteration. The update of the Lagrange multipliers d_k follows a traditional scheme which includes the penalty parameter. One of the challenges is that if the instance to be solved does not have a feasible dual solution, then no certificate of infeasibility is generated.

Therefore, we developed a first stage algorithm to check on the existence of a feasible point solving a nonnegative convex quadratic optimization problem which generates not necessarily a vertex solution in Algorithm 3. If no feasible point exists, it provides a direction d of the primal problem with $A^T d \geq 0$ and $c^T d < 0$ as a certificate of infeasibility of the dual. If a feasible point y_0 exists, it is used as a starting point in the AL minimization in a Polyak-Tretiakov like iterative scheme generating a basic solution in a finite number of steps.

Algorithm 3. First Stage added (A, c, b, ω)

Require: A: matrix
    c and b: vectors
    $\omega > 1$: multiplication parameter
1: $y_0 \in \text{argmin}_{y \geq 0} \frac{1}{2}(c - Ay)^T(c - Ay)$
2: $d_0 = -(c - Ay_0)$
3: **if** $\|d_0\| \geq 10^{-6}$ **then**   ▶ no feasible point exists
4:     **return** d_0
5: **else**   ▶ y_0 is feasible, but not necessarily basic solution
6:     Initialize $k = 0, \rho_0 > 0$ ▶ Use y_0 as starting value for the AL optimization
7:     **repeat**
8:         $y_{k+1} \in \text{argmin}_{y \geq 0} \left(-b^T y - d_k^T(c - Ay) + \frac{\rho_k}{2}(c - Ay)^T(c - Ay) \right)$
9:         $d_{k+1} = d_k - \rho_k(c - Ay_{k+1})$
10:        $\rho_{k+1} = \omega \rho_k$ ▶ update ρ
11:        $k = k + 1$
12:     **until** $\|y_k - y_{k-1}\| < \varepsilon$
13:     **return** y_k

In our experiments, we used FMINCON to minimize the quadratic function on the positive orthant. Actually, for the specific case of minimizing a sum of squares on nonnegativity constraints, we have been experimenting with a gradient projection approach from handbook [9, Sect. 16.7], but realized that for reproduction purposes it is easier to use a standard optimization routine.

4 Numerical Experiments

We first illustrate the approaches with two small examples from literature in Sect. 4.1. Then we use several benchmark problems in Sect. 4.2 to compare behaviour. In all experiments, we used FMINCON to minimize the quadratic AL function over nonnegativity constraints with the default setting. We provided the expressions for the gradient to reduce the number of function evaluations. The final accuracy was $\varepsilon = 1.5\ 10^{-8}$.

4.1   Numerical Illustration

Consider the following instance of an LP problem

$$A = \begin{pmatrix} -1 & -1 & -1 & 1 & 0 \\ 0 & -1 & 1 & 0 & -1 \\ -1 & -1 & -2 & 0 & 0 \end{pmatrix}, \ c = \begin{pmatrix} -4 \\ -2 \\ -6 \end{pmatrix}, \ b^T = (-3, -2, -1, 0, 0),$$

with optimal primal solution $x^* = (3, 0, -1)$ and the dual $y^* = (0, 2, 2, 0, 2)$.

We start inspecting the idiot crash variant as outlined in Algorithm 1 called FoGaHa here. We use the multiplication factor $\omega = 3$ as suggested in [3] and use as initial penalty value $\rho = 1.0$. Their pseudocode suggests that subproblems are approximately solved. However, no details are given. Their discussion in an appendix suggests they solve to optimality, which we adopted in our experiments. The algorithm converges in 13 iterations to an approximation of y^*. It is typical that the approximation differs 10^{-5} from the optimum. Notice that the FMINCON is also fed with the explicit gradient expression and requires 427 function evaluations. However, the slack $c - Ay$ is still order of magnitude of 5×10^{-4} in norm off from zero. Using the same accuracy would require 34 iterations and 2234 function evaluations to get closer to the exact optimal value y^*.

The Polyak-Tretiakov variant called PolTre according to Algorithm 2 was also run with a multiplication factor $\omega = 3$. We observe a convergence to the exact solution y^* with an accuracy of 10^{-6} after 4 iterations requiring 79 function evaluations. The order of magnitude of $\|c - Ay\|$ is 8×10^{-8}. Algorithm 3, which we will call GuHeRo, runs first a first stage to find a non-basic (even interior) solution $y_0 = (1.7176, 1.8197, 1.2313, 0.7867, 1.4116)$ using 14 function evaluations corresponding to $\|c - Ay_0\|$ of 3×10^{-8}. From there it starts the second stage which requires 3 iterations and 57 function evaluations to approach y^* with an accuracy of 10^{-6} and $\|c - Ay_4\|$ of 3×10^{-7}. It seems for this instance that running a first stage improves solving the problem compared to running Algorithm 2, called PolTre, without the first stage.

Now we consider a small instance with an unbounded primal problem and consequently an infeasible dual problem. This means we have to find a certificate direction d for the primal problem. Observe that the second and third column are linearly dependent.

$$A = \begin{pmatrix} 1 & 2 & -2 & 1 & 1 & 0 & 0 \\ -2 & 1 & -1 & 0 & 0 & 1 & 0 \\ 1 & 2 & -2 & -3 & 0 & 0 & 0 \\ -1 & -2 & 2 & 1 & 0 & 0 & 1 \end{pmatrix}, \ c = \begin{pmatrix} 1 \\ 4 \\ 0 \\ -1 \end{pmatrix}, \ b^T = (-2, 4, -4, 2, 0, 0, 0)$$

Running the idiot crash provides a point y after 13 iterations and 458 function evaluations towards $y = (0, \alpha, \alpha, \frac{1}{4}, 0, 3.54, 0)^T$, where α is an arbitrary big number corresponding to an infeasible slack of $(c - Ay) = (-\frac{1}{6}, 0, -\frac{1}{6}, -\frac{1}{3})$. However, the direction $d = -\frac{1}{\rho_k}(c - Ay)$ is yielding very small values due to the division by the penalty parameters. Using simply $(c - Ay)$ provides a direction of the feasible area of (P) with a positive objective value $c^T(c - Ay) = \frac{1}{6}$ so does not certify unboundedness of the primal and with that infeasibility of the dual.

Algorithm 2 (Polyak-Tretiakov) generates after two iterations with 40 function evaluations infeasible point $y = (0, 2.3, 1, 84, \frac{1}{4}, 0, 3.54, 0)^T$. Direction $d = -(4, 0, 2, 4)$ does not provide a direction of the feasible area of (P).

Algorithm 3, called GuHeRo, uses the first phase to detect the infeasibility. Basically, the minimum objective function value is $\frac{1}{6} > 0$. It generates a direction into the feasible area of $d = (c - A^T y) = (\frac{1}{6}, 0, \frac{1}{6}, \frac{1}{3})^T$ with an objective $c^T d = -\frac{1}{6} < 0$. As $A^T d > 0$ and $c^T d < 0$ we have a certificate that the primal is unbounded and the dual infeasible.

Table 1. NETLIB test problem instances; #: Bixby number [1]; nnz: number of nonzeros; m and n the number of rows and columns of matrix A.

#	name	optimal value	m	n	nnz(A)	nnz(b)	nnz(c)	nnz(LP)
6	ADLITTLE	−0.22549496316e+6	138	56	424	82	37	543
1	AFIRO	0.46475314286e+3	51	27	102	5	7	114
28	AGG	0.35991767287e+8	615	488	2862	131	432	3425
29	BANDM	0.15862801845e+3	472	305	2494	165	118	2777
9	BLEND	0.30812149846e+2	114	74	522	30	8	560
22	BRANDY	−0.15185098965e+4	303	220	2202	2	54	2258
16	DUISRAEL	−0.89664482186e+6	316	142	2411	171	89	2671
30	E226	0.18751929066e+2	472	223	2768	189	99	3056
23	ISRAEL	0.89664482186e+6	316	174	2443	89	171	2703
14	LOFTI	0.25264706062e+2	366	153	1136	8	49	1193
3	SC50A	0.64575077059e+2	78	50	160	1	10	171
2	SC50B	0.70000000000e+2	78	50	148	1	5	154
4	SC105	0.52202061212e+2	163	105	340	1	20	361
10	SC205	0.52202061212e+2	317	205	665	1	38	704
7	SCAGR7	0.23313898243e+7	185	129	465	133	53	651
19	SCAGR25	0.14753433061e+8	671	471	1725	475	179	2379
31	SCFXM1	−0.18416759028e+5	600	330	2732	23	116	2871
17	SCORPION	−0.18781248227e+4	466	388	1534	282	76	1892
26	SCSD1	−0.86666666743e+1	760	77	2388	760	1	3149
20	SCTAP1	−0.14122500000e+4	660	300	1872	360	154	2386
15	SHARE1B	0.76589318579e+5	253	117	1179	31	103	1313
12	SHARE2B	0.41573224074e+3	162	96	777	36	24	837
8	STOCFOR1	0.41131976219e+5	165	117	501	27	8	536

Table 2. A comparison of three algorithms, MATLAB® R2024b. #: Bixby number; NZ: number of nearly nonzero $|y_i| \geq \varepsilon$; Feas acc: $\|c - Ay\|_2$; Iters: number of iterations; Feval: number of function evaluations; Time: CPU time in seconds.

#	IDIOT CRASH (FOGAHA)					FIRST STAGE ADDED (GUHERO)					POLYAK-TRETIAKOV (POLTRE)				
	NZ	Feas acc	Iters	Feval	Time	NZ	Feas acc	Iters	Feval	Time	NZ	Feas acc	Iters	Feval	Time
6	102	1.44e−04	25	12673	17.4	71	1.96e−09	13	4072	7.4	71	5.37e−10	14	3579	7.5
1	50	2.22e−05	33	4590	1.6	34	1.18e−07	27	2463	0.9	35	3.11e−07	27	2086	0.8
28	601	2.26e+02	480	853573	45976.4	593	4.32e−02	12	23985	957.3	615	1.78e−03	34	65450	1948.3
29	306	6.14e−01	483	827354	28685.4	421	1.15e−05	15	41981	674.0	383	8.19e−02	322	582682	21887.8
9	93	3.54e−03	13	8311	7.4	93	8.68e−06	14	4591	5.5	114	6.97e−08	14	4654	5.1
22	303	1.31e−02	13	13611	99.5	303	2.53e−05	12	11482	77.5	212	1.98e−08	18	14075	120.2
16	114	1.27e+01	478	828634	8329.7	117	2.56e−01	320	560789	6465.4	286	2.20e+00	317	546809	7622.4
30	472	2.37e−05	25	14281	395.8	472	7.69e−06	14	11491	244.5	446	4.33e−06	16	25469	456.0
23	257	2.29e+00	16	15394	128.5	279	3.45e−02	221	290490	667.8	254	5.20e−02	8	9157	92.8
14	366	5.49e−03	335	384864	1186.7	366	7.79e−03	224	258597	930.4	366	6.89e−03	224	274958	782.8
3	78	2.12e−05	37	35859	14.5	78	1.41e−06	22	7030	3.4	78	1.41e−05	17	24973	11.8
2	75	2.84e−06	31	13632	6.2	75	4.86e−07	29	18041	5.6	78	3.60e−06	26	20586	6.9
4	163	1.26e−05	25	44915	61.4	163	6.26e−06	20	16210	18.1	163	1.71e−05	59	80368	79.6
10	317	1.51e−05	353	474825	1187.0	317	1.11e−04	232	320304	989.8	315	2.56e−06	234	302754	3644.8
7	144	1.88e−01	16	11137	26.8	139	1.39e−09	15	8558	20.6	129	2.44e−02	326	556301	1883.6
19	476	3.40e−01	16	27285	902.9	671	3.56e−03	328	596990	102249.3	543	1.62e−03	331	605398	107054.1
31	600	2.75e−01	10	17736	481.9	589	1.20e−06	14	28371	705.3	600	1.83e−04	19	31355	658.1
17	466	3.51e−05	351	405276	2336.9	442	1.41e−02	328	550287	19010.2	297	5.96e−05	233	284138	21040.0
26	550	3.81e−05	40	32103	797.8	760	2.93e−07	21	27293	2250.6	116	2.67e−07	29	15176	364.2
20	660	9.81e−05	28	54685	1330.5	660	1.39e+00	320	564598	48527.5	660	2.42e−05	14	28381	874.9
15	253	6.64e−04	19	31162	225.5	253	4.07e−05	15	27779	259.4	253	1.09e−03	23	38017	193.7
12	162	6.38e−03	16	11954	22.8	162	1.02e−07	14	20288	37.4	162	1.67e−08	14	13267	23.1
8	124	3.80e+00	10	5300	8.2	128	7.44e−05	6	4813	7.5	121	2.34e−05	6	4356	6.6

4.2   Benchmark Problems

We run computational experiments using the first 31 smallest NETLIB problems [4] in Table 1. From them we have selected only those formulated in standard form and/or canonical form. This defines a test benchmark of 23 LPs in pure inequality form.

Note that DUISRAEL is relatively new. Following the reasoning of the Bixby numbers it has Bixby number 16 due to the number of nonzeros. Moreover, according to [1], we are aware of the fact that the order used in Table 1 is not most logical, but we guess it is easier to find the details of a particular LP by only focusing on its name. Table 2 shows the results obtained by the three algorithms comparing each instance individually. For example one can observe that for instances BANDM and SCAGR7, the algorithm GuHeRo provides far more accuracy with much fewer function evaluations than the other algorithms. To have a more global comparison of the performance of the three algorithms, we use performance profiles as described in Dolan and Moré's paper [2].

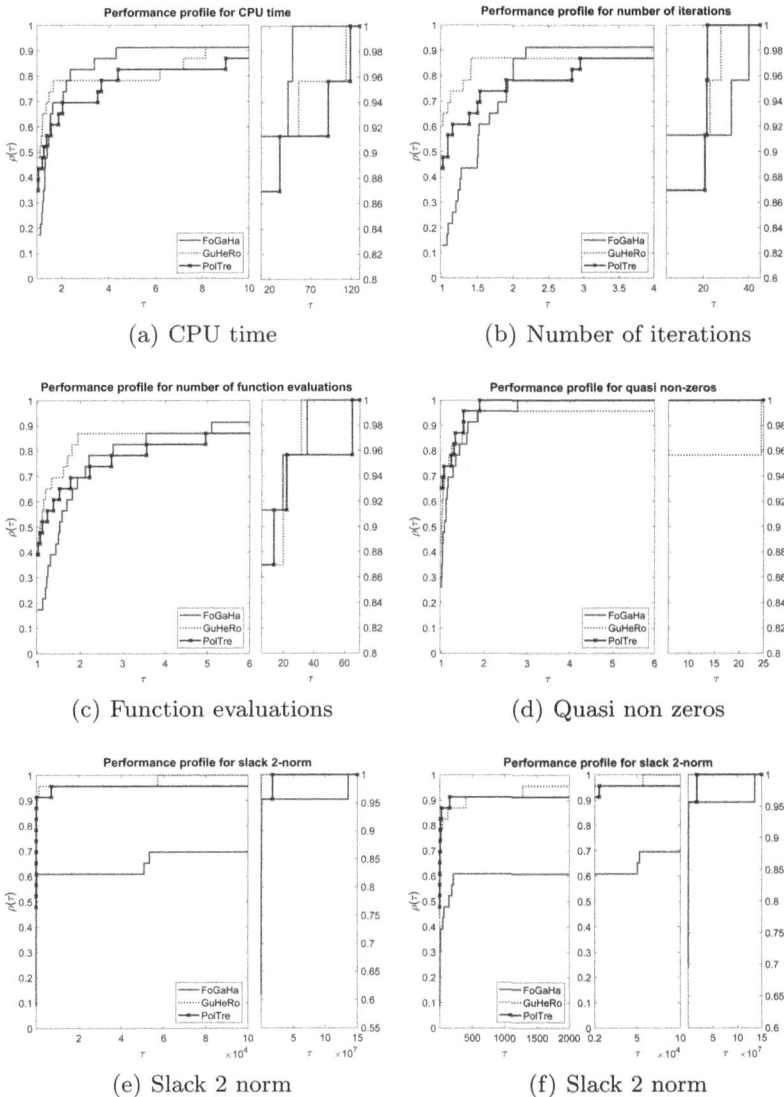

(a) CPU time   (b) Number of iterations

(c) Function evaluations   (d) Quasi non zeros

(e) Slack 2 norm   (f) Slack 2 norm

Fig. 1. Performance profiles, 5 metrics, 3 algorithms: FoGaHa in red; GuHeRo in green, PolTre in blue (Color figure online)

4.3   Comparison Based on Performance Profiles

The performance profiles are based on minimizing a certain performance metric to compare the performance of solvers. These are based on observations of running algorithm $s \in \mathcal{S}$ for solving problem instance $p \in \mathcal{P}$. In our case, the metric data are provided by Table 2. Let $m_{p,s}$ be the value of the metric when solving problem instance $p \in \mathcal{P}$ by solver $s \in \mathcal{S}$. The comparison is based on performance ratios defined by

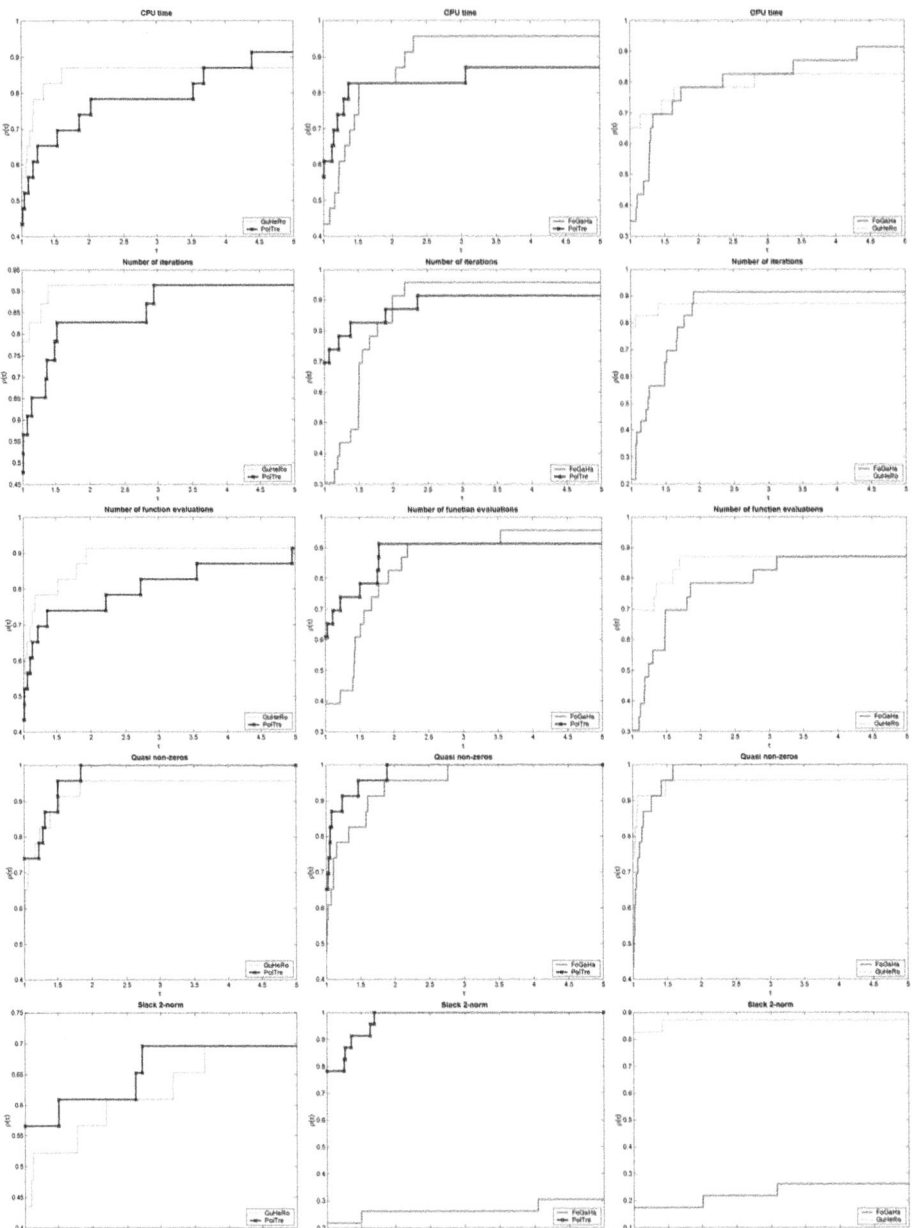

Fig. 2. Performance profiles one-versus-one comparison, 5 metrics, three algorithms: FoGaHa in red; GuHeRo in green, PolTre in blue (Color figure online)

$$r_{p,s} = \frac{m_{p,s}}{\min\{m_{p,s} : s \in \mathcal{S}\}}.$$

The overall assessment of the performance of the solver s is given by

$$\rho_s(\tau) = \frac{\text{number of instances with } r_{p,s} \leq \tau}{\text{total number of instances}}.$$

Following a probabilistic perspective, $\rho_s(\tau)$ gives the probability (for $s \in \mathcal{S}$) that $r_{p,s}$ is within a factor $\tau \in \mathbb{R}$ of the best possible ratio.

The value of $\rho_s(1)$ gives the probability that a particular solver, s, will have a better performance than the others. Thus, to see which solver has the least value of the metric most of the times, $\rho_s(1)$ should be compared for all the solvers. The higher the value of ρ_s the better the solver is. In this interpretation, $\rho_s(\tau)$ measures for large values of τ the solver robustness.

Figure 1 shows the performance profiles based on the selected metrics. We do not only focus on efficiency metrics as computational effort in terms of CPU time, number of iterations and objective function evaluations, but also the effectiveness measured as quality of the feasible point obtained in terms of accuracy and sparsity. The hypothesis is that the "idiot crash" algorithm as described by Forrest, Galabova and Hall in their pseudocode can be outperformed when subproblems are solved to optimality rather than approximately. Moreover, we want to measure the importance of a good initialization step in a first stage when added to the Polyak-Tretiakov algorithm.

Consider first the computational effort. From Fig. 1(a) we can observe that GuHeRo is faster than PolTre in the whole test set. There are some instances for which FoGaHa is faster. However, having a more detailed look at the results of FoGaHa for instances SCFXM1 (#31) and SCAGR25 (#19) in Table 2, one can observe that indeed computation is faster, but FoGaHa reaches an accuracy less than at least two orders of magnitude compared to GuHeRo. From Fig. 1(b) we can observe that GuHeRo requires less iterations than PolTre in the whole test set. FoGaHa only performs better for several instances against reaching a lower accuracy as described above. From Fig. 1(c) we can observe that GuHeRo requires less function evaluations than both PolTre and FoGaHa in the whole test set. FoGaHa performs better than PolTre on half the test set. Furthermore, GuHeRo appears slightly robuster than FoGaHa when considering this metric.

We now focus on the quality of the obtained feasible point. Figure 1(d) illustrates that PolTre reaches sparser feasible points i.e., those with a smaller number of nonzeros. Notice that the addition of the first stage of GuHeRo does not improve this performance. However, GuHeRo reaches sparser results than FoGaHa for nearly the whole test set. Figures 1(e) and 1(f) focus on the Euclidean norm of the slack $s := c - Ay$. We can observe that both GuHeRo and PolTre reach tighter solutions than FoGaHa. Focusing further on the difference between GuHeRo and PolTre, we provide both a 2-zoom and a 3-zoom performance profile, which illustrate that GuHeRo is most robust according to this metric.

To strengthen the observations before, we also provide 15 performance profiles for the 5 metrics considered for one-versus-one comparisons as suggested by

[5], see Fig. 2. In this case we have restricted the analysis to a factor $\tau \le 5$ to improve readability, since the limiting behaviour was already analyzed before. The second and third column show that PolTre and GuHeRo provide better performance than FoGaHa in all metrics. The first column suggests a smaller computational effort of GuHeRo, whereas PolTree slightly outperforms GuHeRo with respect to the quality of the obtained feasible point.

5   Conclusions

This paper focuses on the generation of a feasible dual point of a potentially sparse LP problem. As a basis, we took two algorithms from literature, the Polyak and Tretiakov algorithm from early 70 s and the so-called "idiot crash" algorithm of Forrest analysed recently by Galabova and Hall. As an alternative, we added to the first algorithm a first stage initialization to generate a starting point. This first stage initialization step has the advantage that it generates a certificate of infeasibility when the instance to be solved has an unbounded solution and the corresponding dual is infeasible.

First of all, the described algorithms have been embedded in a common framework. Two illustrative small examples show the difference among the algorithms. A comparative computational study on the smallest Netlib sparse LP problems has been used to generate performance profiles on five metrics; CPU time, number of iterations, number of function evaluations, the accuracy of the solution as the Euclidean size of the slack and the sparsity. Subproblems are solved up to optimality with FMINCON from the MATLAB® Optimization Toolbox. The experiments show the advantage of the introduced algorithm. For most cases, the novel algorithm is faster than the original Polyak Tretjakov algorithm and provides better (more accurate) solutions than the idiot crash algorithm.

References

1. Bixby, R.E.: Implementing the simplex method: the initial basis. ORSA J. Comput. **4**(3), 267–284 (1992)
2. Dolan, E.D., Moré, J.J.: Benchmarking optimization software with performance profiles. Math. Program. **91**, 201–213 (2002)
3. Galabova, I., Hall, J.: The 'idiot' crash quadratic penalty algorithm for linear programming and its application to linearizations of quadratic assignment problems. Optim. Methods Softw. **35**(3), 488–501 (2020)
4. Gay, D.M.: Electronic mail distribution of linear programming test problems. Committee on Algorithms (COAL) Newslett. **13**, 10–12 (1985)
5. Gould, N., Scott, J.: A note on performance profiles for benchmarking software. ACM Trans. Math. Softw. **43**(2), 15(1–5) (2017)
6. Guerrero-García, P., Hendrix, E.M.T.: On active-set LP algorithms allowing basis deficiency. In: Gervasi, O., Murgante, B., Misra, S., Rocha, A., Garau, C. (eds.) Computational Science and Its Applications–Proceedings of the ICCSA 2022 Workshops, Part II, LNCS, vol. 13378, pp. 174–187. Springer International Publishing, Cham (2022). https://doi.org/10.1007/978-3-031-10562-3_13

7. Guerrero-García, P., Hendrix, E.M.T.: Experiments with active-set LP algorithms allowing basis deficiency. Computers **12**(3), 1–23 (2023). https://doi.org/10.3390/computers12010003
8. Güler, O.: Augmented Lagrangian algorithms for linear programming. J. Optim. Theory Appl. **75**, 445–470 (1992)
9. Nocedal, J., Wright, S.J.: Numerical Optimization, 2e edn. Springer, New York, NY, USA (2006). https://doi.org/10.1007/978-0-387-40065-5
10. Polyak, B.T., Tretjakov, N.V.: An iterative method of linear programming and its economic interpretation. Ekon. Mat. Metody **8**(5), 740–751 (1972). in Russian

Analysis of the Effect of Global and Local Objectives in Multi-objective Distributed Job Shop Scheduling Problems

Francisco dos Santos[1,2]($\boxtimes$) (ID), Lino Costa[1,3] (ID), and Leonilde Varela[1,3] (ID)

[1] ALGORITMI Research Centre/LASI, University of Minho, Braga, Portugal
[2] Polytechnic Institute, Kimpa Vita University, Uíge, Angola
francisco_dos_santos@outlook.pt
[3] Department of Production and Systems, University of Minho, Braga, Portugal
{lac,leonilde}@dps.uminho.pt

Abstract. In distributed manufacturing systems, the goal is to process jobs on several factories with different number of machines. Each machine has given processing and setup times that depend on the jobs. The problem of seeking solutions minimizing total production time (makespan), reducing tardiness, or maximizing resources utilization is known as Job Shop Scheduling problem. However, in this problem, each factory may have specific priorities or local objectives. On the other hand, global objectives of the organization can also exist. Thus, this paper studies the effect of these factory local objectives in Distributed Job Shop Scheduling Problems (DJSS). Some instances of the DJSS problems are solved using NSGA-III considering various combinations of local objectives with global ones in a multi-objective context. The trade-off solutions obtained are compared and analyzed. These preliminary results indicate the usefulness and validity of this approach.

Keywords: Distributed job shop scheduling problem · global and local objectives · multi-objective optimization · evolutionary algorithms

1 Introduction

The growing complexity of distributed manufacturing systems has revealed the need for efficient approaches to optimizing multiple objectives in distributed factory environments [13]. In the context of distributed job shop scheduling problems, each factory may have different priorities, such as minimizing total production time (makespan), reducing tardiness or maximizing resource utilization, among others. The existence of divergent objectives between factories introduces significant challenges, since local decisions can have a negative impact on the overall performance of the system. In this scenario, coordination between factories is crucial to ensure that individual goals are achieved without compromising collective efficiency.

This work has been supported by FCT - Fundação para a Ciência e Tecnologia within the R&D Unit Project Scope UID/00319/Centro ALGORITMI (ALGORITMI/UM).

Currently, distributed production systems have been widely adopted in industrial production processes, and in recent years many studies have been carried out on the modeling and optimization of distributed job shop scheduling problems [6]. The Distributed Job Shop Scheduling (DJSS) problem extends the traditional Job Shop Scheduling (JSS) problem by introducing a set of geographically distributed factories, each equipped with a specific number of machines. In this scenario, a certain number of jobs must be processed in these factories. DJSS problems are more complex and challenging than traditional JSS problems, as they require the simultaneous resolution of two interconnected sub-problems: assigning jobs to machines within each factory and determining the optimal sequence of jobs in each factory [3,8]. Like traditional JSS problems, the main objective of DJSS is to find a job distribution and sequencing strategy that minimizes the makespan [15], which remains the most widely used optimization criterion in JSS problems.

Previous works considered objectives such as makespan [1,11,15], the average completion time of the jobs [7,11,14], standard deviation of completion times and the total tardiness [9,15] among others. Some of these works considered DJSS as a single objective optimization problem. However, DJSS problems involve more than one objective to optimize simultaneously. This kind of problems require advanced optimization techniques [12,14], capable of dealing with multiple conflicting objectives [10]. In [11], a multi-objective distributed job shop scheduling model with unrelated parallel machines and sequence-dependent setup times was used to solve small instances using NSGA-III [4], considering the makespan and the average completion time as objectives in a global perspective.

However, it is important to study the effects of considering priorities or local objectives for factories. It should be stressed the relevance of considering the heterogeneity of factories in distributed production systems and therefore, in finding solutions that efficiently balance local and global requirements. Thus, objectives must be reformulated in order to take into account the diversity of factories goals and the interdependence between factories.

Thus, in this paper, an approach for optimizing different objectives in distributed manufacturing systems with global objectives for the entire system and local objectives for factories is proposed. The methodology developed aims to find solutions that harmonize the individual priorities of each factory, while guaranteeing the overall efficiency of the system. Several global and local objectives are formulated. A set of DJSS instances with unrelated parallel machines and sequence-dependent setup times are solved using NSGA-III [4]. The effect of global and local objectives on the solutions obtained is then studied and analyzed.

The structure of the document is as follows. Section 2 briefly presents the distributed job shop scheduling framework, including the description of the general framework implemented and the formulation of global and local objectives. In Sect. 3, the results of several combinations of global and local objectives using

NSGA-III on a set of DJSS instances are analyzed and discussed. Finally, in Sect. 4, some conclusions and future work are addressed.

2 Distributed Job Shop Scheduling Framework

2.1 Framework Description

A general framework for solving Distributed Job Shop Scheduling (DJSS) and Job Shop Scheduling (JSS) problems was developed and implemented in Python programming language. In Fig. 1, it is presented a diagram that describes this general framework. First, the user must define the DJSS problem by indicating the number of factories, the number of machines in each factory, and the number of jobs to be processed. This way, the distributed production systems is defined. It should be noted that a JSS problem can be also defined by indicating a number of factories equal to one, i.e., it is a particular case of a DJSS where the number of factories is one. Next, the number of objectives, type of global or local objectives must be defined. DJSS problems can be formulated with one or more conflicting objectives, this latter case correspond to a multi-objective problem. Moreover, objectives can express global and local goals. Global objectives refer to the overall objectives of the organization. On the other hand, local objectives are related with local criteria of each factory of the organization. Finally, specific problem data have to be provided, namely the setup times (order dependent), the processing times of each job on each machine of each factory, and the transportation times of each job to each factory. All problem data is saved in a file that will be read later by the optimization algorithm.

Afterwards, an optimization algorithm (e.g., GA, NSGA-II, NSGA-III among others) has to be selected taking into account the characteristics or properties of the problem being solved. Meta-heuristics such as evolutionary algorithms [5] are often used to solve these DJSS optimization problems that are combinatorial in nature. Evolutionary algorithms are inspired by the genetic process of biological organisms, which evolve through natural selection. These algorithms are particularly suited to solve combinatorial problems since permutation representation of solutions and specific genetic operators can be used. Furthermore, in general, several conflicting objectives exist and evolutionary algorithms that work with a population of solutions can find an approximation of the Pareto optimal frontier. In this implementation, the optimization algorithms have to be selected by the user from the PyMOO [2] framework.

For all algorithms, the user can modify their parameters and stopping criteria or use the default setup (in this case, default algorithm parameters are used). Next, the optimization algorithm runs and the results are stored in an output file. This file contains data regarding the solutions of the problem and the respective objective functions values. Other data related with the optimization process can be also stored. Finally, a set of tools can be selected to present and visualize the results such as Gantt charts to represent solutions, graph representations of the

Pareto optimal frontier or parallel coordinate plots to identify trade-offs. These visualization tools intend to facilitate the analysis of solutions and also facilitate the decision-making process.

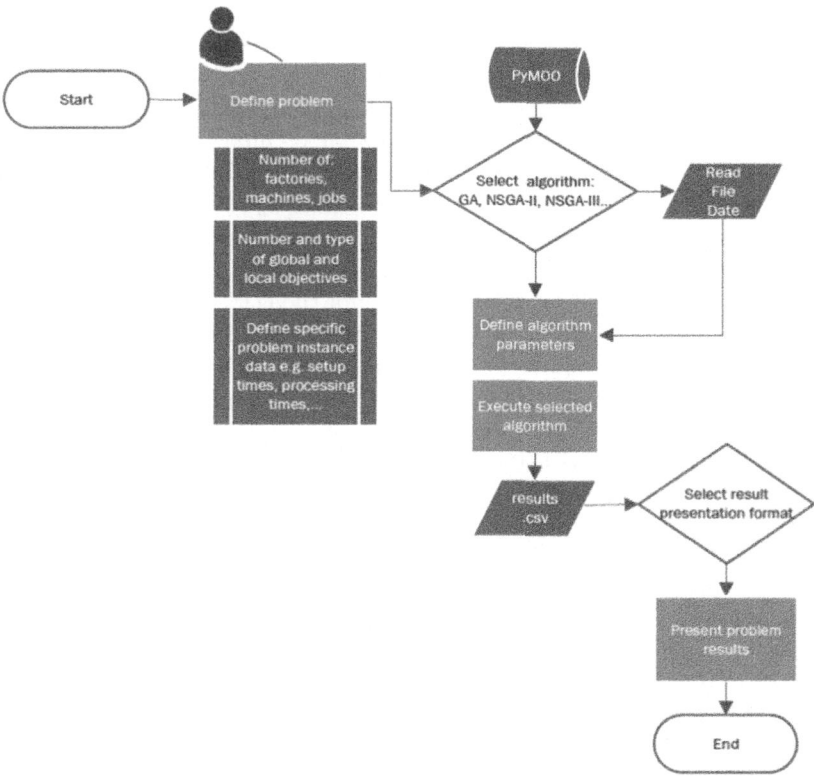

Fig. 1. Diagram of the implemented system for solving DJSS problems.

2.2   Global and Local Objectives Formulation

In DJSS problems, machines are distributed across multiple factories located in different geographic locations. This adds an extra layer of complexity to the problems, differing from traditional JSS problems in that factors such as transportation times of raw materials between factories, as well as processing and setup times for jobs on machines of each factories must be considered. Each factory is considered autonomous and capable of performing any job. Therefore, in order to formulate the optimization problem with global and local objectives, the user must indicate all information to describe the distributed manufacturing system.

First, the following sets must be defined by the user in order to characterize the DJSS problem:

- $\mathbb{N}$ is the set of N jobs, i.e., $\mathbb{N} = \{n_1, n_2, n_3, ... n_N\}$;
- $\mathbb{F}$ is the set of F factories, i.e. $\mathbb{F} = \{f_1, f_2, f_3, ... f_F\}$;
- $\mathbb{M}_u$ of M_u is the set of of machines for each factory $u \in \mathbb{F}$, i.e. $\mathbb{M}_1 = \{m_{1,1}, ..., m_{1,M_1}\}, \mathbb{M}_2 = \{m_{2,1}, ..., m_{2,M_2}\}, ..., \mathbb{M}_F = \{m_{F,1}, ..., m_{1,M_F}\}$.

The following assumptions are considered: for each factory u, each machine M_u can only execute one job N at each instant; all machines are always available; there is no precedence in the N jobs, each of them being independent; all jobs are available to be executed at the initial moment; and, no preemption is allowed, i.e., the processing of a job in a machine cannot be interrupted.

The following data must defined by the user: processing times $p_{u,i,j}$ for each machine i on factory u, and each job j; setup times $s_{u,i,j,k}$ for each machine i on factory u, to process job j after job k; and, transportation times $t_{u,j}$ to transport job j to factory u.

The following nomenclature and notation for the DJSS problem is considered: π is the feasible sequence of all jobs assigned to machines in each factory, i.e., the vector of all feasible subsequences $\pi_{u,i}$ on each machine $i \in \mathbb{M}_u$ of factory $u \in \mathbb{F}$; and $c_{u,i}(\pi)$ is the total completion time of jobs on machine $i \in \mathbb{M}_u$ of factory $u \in \mathbb{F}$ for the feasible sequence π. So, the goal in a DJSS optimization problem is to determine a feasible sequence of jobs on each machine in the different factories, in order to simultaneously minimize one or more objectives or criteria.

Therefore, after indicating all parameters of the DJSS problem, it is required to formulate objectives, such as minimizing the maximum completion time (makespan), minimizing the average completion times, minimizing the standard deviations of completion times, minimizing the total delay, minimizing the average delay, among others. In general, these objectives are formulated aiming to optimize the overall efficiency and performance of the distributed system, i.e., they can be regarded as global objectives across all factories. In [11], the makespan and the average completion time of the jobs were considered as objectives in a global perspective. However, local objectives for factories can be different due to its heterogeneity in distributed production systems. Thus, it is crucial to formulate objectives that considers these two perspectives and allow to find solutions that efficiently balance local and global requirements.

The following nomenclature is adopted to facilitate the formulation of objectives that considers both global and local objectives of the DJSS problems: C_G^L represents an objective in which G is the global objective and L is the local objective of completion times. Several different functions can be defined for G and L. In this work, $G, L \in \{\max, \mu, \sigma\}$ where max, μ and σ are the maximum, average and standard deviation functions, respectively. For instance, in [11], the objectives considered were minimizing the maximum completion time (makespan), and minimizing the average completion times, i.e., $\min C_{\max}^{\max}(\pi) = c_{\max}(\pi)$ and $\min C_\mu^\mu(\pi) = \bar{c}(\pi)$, respectively.

Let us start by defining objectives in which global and local objectives coincide. These objectives can be expressed by the following equations:

$$C_{\max}^{\max}(\pi) = c_{\max}(\pi) = \max_{u=1,...,F}\left(\max_{i=1,...,M_u}(c_{u,i}(\pi))\right) \tag{1}$$

$$C_\mu^\mu(\pi) = \bar{c}(\pi) = \sum_{u=1}^{F} \frac{1}{M_u} \sum_{i=1}^{M_u} c_{u,i}(\pi) \tag{2}$$

$$C_\sigma^\sigma(\pi) = c_\sigma(\pi) = \sqrt{\frac{\sum_{u=1}^{F} \sum_{i=1}^{M_u} (c_{u,i}(\pi) - \bar{c}_u(\pi))^2}{\sum_{u=1}^{F} M_u}} \tag{3}$$

for the maximum completion time (makespan), the average completion time, and the standard deviation completion time, respectively. It should be noted that in each of these equations the global and local objectives are the same.

Let us now consider situations in which global and local objectives are different. Several combinations of global and local can be defined. For instance, the following objective combines the makespan as global objective with the average completion time as local objective for factories:

$$C_{\max}^\mu(\pi) = \max_{u=1,\dots,F} \left(\frac{1}{M_u} \sum_{i=1}^{M_u} c_{u,i}(\pi) \right) \tag{4}$$

On the other hand, the following objective combines the makespan as global objective with the standard deviation of the completion time as local objective for factories:

$$C_{\max}^\sigma(\pi) = \max_{u=1,\dots,F} (\sigma_u(\pi)) = \max_{u=1,\dots,F} \left(\sqrt{\frac{\sum_{i=1}^{M_u} (c_{u,i}(\pi) - \bar{c}_u(\pi))^2}{M_u}} \right) \tag{5}$$

Other combinations of global and local objectives can be defined. In the above examples, the local objectives are equal for all factories. However, it should be noted that a different local objective for each factory could be defined. Different combinations of these objectives result in different single objective or multi-objective DJSS problems.

3   Experimental Results

3.1   Implementation Details

In this paper, some DJSS problem instances were taken from a previous work [11] in order to study the effect of global and local objectives. The instances are P_1, P_2 and P_3, and their characteristics are summarized below:

- P_1 - instance with 2 factories, both with 2 machines, and 6 jobs ($F = 2$, $M_1 = 2$, $M_2 = 2$, and $N = 6$);
- P_2 - instance with 2 factories, one with 2 machines and the other with 4 machines, and 11 jobs ($F = 2$, $M_1 = 2$, $M_2 = 4$, and $N = 11$);
- P_3 - instance with 3 factories, two of them with 2 machines and the other with 4 machines, and 11 jobs ($F = 3$, $M_1 = 2$, $M_2 = 2$, $M_3 = 4$, and $N = 11$).

The following four bi-objective DJSS problems were considered for instances P_1, P_2 and P_3:

$$\min \mathbf{F_1}(\pi) = \left(C_{\max}^{\max}(\pi), C_\mu^\mu(\pi)\right)^T \tag{6}$$

$$\min \mathbf{F_2}(\pi) = (C_{\max}^{\max}(\pi), C_{\max}^\mu(\pi))^T \tag{7}$$

$$\min \mathbf{F_3}(\pi) = (C_{\max}^{\max}(\pi), C_\sigma^\sigma(\pi))^T \tag{8}$$

$$\min \mathbf{F_4}(\pi) = (C_{\max}^{\max}(\pi), C_{\max}^\sigma(\pi))^T \tag{9}$$

where π is a feasible sequence belonging to the feasible set Ω (the set of all possible permutations) and $\mathbf{F_1}(\pi)$, $\mathbf{F_2}(\pi)$, $\mathbf{F_3}(\pi)$, and $\mathbf{F_4}(\pi)$ are the vectors of objective functions defined in the objective space for each problem.

As in [11], NSGA-III was selected from PyMOO [2] framework to solve all DJSS problems. The population size was 100 chromosomes. The feasible sequence of jobs on the machines in different factories, i.e. the π sequence, is represented by a chromosome as a permutation of size $N + \sum_{u=1}^{F} M_u - 1$. Positions in the chromosome with genes larger than N divide the chromosome into subsequences ($\pi_{u,i}$) representing the set of jobs and the corresponding order assigned to each machine $i \in \mathbb{M}_u$ in the factory $u \in \mathbb{F}$. The genetic operators used were similar to the ones used in [11], i.e., binary tournament selection operator to select chromosomes for reproduction, and the order-based crossover and the inversion mutation to generate offspring from parents. All genetic operators guarantee the feasibility of all solutions during the search. The stopping criteria was the same used in [11], i.e., a maximum number of generations of 10,000 and a period at 100 generations for testing the nonexistence of improvement in the search. Due to stochasticity of the NSGA-III, 20 independent runs were performed.

3.2   Results for F_1 and F_2 Problems

In this section, the results for instances P_1, P_2, and P_3 for F_1 and F_2 problems are presented and discussed. In these problems, one of the objectives correspond to the minimization of the makespan both globally and locally ($C_{\max}^{\max}$). The other objective is the minimization of the average completion time globally and locally (problem F_1) or the makespan globally and the average completion time locally (problem F_2). Figure 2, Fig. 3, and Fig. 4 show the approximations to the Pareto optimal frontier for P_1, P_2, and P_3 instances, respectively. In all these figures, the X-axis corresponds to $C_{\max}^{\max}$ objective and the Y-axis indicates the values of C_μ^μ and $C_{\max}^\mu$ objectives. All these figures also includes two pay-off tables indicating the values of the objectives for each solution for F_1 and F_2 problems. The table closest to the top right corner of the graph is the pay-off table for problem F_1 (the other is for problem F_2). The best approximations to the Pareto optimal set obtained by NSGA-III are presented. So, the solutions obtained in the run with the highest hypervolume (i.e., the best approximation to the Pareto optimal set) among the 20 independent runs are shown.

Instance P_1 In Fig. 2, the approximations to the Pareto optimal frontier for F_1 and F_2 problems for instance P_1 are represented. In this instance, for the objectives of F_1 problem, three different non-dominated solutions (solutions A, B, and C) were obtained. For the objectives of F_2 problem, four non-dominated solutions were obtained (solutions D, E, F and G). When comparing these two sets of solutions as a whole, it can be said that solutions D to G are dominated by solutions A to C.

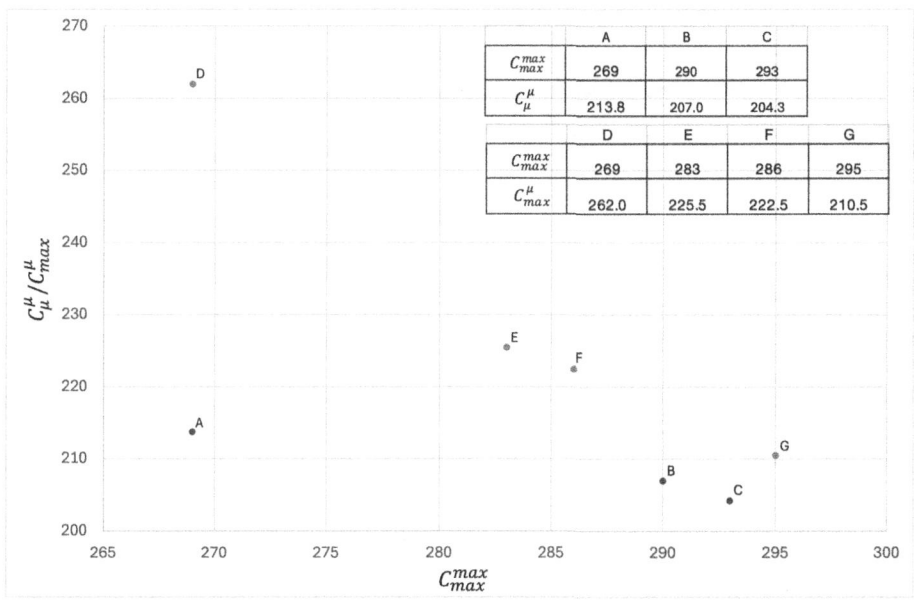

Fig. 2. Representation of the Pareto optimal frontier approximation for F_1 and F_2 problems for instance P_1.

It is worth analyzing with more detail solutions A and D since they have the same value of $C_{\max}^{\max}$. However, solution A results of prioritizing the global goal of reducing the overall average of completion times in all the manufacturing system, while solution B aims to locally reduce this value in each factory. Let us inspect the sequences of jobs assigned to each machine of each factory. Since this instance has two factories ($F = 2$), each one with two machines ($M_1 = M_2 = 2$), this sequence can be expressed as $\pi = \langle < \pi_{1,1}, \pi_{1,2} >, < \pi_{2,1}, \pi_{2,2} > \rangle$. So, solution A and solution D correspond to the following sequences of jobs, completion times, and objective values:

- Solution A: $\pi^A = \langle < [4,1], [2,6] >, < [3], [5] > \rangle$ with total completion times of $c_{1,1}(\pi^A) = 255$, $c_{1,2}(\pi^A) = 269$, $c_{2,1}(\pi^A) = 205$ and $c_{2,2}(\pi^A) = 126$, and therefore $C_{\max}^{\max}(\pi^A) = 269$, and $C_\mu^\mu(\pi^A) = 213.75$;

– Solution D: $\pi^D = \langle < [4,1], [2,6] >, < [5], [3] > \rangle$ with total completion times
are $c_{1,1}(\pi^D) = 255$, $c_{1,2}(\pi^D) = 269$, $c_{2,1}(\pi^D) = 185$ and $c_{2,2}(\pi^D) = 174$, with
$C_{\max}^{\max}(\pi^D) = 269$, and $C_{\max}^{\mu}(\pi^D) = 262$.

Solutions A and D are very similar, differing just in the assignment of jobs
in the machines of factory 2. When these solutions are evaluated in terms the
other objectives, solution A has $C_{\max}^{\mu}(\pi^A) = 262$ and solution D has $C_{\mu}^{\mu}(\pi^D) = 220.75$. Thus, solution D is dominated by solution A in a global perspective
since $C_{\mu}^{\mu}(\pi^A) < C_{\mu}^{\mu}(\pi^D)$. The opposite can not be stated, i.e., solution D does
not dominate solution A locally due to $C_{\max}^{\mu}(\pi^A) = C_{\max}^{\mu}(\pi^D)$.

Instance P_2. Figure 3 shows the approximations to the Pareto optimal frontier
for F_1 and F_2 problems for instance P_2. Solutions A to D are the non-dominated
solutions for problem F_1. Solutions E to G are the non-dominated solutions
obtained for problem F_2. Taking into account the comparison of these two sets
of solutions as a whole, t can be said that solutions F and G are dominated by
solution A. However, solution E is not dominated by any other.

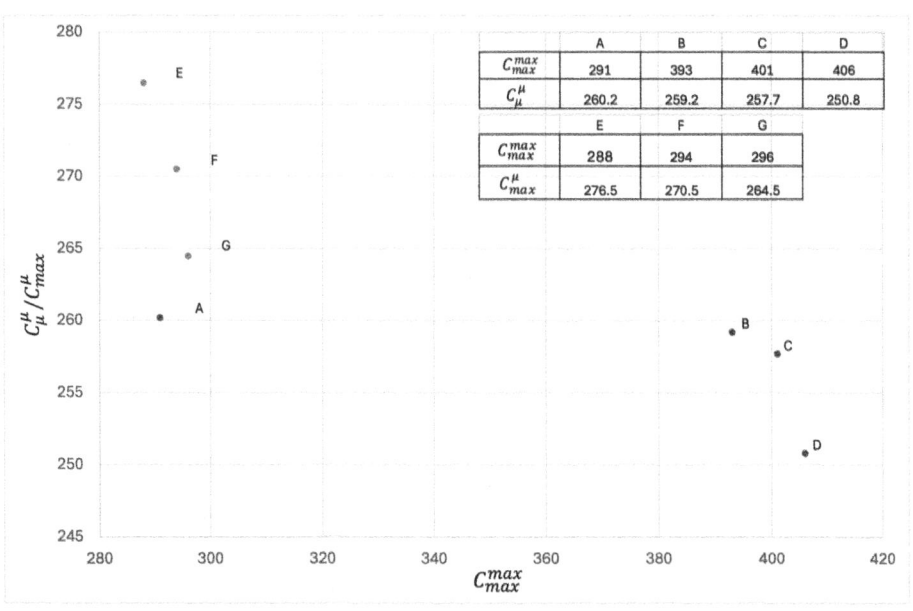

Fig. 3. Representation of the Pareto optimal frontier approximation for F_1 and F_2
problems for instance P_2.

Solution E is the solution with lower value of $C_{\max}^{\max}$ (even inferior to the
one of solution A). It is interesting to inspect the scheduling plans defined the
sequences of these two solutions. This instance P_2 has two factories ($F = 2$), one
with two machines ($M_1 = 2$) and the other with four machines ($M_2 = 4$), this
sequence can be expressed as $\pi = \langle < \pi_{1,1}, \pi_{1,2} >, < \pi_{2,1}, \pi_{2,2}, \pi_{2,3}, \pi_{2,4} > \rangle$:

- Solution A: $\pi^A = \langle < [4,8], [7,10] >, < [1], [3,2], [11,9], [5,6] > \rangle$;
- Solution E: $\pi^E = \langle < [4,5], [7,10] >, < [8,1], [2], [11,9], [3,6] > \rangle$.

As expected, it can be observed that there exist some similarities between the two solutions. On the other hand, it is worth emphasizing that, in this case, using a local perspective allows to obtain a solution that is better in terms of C_{max}^{max}.

Instance P_3. Figure 4 shows the approximations to the Pareto optimal frontier for F_1 and F_2 problems for instance P_3. Solutions A to D and solutions E to H are the non-dominated solutions for F_1 and F_2 problems, respectively.

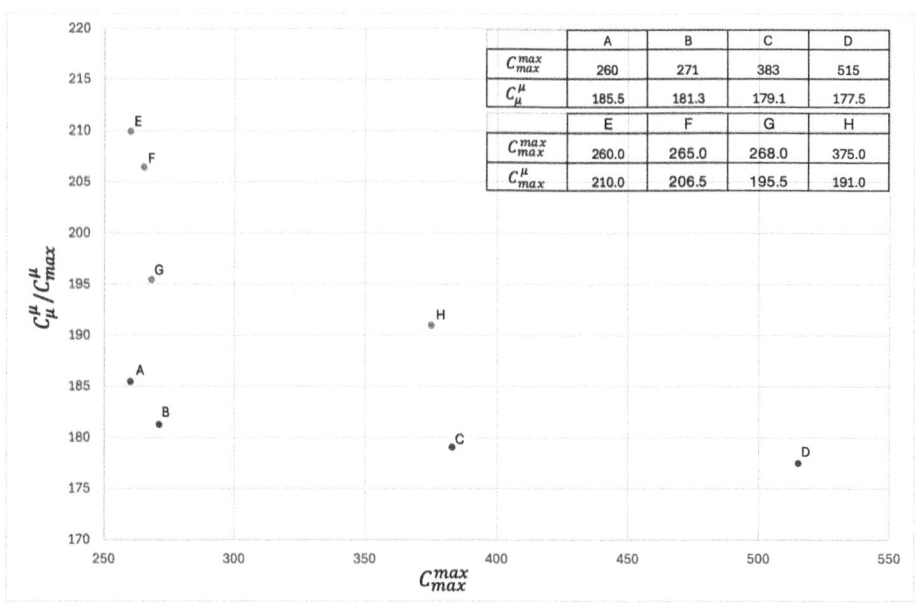

	A	B	C	D
C_{max}^{max}	260	271	383	515
C_μ^μ	185.5	181.3	179.1	177.5
	E	F	G	H
C_{max}^{max}	260.0	265.0	268.0	375.0
C_{max}^μ	210.0	206.5	195.5	191.0

Fig. 4. Representation of the Pareto optimal frontier approximation for F_1 and F_2 problems for instance P_3.

When comparing the two sets of solutions, it can be seen that solutions of F_1 problem dominate solutions of F_2 problem. Nevertheless, it is worth analyzing solutions A and E since they have the same value of C_{max}^{max}. For instance P_3, the sequences of jobs assigned to each machine of each factory can be expressed as $\pi = \langle < \pi_{1,1}, \pi_{1,2} >, < \pi_{2,1}, \pi_{2,2} >, < \pi_{3,1}, \pi_{3,2}, \pi_{3,3}, \pi_{3,4} > \rangle$:

- Solution A: $\pi^A = \langle < [7,2], [8] >, < [1,6], [9] >, < [3], [5,4], [10], [11] > \rangle$;
- Solution E: $\pi^E = \langle < [7,3], [1] >, < [9,11], [2] >, < [6], [5,4], [8], [10] > \rangle$.

These two solutions does not have any subsequences in common, except for the second machine of the third factory. In a global perspective, solution A seems to be preferable.

3.3   Results for F_3 and F_4 Problems

The results for instances P_1, P_2, and P_3 for F_3 and F_4 problems are presented and discussed in this section. Like in F_1 and F_2 problems, one of the objectives is the minimization of the makespan both globally and locally (C_{max}^{max}). However, the other objective is the minimization of the standard deviation of the completion time both globally and locally (problem F_3) or the makespan globally and the standard deviation of the completion time locally (problem F_4). Figure 5, Fig. 6, and Fig. 7 depict the approximations to the Pareto optimal frontier for P_1, P_2, and P_3 instances, respectively. As before, in all these figures, the X-axis corresponds to C_{max}^{max} objective, but now the Y-axis indicates the values of C_σ^σ and C_{max}^σ objectives. In each figure, the two pay-off tables indicate the values of the objectives for each solution for F_3 and F_4 problems. The approximations to the Pareto optimal set obtained by NSGA-III with highest hypervolume among the 20 independent runs are presented.

Instance P_1. Figure 5 shows the approximations to the Pareto optimal frontier for F_3 and F_4 problems for instance P_1. There are two non-dominated solutions for problem F_3 (solutions A and B). Solutions C to F are the non-dominated solutions for problem F_4. The solutions with the smallest values of C_{max}^{max} are solutions C and A. However, globally, the set of solutions A and B are dominated by the set of solutions C to F. It should be noted that the maximum standard deviation of the completion times is zero. This means that the load associated to the jobs is balanced between machines in the two factories. Overall, in this instance, it can be observed that local prioritization allowed to achieve solutions the correspond to better balance of loadings between machines in each factory.

Instance P_2. In Fig. 6, the approximations to the Pareto optimal frontier for F_3 and F_4 problems for instance P_2 are shown. Four non-dominated solutions were found for problem F_3. For problem F_4, two solutions were obtained. These two solutions have extrema values of C_{max}^{max}. When the two sets of solutions for F_3 and F_4 problems are compared, it can be seen that they are incomparable each other. So, neither set dominates the other. Overall, in this instance, solution E has the lowest makespan. Conversely, solution F has the worst makespan, but the best workload balance.

Instance P_3. The approximations to the Pareto optimal frontier for F_3 and F_4 problems for instance P_3 are represented on Fig. 7. For problem $F3$, a single solution was found (solution A). This means that the two objectives of problem F_3 are not conflicting in this instance. Nevertheless, for problem F_4, this conflict exist since four solutions (solutions B to E) were achieved. Solutions A and B have the same makespan value, but first one seems to be preferable in terms workload balance. Solutions D and E have large makespan values when compared with the remaining ones.

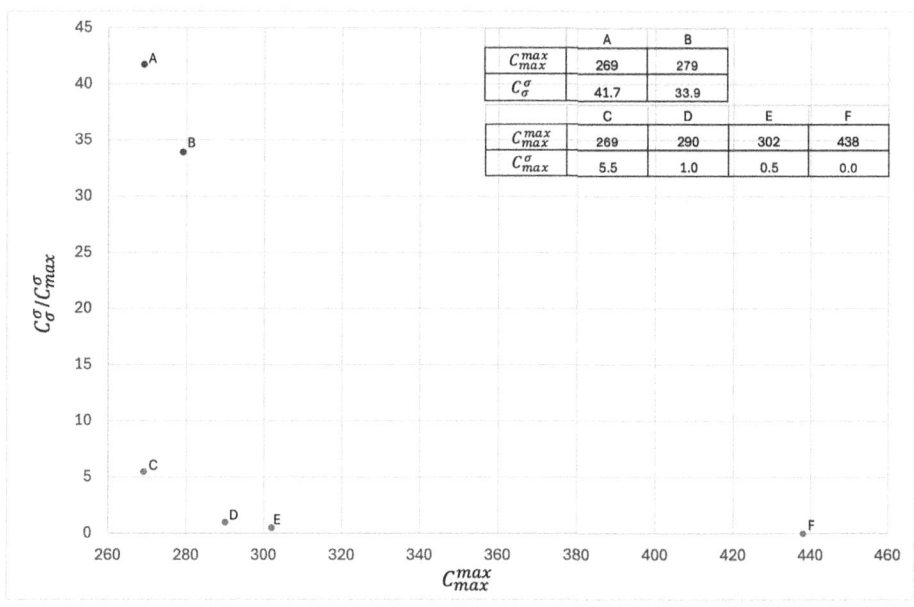

Fig. 5. Representation of the Pareto optimal frontier approximation for F_3 and F_4 problems for instance P_1.

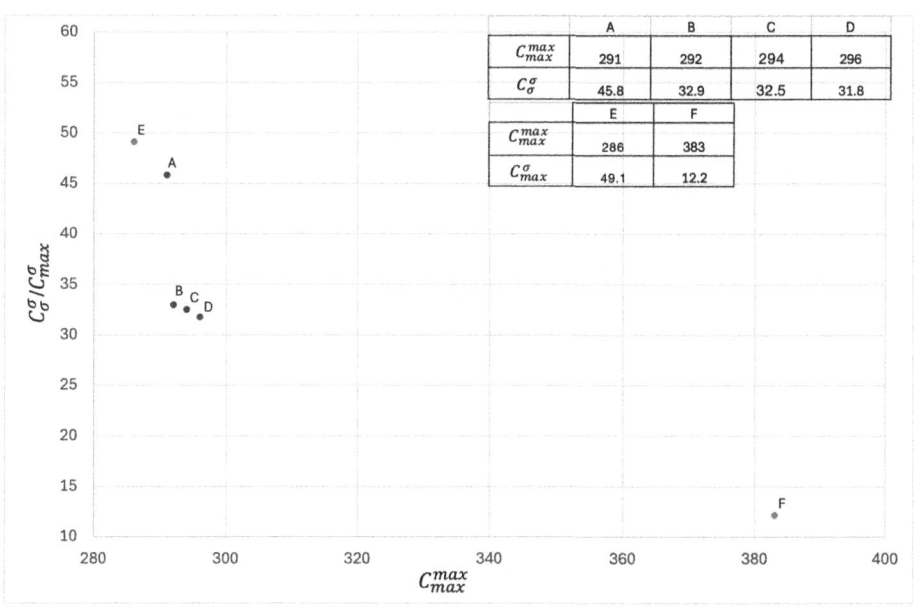

Fig. 6. Representation of the Pareto optimal frontier approximation for F_3 and F_4 problems for instance P_2.

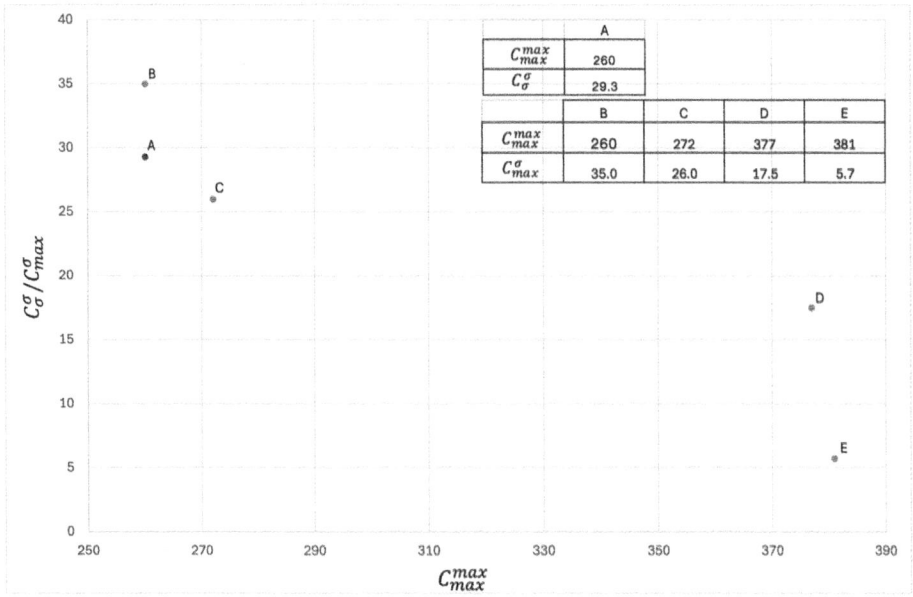

Fig. 7. Representation of the Pareto optimal frontier approximation for F_3 and F_4 problems for instance P_3.

4 Conclusions and Future Work

In this paper, a DJSS framework is proposed to tackle DJSS problems. In particular, the effect of global and local objectives in DJSS problems is studied. Several optimization objectives are formulated and proposed to reflect global and/or local goals related with the distributed manufacturing systems. Some DJSS instances (borrowed from [11]) with unrelated parallel machines and sequence-dependent setup times were solved using NSGA-III to test and analyze how the objectives affect the solutions obtained for the distributed manufacturing system. For this purpose, various combinations of global and local objectives were considered, namely related with makespan, average completion times and standard deviation of the completion times.

The preliminary results indicate that this approach can be useful for decision-making since combines global and local goals, i.e., takes into account simultaneously a global perspective of the organization as a whole system and the particular priorities of the factories. As shown by the results, the solutions have meaning and represent different alternatives that can not be assessed by the decision-maker if just global objectives were formulated.

Moreover, it is clear that the decision-making process is facilitated and may involve both global and local decision-makers. They can analyze trade-offs both in terms of global and local objectives and the scheduling plans they represent.

Future work will include formulating more objectives expressing other priorities both global and local, involving local decision-makers in the process, applying this framework to other instances of DJSS problems, and investigating the use of bi-level approaches for DJSS problems.

References

1. Abdelmaguid, T.F.: Representations in genetic algorithm for the job shop scheduling problem: a computational study. J. Softw. Eng. Appl. **3**(12), 1155 (2010)
2. Blank, J., Deb, K.: Pymoo: multi-objective optimization in Python. IEEE Access **8**, 89497–89509 (2020)
3. Chan, F.T., Chung, S.H., Chan, L., Finke, G., Tiwari, M.: Solving distributed FMS scheduling problems subject to maintenance: Genetic algorithms approach. Robot. Comput.-Integr. Manufact. **22**(5–6), 493–504 (2006)
4. Deb, K., Jain, H.: An evolutionary many-objective optimization algorithm using reference-point-based nondominated sorting approach, part i: Solving problems with box constraints. IEEE Trans. Evol. Comput. **18**(4), 577–601 (2014)
5. Deb, K., Pratap, A., Agarwal, S., Meyarivan, T.: A fast and elitist multiobjective genetic algorithm: NSGA-II. IEEE Trans. Evol. Comput. **6**(2), 182–197 (2002)
6. Fu, Y., Hou, Y., Wang, Z., Wu, X., Gao, K., Wang, L.: Distributed scheduling problems in intelligent manufacturing systems. Tsinghua Sci. Technol. **26**(5), 625–645 (2021). 10.26599/TST.2021.9010009
7. González-Neira, E.M., Urrego-Torres, A.M., Cruz-Riveros, A.M., Henao-García, C., Montoya-Torres, J.R., Molina-Sánchez, L.P., Jimenez, J.F.: Robust solutions in multi-objective stochastic permutation flow shop problem. Comput. Indust. Eng. **137**, 106026 (2019)
8. Lohmer, J., Lasch, R.: Production planning and scheduling in multi-factory production networks: a systematic literature review. Int. J. Prod. Res. **59**(7), 2028–2054 (2021)
9. Ruiz, R., Allahverdi, A.: Minimizing the bicriteria of makespan and maximum tardiness with an upper bound on maximum tardiness. Comput. Oper. Res. **36**(4), 1268–1283 (2009)
10. dos Santos, F., Costa, L., Varela, L.: Multi-objective optimization of the job shop scheduling problem on unrelated parallel machines with sequence-dependent setup times. In: International Conference on Computational Science and its Applications, pp. 495–507. Springer (2023)
11. dos Santos, F., Costa, L., Varela, L.: A multi-objective approach for solving distributed job shop scheduling problems. In: International Conference on Optimization, Learning Algorithms and Applications, pp. 326–339. Springer (2024)
12. dos Santos, F., Costa, L.A., Varela, L.: A systematic literature review about multi-objective optimization for distributed manufacturing scheduling in the industry 4.0. In: Computational Science and Its Applications–ICCSA 2022 Workshops: Malaga, Spain, July 4–7, 2022, Proceedings, Part II, pp. 157–173. Springer (2022)
13. dos Santos, F., Costa, L.A., Varela, L.: Multiobjective optimization in distributed industry and environmental sustainability: a systematic literature review. Revista Angolana de Ciências **5**(2), e050210 (Abr 2024)
14. dos Santos, F., Costa, L.A., Varela, L.: Performance comparison of NSGA-II and NSGA-III on bi-objective job shop scheduling problems. In: International Conference on Optimization, Learning Algorithms and Applications, pp. 531–543. Springer (2024)
15. Yenisey, M.M., Yagmahan, B.: Multi-objective permutation flow shop scheduling problem: literature review, classification and current trends. Omega **45**, 119–135 (2014)

Relationship Between Operational, Economic, and Financial Efficiencies and User Satisfaction at the Health Centers of Praia City

Helder Correia[1], Jorge Alves[2] ⓘ, and Clara B. Vaz[3](✉) ⓘ

[1] Instituto Politécnico de Bragança, 5300-253 Bragança, Portugal
heldercorreia.enf@gmail.com
[2] UNIAG, Instituto Politécnico de Bragança, 5300-253 Bragança, Portugal
jorge@ipb.pt
[3] CeDRI, SusTEC, Instituto Politécnico de Bragança, 5300-253 Bragança, Portugal
clvaz@ipb.pt

Abstract. This study aims to contribute to a better understanding of the current state of Primary Health Care, specifically in terms of efficiency and user satisfaction at 8 Health Centers in Praia City, Cape Verde, observed in 2017, 2018, 2020 and 2021. The Data Envelopment Analysis (DEA) model with input orientation and Constant Returns of Scale (CRS) is used to measure operational efficiency, and the income to expenditure ratio is used to measure economic and financial efficiency. User satisfaction is assessed using a questionnaire survey involving 408 respondents. The results indicate that 8 Decision-Making Units (DMUs) are operationally efficient. Regarding economic and financial efficiency, the ratios observed were generally higher than 1 in the different Health Centers analyzed. The satisfaction results show that most users are satisfied with the organization and services provided by the Health Centers. However, some improvements are needed in all the categories evaluated. A positive association between operational efficiency and the economic and financial efficiency ratio stands out as a result of comparing the different types of efficiency. Operational efficiency shows a negative relationship with the dimensions of satisfaction related to organization, service process, medical and nursing services, but this relationship is only statistically significant for the service process.

Keywords: Efficiency · DEA · Primary Health Care · Survey · Satisfaction

1 Introduction

When analyzing the health sector from an economic and operational perspectives, all the decisions made by managers or agents linked to the sector must be considered. It is relevant to study the health sector because of its growing importance in developed economies and because it deals with human lives [1]. It is a sector with high expenditure, and the percentage of the budget of the Ministry of Health of Cape Verde for 2021 was 10,93%, representing an increase of 2,22% compared to 2020. For example, the Health Authority of Praia City, responsible for managing the Health Centers, recorded 65.788.582,00 escudos as expenditure in 2021 [2]. For these and other reasons, it is essential to analyze whether the health system produces efficiently or wastes resources. Efficiency is the relationship between what has been produced and what could be produced using the same available resources, i.e., maximizing the relationship between inputs and outputs. Following this line of reasoning, an organization is considered efficient when it obtains a certain level of results with a considerable degree of quality, using a minimum combination of resources [3–5]. Similarly, the organization's efficiency can be closely linked to its productivity since its definition involves inputs and outputs [6].

Many studies have analyzed hospital efficiency, although the various stakeholders have not prioritized the efficiency of Health Centers. In Portugal, there are few studies evaluating efficiency in Health Centers. As far as we know, there is no record of such studies in Cape Verde.

Efficiency can be categorized as economic, allocative and technical. Based on the seminal definitions of Farrel [7], technical efficiency consists of producing the maximum amount of output from a given amount of input (output-orientation) or, conversely, producing a given output with a minimum amount of input (input-orientation) so that when a company is technically efficient, it operates on its production frontier. Economic efficiency is seen in Farrel's [7] perspective as being a broader efficiency, and for an organization to be classified as economically efficient, it must meet three fundamental criteria: maximize profit, minimize costs, and maximize customer satisfaction with the organization's products or services.

For this study, the Data Envelopment Analysis (DEA) technique is used, which has a non-parametric nature that does not require the definition of a functional form in the relationship between inputs and outputs, relating these variables through the comparative measurement of the efficiency of Decision-Making Units (DMUs) using the best practices units as a reference. Therefore, DEA enables the assessment of the relative efficiency of production units using multiple inputs and outputs, mediated by the definition of an empirical production function defined as the efficiency frontier [3, 4, 8, 9]. The DEA model, initially introduced by Charnes et al. [10], allows each unit to be evaluated against constant returns to scale (CRS) frontier, which means that for each change in the value of inputs in a DMU, there will be an equal change in outputs. The model introduced by Banker et al. [11] has variable returns to scale (VRS), which makes it possible to accommodate different sizes of DMU. This means that a unit is evaluated against a frontier with variable returns to scale, distinguishing between technical and scale efficiency.

Another critical issue in assessing the performance of health centers involves knowing user satisfaction, which is seen as a fundamental aspect of any health unit, leading to quality care [12]. The National Health Service (SNS) Health Centers serve as the primary entry point for users into the system. Chaves et al. [12] show that the concept of satisfaction extends beyond a simple feeling of liking or disliking. In healthcare, it relates to various factors, particularly users' past experiences with health services, and is reflected in their overall well-being.

Assessing user satisfaction in the health sector is different and unique from other sectors, as it requires a more targeted approach to users and the professionals who provide care, as measuring user satisfaction is complex. This complexity is justified because health services deal directly with human lives, and users often find it challenging to understand the complexity of the technologies used to provide care [13]. A widely used way of measuring satisfaction beyond the questionnaire is by analyzing user complaints, which most health systems consider to be a good direct indicator of user satisfaction.

In addition to this introduction, which describes the main concepts, this paper is organized into three more sections. The following section presents the methodology used in this research, such as the selection of the DMUs and variables to be used, the DEA models, and the selection of the study samples. Afterwards, the analysis of the results is presented, starting with a general analysis and then addressing the more specific issues with the results obtained from the two models used to analyze efficiency and assessment satisfaction. This section also presents the results of comparing the efficiency assessment with those obtained from the satisfaction evaluation. The last section presents the main conclusions, suggestions, and recommendations for future developments.

2   Methodology, Data Collection and Sample

This study uses the DEA technique to assess the operational efficiency of Health Centers in Praia City, Cape Verde. In addition, users' satisfaction with the different Health Centers will be assessed and compared with their operational and economic performance. The data of Health Centers were preprocessed in Excel, and RStudio version 4.4.1 was used to run the DEA models to assess the operational efficiency of the Health Centers.

The DEA technique enables efficiency measurement by identifying the Health Centers that serve as benchmarks and should be models for inefficient Health Centers. Another important advantage of the DEA is that it can work simultaneously with multiple inputs and outputs. Furthermore, another advantage of the DEA is that it allows a group of benchmarks to be identified for each inefficient DMU that corresponds to a group of units with best practices [14].

The most appropriate model should be determined by the characteristics of the process of transforming inputs into outputs of the DMUs. Thus, for this study, we used two models, the Charnes, Cooper and Rhodes (CCR) model [10] and the Banker, Charnes and Cooper (BCC) model [11], since the Health Centers, which are the DMUs, have different dimensions related to the regional dimension, as can be seen from the distribution of the population, among other characteristics [15].The input orientation model is best suited to this study, as managers can control the resources which are limited. As emphasized by Dyson et al. [14], the choice of model orientation depends on managers' ability to control resources and the production process. Since the input orientation allows managers to have greater control over resources, emphasis is placed on reducing inputs for a given level of services provided, aiming to increase efficiency [16].

This study intends to evaluate the operational and economic efficiency of the Health Centers in Praia City for the years 2017, 2018, 2020 and 2021. These data were obtained from the Health Authority of Praia City between January and March 2024. The data for 2019 was not published, according to the Health Authority, due to the COVID-19 pandemic. As a result, it was only possible to work in the four years mentioned. Thus, the annual activity reports and the financial data of the Health Authority were used. The Health Authority of Praia City manages the Health Centers located in Ponta d'Água

(PD), Fazenda (FZ), Achada Santo António (ASA), Achada Grande Trás (AGT), and Tira Chapéu (TC), owning their coverage area.

Based on the literature review, data availability and relevance to the research, three inputs were selected to assess the operational efficiency of Health Centers: number of doctors (N_MED), number of nurses (N_ENF), and number of beds (N_CM) and three outputs: number of outpatient appointments (C_EXT), number of general medical appointments (CCG) and number of nursing appointments and treatments (C_ENF_C). Total revenue was selected as the input and total expenditure as the output to assess economic and financial efficiency. The data can be seen in Table 1.

Table 1. Identification of variables (inputs and outputs)

Operational efficiency		Economic and financial efficiency	
Inputs	Outputs	Input	Output
No. of doctors No. of nurses No. of beds	No. of outpatient appointments No. of general medical appointments No. of nursing appointments and treatments	Total revenue	Total expenditure

The sample for the satisfaction assessment was calculated based on the data collected by the Health Authority for 2020, using data from the population of Praia City, which comprises all the users of the five Health Centers. According to the statistical procedure, a sample of 408 respondents was obtained and distributed proportionally among the five Health Centers. Thus, 89, 48, 119, 48, and 104 responses were collected from the TC, ASA, FZ, AGT, and PD centers, respectively. The questionnaire survey allows for measurement of satisfaction using a 5-point Likert scale, where users select a value from 1 to 5 based on their level of satisfaction, which 1 means 'very little', 2 'little', 3 'reasonable', 4 'good' and 5 'very good', with 6 used for situations that are not applicable.

3   Results

3.1   Data Analysis

Analyzing the descriptive statistics of the data on operational efficiency, there were no major changes in the first 3 years, either in terms of inputs or outputs, with the most significant change occurring from 2020 to 2021, where there were increases in both the input and output variables, as can be seen in Table 2.

The economic and financial efficiency analysis was carried out based on the ratio of revenue to expenditure, in which most of the Health Centers obtained a value greater than 1, indicating that their revenue is greater than their expenditure. In the first 2 years, the FZ Health Center had the highest ratio, and the PD Health Center had the lowest ratio. In the last two years, the TC Health Center had the highest ratio and the AGT Health Center had the lowest ratio, as shown in Table 3.

Table 2. Descriptive statistics for the indicators used to assess operational efficiency.

Inputs				Outputs		
Year 2017	N_MED	N_ENF	N_CM	C_EXT	CCG	C_ENF_C
Minimum	4	5	2	2398	9321	3758
Maximum	7	10	4	4791	19958	18317
Average	4,80	6,40	3,00	3732,40	13732,20	9582,40
Standard deviation	1,304	2,191	1,000	860,541	4446,772	5492,128
Year 2018						
Minimum	4	5	2	1788	6055	4982
Maximum	7	10	5	2801	19618	14917
Average	4,80	6,40	3,20	2248,20	13871,40	10781,60
Standard deviation	1,304	2,191	1,304	404,665	4936,059	4011,409
Year 2020						
Minimum	4	5	2	541	3630	3224
Maximum	6	12	5	3993	11321	13398
Average	4,60	8,00	3,20	1754,00	7523,20	7193,60
Standard deviation	0,894	2,550	1,304	1427,809	3515,932	4194,131
Year 2021						
Minimum	4	7	2	433	946	8450
Maximum	8	15	6	11858	15301	17078
Average	5,00	9,80	3,80	4583,40	8294,40	11801,80
Standard deviation	1,732	3,347	1,483	4567,616	5723,302	3447,640

As a first step, the efficiency of the DMUs was analyzed for each year, and the BCC and CCR models with input orientation were applied. As explained above, this analysis mainly seeks to construct an efficient frontier, which will comprise the DMUs with the best practices, where an efficiency score is assigned to each DMU, based on its distance from the frontier. With these results, the efficient and inefficient DMUs are identified, enabling the determination of the benchmarks for each inefficient Health Center and serving as models for the inefficient ones to reach the efficiency frontier. Table 4 shows the results of the operational efficiency analysis based on the CCR model and input orientation.

In general, analyzing the 5 Health Centers over the 4 years corresponding to the 20 DMUs, it was observed that 40% of the DMUs are operationally efficient based on the CCR model and input orientation. The average and standard deviation of the operational efficiency of each Health Center over the 4 years were also analyzed, followed by an analysis of all 5 Health Centers by year. The results indicate that 3 Health Centers were efficient in 2017 and 3 in 2018. In 2020, none of the 5 Centers were efficient, and in 2021, only 2 were efficient. These results can be seen in the Fig. 1.

Table 3. Economic and financial data for Health Centers of Praia City.

		TC	ASA	FZ	AGT	PD
2017	Revenue	6054821	7172372	4425375	5255737	3994442
	Expenditure	6023062	6872372	1593633	4432389	3994925
	Ratio	1,005	1,044	2,777	1,186	0,999
2018	Revenue	6054821	7172372	4425375	5255737	4425375
	Expenditure	6023062	6872372	1593633	4432389	4432389
	Ratio	1,005	1,044	2,777	1,186	0,998
2020	Revenue	5013062	5845515	7721887	4556719	4556719
	Expenditure	4764518	5772382	9285048	6092226	4764518
	Ratio	1,052	1,013	0,832	0,748	0,956
2021	Revenue	8274932	5845515	21295986	4556719	5573580
	Expenditure	5321250	5772382	22053795	6092226	5436795
	Ratio	1,555	1,013	0,966	0,748	1,025

Table 4. Results of operational efficiency with the CCR model.

DMU	2017	2018	2020	2021	Mean	Standard deviation
TC	100%	100%	89,98%	100%	97,50%	4,34%
ASA	96,95%	100%	67,58%	60,19%	81,18%	17,52%
FZ	100%	100%	61,50%	100%	90,38%	16,67%
AGT	97,31%	66,02%	45,00%	46,13%	63,62%	21,17%
PD	100%	86,12%	34,45%	69,10%	72,42%	24,50%
Mean	98,85%	90,43%	59,70%	75,08%		
Standard deviation	1,41%	13,34%	19,16%	21,62%		

Operational efficiency was also analyzed using the BCC model. However, the results show that almost all DMUs are efficient, which prevents the use of the BCC model. Thus, when comparing each DMU with similar units in terms of scale, almost all DMUs are efficient. The results of the DEA can be biased when the sample size is small [17]. In such cases, there is a trend for almost all DMUs to appear efficient, as a larger number of inputs and outputs reduces the discrimination of the efficiency score among the DMUs [14].

Based on the CCR model, we can compare the results between the variables of the efficient DMUs and the inefficient DMUs, as can be shown in the Fig. 2. The N_MED and N_ENF inputs have a higher average in the benchmarks than in the inefficient DMUs.

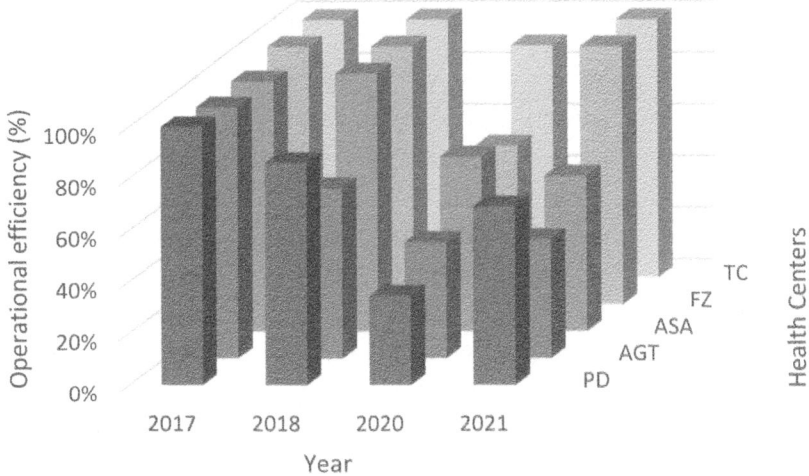

Fig. 1. Evolution of the efficiency of Health Centers over the 4 years.

In comparison, the N_CM input has a higher average in the inefficient DMUs than in the benchmarks. When analyzing the outputs, it can also be seen that the benchmark DMUs' averages are higher than those of the inefficient DMUs. These results show that inefficient units can readjust their capacity in terms of beds and possibly manage their human resources better to achieve a high level of service closer to that of efficient units.

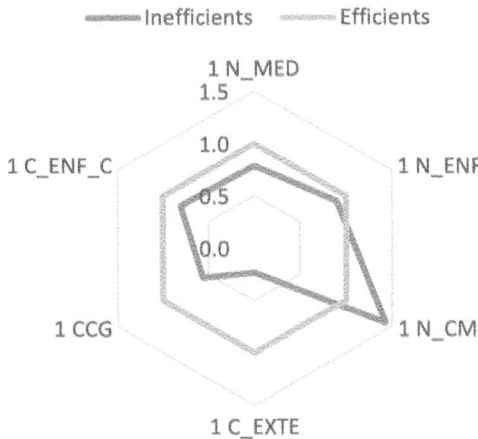

Fig. 2. Comparison of the average variables between efficient and inefficient DMUs.

The results of the evaluation of user satisfaction were based on 408 valid responses, which guarantees the necessary sample. Most respondents were female, representing 73% of 408 valid questionnaires. The predominant age was between 20 and 59 years old; 66% had a minimum of secondary school, and 94% had come to the Health Center for an appointment. These results can be seen in Table 5.

Regarding the satisfaction evaluation of the Health Centers, the following aspects were analyzed: the general organization of the centers, the service process at the Health Centers, the medical services provided at each of the centers, and the nursing services. Finally, a question was asked to assess the satisfaction concerning the general organization of the Health Centers from years 2017 to 2021. The result of Cronbach's alpha coefficient is 0,91, considering the items that assess the four dimensions of satisfaction (organization, service process, medical and nursing services). This value indicates excellent internal consistency among the variables in the scale [18].

The Kruskal-Wallis test is also used to assess the equality of median satisfaction levels across the five Health Centers, with respect to the four dimensions of service such as organization, service process, medical services and nursing services. Significant differences in satisfaction levels were observed among Health Centers for each service dimension (at the 0,01 level) shown in Table 6 and Table 7.

Regarding the users' evaluation of the general organization of health Centers, the average of the users' responses shows that almost all centers obtained an average above 4, which is good because most users are satisfied with this organization as shown in Table 6. On the question of satisfaction with the service process at the Health Centers, the ASA, FZ, AGT and PD Health Centers obtained an average above 3, as presented in Table 6, which means that users are not dissatisfied with the service process, but it needs to be improved.

When analyzing the minimum values, some users from TC, ASA, and FZ Health Centers rated the service process as very poor, which means that these users are dissatisfied with the service at these Centers. The TC Health Center, on the other hand, had the worst evaluation among the Health Centers.

According to the data presented in Table 7, it can be seen in the evaluation of user satisfaction with the medical services provided in each of the centers, that TC Health Center received the worst evaluation, with an average of 2,77, which shows that users are not satisfied, and a minimum of 1, which means that there is a group of users who are dissatisfied with this service. The other four Health Centers obtained an average above 3, which means that a good proportion of users are satisfied with the medical services. Lastly, evaluating user satisfaction with nursing services, the ASA, FZ, AGT, and PD Health Centers obtained an average above 3, showing that users are not dissatisfied but want improvements. However, when analyzing their minimum values, the TC Health Center had the worst evaluation since a group of users said they were dissatisfied with these services, owning an average of 2,77.

3.2 Results Discussion

When comparing the results, the TC Health Center was operationally efficient and had the highest economic efficiency ratio. It also had one of the best averages regarding user satisfaction with the organization. However, this center had the worst ratings in the other three dimensions: satisfaction with service, medical and nursing services. On the other hand, the AGT Health Center was the worst in terms of efficiency, as it has the lowest average in operational and economic efficiency. Its users are only satisfied

Table 5. Characterization of the sample.

Health Center		TC	ASA	FZ	AGT	PD	Total
Age	< 19 years old	2%	0%	7%	4%	5%	4%
	20 to 39 years old	29%	23%	39%	46%	39%	36%
	40 to 59 years old	63%	73%	52%	50%	55%	57%
	> 60 years old	6%	4%	2%	0%	1%	2%
Total		100%	100%	100%	100%	100%	100%
Gender	Male	40%	31%	23%	27%	20%	27%
	Female	60%	69%	77%	73%	80%	73%
Total		100%	100%	100%	100%	100%	100%
Education level	No qualifications	9%	6%	3%	8%	5%	6%
	Primary school	6%	15%	8%	23%	13%	12%
	Secondary school	67%	54%	75%	58%	64%	66%
	University	18%	25%	14%	10%	17%	17%
Total		100%	100%	100%	100%	100%	100%
Reason for visiting the Health Center	Urgency	3%	6%	3%	4%	0%	3%
	Appointment	96%	90%	92%	92%	98%	94%
	Treatment	1%	4%	6%	4%	1%	3%
	Other	0%	0%	0%	0%	1%	0%
	Total	100%	100%	100%	100%	100%	100%
Sample size		89	48	119	48	104	408

with how it is organized, as it was assessed as reasonable in the other dimensions. Therefore, responsible managers should better evaluate how their resources are allocated and utilized. In this way, they can improve operating practices compared to benchmarks and control costs, increasing the economic and financial efficiency ratio.

The users who frequent the Health Centers the most were female (72%). This percentage can be explained by women playing an essential role in the family and community [19].

When analyzing the overall satisfaction data of the Health Centers, in terms of organization and service, it can be said that the centers are doing a good job, as they record a good average in terms of the satisfaction of their users. Organizing services is essential when assessing their quality [20]. However, the service issue did not receive as good rating as the organization evaluation, given that most users consider that the Health Centers provide reasonable service, as the average for most Centers was above 3. According to Santos et al. [21], some fundamental aspects are often seen as barriers between users and Health Centers, leading to dissatisfaction. These include accessibility issues such as location, opening hours and other aspects that frequently cause users to miss appointments and subsequently give the Health Center a low rating.

Table 6. Satisfaction with the organization and service of the Health Center.

Satisfaction with the general organization of Health
Centers

Health Centers	TC	ASA	FZ	AGT	PD
Mean	4,13	4,03	3,91	4,15	4,18
Standard deviation	0,670	0,490	0,488	0,495	0,375
Maximum	5	5	5	5	5
Minimum	2	3	2	3	2

Satisfaction with the service process at Health Centers

Health Centers	TC	ASA	FZ	AGT	PD
Mean	2,91	3,35	3,31	3,61	3,41
Standard deviation	0,711	0,572	0,437	0,535	0,370
Maximum	4	5	4	4	4
Minimum	1	1	1	2	2

Table 7. Satisfaction with medical and nursing services.

Satisfaction with medical services

Health Centers	TC	ASA	FZ	AGT	PD
Mean	2,77	3,64	3,62	3,81	3,81
Standard deviation	0,584	0,654	0,510	0,580	0,341
Maximum	5	5	5	5	4
Minimum	1	2	2	2	3

Satisfaction with nursing services

Health Centers	TC	ASA	FZ	AGT	PD
Mean	2,77	3,60	3,42	3,24	3,28
Standard deviation	0,670	0,650	0,416	0,530	0,331
Maximum	5	5	5	4	4
Minimum	1	2	2	2	2

Users' satisfaction with the medical services was considered satisfactory, with an average score above 3. On the other hand, user satisfaction with the services provided by the nurses was lower, as most respondents rated the services as reasonable, with an average score slightly above 3. According to Santos et al. [21], health professionals are important in determining users' satisfaction with Health Centers.

Concerning the association between efficiency and satisfaction, Table 8 shows the Spearman correlation coefficients between operational efficiency, the economic and financial efficiency ratio, and the dimensions of satisfaction (organization, service process, medical services and nursing services).

According to the correlation analysis shown in Table 8, it can be seen that operational efficiency shows a strong (absolute score from 0,71 to 0,90 [22]) negative correlation [18] with user satisfaction regarding medical services and also with the Health Center's service process, implying that the more satisfied users are with medical care and services, the lower the average operational efficiency will be, and vice versa. However, this correlation is only statistically significant for satisfaction in the service process. There is also a positive correlation between operational efficiency and the economic and financial efficiency ratio, which shows that the more efficient the Health Center is at an operational level, the higher its economic and financial efficiency ratio will be and vice versa. However, this correlation is not statistically significant. It is also worth noting that there is a very strong (absolute score higher than 0,9 [22]), positive, and statistically significant correlation between user satisfaction with the Health Center's service process and the doctors' service. The Spearman correlation coefficients shown in Table 8 are based on the average of each satisfaction item, calculated from the average of the answers to the questions used to assess each item. Thus, there is only one observation for each Health Center, i.e. five observations.

Table 8. Spearman correlation test of variables.

Variables	EFOP	EFEC	SO	SA	SSM	SSE
EFOP	1,000	0,564	−0,410	−0,872*	−0,789	−0,154
EFEC		1,000	0,200	−0,600	−0,462	−0,300
SO			1,000	0,600	0,667	−0,500
SA				1,000	0,975**	0,100
SSM					1,000	0,154
SSE						1,000

Notes: 1) * The correlation is significant at the 0,1 level (two-sided). 2) ** The correlation is significant at the 0,01 level (two-sided). 3) Definition of variables: operational efficiency (EFOP), economic and financial efficiency (EFEC), satisfaction in the organization (SO), satisfaction in service process (SA), satisfaction in medical services (SSM), and satisfaction in nursing services (SSE)

4 Conclusion

This study evaluates the efficiency of the Health Centers in Praia City using the DEA technique, focusing on operational, economic and financial efficiency. In addition, users' satisfaction with the Health Centers in Praia City was evaluated. The DEA technique assessed the operational efficiency using the CCR model and input orientation.

The results obtained show that 8 out of the 20 DMUs are efficient. Therefore, the 8 efficient DMUs are considered the benchmarks, which should serve as a model for inefficient Health Centers to improve their practices. When comparing the results of the benchmarks with the other inefficient DMUs, it was found that the inputs N_MED and N_ENF have a higher average in the benchmarks than in the inefficient DMUs, and the input N_CM has a higher average in the inefficient DMUs than in the benchmarks. When analyzing the outputs, it can be noted that the averages of efficient DMUs are higher than those of inefficient DMUs. The conclusion that can be drawn is that inefficient units can benefit from adjusting their capacity in terms of beds and eventually improving personnel management to achieve a level of services closer to the level observed in efficient units.

The economic and financial efficiency was evaluated with a single input and a single output. The results showed that the FZ Health Center had the best performance in the first two years, while the TC Health Center ranked highest in the last two. The PD Health Center had the lowest performance in the first two years, while the AGT Health Center ranked lowest in the last two. This shows that the Health Centers with the worst rates must improve their policies regarding obtaining revenue and controlling expenses to improve their economic and financial efficiency rates.

Regarding user satisfaction, all Health Centers had a reasonable and acceptable average, except the TC Health Center, which had the lowest average satisfaction. However, there is still much to improve regarding user satisfaction and efficiency. The Health Centers must work more effectively to optimize available resources and ensure the provision of quality services to users.

Additionally, it would be valuable to extend the analysis to all Health Centers in the country, which would provide a much broader sample and more discriminating results in terms of efficiency. Furthermore, it could be important to compare the country's islands to identify which is the best prepared in terms of management, organization of Health Centers, and user satisfaction.

Acknowledgments. This work was supported by national funds: UID/05757 - Research Centre in Digitalization and Intelligent Robotics (CeDRI); and LA/P/0007/2020 (DOI: https://doi.org/10.54499/LA/P/0007/2020).

Disclosure of Interests. The authors have no competing interests to declare that are relevant to the content of this article.

References

1. Barbosa da Costa, B.: Fatores que determinam a eficiência produtiva dos sistemas de saúde de alguns países da OCDE. Master, Universidade do Porto (2021)
2. Ministério Saúde e Segurança Social: Plano Nacional de Desenvolvimento Sanitário 2017–2021. Praia (2018)
3. Guillon, M., Mathonnat, J., Narantuya, B., Dorjmyagmar, B., Enkhtsetseg, E.: Exploring the efficiency of primary health care provision in rural and sparsely populated areas: a case study from Mongolia. Health Policy Plan. **37**, 822–835 (2022). https://doi.org/10.1093/heapol/czac042

4. Nyawira, L., et al.: Management of human resources for health: implications for health systems efficiency in Kenya. BMC Health Serv. Res. **22**, 1046 (2022). https://doi.org/10.1186/s12913-022-08432-1
5. Moreira AA de, S.: Análise de Eficiência das Unidades Locais de Saúde: uma aplicação da Data Envelopment Analysis. Master, Universidade do Porto (2016)
6. Pinto, N.G.M., Coronel, D.A.: Efficiency and effectiveness in administration: the proposal of quantitative models. 6 (2017)
7. Farrell, M.J.: The measurement of productive efficiency. J. R. Stat. Soc. Ser. A **120**, 253 (1957). https://doi.org/10.2307/2343100
8. Garmatz, A., Vieira, G.B.B., Sirena, S.A.: Assessing the technical efficiency of brazil's teaching hospitals using data envelopment analysis. Ciencia e Saude Coletiva **26**, 3447–3457 (2021). https://doi.org/10.1590/1413-81232021269.2.34632019
9. Silva, C.M.D., Silva, S.E., Gonçalves, M.A., Gonçalves, C.A.: Data Envelopment Analysis (DEA) em Estudos Sobre Saúde e Educação **18**, 214–239 (2021)
10. Charnes, A., Cooper, W.W., Rhodes, E.: Measuring the efficiency of decision making units. Eur. J. Oper. Res. **2**, 429–444 (1978). https://doi.org/10.1016/0377-2217(78)90138-8
11. Banker, R.D., Charnes, A., Cooper, W.W.: Some models for estimating technical and scale inefficiencies in data envelopment analysis. Manage. Sci. **30**, 1078–1092 (1984). https://doi.org/10.1287/mnsc.30.9.1078
12. Chaves, C., Duarte, J., Amaral, O., Coutinho, E., Nelas, P.: Satisfaction of users of primary health care with nursing care : sample of the central region of Portugal. Int. J. Dev. Educ. Psychol. Revista INFAD de Psicología **1**, 339 (2016). https://doi.org/10.17060/ijodaep.2016.n2.v1.582
13. Jacinto Monteiro Fortes Pimentel, H.: Avaliação da satisfação dos utentes em relação aos centros de saúde do Serviço Regional de Saúde dos Açores. Açores (2010)
14. Dyson, R.G., Allen, R., Camanho, A.S., Podinovski, V.V., Sarrico, C.S., Shale, E.A.: Pitfalls and protocols in DEA. Eur. J. Oper. Res. **132**, 245–259 (2001). https://doi.org/10.1016/S0377-2217(00)00149-1
15. Nascimento, É.S., Melo Carvalho, F., Carvalho Benedito, G., Willer Prado, J.: Determinantes da Eficiência Relativa da Gestão Pública da Saúde. Viçosa (2023)
16. Cláudia de Castro Ferreira Carriço, A.: Uma abordagem por data envelopment analysis engenharia biomédica. Master (2012)
17. Marques, R.C., Silva, D.: Inferência Estatística dos Estimadores de Eficiência obtidos com a Técnica Fronteira Não Paramétrica de DEA. Uma Metodologia de Bootstrap. Investigação Operacional **26**, 89–110 (2006)
18. George, D., Mallery, P.: IBM SPSS Statistics 23 Step by Step A Simple Guide and Reference, 14th edn. Routledge (2016)
19. Oliveira, C.: Saúde do Homem: um Desafio para os Serviços de Saúde. Universidade Federal de Minas Gerais (2016)
20. Sandi, A.A.: A importância dos Sistemas de Informação em Saúde-Estudo de caso na USF CelaSaúde. Master, Universidade de Coimbra (2015)
21. Santos, O., et al.: Os Centros de Saúde em Portugal Missão para os Cuidados de Saúde Primários, 1ª Edição. Ministério da Saúde, Lisboa (2007)
22. Miot, H.A.: Correlation analysis in clinical and experimental studies Análise de correlação em estudos clínicos e experimentais. Out-Dez **17**, 275–279 (2018). https://doi.org/10.1590/1677-5449.174118

Multifractal Analysis of Gold as a Hedge Against Geopolitical Risk

Jorge Moreira[1]🅘, Rui Pascoal[2]🅘, and Humberto Rocha[2](✉)🅘

[1] University of Coimbra, DMUC, 3001–501 Coimbra, Portugal
[2] University of Coimbra, CeBER, FEUC, 3004–512 Coimbra, Portugal
{ruiapsp,hrocha}@fe.uc.pt

Abstract. This study investigates the efficacy of gold as a hedge against geopolitical risk through a Multifractal Detrended Cross-Correlation Ana- lysis (MF-DCCA). Daily price data of gold, S&P500, DAX40, DXY, Nikkei225, and WTI from 2006 to 2022 is analyzed as well as the performance of these assets during periods of heightened Geopoliti- cal Risk Index. Three hypotheses are tested: whether gold loses its safe haven attributes during times of increased geopolitical risk, whether its ability to offset downside risk is lower than other assets, and whether cross-correlations between assets and geopolitical risk present multifrac- tal properties. The findings suggest that all assets exhibit a long-range correlation with the geopolitical risk index, confirming the presence of multifractality. This study demonstrates significant temporal variations across different market regimes, illustrating the relation of gold with geopolitical risk evolving from the 2008–2009 financial crisis through the COVID pandemic. In the full period analysis, gold reveals more pro- nounced anti-persistence than most other assets (except S&P500), indi- cating more rapid mean-reverting behavior in response to geopolitical shocks. This stronger anti-persistence suggests gold functions effectively as a short-term hedge where investors quickly move to gold during crises but is sold once the situation begins to stabilize. The pattern varies across different market regimes. However, gold's behavior during the COVID crisis challenge traditional safe haven narratives. These find- ings align with recent research showing that gold has a cross correlation with financial markets that may shift significantly during extreme market conditions. This shows that the safe haven character of gold is context- dependent and varies based on the specific nature of the crisis. Overall, this study reveals a more nuanced understanding of gold's relationship with geopolitical risk than traditionally understood, while still affirm- ing its generally superior position relative to other assets during most periods of geopolitical uncertainty.

Keywords: Multifractal Analysis of Asset Returns · Self-Affinity · Geopolitical Risk · Gold

ⓒ The Author(s), under exclusive license to Springer Nature Switzerland AG 2026
O. Gervasi et al. (Eds.): ICCSA 2025 Workshops, LNCS 15888, pp. 207–224, 2026.
https://doi.org/10.1007/978-3-031-97596-7_14

1   Introduction

The world of finance has always been influenced by various factors, including economic, political, and social conditions. In recent times, the impact of geopolitical risks on the financial market has gained significant attention from researchers and investors alike. Gold, being one of the most sought-after precious metals for the reasons listed below, is no exception to this trend.

Gold has long been considered a safe haven asset [1], meaning that it is often sought-after by investors during times of economic uncertainty or geopolitical risk. This is because gold is seen as a stable store of value and a hedge against inflation, making it an attractive investment option in times of market volatility and it is often used as diversification tool for portfolios by analysts due to its low correlation with other commodities and stocks [2].

When geopolitical risk is high, investors often seek safe havens for their money, and gold can be an attractive option. In times of political instability or military conflict, demand for gold may increase as investors look to protect their wealth. Similarly, geopolitical events can affect the global economy and, in turn, the demand for gold. For example, during times of economic uncertainty, gold may be seen as a more stable and reliable investment than stocks or other financial assets. Additionally, gold is not tied to any particular country or political system, which makes it not suffer as heavily due to regional conflicts, making it a relatively neutral option for investors. These factors can make gold an appealing choice in times of geopolitical risk.

The purpose of this study is to investigate and attempt to test 3 hypothesis. First, if the gold loses its safe haven attributes during periods of increased geopolitical risk. Secondly, if its ability to offset risk during riskier periods is lower than other assets. Lastly, the final hypothesis being tested is if the cross-correlation between the different assets and the geopolitical risk index present multifractal properties. The method being used to test the hypothesis laid out will be a multifractal detrended cross-correlation analysis (MF-DCCA). This method quantifies nonlinear and long-range correlation between two time series. By using MF-DCCA, this study aims to shed light on the intricate connection between gold prices and geopolitical risks and the results of this analysis should provide valuable insights for investors to manage and mitigate the impact of geopolitical risks on their investments. Additionally, the use of multifractal analysis facilitates a comprehensive analysis of the gold market. Unlike traditional methods that assume a linear relationship between two time series, multifractal analysis takes the multifractal nature of financial markets into account. This leads to an accurate representation of the underlying dynamics. If the belief that gold is a safe haven for geopolitical risk and that markets are rational holds true, then the expected result should be that gold maintains its safe haven attributes and that its ability to offset risk should be greater than the other assets. Furthermore, there should not be any multifractal properties in the cross-correlation between the assets and geopolitical risk since that would indicate an inefficient market that could be exploited by rational players.

2   Methodology

Financial markets are institutions and mechanisms that facilitate the buying and selling of financial securities, such as stocks, bonds, and derivatives. These markets play a crucial role in allocating capital and managing risk, and are integral to the functioning of modern economies. To study the behavior of these markets, financial analysts often use financial time series, such as stock prices. These series are often characterized by a high level of volatility and complexity, making them difficult to predict using traditional statistical models.

To understand these complex systems better, researchers have turned to mathematical and computational tools, including fractal theory and multifractalism. Fractal theory, first introduced by Benoit Mandelbrot in the 1960 s, is a mathematical framework for studying self-similarity in complex systems [3]. Multifractalism is a further development of fractal theory, which allows for the characterization of complex systems that exhibit self-similarity at multiple scales. In finance, multifractal models have been used to study scaling properties of financial time series, such as stock market indices and exchange rates. These models have been used to gain insights into the underlying dynamics of financial markets and to develop new trading strategies. It is important to mention that not all systems exhibit multifractal behavior. Some systems are monofractal, meaning that they exhibit self-similarity with a single scaling exponent.

By understanding the multifractal nature of financial markets, investors and traders can gain a better understanding of market behavior, and make more informed investment decisions. This multifractal framework has been applied to analyze financial time series and detect patterns in volatility, return and correlation, providing a more comprehensive view of the market. This is demonstrated by the works of Gunay [4], Xu *et al.* [5] and many other researchers, who have used multifractal analysis to gain new insights into the behavior of financial markets.

2.1   Monofractalism

A self-similar stochastic process is a process that is statistically similar to a part of itself. In formal terms, let $(X_t, t \in T)$ be a stochastic process, q a constant that we call the scale exponent and H a constant call the Hurst exponent, then

$$X_{qt} = q^H X_t. \tag{1}$$

The definition is also extended for self-affine time series, which is the basis of fractal analysis. Note that we can get relevant information of a process depending on both the scaling constant and the Hurst exponent. The Hurst exponent is a real number bounded between 0 and 1, with $H < 0.5$ indicating an anti-persistent series, $H > 0.5$ indicating a persistent series and $H = 0.5$ indicating that the series behaves like a random walk, or can be thought of as a non existent persistence. Note that persistence can represent a myriad of definitions that can entail covariance or correlation, but we are using it to the behavior of the series.

For $H > 0.5$, we can say that the process displays long memory, meaning it displays persistency, which will be key for the study presented in this study.

In this study, the focus is on analyzing asset prices, where the data represents the price of an asset. Consequently, the axes of the data, namely the X and Y axes, represent distinct values. In this context, as shown by Kantelhardt [6], self-affinity, which refers to the property of a time series where it exhibits similar patterns at different scales, is what will be used to characterize a stochastic process as a monofractal alongside the definition shown in (1).

2.2   Multifractalism

Expanding upon the definition of monofractalism, we can describe complex systems where a single scaling exponent is not enough to describe the system [7]. For that, we find that we need multiple scaling exponents to provide a thorough analysis of the complex system. In such case, we can define a multifractal system as

$$X_{qt} = q^{h(q)} X_t,$$ (2)

where $h(q)$ is the generalized Hurst exponent. This exponent is a value that ranges between 0 and 1 and is calculated by looking at different moments of the time series.

In informal terms, multifractalism can be thought of as an interwoven set of monofractals, where each monofractal represents a different scaling behavior within the overall system. In other words, a multifractal system can be thought of as consisting of multiple monofractals, each exhibiting a particular degree of complexity [6]. This implies that the conclusion that if $h(q)$ is constant, then the above equation simplifies into the definition of a monofractal. In the case of financial time series, each monofractal characterizes the behavior of fluctuation of a particular size.

By adding stricter stationarity as a requirement for the time series, we have the following scaling rule

$$E(|X_t|^q) = c(q) t^{\tau(q)+1},$$ (3)

where $E(|X_t|^q)$ is the q-th moment of the absolute value of the time series, $c(q)$ a function of q, t is the time scale, and $\tau(q)$ is the scaling exponent. With the above equation, two things becomes apparent. First, most of the work will now revolve around the function $\tau(q)$, which is called the scaling function or the Renyi exponent, defined as

$$\tau(q) = h(q)q - 1.$$ (4)

Second, for $q > 0$, the larger values of the time series are given more weight. This means that the calculation of the generalized Hurst exponent will be more sensitive to larger fluctuations in the time series. Intuitively this can be seen as having a positive value of q implying that the variable is raised to a positive power, which amplifies the larger values of the variable and de-emphasises the smaller values. By applying the same interpretation as in the monofractal case, $h(q) > 0.5$ is an indication of a persistent time series, $h(q) < 0.5$ an anti-persistent time series and for $h(q) = 0.5$ an absence of long range correlations [8]. The situation for $q < 0$ is analogous.

Focusing on the interpretation of the scaling function $\tau(q)$, if the time series is a multifractal system, then the scaling function is nonlinear and concave [9]. The function is linear when $h(q)$ is a constant, which means that all the moments of the time series have the same scaling exponent. In this case, the time series is a monofractal, since it has only one fractal scaling exponent.

If we want to characterize the properties of a multifractal system, we look into its spectrum, which we will denote as $f(\alpha)$. One may think of the multifractal as an interwoven set of fractals of different dimensions α, called the Hölder exponent, where $f(\alpha)$ is a measure of their relative strength and frequency. From this concept, we can find powerful tools that will help further in studying the self-similarity in time series [10].

2.3   Development of Multifractal Analysis in Financial Markets

The application of multifractal analysis to financial markets has its roots in the work of Mandelbrot, who demonstrated that price changes exhibit scaling properties inconsistent with normal distributions [3].

Multifractal analysis extends beyond traditional financial theories by characterizing complex systems through local scaling properties that vary across different regions of the system. Unlike monofractal analysis, which assumes uniform scaling properties described by a single scaling exponent (the Hurst exponent), multifractal analysis reveals how scaling behavior changes across different magnitudes of fluctuations, providing deeper insights into market dynamics. This is particularly important, because financial markets exhibit different statistical properties during periods of stability versus periods of crisis, which cannot be adequately captured by conventional models assuming stationarity and Gaussian distributions [11].

The multifractal approach offers several key advantages for financial analysis: (1) it captures both short and long-range dependence in time series; (2) it characterizes the degree of heterogeneity in scaling behavior; (3) it provides measures of market complexity and inefficiency; and (4) it enables the identification of structural changes in market behavior that may precede significant events [12]. These capabilities make multifractal analysis especially valuable for investigating safe haven assets like gold, whose behavior during market stress often deviates significantly from normal conditions.

Methodological advances have been substantial. Peng et al. introduced the original Detrended Fluctuation Analysis (DFA), providing a foundational method for analyzing long-range correlations in non-stationary time series while eliminating trends [13]. Building upon this work, Kantelhardt et al. developed the MF-DFA method [7], extending DFA to analyze multifractal properties of non-stationary time series by examining how fluctuation functions scale differently for various q-order statistical moments, effectively capturing the multifractal spectrum.

Further methodological developments saw Podobnik and Stanley introduce the Detrended Cross-Correlation Analysis (DCCA), which extends DFA to measure cross-correlations between two non-stationary time series [14]. Subsequently, Zhou advanced this approach by developing the Multifractal Detrended Cross-Correlation Analysis (MF-DCCA), which combines the multifractal approach with cross-correlation analysis, enabling the study of how cross-correlations between different time series vary across multiple time scales and fluctuation magnitudes [15].

While existing literature has established both gold's safe haven properties and the presence of multifractal characteristics in financial markets, there remains a significant gap in understanding how these properties interact specifically during periods of heightened geopolitical risk. Most studies have focused either on gold's safe haven properties or on market multifractality, but few have combined these approaches to analyze their joint dynamics during geopolitical events. The application of MF-DCCA to study these relationships offers potential new insights into market dynamics that traditional correlation analyses might miss.

2.4   Multifractal Formalism

The multifractal formalism is a mathematical framework used to understand complex systems that show multiple fractal scaling exponents. In this particular formalism, we will be basing upon the works of Salat et al. where one quantifies the self-similarity present in a system at different scales [10]. The analysis can be approached through two main methods: moment methods and histogram methods. To effectively compute the multifractal spectrum, the moment method is employed by raising the probability measure p_i to different moments q. This technique forces only one value of α for each moment q to make a significant contribution to the total value of the measure. In contrast, histogram methods focus on counting occurrences at different levels of aggregation, with box-counting being the most commonly implemented approach, which uses square grids of increasing resolutions to analyze the data. Alternative aggregation methods include ball neighborhoods, gliding boxes, and regular unit shapes.

In this framework, a grid of unit r is used to cover a domain D and a phenomenon occurring N times in D. The probability measure is represented by μ and p_i is defined as the number of times the phenomenon occurs in the ith box divided by the total number of times the event occurs in D, represented as:

$$p_i := \frac{N_i}{N} = \int_{i^{th}\ box} d\mu(x). \tag{5}$$

This verifies $p_i \sim r^{\alpha_i}$, where α_i is the Hölder dimension calculated as

$$\alpha_i = \lim_{r \to 0} \frac{\log(\mu_i(r))}{\log(r)}. \tag{6}$$

The number of times α occurs in each interval $[\alpha_i, \alpha_i + d\alpha_i]$ is represented by $N(\alpha_i)$ and verifies:

$$N(\alpha_i) \sim \rho(\alpha_i) r^{-f(\alpha_i)} d\alpha_i. \tag{7}$$

The moment method is used to compute f. By raising p_i to different moments, p_i^q, at each q one single value of α is forced to contribute to the total value of the measure. This is represented by:

$$Z(q) := \sum_i p_i^q \sim \sum_i r^{\alpha_i q} \sim \int_\alpha N(\alpha) r^{\alpha q} \sim \int \rho(\alpha) r^{\alpha q - f(\alpha)} d\alpha, \tag{8}$$

where $Z(q)$ is a partition function. For small enough r, the value of $Z(q)$ is almost entirely determined by the α that minimizes $\tau(q) = \alpha q - f(\alpha)$. This minimal value of α is defined as $\alpha(q)$ and can be calculated using the Legendre transform:

$$\alpha(q) = \frac{d\tau(q)}{dq} \tag{9}$$

$$f(\alpha(q)) = \alpha(q) q - \tau(q).$$

Since q represents the moments order of the distribution, the influence of q on the nature of the fluctuations can be described as follows as shown by [10]:

- Higher values of q indicate larger fluctuations. When q is large, the partition function $Z(q)$ is dominated by contributions from regions with higher values of the measured quantity (such as the probability p_i). Thus, large q values emphasize the impact of rare, significant fluctuations.
- Lower values of q indicate smaller fluctuations. When q is small, the contributions to $Z(q)$ are more evenly distributed, capturing more typical, smaller fluctuations.

This relationship also shows that each moment q corresponds to a particular value of α, characterizing the nature of the fluctuations in the system. By analysing $Z(q)$ across a range of q values, one can understand how fluctuations of different magnitudes contribute to the overall system, with each q highlighting a specific aspect of these fluctuations and their corresponding α.

Computing $\tau(q)$ from $Z(q)$ for each q between $]-\infty, +\infty[$ provides the full spectrum.

2.5 Multifractal Detrended Cross-Correlation Analysis

The Multifractal Detrended Cross-Correlation Analysis (MFD-CCA) is a method that evaluates the relationship between two time series, $x(i)$ and $y(i)$, where i ranges from 1 to N. The steps involved in this method are as follows and are based upon the works of Podobnik and Stanley [14], which were further expanded by Zhou [15].

Step 1 - Construct the profiles: The profiles $X(i)$ and $Y(i)$ are calculated by summing the cumulative values of each time series after subtracting their respective average, as follows:

$$X(i) = \sum_{t=1}^{i}(x(t) - \bar{x})$$

$$Y(i) = \sum_{t=1}^{i}(y(t) - \bar{y})$$

(10)

Notice that if the two time series are equal, then MFD-CCA is the same as Multifractal Detrended Fluctuation Analysis (MF-DFA) [6].

Step 2 - Partition of the profiles into windows: The profiles $X(i)$ and $Y(i)$ are partitioned into $2N_s$ non-overlapping windows of equal length s. This is achieved by dividing each profile into $[N/s]$ windows and then repeating the same procedure starting from the reverse end of each profile.

Step 3 - Evaluate local trends: The local trends $X_\nu(i)$ and $Y_\nu(i)$ for each segment ν, where ν ranges from 1 to $2N_s$, are evaluated by performing a least squares fit on the data for each segment. The detrended covariance is then determined using the following equation:

$$F^2(s,v) = \frac{1}{s}\sum_{i=1}^{s}|((\nu-1)s+i) - X_v(i)||Y((\nu-1)s+i) - Y_v(i)| \qquad (11)$$

for each segment ν such that $v = 1, 2, ..., N_s$.

$$F^2(s,v) = \frac{1}{s}\sum_{i=1}^{s}|X(N-(v-N_s)s+i)-x_v(i)||Y(N-(v-N_s)s+i)-y_v(i)| \quad (12)$$

for each segment ν such that $v = N_{s+1}, N_{s+2}, ..., 2N_s$. The trends $x_v(i)$ and $y_v(i)$ are represented by a fitting polynomial with order m.

Step 4 - Obtain the order q fluctuation: The order q fluctuation function is calculated as follows:

$$F_q(s) = \left[\frac{1}{2N_s}\sum_{v=1}^{2N_s}[F^2(s,v)]^{q/2}\right]^{1/q} \qquad (13)$$

and, if $q \neq 0$, the q-th order fluctuation function would be

$$F_0(s) = \exp\left[\frac{1}{4N_s}\sum_{v=1}^{2N_s}\ln[F^2(s,v)]\right] \qquad (14)$$

Note that when $q = 2$, the MF-DCCA is equivalent to a traditional cross-correlation analysis (CCA) [17].

Step 5 - Analyze the results: The scaling behavior of the fluctuations is analyzed by plotting logarithmic graphs of $F_q(s)$ versus s for each value of q. If the two series are long-range cross-correlated, then $F_q(s)$ will increase for larger values of s, and the relationship can be represented as a power law:

$$F_q(s) \sim s^{H_{xy}(q)} \tag{15}$$

which can be simplified into

$$\log F_q(s) \sim H_{xy}(q) \log(s) \tag{16}$$

Here, $H_{xy}(q)$ is known as the generalized cross-correlation Hurst exponent, which describes the power-law relationship between the two series.

Focusing now on $q = 2$, the covariance of the fluctuations of the multifractal behavior [18], which will be important during the analyses of the data. If $H_{xy}(q = 2) > 0.5$, the cross-correlation between the return fluctuations of the two series related to q are long-range persistent. If $H_{xy}(q = 2) < 0.5$, the cross-correlations between the return fluctuations of the two series are anti-persistent. If $H_{xy}(q = 2) = 0.5$, there is no cross-correlation between the two series.

The Renyi function $\tau_{xy}(q)$ is used to characterize the multifractal nature of the time series, which was previously defined as (4) now takes the shape of

$$\tau_{xy}(q) = H_{xy}(q)q - 1 \tag{17}$$

If the Renyi function $\tau_{xy}(q)$ is linear, we can conclude that the cross-correlation between the two series is monofractal, otherwise, it is multifractal.

As proposed by Yuan *et al.* [16], the strength of the multifractality, meaning the degree of multifractality present and it can be estimated with ΔH and it is given by

$$\Delta H = H_{max}(q) - H_{min}(q) \tag{18}$$

The multifractal spectra $f_{xy}(\alpha)$ could be derived through the Legendre transform [10,17]:

$$\alpha_{xy}(q) = H_{xy}(q) + qH'_{xy}(q) \tag{19}$$

$$f_{xy}(\alpha) = q(\alpha_{xy} - H_{xy}(q)) + 1 \tag{20}$$

where H'_{xy} denotes the first derivative of H_{xy} with respect to q.

Using the multifractal spectrum, one can measure its width to examine the multifractal level [19], given by:

$$\Delta\alpha = \max(\alpha_{xy}) - \min(\alpha_{xy}) \tag{21}$$

Using this parameters will be key to further understand the nature of the multifractal behavior, with a larger $\Delta\alpha$ indicating a more complex, varied structure, while a smaller $\Delta\alpha$ suggests a more uniform structure.

3   Empirical Results

3.1   Dataset

The dataset analyzed in this study consists of the spot price of Gold in dollars[1], the S&P500 index[2], the DAX40[3], the dollar index (DXY)[4], the Nikkei225[5] and the crude Oil commodity (WTI)[6]. For each of these assets, we calculate the logarithmic daily returns using the formula $r_t = ln(P_t/P_{t-1})$, where P_t is the closing price at time t and P_{t-1} is the closing price at time $t-1$. The choice of logarithmic returns over simple returns or raw prices is motivated by several factors. First, log returns are more likely to be additive over time and tend to be more normally distributed than simple returns, which makes them more suitable for statistical analysis. Second, unlike raw prices or cumulative returns which can exhibit strong trends and non-stationarity, daily log returns are more likely to be stationary, a crucial property that as we discussed before, is a necessary condition for the application of multifractal analysis.

All the price data comes from investing.com, and consists of daily prices from January 1st, 2006 to December 31st, 2022. The selection of daily frequency, as opposed to weekly or monthly data is that it captures more granular market movements and immediate responses to geopolitical events. This is particularly important as geopolitical events can have rapid, sometimes intraday impacts on financial markets. Since we are analyzing commodities, forex and indices from different countries, we encounter the problem where some days some assets may be tradable and others are not, due to national holidays or other issues. To mitigate this problem, we have normalised the data so we only analyze the assets on the same days. This is also important since we are going to be analyzing these assets against the Geopolitical Risk Index[7]. For the Geopolitical Risk Index, we also considered growth rates to ensure consistency with the return-based approach used for financial assets and to maintain stationarity in the data series, which is essential for our multifractal analysis framework.

Each asset in our dataset represents a different aspect of the global financial market:

- Gold (XAU/USD): Traditionally viewed as a safe-haven asset and hedge against geopolitical uncertainty
- S&P500: The benchmark U.S. equity index, representing the performance of the largest U.S. companies
- DAX40: The primary German stock index, representing Europe's largest economy

---

[1] https://www.investing.com/currencies/xau-usd.
[2] https://www.investing.com/indices/us-spx-500.
[3] https://www.investing.com/indices/germany-30.
[4] https://www.investing.com/indices/usdollar.
[5] https://www.investing.com/indices/japan-ni225.
[6] https://www.investing.com/commodities/crude-Oil.
[7] https://www.matteoiacoviello.com/gpr.htm.

Fig. 1. Cumulative Gains of Assets

- Dollar Index (DXY): A measure of the U.S. dollar's strength against a basket of major currencies
- Nikkei225: Japan's primary stock index, representing the Asian market perspective
- Crude Oil (WTI): A key commodity highly sensitive to geopolitical events, particularly in oil-producing regions

The data from geopolitical risk is based on computerized text searches from the archives of ten newspapers (Chicago Tribune, The Daily Telegraph, Financial Times, The Globe and Mail, The Guardian, The Los Angeles Times, The New York Times, USA Today, The Wall Street Journal, and The Washington Post) [20]. It tracks the number of times per day that adverse geopolitical events took place and takes into consideration: war threats, peace threats, military buildups, nuclear threats, terror threats, beginning of war, escalation of war, and terror acts.

One can see from Fig. 1 that during the timeline being analyzed, Gold was indeed one of the best performing assets, with a return of 241.90%, beating the S&P500 and the DAX40 (formerly DAX30), which had a return of 202.61% and 154.98% respectively. Meanwhile, Oil and the DXY end up with the a return of 26.88% and 16.88% respectively while the Nikkei225 had a return of 59.44%

From a superficial level, by analyzing the data, one can also see that Gold had a significantly better performance during some periods of crisis, namely a very quick recovery during the 2008 financial crisis and the COVID19 pandemic, where, due to logistical reasons and lack of demand, Oil futures went into negative territories. One can also observe a stagnation between those 2 time periods while the DAX40 and S&P500 experienced an upward trend which, on the surface level, means that Gold was indeed outperforming the other indices during periods of crisis. However, one can also verify that Gold, along side the other

Table 1. Descriptive Statistic Analysis of prices from 2006 to 2022

	Mean	SD	Median	Min	Max	Skewness	Kurtosis	Jarque Bera
Gold	1292.979	364.5634	1281.52	525.05	2063.81	−0.18270	−0.69140	2204.459
DXY	88.22696	8.970505	87.555	71.33	114.11	0.187923	−0.91754	2481.376
S&P500	2125.139	1002.838	1894.47	676.53	4793.54	0.910085	−0.14018	2110.54
Nikkei225	17129.69	6102.594	16764.36	7054.98	30670.1	0.295492	−0.84842	2428.692
DAX40	9490.028	3159.364	9452.875	3666.41	16271.75	0.222918	−1.15141	2792.91
Oil	72.27448	22.77575	70.335	-37.63	145.29	0.233772	−0.42753	1917.147

Table 2. Descriptive Statistic Analysis of the daily returns from 2006 to 2022

2006–2022								
	Mean	SD	Median	Min	Max	Skewness	Kurtosis	Jarque Bera
Gold	0.000211	0.0112	0.000416	−0.08459	0.112227	−0.13669	6.629835	2122.831
DXY	0.0000033	0.004626	0	−0.02996	0.024038	−0.074	2.264713	90.12574
S&P500	0.000156	0.011181	0.000599	−0.08723	0.10789	−0.40375	9.706802	7310.828
Nikkei225	−0.00017	0.010833	−0.0001	-0.10025	0.123649	−0.37202	14.94745	22957.1
DAX40	−0,0000060	0.0111877	0.000408	−0.07125	0.117856	0.008130	6.616755	2095.7148
Oil	−0.00134	0.062373	0.00063	−3.12239	0.204604	−38.0117	1778.752	5.06E+08

assets, had a short crash immediately following said crisis, which puts in question the stability of Gold as a short term stable asset.

By doing a descriptive statistical analysis, Table 1, one can see that Gold is the only asset with a negative skewness, which indicates that the distribution of Gold prices is skewed to the left. This means that the tail of distribution is heavier on the left side. This means that Gold has a tendency for larger downward movements, however, since the value of skewness is not highly pronounced, the asymmetry is relatively small. This is the opposite for all other assets being analyzed. Furthermore, by performing the Jarque-Bera test, which is a statistical test that assesses whether the data has skewness and kurtosis matching a normal distribution, one can find that the Jarque-Bera values for the assets prices are all above the usual significance levels, we can see in this case testing for $\alpha = 0.05$, we can reject the null hypothesis that none of the pricing distribution follows a normal distribution.

By focusing now on the daily returns of the assets, Table 2, one can see that all assets but the DAX40 have negative skewness, meaning that they have more negative daily returns than positive returns. This indicates that the COVID19 crisis and the flash crash of Oil futures prices into negative territory had a significant impact in Oil returns. One can also observe that all assets' returns present positive kurtosis and that with the exception of DXY. The daily returns of each asset present leptokurtic distribution, with Gold and the DAX40 daily returns having the smallest kurtosis from the leptokurtic assets. This means that, although their distribution present heavier tails, compared to the other assets, they are less likely to present heavier fluctuations in daily returns. Once again, considering the value of the Jarque-Bera test, none of the daily returns of the assets follow a normal distribution.

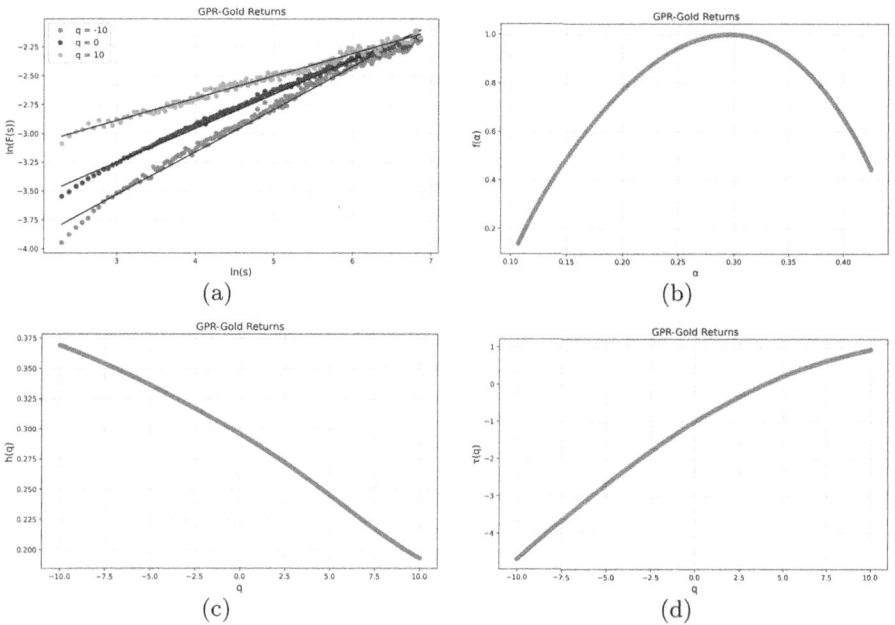

Fig. 2. MF-DCCA for geopolitical risk index and Gold

3.2   Multifractal Dentrended Cross Correlation Analysis

By employing now the MF-DCCA between each asset and the Geopolitical Risk Index, one can calculate the scaling exponents $h_{XY}(q)$ of q ranging from -10 to 10. Note that using those ranges, one can provide enough coverage to observe both the local and global scaling behavior. The main hypothesis being tested are:

H_1: Gold loses its safe haven attributes during times of increased Geopolitical risk

H_2: Its ability to offset downside risk is lower than the other assets

H_3: The cross-correlation between the different assets and the geopolitical risk index present multifractal properties.

Figure 2 represent a MC-DCCA analysis between the daily returns of gold and geopolitical risk. The figure shows: (a) the log-log of the fluctuation $F_q(s)$ versus s, (b) the multifractal spectrum, $f(\alpha)$ with dependencies for $q \in [-10, 10]$, (c) the generalized Hurst exponent H_{xy} and (d) the Reyni function τ, respectively. The code implemented in python was based on the Fathon library [21], a detrendend fluctuation analysis library that was modified to be used for the dataset we have. The same analysis was performed for the remaining assets.

From the results, the log-log plots demonstrate clear power-law scaling behavior between the $F_q(s)$ and the scale s for different values of q. Notably, the $q = -10$ line (red, representing smaller fluctuations) consistently shows a steeper slope than the $q = 0$ line (blue), which in turn has a steeper slope than the

$q = 10$ line (green, representing larger fluctuations). This pattern indicates that the scaling properties depend on the magnitude of the fluctuations, with smaller market movements exhibiting stronger scaling behavior.

The Hurst exponent, $H_{xy}(q)$, for all pairs is not constant and exhibits a systematic decrease as q ranges from -10 to 10. This declining trend indicates that the cross-correlation between geopolitical risk and financial assets shows stronger persistence for smaller fluctuations (negative q values) and weaker persistence for larger fluctuations (positive q values).

Since the Hurst exponent depends on q and is not constant, it confirms that the cross-correlation between the different assets and the geopolitical risk index presents multifractal properties, validating the third hypothesis. This conclusion is further supported by the multifractal spectrum $f(\alpha)$ plots, which show a clear inverted parabolic shape, and by the Renyi function $\tau(q)$, which exhibits nonlinear behavior, both characteristic signatures of multifractality in the cross-correlation structure.

In our MF-DCCA framework, the generalized Hurst exponent at $q = 2$, denoted as $H_{xy}(2)$, is particularly significant as it quantifies the degree of persistence in the cross-correlations. According to the formalism described before, values of $H_{xy}(2)$ below 0.5 indicate anti-persistent relationships, while values above 0.5 indicate persistent relationships. Examining Table 3 we observe that all $H_{xy}(2)$ values fall below 0.5, confirming anti-persistent cross-correlations. There is a tendency to invert the correlation between asset returns and geopolitical growth rates. Notably, Gold demonstrates more pronounced anti-persistence (0.277) compared to most other assets except S&P500 (0.274), with DXY

Table 3. Cross correlation generalized Hurst exponent of order q between Geopolitical Risk and different assets

q	GPR GOLD	GPR DXY	GPR SP500	GPR Nikkei225	GPR DAX40	GPR Oil
-10	0.36938978	0.38388519	0.35755061	0.37977183	0.38702615	0.38714654
$--9$	0.36358157	0.37738052	0.35262529	0.37478466	0.38086403	0.38078975
-7	0.35079828	0.36309373	0.34150839	0.36368922	0.36692152	0.36718170
-6	0.34386611	0.35564659	0.33532631	0.35759318	0.35930896	0.36036595
-5	0.33660801	0.34829446	0.32876212	0.35115432	0.35148181	0.35389229
-4	0.32904682	0.34121358	0.32186352	0.34439859	0.34362745	0.34795635
-3	0.32119721	0.33447774	0.31469023	0.33735525	0.33588802	0.34262257
-2	0.31306135	0.32806651	0.30729518	0.33005053	0.32831591	0.33781699
-1	0.30462457	0.32189258	0.29968962	0.32249688	0.32085423	0.33335355
0	0.29585169	0.31582122	0.29180174	0.31467663	0.31334217	0.32896083
1	0.28668687	0.30968295	0.28346188	0.30652169	0.30554588	0.32430153
2	**0.27706266**	**0.30328708**	**0.27445828**	**0.29789942**	**0.29721907**	**0.31900112**
3	0.26692468	0.29644343	0.26467580	0.28862834	0.28819528	0.31271061
4	0.25627378	0.28900087	0.25424628	0.27855442	0.27849031	0.30521953
5	0.24521316	0.28090584	0.24357511	0.26768523	0.26835130	0.29658919
6	0.23396919	0.27225802	0.23319014	0.25629441	0.25819280	0.28719896
7	0.22285653	0.26330976	0.22353407	0.24487355	0.24844690	0.27761391
8	0.21219723	0.25438766	0.21485374	0.23394280	0.23943148	0.26836134
9	0.20224269	0.24579140	0.20721114	0.22387693	0.23130551	0.25978838
10	0.19313828	0.23773290	0.20054979	0.21485242	0.22409616	0.25205037

Table 4. Generalized Hurst exponents $H_{xy}(2)$ and multifractal strength ΔH [in brackets] for the cross-correlation between GPR and financial assets across different market regimes

Asset	$H_{xy}(2)$ [Multifractal Strength ΔH]				
	Pre-Crisis	Financial Crisis	European Debt Crisis	Post-Crisis	COVID Crisis
Gold	0.46104 [0.458]	0.40057 [0.305]	0.40467 [0.263]	0.35643 [0.223]	0.28488 [0.321]
DXY	0.42126 [0.779]	0.39836 [0.619]	0.42132 [0.137]	0.32571 [0.136]	0.32077 [0.353]
S&P500	0.24057 [0.550]	0.30776 [0.717]	0.36503 [0.245]	0.29020 [0.229]	0.46002 [0.286]
Nikkei225	0.44996 [0.638]	0.27941 [0.710]	0.43966 [0.295]	0.30576 [0.229]	0.35212 [0.111]
DAX40	0.39145 [0.468]	0.28287 [0.932]	0.46470 [0.115]	0.32400 [0.162]	0.41143 [0.352]
Oil	0.37580 [0.448]	0.36001 [0.653]	0.41165 [0.288]	0.37213 [0.092]	0.42463 [0.361]

(0.303), Nikkei225 (0.298), DAX40 (0.297), and Oil (0.319) all showing less anti-persistence. This stronger anti-persistence suggests that Gold exhibits more rapid mean-reverting behavior in response to geopolitical shocks, making it particularly effective as a short-term hedge where investors rush to Gold during crises but sell once the situation begins to stabilize. This rapid mean-reversion characteristic offers a different kind of protection than assets with less pronounced anti-persistence, which tend to show less anti-persistent directional movements in response to geopolitical events.

However, these broad patterns mask significant variations across different market regimes. To investigate this further, a sub-period analysis covering distinct economic phases: Pre-Crisis (2006–2007), Financial Crisis (2008–2009), European Debt Crisis (2010–2012), Post-Crisis (2013–2019), and COVID Crisis (2020–2021), was conducted. The sub-period analysis reveals significant temporal variations in the relationship between Gold and geopolitical risk across different market regimes. Table 4 presents the generalized Hurst exponents at $q = 2$ and the multifractal strength parameters across these periods.

The temporal analysis demonstrates that Gold's relationship with geopolitical risk is not constant but varies substantially across different market regimes. During the 2008–2009 financial crisis, Gold showed relatively stable multifractal properties compared to equity markets, supporting its safe haven reputation during financial turbulence. However, during the COVID crisis, Gold displayed heightened negative sensitivity to geopolitical risks, likely because unprecedented monetary interventions and the unique nature of the pandemic created market conditions where traditional relationships were distorted. Our findings align with Bentes, who applied MF-DCCA to CIVETS emerging markets during 2018–2023 and discovered that Gold's cross-correlations with financial markets shifted from negative before the pandemic to positive during the COVID-19 and Russia-Ukraine war crises, demonstrating that Gold lost its safe haven attributes during these extreme market conditions [19].

4   Conclusion

Gold is widely regarded as a safe-haven asset during geopolitical uncertainty [1]. Its intrinsic value, scarcity, and historical role as a store of wealth make it attractive during crises, offering stability and wealth preservation in turbulent times. Our research reveals this relationship is more nuanced and context-dependent than traditionally understood.

In order to understand these connections, we applied MF-DCCA to the daily returns of gold and from other assets, from the 1st of January 2006 to the 31st of December 2022. However, considering that the assets are from different countries and different sectors, the data had to be normalized for a fair comparison. Our research was guided by three central hypotheses: whether Gold loses its safe haven attributes during times of increased geopolitical risk (H1), whether its ability to offset downside risk is lower than other assets (H2), and whether the cross-correlations between assets and the geopolitical risk index present multifractal properties (H3).

This study found that all the assets we examined, when compared to geopolitical risk index, present long-range correlations, indicating the presence of multifractality, which supports our third hypothesis (H3). The non-linear dependency of the Hurst exponent on q, the inverted parabolic shape of the multifractal spectrum $f(\alpha)$, and the non-linear Renyi function $\tau(q)$ all confirm this multifractality. However, the strength of multifractality in the cross-correlation varies across all pairs. The complexity parameters (ΔH and $\Delta \alpha$) quantify this multifractality across all assets and time periods. All the assets showed anti-persistent cross-correlation with GPR, with Hurst exponent values below 0.5.

Regarding our first hypothesis (H1), our findings indicate it is partially true and significantly dependent on the nature of the crisis. During the 2008–2009 financial crisis, Gold maintained relatively stable multifractal properties compared to equity markets, supporting its traditional safe haven reputation. However, during the COVID crisis, Gold exhibited heightened negative sensitivity to geopolitical risks, with its Hurst exponent dropping to 0.28488. This aligns with recent research by Bentes, who found that Gold's cross-correlations with financial markets shifted from negative before the pandemic to positive during the COVID-19 and Russia-Ukraine war crises [19].

For our second hypothesis (H2), our analysis largely rejects the notion that Gold's ability to offset downside risk is lower than other assets, but for more nuanced reasons than initially hypothesized. In the full period analysis (2006–2022), Gold actually demonstrates more pronounced anti-persistence compared to most other assets (except S&P500), indicating more rapid mean-reverting behavior in response to geopolitical shocks. This stronger anti-persistence suggests that Gold functions as an effective short-term hedge where investors quickly move to Gold during crises but sell once the situation begins to stabilize. This rapid reaction characteristic differs from traditional views of Gold's stability but nonetheless confirms its special role during periods of geopolitical instability [1]. The pattern varies across different market regimes, however. During the financial crisis, Gold maintained a higher Hurst exponent (0.40057) than major equity indices, suggesting more stable behavior during this specific type of market turbulence. Only during the unprecedented conditions of the COVID crisis did Gold's hedging dynamics change dramatically, with the S&P500 showing a remarkable reversal in behavior.

Our study found that Hurst values for all assets exhibited a systematic decrease as q ranges from -10 to 10. This declining trend indicates that the cross-correlation between geopolitical risk and financial assets shows weaker anti-persistence for smaller fluctuations and stronger anti-persistence for larger fluctuations. This pattern suggests complex market behavior where the scaling properties depend on the magnitude of the fluctuations.

A particularly important finding of our research is the significant temporal variation in the relationship between Gold and geopolitical risk across different market regimes. During the pre-crisis period (2006–2007), Gold exhibited a Hurst exponent of 0.46104, very close to 0.5, indicating an almost random walk relationship with geopolitical risk. This relationship evolved through various market regimes, with each period showing distinct patterns in the cross-correlations [18].

Overall, our research shows that gold is indeed generally one of the better hedges against geopolitical risk compared to other financial assets, except during the COVID crisis when traditional relationships were distorted [22]. Although this does not mean that it presented positive returns during times of uncertainty, but rather that its relative performance in relation to Geopolitical Risk was typically better than other assets.

In addition to the findings presented, it is essential to recognize that Gold price movements are influenced by factors beyond those captured in the GPR index. Interest rate expectations, central bank balance sheet expansions, inflation concerns, and currency debasement fears significantly impact Gold prices but are not explicitly measured in geopolitical risk metrics. During 2020-2021, Gold reached all-time highs despite showing strong anti-persistent behavior with geopolitical risk, suggesting dominant influence from monetary policy expectations and inflation concerns.

Acknowledgments. This work was supported by the FCT - Fundação para a Ciência e a Tecnologia, I.P., under Grant PTDC/MAT-APL/1286/2021 (RiskBigData project: Complex Risk Management in the Big Data Regime), Grant UIDB/05037/2020 with DOI 10.54499/UIDB/05037/2020, and Grant UIDB/00324/2020 with DOI 10.54499/UIDB/00324/2020.

References

1. Baur, D.G., McDermott, T.K.: Is gold a safe haven? Int. Evid. J. Bank. Finance **34**, 1886–1898 (2010)
2. Baur, D.G., Lucey, B.M.: Is gold a hedge or a safe haven? An analysis of stocks, bonds and gold. Financ. Rev. **45**, 217–229 (2010)
3. Mandelbrot, B.: Forecasts of future prices, unbiased markets, and "martingale" models. J. Bus. **39**, 242–255 (1966)

4. Gunay, S.: Fractal structure of the stock markets of leading Asian countries. J. East Asian Econ. Integr. **18**, 367–394 (2014)
5. Xu, N., Li, S., Hui, X.: Multifractal analysis of COVID-19's Impact on China's stock market. Fractals **20**, 2150213 (2021)
6. Kantelhardt, J.W.: Fractal and multifractal time series. arXiv **0804**, 0747 (2008)
7. Kantelhardt, J.W., Zschiegner, S.A., Koscielny-Bunde, E., Havlin, S., Bunde, A., Stanley, H.E.: Multifractal detrended fluctuation analysis of nonstationary time series. Phys. A: Stat. Mech. Appl. **316**, 87–114 (2002)
8. Fang, S., Lu, X., Li, J., Qu, L.: Multifractal detrended cross-correlation analysis of carbon emission allowance and stock returns. Phys. A: Stat. Mech. Appl. **509**, 551–566 (2018)
9. Mandelbrot, B. B., Fisher, A. J., Calvet, L. E.: A multifractal model of asset returns. Cowles Foundation Discussion Paper No. 1164, Sauder School of Business Working Paper (1997)
10. Salat, H., Murcio, R., Arcaute, E.: Multifractal methodology. Phys. A: Stat. Mech. Appl. **473**, 467–487 (2017)
11. Calvet, L., Fisher, A.: Multifractality in asset returns: theory and evidence. Rev. Econ. Stat. **84**, 381–406 (2002)
12. Jiang, Z,-Q., Xie, W.-J., Zhou, W.-X., Sornette, D.: Multifractal analysis of financial markets: a review. Rep. Prog. Phys. **82**, 125901 (2019)
13. Peng, C.-K., Buldyrev, S.V., Havlin, S., Simons, M., Stanley, H.E., Goldberger, A.L.: Mosaic organization of DNA nucleotides. Phys. Rev. E **49**, 1685 (1994)
14. Podobnik, B., Stanley, H.E.: Detrended cross-correlation analysis: a new method for analyzing two nonstationary time series. Phys. Rev. Lett. **100**, 084102 (2008)
15. Zhou, W.-X.: Multifractal detrended cross-correlation analysis for two nonstationary signals. Phys. Rev. E **77**, 066211 (2008)
16. Yuan, Y., Zhuang, X., Jin, X.: Measuring multifractality of stock price fluctuation using multifractal detrended fluctuation analysis. Phys. A: Stat. Mech. Appl. **388**, 2189–2197 (2009)
17. Pal, M., Rao, P.M., Manimaran, P.: Multifractal detrended cross-correlation analysis on gold, crude oil and foreign exchange rate time series. Phys. A: Stat. Mech. Appl. **416**, 452–460 (2014)
18. Kristoufek, L.: Multifractal height cross-correlation analysis: A new method for analyzing long-range cross-correlations. Europhys. Lett. **95**, 68001 (2011)
19. Bentes, S.R.: Is gold a safe haven for the CIVETS countries under extremely adverse market conditions? Some new evidence from the MF-DCCA analysis. Phys. A: Stat. Mech. Appl. **623**, 128898 (2023)
20. Caldara, D., Iacoviello, M.: Measuring geopolitical risk. Am. Ec. Rev. **112**, 1194–1225 (2022)
21. Bianchi, S.: fathon: A Python package for a fast computation of detrendend fluctuation analysis and related algorithms. J. Open Source Softw. **5**, 1828 (2020)
22. Goodell, J.W.: COVID-19 and finance: Agendas for future research. Fin. Res. Lett. **35**, 101512 (2020)

A Study on the Effects of Model Simplifications for Generating Human-Like Robot Movements in Refill Tasks

Daniel Rodrigues[1]([✉]) [iD], Eliana Costa e Silva[1,2] [iD], Gianpaolo Gulletta[1] [iD],
Pedro Ribeiro[1] [iD], Inês Costa[1] [iD], Wolfram Erlhagen[3] [iD], Cátia Ferreira[4],
Luís Louro[1] [iD], and Estela Bicho[1] [iD]

[1] Center Algoritmi/Department of Industrial Electronics, University of Minho,
Braga, Portugal
{pg47125,a84489,pg50435}@alunos.uminho.pt,
{d6468,estela.bicho}@dei.uminho.pt, luislouro@algoritmi.uminho.pt
[2] CIICESI, ESTG, Polytechnic of Porto, Porto, Portugal
eos@estg.ipp.pt
[3] Center of Mathematics/Department of Mathematics, University of Minho,
Braga, Portugal
wolfram.erlhagen@math.uminho.pt
[4] MC SONAE, Matosinhos, Portugal
catsferreira@mc.pt

Abstract. In the present work, the optimization problems arising during the generation of human-like movements for an anthropomorphic robot performing shelf replenishment tasks are evaluated in detail. Specifically, a set of movements that involve grasping five objects from a support table and transporting each object to a shelf is analyzed. These movements are formulated as nonlinear optimization problems, with various constraints related to the posture of the arm and the objects in the workspace. The impact of different model simplifications on the computational time necessary for the Interior Point OPTimizer (IPOPT) solver to obtain an optimal solution is explored. The optimization problems are modeled using the A Mathematical Programming Language (AMPL) modeling language and different levels of presolve are used. Our results demonstrate that increasing the presolve level enhances computational efficiency. However, excessively high presolve may negatively affect performance for some problems when compared to lower levels. This research highlights the importance of selecting an appropriate presolve level to optimize both problem formulation and solution time.

Keywords: Nonlinear optimization · Motion planning · Statistical analysis · Retail · Robotic manipulation

1 Introduction

The Human-like Upper-limb motion planner (HUMP) is a motion planning algorithm developed to generate collision-free trajectories with human-like characteristics for anthropomorphic robotic arms [1, 2]. In this, the underlying nonlinear

O. Gervasi et al. (Eds.): ICCSA 2025 Workshops, LNCS 15888, pp. 225–240, 2026.
https://doi.org/10.1007/978-3-031-97596-7_15

constrained optimization problems were modeled using AMPL [3] and solved using the IPOPT solver [4]. The performance of HUMP, in terms of computation time and quality of the solution found, is affected by IPOPT's ability to solve the underlying optimization problems. IPOPT is a widely used interior point optimization solver for large-scale nonlinear programming problems [5]. Its performance depends on several aspects that will be summarized next. The choice of the linear solver affects IPOPT's performance, with parallel solvers potentially improving scalability for certain problem classes [5]. The mathematical formulation affects IPOPT's performance, as demonstrated by a new spherical coordinates model for progressive lens design, which exhibited better convexity properties than previous Cartesian models [6]. To improve robustness for problems without constraint qualifications, an l1-exact penalty-barrier phase was implemented in IPOPT, showing favorable performance for degenerate nonlinear programs [7]. For problems with nonconvex constraints, a new interior point method was developed that finds approximate Fritz John points with improved iteration bounds, representing a significant advancement in complexity analysis for such methods [8]. Scaling the linear system before solving can also improve performance in some cases [9]. The type of optimization problem, such as compliance minimization or stress-constrained mass minimization, affects solver performance [10]. Problem size, mesh structure, and design domain complexity can also influence IPOPT's effectiveness [10]. Comparative studies using benchmark problems have shown that different solvers may perform better for specific types of problem, highlighting the importance of selecting appropriate algorithms based on the problem characteristics [5,10].

Using the presolve option in AMPL can enhance IPOPT's performance by simplifying the optimization problem, leading to faster and more stable solutions. It is generally recommended to enable presolve and test its impact on specific problems. In this work, an empirical test is conducted on a set of 46 nonlinear constrained optimization problems related to the generation of reaching and grasping movements for five objects, followed by their placement on shelves. The objective is to perceive how the problem formulation affects the problem resolution in terms of computing time.

Section 2 introduces the language used to formulate the problems and provides an overview of the solver employed. Section 3 outlines the task under analysis and details the experimental procedure. Section 4 presents the results, with Sect. 4.1 examining the dimensionality of the optimization problems, particularly focusing on the number of inequality constraints. Section 4.2 discusses the influence of different presolve levels on the solving time of the optimization problems. Section 5 presents the conclusions drawn from the work undertaken.

2   Methods

The solver used is IPOPT, which is a powerful open-source solver for large-scale nonlinear optimization, developed by Andreas Wächter and Lorenz T. Biegler.

It uses a primal-dual interior point method, making it particularly effective for handling large, sparse problems with high precision and reliability. IPOPT supports various linear solvers, such as MUMPS, HSL, and Pardiso, and integrates seamlessly with AMPL, making it a robust and efficient choice for nonlinear optimization.

AMPL is a modeling language designed to solve large-scale optimization problems in mathematical computing. It supports linear, nonlinear, and integer optimization, using syntax that closely mirrors mathematical notation to clearly express constraints, variables, and objectives. AMPL integrates seamlessly with a wide range of solvers, including CPLEX, MINOS, IPOPT, SNOPT, and KNITRO, by transmitting problems through .nl files generated from its model and data files. Its primary strengths lie in its user-friendly design, exceptional flexibility, and smooth integration with solvers. Additionally, AMPL supports the use of trigonometric functions in problem descriptions, making it particularly effective for modeling the kinematics of robotic arms [11].

Presolve is a preprocessing step intended to simplify optimization problems before solving. It removes redundant constraints, fixes variables by deducing their values from constraints, and simplifies equations to eliminate unnecessary variables and constraints. These reductions decrease problem size, lower computational effort, and enable faster, more efficient problem resolution. For a detailed explanation of the presolve algorithm used in AMPL, it is recommended to see the work [14].

In addition to problem simplification, presolve enhances numerical stability and overall solver performance. By identifying and removing poorly scaled or redundant constraints, it improves convergence properties and reduces memory usage during optimization [12]. For instance, in [13], presolve reduced model complexity by an average of 52.8% and identified infeasibility in 20% of cases. These reductions help solvers like IPOPT achieve faster and more efficient convergence. The performance benefits of presolve are particularly significant for larger, more structured problems, which tend to see the greatest reductions. However, the extent of presolve's impact also depends on the quality of the initial problem formulation in AMPL. In order to ascertain how this preprocessing step affects the solving of nonlinear optimization problems by IPOPT, different levels of presolve are used on the same problem. The differences in the problem formulation and the solving process are then analyzed.

3   Experimental Setup

The scenario under examination comprises the anthropomorphic robot RAMBO (Robotic Anthropomorphic Manipulator for Bimanual Operations) [15], which is tasked with restocking a shelving unit with various products. In particular, the process of restocking five products on a rotative shelf using the right arm will be analyzed in detail (see Fig. 1). The task begins with the robot in its home position. The robotic arm initiates the process by grasping the first object from the table and placing it onto the bottom shelf. It then returns to the table to retrieve the second object, which is placed on the second shelf. Next, it picks up the third object and places it on the top shelf, followed by the fourth object, which is positioned on the third shelf. Finally, the arm collects the fifth object from the table and places it on the third shelf as well. Once all objects have been restocked, the arm returns to its home position.

Fig. 1. RAMBO robotic platform restocking a shelving unit with products placed on a support table to the right of the robot.

For planning the robotic arm's movements, the HUMP [2] motion planner was used, which offers a global approach for generating obstacle-free, human-like trajectories of robotic arms. The refilling process is divided into two main stages: (i) picking the product from a support table, and (2) placing it on a shelf. The pick and place movements can be subdivided into three objected-directed primitives, designated as transport, approach, and retreat, whereas move movements, which consist of moving the arm without any object manipulation, only have the transport phase, as depicted in Fig. 2. To generate the pick-and-place movements, it is necessary to determine two key sets of postures: the target posture and the bounce posture. The determination of these postures involves addressing nonlinear optimization problems with different characteristics (for details on the nonlinear optimization problems see [2]). The target posture problem computes a posture that, given a desired position and orientation for the robot's hand, guarantees there are no collisions with obstacles in the workspace, provided the movement is feasible. Additionally, it ensures that the physical joint limits are respected while minimizing joint displacement from the initial to the target posture. Once the target posture is determined, a trajectory – referred to as the direct movement – is generated, guiding the robot from the starting posture to the calculated target posture. The bounce posture, on the other hand, is determined by checking for potential collisions at multiple discrete points along the trajectory, while again ensuring that joint limits are maintained and joint displacement is minimized. This posture facilitates the creation of a back-and-forth movement. To avoid collisions with obstacles, this back-and-forth movement is superimposed on the direct movement, producing a composite movement that ensures there are no collisions with obstacles over the duration of the movement.

In regard to the pick movement to determine the trajectories for each stage it is necessary to calculate four postures: (i) pre-approach posture, which involves moving the arm to a position near the selected product; (ii) bounce posture, which is responsible for ensuring that the trajectory generated does not have collisions with any obstacles present in the workspace of the robot; (iii) approach posture that corresponds to the posture of grasping the product; (iv) retreat posture that lifts the product from the table.

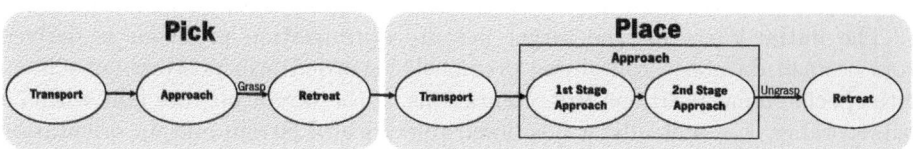

Fig. 2. Movement segmentation (for details it is recommended to see the work by [2]).

Conversely, the place movement comprises the determination of five distinct postures: (i) pre-approach posture, is characterized by the positioning of the product in close proximity to its intended location on the shelf; (ii) bounce posture, ensures that the robotic arm and the product being manipulated do not collide with any objects present in the scenario; (iii) first approach posture, which entails positioning the object just above its intended placement position; (iv) second approach posture, involves placing the product in its designated location; (v) retreat posture is the posture that takes the hand away from the product. Finally, there is a move movement that returns the robotic arm to its home posture. This movement only requires the calculation of the bounce posture, as the target posture is predefined as the arm's home position. The move movement may need a target posture selection problem if the intention is for the robotic arm to reach a pose other than its predefined home posture. The postures calculated in each stage of each movement are summarized in Table 1.

Table 1. Optimization problems solved on each movement.

Movement	Phase	Target Posture Selection	Bounce Posture Selection
Pick	Transport	✓	✓
	Approach	✓	×
	Retreat	✓	×
Place	Transport	✓	✓
	Approach	✓	×
	Retreat	✓	×
Move	Transport	×	✓

In all planned movements, the robot's body, the table, and the products to be replenished on the right side are modeled as obstacles using ellipsoids. However, during the pick movement, due to the geometry of the shelving unit and to simplify the optimization problems, ellipsoids are not used. Instead, a constraint is imposed that prevents any point of the robotic arm from exceeding the distance between the torso and the shelving unit, effectively avoiding collisions. For the place movement, this constraint is only considered for the transport phase. In the approach and retreat phases, individual shelves are modeled as ellipsoids, allowing the robot's hand to enter the shelf for a precise product placement.

The initial guess for the target posture optimization problems is derived from a small database containing previously recorded arm postures associated with specific hand positions and orientations. If the target posture falls within a defined range – specifically, a positional tolerance of 50 mm and an orientation tolerance of 5°C – of a stored posture, the corresponding posture is used as the initial guess. Otherwise, the arm's default initial configuration is used as the starting point. For the bounce posture optimization problems, the initial configuration of the arm is used as initial guess.

The refilling task consists of restocking five different products on the shelf. To accomplish this, the system must plan five pick movements, five place movements, and one move movement. As previously explained, each pick movement requires determining four distinct postures, while each place movement involves calculating five postures. The move movement, on the other hand, requires the computation of a single posture. Table 2 provides a breakdown of the 46 optimization problems organized by movement type.

Table 2. Number of optimization problems for the different type of movements.

Action	Pick	Place	Move
1	Vinegar	4th Shelf	-
2	Coffee	2nd Shelf	-
3	Conditioner	1st shelf	-
4	Can of beans	3rd shelf	-
5	Can of tomatoes	3rd shelf	-
6	-	-	Home
N. Target prob.	15	20	0
N. Bounce prob.	5	5	1

For evaluating the influence of the formulation on the CPU time on these problems, three presolve levels are considered, namely:

- 0, presolve is disabled, however AMPL may perform substitutions;
- 1, part one of the presolve is enabled, in this AMPL assigns the bounds to each variable and then tries to deduce tighter bounds. At the same time, it tries to detect variables that can be fixed and constraints that can be dropped;

– 10, both parts of the presolve are enabled, where several iterations of the problem are performed in order to deduce tighter bounds for the variables bounds and linear constraints for the current bounds.

4 Results

The evaluation of nonlinear optimization problems is based on three metrics: the number of variables, the number of inequality constraints, and the total CPU time required by the solver to reach a solution.

4.1 Dimension of the Optimization Problems

Table 3 summarizes the statistics on the number of inequality constraints for each optimization problem solved, during the task of restocking five products, considering three presolve levels: 0, 1, and 10. The data is divided by movement type and problem type(target or bounce). For the target posture problems, the number of decision variables is seven, corresponding to the seven joints of the robotic arm. In contrast, for bounce posture problems, the number of variables increases to eight, as the hand aperture is also considered.

Table 3. Statistics of the number of inequality constraints.

Movement	Type	Presolve	Variables	Min	Median	Max	Count
Pick	Target	0	7	17	37	73	15
		1					
		10					
Pick	Bounce	0	8	656	1301	1616	5
		1		599	1196	1463	
		10		455	1028	1319	
Place	Target	0	7	5	68	135	20
		1					
		10					
Place	Bounce	0	8	501	1197	1751	5
		1		454	1098	1578	
		10		321	944	1452	
Move	Bounce	0	8	257			1
		1		221			
		10		149			

In optimization problems involving the selection of target postures for both pick and place movements, the number of variables and constraints remains small. Additionally, the presolve level has no impact on the number of constraints. Specifically, for pick movements, the number of constraints ranges from 17 to 73, with half of the problems involving 37 or fewer constraints. However, when bounce postures are selected, the number of constraints increases significantly. At presolve level 0, the number of constraints range from 656 to

1616, with half of the problems having 1301 or fewer constraints. Increasing the presolve level to 1 and 10 reduces the number of constraints. At presolve level 10, the number of inequality constraints ranges from 455 to 1319, with half of the problems having 1028 or less constraints. This demonstrates that higher presolve levels consistently reduce inequality constraints in bounce posture problems. For place movements, the target posture problems have the same number of constraints across all presolve levels, with a range from 5 to 135, indicating no effect from presolve. However, for bounce posture problems, the number of constraints is much higher. At presolve level 0, the constraints range from 501 to 1751, with half of the problems having 1197 or fewer constraints. As the presolve level increases to 1 and 10, the number of constraints decreases, with presolve level 10 yielding values ranging from 321 to 1452, and half of the problems having 944 constraints or less. For the move movement, the number of constraints consistently decreases as the presolve setting increases. At presolve level 0, the constraints are fixed at 257, while presolve level 1 reduces this to 221, and presolve level 10 further reduces it to 149.

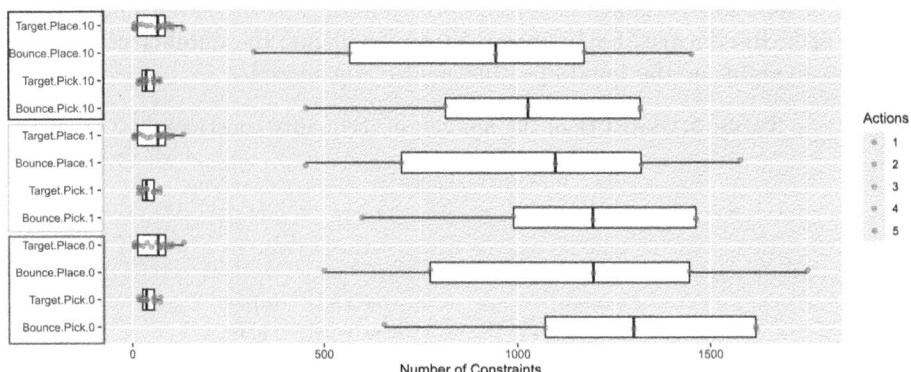

Fig. 3. Distribution of the number of inequality constraints.

Overall, the presolve process effectively reduces inequality constraints for the bounce type problems, with the most significant reductions seen at higher presolve values. In contrast, the target posture problems are less affected by presolve, with place movements showing no changes at all. The move movement shows uniform reductions in constraints with higher presolve levels but no variability. The number of inequality constraints for each solved problem is depicted in Fig. 3. Due to the significant differences in the problem formulation between target posture problems and bounce posture problems, they were categorized into these two distinct groups.

Changing the presolve level in target posture problems had no effect, as the number of inequality constraints remained unchanged. This is likely because the problems associated with the target postures are simpler in nature.

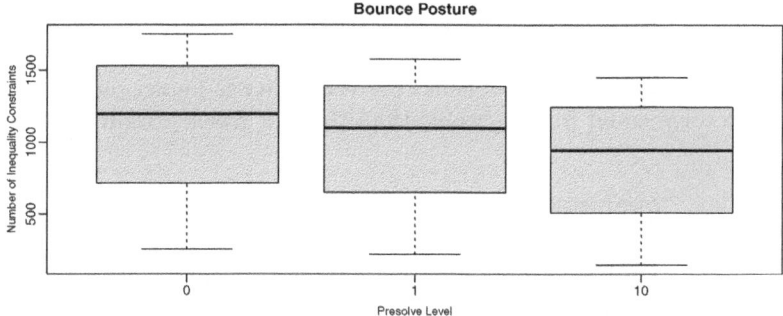

Fig. 4. Distribution of the number of constraints for different presolve levels of bounce posture problems.

On the other hand, when calculating the bounce posture, increasing the presolve level results in a reduction of the dimension of the associated optimization problems, more precisely, in the number of inequality constraints. This might be explained by the fact that the selection of the bounce posture is such that a collision-free trajectory of the arm and hand is obtained. There are constraints representing each object in the robot's workspace and for each point of the robot at every step of the trajectory. As a result, the problem is more complex compared to the target posture problems. Figure 4 illustrates the relationship between presolve levels and the number of inequality constraints in the optimization problems solved to determine the bounce posture.

To determine whether the observed decrease in the number of inequality constraints with an increase in the presolve level is statistically significant, a Kruskal-Wallis rank sum test was conducted to infer if there are significant differences in the median number of constraints for each presolve level. Since p-value=0.4211 > 5% ($\chi^2 \simeq 1.73$), for a significance level of 5%, there are no significant differences in the median number of inequality constraints in the bounce posture problems. Therefore, there is no evidence to support a significant effect of the presolve on the number of inequality constraints.

4.2 Computational Time

For each presolve level, each of the nonlinear optimization problems was executed 30 times to ensure the reliability of the results. Data regarding computation time and other pertinent metrics were gathered in a systematic manner across these trials with the objective of evaluating the influence of presolve on the overall efficiency of solving the optimization problems.

Nevertheless, it is important to note that, in some cases, the correlation between presolve and computation time may not be straightforward. This suggests that the complexity and structure of the problem may impact the effectiveness of presolve in optimizing performance. The data raises the question of whether increasing the presolve level could prove detrimental to the resolution of the problem. When plotting the computation time for different presolve levels of target posture problems (Fig. 5), there is minimal variation between levels. However, in bounce posture problems, the variability is higher, and the median value for presolve equal to 10 is worse than that for lower presolve settings.

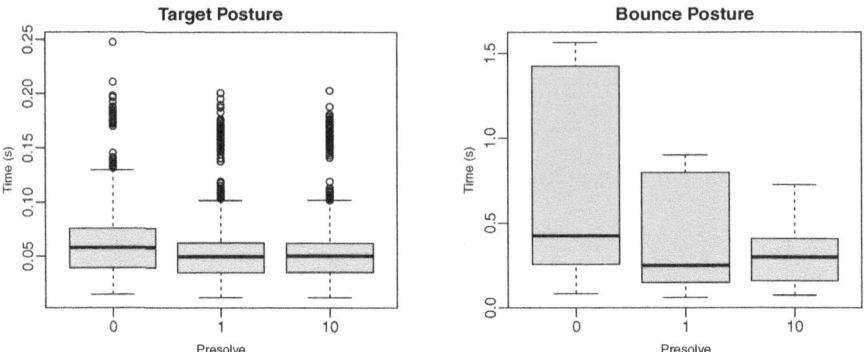

Fig. 5. Distribution of the time computation for optimization problems for different presolve levels.

Since the optimization problems solved for determining the bounce posture depend also on the spatial distribution of the objects on the robot's workspace and on the specific objects of the target-oriented movements, a closer examination was conducted on its computation. Figure 6 illustrates the computation times of bounce posture problems for different types of movements under various levels of presolve. The horizontal axis presents the computation time in seconds, while the vertical axis displays the types of movement that are planned. The initial five actions represent the reaching and placement of a product on the shelves, while action 6 represents a move movement, which corresponds to the arm returning to its home posture. As can be observed in Fig. 5, higher presolve levels generally result in shorter computation times.

The analysis is complemented with the information in Table 4 and Table 5, which present computation times for selecting target and bounce postures under different presolve settings (0, 1, 10) for pick, place, and move type movements. For the computation of the optimal bounce posture of each pick movement, presolve has a significant impact, half of the problems present computational times less than or equal to 1.046 s, while for presolve 1 this time reduces by 41% to 0.619 s, and presolve 10 reduces the time by 34% compared to presolve 1. For bounce posture problems, in place movements, half of the problems present a computational time of 0.422 s or less. When using presolve 1 the computation time reduces by 42%, however, when using a presolve 10, the computation time for half of the problems was not greater than 0.408 s, which represents an increase of 65% in relation to the previous level and a decrease of only 2% compared to presolve 0. For the move movement, computation times are generally lower, as

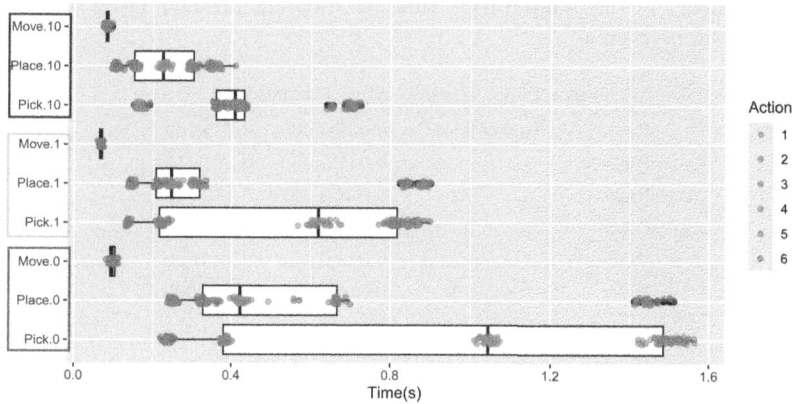

Fig. 6. Distribution of the computational time, in seconds, for selecting the bounce posture for restocking five products (Actions 1,2,3,4, and 5) in a shelving unit and return to home position (Action 6).

this movement only moves the arm from the third shelf to its home position, with presolve 1 offering the greatest reduction of 31%, while presolve 10 presents only a reduction of 14%. For target posture problems, computation times remain stable across different presolve levels, with a maximum decrease of about 2%. Increasing the presolve level reduces computation times for bounce posture problems, while having little impact on the computation time of target posture problems. This suggests the existence of differences in the computational time required by the solver to compute the bounce posture at different presolve levels for pick and place movements. To infer if these differences are significant, two Kruskal-Wallis tests were performed (see Table 6), namely to test whether there are differences in the median computational times using the three presolve levels for (i) pick

Table 4. Statistics of the computation time for different presolve levels of the bounce posture selection problems.

Movement	Type	Presolve	Min	Median	Max	N
Pick	Bounce	0	0.220	1.046	1.564	150
Pick		1	0.132	0.619	0.899	150
Pick		10	0.152	0.408	0.725	150
Place		0	0.237	0.422	1.513	150
Place		1	0.138	0.247	0.901	150
Place		10	0.152	0.408	0.725	150
Move		0	0.082	0.097	0.112	30
Move		1	0.059	0.067	0.075	30
Move		10	0.073	0.083	0.097	30

Table 5. Statistics of the computation time for different presolve levels of the target posture selection problems.

Movement	Type	Presolve	Min	Median	Max	N
Pick	Target	0	0.027	0.065	0.145	450
Pick		1	0.017	0.059	0.201	450
Pick		10	0.024	0.057	0.179	450
Place		0	0.015	0.049	0.248	600
Place		1	0.012	0.043	0.183	600
Place		10	0.012	0.045	0.203	600

and (ii) place movements. For (i) p-value=$4.2e - 11 < 5\%$ ($\chi^2 \simeq 47.78$), while for (ii) p-value=$2.2e - 16 < 5\%$ ($\chi^2 \simeq 142.43$). Therefore, for a significance level of 5%, the null hypothesis that there are no significant differences is rejected. These results imply that the choice of presolve level has a significant impact on computation performance for both groups, but the effect appears even more pronounced in the computation of the bounce posture, as indicated by the higher χ^2 statistic.

Table 6. Kruskal-Wallis test.

Movement	Type	χ^2	p-value
Target	Pick	28.81	5.547e-07
	Place	70.348	5.298e-16
Bounce	Pick	47.783	4.209e-11
	Place	142.43	2.2e-16

Subsequently, Pairwise Wilcox tests were conducted to assess whether the differences between the various presolve levels were statistically significant. From the p-values shown in Table 7, it can be inferred that to determine the bounce posture for pick movements, there are differences in the computation times between level 0 and levels 1 (p-value=$6.7e-14 < 5\%$) and 10 (p-value=$8.9e-11$), and also level 1 and level 10 (p-value=$0.0024 < 5\%$). The same applies to bounce posture problems in place movements, where it is possible to infer that there are differences in computation times between level 0 and levels 1 (p-value=$2e-16 < 5\%$) and 10 (p-value=$2e-16 < 5\%$), and also level 1 and level 10 (p-value=$0.0037 < 5\%$). For target posture problems, in pick movements there are differences in the computation time between level 0 and levels 1 (p-value=$4.7e-05 < 5\%$) and 10 (p-value=$2e-06 < 5\%$), but there are no significant differences between presolve level 1 and 10 (p-value=$0.46 > 5\%$). In place movements there are differences in the computation time between level 0 and levels 1 (p-value=$1e-09 < 5\%$) and 10 (p-value=$3.9e-8 < 5\%$), but there are no significant differences between presolve level 1 and 10 (p-value=$0.41 > 5\%$).

Table 7. P-values of the Pairwise Wilcox tests.

	Pick				Place			
	Target		Bounce		Target		Bounce	
Presolve	0	1	0	1	0	1	0	1
1	4.7e-05	-	6.7e-14	-	1.0e-09	-	2e-16	-
10	2.0e-06	0.46	8.9e-11	0.0024	3.9e-08	0.41	2e-16	0.0037

In Fig. 6, it is also possible to observe, in different colors, the computational times to determine the bounce postures for picking and placing each of the five products on the shelves (actions 1–5) and moving the arm to the home position (action 6). It suggests differences for different actions. Actions 4 and 5 are comparable, as the pick movement occurs in a similar position and the place movement for these objects is to the same shelf, placed next to each other. In order to gain insight into the differences between similar movements, actions 4 and 5 are subjected to analysis. As previously observed, the target posture problems exhibit minimal variability between them. Table 8 displays data on the number of inequality constraints of these problems, the number of iterations required by IPOPT to reach an optimal solution, the discretization steps used for collision checking, and the minimum, median, and maximum computation times for the pick-and-place movements of two objects (actions 4 and 5) under different presolve settings.

Action 4 consistently has more inequality constraints than action 5 in both pick and place movements. In the pick movement, action 4 has 1071 inequalities with presolve 0, compared to action 5's 656, and this trend persists across all presolve levels. Similarly, in the place movement, action 4 has 774 inequalities with presolve 0, while action 5 has 501. Despite the reductions with an increase in the presolve, action 4 maintains more constraints in both movements. Iteration counts are similar between the actions, but the higher number of inequality constraints for action 4, especially in the pick movement, suggest greater complexity.

Following this, the time to reach an optimal solution for the bounce posture is studied. When comparing the computation time of the bounce posture problems in pick movements between actions 4 and 5, distinct differences emerge both in overall times and in the impact of varying presolve settings. In action 4, the bounce problem of the pick movement without presolve (presolve 0) takes significantly longer, taking a computation time 4.35 times greater than action 5. Specifically, action 4 has a median time of 1.046 s compared to 0.240 s for action 5. This indicates that the picking phase in action 4 is initially much more time-consuming. The difference can be explained by the starting positions: in action 4, the arm begins near the third shelf, while in action 5, the arm starts closer to the top shelf, resulting in a longer and more complex path for the robotic arm. When presolve is applied, action 4 shows considerable improvement. With presolve 1, the median computation time drops by 41% to 0.620 s, and further decreases to

Table 8. Statistics computation time with different presolve settings for the bounce posture in pick and place movements of object 4 and 5.

				Number of			Time (s)			
Action	Type	Mov	Presolve	Ineq	Iter	Nsteps	Min	Median	Max	N
4	Bounce	Pick	0	1071	40	23	1.011	1.046	1.075	30
		Pick	1	990	40	23	0.568	0.620	0.676	30
		Pick	10	814	11	23	0.152	0.165	0.191	30
		Place	0	774	25	20	0.407	0.422	0.493	30
		Place	1	701	25	20	0.231	0.247	0.277	30
		Place	10	568	25	20	0.209	0.225	0.249	30
5	Bounce	Pick	0	656	15	19	0.220	0.240	0.257	30
		Pick	1	599	15	19	0.132	0.137	0.146	30
		Pick	10	455	44	19	0.352	0.364	0.391	30
		Place	0	501	29	20	0.311	0.333	0.397	30
		Place	1	454	29	20	0.201	0.210	0.234	30
		Place	10	312	15	20	0.095	0.106	0.138	30

0.165 s with presolve 10. In contrast, action 5 follows a different pattern. While presolve 1 reduces the median time to 0.137 s, presolve 10 unexpectedly increases it to 0.364 s. This suggests that for action 4, increasing presolve consistently improves performance, while in action 5, higher presolve values do not offer the same benefit and may even hinder performance at the highest setting. For the place movements, the comparison between actions 4 and 5 is also noteworthy. Without presolve, action 4 has a median computation time of 0.422 s, which is slightly higher than action 5 where half of the problems have a solving time of 0.333 s or less. However, when presolve is applied, both actions see improvements, but to different extents. In action 4, the median time drops by 47% to 0.247 s with presolve 1, and further to 0.225 s with presolve 10. In action 5, the reduction is even more pronounced, with a 37% decrease to 0.210 s with presolve 1, and a reduction to 0.106 s with presolve 10.

A Kruskal-Wallis rank sum test was performed using the data of the bounce postures problems of actions 4 and 5, for different levels of presolve. It was obtained a p-value=2.2e-16<5% ($\chi^2 \simeq 108.98$), therefore there are significant differences in the computation time using different presolve settings to solve the bounce posture selection problems.

5   Conclusions

In general, the most efficient model simplifications obtained using the presolve algorithm implemented in AMPL were obtained for presolve level 1. For this, the computation time for both pick and place movements, presented significant reductions. In contrast, although presolve level 10 presented larger reductions on the number of constraints of the optimization problems, does not consistently improve performance. Specifically, for pick movements, it increases both the number of iterations and computation time. Moderate presolve levels, such as level 1, may provide the best balance between constraint reduction and solver efficiency. Higher presolve levels, however, may degrade solver performance in certain cases.

Future work could focus on developing an algorithm to determine the most efficient presolve level for a given problem. Additionally, exploring how different parameters of the optimization problem, such as the initial guess, approach and retreat distances, or obstacle tolerances, affect the solving time, solution quality and complexity of the movement, could lead to a more effective parameter tuning for better results.

Acknowledgments. This work was supported by the project PT SMART RETAIL (ref. PRR 02/C05-i01.01/2022.PC645440011-00000062).

Disclosure of Interests. The authors have no competing interests to declare that are relevant to the content of this article.

References

1. Costa e Silva, E., Costa, F., Bicho, E., Erlhagen, W.: Nonlinear optimization for human-like movements of a high degree of freedom robotics arm-hand system. In: Murgante, B., Gervasi, O., Iglesias, A., Taniar, D., Apduhan, B.O. (eds.) ICCSA 2011. LNCS, vol. 6784, pp. 327–342. Springer, Heidelberg (2011). https://doi.org/10.1007/978-3-642-21931-3_26
2. Gulletta, G., Silva, E.C.e., Erlhagen, W., Meulenbroek, R., Costa, M.F.P., Bicho, E.: A human-like upper-limb motion planner: generating naturalistic movements for humanoid robots. Int. J. Adv. Robot. Syst. **18**(2) (2021)
3. AMPL Optimization: AMPL APIs. https://ampl.com/products/ampl/apis/. Accessed 27 Sept 2024
4. Wächter, A., Biegler, L.T.: On the implementation of an interior-point filter line-search algorithm for large-scale nonlinear programming. Math. Program. **106**, 25–57 (2006)
5. Tasseff, B., Coffrin, C., Wächter, A., Laird, C.: Exploring benefits of linear solver parallelism on modern nonlinear optimization applications. arXiv preprint arXiv:1909.08104 (2019)
6. Casanellas, G., Castro, J.: Using interior point solvers for optimizing progressive lens models with spherical coordinates. Optim. Eng. **21**(4), 1389–1421 (2020)
7. Thierry, D., Biegler, L.: The l1-exact penalty-barrier phase for degenerate nonlinear programming problems in ipopt. IFAC-PapersOnLine **53**(2), 6496–6501 (2020)
8. Hinder, O., Ye, Y.: A one-phase interior point method for nonconvex optimization. arXiv preprint arXiv:1801.03072 (2018)
9. Hogg, J.D., Scott, J.A.: On the effects of scaling on the performance of ipopt. arXiv preprint arXiv:1301.7283 (2013)
10. Kennedy, G., Fu, Y.: Topology optimization benchmark problems for assessing the performance of optimization algorithms. In: AIAA Scitech 2021 Forum. p. 1357 (2021)

11. Guamán, W., Pesántez, G., Falcones, S., Urquizo, J., et al.: Optimal dynamic reactive power compensation in power systems: Case study of ecuador-perú interconnection. Electric Power Syst. Res. **218**, 109191 (2023)
12. Puranik, Y., Sahinidis, N.V.: Domain reduction techniques for global NLP and minlp optimization. Constraints **22**(3), 338–376 (2017)
13. Jusevičius, V., Paulavičius, R.: Web-based tool for algebraic modeling and mathematical optimization. Mathematics **9**(21), 2751 (2021)
14. Fourer, R., Gay, D.M.: Experience with a primal presolve algorithm. Large Scale Optimization: State of the Art pp. 135–154 (1994)
15. Ribeiro, N., et al.: Rambo–robotic anthropomorphic manipulator for bimanual operations. In: 2024 IEEE International Conference on Autonomous Robot Systems and Competitions (ICARSC), pp. 157–164. IEEE (2024)

Characterization of Key Processes
for Production Systems Optimization

Denisa Borges[1,2(✉)] (iD), Luís M. S. Dias[1,2] (iD), Ricardo J. Machado[1,2] (iD),
and Marcelo F. N. Henriques[1,2] (iD)

[1] CCG/ZGDV Institute, University of Minho, Azurém Campus, 4800-058 Guimarães, Portugal
denisa.borges@ccg.pt
[2] ALGORITMI Research Centre, University of Minho, 4710-057 Braga, Portugal

Abstract. Several fields of knowledge have been invited to collaborate on production systems, in order to (a) answer to a growing system complexity, (b) offer organizations holistic solutions, and (c) obtain more resilient results to future changes. Examples of this are the collaborations between simulation, machine learning, and data engineering with multiple domains, for example production system – the focus of this research. Hence, this research aims to provide a holistic view of production systems, characterizing the key processes and concepts of production systems, to offer a clear and integrated understanding for newcomers into this field. The main processes are examined, such as: Production planning and control, Industrial processes, Logistics, Quality management, Maintenance, and Sustainability. The latter is structured around three core dimensions: environmental, social, and governance (ESG), representing an emerging differentiator among organisations. One notable example is green manufacturing, which focuses on minimising waste and promoting sustainable practices throughout the production process. Moreover, different production system models are reviewed, such as: Lean manufacturing, Just-in-time, and Mass production. At the end, a detailed analysis of each of these processes and models is provided, highlighting the relevance of a strategic and sustainable approach to success in contemporary production systems, promoting their optimization.

Keywords: Production system · Processes and models · Optimization

1 Introduction

Production systems are a framework within which production activities develop [1, 2]. A production system encompasses attributes – which may include people, machines, or tools – with the function of transforming raw materials into desired and forecasted goods and services. It is a quite complex concept, involving a series of activities and stakeholders, and thus must be treated with a certain level of seriousness.

Among the various types of production systems, Lean Manufacturing, Just-In-Time, and Mass Production stand out [3]. However, to gain a comprehensive understanding of these systems, it is essential to examine their core processes: production planning

O. Gervasi et al. (Eds.): ICCSA 2025 Workshops, LNCS 15888, pp. 241–257, 2026.
https://doi.org/10.1007/978-3-031-97596-7_16

and control, production processes, logistics, quality management, maintenance, and sustainability.

Most of these concepts were defined many years ago, and their constructs are described in books. The objective is to condense this information into a single paper, so that newcomers in this area can develop a holistic view of the production system.

This research is, therefore, relevant not only because of the review and synthesis of already established concepts but also due to the opportunity to apply these concepts in the current context of organizations. By analysing the main processes and practices, the study aims to offer a clearer understanding of how these elements interconnect, with the goal of promoting more efficient management aligned with contemporary needs. Thus, this study seeks to provide a detailed view of production systems, as well as generate valuable insights for innovation and the advancement of production practices in organizations.

This research is structured into four sections. The first refers to the current subsection, where the opportunities of the developed research are explained, along with the research questions and objectives that prompted the development of the work, and the methodology used for its development. The second subsection provides a brief review of the various types of production systems and describes the main processes within the production system: Production Planning and Control, Production Process, Logistics, Quality Management, Maintenance, and Sustainability. The third subsection makes a brief discussion, and finally, the fourth subsection describes the main conclusions of the developed work, as well as suggestions for future research.

1.1 Research Questions and Objectives

Table 1. Research questions and objectives

Research Questions	Research Objectives	Research Strategy
1: What are the types of production systems?	RO2: Analyse the various types of production systems	Systematic Literature Review
2: What are the main processes inherent to production systems?	RO2: Investigate the main processes inherent to production system	Systematic Literature Review

This research aims to answer a set of research questions, from which a set of research objectives were derived. For each one, a research strategy was defined, and all are listed on Table 1.

1.2 Methodology

The strategy used to answer both RO1 and RO2 was a systematic literature review, developed to each of them separately. According to [4], systematic literature reviews should be rigorous and relevant, as they can foster scientific knowledge. Furthermore, they should be reliable and repeatable [5] in order to enlighten the reader on what has been learned.

Based on the framework proposed by [6], the PRISMA was used to guide the article selection process. The complete details of the process can be accessed via the following link: https://tinyurl.com/yc8d5uu6. Initially, the selected databases were: Scopus, Google Scholar, and Web of Science (WoS). A filtering process was then applied to journal articles, conference papers, and books. The keywords used to obtain articles were previously defined, and are available at the following link: https://tinyurl.com/paf syjh7. Subsequently, a filter for publication year was applied, from 2013 to 2025. An exception was made for studies identified through the snowballing technique, due to its relevance on the subject. The search results were ordered by relevance, and filtered by reading their abstracts.

The snowball technique was employed when a retrieved article, from the systematic review, cited another article, from which it was identified as the original source of the fundamental concepts for production system.

2 Production System and Its Models

The evolution of production systems reflects changes in technological advancements, market needs, and the growing ambition for efficiency in production. Mass production emerged in the early 20th century, as a response to the increasing demand, leading to the introduction of the assembly line, popularized by Henry Ford in the automotive industry. Mass production significantly reduced costs and increased output, becoming the dominant model for much of the 20th century [7], with a single goal: maximize production output [8].

As product diversity expanded and consumer demand increased, new production models began to gain prominence. Batch production, or mass customization, emerged as viable alternatives, allowing for a balance between mass production and a degree of customization. This model became common in industries such as semiconductors, automotive, and textiles; responding to the growing demand for customization without compromising efficiency [9, 10].

With the advent of the third Industrial Revolution, also known as the Digital Revolution, made-to-order production has been gaining ground, especially with the advancement of technologies such as CAD (computer-aided design), CAM (computer-aided manufacturing), and numerical control; which enabled the production of personalized goods in smaller batches, aiming at reducing that impact on production efficiency, therefore on the end-product's price. This model has allowed organizations to offer highly customized products tailored to the specific needs of each customer [11].

Despite these advantages, continuous production continues to be fundamental in some industries, such as petrochemical and metallurgical. These are characterized by an uninterrupted manufacturing process, making it particularly suitable for large-scale production of homogeneous products. This type of production offers great stability in product quality and operation efficiency, especially on complex production systems [12, 13].

After the 1973 oil crisis, demand decreased, and, consequently, economic growth slowed. As a response, mainly to induce demand, the need for product diversification arose. As such, the Just-In-Time (JIT) production system gained prominence as a recession-resistant model, due to its drastic reduction in Work-In-Process (WIP) and stock levels. JIT influences the production flow timing, where materials are delivered to the production system at the right moment, in the required quantities, to the production processes where they are needed. Materials need to arrive within minutes – not days or weeks – before being used on the production line. Hence, JIT reduces different types of waste, such as WIP, stock, overproduction, and delays in delivery times. The lead time will, in principle, be shorten. The JIT production system is market-oriented, entirely based on customer satisfaction [14, 15]. According to [16], JIT can also be understood as a production philosophy applied to production systems, with the goal of delivering a high-quality final product.

When discussing the JIT production system, the concept of Kanban immediately comes up, a component created by Toyota to enhance production efficiency. The term "Kanban" – which means "visual signal" or "card", in Japanese – is used to indicate the next stages in the production process. In a conventional Kanban system, whenever a material is used on the production line, a Kanban card is sent to the previous process to indicate the need for a replacement. This (a) facilitates inventory management and (b) ensures that materials are produced or moved only when necessary; therefore reducing waste and increasing flow efficiency [14].

The Lean Manufacturing production system originates from the Toyota Production System (TPS), based on the principles of JIT (Just-In-Time), meaning that materials should be requested when they are needed, the process should only initiate when needed, and the product should be manufactured when ordered, entirely based on consumer demand. Lean Manufacturing is grounded in the Kaizen philosophy of continuous process improvement, standardization of work procedures, and maintaining the improvements achieved. As a result, changes are expected, focusing on waste reduction, process enhancement, and increased value creation. Lean Manufacturing balances production speed according to demand [3].

The different production models mentioned above summarize the various approaches organizations have been adopting throughout the past decades, mainly to adapt to market demand, balancing factors such as production efficiency, flexibility, and customization. The choice of the adequate production system will depend on several factors, including the nature of the product, production volume, and consumer expectations.

2.1 Main Processes

A production line is a complex system, encompassing several concepts and elements, hence, it shall not be treated lightly. Characterizing the main processes of production systems is essential to better understand how organizations transform materials into products. Moreover, it is also relevant to understand the processes that indirectly influence the product and processes, e.g., maintenance. These (indirect) processes are crucial because, through them, we can promote better product quality. Arguably, it is an essential process in any production system, maintenance is often neglected.

This section focuses on the main processes of production systems, namely: production planning and control, industrial processes, logistics, quality management, maintenance, and sustainability.

Production Planning and Control

Production planning encompasses a multitude of elements, with a focus on the daily activities of the team, as well as meeting delivery deadlines. According to Henry Fayol, planning involves deciding the best strategy from a set of options [17].

When discussing production planning, aggregate production planning (APP), shall not be overlooked. APP consists of determining the optimal production levels and workforce for each period within the medium-term planning horizon. Its goal is to define the general production levels for each product family, to meet fluctuating demand in the near future. Among the existing APP models, stochastic models stand out. These models are typically based on the concept of randomness and probability theory, being limited in handling uncertainties through probability distributions [18]. Included in these models, stochastic simulation is becoming one of the main techniques applied to production systems, due to its capability of evaluating the performance of systems with random behaviours, which are mathematically intractable through a deterministic approach [19].

Regarding production control, according to Henry Fayol, it involves checking whether everything is running according to the adapted plans – the issued instructions, and the estimated principles. Its main objective is to identify deviations, to uncover weaknesses and errors, so they can be avoided or corrected in the future [17].

Production planning and control (PPC) encompasses a series of decisions aimed at defining what, how much, and when to produce, order, and deliver – to allow for operations to be carried out according to predefined schedules [17]. PPC activities are developed not only based on the restrictions and goals set by top management, but also on customer orders, demand forecasting, and stock [20]. According to [17], PPC should be tailored to the type and volume of production, developing simple techniques for organisations that manufacture high volumes of customised products, while balancing the level of control with associated costs. It is for this reason that each organisation has its own PPC technique, resulting from several insights from other organisations (e.g., Toyota and TPS), and continuous improvement.

The main PPC objectives include: minimising downtime (man vs. machine), reducing stock turnover time, maximising product quality and customer satisfaction, maintaining low inventory levels, ensuring short setup and lead times, preventing bottlenecks in the production flow, and planning material orders in advance. This last objective is achievable making use of the Bill of Materials (BOM), which details all components and consumables required to produce the final product.

A commonly used technique in PPC is (demand) forecasting, which involves using past demand patterns to forecast future demand. Typically, forecasting is more accurate in short-term planning. Demand forecasting is riskier upon increasing the planning horizon, due to the high scope of the current economical interdependency. Regardless, every forecasting should always include an error estimate [21].

Forecasting can be categorized from a period perspective: short-term, medium-term, and long-term forecasting. Short-term forecasting (up to 1 year) is necessary for personnel scaling, production, transportation, and demand forecasting. Medium-term forecasting (up to 5 years) is necessary to determine future requirements for material purchases, hiring personnel, or purchasing machinery and equipment. Long-term forecasting (over 5 years) is used in strategic planning, e.g., acquiring land, expanding facilities, establishing in a different country. The latter must take into account market opportunities, environmental factors, and internal resources [17].

MRP

Material Requirements Planning (MRP) is a key inventory management technique which allows to schedule materials, aligned with the Master Production Schedule (MPS). Its main objective is to ensure the right type and quantity of materials is available at the right time, avoiding both waiting times and WIP. MRP defines when to release and receive material orders, supporting the effective implementation of the MPS. In turn, the MPS guides production by coordinating inputs from different departments to determine what and when to produce, ensuring demand is met efficiently [22]. For each planning order, the MRP determines the materials based on the product BOM. When there is insufficient material stock, and no planned delivery, the MRP generates a replenishment proposal, alerting the need to order or produce said material [23, 24].

Due to the lot-sizing rule of the MRP technique, changes in higher-level schedules cause significant changes in lower-level schedules. For instance, a small change in the MPS may result in significant changes in the time or quantity of a given material at a production cell. The causes of MRP instability (or 'nervousness') include: changes in the MPS, fluctuations in supplier lead times, poor material quality, record errors, unplanned transactions, among others. Approaches to reduce MRP nervousness include: improving both customer and supplier relationships, as well as greater data processing efficiency [25].

MRP II

Manufacturing Resource Planning (MRP II) is an extension of the Material Requirements Planning (MRP). MRP II is an advancement which integrates various processes, such as: business and production planning, scheduling, and capacity management. It also supports execution, and links production data with financial planning – making it a broader extension of the closed-loop MRP system [24].

MRP II helps industrial engineers to plan all the resources needed for production, including: equipment, labour, production planning and control, costs, and more. MRP II provides industrial engineers with detailed information at the right time on what, how much, and when to produce; as well as generating new orders and reschedule previously planned orders. Hence, MRP II enables a more efficient response to volatile demand [17].

ERP

Enterprise Resource Planning (ERP) systems are intra-organization systems which support core business processes across various organizations. They include MRP II functionality for manufacturing organizations and general management features, e.g., accounting, financial planning, and human resources; applicable to all types of organizations. ERP systems serve as the backbone of business information processing, enabling integrated management of major business processes and recording most business transactions [26]. ERP systems can significantly reduce operational costs while improving efficiency, productivity, and data quality – when implemented correctly. They contribute to internal integration, as well as supply chain integration [18, 27].

Digital Twin

Production planning and control (PPC) involves managing the processes necessary to produce goods and services [28]. As such processes are quite different among organizations, the PPC varies by organization. Despite this, the need to determine production schedules is universal [29].

Consumer, competition, and technology pressures are constantly evolving, requiring updates to processes, therefore, to the design of PPC systems. As a result, PPC systems must be responsive, supporting high-quality production, small lots, customization, customer commitment, and sustainable practices [20].

Research is being developed in Digital Twin technology for production systems to address PPC activities and modelling [30]. PPC is evolving with Industry 4.0 principles, focusing on self-managed, automated, and autonomous systems [20]. Industry 4.0 merges digital technologies, organizational concepts, and management principles to provide more economical, responsive, resilient, and sustainable operations [31].

Industrial Processes

A production process consists of a series of planned actions that cause physical or chemical changes in a material, with the purpose of adding value. Generally, a production process is carried out as a unit operation, i.e., it is a single step within a set of operations which are necessary to transform one or more materials into one or mode final products [32].

According to [33], a production process generally involves a sequence of fundamental steps, which form the material flow. This sequence can be divided into three main phases: (1) the first phase refers to processes that prepare the material by adjusting its geometry or properties, e.g., heating, melting, cutting, sawing; to make it suitable for the changes that will occur in the subsequent phases. (2) The second phase involves processes that modify the geometry or properties of the material, creating the desired shape for the component. (3) The third, and last, phase consists of processes that finish the component, bringing it to the final desired state, through actions, e.g., solidification, cooling, and deburring.

By contrast, [32] presents a more Boolean view of production processes, at a high-level. According to the author, production operations can be divided into two main types: (a) processing operations, and (b) assembly operations.

a) Processing Operations.

A processing operation uses energy to modify the shape, properties, or appearance of a material, adding value to the material. Energy sources include: mechanical, thermal, electrical, and chemical; applied by machines or tools. Human energy may also be required, typically for operating machines, supervising processes, or handling materials.

The general model of processing involves material entering the process, energy being applied to modify it, and the final piece exiting. Most operations generate waste or scrap, either as a by-product (e.g., material removal in machining) or defective pieces; and reducing waste is critical in these processing operations.

Usually, processing operations are applied to individual materials, but some can also be carried out on materials which have already been assembled (e.g., painting a vehicle body that has already been welded).

Typically, multiple operations are needed to transform the material into the final desired state, performed in a specific sequence, based on design requirements. Processing operations are classified into three categories: (i) shaping operations (e.g., casting, forging, machining), (ii) property improvement operations (e.g., tempering), and (iii) surface processing operations (e.g., galvanizing, painting).

b) Assembly Operations.

The assembly process occurs when two or more separate materials are joined to form a new, assembled, one. The materials of the resulting assembly can be joined permanently or semi-permanently. Permanent joining processes include welding, brazing, and gluing; which create a junction between components that cannot be easily separated. There are also mechanical assembly methods which allow two (or more) parts to be fixed in such a way that the assembly can be conveniently disassembled. The use of bolts, nuts, and other threaded fasteners are important traditional methods in these operations. Subassembly, the name can demonstrate the assembly process itself, e.g., a welded assembly is the result of a welding assembly operation.

Logistics

Transportation is an integral, and investable, part of the logistics system, as it is the physical link that connects materials, final products, customers, and suppliers [34]. Transportation can be grouped into two types: short-distance and long-distance transportation. Short-distance transportation refers to the movement between points relatively close to each other, within a specific area; while long-distance transportation involves the movement between distant points [35].

When discussing transportation, it is also important to consider the associated costs, making it crucial to distinguish between marginal costs and average costs. In this context, marginal cost refers to the additional expense incurred when transporting one extra unit, while average cost represents the total transportation cost divided by the number of units transported [36].

Inventory management is a critical component of logistics, allowing organizations to ensure customer service levels and support logistical and production activities, especially in situations where purchasing or producing items cannot immediately meet demand. Inability to respond to demand in a timely manner can occur, due to acquisition or production lead times, or the inability to supply the necessary quantities without pre-existing stock. The size of the logistics inventory is influenced, and often determined, by the chosen transportation methods and the resulting delivery lot size. Changing the delivery method can influence stock levels [37]. Furthermore, some materials might be perishable, i.e., tend to deteriorate over time, due to their characteristics. Hence, a proper inventory strategy might be required to ensure that those perishable materials are not wasted. E.g., FEFO (First-Expire, First-Out) prioritizes the retrieval of materials with the earliest expiration date.

Quality Management

For many, quality is seen as meeting pre-defined specifications. However, some argue that quality is subjective and depends on each individual's perception [38]; in other words, quality has different meanings for different people. The definition of quality, in the context of production, processes and service industries is as follows [39]: meeting customer needs, suitability for use, compliance with requirements and degree of excellence at an acceptable price.

The International Organization for Standardization (ISO) defines quality as "the totality of characteristics of an entity that influences its ability to satisfy explicit or implicit needs", and provides an explanation of the various quality management principles, which are essential for facilitating the application of the ISO 9001:2015 standard [39].

Quality in a production system is achieved through a sequence of processes in which materials and labour are transformed to create the final product. The product is monitored throughout the system, by inspections and tests at different stages. If a product fails to meet the defined requirements, it is repaired, reworked, or discarded; and actions are taken to eliminate the root causes of the issue. For this, statistical process control methods are typically employed control the process, with the objective of reducing process variability and increase process efficiency [39].

Quality management is essential to ensure that objectives are achieved with the desired level of excellence, making the organization competitive in the market [39]. Over the past decade, quality management has promoted significant and valuable improvements in operations and supply chain systems [38].

The quality management principles are essential in the implementation of the ISO 9001:2015 standard. Albeit, they are not complete, nor do they have a clear theoretical or conceptual basis; being simply a list without prioritization and interconnections. Below are the seven principles contained in the ISO 9000:2015 Quality management systems - Fundamentals and vocabulary [40]:

- Customer Focus: Customer focus is seen as the central goal of quality management. The organization must understand customer expectations in order to respond to them and even exceed them, which will ultimately lead to higher customer satisfaction;
- Leadership: According to the Total Quality Management (TQM) philosophy, organization leaders should be role models in quality matters, engaging and empowering employees in quality improvement processes. Leadership is responsible for the implementation of quality management;
- Engagement of People: Employee engagement and qualification are directly related to leadership. Quality management requires skilled employees, who must be trained for the tasks they are assigned. Resources and tools, such as surveys, training, and internal communication programs, should be provided for this purpose;
- Process Approach: Quality management should analyse the organization's process flows. All processes must be coordinated and controlled, to avoid errors at different stages. This requires careful and systematic planning of individual processes;
- Improvement: The focus is on continuous improvement processes, which aim to optimize performance, processes, and products. These processes should be addressed systematically, using tools such as error analyses, quality circles, improvement suggestions, and feedback from market actors;

- Evidence-Based Decision Making: Professional quality management seeks to avoid excessive subjective evaluations of quality issues, such as causes, effects, and risks. Decision-making should be based on facts, provided by information, data, numbers, and evidence. Tools like key indicators, statistical surveys, and experiments are used;
- Relationship Management: For successful and long-term quality management, as many stakeholders as possible should be involved. The goal is not to achieve short-term advantages, but to build, maintain, and strengthen partnership relationships, also analysing the use of shared resources through cooperation with the appropriate market players.

The integration of business and production operations with quality practices and technological advancements can help achieve higher levels of maturity. As a result, it enables the optimization of production process performance and product quality, improves supply chain reliability, and promotes continuous and proactive improvement [41].

Maintenance

In the production context, maintenance plays a vital role across various sectors, including manufacturing and transportation. It both influences and is influenced by other organizational functions, such as: production, quality, inventory management, marketing, and human resources.

Although traditionally analysed in isolation, its integration with other departments – and the broader supply chain – has become increasingly essential. Within the production system, maintenance is one of the most complex processes, as it requires the reduction of costs, increase of asset value, and enhancement of product quality. Its impact on organizational success is undeniable, particularly in the manufacturing sector, where it has become a leading factor in advancing development in this sector [42].

Maintenance can be classified into three types:

- Corrective Maintenance: it is a maintenance task performed to identify and correct the causes of system failures. This type of maintenance occurs when equipment malfunctions and is unable to continue its intended operation, leading to unscheduled production downtimes [43, 44]. Corrective maintenance requires human involvement. When a system experiences downtime, the operator observes the system, analyses the failure (diagnostics), and takes corrective action to eliminate the cause of the failure. With the rise of technologies triggered by Industry 4.0, the complexity of production systems has increased, and, as a result, the occurrence of human errors during corrective maintenance has also risen [45]. Moreover, as it is human dependant, especially in terms of diagnosis, it benefits from training and experience.
- Preventive Maintenance: it is a programmed maintenance, consisting of activities initiated at predetermined intervals or based on prescribed criteria, aimed at reducing the likelihood and severity of failure [46, 47]. Preventive maintenance tasks can be performed during non-production periods, to avoid unexpected production downtimes [48]. According to [49], some researchers argue that preventive maintenance does not fully restore the system to an ideal state, but instead brings it to a state where it can perform its functions within what is possible.

- Predictive Maintenance: is a strategy that leverages real-time data to anticipate equipment failures before they occur, enabling scheduled interventions and preventing unexpected production downtimes. Unlike preventive maintenance, which operates on fixed intervals, predictive maintenance is based on the actual condition of the equipment, optimising resources and reducing operational costs [50]. This approach is particularly effective on specific equipment's, with predictable failure modes. For instance, predictive inspections may utilise existing equipment such as voltmeters and other measuring instruments [51], or new ones installed on older machinery. E.g., changes on a pump vibration patterns, caused by a failing bearing, can trigger a repair operation. It is relevant to note that such approach requires investment in infrastructure and technology, some of them linked to Industry 4.0 and the Digital Twin. The benefits are similar to Preventive Maintenance, adding the reduction in time and costs associated with excessive repair operations – as each repair operation is "predicted", based on data collected from the equipment itself. In cases of catastrophic system failures, predictive maintenance plays a crucial role in preventing significant damage to infrastructure or machinery, as well as mitigating potential risks to operators working on the system [52].

Sustainability

Sustainability defines the foundation of the human-nature relationship, encompassing issues such as equal access to resources, not only for present generations, but also for future generations [53]. It defines behaviours and attitudes that do not compromise the ability of future generations to meet their needs. Sustainable development intervenes in various areas, being highly dynamic and reactive, and interpreted in different ways, by different people, and in different contexts.

In this context, ESG (Environmental, Social, and Governance) emerges as a set of criteria that assess an organization's impact in three main areas: environmental, social, and governance, aiming to promote responsible and sustainable practices that ensure the preservation of natural resources, social well-being, and good corporate governance [6].

Sustainability is a concept that dates back to green manufacturing, which represents ecological sustainability. It encompasses various concerns, such as air, water, and soil pollution, waste recycling, as well as the use of more sustainable energy sources.

For some authors, green manufacturing is seen as a philosophy, not just a process; it is a production method that minimizes waste and pollution through product and process design. However, to achieve this, continuous improvement in production processes is necessary [54].

The goal of green manufacturing is to minimize the environmental impact caused by human activities. Several organizations have started adopting these initiatives in their operations due to rising energy costs and the growing demand for "green" products [55, 56]. Therefore, it is expected that manufacturing organizations will implement green manufacturing and increase product complexity at a competitive price [57].

Both governmental and non-governmental organizations are increasingly concerned with sustainability issues, such as: reducing the consumption of natural resources, using those resources sustainably, and utilizing renewable energy sources. This is possible through technologies that enhance the generation of renewable energies, such as photovoltaic panels, wind turbines, bioreactors, biofiltration, bioremediation, and energy conservation [53, 56]. It is also important to highlight those socioeconomic issues, such as the creation of new jobs, are intrinsically linked to sustainability.

3 Discussion

It is widely recognized that organizations have to deal with an increasingly volatile marked, which will be reflected on their production system, through its processes, machinery, techniques, and technologies; which promotes the inclusion of new solutions [58].

Production planning and control should include the following activities: decomposition of all product tasks, product requirement analysis (technical and human resources), operation sequencing, and task progress real-time monitoring and control. It is a multi-departmental effort, meaning, it involves several expertise, e.g., product development, maintenance, customer service [59].

Therefore, the solutions employed on production systems – being machinery, technologies, or tools –must ensure both (a) interoperability among the multitude of digital assets already in place; and (b) attend to the different departmental requirements.

As a result, production systems are becoming increasingly complex and interoperable. In line, the need for maintenance on production systems is emphasized, to correct, but specially to prevent or predict failures; therefore, avoiding unscheduled production interruption.

This is mainly because the success of organizations is closely linked to the performance of their production systems, in terms of quantity, quality, and safety. This performance can only be achieved through a highly effective and efficient production system, capable of ensuring high manufacturing equipment availability, ensuring long-term reliability, and preserving asset value and human safety [42].

Quality management is an important part of the production processes, as it is closely linked to the organization credibility, in its processes, and products or services. Often, quality management is mandatory to be part of certain supply chains, e.g., automotive, aviation, food, medical. I.e., if organizational processes do not attend certain criteria, products do not meet certain specifications or attend the defined requirements; organization will not be eligible to supply parts (automotive and aviation) or even to operate (food and medical). Moreover, its credibility may be negatively impacted if a single aspect is not met. A plane crash, or a drug incident, may at minimum discourage consumers, or at maximum stop an organization from operating.

Many organizations are resorting to advanced technologies to ensure material and product quality, inventory optimization, production system availability, and supply chain integration [60]. These work to both increase organization efficiency, and also to avoid incidents.

Regarding logistics, it should be seen as a network in which all processes and organizational resources are interconnected, and communicate with each other [61]. Several initiatives are being researched to implement more sustainable and efficient solutions in terms of logistics transportation [60]. The use of AMRs (Autonomous Mobile Robots) inside facilities, to reduce the amount of peripherals and deadlocks typically associated with AGVs (Automated Guided Vehicle) is an example, as well as self-driving semitrucks or hydrogen-powered airplanes.

Industrial organizations must adapt to changes, while consistently integrating sustainability principles into all their processes. In this context, Green manufacturing emerged, aiming to minimize waste and environmental impact throughout the production process [58, 60]. However, rather than relying solely on traditional frameworks, some authors argue that it is more effective to adopt the Environmental, Social, and Governance (ESG) criteria. ESG provides a structured framework for assessing and implementing sustainable practices, aligning with global initiatives, such as the SDG (Sustainable Development Goals, a United Nations Development Programme) and The European Green Deal (approved by the European Commission). This shift towards ESG ensures a more comprehensive and forward-looking approach to sustainability.

4 Conclusions and Future Work

Production systems involve a high level of complexity, making it vital to focus on their core processes to optimise performance. Different types of production systems exist to serve varying operational needs, and selecting the appropriate one depends on the strategic objectives of the organisation. To remain competitive, organizations must monitor broader economic shifts, stay attuned to evolving customer preferences, and continuously embrace innovation to ensure their products and services align with market demands.

In order to take full advantage of new technologies and tools which unlock greater integration and efficiency within and among organizations, all the stockholders should understand the core business. Indeed, the same is true regarding production system. Hence, this research provides a characterizing of the key processes and concepts of production systems, to offer a clear and integrated understanding for newcomers into this field. By doing so, we intend to promote an effective and efficient addition of specialists in different fields of knowledge, such as: simulation, machine learning and data engineering; in order to further advance production system optimization through collaboration efforts.

Through collaborative efforts, a set of advantages are unlocked, namely: (a) answer to a growing system complexity, (b) offer organizations holistic solutions, and (c) obtain more resilient results to future changes.

Moreover, the review of production systems allows for establishing a crucial connection for subsequent research on the fundamental building blocks structuring (source, server, combiner, separator, among others); which are essential for the construction of simulation models. This process eases the identification of critical production systems building blocks. The source, for example, can be applied in raw material input, adjusting times according to demand. The server, in turn, can be used to mimic the processing of raw materials. The combiner can be employed to replicate the assembly or palletization. By contrast, the separator can be used to separate components or to remove from a pallet. At last, there are elements which will link the previously mentioned building blocks, e.g., paths, conveyors.

Through this research, the main production processes and models were detailed, and the key building blocks were identified. This enables the collaboration among different fields of knowledge, promoting production system optimization. Particularly, regarding simulation, one of the authors' research topics, this effort is intended to feed future developments to promote the use of simulation as an optimization in decision-support systems (DSS).

Acknowledgements. Acknowledgements. This work has been supported by the European Union under the NextGenerationEU, through a grant of the Portuguese Republic's Recovery and Resilience Plan (PRR) Partnership Agreement, within the scope of the program "Missão Interface", aiming at financing the base component of CCG/ZGDV Institute (Operation code nr. 03/C05-i02/2022.P5; Total Grant: 4 037 440,23 Euros).

References

1. Das, S., Patnaik, A.: Production planning in the apparel industry. In: Garment Manufacturing Technology, pp. 81–108. Elsevier (2015). https://doi.org/10.1016/B978-1-78242-232-7.000 04-7
2. Jacobs, F.R., Chase, R.: Operations and Supply Chain Management. McGraw-Hill/Irwin. McGraw-Hill/Irwin, New York, USA (2018)
3. Vinodh, S.: Lean Manufacturing: Fundamentals, Tools, Approaches, and Industry 4.0 Integration. CRC Press, New York (2022). https://doi.org/10.1201/9781003190332
4. Paré, G., Trudel, M.-C., Jaana, M., Kitsiou, S.: Synthesizing information systems knowledge: a typology of literature reviews. Inf. Manage. **52**, 183–199 (2015). https://doi.org/10.1016/j.im.2014.08.008
5. Xiao, Y., Watson, M.: Guidance on conducting a systematic literature review. J. Plan. Educ. Res. **39**, 93–112 (2019). https://doi.org/10.1177/0739456X17723971
6. Martiny, A., Taglialatela, J., Testa, F., Iraldo, F.: Determinants of environmental social and governance (ESG) performance: a systematic literature review. J. Clean. Prod. **456**, 142213 (2024). https://doi.org/10.1016/j.jclepro.2024.142213
7. Marsh, P.: The new industrial revolution: consumers, globalization and the end of mass production. Yale University Press, New Haven (2012)
8. Gundlach, T.: Lean Empowerment and Respect for People: The Evolution of Lean Production Systems. Productivity Press, New York (2024). https://doi.org/10.4324/9781032644134
9. Hu, J., Jiang, Z., Liao, H.: Preventive maintenance of a batch production system under time-varying operational condition. Int. J. Prod. Res. **55**, 5681–5705 (2017). https://doi.org/10.1080/00207543.2017.1330565
10. Mönch, L., Uzsoy, R., Fowler, J.W.: A survey of semiconductor supply chain models part III: master planning, production planning, and demand fulfilment. Int. J. Prod. Res. **56**, 4565–4584 (2018). https://doi.org/10.1080/00207543.2017.1401234
11. Suri, R.: The practitioner's guide to POLCA: the production control system for high-mix, low-volume and custom products. CRC Press, Boca Raton, FL (2018)
12. Chinwanitcharoen, C., Kanoh, S., Yamada, T., Tada, K., Hayashi, S., Sugano, S.: Preparation and shelf-life stability of aqueous polyurethane dispersion. Macromol. Symp. **216**, 229–240 (2010). https://doi.org/10.1002/masy.200451222
13. Rakmai, J., Cheirsilp, B.: Continuous production of β-cyclodextrin by cyclodextrin glycosyltransferase immobilized in mixed gel beads: Comparative study in continuous stirred tank reactor and packed bed reactor. Biochem. Eng. J. **105**, 107–113 (2016). https://doi.org/10.1016/j.bej.2015.09.011

14. Hirano, H.: JIT Implementation Manual (2009)
15. Sugimori, Y., Kusunoki, K., Cho, F., Uchikawa, S.: Toyota production system and Kanban system Materialization of just-in-time and respect-for-human system. Int. J. Prod. Res. **15**, 553–564 (1977). https://doi.org/10.1080/00207547708943149
16. García Alcaraz, J.L., Macías, A.A.M.: Just-in-Time Elements and Benefits. Springer International Publishing, Cham (2016). https://doi.org/10.1007/978-3-319-25919-2
17. Kiran, D.R.: Production planning and control. a comprehensinve approach. In: Production Planning and Control. pp. i–iii. Elsevier (2019). https://doi.org/10.1016/B978-0-12-818364-9.00036-6
18. Cheraghalikhani, A., Khoshalhan, F., Mokhtari, H.: Aggregate production planning: A literature review and future research directions. Int. J. Ind. Eng. Comput. 309–330 (2019). https://doi.org/10.5267/j.ijiec.2018.6.002
19. Corlu, C.G., Akcay, A., Xie, W.: Stochastic simulation under input uncertainty: a review. Oper. Res. Perspect. **7**, 100162 (2020). https://doi.org/10.1016/j.orp.2020.100162
20. Esteso, A., Peidro, D., Mula, J., Díaz-Madroñero, M.: Reinforcement learning applied to production planning and control. Int. J. Prod. Res. **61**, 5772–5789 (2023). https://doi.org/10.1080/00207543.2022.2104180
21. Chapman, S.N.: The fundamentals of production planning and control. Pearson, Upper Saddle River, NJ (2008)
22. Mukhopadhyay, S.K.: Production Planning and Control (2015)
23. Almeida, C.: Material Requirements Planning with SAP S/4HANA. (2020)
24. Ptak, C.A., Smith, C., Orlicky, J.: Orlicky's material requirements planning. McGraw-Hill, New York (2011)
25. Axsäter, S.: Inventory Control. Springer International Publishing, Cham (2015). https://doi.org/10.1007/978-3-319-15729-0
26. Kurbel, K.E.: Enterprise Resource Planning and Supply Chain Management: Functions, Business Processes and Software for Manufacturing Companies. Springer Berlin Heidelberg, Berlin, Heidelberg (2013). https://doi.org/10.1007/978-3-642-31573-2
27. Caserio, C., Trucco, S.: Enterprise Resource Planning and Business Intelligence Systems for Information Quality. Springer International Publishing, Cham (2018). https://doi.org/10.1007/978-3-319-77679-8
28. Kuhnle, A., Kaiser, J.-P., Theiß, F., Stricker, N., Lanza, G.: Designing an adaptive production control system using reinforcement learning. J. Intell. Manuf. **32**, 855–876 (2021). https://doi.org/10.1007/s10845-020-01612-y
29. Bonney, M.: Reflections on production planning and control (PPC). Gest. Produção. **7**, 181–207 (2000). https://doi.org/10.1590/S0104-530X2000000300002
30. Kritzinger, W., Karner, M., Traar, G., Henjes, J., Sihn, W.: Digital Twin in manufacturing: a categorical literature review and classification. IFAC-Pap. **51**, 1016–1022 (2018). https://doi.org/10.1016/j.ifacol.2018.08.474
31. Mula, J., Bogataj, M.: OR in the industrial engineering of Industry 4.0: experiences from the Iberian Peninsula mirrored in CJOR. Cent. Eur. J. Oper. Res. 29, 1163–1184 (2021). https://doi.org/10.1007/s10100-021-00740-x
32. Groover, M.P.: Fundamentals of Modern Manufacturing Materials, Processes, and Systems (2019)
33. Aitihg, L.: Manufacturing Engineering Processes; Second Edition, Revised and Expanded. (1994)
34. Bitkowska, A., Tyszkiewicz, R.: Intermodal transport as an integral part of logistics system. Prod. Eng. Arch. 11, 31–35 (2016). https://doi.org/10.30657/pea.2016.11.08
35. NOWOTYŃSKA, I., KUT, S., KRAUZ, M.: Autobusy Tech. Eksploat. Syst. Transp. (2017)

36. Mostert, M., Limbourg, S.: External costs as competitiveness factors for freight transport — a state of the art. Transp. Rev. **36**, 692–712 (2016). https://doi.org/10.1080/01441647.2015.113 7653
37. Wild, T.: Best Practice in Inventory Management. Taylor and Francis, Hoboken (2007)
38. Kuei, C., Lu, M.H.: Integrating quality management principles into sustainability management. Total Qual. Manag. Bus. Excell. **24**, 62–78 (2013). https://doi.org/10.1080/14783363.2012.669536
39. Rumane, A.R.: Quality management: how to achieve sustainability in projects. CRC Press, Boca Raton (2023). https://doi.org/10.1201/9781003377375
40. Bruhn, M.: Quality Management for Services: Handbook for Successful Quality Management. Principles – Concepts – Methods. Springer Berlin Heidelberg, Berlin, Heidelberg (2023). https://doi.org/10.1007/978-3-662-67032-3
41. Rodriguez-Perez, J.: (Pepe): Quality Risk Management in the FDA-Regulated Industry. Quality Press, La Vergne (2024)
42. Al-Turki, U.M., Ayar, T., Yilbas, B.S., Sahin, A.Z.: Integrated Maintenance Planning in Manufacturing Systems. Springer International Publishing, Cham (2014). https://doi.org/10.1007/978-3-319-06290-7
43. Costa, A.L.B., Balduino, Â.R.: The importance of preventive and corrective maintenance in works. Int. J. Adv. Eng. Res. Sci. 5, 72–76 (2018). https://doi.org/10.22161/ijaers.5.5.10
44. Wang, Y., Deng, C., Wu, J., Wang, Y., Xiong, Y.: A corrective maintenance scheme for engineering equipment. Eng. Fail. Anal. **36**, 269–283 (2014). https://doi.org/10.1016/j.engfai lanal.2013.10.006
45. Vathoopan, M., Johny, M., Zoitl, A., Knoll, A.: Modular fault ascription and corrective maintenance using a digital twin. IFAC-Pap. **51**, 1041–1046 (2018). https://doi.org/10.1016/j.ifa col.2018.08.470
46. Lee, H., Cha, J.H.: New stochastic models for preventive maintenance and maintenance optimization. Eur. J. Oper. Res. **255**, 80–90 (2016). https://doi.org/10.1016/j.ejor.2016.04.020
47. Linear and Nonlinear Preventive Maintenance Models: Shaomin Wu, Zuo, M.J. IEEE Trans. Reliab. **59**, 242–249 (2010). https://doi.org/10.1109/TR.2010.2041972
48. Ni, J., Gu, X., Jin, X.: Preventive maintenance opportunities for large production systems. CIRP Ann. **64**, 447–450 (2015). https://doi.org/10.1016/j.cirp.2015.04.127
49. Gouiaa-Mtibaa, A., Dellagi, S., Achour, Z., Erray, W.: Integrated maintenance-quality policy with rework process under improved imperfect preventive maintenance. Reliab. Eng. Syst. Saf. **173**, 1–11 (2018). https://doi.org/10.1016/j.ress.2017.12.020
50. Motaghare, O., Pillai, A.S., Ramachandran, K.I.: Predictive maintenance architecture. In: 2018 IEEE International Conference on Computational Intelligence and Computing Research (ICCIC), pp. 1–4. IEEE, Madurai, India (2018). https://doi.org/10.1109/ICCIC.2018.8782406
51. Levitt, J.: Complete Guide to Preventive and Predictive Maintenance. Industrial Press Inc, New York (2011)
52. Lughofer, E., Sayed-Mouchaweh, M. eds: Predictive Maintenance in Dynamic Systems: Advanced Methods, Decision Support Tools and Real-World Applications. Springer International Publishing, Cham (2019). https://doi.org/10.1007/978-3-030-05645-2
53. Avikal, S., Singh, A.R., Ram, M.: Sustainability in Industry 4.0: Challenges and Remedies. CRC Press, Boca Raton (2021). https://doi.org/10.1201/9781003102304
54. Maruthi, G.D., Rashmi, R.: Green manufacturing: it's tools and techniques that can be implemented in manufacturing sectors. Mater. Today Proc. **2**, 3350–3355 (2015). https://doi.org/10.1016/j.matpr.2015.07.308
55. Bhattacharya, A., Jain, R., Choudhary, A.: Green manufacturing: energy, products and processes. In: The Green manufacturing report by The Boston Consultancy Group for Confederation of Indian Industry (2011)

56. Paul, I.D., Bhole, G.P., Chaudhari, J.R.: A review on green manufacturing: it's important, methodology and its application. Procedia Mater. Sci. **6**, 1644–1649 (2014). https://doi.org/10.1016/j.mspro.2014.07.149

57. Singh, C.D., Kaur, H.: Sustainable Green Development and Manufacturing Performance through Modern Production Techniques. CRC Press, Boca Raton (2021). https://doi.org/10.1201/9781003189510

58. Thomas, D.S.: The costs and benefits of advanced maintenance in manufacturing. National Institute of Standards and Technology, Gaithersburg, MD (2018). https://doi.org/10.6028/NIST.AMS.100-18

59. Zhang, J.: Multi-agent based production planning and control. John Wiley & Sons Inc, Hoboken, NJ, USA (2017)

60. Ammar, M., Haleem, A., Javaid, M., Walia, R., Bahl, S.: Improving material quality management and manufacturing organizations system through Industry 4.0 technologies. Mater. Today Proc. **45**, 5089–5096 (2021). https://doi.org/10.1016/j.matpr.2021.01.585

61. Barreto, L., Amaral, A., Pereira, T.: Industry 4.0 implications in logistics: an overview. Procedia Manuf. **13**, 1245–1252 (2017). https://doi.org/10.1016/j.promfg.2017.09.045

62. Tadić, S., Zečević, S., Krstić, M.: A novel hybrid MCDM model based on fuzzy DEMATEL, fuzzy ANP and fuzzy VIKOR for city logistics concept selection. Expert Syst. Appl. **41**, 8112–8128 (2014). https://doi.org/10.1016/j.eswa.2014.07.021

Computational Astrochemistry 2025 (CompAstro 2025)

Theoretical Study of the NaO + HCl Reaction: A Potential Formation Route of NaCl in the Interstellar Medium

Andrea Giustini[1], Gabriella Di Genova[2], Nadia Balucani[2]([✉]),
Cecilia Ceccarelli[3], Albert Rimola[4], Piero Ugliengo[5], and Marzio Rosi[1]

[1] Dipartimento di Ingegneria Civile ed Ambientale, Università degli Studi di Perugia,
via G. Duranti 93, 06125 Perugia, Italy
{andrea.giustini,marzio.rosi}@unipg.it
[2] Dipartimento di Chimica, Biologia e Biotecnologie, Università degli Studi di
Perugia, via Elce di Sotto 8, 06123 Perugia, Italy
nadia.balucani@unipg.it
[3] University Grenoble Alpes, CNRS, IPAG, 38000 Grenoble, France
[4] Departament de Quimica, Universitat Autònoma de Barcelona, Bellaterra 08193,
Catalonia, Spain
[5] Dipartimento di Chimica, Università di Torino, via Pietro Giuria 7,
10125 Torino, Italy

Abstract. A preliminary theoretical characterization of the reaction
NaO + HCl in the gas phase and in the presence of a cluster of seventeen water molecules has been carried out. The purpose of this explorative study is to investigate the NaCl + OH reaction for the formation
of interstellar NaCl, both in the gas phase and on the surface of amorphous ice of interstellar grains. The reaction was seen to occur without
entrance barriers to form an adduct that easily evolves into the NaCl +
OH products both in the gas phase and in the presence of the cluster of
water molecules. In the case of the cluster reaction, we have simulated an
Eley-Rideal mechanism in which HCl approaches, from the gas phase, the
NaO radical bound to the 17-water-molecules cluster. Both the gas and
ice reactions are strongly exothermic and feasible from a thermodynamic
standpoint. Furthermore, being barrierless, they are also expected to be
fast under the typical conditions of the interstellar medium. Therefore,
this process can be added to the list of reactions to be considered as possible formation routes of the diatomic NaCl molecule in the interstellar
medium. More work is needed to better describe this system and other
similar reactions, such as those leading to KCl, which is also observed in
the interstellar medium.

Keywords: Astrochemistry · Gas Phase · Extraterrestrial Ice ·
Chlorine · Sodium Chloride · Water-Molecules Cluster

© The Author(s), under exclusive license to Springer Nature Switzerland AG 2026
O. Gervasi et al. (Eds.): ICCSA 2025 Workshops, LNCS 15888, pp. 261–271, 2026.
https://doi.org/10.1007/978-3-031-97596-7_17

1   Introduction

The NaCl molecule has been detected in carbon-rich and oxygen-rich stellar atmospheres [1–7], as well as in the high-mass protostellar disc around Orion Source I [8] and toward the massive proto-binary system IRAS 16547-4247 [9]. In this last study, the authors suggested that molecular lines of NaCl and other alkali halides can play an important role as tracers of the innermost part of the disc, thus allowing the disc to be separated from its envelope. For this reason, it is quite important to understand their formation routes. However, at present, NaCl detection in solar-type star-forming regions and cold clouds remains elusive. The chemistry leading to NaCl has recently been considered in a gas-grain astrochemical model by Acharyya et al. [10], where both gas-phase formation routes and grain chemistry have been considered. All known processes have been reviewed, new ones have been suggested, and the binding energy of several Na-bearing molecules has been estimated [10]. According to that study [10], $NaCl_{(g)}$ can be formed in the gas phase by the radiative association of $Na_{(g)}$ and $Cl_{(g)}$, a process recently characterized by Šimsová et al. [11]. In addition to radiative association, NaCl can be synthesized by a number of reactions between sodium atoms and the Cl-bearing species identified so far in the interstellar medium, including HCl (which is considered one of the main chlorine reservoirs in the interstellar medium [12–14]), or starting from NaH and NaOH [10]. Despite the very large binding energy derived for NaCl on water ice, its formation on the ice surface is considered the dominant process when assuming that 50% of NaCl produced in ice is released in the gas phase by reactive desorption. This suggestion was made in line with the experimental data by Minissale et al. [15] for other diatomic species. Reactions involving sodium monoxide, NaO, have not been considered yet. However, although not detected, NaO is considered a species likely to have astronomical significance due to observational evidence [16] and its presence in several regions of the interstellar medium is indeed plausible since other metal monoxides have been detected (e.g. $FeO_{(g)}$, $AlO_{(g)}$, $TiO_{(g)}$, $CrO_{(g)}$, $VO_{(g)}$, $CaO_{(g)}$ [17–21]). For this reason, we have decided to explore its chemistry with $HCl_{(g)}$ to verify whether NaCl can be readily formed by this process as well. Our choice is also dictated by the fact that sodium atoms might react with water when in contact with numerous water molecules. In fact, some evidence of NaOH formation was obtained when more than one Na atom is adsorbed by a cluster of water molecules or if the water molecules are vibrationally excited ([22,23]).

In this contribution, we present a first explorative study using a density functional theory (DFT) approach to gain a first look at the global potential energy surfaces (PES) of two new possible routes of formation of NaCl, that is, the reaction NaO + HCl in the gas phase:

$$NaO_{(g)} + HCl_{(g)} \rightarrow NaCl_{(g)} + OH_{(g)} \tag{1}$$

and on interstellar amorphous ice simulated by considering a cluster of seventeen water molecules and assuming an Eley-Rideal mechanism in which HCl lands [10] on the NaO radical adsorbed on ice:

$$NaO_{(ice)} + HCl_{(g)} \rightarrow NaCl_{(ice)} + OH_{(ice)} \tag{2}$$

2 Theoretical Methods

The PESs for the two reactions (1) and (2) have been obtained by performing electronic structure calculations at the DFT level of theory. More specifically, all local minima and transition states were optimized using the ωB97XD functional [24], which is known to be suitable for calculating intermolecular interactions such as hydrogen bonds and dispersion forces. For open-shell species, such as NaO, the unrestricted Hartree-Fock (UHF) formalism has been adopted to define the electronic wave function, while the RHF formalism has been used for closed-shell species. The split valence triple zeta polarized basis set 6-311G(d) [25, 26], where polarization functions are added for heavy atoms [27], has been used. Calculations were performed using the GAUSSIAN09 program package [28]. The resulting total electronic energies were corrected by adding the zero-point energy (ZPE) and hence obtain enthalpy values at 0 K. Frequency analysis was carried out to assure that the optimized geometries are minima stationary points of the potential energy surfaces. The approach is the same successfully used for other reactions, see Ref. [29–35].

3 Results and Discussion

3.1 The $NaO_{(g)} + HCl_{(g)}$ Reaction

The structures of the reactants and products resulting from our calculations are shown in Fig. 1. The energy and bond lengths compare nicely with the accepted values. For instance, the NaCl and NaO bond lengths are 2.40 and 2.05(6) Å to be compared with the accepted values of 2.36 and 2.05 Å [16, 36]. According to our calculations, the gas-phase reaction proceeds with the H-atom transfer from the chlorine atom to the oxygen atom of NaO while, at the same time, a strong interaction between Cl and Na is established. The adduct with the structure reported in Fig. 1(e) is formed via this concerted mechanism in a barrierless process. Notably, even though Na participates in the newly-formed Na-Cl bond, it is still interacting with the oxygen atom that now belongs to the OH group. A small increase of the Na$-$O bond length can be appreciated (see Fig. 1), while the chemical bond between Na-Cl is almost formed. The adduct is more stable than the reactants by 246.7 kJ/mol at this level of theory. For the isolated system, the large amount of energy released by the adduct formation cannot be dissipated, and the adduct undergoes Na-O bond fission with the formation of the products NaCl + OH. This reactive channel is globally exothermic by 156.9 kJ/mol with respect to the initial NaO + HCl reactants. The calculated reaction enthalpy at 0 K is in reasonable agreement with the value of -142.6 kJ/mol that can be obtained when using the tabulated enthalpies of formation of reactants and products (see Ref. [37]).

In conclusion, according to our calculations, this barrierless and exothermic reaction is a plausible formation route of interstellar NaCl directly in the gas phase.

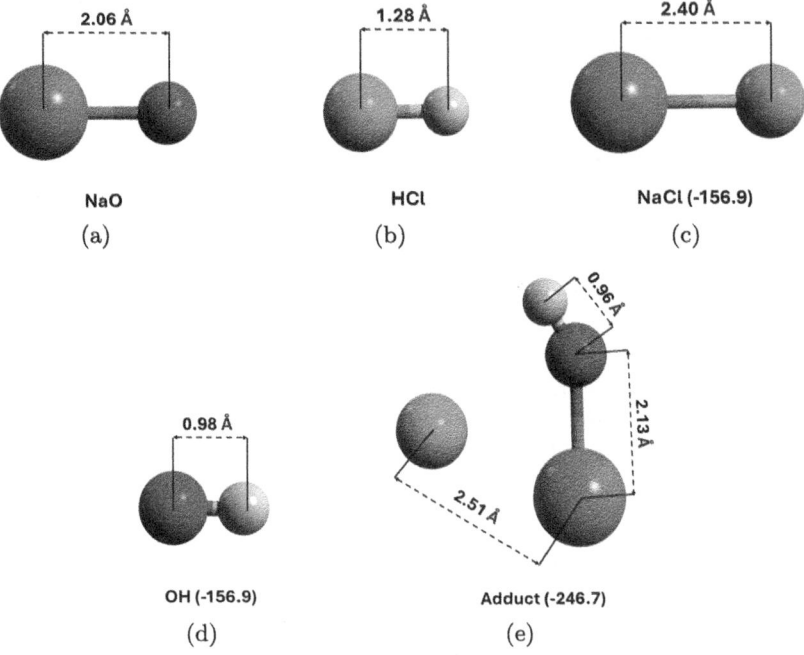

Fig. 1. ωB97XD/6-311G(d) optimized structure and energy (in hartree) of (a) NaO, (b) HCl, (c) NaCl, (d) OH, and (e) the adduct formed in the NaO$_{(g)}$ + HCl$_{(g)}$ reaction. Bond distances in Ångström; energies in parentheses are expressed in kJ/mol with respect to NaO + HCl, regarded as reactants.

3.2   The NaO + HCl Reaction in a Group of 17 Water Molecules

As anticipated, we have simulated an Eley-Rideal mechanism in which HCl, from the gas phase, interacts with NaO adsorbed on the surface ice, which we simulate with a cluster of water molecules. The 17-water-molecules cluster has been built following a previously derived cluster of 18-water-molecules, used to simulate reactions that occur on amorphous ice covering interstellar grains [38–41]. In this work, the number of water molecules in the cluster was due to the replacement of one external water molecule with NaO. Only the most stable NaO adsorption site has been considered here. Its ωB97XD/6-311G(d) optimized structure (17-WMC-NaO) is shown in Fig. 2(a). Interestingly, the Na—O bond distance, calculated to be 2.29 Å, is larger than the same bond distance for the isolated molecule depicted in Fig. 1(a). This is in line with what is expected because of the increased ionic character of the NaO bond in the presence of the polar water molecules of the cluster. Indeed, as indicated by the Mulliken partial atomic charges with respect to those of the isolated NaO, a slightly higher ionic degree of the sodium/oxygen pair ($-0.621/0.630\ e$) is computed. The optimized structure of NaCl embedded in the 17-water-molecules cluster (17-WMC-NaCl) is shown in Fig. 2(d). We have determined this structure as a reference point to establish if the interaction between $HCl_{(g)}$ and $NaO_{(ice)}$ produces the expected NaCl product. Also in this case, the bond distance between sodium and chlorine, calculated to be 2.65 Å, is larger than the same atomic distance of the isolated molecule depicted in Fig. 1(a) and an examination of the Mulliken charge distribution reveals a larger charge separation ($-0.854/0.666\ e$) with respect to the isolated NaCl ($-0.652/0.652\ e$). When considering the interaction of $HCl_{(g)}$ with $NaO_{(ice)}$, our calculations identified two stationary points that unveil the ongoing reaction mechanism. A first intermediate (17-WMC1, see Fig. 2(b)) is formed, more stable than the reactants by 45.3 kJ/mol. The approaching HCl molecule has oriented itself in such a way that chlorine interacts with the Na atom of NaO, while the H atom interacts with a lone pair of a water molecule. This first intermediate can easily evolve (without an energy barrier) into another structure (17-WMC2, see Fig. 2(c)) that can be taken as the ending point of the reaction. Indeed, the NaCl bond distance (2.60 Å) has a value comparable to that of the optimized structure of NaCl in the water cluster (2.65 Å). Nevertheless, the sodium atom is still considerably interacting with the O atom (the bond distance has only increased from 2.29 to 2.31 Å) while the H—Cl bond length has significantly increased (from 1.28 Å of the isolated gas-phase molecule to 1.36 Å in 17-WMC1 up to 1.85 Å in the product-like final structure 17-WMC2). The global energy gain with respect to the reactants is 71.2 kJ/mol, making this mechanism exothermic. We did not explore that further, but it is probable that a proton relay process occurs at this stage, eventually leading to the OH coproduct. It is interesting to note that, while in many other cases the presence of water molecules [31,38–44] stabilizes the reaction intermediates with respect to the reactants, here the opposite is true. This simply means that the stabilizing effect of the cluster of seventeen water molecules is smaller for the intermediate and the products than for $NaO_{(ice)}$. However, the overall reaction remains exothermic and the reactants are easily converted into NaCl. The hydrogen bonds provide a stabilizing effect: when the NaO radical is considered on the water cluster, the binding energy is on the order of hundreds kJ/mol (ca. 250 kJ/mol). Notably, Eley-Rideal mechanisms (that is, processes in which one of the reactants is adsorbed on the ice surface with the other coming from the gas phase) are considered important mechanisms in interstellar regions characterized by high atomic densities [45,46].

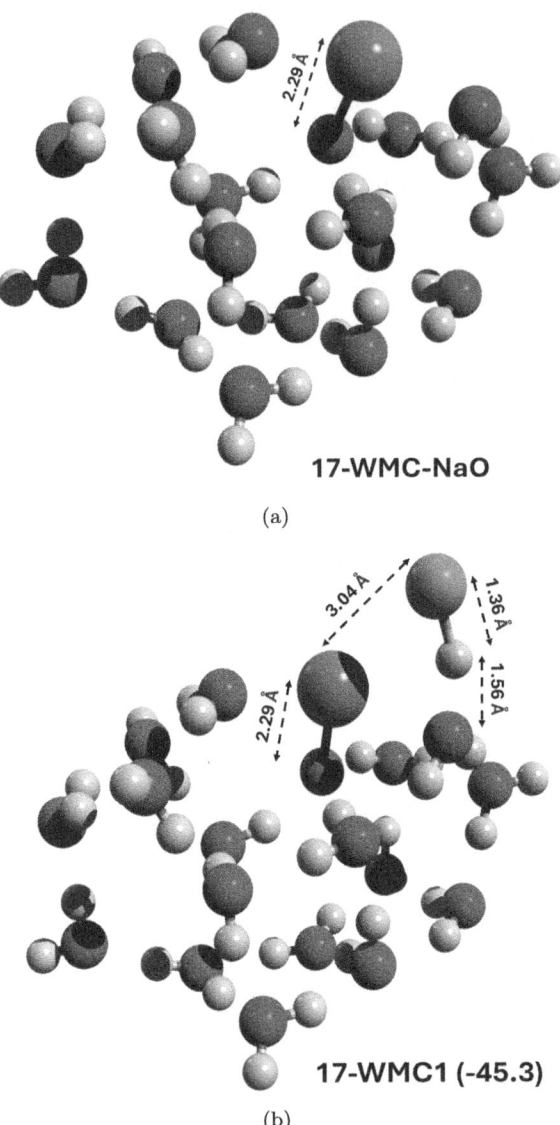

17-WMC-NaO

(a)

17-WMC1 (-45.3)

(b)

Fig. 2. ωB97XD/6-311G(d) optimized structure and energy of (a) NaO adsorbed in the 17-water-molecules cluster (the most stable arrangement); (b) the intermediate arising from the reaction between NaO adsorbed in the 17-water-molecules cluster with HCl from the gas phase; (c) the post-reaction structure arising from the establishment of the Na–Cl bond and H-transfer from the Cl atom to one of the O atoms of the 17-water-molecules cluster; (d) the optimized structure of NaCl adsorbed on the 17-water-molecules cluster. Bond distances in Ångström; energies in parentheses are expressed in kJ/mol with respect to the 17-WMC-NaO +HCl$_{(g)}$.

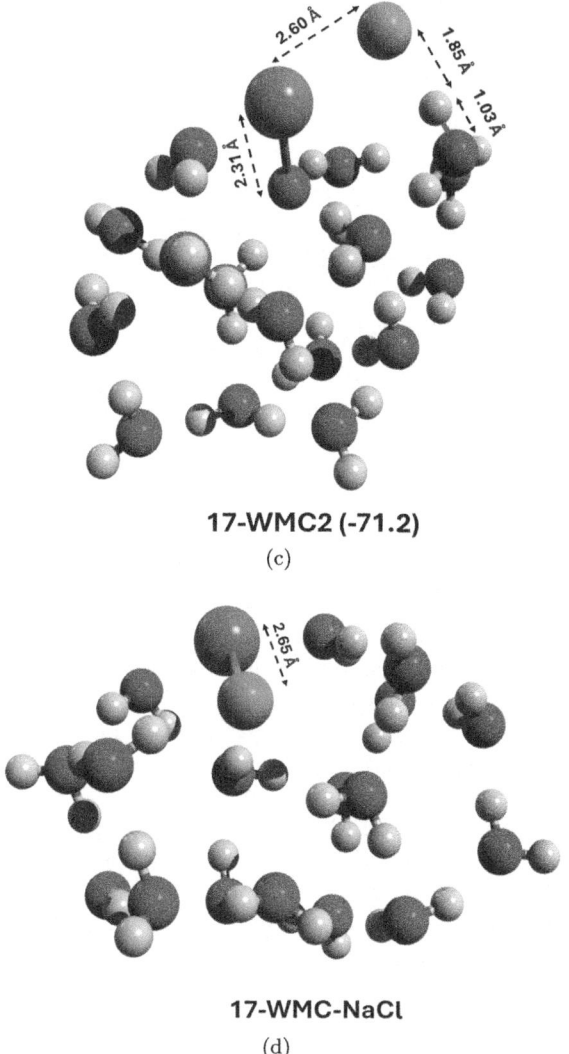

17-WMC2 (-71.2)

(c)

17-WMC-NaCl

(d)

Fig. 2. (*continued*)

4   Conclusion and Implications in Astrochemistry

In this work, the reaction between NaO and HCl has been investigated considering the two possible media where reactions can occur in interstellar environments, that is, the gas phase and the icy mantles of interstellar grains. Grain chemistry has been simulated by considering a cluster of seventeen water molecules as a model for amorphous ice and an Elay-Rideal mechanism in which HCl comes from the gas phase. The presence of the water molecules does not significantly alter the reaction mechanism. In both cases, the reactions are barrierless and evolve through intermediates located well below the energy asymptote of the reactants. We have planned further calculations to better describe these systems at a higher level of theory to confirm the results of this preliminary investigation.

Concerning the possible implications in astrochemistry, our study indicates that the gas-phase $NaO_{(g)}$ + $HCl_{(g)}$ reaction is another possible formation route of NaCl directly in the gas phase where it has been observed. We have not derived the rate coefficient, but being barrierless in the entrance channel and very exothermic, reaction (1) is expected to have a rate coefficient in the gas-kinetics limit, that is, around 10^{-10} cm^3 s^{-1}. Therefore, it is as efficient as the other gas-phase reactions considered in the model by Acharyya et al. [10], that is, $NaOH_{(g)}$ + $HCl_{(g)}$, $NaH_{(g)}$ + $Cl_{(g)}$, and $Na_{(g)}$ + $HCl_{(g)}$. The importance of these reactions, therefore, depends on the abundance of the reactants. $NaOH_{(g)}$ and $NaH_{(g)}$, as well as $NaO_{(g)}$, have not yet been detected, and therefore it is difficult to judge their relative importance.

As regards the reactions on ice, according to the model by Acharyya et al. [10], the dominant processes are $Na_{(ice)}$ + $Cl_{(ice)}$ → $NaCl_{(ice)}$ and $NaH_{(ice)}$ + $Cl_{(ice)}$ → $NaCl_{(ice)}$ + $H_{(ice)}$. The $Na_{(ice)}$ + $Cl_{(ice)}$ reaction is dominant up to 10^5 years. Hydrogenation of $Na_{(ice)}$ and $Cl_{(ice)}$ are competing processes that could suppress the importance of $Na_{(ice)}$ + $Cl_{(ice)}$ → $NaCl_{(ice)}$. Furthermore, Na can react with water in large water clusters or in the presence of more than one Na atom [22,23]. Furthermore, in the astrochemical model by [10], this specific formation route of NaCl in ice is so important because it is assumed that 50% of it is released in the gas phase by reactive desorption. This suggestion was made upon the indications of the experimental work by Minissale et al. [15] for other diatomic species that, however, are very different with respect to NaCl (e.g., O2, N2). Indeed, their conclusion was that chemical desorption is a favorable process for diatomic molecules with low binding energies formed by recombination reactions. This is also confirmed by ab initio molecular dynamics simulations of H_2 formation on periodic crystalline and amorphous ice surface models ([47]). However, NaCl is characterized by a very large binding energy of 14000 K [10] and, therefore, it is quite different compared to the cases analyzed by Minissale et al. [15]

The characterization of NaCl formation pathways in the interstellar medium is still in its infancy. More theoretical and experimental data are needed.

Acknowledgments. GDG, NB, CC, and PU thank the MUR PRIN2020 (2020AFB3FX-Astrochemistry beyond the second-period elements) and the European Union's Horizon 2020 research and innovation program from the European Research Council (ERC) project 'The Dawn of Organic Chemistry' (DOC), grant agreement no 741002) for support. AG and MR thank financial support under the National Recovery and Resilience Plan (NRRP), Mission 4, Component 2, Investment 1.1, Call for tender No. 104 published on 2.2.2022 by the Italian Ministry of University and Research (MUR), funded by the European Union - NextGenerationEU - Project Title 2022JC2Y93 ChemicalOrigins: linking the fossil composition of the Solar System with the chemistry of protoplanetary disks - CUP J53D23001600006 - Grant Assignment Decree No. 962 adopted on 30/06/2023 by the Italian Ministry of University and

Research (MUR). NB and PU acknowledge support from the Italian Space Agency (Bando ASI Prot. n. DC-DSR-UVS-2022-231, Grant no. 2023-10-U.0 MIGLIORA). AR thanks the European Union's Horizon 2020 research and innovation program from the European Research Council (ERC) for the project 'Quantum Chemistry on Interstellar Grains' (QUANTUMGRAIN), grant agreement no. 865657. PU acknowledges support from the Project CH4.0 under the MUR program "Dipartimenti di Eccellenza 2023-2027" (CUP: D13C22003520001).

Disclosure of Interests. None of the authors have any conflicts of interest to declare.

References

1. Cernicharo, J., Guelin, M.: Metals in IRC +10216: detection of NaCl, AlCl, and KCl, and tentative detection of AlF. Astron. Astrophys. **183**, L10–L12 (1987)
2. Danilovich, T., et al.: The salty emission of the intermediate-mass AGB star OH 30.1-0.7. Montly Notices of the Roya Astronomical Society **536**(1), 684–713 (2025)
3. Qiu, J.J., Zhang, Y., Zhang, J.S., Nakashima, J.I.: Molecules in the carbon-rich protoplanetary nebula crl 2688. Astrophys. J. Supplement Series **259**(2), 56 (2022)
4. Coenegrachts, A., Danilovich, T., De Ceuster, F., Decin, L.: The unusual 3D distribution of NaCl around the asymptotic giant branch star IK Tau. Astron. Astrophys. **678**, A85 (2023)
5. Agúndez, M., Fonfría, J.P., Cernicharo, J., Kahane, C., Daniel, F., Guélin, M.: Molecular abundances in the inner layers of IRC +10216. Astron. Astrophys. **543**, A48 (2012)
6. Milam, S.N., Apponi, A.J., Woolf, N.J., Ziurys, L.M.: Oxygen-rich mass loss with a pinch of salt: NaCl in the circumstellar gas of IK Tauri and VY Canis Majoris. Astrophys. J. **668**(2), L131 (2007)
7. Kamiński, T., Gottlieb, C.A., Young, K.H., Menten, K.M., Patel, N.A.: An interferometric spectral line and imaging survey of VY Canis Majoris in the 345 Ghz band. Astrophys. J. Suppl. Ser. **209**(2), 38 (2013)
8. Ginsburg, A., McGuire, B., Plambeck, R., Bally, J., Goddi, C., Wright, M.: Orion SrcI's disk is salty. Astrophys. J. **872**(1), 54 (2019)
9. Tanaka, K., et al.: Salt, hot water, and silicon compounds tracing massive twin disks. Astrophys. J. Letters **900**(1), L2 (2020)
10. Acharyya, K., Woon, D.E., Herbst, E.: Formation of sodium-bearing species in the interstellar medium. Mon. Not. R. Astron. Soc. **527**(2), 1722–1732 (2023)
11. Šimsová-Zámecníková, M., Soldán, P., Gustafsson, M.: Formation of NaCl by radiative association in interstellar environments. Astron. Astrophys. **664**, A5 (2022)
12. Blake, G.A., Keene, J., Phillips, T.G.: Chlorine in dense interstellar clouds - the abundance of HCL in Omc-1. Astrophys. J. **295**, 501 (1985)
13. Federman, S.R., Cardell, J.A., van Dishoeck, E.F., Lambert, D.L., Black, J.H.: Vibrationally excited H2, HCL, and NO(+) in the diffuse clouds toward zeta Ophiuchi. Astrophys. J. **445**, 325 (1995)
14. Cemicharo, J., et al.: Detection of anhydrous hydrochloric acid, HCl, in IRC +10216 with the Herschelspire and PACS spectrometers: Detection of HCl in IRC +10216. Astrophys. J. **518**, L136 (2010)
15. Minissale, M., Dulieu, F., Cazaux, S., Hocuk, S.: Dust as interstellar catalyst. I. Quantifying the chemical desorption process. Astron. Astrophys. **585**, A24 (2016)

16. Mitev, G.B., Taylor, S., Tennyson, J., Yurchenko, S.N., Buchachenko, A.A., Stolyarov, A.V.: Exomol molecular line lists – xliii. rovibronic transitions corresponding to the close-lying X2π and A$2\sigma+$ states of NaO. Monthly Notices of the Royal Astron. Society **511**(2), 2349–2355 (2022)

17. Walmsley, C.M., Bachiller, R., Pineau des Forêts, G., Schilke, P.: Detection of FeO toward Sagittarius B2. The Astrophys. J. Letters **566**(2), L109–L112 (2002)

18. Tenenbaum, E.D., Ziurys, L.M.: Millimeter Detection of AlO (X $^2\Sigma^+$): Metal Oxide Chemistry in the Envelope of VY Canis Majoris. Astrophys. J. Letters **694**(1), L59–L63 (2009)

19. Humphreys, R.M., et al.: The unexpected spectrum of the innermost ejecta of the red hypergiant VY CMa. Astrophys. J. Letters **874**(2), L26 (2019)

20. Kamiński, T., Mason, E., Tylenda, R., Schmidt, M.R.: Post-outburst spectra of a stellar-merger remnant of V1309 Scorpii: from a twin of V838 Monocerotis to a clone of V4332 Sagittarii. Astron. Astrophys. **580**, A34 (2015)

21. Rey-Montejo, M., et al.: Discovery of MgS and NaS in the Interstellar Medium and Tentative Detection of CaO. Astrophys. J. **975**(2), 174 (2024)

22. Buck, U., Steinbach, C.: Formation of sodium hydroxyde in multiple sodium-water cluster collisions. J. Phys. Chem. A **102**(38), 7333–7336 (1998)

23. Cwiklik, L., Kubisiak, P., Kulig, W., Jungwirth, P.: Reactivity of a sodium atom in vibrationally excited water clusters: an ab initio molecular dynamics study. Chem. Phys. Lett. **460**(1), 112–115 (2008)

24. Chai, J.D., Head-Gordon, M.: Long-range corrected hybrid density functionals with damped atom–atom dispersion corrections. Phys. Chem. Chem. Phys. **10**(44), 6615 (2008)

25. McGrath, M.P., Radom, L.: Extension of gaussian-1 (g1) theory to bromine-containing molecules. J. Chem. Phys. **94**(1), 511–516 (1991)

26. Curtiss, L.A., McGrath, M.P., Blaudeau, J.P., Davis, N.E., Binning, R.C., Radom, L.: Extension of gaussian-2 theory to molecules containing third-row atoms Ga-Kr. J. Chem. Phys. **103**(14), 6104–6113 (1995)

27. Dunning Jr, T.H., Peterson, K.A., Wilson, A.K.: Gaussian basis sets for use in correlated molecular calculations. x. the atoms aluminum through argon revisited. J. Chem. Phys. **114**(21), 9244–9253 (2001)

28. Frisch, M., et al.: Gaussian 09, Revision A. 02, Gaussian. Inc., Wallingford CT (2009)

29. Liang, P., et al.: OH (2π)+ C2H4 reaction: a combined crossed molecular beam and theoretical study. J. Phys. Chem. A **127**(21), 4609–4623 (2023)

30. Pannacci, G., et al.: A combined crossed molecular beam and theorerical study of the O (^{3}P, ^{1}D)+ acrylonitrile (CH2CHCN) reactions and implications for combustion and extraterrestrial environments. Phys. Chem. Chem. Phys. **25**(30), 20194–20211 (2023)

31. Giustini, A., Di Genova, G., Skouteris, D., Ceccarelli, C., Rosi, M., Balucani, N.: Gas-phase and model ice-surface reactions of S(^{1}D) with water and methanol: A computational investigation and implications for cosmochemistry/astrochemistry. ACS Earth Space Chem. **8**(11), 2318–2333 (2024)

32. Marchione, D., et al.: Unsaturated dinitriles formation routes in extraterrestrial environments: A combined experimental and theoretical investigation of the reaction between cyano radicals and cyanoethene (C2H3CN). J. Phys. Chem. A **126**(22), 3569–3582 (2022)

33. Vanuzzo, G., et al.: Reaction N(^{2}D) + CH2CCH2 (allene): an experimental and theoretical investigation and implications for the photochemical models of titan. ACS Earth Space Chem.y **6**(10), 2305–2321 (2022)

34. Balucani, N.: An experimental and theoretical investigation of the $N(^2D)$ + C6H6 (benzene) reaction with implications for the photochemical models of titan. Faraday Discuss. **245**, 327–351 (2023)
35. Giani, L., et al.: A comprehensive study of the gas-phase formation network of hc5n: theory, experiments, observations and models. Monthly Notices of the Royal Astronomical Society, p. staf189 (2025)
36. National Institute of Standards and Technology (2001) Security Requirements for Cryptographic Modules. Tech. Rep. Federal Information Processing Standards Publications (FIPS PUBS) 140-2, Change Notice 2 December 03, 2002, U.S. Department of Commerce, Washington, D.C. (2001). https://doi.org/10.6028/nist.fips.140-2
37. Burkholder, J., et al.: Chemical kinetics and photochemical data for use in atmospheric studies. Evaluation No. 19, JPL Publication 19-5 **19** (2020). http://jpldataeval.jpl.nasa.gov
38. Rimola, A., Taquet, V., Ugliengo, P., Balucani, N., Ceccarelli, C.: Combined quantum chemical and modeling study of co hydrogenation on water ice. Astron. Astrophys. **572**, A70 (2014)
39. Rimola, A., et al.: Can formamide be formed on interstellar ice? an atomistic perspective. ACS Earth and Space Chemi. **2**(7), 720–734 (2018)
40. Perrero, J., Rimola, A.: Synthesis of urea on the surface of interstellar water ice clusters. a quantum chemical study. Icarus **410**, 115848 (2024)
41. Di Genova, G., Perrero, J., Rosi, M., Ceccarelli, C., Rimola, A., Balucani, N.: Hot sulfur on the rocks: the reaction of electronically excited sulfur atoms with water in an ice-surface model. ACS Earth Space Chem. (2025)
42. Giustini, A., Di Genova, G., Balucani, N., Ceccarelli, C., Rosi, M., Lombardi, A.: Theoretical Insights on the $S(^1D)$ + H2O Reaction and Implications on the Chemistry at the Surface of Ice in Extraterrestrial Environments, pp. 274–282. Springer Nature Switzerland (2024)
43. Enrique-Romero, J., Ceccarelli, C., Rimola, A., Skouteris, D., Balucani, N., Ugliengo, P.: Theoretical computations on the efficiency of acetaldehyde formation on interstellar icy grains. Astron. Astrophys. **655**, A9 (2021)
44. Enrique-Romero, J., Rimola, A., Ceccarelli, C., Ugliengo, P., Balucani, N., Skouteris, D.: Quantum mechanical simulations of the radical-radical chemistry on icy surfaces. Astrophys. J. Suppl. Ser. **259**(2), 39 (2022)
45. Le Bourlot, J., Le Petit, F., Pinto, C., Roueff, E., Roy, F.: Surface chemistry in the interstellar medium: I. H2 formation by langmuir-hinshelwood and eley-rideal mechanisms. Astron. Astrophys. **541**, A76 (2012)
46. Ruaud, M., Loison, J., Hickson, K., Gratier, P., Hersant, F., Wakelam, V.: Modelling complex organic molecules in dense regions: Eley-rideal and complex induced reaction. Mon. Not. R. Astron. Soc. **447**(4), 4004–4017 (2015)
47. Pantaleone, S., et al.: H2 formation on interstellar grains and the fate of reaction energy. Astrophys. J. **917**(1), 49 (2021)

Modeling Polymer Degradation by Atomic Oxygen in Low Mars and Earth Orbits: Are Diffuse Functions Necessary?

Dario Campisi[1]([✉]) [iD], Giacomo Pannacci[2] [iD], Nadia Balucani[2] [iD],
and Marzio Rosi[3,4] [iD]

[1] Engineering Department, University of Perugia, via Duranti 93, 06125 Perugia,
Italy
dario.campisi@unipg.it, darcampisi@outlook.com
[2] Department of Chemistry, Biology and Biotechnology, University of Perugia, via
dell' Elce di Sotto 8, 06123 Perugia, Italy
[3] Department of Civil and Environmental Engineering, University of Perugia, via
Duranti, 93, 06125 Perugia, Italy
[4] Istituto CNR di Scienze e Tecnologie Chimiche "Giulio Natta" (CNR-SCITEC), via
dell' Elce di Sotto 8, 06123 Perugia, Italy

Abstract. Materials used in satellites, often composed of organic polymers, are subject to degradation by highly reactive atomic oxygen in low Earth and Mars orbits. The local structures of these polymers often feature fused aromatic rings, resembling small polycyclic aromatic hydrocarbons (PAHs). Computational chemistry calculations, such as density functional theory (DFT), provide a method for estimating the chemical resistance of these moieties. The choice of basis sets in DFT calculations is a critical factor in accurately describing the molecular electronic density in the fragmentation pathways of PAH degradation. In particular, the inclusion of diffuse functions in the basis set is necessary for capturing long-range interactions and charge transfer effects. However, when modeling PAHs, computational limitations become a challenge.

Here, we assess the accuracy of Pople basis sets, polarization-consistent contracted basis sets (pcseg-n), and correlation-consistent basis sets (cc-pVnZ) using the established ωB97X-D3BJ long-range DFT functional. Additionally, we evaluate the impact of including diffuse functions on the performance of the calculations in terms of energy accuracy and computational cost. These basis sets were tested on two PAH samples, naphthalene and phenanthrene. We found that diffuse functions do not significantly affect the performance of the ωB97X-D3BJ functional, and that cc-pVTZ provides the best balance of accuracy and computational efficiency.

Keywords: Basis Sets · DFT · Polymers

O. Gervasi et al. (Eds.): ICCSA 2025 Workshops, LNCS 15888, pp. 272–288, 2026.
https://doi.org/10.1007/978-3-031-97596-7_18

1   Introduction

The interaction of atomic oxygen $O(^3P)$ with polymers (Fig. 1) is a key factor in determining the durability of materials used in satellite missions, particularly in low Earth orbit (LEO) and low Mars orbit (LMO), that extend up to 2000 km above the planets. Due to the high reactivity of atomic O in these environments, polymeric surfaces of satellites undergo significant erosion, necessitating a fundamental understanding of the underlying chemical processes. [1]

Aerospace applications frequently rely on polymeric films, advanced composites, and thermoplastic materials due to their insulation, low weight and high flexibility. Exposure of these materials to LEO and LMO conditions, which are highly oxidative environments, causes polymer erosion, significantly reducing their durability and functional effectiveness over time. However, the erosion rate of polymers varies, as it depends on their physical and chemical properties, which, in turn, are influenced by the polymer's electronic structure. [2] The LEO exposition of 40 different polymers and graphite, including those used in space missions and polymers with various chemical structures for different applications, has resulted in the development of a database of erosion rates. [3] These experiments have shown that polymers capable of enduring decades of exposure to $O(^3P)$ quickly degrade and break down into CO or other volatile molecules. To protect them, polymers are now shielded by coatings made of materials resistant to degradation by atomic $O(^3P)$. However, imperfections in the coating, either from the deposition process or physical damage occurring during orbit, cause erosion of the polymer substrates. Even though self-healing polymers have been developed, they still have an Achilles' heel, as their structural chains might have weak bonds that can be broken by O. [4]

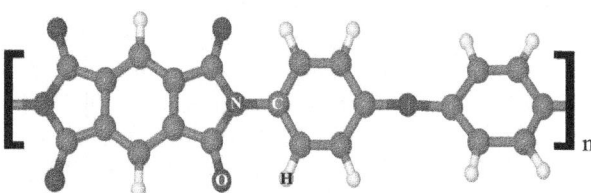

Fig. 1. Example of a polymer material used in satellites: Kapton (poly-oxydiphenylene-pyromellitimide) molecular unit (n > 1). Atomic labels are provided for selected atoms and correspond to all atoms of the same color category.

Despite the availability of ground-based simulation and exposure data, the reaction mechanism at the microscopic level remains obscure. Given the complexity of the systems, theoretical studies remained confined to molecular dynamics simulations [5–7] that, however, did not treat important aspects that strongly affect O reactions with organic compounds like intersystem crossing (ISC) to the underlying singlet potential energy surface. Previous combined experimental and theoretical work from our laboratory on the bimolecular reactions of atomic oxygen with organic compounds, including several aromatics, demonstrated that the extent of ISC strongly depends on the characteristics of the triplet and singlet PESs and their coupling terms. [8–19] To further explore this, we have initiated a systematic investigation of the reactions between atomic oxygen and aromatic compounds bearing different functional groups that mimic the local structure of space polymers. By integrating experimental data with theoretical calculations of the adiabatic singlet and triplet PESs, as well as product branching fractions, we aim to quantitatively estimate the extent of ISC in a semi-empirical manner, thereby alleviating the challenges associated with a rigorous theoretical treatment of ISC. This will, in turn, allow us to identify the most vulnerable moieties in the polymer skeleton.

Density functional theory (DFT), a quantum chemistry methodology, has been employed to characterize the PES of the O atom reacting with organic molecules due to its computational feasibility. [20] DFT is the ground for characterizing the main intermediates and barriers, which are then used in conjunction with higher-level post-Hartree-Fock (post-HF) methodologies (e.g., CCSD(T) and CASPT2 methods) to compute more accurate energies. [8] However, post-Hartree-Fock methods are feasible for molecular species with fewer than 10 atoms. [21] The problem arises when larger molecular species need to be considered, such as polycyclic aromatic hydrocarbons (PAHs). [22] Nevertheless, for studies based on cross-beam experiments, branching fractions are required to derive the mechanism. These fractions are not sensitive to the exact value of the barriers but rather to the relative variation in energy. [9,23,24]

PAHs are also of interest because they are ubiquitous in interstellar space [25,26] and planetary systems [27–29] due to their easy formation in combustion processes or processes akin to sooting flames in interstellar space. [22,30,31] They are highly resistant to destruction because of their large bond energies, which prevent degradation. [29] However, due to their large structure, post-HF methods are not feasible. Therefore, understanding the accuracy of DFT methodologies is needed to accurately reproduce experimental data. [20] DFT methodologies rely on the accuracy of two important factors: the exchange-correlation (XC) functionals and the basis sets. XC functionals are dependent on specific factors, and several types have been developed over the years to reproduce properties of interest. [22,32] In the case of O-attack on aromatic molecules, the range-separated ωB97X exchange-correlation functional, [33] in conjunction with the Grimme dispersion correction, [34] has been shown to accurately reproduce the PES of O reacting with several organic molecules for both the triplet and singlet states, compared to experiments. [13,14,17,20,35]

Another critical aspect of such calculations is the choice of basis sets, which define the level of accuracy in representing the molecular wave function. [36,37] The inclusion of diffuse functions is often essential, [38] particularly when dealing with open-shell species like atomic oxygen or when modeling weakly bound intermediates and transition states. Diffuse functions extend the spatial flexibility of the basis set by introducing low-exponent Gaussian functions, improving the description of electron density in the outer regions of atoms and molecules. This refinement is crucial for accurately capturing charge distributions and long-range interactions. [39,40] However, the addition of diffuse functions significantly increases the computational cost, as the number of integrals grows due to the enhanced treatment of long-range electron interactions. Large basis sets increase the number of variational parameters in the wave function, leading to higher memory requirements and longer computation times. For large molecules or polymeric systems, this can pose convergence challenges, making some basis sets impractical for routine calculations. [38,41] To address the computational bottleneck associated with large basis sets, the Resolution of Identity (RI) approximation is often employed. [42] RI reduces the computational scaling of electron repulsion integrals by introducing an auxiliary basis set, effectively simplifying the four-center integrals into three-center terms. This approximation significantly speeds up calculations, particularly in DFT and post-HF methods, without substantially compromising accuracy. However, when large basis sets are used in conjunction with RI, convergence problems can arise due to the linear dependence of the auxiliary basis set. These issues become more pronounced as the basis set limit is approached, leading to numerical instabilities in wave function optimization. [43] This raises an important question: Is it always necessary to use highly diffuse basis sets to obtain reliable results, or can a judiciously chosen, more compact basis set provide a sufficient balance between accuracy and computational efficiency?

To address this, we evaluate different types of basis sets, both with and without diffuse functions, by assessing their performance in calculating the entrance barrier of an oxygen atom interacting with two small PAHs—naphthalene and phenanthrene—for which the use of diffuse functions is still affordable. [44,45]

2   Theoretical Methods

All the density functional theory (DFT) calculations were conducted using the ORCA [46] code with the ωB97X exchange-correlation functional [33,34] with Grimme's D3BJ dispersion correction. [47,48] Different types of basis sets were tested for this work, detailed as follows:

Pople's 6-311++G(3df,3pd) and 6-311G(3df,3pd) basis sets were used. [49–51] Pople's basis sets incorporate a triple-zeta split-valence representation, diffuse functions on both heavy atoms and hydrogen, and higher-order polarization functions (including three sets of d-functions and one set of f-functions for heavy atoms, as well as three sets of p-functions and one set of d-functions for hydrogen). Correlation-consistent polarized valence basis sets, such as cc-pVTZ and aug-cc-pVTZ, developed by Dunning and co-workers [52], are designed to accurately describe electron correlation and molecular properties. The cc-pVTZ basis set incorporates a triple-zeta representation for the valence orbitals, with three sets of functions for each orbital, along with polarization functions on heavy atoms to improve the description of bonding and electron distribution. The aug-cc-pVTZ basis set extends the cc-pVTZ set by adding diffuse functions on both heavy atoms and hydrogen. Polarized correlation-consistent Gaussian basis sets, such as pcseg-2 and aug-pcseg-2, developed by Peterson and co-workers [53], are optimized for accurate DFT calculations. The pcseg-2 basis set incorporates a triple-zeta representation for the valence orbitals, along with polarization functions on heavy atoms to improve the description of bonding and electron distribution. The aug-pcseg-2 basis set extends the pcseg-2 set by including diffuse functions on both heavy atoms and hydrogen.

All calculations were performed using the resolution-of-identity (RI) method with an auto-generated auxiliary basis set. [54,55] They were optimized using a very tight self-consistent field (SCF) convergence criterion of 1×10^{-09} a.u. Minima were optimized using the Broyden–Fletcher–Goldfarb–Shanno (BFGS) method. [56] The minima were considered optimized when the maximum gradient was lower than 3×10^{-5} a.u. per Bohr radius. Transition states were optimized using an eigenvalue-following transition state-finding algorithm in ORCA and were considered optimized when the maximum gradient was less than 1×10^{-4} a.u. per Bohr radius. Harmonic vibrational frequencies were calculated to characterize local minima (no negative frequencies) and saddle points (one imaginary frequency only). The energies of the minima and transition states are all referenced to the reactants at infinite distance (naphthalene or phenanthrene and $O(^3P)$). All the electronic energies are corrected for the vibrational zero-point energy (ZPE).

3   Results

To evaluate the role of diffuse functions in the basis sets for the reaction of $O(^3P)$ with aromatic monomers, we report the potential energy surface for the entrance reaction of $O(^3P)$ with naphthalene and phenanthrene, as well as analyze the computational time required for each basis set.

3.1 $O(^3P)$+Naphthalene

The ωB97X-D functional [33,34], in conjunction with dispersion correction and the Pople basis sets has been shown in prior studies to adequately describe the reactivity of $O(^3P)$ with monocyclic aromatics such as benzene. [8,14] However, this approach is computationally expensive and may become impractical when modeling larger molecules such as naphthalene or phenanthrene.

Here, as shown in Fig. 2, we report results for the addition of an $O(^3P)$ to naphthalene to form the O-PAH adduct in the triplet spin state (the product). We tested the most commonly employed basis sets (e.g., cc-pVTZ and pcseg-2) and evaluated whether adding diffuse functions is necessary for modeling the attack of $O(^3P)$. Here, we employed ωB97X-D3BJ, as the older ωB97X-D is based on the earlier Grimme dispersion correction (D2), [57] whereas here we use the more accurate D3BJ in this work. [48]

To investigate the $O(^3P)$ addition onto naphthalene, we have selected the carbon of the C-H group located next to the inner carbons (which lack hydrogen),

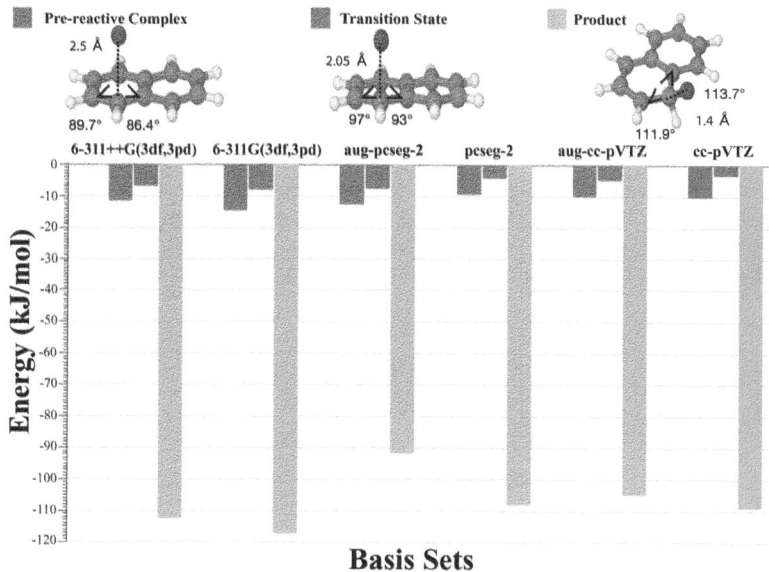

Fig. 2. Energy differences of the pre-reactive complex, transition state, and product, respectively, for different Basis Sets, relative to O(^{3}P) and naphthalene at infinite distance. The molecular structures of O(^{3}P) and naphthalene at the minima and saddle point are also reported including C-O distances and $C - \overbrace{C - O}$ angles.

as previous studies [23,58] have shown that this position is particularly receptive to radical attachment (see Fig. 2). The addition of O(^{3}P) to naphthalene (Fig. 2) proceed with the formation of a weak pre-reactive complex, with a C-O distance of 2.54 Å, as shown in the first bar (blue color) for each basis set at ωB97X-D3BJ. The reaction then proceeds, at the same level of theory, by overcoming barriers, characterized by a partial bond formation and located at C-O distance of 2.05 Å, which are submerged considering the reactants at infinite distance (O+PAH). Once the barrier is passed, the product consists in the PAH-O adduct, with a C-O bond distance of 1.37 Å, as shown in the reaction depicted in Fig. 2.

Figure 2 shows the effect of diffuse functions when using different basis sets. The pre-reactive complex well ranges from −10 kJ/mol to −15 kJ/mol, with the removal of the diffuse functions leading to a slightly larger well, approximately 4 kJ/mol deeper, compared to the 6-311++G(3df,3pd) basis set. For the pcseg-2 series, we observe a different behavior: the pcseg-2 result yields a pre-reactive complex of −9 kJ/mol, which is lower than that of the aug-pcseg-2 basis set, which results in a well of about −13 kJ/mol. We did not find any differences for the cc-pVTZ basis set, where the presence of diffuse functions does not affect the pre-reactive complex, which remains at −10 kJ/mol. Overall, the Pople basis set overestimates the pre-reactive complex depth by a few kJ/mol compared to the other basis sets. All the barrier results are submerged due to the presence of a favorable pre-reactive complex. These submerged barriers are reported in Table 2 and compared with literature values.

Table 1. Submerged barrier (E_{sub}) values, in kJ/mol, referenced to the pre-reactive complex, for the addition of O(^{3}P) to naphthalene (see PES in Fig. 2) computed at ωB97X-D3BJ using different basis sets in this work. These values are compared with literature (Lit.) data from theoretical studies conducted at BH&HLYP/6-31G(3d,3p)//B3LYP/6-311G(d,p) (Lit. [59]), M06-2X/cc-pVTZ//M06-2X/6-311G(d,p) (Lit. a [60]), M06-2X/6-311G(d,p) (Lit. b [60]) and CBS-QB3 (Lit. [23]).

Level of Theory	E_{sub}
6-311++G(3df,3pd)	4.83
6-311G(3df,3pd)	6.62
aug-pcseg-2	5.16
pcseg-2	5.12
aug-cc-pVTZ	5.10
cc-pVTZ	7.00
Lit. [59]	8.37
Lit. a [60]	4.25
Lit. b [60]	6.74

The submerged barrier values (Table 1) obtained with ωB97X-D3BJ are perfectly in line with those found in the literature at DFT level. [59,60] Regarding the barrier height, the effect of the diffuse function is such that 6-311++G(3df,3pd), in agreement with the values reported by Scapinello *et al.* [60] using the M06-2X/cc-pVTZ//M06-2X/6-311G(d,p) level of theory, underestimates the barrier height compared to when diffuse functions are included. The diffuse function in the pcseg-2 basis set does not impact the submerged barrier height, whereas the cc-pVTZ basis set results in a larger submerged barrier—similar to what is observed for the Pople-type basis sets—by about 2 kJ/mol. Overall, a 2 kJ/mol difference is small compared to the typical intrinsic errors of DFT functionals. [61] Therefore, for the barrier height and pre-reactive complex, diffuse functions do not have a major impact on the accuracy of the basis set within the uncertainty of the method. [61]

The reaction energy for product formation (Fig. 2) ranges from approximately −90 kJ/mol to -118 kJ/mol. Reported literature values are −92.27 kJ/mol at the M06-2X/6-311G(d,p) level of theory [60] and −93.3 kJ/mol at the BH&HLYP/6-31G(3d,3p)//B3LYP/6-311G(d,p) level. [59] Among the tested methods, only ωB97X-D3BJ/aug-pcseg-2 provides values in perfect agreement with the literature. In contrast, other basis sets overestimate the reaction energy for product formation by approximately 20 kJ/mol with respect to the literature values.

[59,60] The role of diffuse functions is more significant in the formation of the product, as indicated by differences larger than 2 kJ/mol between basis sets with and without diffuse functions (Fig. 2). Specifically, the 6-311++G(3df,3pd) and 6-311G(3df,3pd) basis sets yield values of −112 kJ/mol and −117 kJ/mol, respectively, resulting in a difference of 5 kJ/mol. Similarly, the aug-pcseg-2 and pcseg-2 basis sets predict values of −92 kJ/mol and −108 kJ/mol, respectively, with a difference of 16 kJ/mol. In contrast, the cc-pVTZ basis sets exhibit smaller discrepancies, yielding values of −105 kJ/mol and −109 kJ/mol, with a difference of only 4 kJ/mol.

The reported results in Fig. 2 are based on full optimization at each basis set type and include ZPE correction. To fully understand the observed discrepancies, we also report the values as single-point energies, without ZPE correction, using the ωB97X-D3BJ/6-311G(3df,3dp) geometry as a reference. This allows us to evaluate whether the observed discrepancies arise not only from the choice of basis set but also from the optimization of the geometry.

For the pre-reactive complex, the 6-311G(3df,3pd) basis set (Fig. 3) gives the lowest energy (−16.7 kJ/mol), while the highest value is obtained with pcseg-2 (−10.3 kJ/mol). The aug-pcseg-2 and aug-cc-pVTZ basis sets yield nearly identi-

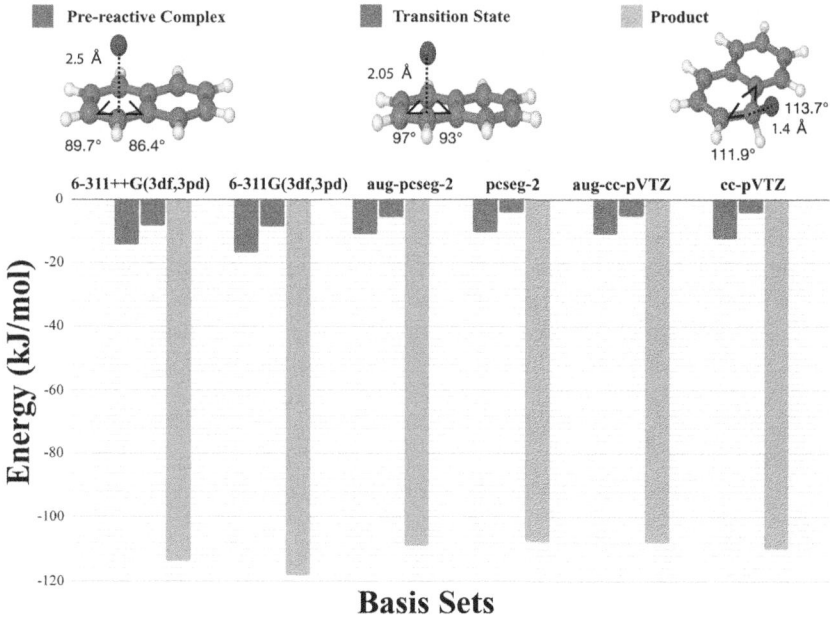

Fig. 3. Energy evaluation using the same geometry for all basis sets to study the energy differences due to the change of Basis Set types for the reaction of O(^{3}P) with naphthalene. Those geometries are single-point energy evaluations, without ZPE correction, of the optimized geometries of the pre-reactive complex, transition state, and product at the ωB97X-D3BJ/6-311G(3df,3dp) level. The molecular structures of minima and saddle points are shown including C-O distances and $C \overarc{- C -} O$ angles.

cal values (−10.9 kJ/mol), suggesting that augmentation with diffuse functions has little impact on the energy at this stage of the reaction. The difference between 6-311G(3df,3pd) and 6-311++G(3df,3pd) (−16.7 vs. −14.2 kJ/mol) indicates a small effect of additional diffuse functions in this case.

At the transition state, all basis sets predict similar energies, ranging from −8.6 kJ/mol (6-311G(3df,3pd)) to −4.0 kJ/mol (cc-pVTZ). The pcseg-2 basis set gives a similar result (−4.1 kJ/mol), showing the highest value among the segment-contracted sets. The difference between the highest and lowest values is about 4.6 kJ/mol, which suggests that while basis set choice does influence the computed barrier height, the effect is less pronounced than in the pre-reactive complex or product.

For the product, the computed energies range from −107.5 kJ/mol (pcseg-2) to −118.2 kJ/mol (6-311G(3df,3pd)). The differences among the basis sets are more significant in this case, with a spread of approximately 10.7 kJ/mol. This variation suggests that the description of the electronic structure of the product is more sensitive to basis set choice than that of the transition state. Overall, while all basis sets capture the general trend of the reaction pathway, the computed energy differences depend on the choice of basis set. The largest differences are observed in the pre-reactive complex and the product, whereas the transition state energies remain relatively close across all methods. These variations highlight the impact of basis set selection on the computed reaction profile.

3.2   O(^{3}P)+Phenanthrene

To understand the size effect on the tested basis sets (see prior section), we computed the addition of O(^{3}P) to phenanthrene (Fig. 4) using the same basis sets employed for naphthalene at the ωB97X-D3BJ level. The attack was conducted on the most reactive carbons as report by prior studies. [23,58] However, for the phenanthrene case, we could not include diffuse functions in the pcseg-2 and cc-pVTZ basis sets due to convergence problems caused by linear dependence in the basis, which arises when the basis set limit is reached, leading to convergence issues. Nevertheless, this is not a concern, as for naphthalene, we have observed that including diffuse functions in these basis sets does not significantly affect the results.

The results of the O(^3P) reaction with phenanthrene are reported in Table 2. In the pre-reactive complex, the difference between the 6-311++G(3df,3pd) and the 6-311G(3df,3pd) basis set is 3 kJ/mol, while the difference between the pcseg-2 and cc-pVTZ basis sets is 1 kJ/mol. There are no significant differences between pcseg-2 and cc-pVTZ, whereas the inclusion of diffuse functions increases the energy of the pre-reactive complex by 4.5 kJ/mol for cc-pVTZ and 5.5 kJ/mol for pcseg-2 compared to 6-311++G(3df,3pd). The 6-311G(3df,3pd) basis set shows larger discrepancies, with a difference of 5.5 kJ/mol relative to pcseg-2 and 4.5 kJ/mol relative to cc-pVTZ.

For the transition state, all basis sets show a submerged barrier, except for cc-pVTZ, which is slightly emerged by 0.2 kJ/mol. The 6-311++G(3df,3pd) basis

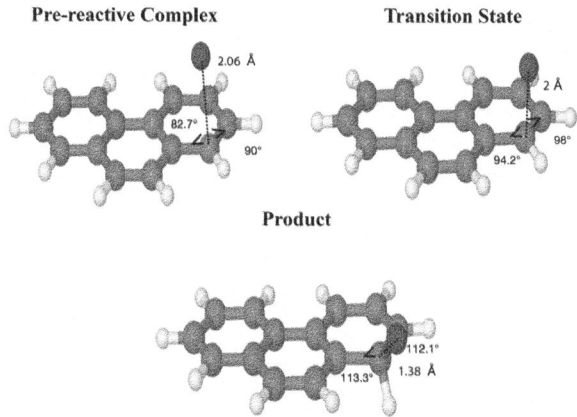

Fig. 4. Molecular structures, including C-O distances and $C - \widehat{C - O}$ angles, of the pre-reactive complex, transition states, and products of the $O(^3P)$ + Phenanthrene reaction.

set agrees closely with pcseg-2, with a difference of 0.1 kJ/mol, while it diverges from 6-311G(3df,3pd) by 3.7 kJ/mol and by 1.1 kJ/mol relative to cc-pVTZ. The 6-311G(3df,3pd) basis set shows differences of 3.8 kJ/mol compared to pcseg-2 and 4.8 kJ/mol compared to cc-pVTZ. A difference of 1 kJ/mol is negligible compared to the error of the method. [61]

The phenanthrene-O (product), computed using the 6-311++G(3df,3pd) basis set, shows very small differences (Table 2) compared to pcseg-2 and cc-pVTZ, with deviations of 2.1 kJ/mol and 1.1 kJ/mol, respectively. The 6-311G(3df,3pd) basis set overestimates the reaction energy for product formation by approximately 7.2 kJ/mol compared to 6-311++G(3df,3pd), 9.3 kJ/mol compared to pcseg-2, and 8.3 kJ/mol compared to cc-pVTZ.

Overall, the phenanthrene results align with the trend observed for naphthalene.

Table 2. PES of the addition of $O(^3P)$ to phenanthrene, showing energy differences with respect to the reactants at infinite distance ($O(^3P)$ + phenanthrene). The reported energies, in kJ/mol, are calculated at the wB97-D3BJ level of theory and include ZPE correction.

	6-311++G(3df,3pd)	6-311G(3df,3pd)	pcseg-2	cc-pVTZ
Pre-reactive complex	−11.7	−14.7	−9.2	−10.2
TS	−0.9	−4.6	−0.8	0.2
Product	−99.4	−106.6	−97.3	−98.3

3.3   Computational Time

To evaluate the computational time of the selected basis set types (Fig. 5), we tested them for the case of naphthalene + O(^{3}P), considering both the computational time required and the number of self-consistent field (SCF) iterations needed to achieve convergence.

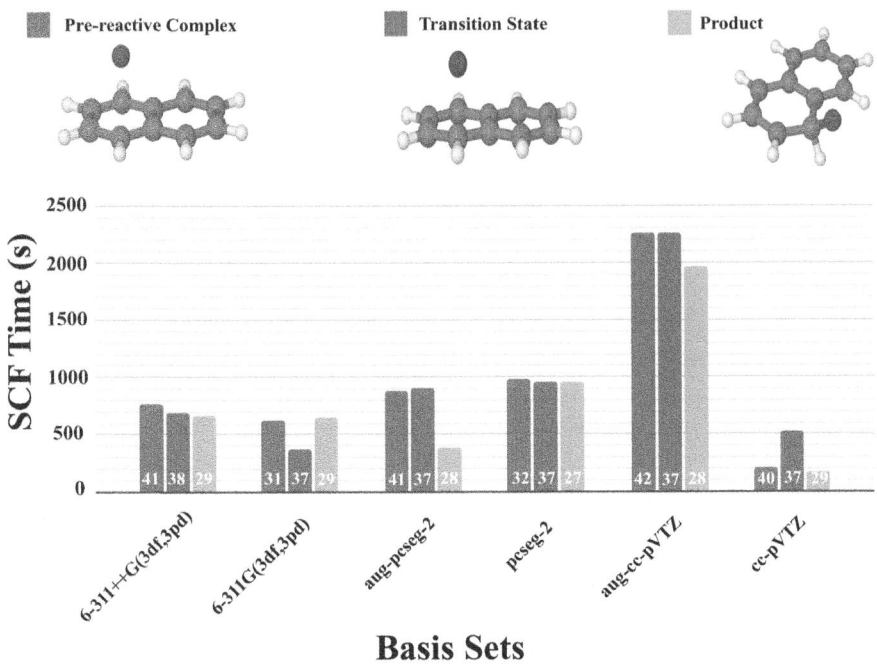

Fig. 5. SCF Time, for only one converged cycle, in seconds (s), for the reaction of O(^{3}P) to naphthalene in the pre-reactive complex, transition state, and product, using various basis sets, and reported in the same order for each basis set. The number of SCF cycles required to reach convergence is reported above each bar.

Examining the time to converge one SCF (Fig. 5), significant differences emerge among the basis sets. The computational cost varies considerably, with the largest times observed for the augmented correlation-consistent basis set (aug-cc-pVTZ). Specifically, for the pre-reactive complex and transition state (TS), this basis set results in the highest SCF times, 2255 s and 2267 s, respectively. The second most time-consuming basis set is pcseg-2, which consistently requires nearly 950–990 s across all species. On the other hand, the cc-pVTZ basis set displays the lowest computational times, particularly for the product, where the SCF time is only 169 s. Similarly, 6-311++G(3df,3pd) and 6-311G(3df,3pd) show moderate computational costs, with times generally below 800 s. Despite variations in computational time, the number of SCF iterations required to achieve convergence remains relatively consistent across basis sets.

The transition state (TS) exhibits a nearly uniform behavior, requiring 37 iterations in all cases except for 6-311++G(3df,3pd), which converges in 38 iterations. The pre-reactive complex generally demands a higher number of iterations, with the aug-cc-pVTZ basis set reaching the highest count at 42 iterations, while the pcseg-2 and 6-311G(3df,3pd) basis sets require slightly fewer iterations (32 and 31, respectively). For the product, a slightly lower number of iterations is observed, ranging from 27 (pcseg-2) to 29 (most other basis sets). These results suggest that computational time does not directly correlate with the number of SCF iterations. For instance, aug-cc-pVTZ and pcseg-2 require more time despite having iteration counts comparable to other basis sets. This discrepancy can be attributed to the intrinsic complexity and size of the basis sets, which increase the computational burden per iteration. Augmented basis sets such as aug-cc-pVTZ include diffuse functions, which can lead to more complex integral evaluations and slower matrix operations, explaining the extended SCF times. Similarly, the segmented-contracted pcseg-2 basis set may involve additional computational overhead despite converging in fewer iterations than aug-cc-pVTZ. Conversely, cc-pVTZ, which is a non-augmented correlation-consistent basis set, exhibits the shortest SCF times across all cases while maintaining iteration counts comparable to other basis sets. This highlights its computational efficiency, making it an attractive choice when balancing accuracy and cost. Overall, the results underscore the trade-off between basis set complexity and computational expense. While larger basis sets offer improved accuracy, they also come with significant computational costs, which must be carefully considered when modeling large systems.

4 Conclusions

Modeling the $O(^3P)$ reaction with large aromatic compounds, such as naphthalene and phenanthrene, as well as polymers, to study the degradation of these materials in space requires a careful selection of basis sets that balance efficiency and computational cost. In this work, we tested several basis sets with and without diffuse functions (6-311++G(3df,3pd), 6-311G(3df,3pd), aug-pcseg-2, pcseg-2, aug-cc-pVTZ, and cc-pVTZ) at the ωB97X-D3BJ DFT level.

We found that the addition of diffuse functions for the reaction of $O(^3P)$ with naphthalene and phenanthrene does not significantly affect the performance of the basis sets in terms of energy pathways, although it increases the computational burden. For the addition of $O(^3P)$ to phenanthrene, the use of diffuse functions in pcseg-2 and cc-pVTZ is prohibitive due to linear dependence of the basis set as it reaches the basis set limit.

Overall, cc-pVTZ achieved the lowest computational cost while maintaining accuracy comparable to basis sets that include diffuse functions, such as 6-311++G(3df,3pd), for both naphthalene and phenanthrene cases. It is also important to note that basis set superposition error (BSSE) was not explicitly addressed, as triple-zeta basis sets generally lead to BSSE values smaller than the typical errors associated with DFT functionals. Moreover, theoretical studies by Mentel *et al.* [62] indicates that applying counterpoise corrections can sometimes introduce new imbalances, rather than improve agreement with basis set limit results. To avoid this potential source of bias—particularly when comparing the influence of diffuse functions across different basis sets—counterpoise corrections were not employed. Additionally, we did not adopt a computational strategy involving geometry optimization with triple-zeta basis sets followed by single-point calculations using their augmented counterparts. Although this approach can lower computational cost, our results show that the presence of diffuse functions has minimal impact on the potential energy surface (PES). Finally, to ensure consistency and allow for fair comparisons, all calculations were performed on the same computer node, using identical CPU and memory configurations when measuring the SCF time.

The present results show that the inclusion of diffuse functions is not always necessary and requires careful consideration, as in the case of neutral PAHs, where it does not affect accuracy but increases computational cost. The latter could be prohibitive when modeling $O(^3P)$ reactions with large monomers and/or polymers to evaluate the efficiency of these materials in satellite applications in LEO and LMO environments.

Acknowledgments. D.C. acknowledges the CINECA award under the ISCRA initiative, for the availability of high performance computing resources and support. We acknowledge financial support under the National Recovery and Resilience Plan (NRRP),Mission 4, Component 2, Investment 1.1, Call for tender No. 1409 published on 14.09.2022 by the Italian Ministry of University and Research (MUR), funded by the European Union – NextGenerationEU – Project Title P20223H8CK Degradation of space-technology polymers by thermospheric oxygen atoms and ions: an exploration of the reaction mechanisms at an atomistic level (ThermOPoly) – CUP J53D23014440001 – Grant Assignment Decree No. 1386 adopted on 01.09.2023 by the Italian Ministry of University and Research (MUR). We acknowledges COLONIZE project from the University of Perugia: indagini preliminari su risposte biologiche, materiali cementizi alternativi e nuove fonti energetiche per affrontare la colonizzazione infrastrutturale dello Spazio.

Disclosure of Interests. The authors have no competing interests to declare that are relevant to the content of this article.

References

1. Grossman, E., Gouzman, I.: Space environment effects on polymers in low earth orbit. Nucl. Instrum. Methods Phys. Res. B **208**, 48–57 (2003). https://doi.org/10.1016/S0168-583X(03)00640-2
2. Strganac, T.W., Letton, A., Rock, N.I., Williams, K.D., Farrow, D.A.: Characterization of polymer films retrieved from Nasa's long duration exposure facility. J. Spacecr. Rockets **32**(3), 502–506 (1995). https://doi.org/10.2514/3.26643
3. Groh, K., Banks, B.A., Mccarthy, C.E., Rucker, R.N., Roberts, L.M., Berger, L.A.: Misse 2 peace polymers atomic oxygen erosion experiment on the international space station. High Perform. Polym. **20**(4–5), 388–409 (2008). https://doi.org/10.1177/0954008308089705

4. Minton, T.K., et al.: Atomic oxygen effects on POSS polyimides in low earth orbit. ACS Appl. Mater. Interfaces. **4**(2), 492–502 (2012). https://doi.org/10.1021/am201509n

5. Rahnamoun, A., van Duin, A.: Reactive molecular dynamics simulation on the disintegration of Kapton, POSS polyimide, amorphous silica, and Teflon during atomic oxygen impact using the ReaxFF reactive force-field method. J. Phys. Chem. A **118**(15), 2780–2787 (2014). https://doi.org/10.1021/jp4121029

6. Zhang, Y., et al.: The effects of atomic oxygen and ion irradiation degradation on multi-polymers: a combined ground-based exposure and ReaxFF-MD simulation. Polym. Degrad. Stab. **205**, 110134 (2022). https://doi.org/10.1016/j.polymdegradstab.2022.110134

7. Zeng, F., Peng, C., Liu, Y., Qu, J.: Reactive molecular dynamics simulations on the disintegration of PVDF, FP-POSS, and their composite during atomic oxygen impact. J. Phys. Chem. A **119**(30), 8359–8368 (2015). https://doi.org/10.1021/acs.jpca.5b03783

8. Cavallotti, C., et al.: Theoretical study of the extent of intersystem crossing in the $O(^3P)$ + C_6H_6 reaction with experimental validation. J. Phys. Chem. Lett. **11**(22), 9621–9628 (2020). https://doi.org/10.1021/acs.jpclett.0c02866

9. Cavallotti, C., et al.: Crossed-beam and theoretical studies of multichannel nonadiabatic reactions: branching fractions and role of intersystem crossing for $O(^3P)$ + 1,3-butadiene. Faraday Discuss. **238**, 161–182 (2022). https://doi.org/10.1039/D2FD00037G

10. Gimondi, I., Cavallotti, C., Vanuzzo, G., Balucani, N., Casavecchia, P.: Reaction dynamics of $O(^3P)$ + propyne: II. primary products, branching ratios, and role of intersystem crossing from Ab initio coupled triplet/singlet potential energy surfaces and statistical calculations. J. Phys. Chem. A **120**(27), 4619–4633 (2016). https://doi.org/10.1021/acs.jpca.6b01564

11. Leonori, F., et al.: Experimental and theoretical studies on the dynamics of the $O(^3P)$ + propene reaction: primary products, branching ratios, and role of intersystem crossing. J. Phys. Chem. C **119**(26), 14632–14652 (2015). https://doi.org/10.1021/jp512670y

12. Fu, B., et al.: Intersystem crossing and dynamics in $O(^3P)$ + C_2H_4 multichannel reaction: experiment validates theory. Proc. Natl. Acad. Sci. U.S.A. **109**(25), 9733–9738 (2012). https://doi.org/10.1073/pnas.1202672109

13. Recio, P., et al.: Intersystem crossing in the entrance channel of the reaction of $O(^3P)$ with pyridine. Nat. Chem. **14**(12), 1405–1412 (2022). https://doi.org/10.1038/s41557-022-01047-3

14. Vanuzzo, G., et al.: Crossed-beam and theoretical studies of the $O(^3P,\ ^1D)$ + benzene reactions: primary products, branching fractions, and role of intersystem crossing. J. Phys. Chem. A **125**(38), 8434–8453 (2021). https://doi.org/10.1021/acs.jpca.1c06913

15. Ramasesha, K., Savee, J.D., Zádor, J., Osborn, D.L.: A new pathway for intersystem crossing: unexpected products in the $O(^3P)$ + cyclopentene reaction. J. Phys. Chem. A **125**(45), 9785–9801 (2021). https://doi.org/10.1021/acs.jpca.1c05817

16. Liang, P., et al.: Reactions $O(^3P,\ ^1D)$ + $HCCCN(X^1\Sigma^+)$ (cyanoacetylene): crossed-beam and theoretical studies and implications for the chemistry of extraterrestrial environments. J. Phys. Chem. A **127**(3), 685–703 (2023). https://doi.org/10.1021/acs.jpca.2c07708

17. Balucani, N., et al.: Crossed molecular beam experiments and theoretical simulations on the multichannel reaction of toluene with atomic oxygen. Faraday Discuss. **251**, 523–549 (2024). https://doi.org/10.1039/D3FD00181D

18. Piergiorgio Casavecchia, F.L., Balucani, N.: Reaction dynamics of oxygen atoms with unsaturated hydrocarbons from crossed molecular beam studies: primary products, branching ratios and role of intersystem crossing. Int. Rev. Phys. Chem. **34**(2), 161–204 (2015). https://doi.org/10.1080/0144235X.2015.1039293

19. Balucani, N., Leonori, F., Casavecchia, P., Fu, B., Bowman, J.M.: Crossed molecular beams and Quasiclassical trajectory surface hopping studies of the multichannel nonadiabatic $O(^3P)$ + ethylene reaction at high collision energy. J. Phys. Chem. A **119**(50), 12498–12511 (2015). https://doi.org/10.1021/acs.jpca.5b07979

20. Rosi, M., Balucani, N., Casavecchia, P., Mancini, L., Pannacci, G., Vanuzzo, G.: A computational strategy for the theoretical investigation of the reactions between atomic oxygen and aromatic compounds. In: Computational Science and Its Applications – ICCSA 2024 Workshops, vol. 14818, pp. 71–83 (2024). https://doi.org/10.1007/978-3-031-65273-8_5

21. Catlow, R., Burke, P., Goodfellow, J., Tildesley, D., Wilson, M., Morokuma, K.: New challenges in quantum chemistry: quests for accurate calculations for large molecular systems. Philos. Trans. R. Soc. A **360**(1795), 1149–1164 (2002). https://doi.org/10.1098/rsta.2002.0993

22. Campisi, D.: Interstellar catalysts and the PAH universe. Scolarly Publications Leiden University (2021). https://hdl.handle.net/1887/3210124

23. Kayanuma, M., Suzuki, S., Choe, Y.K., Shimoi, Y.: Structure dependency of the reactivity of aromatic hydrocarbons involving the formation of oxygenated polycyclic aromatic hydrocarbons (OPAHs). Chem. Phys. Lett. **754**, 137652 (2020). https://doi.org/10.1016/j.cplett.2020.137652

24. Frerichs, H., Tappe, M., Wagner, H.G.: Comparison of the reactions of mono- and polycyclic aromatic hydrocarbons with oxygen atoms. Ber. Bunsenges. Phys. Chem. **94**(11), 1404–1407 (1990). https://doi.org/10.1002/bbpc.199000043

25. Campisi, D., et al.: Superhydrogenation of pentacene: the reactivity of zigzag-edges. Phys. Chem. Chem. Phys. **22**, 1557–1565 (2020). https://doi.org/10.1039/C9CP05440E

26. Campisi, D., Candian, A.: Do defects in PAHs promote catalytic activity in space? stone-wales pyrene as a test case. Phys. Chem. Chem. Phys. **22**, 6738–6748 (2020). https://doi.org/10.1039/C9CP06523G

27. Campisi, D., Lamberts, T., Dzade, N.Y., Martinazzo, R., ten Kate, I.L., Tielens, A.: Interaction of aromatic molecules with forsterite: accuracy of the periodic DFT-D4 method. J. Phys. Chem. A **125**(13), 2770–2781 (2021). https://doi.org/10.1021/acs.jpca.1c02326

28. Campisi, D., Tielens, A., Dononelli, W.: The role of point defect reconstructions and polycyclic aromatic hydrocarbons in silicate dust preservation. Mon. Not. R. Astron. Soc. **533**(2), 2282–2293 (2024). https://doi.org/10.1093/mnras/stae1962

29. Campisi, D., Lamberts, T., Dzade, N.Y., Martinazzo, R., ten Kate, I.L., Tielens, A.: Adsorption of polycyclic aromatic hydrocarbons and C_{60} onto forsterite: C-H bond activation by the Schottky vacancy. ACS Earth Space Chem. **6**(8), 2009–2023 (2022). https://doi.org/10.1021/acsearthspacechem.2c00084

30. McCabe, M.N., et al.: Formation of phenylacetylene and benzocyclobutadiene in the ortho-benzyne + acetylene reaction. Phys. Chem. Chem. Phys. **24**, 1869–1876 (2022). https://doi.org/10.1039/D1CP05183K

31. Tielens, A.: Interstellar polycyclic aromatic hydrocarbon molecules. Annu. Rev. Astron. Astrophys. **46**, 289–337 (2008). https://doi.org/10.1146/annurev.astro.46.060407.145211

32. Parr, R.G.: Density functional theory. Annu. Rev. Phys. Chem. **34**, 631–656 (1983). https://doi.org/10.1146/annurev.pc.34.100183.003215

33. Chai, J.D., Head-Gordon, M.: Systematic optimization of long-range corrected hybrid density functionals. J. Chem. Phys. **128**(8), 084106 (2008). https://doi.org/10.1063/1.2834918

34. Chai, J.D., Head-Gordon, M.: Long-range corrected hybrid density functionals with damped atom-atom dispersion corrections. Phys. Chem. Chem. Phys. **10**, 6615–6620 (2008). https://doi.org/10.1039/B810189B

35. Caracciolo, A., Vanuzzo, G., Balucani, N., Stranges, D., Cavallotti, C., Casavecchia, P.: Observation of H displacement and H_2 elimination channels in the reaction of $O(^3P)$ with 1-butene from crossed beams and theoretical studies. Chem. Phys. Lett. **683**, 105–111 (2017). https://doi.org/10.1016/j.cplett.2017.02.036

36. Ahlrichs, R., Taylor, P.R.: The choice of gaussian basis sets for molecular electronic structure calculations. J. Chim. Phys. **78**, 315–324 (1981). https://doi.org/10.1051/jcp/1981780315

37. Schuchardt, K.L., et al.: Basis set exchange: a community database for computational sciences. J. Chem. Inf. Model. **47**(3), 1045–1052 (2007). https://doi.org/10.1021/ci600510j

38. Lynch, B.J., Zhao, Y., Truhlar, D.G.: Effectiveness of diffuse basis functions for calculating relative energies by density functional theory. J. Phys. Chem. A **107**(9), 1384–1388 (2003). https://doi.org/10.1021/jp021590l

39. Jensen, F.: Polarization consistent basis sets. III. the importance of diffuse functions. J. Chem. Phys. **117**(20), 9234–9240 (2002). https://doi.org/10.1063/1.1515484

40. Papajak, E., Zheng, J., Xu, X., Leverentz, H.R., Truhlar, D.G.: Perspectives on basis sets beautiful: seasonal plantings of diffuse basis functions. J. Chem. Theory Comput. **7**(10), 3027–3034 (2011). https://doi.org/10.1021/ct200106a

41. Papajak, E., Truhlar, D.G.: Efficient diffuse basis sets for density functional theory. J. Chem. Theory Comput. **6**(3), 597–601 (2010). https://doi.org/10.1021/ct900566x

42. Skylaris, C.K., Gagliardi, L., Handy, N., Ioannou, A., Spencer, S., Willetts, A.: On the resolution of identity coulomb energy approximation in density functional theory. J. Mol. Struct. THEOCHEM **501–502**, 229–239 (2000). https://doi.org/10.1016/S0166-1280(99)00434-0

43. Pedersen, T.B., Aquilante, F., Lindh, R.: Density fitting with auxiliary basis sets from Cholesky decompositions. Theor. Chem. Acc. **124**(1), 1–10 (2009). https://doi.org/10.1007/s00214-009-0608-y

44. Qu, X.W., Zuo, P.P., Li, Y.M., Li, N., Shen, W.Z.: Mechanism for the catalytic thermal polycondensation of naphthalene at low temperature. J. Fuel Chem. Technol. **50**(10), 1259–1270 (2022). https://doi.org/10.1016/S1872-5813(22)60021-5

45. Hanemann, T., Böhm, J., Honnef, K., Ritzhaupt-Kleissl, E., HauSSelt, J.: Polymer/phenanthrene-derivative host-guest systems: rheological, optical and thermal properties. Macromol. Mater. Eng. **292**(3), 285–294 (2007). https://doi.org/10.1002/mame.200600409

46. Neese, F., Wennmohs, F., Becker, U., Riplinger, C.: The ORCA quantum chemistry program package. J. Chem. Phys. **152**(22), 224108 (2020). https://doi.org/10.1063/5.0004608

47. Grimme, S., Antony, J., Ehrlich, S., Krieg, H.: A consistent and accurate ab initio parametrization of density functional dispersion correction (DFT-D) for the 94 elements H-Pu. J. Chem. Phys. **132**(15), 154104 (2010). https://doi.org/10.1063/1.3382344

48. Grimme, S., Ehrlich, S., Goerigk, L.: Effect of the damping function in dispersion corrected density functional theory. J. Comput. Chem. **32**(7), 1456–1465 (2011). https://doi.org/10.1002/jcc.21759

49. Krishnan, R., Binkley, J.S., Seeger, R., Pople, J.A.: Self-consistent molecular orbital methods. XX. a basis set for correlated wave functions. J. Chem. Phys. **72**(1), 650–654 (1980). https://doi.org/10.1063/1.438955

50. McLean, A.D., Chandler, G.S.: Contracted gaussian basis sets for molecular calculations. I. second row atoms, Z=11-18. J. Chem. Phys. **72**(10), 5639–5648 (1980). https://doi.org/10.1063/1.438980

51. Frisch, M.J., Pople, J.A., Binkley, J.S.: Self-consistent molecular orbital methods 25. supplementary functions for gaussian basis sets. J. Chem. Phys. **80**(7), 3265–3269 (1984). https://doi.org/10.1063/1.447079

52. Dunning, T.: Gaussian basis sets for use in correlated molecular calculations. I. The atoms boron through neon and hydrogen. J. Chem. Phys. **90**(2), 1007–1023 (1989). https://doi.org/10.1063/1.456153

53. Jensen, F.: Unifying general and segmented contracted basis sets. segmented polarization consistent basis sets. J. Chem. Theory Comput. **10**(3), 1074–1085 (2014). https://doi.org/10.1021/ct401026a

54. Neese, F.: An improvement of the resolution of the identity approximation for the formation of the coulomb matrix. J. Comput. Chem. **24**(14), 1740–1747 (2003). https://doi.org/10.1002/jcc.10318

55. Stoychev, G.L., Auer, A.A., Neese, F.: Automatic generation of auxiliary basis sets. J. Chem. Theory Comput. **13**(2), 554–562 (2017). https://doi.org/10.1021/acs.jctc.6b01041

56. Head, J.D., Zerner, M.C.: A Broyden–Fletcher–Goldfarb–Shanno optimization procedure for molecular geometries. Chem. Phys. Lett. **122**(3), 264–270 (1985). https://doi.org/10.1016/0009-2614(85)80574-1

57. Grimme, S.: Accurate description of van der Waals complexes by density functional theory including empirical corrections. J. Comput. Chem. **25**(12), 1463–1473 (2004). https://doi.org/10.1002/jcc.20078

58. Santos, R.C., Agapito, F., Gonçalves, E.M., Martinho Simões, J.A., Borges dos Santos, R.M.: Energetics of H-atom addition to naphthalene: a thermochemical cycle from tetralin to naphthalene. J. Chem. Thermodyn. **61**, 83–89 (2013). https://doi.org/10.1016/j.jct.2013.01.028

59. Orrego, J.F., Truong, T.N., Mondragón, F.: A linear energy relationship between activation energy and absolute hardness: a case study with the $O(^3P)$ atom-addition reactions to polyaromatic hydrocarbons. J. Phys. Chem. A **112**(36), 8205–8207 (2008). https://doi.org/10.1021/jp805012f

60. Scapinello, M., Martini, L.M., Tosi, P., Maranzana, A., Tonachini, G.: Molecular growth of PAH-like systems induced by oxygen species: experimental and theoretical study of the reaction of naphthalene with HO $(^2\Pi_{3/2})$, $O(^3P)$, and $O_2(^3\Sigma_g^-)$. RSC Adv. **5**, 38581–38590 (2015). https://doi.org/10.1039/C5RA05129K

61. Mardirossian, N., Head-Gordon, M.: How accurate are the Minnesota density functionals for noncovalent interactions, isomerization energies, thermochemistry, and barrier heights involving molecules composed of main-group elements? J. Chem. Theory Comput. **12**(9), 4303–4325 (2016). https://doi.org/10.1021/acs.jctc.6b00637

62. Mentel, M., Baerends, E.J.: Can the counterpoise correction for basis set superposition effect be justified? J. Chem. Theory Comput. **10**(1), 252–267 (2014). https://doi.org/10.1021/ct400990u

Formation Routes of Interstellar Metal Oxides: A Computational Chemistry Approach

Marzio Rosi[1,2]([✉]) [iD], Dario Campisi[3] [iD], Gabriella Di Genova[4] [iD],
Osvaldo Gervasi[5] [iD], Cecilia Ceccarelli[6] [iD], and Nadia Balucani[4] [iD]

[1] Dipartimento di Ingegneria Civile ed Ambientale, Università di Perugia, 06125 Perugia, Italy
marzio.rosi@unipg.it

[2] Istituto CNR di Scienze e Tecnologie Chimiche "Giulio Natta" (CNR-SCITEC), 06123 Perugia, Italy

[3] Dipartimento di Ingegneria, Università di Perugia, 06125 Perugia, Italy
dario.campisi@unipg.it

[4] Dipartimento di Chimica, Biologia e Biotecnologie, Università di Perugia, 06123 Perugia, Italy
gabriella.digenova@dottorandi.unipg.it, nadia.balucani@unipg.it

[5] Dipartimento di Matematica e Informatica, Università di Perugia, 06123 Perugia, Italy
Osvaldo.gervasi@unipg.it

[6] Univ. Grenoble Alpes, CNRS, IPAG, 38000 Grenoble, France
cecilia.ceccarelli@univ-grenoble-alpes.fr

Abstract. We have investigated possible formation routes of interstellar oxides in gas phase via the reactions of the atoms of several metals (Mg, Ca, Al, Fe) with the OH radical and the reaction of atomic Ti with the HO_2 radical in a first explorative computational study based on DFT calculations. The aim is to understand if investing more effort in a higher-level theoretical characterization of these reactions can help to solve open issues on the formation of metal oxides in circumstellar envelopes (CSE) of O-rich AGB stars. The reactions of Ca and Fe with OH are blandly endothermic and can only occur at high temperature or if vibrationally excited OH radicals are involved. The reaction Mg + OH is too endothermic to be significant in the CSE chemistry, while the Al + OH reaction is exothermic and barrierless. Therefore, it is expected to be an efficient AlO formation route, also in other low temperature media.

The reaction $Ti + HO_2 \rightarrow TiO_2 + H$ is strongly exothermic and barrierless. It is, therefore, very efficient and able to establish a direct connection between TiO_2 and Ti atoms, provided that HO_2 has a non-negligible abundance, in the circumstellar envelopes of AGB stars. A competitive channel leads to the TiO + OH products.

From a computational perspective, the present computational approach, based on DFT, nicely reproduces the structures of the investigated species and provides a general view of the reaction mechanism. However, more accurate methods are needed to derive the energy of intermediates and transition states to be used in the calculations of the reaction rate coefficients.

Keywords: Computational chemistry · Density Functional Theory · Metal oxides · Interstellar Medium - ISM

© The Author(s), under exclusive license to Springer Nature Switzerland AG 2026
O. Gervasi et al. (Eds.): ICCSA 2025 Workshops, LNCS 15888, pp. 289–299, 2026.
https://doi.org/10.1007/978-3-031-97596-7_19

1 Introduction

The analysis of pre-solar dust grains in meteorites indicates that the refractory material from which the rocky objects of our solar system originated came from dying stars [1, 2]. In particular, the isotopic composition of those grains allows us to trace their origins back to either massive stars that exploded in core-collapse supernova events or to less massive stars that lose a considerable portion of their mass through stellar winds during the last stage of their evolution, that is, when they enter into the asymptotic giant branch (AGB) phase after having consumed most of the hydrogen and helium in their cores (see [1, 2] and references therein). The dust produced by late AGB stars plays a crucial role being the most important source of interstellar dust particles (accounting up to 70%). The role of interstellar dust is essential since it regulates the radiative transfer of photons and dominates the spectral energy distribution of galaxies and the heating of the gas in diffuse clouds and photodissociation regions. In addition, dust grains provide the surfaces for interstellar heterogeneous chemistry to occur and are the bricks from which planetesimals, and then new planets, are formed around young stars [2–4].

Infrared emission of circumstellar dust in oxygen-rich AGB stars indicates that their major components are amorphous Mg-Fe-silicates. However, is not trivial to reconstruct the processes that lead from gas-phase matter to solid matter. The gas-phase molecules identified in the dust-forming regions might help to unravel the chemical processes at play. In oxygen-rich AGB stars, metal oxides and hydroxides, such as SiO, AlO, AlOH, TiO, and TiO_2, have been detected as isolated molecules (see, for instance, [5–9]). In the inner edge where dust is observed the temperature still exceeds 1000 K, thus implying that the seeds of dust are formed before, closer to the central star with temperatures as high as 1200 K. Gail & Sedlmayr [10, 11] suggested that the direct nucleation of Mg, Fe and SiO from the gas phase cannot occur at temperatures above 1000 K (they estimated that SiO nucleation can only occur below 600 K). Considering their abundance and their bond energies, TiO and AlO emerge as good candidates to start nucleation at higher temperatures [10–12]. In particular, solid Ti/O species can be formed at temperature below 1500 K in rarefied gas at a pressure similar to the one of the circumstellar condensation zone [10–12]. However, it is not yet known for certain if TiO and TiO_2 are responsible for the formation of the seeds of nucleation [13]. TiO_2 emission extends well beyond the dust condensation radius and Ti atoms are observed even farther [5]. Therefore, either a large fraction of Ti is retained in the gas phase (thus questioning its role as one of the main drivers of the formation of nucleation seeds [5]) or Ti, TiO and TiO_2 are released back to the gas-phase by shocks.

Furthermore, even the chemistry that leads to the gas-phase oxides and hydroxides is uncertain and most of the above suggestions come from studies of equilibrium systems [13]. Considering circumstellar envelopes as equilibrium systems is questionable. A kinetics description is, instead, hampered by the missing information on the relevant processes. As an example, a few reactions leading to TiO are considered in the UMIST database [14] (data from one of the few experimental studies available [15]) and none in the KIDA database [16]. A recent model on TiO and TiO_2 formation proposed a series of reactions by analogy with SiO reactions and using the same kinetic parameters [17]. However, the bond energy of SiO (799.6 kJ/mol) and TiO (672.4 kJ/mol) are significantly different and there is no reason to expect a similar chemistry and, especially, the same rate coefficients for their bimolecular reactions.

In this contribution, by using a computational chemistry approach (already employed in the past for other systems [18–21]) we analyzed the reactions of several metal atoms (Mg, Ca, Fe, Al) with the OH radical and the reaction of Ti atoms with the hydroperoxyl radical (HO$_2$) to verify if they are feasible formation routes of interstellar MgO, CaO, FeO, AlO and TiO$_2$. OH is an abundant radical in circumstellar envelopes where it was also seen in vibrationally excited states [22, 23]. HO$_2$, instead, has not been identified in circumstellar envelopes yet. So far, HO$_2$ has been detected only toward Ophiuchi A [24] where also H$_2$O$_2$ and O$_2$ have been identified [25, 26]. These species, and especially H$_2$O$_2$, were searched for as confirmation that water is produced on interstellar ice in star-forming regions, but several attempts have failed so far [27, 28]. In the conditions of AGB stars, where the pressure can be high enough to allow termolecular reactions, HO$_2$ could be formed by the association of H (always present) and O$_2$, a species predicted to be formed by all astrochemical models of O-rich circumstellar envelopes. HO$_2$ is an important radical in combustion and atmospheric chemistry being the leading oxidizing radical together with OH [29]. Its chemistry in the interstellar medium has not been explored much to date.

2   Theoretical Methods

The optimization of the stationary points of the potential energy surface (PES) of the investigated species has been performed applying a computational strategy already adopted in the past and recent studies [30–37]. In particular, in this first explorative study, the geometry optimizations and energy evaluations have been limited to a Density Functional Theory (DFT) approach using the ωB97X-D [38, 39] functional, and the 6−311 + G(d,p) basis set [40, 41]. In order to assign the saddle points to the relative reactants and products we performed intrinsic reaction coordinate (IRC) calculations [42, 43]. All the energies were corrected to 0 K by adding the zero point energy correction computed using the frequencies evaluated at DFT level. All the calculations were performed using Gaussian 09 [44], while the analysis of the vibrational frequencies was performed using Molekel [45, 46].

3   Results and Discussion

3.1   Formation of Metal Monoxides

We considered the reactions between metal atoms M and the OH radical leading to the metal oxide and hydrogen for M = Mg, Ca, Fe, Al.

In Table 1 we have reported the ΔH_0 values for the metal oxides formation reactions computed at DFT level using the ωB97X-D functional in conjunction with the 6−311 + G(d,p) basis set. These values are computed at 0 K and include the zero point energy corrections (ZPE). Let us consider the different oxide formation reactions in details. To be noted that, in most cases, the accepted value of the enthalpy of formation of metal oxides have been derived with indirect ways and there is a considerable uncertainty.

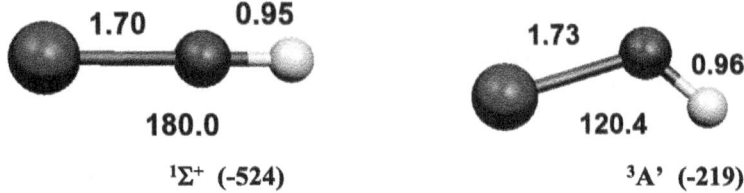

Fig. 1. Optimized geometries of the singlet and triplet AlOH minima. Relative energies (kJ/mol), with respect to the Al + OH reactants, are reported in parentheses. The exit channel, AlO + H, is −46 kJ/mol under the reactants. Bond lengths in Å, angles in degrees.

Table 1. ΔH_0 (kJ/mol, 0 K) and R(M-O) (Å) computed at ωB97X-D/6–311 + G(d,p) level for the reactions of formation of the metal oxides investigated. All the energies include zero-point energy correction. In parentheses the experimental values of the M-O distances obtained from NIST Chemistry Webbook [47, 48].

	ΔH^0_0	R(M-O)
Mg + OH ($^2\Pi$) → MgO ($^1\Sigma^+$) + H	238	1.755 (1.749)
Ca + OH ($^2\Pi$) → CaO ($^1\Sigma^+$) + H	37	1.826 (1.822)
Fe + OH ($^2\Pi$) → FeO ($^5\Delta$) + H	29	1.605 (1.57)
Al + OH ($^2\Pi$) → AlO ($^2\Sigma^+$) + H	−46	1.636 (1.618)
Ti + HO$_2$ (^{2}A") → TiO$_2$ (^{1}A$_1$) + H	−534	1.627 (1.658)

MgO. The ground state of MgO is the singlet $^1\Sigma^+$, the Mg ground state is a singlet while the radical OH has a doublet ground state. The reaction therefore evolves on a doublet PES. According to our DFT calculations, this reaction is strongly endothermic by 238 kJ/mol. The estimated enthalpy of reaction is 90 kJ/mol when using the accepted enthalpies of formation [47]. Therefore, there is a strong discrepancy with the calculated value, suggesting that further investigations with a different theoretical methodology are required. The optimized geometry of MgO shows a Mg-O distance of 1.755 Å in very good agreement with the experimental value of 1.749 Å [48].

CaO. There has been a tentative detection of CaO toward the Galactic center molecular cloud G + 0.693−0.027 [49]. It was suggested that the radiative association of Ca$^+$ with O or O$_2$ could be responsible for its formation upon electron ion recombination. The reactions of Ca atoms with OH or O$_2$ have also been invoked [49]. The ground state of CaO is the singlet $^1\Sigma^+$, also Ca has a singlet ground state while the radical OH has a doublet ground state. The reaction therefore evolves on a doublet surface. This reaction is endothermic by 37 kJ/mol which can be compared with the estimate of 40 kJ/mol obtained from the values by Gurvich et al. [50] for $\Delta H°_{f,0}K$(CaO) and NIST [47] for the other species. The optimized geometry of CaO shows a Ca-O distance of 1.826 Å in very good agreement with the experimental value of 1.822 Å [48]. Given its endothermicity, this reaction cannot occur unless vibrationally excited OH (or other sources of energy) are available. Interestingly, vibrationally excited OH radicals have been detected in several AGB systems [22, 23]. Therefore, it is conceivable that CaO is formed in those conditions, if Ca atoms are available.

FeO. The ground state of FeO is the quintet $^5\Delta$, also Fe has a quintet ground state while the radical OH has a doublet ground state. The reaction therefore evolves on a quartet surface. According to our calculations, this reaction is endothermic by 29 kJ/mol which can be compared with the estimate of 15 kJ/mol obtained from the NIST values of enthalpies of formation [47]. Therefore, this reaction can occur only in warm interstellar environments or with vibrationally excited OH. The optimized geometry of FeO shows a Fe-O distance of 1.605 Å in reasonable agreement with the experimental value of 1.57 Å [48].

AlO. The ground state of AlO is the doublet $^2\Sigma^+$, also Al has a doublet ground state as well as the radical OH. The reaction therefore can evolve on a singlet or triplet surface. The singlet PES has already been characterized by Gobrecht et al. [51] at the higher level of theory CBS-QB3. According to our calculations, this reaction is exothermic by 46 kJ/mol which can be compared with the estimate of 84 kJ/mol obtained from the experimental enthalpies of formation [47] and with the value of 72 kJ/mol derived by Gobrecht et al. [51]. Also in this case, it is clearly necessary to use a higher level of theory. The optimized geometry of AlO shows an Al-O distance of 1.636 Å in good agreement with the experimental value of 1.6179 Å [48] and the value of 1.630 Å by Gobrecht et al. [51]. The interaction of Al with OH leads to an intermediate AlOH both in the singlet and in the triplet PESs. The geometries of these species are reported in Fig. 1, together with their relative energies with respect to the reactants Al + OH. The singlet $^1\Sigma^+$ is linear and is more stable with respect to the reactants by 524 kJ/mol, in line with the value of 554 kJ/mol obtained by Gobrecht et al. [51]. The AlOH intermediate dissociates to AlO + H without any barrier. The triplet ^{3}A' shows an Al-O-H angle of 120.4° and is more stable than the reactants by 219 kJ/mol. The triplet intermediate also evolves towards the products in a barrierless process.

3.2 Formation of TiO$_2$

We considered the reactions between Ti atoms and the HO$_2$ radical to verify if TiO$_2$ can be formed directly from Ti atoms without the intermediacy of TiO formation. The spatial distributions TiO and TiO$_2$ were seen to be quite different in the case of VY Canis Majoris, while the emission of Ti is extended farther [52].

The ground state of TiO$_2$ is the singlet ^{1}A$_1$, while Ti has a triplet ground state and the radical HO$_2$ has a doublet ground state. The reaction therefore evolves on a doublet surface. We considered only this potential energy surface, since we were interested on the formation of TiO$_2$ in its ground state. We will discuss the quartet surface elsewhere. The channel leading to TiO$_2$ + H is strongly exothermic with an enthalpy variation of 534 kJ/mol (to be compared with the estimate of −563 kJ/mol obtained from the experimental enthalpies of formation [47]). The competitive channel leading to TiO + OH is, instead, exothermic by 265 kJ/mol. The optimized distance of Ti-O in TiO$_2$ is 1.627 Å in reasonable agreement with the experimental value of 1.658 Å [47].

The interaction of Ti with the radical HO_2 gives rise, in a barrierless addition process, to a first minimum (MIN1) which is more stable than the reactants by 292 kJ/mol. The geometry of MIN1 is reported in Fig. 2. By overcoming a very small barrier of 6 kJ/mol (corresponding to the transition state, TS, shown in Fig. 2), MIN1 easily evolves to a second minimum (MIN2) which is much more stable (-833 kJ/mol with respect to the energy of the reactants). Because of the large internal energy content, MIN2 decomposed into the $TiO_2 + H$ or into $TiO + OH$ products without any exit barrier.

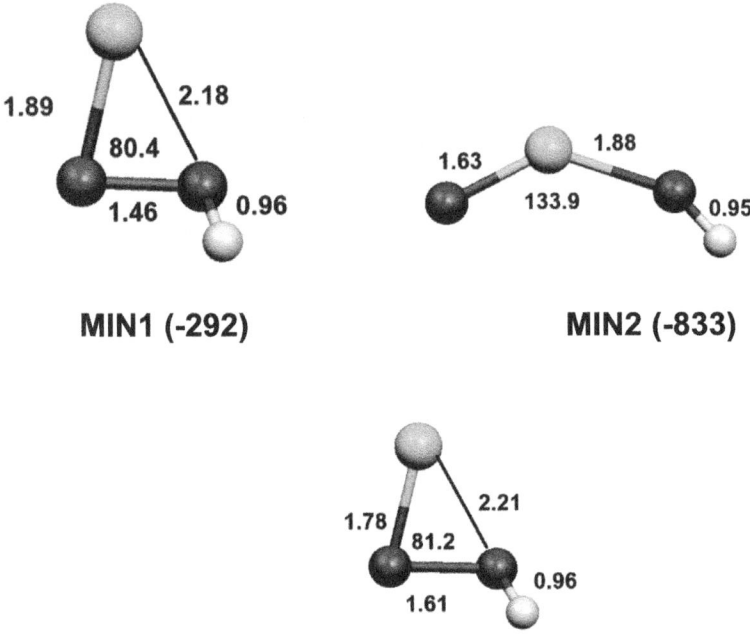

Fig. 2. Optimized geometries of the minima and the transition state obtained for the reaction of Ti with HO_2. Relative energies (kJ/mol), with respect to the reactants, are reported in parentheses. The exit channel, $TiO_2 + H$, is -534 kJ/mol below the energy of the reactants. Bond lengths in Å, angles in degrees.

4   Conclusions and Astrochemical Implications

In this first explorative computational study, we have investigated possible formation routes of interstellar oxides via the reactions of the atoms of several metals (Mg, Ca, Al, Fe) with the OH radical and the reaction of Ti atoms with HO_2 radicals. The main aim was to understand if it is worth investing more effort in a higher-level theoretical characterization of these reactions. The results are encouraging overall. From a computational perspective, it is clear that the computational approach we have used, based on DFT, is not accurate enough for the calculation of the energy variations and much more accurate methods as, for instance, CCSD(T)/CBS are necessary, while the structure of the investigated species is in line with experimental determinations or previous calculations.

As far as the feasibility of the investigated reactions is concerned, it is quite obvious that CaO cannot be formed by the reaction between Ca and OH, unless OH is present in vibrationally excited state (the energy content of $v_{OH} = 1$ is 44.7 kJ/mol). This can actually be the case for AGB stars, while it is quite improbable in the case of the molecular cloud G + 0.693−0.027. Incidentally, also the other neutral-neutral reaction suggested by Rey-Montejo et al. [49], i.e. $Ca + O_2 \rightarrow CaO + O$, is endothermic by 110 kJ/mol [47] and, therefore, cannot occur in cold regions of the interstellar medium [53]. The $Mg + OH \rightarrow MgO + O$ is even more endothermic and, therefore, it is improbable that it plays any role. The reaction $Fe + OH \rightarrow FeO + H$ is instead a blandly endothermic reaction that can occur in high-temperature environments or in the presence of vibrationally excited OH. The role of excited OH was invoked by Decin et al. [5] in their model to account for the FeO formation in R Dor (they derive a column density N(FeO) of $1.1 \pm 0.9 \times 10^{15}$ cm^{-2} corresponding to a fractional abundance [FeO/H] $\sim 1.5 \times 10^{-8}$; upper limits for the abundance of CaO and MgO were also provided). Finally, our results on Al + OH are in line with a similar investigation at a higher level of theory that, however, did not consider the triplet PES [50].

Concerning the reaction $Ti + HO_2 \rightarrow TiO_2 + H$, we can conclude that it establishes a direct connection between TiO_2 and Ti atoms, provided that HO_2 (still undetected in the circumstellar envelopes of O-rich AGB stars, but plausibly present) has a non-negligible abundance. It can be an alternative pathway to TiO_2 formation without passing through TiO and its reaction with the OH radical or O_2. Kaminski et al. [4] clearly showed that in VY Canis Majoris not all titanium is depleted into dust particles and the emission of TiO and especially of TiO_2 extends outside the dust formation regions. Most models predict that Ti is converted to oxides in the inner outflow, but emission features of atomic Ti extend farther from the star than the gas with highest TiO abundance [52]. Ti is considered to be highly depleted in the diffuse interstellar medium. The observed optical emission of Ti is further evidence that the condensation of Ti species in VY Canis Majoris is not as efficient as previously estimated or that Ti atoms are originated by the dust destruction. However, in this last case, one would expect to see TiO and TiO_2, also released by dust destruction, at the same location which is not the case.

Clearly, a better understanding of the chemistry at play will help solving this and other open questions.

Acknowledgments. The authors thank the MUR PRIN2020 (2020AFB3FX-Astrochemistry beyond the second-period elements) and the European Union's Horizon 2020 research and innovation program from the European Research Council (ERC) project 'The Dawn of Organic Chemistry' (DOC), grant agreement n° 741002) for support. MR thanks financial support under the National Recovery and Resilience Plan (NRRP), Mission 4, Component 2, Investment 1.1, Call for tender n° 104 published on 2.2.2022 by the Italian Ministry of University and Research (MUR), funded by the European Union – NextGenerationEU – Project Title 2022JC2Y93 Chemical Origins: linking the fossil composition of the Solar System with the chemistry of protoplanetary disks – CUP J53D23001600006 - Grant Assignment Decree No. 962 adopted on 30/06/2023 by the Italian Ministry of University and Research (MUR). Support from the Project of the University of Perugia "COLONIZE. Indagini preliminari su risposte biologiche, materiali cementizi alternativi e nuove fonti energetiche per affrontare la colonizzazione infrastrutturale dello Spazio" is also acknowledged.

References

1. Höfner, S., Olofsson, H.: Mass loss of stars on the asymptotic giant branch: mechanisms, models and measurements. Astron. Astrophys. Rev. **26**(1), 1 (2018). https://doi.org/10.1007/s00159-017-0106-5
2. Tielens, A.G.: The Physics and Chemistry of the Interstellar Medium. Cambridge University Press (2005). https://doi.org/10.1017/CBO9780511819056
3. Plane, J.M.C.: On the nucleation of dust in oxygen-rich stellar outflows. Philos. Trans. R. Soc. A Math. Phys. Eng. Sci. **371**(1994), 20120335 (2013). https://doi.org/10.1098/rsta.2012.0335
4. Tielens, A.G.: Dust formation in astrophysical environments: the importance of kinetics. Front. Astron. Astrophys. **9**, 908217 (2022). https://doi.org/10.3389/fspas.2022.908217
5. Kamiński, T., et al.: Pure rotational spectra of TiO and TiO_2 in VY Canis Majoris. Astron. Astrophys. **551**, A113 (2013). https://doi.org/10.1051/0004-6361/201220290
6. Decin, L., et al.: Constraints on metal oxide and metal hydroxide abundances in the winds of AGB stars: Potential detection of FeO in R Dor. Astrophys. J. **855**(2), 113 (2018). https://doi.org/10.3847/1538-4357/aaab6a
7. Danilovich, T., et al.: Rotational spectra of vibrationally excited AlO and TiO in oxygen-rich stars. Astrophys. J. **904**(2), 110 (2020). https://doi.org/10.3847/1538-4357/abc079
8. Tenenbaum, E.D., Ziurys, L.M.: Millimeter detection of AlO (X $^2\Sigma^+$): metal oxide chemistry in the envelope of VY Canis Majoris. **694**(1), L59–L63 (2009). https://doi.org/10.1088/0004-637X/694/1/L59
9. Agúndez, M., Fonfría, J.P., Cernicharo, J., Kahane, C., Daniel, F., Guélin, M.: Molecular abundances in the inner layers of IRC +10216. Astron. Astrophys. **543**, A48 (2012). https://doi.org/10.1051/0004-6361/201218963
10. Gail, H.P., Sedlmayr, E.: Inorganic dust formation in astrophysical environments. Faraday Discuss. **109**, 303–319 (1998). https://doi.org/10.1039/A709290C
11. Gail, H.P., Sedlmayr, E.: Dust formation in M stars. Int. Ser. Astron. Astrophys. **4**, 285 (1998)
12. Sharp, C., Huebner, W.: Molecular equilibrium with condensation. Astrophys. J. Suppl. Ser. **72**, 417–431 (1990). https://doi.org/10.1086/191422
13. Gobrecht, D., Cherchneff, I., Sarangi, A., Plane, J.M.C., Bromley, S.T.: Dust formation in the oxygen-rich AGB star IK Tauri. Astron. Astrophys. **585**, A6 (2016). https://doi.org/10.1051/0004-6361/201425363
14. Millar, T.J., Walsh, C., Van de Sande, M., Markwick, A.J.: The UMIST database for astrochemistry 2022. Astron. Astrophys. **682**, 109 (2024). https://doi.org/10.1051/0004-6361/202346908
15. Campbell, M.L., McClean, R.E.: Kinetics of neutral transition-metal atoms in the gas phase: oxidation reactions of titanium (a3F) from 300 to 600 K. J. Phys. Chem. **97**(30), 7942–7946 (1993). https://doi.org/10.1021/j100132a024
16. Wakelam, V., et al.: The 2014 KIDA network for interstellar chemistry. Astrophys. J. Suppl. Ser. **217**(2), 20 (2015). https://doi.org/10.1088/0067-0049/217/2/20
17. Shaw, G., Ferland, G.J., Stancil, P., Porter, R.: Recent update of gas-phase chemical reactions and molecular lines of TiO in cloudy. Revista Mexicana de Astronomia y Astrofísica **60**, 373–379 (2024). https://doi.org/10.48550/arXiv.2407.20972

18. Troiani, A., Rosi, M., Garzoli, S., Salvitti, C., de Petris, G.: Effective redox reactions by chromium oxide anions: sulfur dioxide oxidation in the gas phase. Int. J. of Mass Spectrom. **436**, 18–22 (2019). https://doi.org/10.1016/j.ijms.2018.11.009

19. Troiani, A., Rosi, M., Salvitti, C., de Petris, G.: The oxidation of sulfur dioxide by single and double oxygen transfer paths. ChemPhysChem **15**(13), 2723–2731 (2014). https://doi. org/10.1002/cphc.201402306

20. Troiani, A., Rosi, M., Garzoli, S., Salvitti, C., de Petris, G.: Sulphur dioxide cooperation in hydrolysis reactions of vanadium oxide and hydroxide cluster dianions. New J. Chem. **42**(6), 4008–4016 (2018). https://doi.org/10.1039/C7NJ05011A

21. Salvitti, C., Rosi, M., Pepi, F., Troiani, A., de Petris, G.: Reactivity of transition metal dioxide anions MO_2^- (M = Co, Ni, Cu, Zn) with sulfur dioxide in the gas phase: an experimental and theoretical study. Chem. Phys. Lett. **776**, 138555 (2021). https://doi.org/10.1016/j.cplett. 2021.138555

22. Baudry, A., et al.: Atomium: probing the inner wind of evolved O-rich stars with new, highly excited H_2O and OH lines. Astron. Astrophys. **674**, A125 (2023). https://doi.org/10.1051/ 0004-6361/20224519

23. Khouri, T., et al.: Detection of highly excited OH towards AGB stars - a new probe of shocked gas in the extended atmospheres. Astron. Astrophys. **623**, L1 (2019). https://doi.org/10.1051/ 0004-6361/201935049

24. Parise, B., Bergman, P., Du, F.: Detection of the hydroperoxyl radical HO_2 toward Ophiuchi A - additional constraints on the water chemical network. Astron. Astrophys. **541**, L11 (2012). https://doi.org/10.1051/0004-6361/201219379

25. Bergman, P., et al.: Detection of interstellar hydrogen peroxide. Astron. Astrophys. **531**, L8 (2011). https://doi.org/10.1051/0004-6361/201117170

26. Larsson, B., et al.: Molecular oxygen in the Ophiuchi cloud. Astron. Astrophys. **466**(3), 999–1003 (2007). https://doi.org/10.1051/0004-6361:20065500

27. Parise, B., Bergman, P., Menten, K.: Characterizing the chemical pathways for water formation – a deep search for hydrogen peroxide. Faraday Discuss. **168**, 349–367 (2014). https:// doi.org/10.1039/C3FD00115F

28. Fuchs, G.W., et al.: Deep search for hydrogen peroxide toward pre- and protostellar objects - testing the pathway of grain surface water formation. Astron. Astrophys. **636**, A114 (2020). https://doi.org/10.1051/0004-6361/201935386

29. De Petris, G., Angelini, G., Ursini, O., Rosi, M., Troiani, A.: Linking ion and neutral chemistry in C—H bond electrophilic activation: generation and detection of HO_2 reactive radicals in the gas phase. Angew. Chem. Int. Ed. **51**, 1455–1458 (2012). https://doi.org/10.1002/anie. 201107224

30. Giani, L., et al.: Revised gas-phase formation network of methyl cyanide: the origin of methyl cyanide and methanol abundance correlation in hot corinos. Mon. Not. R. Astron. Soc. **526**(3), 4535–4556 (2023). https://doi.org/10.1093/mnras/stad2892

31. Rosi, M., et al.: Electronic structure and kinetics calculations for the Si+SH reaction, a possible route of SiS formation in star-forming regions. In: Lecture Notes in Computer Science (including subseries Lecture Notes in Artificial Intelligence and Lecture Notes in Bioinformatics). Lecture Notes in Artificial Intelligence, vol. 11621, pp. 306–315. Springer Verlag (2019). https://doi.org/10.1007/978-3-030-24302-9_22

32. Liang, P., et al.: OH ($^2\Pi$)+ C_2H_4 reaction: a combined crossed molecular beam and theoretical study. J. Phys. Chem. A **127**(21), 4609–4623 (2023). https://doi.org/10.1021/acs.jpca.2c0 8662

33. Skouteris, D., et al.: Interstellar dimethyl ether gas-phase formation: a quantum chemistry and kinetics study. Mon. Not. R. Astron. Soc. **482**(3), 3567–3575 (2019). https://doi.org/10. 1093/mnras/sty2903

34. Recio, P., et al.: A crossed molecular beam investigation of the $N(^2D)$ + pyridine reaction and implications for prebiotic chemistry. Chem. Phys. Letters **779**, 138852 (2021). https://doi.org/10.1016/j.cplett.2021.138852

35. Vanuzzo, G., et al.: Reaction N (^2D) + CH_2CCH_2 (Allene): an experimental and theoretical investigation and implications for the photochemical models of titan. ACS Earth Space Chem. **6**(10), 2305–2321 (2022). https://doi.org/10.1021/acsearthspacechem.2c00183

36. Marchione, D., et al.: Unsaturated dinitriles formation routes in ectraterrestrial environments. A combined experimental and theoretical investigation of the reaction between cyano radicals and cyanoethene (C_2H_3CN). J. Phys. Chem. A **126**(22), 3569–3582 (2022). https://doi.org/10.1021/acs.jpca.2c01802

37. Pannacci, G., et al.: A combined crossed molecular beam and theorerical study of the O $(^3P, ^1D)$+ acrylonitrile (CH_2CHCN) reactions and implications for combustion and extraterrestrial environments. Phys. Chem. Chem. Phys. **25**(30), 20194–20211 (2023). https://doi.org/10.1039/D3CP01558K

38. Chai, J.-D., Head-Gordon, M.: Long-range corrected hybrid density functionals with damped atom-atom dispersion corrections. Phys. Chem. Chem. Phys. **10**, 6615–6620 (2008). https://doi.org/10.1039/B810189B

39. Chai, J.-D., Head-Gordon, M.: Systematic optimization of long-range corrected hybrid density functionals. J. Chem. Phys. **128**, 084106 (2008). https://doi.org/10.1063/1.2834918

40. Krishnan, R., Binkley, J. S., Seeger, R., Pople, J. A.: Self-consistent molecular orbital methods. XX. A basis set for correlated wave functions. J. Chem. Phys. **72**, 650–654 (1980). https://doi.org/10.1063/1.438955

41. Frisch, M. J., Pople, J. A., Binkley, J. S.: Self-consistent molecular orbital methods 28. Supplementary functions for Gaussian basis sets. J. Chem. Phys. **80**, 3265–3269 (1984). https://doi.org/10.1063/1.447079

42. Gonzalez, C., Schlegel, H.B.: An improved algorithm for reaction path following. J. Chem. Phys. **90**, 2154–2161 (1989). https://doi.org/10.1063/1.456010

43. Gonzalez, C., Schlegel, H.B.: Reaction path following in mass-weighted internal coordinates. J. Phys. Chem. **94**, 5523–5527 (1990). https://doi.org/10.1021/j100377a021

44. Frisch, M. J., Trucks, G. W., Schlegel, H. B., et al.: Gaussian 09, Revision A.02. Gaussian, Inc., Wallingford CT (2009)

45. Flükiger, P., Lüthi, H.P., Portmann, S., Weber, J.: MOLEKEL 4.3, Swiss Center for Scientific Computing, Manno (Switzerland) (2000–2002)

46. Portmann, S., Lüthi, H.P.: MOLEKEL: An Interactive Molecular Graphics Tool Chimia **54**, 766–769 (2000). https://doi.org/10.2533/chimia.2000.766

47. Huber, K.P., Herzberg, G.H.: "Constants of Diatomic Molecules" (data prepared by Jean W. Gallagher and Russell D. Johnson, III). In: Linstrom, P.J., Mallard, W.G. (eds.) NIST Chemistry WebBook, NIST Standard Reference Database Number 69, National Institute of Standards and Technology, Gaithersburg MD, 20899 (2025). https://doi.org/10.18434/T4D303

48. Huber, K.P.; Herzberg, G.: Molecular Spectra and Molecular Structure. IV. Constants of Diatomic Molecules, Van Nostrand Reinhold Co. (1979). https://doi.org/10.1007/978-1-4757-0961-2_2

49. Rey-Montejo, M., et al.: Discovery of MgS and NaS in the Interstellar Medium and Tentative Detection of CaO. **975**(2), 174 (2024). https://doi.org/10.3847/1538-4357/ad736e

50. Gurvich, L., Veyts, I., Alcock, C.: Thermodynamic Properties of Individual Substances, 4th edn. Hemisphere Pub. Co., New York (1989)

51. Gobrecht, D., Plane, J.M.C., Bromley, S.T., Decin, L., Cristallo, S., Sekaran, S.: Bottom-up dust nucleation theory in oxygen-rich evolved stars - I. aluminium oxide clusters. Astron. Astrophys. **658**, A167 (2022). https://doi.org/10.1051/0004-6361/202141976

52. Wallerstein, G.: Titanium oxide emission in the spectrum of VY Canis Majoris in december 1983. Astron. Astrophys. **164**(1), 101–103 (1986)
53. Tinacci, L., et al.: The gretobape gas-phase reaction network: the importance of being exothermic. Astrophys. J. Suppl. Ser. **266**(2), 38 (2023). https://doi.org/10.3847/1538-4365/accae9

Synthesis of Chemical Species Relevant in Environmental and Astro Chemistry: Their Production and Characterization by Synchrotron Radiation

Marco Parriani[1,2] , Eleonora Manuali[1], Simonetta Cavalli[2], Michele Alagia[3], Robert Richter[4], Stefano Stranges[5,3], Raimund Feifel[6], and Stefano Falcinelli[1(✉)]

[1] Department of Civil and Environmental Engineering, University of Perugia, Via G. Duranti 93, 06125 Perugia, Italy
stefano.falcinelli@unipg.it
[2] Department of Chemistry, Biology and Biotechnologies, University of Perugia, Via Elce di Sotto 8, 06100 Perugia, Italy
simonetta.cavalli@unipg.it
[3] IOM CNR Laboratorio TASC, 34012 Trieste, Italy
alagia@iom.cnr.it
[4] Sincrotrone Trieste, Area Science Park, 34149 Basovizza, Trieste, Italy
robert.richter@elettra.trieste.it
[5] Department of Chemistry and Drug Technology, University of Rome Sapienza, 00185 Rome, Italy
stefano.stranges@uniroma1.it
[6] Department of Physics, University of Gothenburg, Origovägen 6B, 412 58 Gothenburg, Sweden
raimund.feifel@physics.gu.se

Abstract. In this work, the synthesis performed for neutral precursors (isothiocyanic acid, carbon suboxide and cyanoacetylene) used in studies of double photoionization spectroscopy with synchrotron radiation are presented. They were performed starting from few data present in the literature by modifying the procedure in order to obtain a better yield of the desired product with an optimized timing. All the synthetic procedures are related to chemical species of great relevance from an environmental and astrochemical point of view and not commercially available. They can be easily reproduced by any researcher interested in studying the chemical species that are the subject of this work.

Keywords: Astrochemistry · Double Photoionization · Synchrotron Radiation

1 Introduction

1.1 The Photoionization

A general property in thermodynamics is that all objects tend to seek the minimum energy state with the maximum entropy. Similarly, electrons in atoms and molecules, unless influenced by an external force, are found in an energetic local minimum known as

© The Author(s), under exclusive license to Springer Nature Switzerland AG 2026
O. Gervasi et al. (Eds.): ICCSA 2025 Workshops, LNCS 15888, pp. 300–314, 2026.
https://doi.org/10.1007/978-3-031-97596-7_20

the ground state. According to the Aufbau principle, electrons fill lower-energy orbitals before occupying higher-energy ones. Photoionization studies here discussed investigate processes initiated in ground state molecules when they are exposed to photons in the ultraviolet and X-ray spectral regions using tunable synchrotron radiation. The absorbed photon energy may ionize the molecule by ejecting one or more electrons, causing single or multiple ionization. The resulting ion naturally seeks to minimize its energy, which can be achieved by altering the bond lengths or angles between atoms, or more drastically, by fragmenting into smaller pieces. Photoelectron spectroscopy (PES) is a powerful analytical technique that probes the electronic structure of materials by measuring the kinetic energy of electrons ejected upon photon absorption. This technique has become indispensable in various fields, including surface science, materials science, chemistry, and condensed matter physics, providing detailed insights into the electronic states and chemical composition of a wide array of systems.

The foundation of PES lies in the photoelectric effect, first explained by Albert Einstein in 1905 through the use of the new Planck's quantum theory of radiation [1]. Prior to his work, there had been several observations of the photoelectric effect, from the 1887 experiment of H. R. Hertz on the production and detection of electromagnetic waves [2], to the 1902 experiment of Lenard to understand the light intensity dependency of the photoelectric effect [3]. In few words, when photons with sufficient energy strike a material, they can eject electrons from the surface. The kinetic energy of these ejected electrons, measured in PES, provides direct information about the binding energies of electrons in the material [4, 5].

Furthermore, it has to be noted that in Penning ionization PES provides real spectroscopy of the transition state of chemi-ionization reactions [6, 7].

1.2 The Atomic and Molecular Dications and Their Role in Environmental and Astro Chemistry

When two electrons are stripped from a neutral species, a doubly charged cation, known as a dication, is formed. Molecular dications can remain stable against dissociation in the gas phase, even without the stabilizing influence of solvation. The first discovery and identification of a gas-phase molecular dication, CO^{2+}, occurred in the early 20th century during the development of mass spectrometry [8, 9]. Since then, the unique properties of dications have spurred further research, challenging fundamental concepts in chemistry and bonding [10–16]. Dications can be produced through collisions between atoms or molecules and high-energy particles or photons. They have been observed in various high-energy environments, such as comet tails, planetary and satellite ionospheres, the interstellar medium, and near high-energy photon sources [17]. Atomic dications like N^{2+}, O^{2+}, S^{2+}, Ar^{2+}, and Ne^{2+} have been detected in various nebulae, including those in other galaxies, through emission spectroscopy [18, 19]. The presence of dications can influence reactivity in these cold interstellar environments; for instance, they can undergo Coulomb explosion, fragmenting into two monocations with high kinetic energy. This process can create monocations with translational energies of several eV, allowing reaction barriers to be surpassed at low temperatures [20, 21]. Additionally, metal dications, as Mg^{2+}, are believed to facilitate interstellar processes by lowering reaction barriers [22]. Research has shown that both atomic and molecular dications exhibit significant bimolecular reactivity following collisions with neutral species [23–25]. These collisional processes are expected to be the primary factor limiting the lifetimes of atomic dications in planetary ionospheres [26, 27]. Despite their inherent thermodynamic instability compared to their dissociated charge-separated products, the metastable electronic states of many molecular dications have lifetimes sufficient to allow collisions with other species in planetary environments. For example, the primary loss mechanisms for CO^{2+} and O^{2+} dications in ionospheres are predicted to be bimolecular reactions [28]. The reactive nature of dications, along with their significant presence in ionospheres, suggests that their bimolecular chemistry could play a role in ionospheric chemistry, potentially contributing to the formation of complex molecules. Carbon-carbon coupling reactions have been observed following interactions of aromatic dications with methane [29], ethyne [30], and benzene [31]. Dications from nitrogen-containing compounds, such as pyridine and benzonitrile, have been used in some of these bond-forming reactions, consequently these processes could be relevant to the nitrogen-rich atmosphere of Titan.

By removing two electrons from a neutral species, a formed dication can be an unstable molecule with a variable lifetime that can be long enough to allow the dication to collide with neutral molecules and evolve through a large number of possible processes. However, in general, a molecular dissociation is highly probable: in this case, the dication does not have a lifetime long enough to collide with neutral molecules before its dissociation into fragment ions. In this case, the analysis of emitted electrons and ionic fragments by photoelectron-photoion-photoion coincidence (PEPIPICO) spectroscopy makes it possible to extract fundamental information about the process, such as energy thresholds, kinetic energy released (KERs) and angular distributions of fragment ions [32–35].

A schematic overview of the possible cases that can occur as a result of molecular dication formation in accordance with Eq. (2) below is illustrated in Fig. 1.

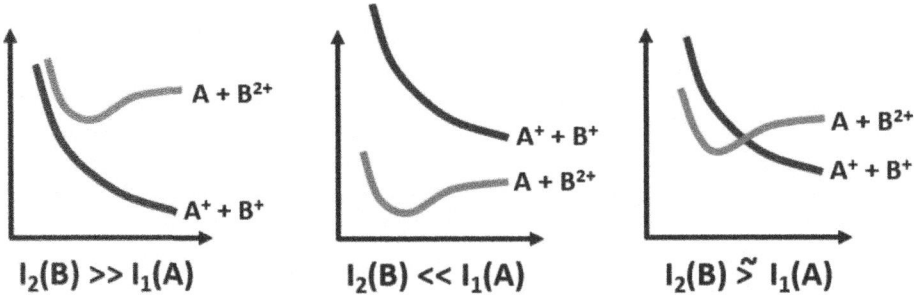

Fig. 1. The scheme of the potential energy curves for the simple case of AB^{2+} diatomic molecular dications. $I_2(B)$ stands for the second ionization potential of the B atom, being the one having the lower electronegativity with respect to A, while $I_1(A)$ is the first ionization potential of the A atom.

Figure 1 shows the scheme of the potential energy curves for the simple case of AB^{2+} molecular dications, in which the first case on the left shows the case of the thermodynamically unstable dications, the center panel the case of stable species that can be detected in gas phase, while the right panel shows molecular dications in a metastable state, as a result of an avoided crossing of the potential energy curves involved. In Fig. 2, is reported the resulting potential energy curve for this latter case, in which is shown the generation of the two A^+ and B^+ fragment ions that generally carry a high relative kinetic energy release. As mentioned above, this dissociation process takes the name of Coulomb explosion and generates monocations with a translational energy content that, in general, ranges from 1 to 10 eV.

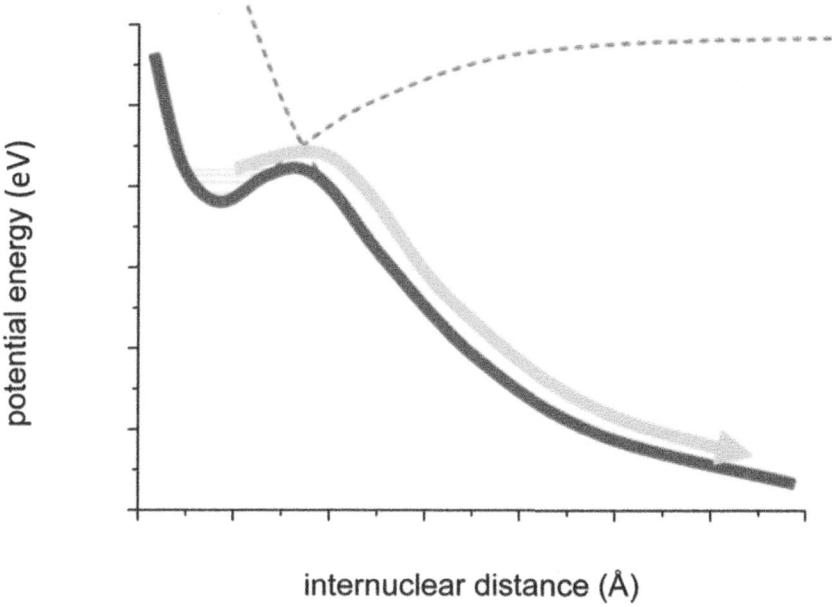

internuclear distance (Å)

Fig. 2. The resulting potential energy curve, typical for the case of metastable molecular dications AB^{2+} (due to an avoided crossing), generating the two A^+ and B^+ fragment ions (dotted lines) having, in general, a kinetic energy content of several eV.

This kind of process is the responsible for the escape of O^+ ions from Mars' ionosphere, which explains the continuous process of erosion to which this planet's atmosphere is subjected [36–38].

The production and characterization of stable and metastable dications are performed by our research group using PES and PEPIPICO techniques coupled with synchrotron radiation at the ELETTRA Synchrotron Facility of Basovizza (Trieste, Italy).

2   The Elettra Synchrotron Facility

The Elettra Synchrotron Facility, located in Trieste, Italy, is a prominent research center dedicated to the exploration and advancement of synchrotron light applications. Since its inauguration in 1993, Elettra has been at the forefront of scientific research, enabling groundbreaking work across a variety of disciplines, including physics, chemistry, biology, and materials science. Operated by "Elettra - Sincrotrone Trieste S.C.p.A.", this facility serves as a critical resource for both academic and industrial researchers from around the world. This third-generation storage ring operates in top-up mode in both 2 and 2.4 GeV user energies. Elettra features 28 beamlines that have been specifically optimized to deliver photons across an energy range from a few eV to several keV. It achieves a spectral brightness of up to 10^{19} photons/s/mm^2/mrad^2 with a 0.1% bandwidth. To maintain its competitiveness with the latest synchrotron light sources, Elettra undergoes continuous upgrades and improvements. In particular, photoionization studies of environmentally and astrochemically relevant molecular precursors are performed at both the GasPhase and CiPo beamlines.

2.1 The GasPhase and CiPo Beamlines

The Gas Phase Photoemission (GAPH) beamline at Elettra is uniquely dedicated to studying gaseous systems (see Fig. 3).

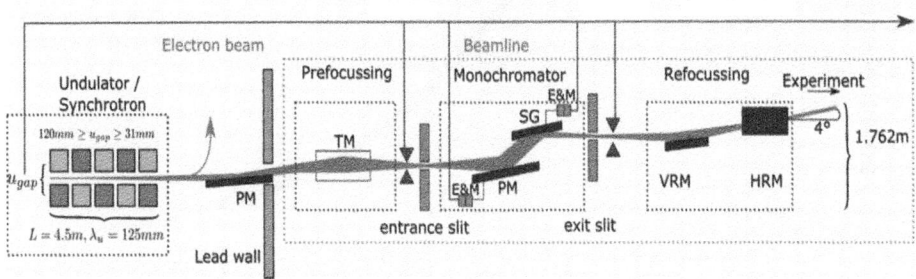

Fig. 3. The Schematic side view of the beamline, reproduced with courtesy of the Elettra Synchrotron Facility (Basovizza, Trieste, Italy).

This beamline offers high-resolution capabilities and provides a high flux across a broad energy range, spanning from 13 to 900 eV. The light beam maintains a stable and nearly circular spot size of approximately 200 μm at the target. An undulator supplies light to the beamline, with energies extending from 13.5 eV to well beyond 900 eV. A "Variable Angle Spherical Grating Monochromator", with fixed slit positions, is used to manage the light's wavelength. The optical design, created by the "Sincrotrone Trieste", incorporates a toroidal prefocusing mirror and two refocusing mirrors-one spherical and the other plane-elliptical. During commissioning, the monochromator not only met but surpassed its design specifications, achieving a resolving power of 60,000 at 48 eV. Even at higher energies, such as 540 eV, it maintains a resolving power above 10,000, and reaches 8,000 at 860 eV, making it the most precise monochromator at Elettra. The inclusion of two refocusing mirrors helps produce a nearly circular beam spot at the sample, with a diameter exceeding 350 μm when using a 20 μm exit slit. This size decreases to under 150 μm as photon energy surpasses 200 eV. The beamline connects to the experimental station through a differential pumping section, ensuring a five-order-of-magnitude pressure difference. This configuration isolates the ultra-high vacuum (UHV) area of the mirror chambers from the higher vacuum region of the experiment. This layout supports a broad energy range (approximately 13 to 900 eV) and maintains a high energy resolution (E/ΔE > 10,000) throughout. The beam delivers a small, nearly circular spot of light (200 μm × 200 μm) with minimal angular divergence (about 3 mrad) at the sample position, located 2.5 m from the last optical component. These design constraints result in an overall monochromator length of about 6 m, featuring two refocusing mirrors. The second mirror has a short exit arm and adjusts the focus to 1.762 m above the floor at a 4°angle. The monochromator also requires entrance and exit slits with adjustable widths ranging from 5 to 200 μm. The monochromator consists of a plane mirror and five spherical gratings to accommodate the extensive energy range. These gratings vary in radius and ruling. The maximum achievable energy resolution with the Variable Angle Spherical Grating Monochromator (VASGM) is limited by the mechanics of the plane mirror and spherical grating movements. However, resolution can be enhanced over short ranges by adjusting the spherical grating to optimize the plane mirror's focus. Moreover, the resolution depends on the exit slit width, which affects the photon flux. More details and schematics can be found in literature and on the official Elettra website [39].

The Circular Polarization (CiPo) beamline at the ELETTRA Synchrotron is notable for its ability to produce synchrotron radiation with variable polarization, ranging from circular to linear, across a wide photon energy spectrum from 11 to 900 eV. At the heart of the CiPo beamline is the Electromagnetic Elliptical Wiggler (EEW), which is engineered to deliver both linearly and circularly polarized light throughout the entire energy range. The EEW can function in both undulator and wiggler modes. A unique aspect of the EEW is its electromagnetic design, which facilitates helicity switching by integrating horizontal and vertical periodic magnets into a single open-side structure. In wiggler mode, the EEW operates with varying horizontal and vertical magnetic field strengths to produce elliptically polarized radiation, offering a continuous emission spectrum from 40 eV to over 1000 eV. It also generates a spectrum of harmonics at the lower end of the photon energy range, below 40 eV. The degree of circular polarization varies with photon energy, starting at 40% at 8.5 eV and reaching 80% at 575 eV. Full circular polarization is achieved when the EEW acts as a pure circular undulator, with equal horizontal and vertical magnetic fields. In undulator mode, the EEW can also produce linearly polarized radiation, with the polarization vector aligned either parallel or perpendicular to the orbit plane. The beamline features two monochromators: a Normal Incidence Monochromator (NIM) for low energies between 5 and 35 eV, and a Spherical Grating Monochromator (SGM) for higher energies. More details and schematics can be found in literature and on the official Elettra website [40].

The used apparatus in our experiments, hosting a PES as well as a PEPICO detector for the characterization of generated molecular dications is the ARPES (Angle Resolved PhotoEmission Spectroscopy)-end station, described in the next subsection.

2.2 The ARPES-End Station

The ARPES-end station used for the experimental measurements on molecular dications is an ion imaging spectroscopy apparatus equipped with a differential pumping system (see Fig. 4). This system allows the use of two interchangeable molecular beam setups: a pyrolytic source and a hypodermic needle. The apparatus enables photoionization studies using a tunable, high- photon flux from a third-generation synchrotron source.

These studies primarily rely on PES and PEPIPICO detectors paired with a time-of-flight (TOF) mass spectrometer, specifically designed to measure the spatial momentum components of ion fragments in double photoionization experiments [40]. In the past, this particular end station has been successfully employed in double photoionization studies of HX molecules (where X = Cl, Br, and I) [14, 41].

Fig. 4. The ARPES-end station apparatus operating at the GasPhase beamline of Elettra Synchrotron Facility (Trieste, Italy).

The experimental procedure and the relative computational analysis of collected observables are fully described in detail in previous papers [42, 43].

Briefly, a stainless-steel needle was used to introduce the sample as an effusive beam into the chamber. During the experiment, synchrotron radiation within the appropriate energy range passes through a monochromator, which uses a 400 lines/mm spherical grating in first-order diffraction. The slits are adjusted to achieve a photon energy resolution of about 1.5 meV. A magnesium filter is used to eliminate spurious ionization effects caused by photons from higher diffraction orders. The radiation then intersects the beam of the target molecule in the extraction region. Electrons are accelerated towards a micro-channel plate (MCP) detector and serve as triggers for ion time-of-flight measurements. Ions are extracted, accelerated through a TOF spectrometer, and mass-selected. The photon flux interacting with the target beam and the gas pressure are continuously monitored. Ion yields are adjusted for fluctuations in pressure and photon flux whenever the photon energy changes. Additionally, the gas inlet source uses a mixture of the target molecule and helium to normalize all ion signals at each photon energy to the total ion yield of helium. Ion impacts create electron clouds that are collected by a position-sensitive detector, which comprises 64 strip anodes (32 vertical and 32 horizontal). Each anode is connected to an independent time-to-digital converter (TDC), allowing for the detection of multiple ion fragments and electrons from a single photoionization event. A discriminator is also connected to the 64 detectors. After an event occurs, the TDC sends signals to a Versa Module Eurocard (VME), which transmits the data to an acquisition computer. This computer records the data, specifically logging the x and y positions of each particle hit, meaning that for each ion, two spatial coordinates and one temporal coordinate are documented. The detected ions are categorized into groups of single, double, triple, and higher-order coincidences for each start electron.

3   Synthesis of Isothiocyanic Acid (HNCS)

The isothiocyanic acid (HNCS, see Fig. 5), the simplest isothiocyanate, is the most stable member of the [H,N,C,S] isomer family. Early experimental work assumed that the NCS chain in HNCS was strictly linear. However, ab initio calculations later challenged this notion, leading to a new evaluation of its structural parameters [44].

HNCS was first detected in the interstellar medium in 1979 within the giant molecular cloud Sgr B2, and since then, its presence in both interstellar and terrestrial environments has been well-established [45], prompting extensive studies on neutral and singly charged HNCS. Photolysis at low temperatures led to the observation of its isomers, HSCN and HSNC. In 1970, Eland characterized the spectral bands of the single ionization photoelectron spectrum of HNCS [46]. Over two decades later, Ruscic and Berkowitz determined the appearance energy of singly charged fragments and the H-NCS bond energy. Gronowski's ab initio calculations further confirmed the existence of neutral HNCS and its cation in the interstellar medium [47].

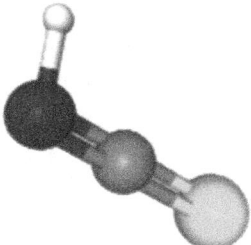

Fig. 5. 3D visualization of the HNCS structure.

The preparation of HNCS has been performed directly in the spectrometer laboratory, due to the high instability of the sample, that tends to autopolymerize in a matter of minutes if not held at a low temperature. The procedure followed was based on the work of John Eland [46], with some modifications in order to optimize time and yield.

The reagents used for the synthesis are potassium thiocyanate (KSCN) and potassium bisulphate (KHSO$_4$), with a 1:1 molar ratio, following the reaction:

$$KHSO_4 + KSCN \rightarrow HSCN + K_2SO_4 \qquad (1)$$

The product of the reaction is formally thiocyanic acid, HSCN, which exists as a tautomer with isothiocyanic acid, HNCS, according to the following reaction:

$$HNCS(g) \leftrightarrow HNCS(g) \qquad (2)$$

In gaseous phase the isothiocyanic acid tautomer tends to dominate with the compound being about 95% of the total.

The preparation scheme is illustrated in Fig. 6, it consists of a glass test tube designed to be connected to the spectrometer through a KF flange, in which are inserted the reagents, previously finely grounded and put in separate vacuum desiccators over phosphorous pentoxide, P$_2$O$_5$, for several days, to remove any trace of water, in which HNCS is soluble.

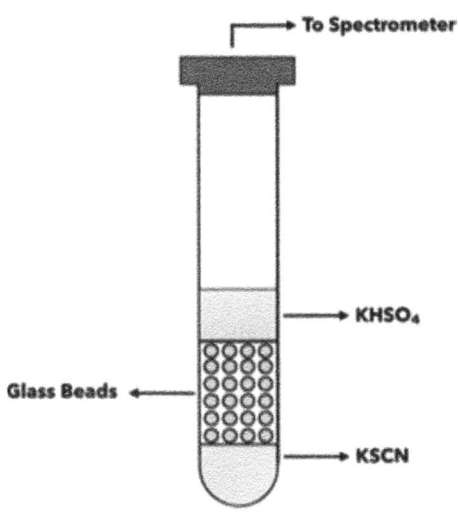

Fig. 6. Scheme of the test tube used in the preparation of gaseous HNCS.

Between the two layers of reagents are placed some glass beads, to maintain the two compounds separated. The test tube has been pumped for 24 h and then immerged in liquid nitrogen (LN$_2$), to prevent the start of the polymerization reaction at room temperature once the reagents are mixed together. The test tube has then been shaken manually to mix the two reagents and quickly put back in LN$_2$, this cycle has been repeated several times to assure a complete mixing of the two compounds. The tube has been attached to the gas inlet system in a slush bath composed of a mixture of LN$_2$ and ethanol, at −80 °C, and pumped again for several minutes; after this cycle, the experimental run has been conducted with the test tube immerged in a slush bath at − 10 °C, in order to slow down the inevitable polymerization reaction and to allow the measurement to run for several hours.

4   Synthesis of Carbon Suboxide (C_3O_2)

The carbon suboxide (see Fig. 7) has been detected in ambient air samples and is considered a potential pollutant and precursor to oxidants, but its atmospheric lifetime and behavior remain largely uncertain. It has been synthesized for the first time by Diels and Wolf in 1906 [48]. At room temperature, this gas is lacrimatory, with a pungent odor that can irritate the eyes, nose, and respiratory system. Structurally, C_3O_2 is a quasi-linear cumulene with the formula $O = C = C = C = O$, featuring a shallow W-shape that easily deforms due to bending vibrations and a weak dipole moment. Although carbon suboxide has some applications in organic synthesis, it also appears as an intermediate in the abiotic degradation of aromatics in soils [49], is released during the incomplete combustion of biofuels and biomass [50], and might exist in extraterrestrial environments [51, 52]. Due to its hydrolysis into malonic acid, which suggested it would not be present in the atmosphere at detectable levels, the chemistry of C_3O_2 in the atmosphere has not been extensively studied yet.

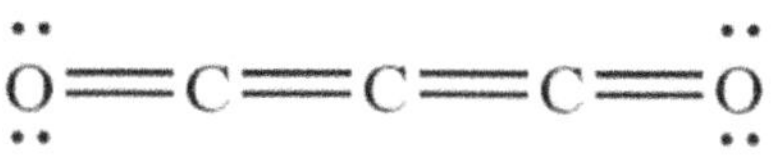

$$\overset{\cdot\cdot}{\underset{\cdot\cdot}{O}} = C = C = C = \overset{\cdot\cdot}{\underset{\cdot\cdot}{O}}$$

Fig. 7. Lewis structure of C_3O_2.

Carbon suboxide has been synthetized through the dehydration of malonic acid with P_2O_5 [48, 53]. The reaction is set to happen at 145 °C and the major product of it is CO_2, with C_3O_2 and acetic acid (CH_3COOH) being the minor products:

$$2C_3H_4O_4 \rightarrow C_3O_2 + CO_2 + CH_3COOH + 2H_2O \tag{3}$$

The setup consists of a two or three necked flask, connected to a thermometer and to a Liebig condenser, without water reflux active, or to a simple bridge, attached to a receiving flask placed in a dewar filled with liquid nitrogen (see Fig. 8). The entire reaction takes place under vacuum ($\approx 10^{-2}$ mbar). 10 to 12 g of malonic acid have been finely grounded and put to dry in a desiccator for a few days, then mixed with 50 g of P_2O_5 and 20 g of roasted sand and added to the main flask, previously cleaned and set under vacuum to remove any trace of moisture. The flask has been placed in a heating mantle with the possibility to control the temperature rising. Despite reaching 145 °C externally, considering the resistance of the glass of the flask the internal temperature has reached a peak of 130 °C. Over the course of two hours, a white solid has condensed into the receiving flask; at the end of the reaction, the receiving flask has been detached from the system, and the product left to thaw under the fume hood, due to the lacrimatory effect that C_3O_2 possess, and transferred when liquid ($C_3O_{2mp} = -110$ °C) in a test tube with a KF junction. The sample has then been purified by being placed in a ethanol/LN_2 bath at -78 °C and pumped for several cycles, in order to remove all the CO_2; regarding acetic acid, very few to no traces have been detected experimentally. In the end, 1 to 1.5 ml of carbon suboxide have been collected, resulting in a yield of about 10%, consistent with the rate reported in literature. Due to its highly unstable nature, every sample has been available for an experimental run for no longer than two days, at room temperature, with the polymerization reaction taking over despite the purification.

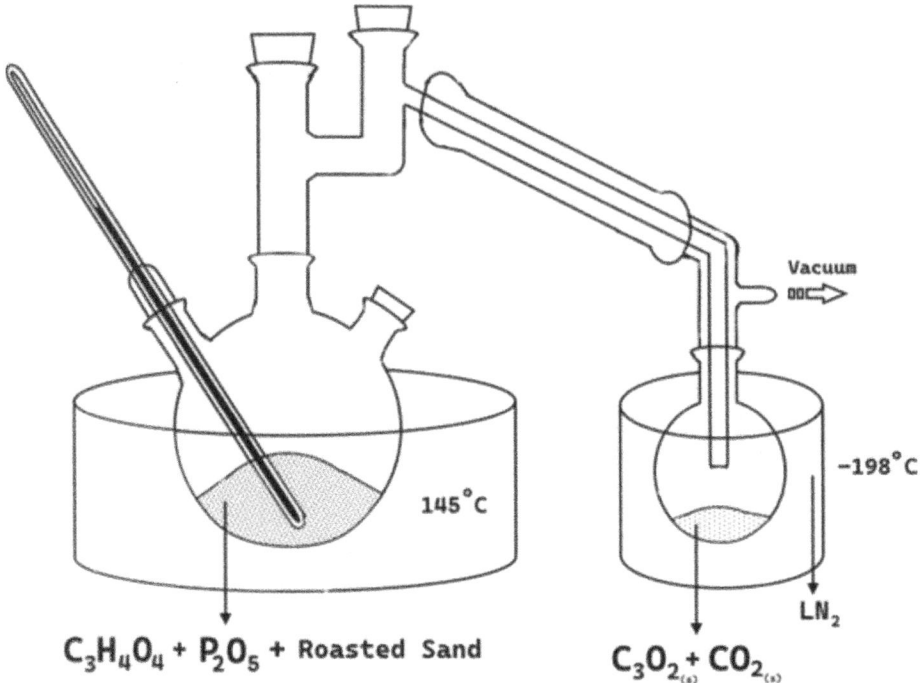

Fig. 8. Scheme of the experimental setup for the synthesis of C_3O_2.

5   Synthesis of Cyanoacetylene (C_3HN)

C_3HN is the simplest cyanopolyne (see Fig. 9).

$$H-C{\equiv}C-C{\equiv}N$$

Fig. 9. Lewis structure of C_3HN.

It has been one of the earliest organic molecules identified in the interstellar medium (ISM) [54, 55]. C_3HN and C_5HN have been also found in abundance within solar-type protostars, as evidenced by recent studies [56]. Notably, C_3HN has been identified in comet C/1995 O1 (Hale-Bopp), suggesting that organic molecules like these may contribute to the interstellar organic chemistry legacy passed on to newly formed solar systems. [57]. Cyanoacetylene plays a crucial role in chain elongation processes, reacting with the C_2H radical to produce C_5HN. Conversely, when cyanoacetylene reacts with the CN radical, it leads to a chain termination reaction, forming dicyanoacetylene (C_4N_2). Although dicyanoacetylene and other higher dicyanopolynes have not been detected in the ISM due to their lack of a permanent electric dipole moment, making them undetectable through rotational spectroscopy, they are believed to be prevalent in interstellar and circumstellar clouds, contributing significantly to the total carbon budget [58]. The reaction between CN radicals and cyanoacetylene is also considered the primary source of C_4N_2, which has been observed in Titan's upper atmosphere, Saturn's largest moon [59–61].

Cyanoacetylene has been synthetized by dehydration of propiolamide (C_3H_3NO) with P_2O_5 at 225 °C [62], following the reaction:

$$C_3H_3NO \rightarrow C_3HN + H_2O \tag{4}$$

The propiolamide has been purchased from Merck. The reaction setup consists in a three- necked round bottom flask connected to a vacuum pump and to a receiver placed in liquid nitrogen, with the whole setup placed under vacuum before the start of the experiment to remove any moisture present (see Fig. 10). 5 g of propiolamide have been mixed with 20 g of P_2O_5 and 20 g of roasted sand, and added to the flask; after that, the temperature has been raised to 225 °C over the course of two hours, and about 3g (60%) of white solid has been collected in the receiving flask and stored under vacuum at −20 °C before using it on the beamline at Elettra. When attached to the spectrometer, the sample has been kept around −30 °C and showed an adequate vapour pressure to perform the experiment for 14 days, with the surplus of the sample that has been put away at −20 °C after the end of the investigation.

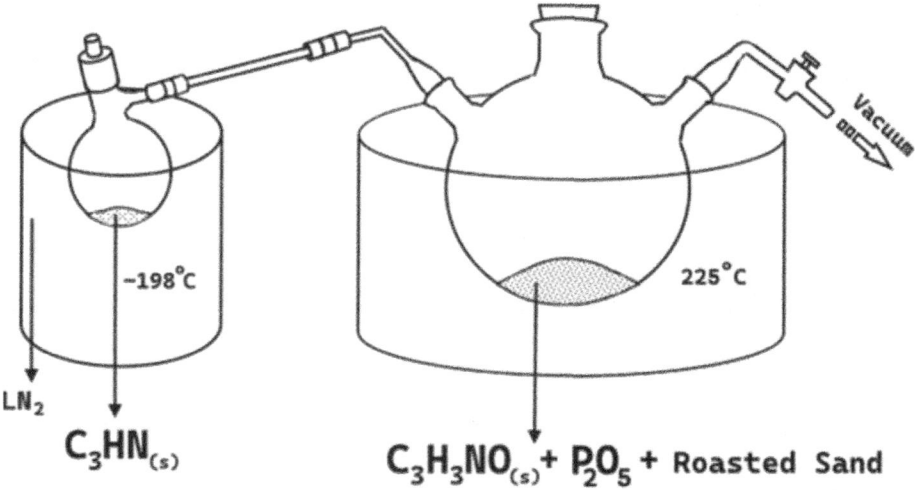

Fig. 10. Scheme of the experimental setup for the synthesis of C_3HN.

Acknowledgments. Dr. Robert Richter, a valued friend and collaborator, died during the preparation of the manuscript. This work and our future efforts are dedicated to him, whose intellectual honesty and genuine love for physics and chemistry continue to inspire our scientific life. This work has been funded by the European Union – NextGenerationEU under the Italian Ministry of University and Research (MUR) National Innovation Ecosystem (grant number ECS00000041) - VITALITY - CUP J97G22000170005. M.P. acknowledges the Italian Space Agency (ASI, DC-VUM-2017–034, Grant no. 2019–3 U.0 Life in Space).

Disclosure of Interests.   The authors have no competing interests to declare that are relevant to the content of this article.

References

1. Einstein, A.: Über einen die Erzeugung und Verwandlung des Lichtes betreffenden heuristischen Gesichtspunkt. Ann. Phys. **322**(6), 132–148 (1905)
2. Jenkin, J.G., Riley, J.D., Liesegang, J., Leckey, R.C.G.: The development of x- ray photoelectron spectroscopy (1900–1960): a postscript. J. Electron Spectrosc. Relat. Phenom. **14**(6), 477–485 (1978)
3. Wheaton, B.R.: Philipp Lenard and the photoelectric effect, 1889–1911. Hist. Stud. Phys. Sci. **9**, 299–322 (1978)
4. Hüfner, S.: Photoelectron Spectroscopy: Principles and Applications, 3rd edn. Springer, Berlin, Heidelberg (2003)
5. Oswald, S.: X-ray photoelectron spectroscopy in analysis of surfaces. Encyclopedia of Analytical Chemistry: Applications, Theory and Instrumentation. John Wiley & Sons, Ltd., Hoboken (2006)
6. Brunetti, B.G., Candori, P., Falcinelli, S., et al.: The stereodynamics of the penning ionization of water by metastable neon atoms. J. Chem. Phys. **139**(16), 164305 (2013)
7. Falcinelli, S., Farrar, J.M., Vecchiocattivi, F., Pirani, F.: Quantum-state controlled reaction channels in chemi-ionization processes: radiative (optical−physical) and exchange (oxidative−chemical) mechanisms. Acc. Chem. Res. **53**(10), 2248–2260 (2020)
8. Conrad, R.: The appearance of doubly positively charged molecules in a beam of canal rays. Phys. Z. **31**, 888–892 (1930)
9. Vaughan, A.L.: Mass spectrograph analyses, and critical potentials for the production of ions by electron impact, in nitrogen and carbon monoxide. Phys. Rev. **38**(9), 1687 (1931)
10. Pauling, L.: The normal state of the helium molecule-ions He_2^+ and He_2^{++}. J. Chem. Phys. **1**, 56–59 (1933)
11. Falcinelli, S., Fernandez-Alonso, F., Kalogerakis, K., Zare, R.N.: Mass spectrometric detection of alkaline earth monohalide dications. Mol. Phys. **88**(3), 663–672 (1996)
12. Brunetti, B., Candori, P., De Andres, J., et al.: Dissociative ionization of methyl chloride and methyl bromide by collision with metastable neon atoms. J. Phys. Chem. A **101**(41), 7505–7512 (1997)
13. Alagia, M., Brunetti, B.G., Candori, P., et al.: Threshold-photoelectron-spectroscopy-coincidence study of the double photoionization of HBr. J. Chem. Phys. **120**(15), 6980–6984 (2004)
14. Alagia, M., Brunetti, B.G., Candori, P., et al.: Low-lying electronic states of HBr^2+. J. Chem. Phys. **120**(15), 6985–6991 (2004)
15. Bartocci, A., Belpassi, L., Cappelletti, D., et al.: Catching the role of anisotropic electronic distribution and charge transfer in halogen bonded complexes of noble gases. J. Chem. Phys. **142**(18), 184304 (2015)
16. Pirani, F., Cappelletti, D., Falcinelli, S., et al.: Selective emergence of halogen bond in ground and excited states of noble-gas—chlorine systems. Angew. Chem. **58**(13), 4195–4199 (2019)
17. Falcinelli, S., Rosi, M.: Production and characterization of molecular dications: experimental and theoretical efforts. Molecules **25**, 4157 (2020)
18. Wilkes, B.J., Ferland, G.J., Hanes, D., Truran, J.W.: On nitrogen abundances of planetary nebulae. MNRAS **197**(1), 1–6 (1981)
19. Greenberg, L.T., Dyal, P., Geballe, T.R.: Detection of forbidden S III fine-structure emission in ionized nebulae. Astrophys. J. **213**, L71–L74 (1977)

20. Böhme, D.K.: Multiply-charged ions and interstellar chemistry. Phys. Chem. Chem. Phys. **13**(41), 18253–18263 (2011)

21. Alagia, M., Candori, P., Falcinelli, S., et al.: Anisotropy of the angular distribution of fragment ions in dissociative double photoionization of N_2O molecules in the 30–50 eV energy range. J. Chem. Phys. **126**(20), 201101 (2007)

22. Thripati, S., Ramabhadran, R.O.: Pathways for the formation of formamide, a prebiotic biomonomer: metal-ions in interstellar gas-phase chemistry. J. Phys. Chem. A **125**(16), 3457–3472 (2021)

23. Tosi, P., Correale, R., Lu, W., et al.: Production of the molecular dication ArN^{2+} in the reaction $Ar^{2+}+N_2$. Phys. Rev. Lett. **82**(2), 450–452 (1999)

24. Price, S.D., Fletcher, J.D., Gossan, F.E., Parkes, M.A.: Bimolecular reactions of the dications and trications of atoms and small molecules in the gas-phase. Int. Rev. Phys. Chem. **36**(1), 145–183 (2017)

25. Ascenzi, D., Aysina, J., Zins, E.-L., et al.: Double ionization of cycloheptatriene and the reactions of the resulting $C_7H_n^{2+}$ dications (n = 6, 8) with xenon. Phys. Chem. Chem. Phys. **13**(41), 18330–18338 (2011)

26. Thissen, R., Witasse, O., Dutuit, O., et al.: Doubly-charged ions in the planetary ionospheres: a review. Phys. Chem. Chem. Phys. **13**(41), 18264–18287 (2011)

27. Falcinelli, S., Pirani, F., Alagia, M., et al.: Molecular dications in planetary atmospheric escape. Atmosphere **7**(9), 112 (2016)

28. Gu, H., Cui, J., Niu, D.D., et al.: Observation of CO_2^{++} dication in the dayside martian upper atmosphere. Earth Planet. Phys. **4**(4), 396–402 (2020)

29. Ricketts, C.L., Schröder, D., Alcaraz, C., Jana Roithová, J.: Growth of larger hydrocarbons in the ionosphere of titan. Chem. A Eur. J. **14**(16), 4779–4783 (2008)

30. Roithová, J. and Schröder, D.: On a possible growth mechanism for poly- cyclic aromatic hydrocarbon dications: $C_7H_6^{2+} + C_2H_2$. Chem. A Eur. J. **13**(10), 2893–2902 (2007)

31. Roithová, J., Schröder, D.: Bond-formation versus electron transfer: C-coupling reactions of hydrocarbon dications with benzene. Phys. Chem. Chem. Phys. J. **9**(6), 731–738 (2007)

32. Alagia, M., Boustimi, M., Brunetti, B.G., et al.: Mass spectrometric study of double photoionization of HBr molecules. J. Chem. Phys. **117**(3), 1098–1102 (2002)

33. Price, S.D.: Coincidence studies of the bond-forming reactivity and reaction dynamics of molecular dications. Int. J. Mass Spectrom. **260**(1), 1–19 (2007)

34. Falcinelli, S., Rosi, M., Candori, P., et al.: Kinetic energy release in molecular dications fragmentation after VUV and EUV ionization and escape from planetary atmospheres. Planet. Space Sci. **99**, 149–157 (2014)

35. Falcinelli, S., Vecchiocattivi, F., Pirani, F., et al.: The fragmentation dynamics of simple organic molecules of astrochemical interest interacting with VUV photons. ACS Earth Space Chem. **3**, 1862–1872 (2019)

36. Witasse, O., Dutuit, O., Lilensten, J., et al.: Prediction of a CO_2^{2+} layer in the atmosphere of Mars. Geophys. Res. Lett. **30**, 1360 (2003)

37. Slattery, A.E., Field, T.A., Ahmad, M., et al.: Spectroscopy and metastability of CO_2^{2+} molecular ions. J. Chem. Phys. **122**, 084317 (2005)

38. Falcinelli, S., Pirani, F., Alagia, M., et al.: The escape of O^+ ions from the atmosphere: an explanation of the observed ion density profiles on Mars. Chem. Phys. Lett. **666**, 1–6 (2016)

39. Blyth, R.R., Delaunay, R., Zitnik, M., et al.: The high resolution gas phase photoemission beamline. Elettra. J. Electr. Spectr. Rel. Phenom. **101**, 959–964 (1999)

40. Lavollée, M.: A new detector for measuring three-dimensional momenta of charged particles in coincidence. Rev. Sci. Instrum. **70**(7), 2968–2974 (1999)

41. Alagia, M., Brunetti, B.G., Candori, P., et al.: The double photoionization of hydrogen iodide molecules. J. Chem. Phys. **124**(20), 204318 (2006)

42. Falcinelli, S., Rosi M., Candori, P., et al.: Modeling the intermolecular interactions and characterization of the dynamics of collisional autoionization processes. In: Murgante, B., et al. (eds.) ICCSA 2013, LNCS, vol. 7971, pp. 69–83. Springer, Heidelberg (2013)

43. Parriani, M., Giustini, A., Alagia, M., et al.: Data analysis of molecular dications fragmentation processes by double photoionization with synchrotron radiation. In: Gervasi, O., et al. (eds.) ICCSA 2024, LNCS, vol. 14818, pp. 55–70. Springer, Heidelberg (2024)

44. Yamada, K., Winnewisser, M., Winnewisser, G., et al.: Ground state spectroscopic constants of $H^{15}NCS$, $HN^{13}CS$, and $HNC^{34}S$, and the molecular structure of isothiocyanic acid. J. Mol. Spectr. **79**(2), 295–313 (1980)

45. Krupa, J., Kosendiak, I., Wierzejewska, M.: New data on photochemistry of the interstellar molecule: HNCS. identification of the S-HCN complex. Phys. Chem. Chem. Phys. **17**(34), 22431–22437 (2015)

46. Eland, J.H.D.: A discussion on photoelectron spectroscopy-the photo- electron spectra of isocyanic acid and related compounds. Philos. Trans. R. Soc. Lond. Ser. A Math. Phys. Sci. **268**(1184), 87–96 (1970)

47. Ruscic, B., Berkowitz, J.: The H-NCS bond energy, ΔH^o(HNCS), ΔH^o(NCS), and IP (NCS) from photoionization mass spectrometric studies of HNCS, NCS, and (NCS)$_2$. J. Chem. Phys. **101**(9), 7975–7989 (1994)

48. Diels, O., Lalin, L.: Über das kohlensuboxyd. Ber. Dtsch. Chem. Ges. **41**(3), 3426–3434 (1908)

49. Huber, S.G., Kilian, G., Schöler, H.F.: Carbon suboxide, a highly reactive intermediate from the abiotic degradation of aromatic compounds in soil. Environ. Sci. Technol. **41**(22), 7802–7806 (2007)

50. Roblee Jr, L.H.S., Agnew, J.T., Wark, K., Jr.: Evidence for carbon suboxide, C_3O_2, as an intermediate product in the cool flame oxidation products of diethyl ether. Combust. Flame **5**, 65–70 (1961)

51. Bennett, C.J., Jamieson, C.S., Kaiser, R.I.: Mechanistic studies on the decomposition of carbon suboxide in a cometary ice analog. Planet. Space Sci. **56**(9), 1181–1189 (2008)

52. Lasne, J., Noblet, A., Szopa, C., et al.: Oxidants at the surface of mars: a review in light of recent exploration results. Astrobiology **16**(12), 977–996 (2016)

53. Long, D.A., Murfin, F.S., and Williams, R.L.: The Raman and infra-red spectra of carbon suboxide. Proc. R. Soc. Lond. Ser. A. Math. Phys. Sci., **223**(1153), 251–266 (1954)

54. Turner, B.E.: Detection of interstellar cyanoacetylene. Astrophys. J. **163**, L35 (1971)

55. Cabezas, C., Agúndez, M., Endo, Y., et al.: Discovery of the interstellar cyanoacetylene radical cation HC_3N^+. Astron. Astrophys. **687**, L22 (2024)

56. Jaber, A., Edhari, A.L., Ceccarelli, C., et al.: History of the solar-type protostar IRAS 16293–2422 as told by the cyanopolyynes. Astron. Astrophys. **597**, A40 (2017)

57. Mumma, M.J., Charnley, S.B.: The chemical composition of comets - emerging taxonomies and natal heritage. Annu. Rev. Astron. Astrophys. **49**(1), 471–524 (2011)

58. Petrie, S., Millar, T.J., Markwick, A.J.: NCCN in TMC-1 and IRC+ 10216. MNRAS **341**(2), 609–616 (2003)

59. Petrie, S. and Osamura, Y.: NCCN and NCCCCN formation in Titan's atmosphere: 2. HNC as a viable precursor. J. Phys. Chem. A **108**(16), 3623–3631 (2004)

60. Mancini, L., Rosi, M., Skouteris, D., Vanuzzo, G., et al.: A computational characterization of the reaction mechanisms for the reactions N (^{2}D) + CH_3CN and HC_3N and implications for the nitrogen-rich organic chemistry of Titan. Comput. Theor. Chem. **1229**, 114341 (2023)

61. Liang, P., Aragão, E., Pannacci, G., et al.: Reactions O (^{3}P, ^{1}D) + HCCCN ($X^1\sum^+$) (cyanoacetylene): crossed-beam and theoretical studies and implications for the chemistry of extraterrestrial environments. J. Phys. Chem. A **127**(3), 685–703 (2023)

62. Miller, F.A., Lemmon, D.H.: The infrared and Raman spectra of di- cyanodiacetylene, NCCCCCN. Spectrochim. Acta A: Mol. Biomol. Spectrosc. **23**(5), 1415–1423 (1967)

Computational Methods for Porous Geomaterials (CompPor 2025)

Multi-GPU Implementation of the Numerical Algorithm Enhancing Discrete Element Modeling Performance

V. D. Chepelenkova$^{(\boxtimes)}$ [iD], D. I. Prokhorov [iD], and V. V. Lisitsa [iD]

Sobolev Institute of Mathematics SB RAS, Novosibirsk, Russia
vchepelenkova@gmail.com

Abstract. This paper presents an algorithm to combine GPU computations for the two-dimensional discrete element method (DEM) with MPI data transfers between computer cluster nodes in distributed-memory systems for one-dimensional domain decomposition. The proposed algorithm redistributes particles between processes, deleting them or adding to the list of particles inside a current subdomain, respectively, in parallel with main GPU calculations to decrease the time loss of calling transferring functions. Strong and weak scaling tests were conducted for the implemented algorithm to show its effectiveness in adding more computational resources to the fixed-size problem and increasing the problem size according to the allocated resources.

Keywords: Multi-GPU · MPI data transfers · Discrete element method

1 Introduction

Modeling crack propagation or contact problems in solid media can be classified as problems with discontinuous properties of a material arising in rock geophysics or any other applications to material science. Continuum-based methods, e.g., finite difference or finite element methods, are the most conventional approach to obtaining a numerical solution in such cases and are widely used for modeling elastoplastic materials. The key feature is in coming down to solving a system of linear equations, which can be easily implemented and parallelized in most cases. However, as reflected in the name of this class of methods, its governing equations are based on principles of continuum mechanics. Therefore, they have common limitations when used to solve discontinuous problems. Firstly, potentially contacting surfaces or the initial placement of a crack must be defined before the simulation starts, and secondly, mesh parts both for contacting surfaces and for fracture lines are required to be compatible to form a continuous mesh.

On the other hand, particle methods, especially the discrete element method, presented in [1], are not based on continuum mechanics, which makes it able to naturally form contacts and fractures without specifying any extra information beforehand. The reason for this is that solid media in DEM is considered a system of small spherical particles bound with elastic springs that can break, thus forming micro-cracks. However, the major drawback in using DEM is its computational intensity: the given medium has to be discretized to a significant number of particles with their elastic properties for each one (memory intensive aspect), which leads to a considerable amount of time-consuming operations when calculating particle pairwise interactive forces within a specific range (time intensive aspect). The way to overcome the aforementioned issues is to use graphics accelerators for more efficient computation and multiple cluster nodes as a distributed memory system exchanging data via MPI. More details on comparing continuum-based and particle methods are given in [2,3].

This paper presents an algorithm to effectively combine multiple-GPU computations for a two-dimensional DEM model that simulates uniaxial tests on porous samples, with MPI data transfers for one-dimensional domain decomposition. Strong and weak scaling tests were conducted to more precisely analyze the implemented program's effectiveness.

2   Discrete Element Modeling

DEM simulations of solid and granular materials are based on a representation of the given medium as a set of spherical (or circular in 2D space) particles interacting by the laws of Newtonian mechanics, so governing equations for particle motion are expressed as

$$m_i \frac{d^2 \boldsymbol{r}_i}{dt^2} = \boldsymbol{f}_i + m_i \boldsymbol{g} - \gamma \boldsymbol{v}_i, \qquad i = 1, ... N \qquad (1)$$

where $\boldsymbol{f}_i = \sum_{j=1}^{N} \boldsymbol{f}_{ij}$ is a total force acting on i-th particle, which is a sum of all pairwise interactions, $\boldsymbol{g}$ is a gravitational constant, and N is the number of particles in a given sample. A term $\gamma \boldsymbol{v}_i$ stands for a dissipative force, the amplitude of which can be altered by changing the value or variable γ. This force is intended to slow particle motion and reach an equilibrium state.

Contacting particles are assumed to have a non-empty yet small overlap region compared to their radii. For instance, if particles i and j have positions $\boldsymbol{r}_i$ and $\boldsymbol{r}_j$ with radii R_i and R_j respectively, the overlap size between them is calculated using formula $\delta = R_i + R_j - \|\boldsymbol{r}_i - \boldsymbol{r}_j\|$. Therefore, we can define a normal to the contact plane vector

$$\boldsymbol{n}_{ij} = \frac{\Delta \boldsymbol{r}_{ij}}{\|\Delta \boldsymbol{r}_{ij}\|}, \qquad \Delta \boldsymbol{r}_{ij} = \|\boldsymbol{r}_i - \boldsymbol{r}_j\|,$$

allowing us to decompose a force of pairwise interactions to $\boldsymbol{f}_{ij} = f_{ij}^n \boldsymbol{n}_{ij} + \boldsymbol{f}_{ij}^t$ (Fig. 1). For ease of notation, indices ij are hereafter omitted.

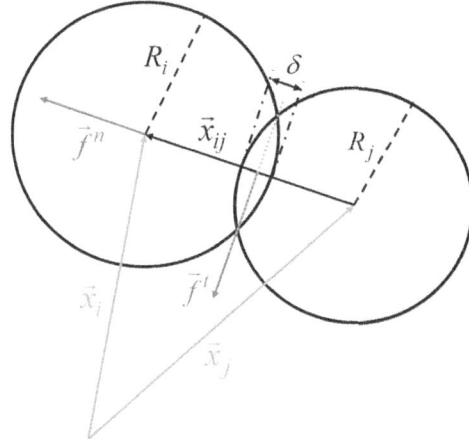

Fig. 1. Normal and tangential components of $\boldsymbol{f}_{ij}$.

There exist multiple force models based on a principle that overlap region is regarded as an elastic spring with stiffness k, connecting two particles [4,5]. In this paper, a linear one is chosen, so for a model used in all further computations, f^n and $\boldsymbol{f}^t$ are defined as follows:

$$
f^n = \begin{cases} k\delta, & \delta > 0, \\ -k|\delta|, & -d_{max} < \delta < 0, \\ 0, & \delta < -d_{max}, \end{cases} \qquad \boldsymbol{f}^t = \begin{cases} \boldsymbol{f}_0^t, & \|\boldsymbol{\xi}\| < d_{max}, \\ \mu f^n \dfrac{\boldsymbol{f}_0^t}{\|\boldsymbol{f}_0^t\|}, & \|\boldsymbol{\xi}\| \geq d_{max}, \end{cases}
$$

where k is the aforementioned stiffness coefficient, μ is a friction coefficient, ξ is a relative displacement of two particles along their contact plane, and $\boldsymbol{f}_0^t = -k^t\boldsymbol{\xi}$ with stiffness k^t. It is assumed that $\boldsymbol{\xi} = 0$ when a new contact is established, then after each time step τ it is updated according to formula $\boldsymbol{\xi}^{(n+1)} = \boldsymbol{\xi}^{(n)} + \tau\boldsymbol{v}^t$. More details on the definition of $\boldsymbol{f}^t$ are given in [6]. Parameter d_{crit} stands for the maximum possible distance particles can move away from each other before the bond between them breaks. From later on, only a repulsive part of f_n can arise, meaning that $f^n = 0$ for $\delta < 0$, and $\boldsymbol{f}^t$ for any contact is limited to sliding friction only, so $f^t = \mu f^n$ for $\delta > 0$.

3   Numerical Approximation

To keep track of i-th particle position $(i = 1, \ldots, N)$ at each time step, we use the Velocity Verlet integration of Eq. 1, which has the form

$$r_i^{n+1} = r_i^n + \tau v_i^n + \frac{\tau^2}{2} \frac{f_i(r^n, v^n)}{m_i},$$

$$v_i^{n+\frac{1}{2}} = v_i^n + \frac{\tau}{2} \frac{f_i(r^n, v^n)}{m_i}, \qquad (2)$$

$$v_i^{n+1} = v_i^{n+\frac{1}{2}} + \frac{\tau}{2} \frac{f_i(r^{n+1}, v^{n+\frac{1}{2}})}{m_i},$$

where m_i denotes i-th particle's position.

The stability criterion for 2 derives from the assumption that any particle can move no further than a distance from the other particle in one time step. It is proposed in [7] that such a condition can be expressed as

$$\tau \leq 0.2 D_{min} \sqrt{\frac{\rho}{K + 4/3G}}, \qquad (3)$$

where D_{min} is the smallest particle diameter, K and G denote a given medium's bulk and shear moduli, and ρ stands for density.

3.1   Optimization of Inter-Particle Force Calculations

The most straightforward way to calculate the total force for each particle is to iterate over all the others. This approach requires N^2 operations, with most of them being redundant since particles placed far away from each other do not interact. Hence, some optimization is needed to limit the area of calculations for each particle.

For this reason, we define a uniform rectangular grid built by the criterion in (3), which means that a particle can move no further than to an adjacent cell in one time step. To do so, let us define a grid cell as

$$C_{kl} = \{(x, y) \in \mathbb{R}^2 \mid kh \leq x \leq (k+1)h, \ lh \leq y \leq (l+1)h\},$$

where the cell size $h = 2R_{max} + d_{max}$ does meet the condition above. A particle i is said to belong to cell C_{kl} if $r_i \in C_k l$. Therefore, for a particle i all possible interactions can only occur inside a domain $J_i = \{C_{k'l'} | k' \in \{k-1, k, k+1\}, \ l' \in \{l-1, l, l+1\}\}$, and an expression $f_i = \sum_{j=1}^{N} f_{ij}$ can be reduced to $f_i = \sum_{j \in J_i} f_{ij}$, which is much less time consuming than complete enumeration.

It is worth mentioning that particles can move in and out of a cell, leading to the necessity of updating corresponding data at each time step, which is, nevertheless, still more efficient than the naive approach if executed on GPU.

4   Implementation of the Algorithm

The execution process of the implemented algorithm contains two major stages. The former generates a sample filled with tightly packed particles and forms bonds between them to create a solid body with given elastic parameters. More details on this stage execution are provided in Sect. 4.1. The latter is a stage of simulating the time-wise evolution of sample characteristics under a specific type of loading.

A flowchart in Fig. 2 presents a brief overview of a modeling stage. All operations inside a loop are executed on GPU without transferring data to CPU and back except occasional writing to file. A stress or strain tensor is measured by averaging all individual particle values over the total sample volume. The only part operating on both CPU and GPU is the subprogram calculating particle positions and velocities, where MPI data transfers are performed in parallel with GPU calculations for the next time step. This process is explained below, in Sect. 4.2.

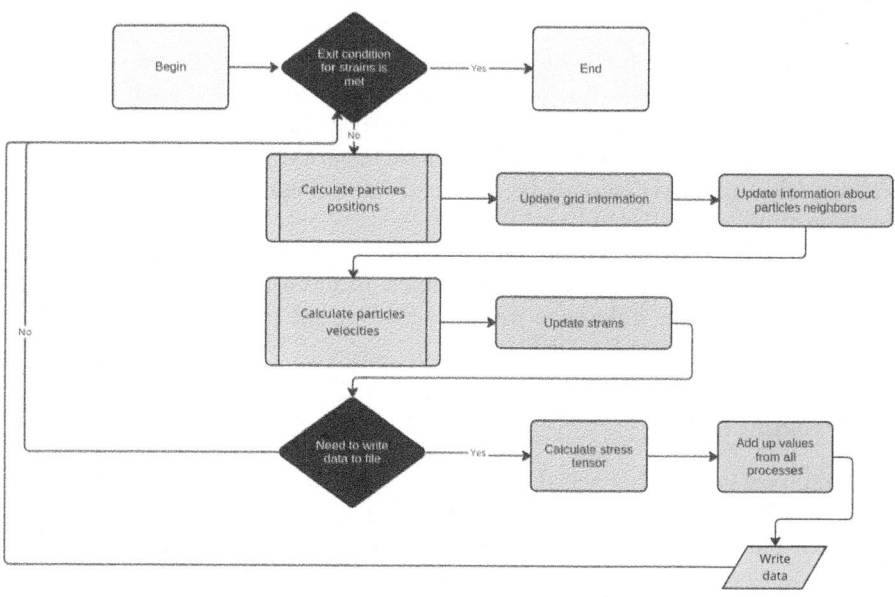

Fig. 2. Flowchart of the implemented algorithm.

Nevertheless, using CUDA and MPI for DEM simulations has some peculiarities. One arises from a particle structure, which contains both value types and pointers to array data stored in other memory locations and, thus, not aligned with the parent structure as shown in Fig. 3. Moreover, all particles in a model are collected in an array, which leads to the problem of transferring data both to

GPU and to another cluster node and back. The most straightforward approach is to send and receive all particles with all their fields separately, sending inner array data instead of pointers. Such a way is the most inefficient one since every transferring operation, either with GPU or with another node, is exceptionally time-consuming and, thus, should be performed as few times as possible.

Representing an array of structures with a sequence of bytes arranged in a certain order, also called serialization, reduces the number of individual calls of transferring functions to just once every time the list particles should be copied to other memory space. The default approach to serialization is to cast a structure to an array of bytes, which is not viable from the point of sending data to a separate memory location because default casting to bytes only preserves pointers to an exact position in RAM and not the values it points to. Thus, after transferring to any other physical device, not only do array data become absent, but all pointers, when deserialized, turn out invalid in the current memory space and lead to a runtime error if dereferenced. In order to avoid this issue, we use deep serialization, which is performed by switching every single particle's pointers to the data they pointed at and aligning them to a byte sequence. A total byte array to be sent consists of byte sequences for all particles placed sequentially together.

It is worth noting that the deserialization process is primarily the opposite of serialization, meaning that for an input byte array using the known data about particle contents and number of particles, we can restore data as a similar array of structures located at another independent memory. For GPU computations, each particle to deserialize can be assigned to a single thread, decreasing the execution time.

The other issue is the requirement to keep track of particles moved through process boundaries on each iteration, which is more complex than a similar exchange in the finite difference method. Section 4.2 provides more details on handling MPI-exchanges for DEM.

4.1 Packing Stage

To obtain a set of tightly packed particles, we use the combination of two methods: generating and moving particles, filling a given domain (rectangular in our case) with particles placed in such a way that every particle has at least two contact points with either a wall or another particle. Figure 4 shows an example of packing for a small amount of particles.

The first step is to generate enough particles to fill the entire domain. To do so, we use Poisson Disk Sampling [8], the general idea of which is to randomly generate a uniformly distributed set of points in such a way that a distance between each pair of them is no less than a particular input value k. In order to ensure a non-zero distance between particles, the value $k = 2R_{max}$ was chosen. After that, each point is used as a center of a circle with radius $r \in 0.1(R_{min}, R_{max})$ picked randomly as well, forming an initial position and size of the particle.

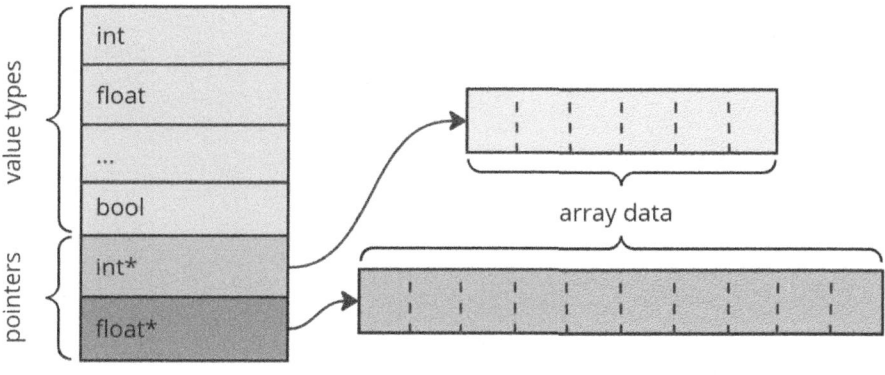

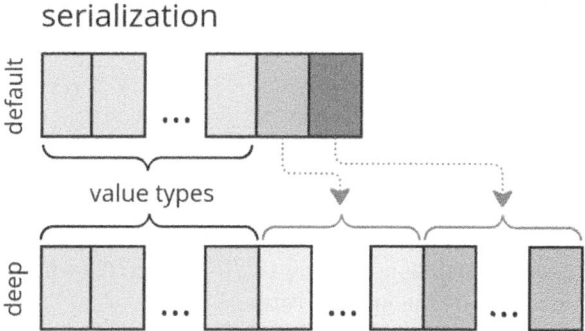

Fig. 3. On the upper part: schematic representation of an individual particle structure. On the lower part: two ways of serialization compared.

The second step is based on a Lubachevsky-Stillinger algorithm [9], which results in densely packed objects within the given domain. The central concept of the algorithm is to use event-driven simulation, which, contrary to time-driven simulations, steps over time not with a fixed time step but with a period from the instant moment to the next closed event.

The process starts with assigning a random velocity v with components in range (0, 1) to each particle. An event, in this case, is considered to be either the collision of two particles or the collision of a particle with any wall.

The major steps of the algorithm are as follows:

1. Predicting the next closest event, obtain the time Δt it will happen, and a pair of particles (or a particle and a wall) taking part in it.
2. Moving particles to the distance defined as $\Delta r = v\Delta t$.
3. Performing the event, i.e., changing particle velocities concerning laws of elastic collision.

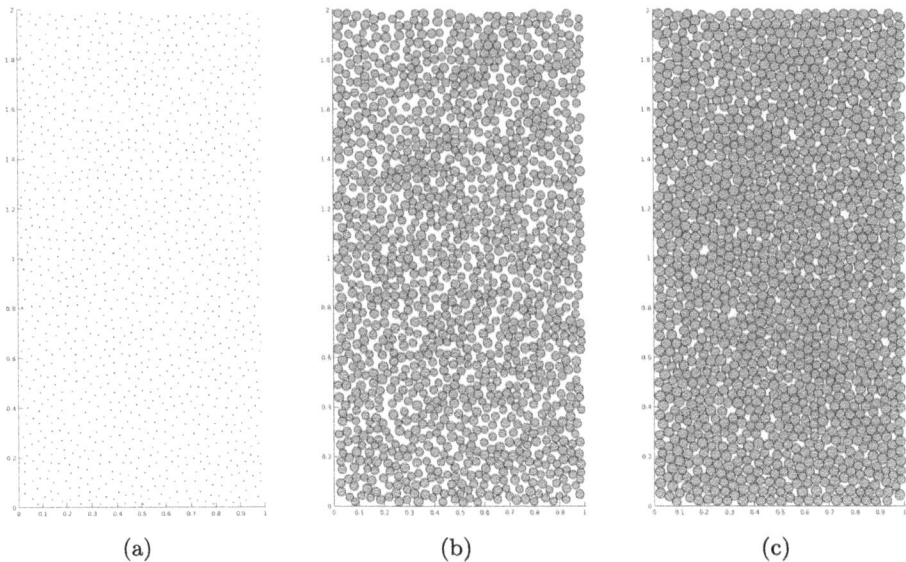

$$(a) \qquad\qquad (b) \qquad\qquad (c)$$

Fig. 4. Packing stages: Output from Poisson Disk Sampling (a), packing with Lubachevsky-Stillinger algorithm in progress (b), ready sample (c).

4. Increase the radius of each particle according to $R^{n+1} = \alpha R^n$, where α is an input parameter defining a particle growth rate.

The process repeats while Δt remains above a certain threshold, meaning that time between events becomes negligible when particles are close enough to treat them as packed and stop the algorithm.

4.2   MPI-Exchanges

Discrete element element is based on a highly memory-intensive algorithm as it requires a significant number of particles to handle a representative sample. At the same time, video random-access memory (VRAM) is limited compared to RAM. A possible solution to this problem is splitting the domain into smaller parts and distributing them to multiple GPUs or nodes of a computer cluster.

Every process has its subgrid with corresponding particles and one row from each adjacent process as halo cells to use information from other processes. In this work, we use 1D decomposition so that each MPI process has only two (one for the first or the last one) rows of halo cells, as depicted in Fig. 5a.

The major peculiarity of using MPI for DEM is the necessity to keep track of particles moving through process boundaries on each iteration, which becomes a more complex task than exchanging data in the finite difference method. In total, there are three possible cases for a particle to move (Fig. 5b):

– Particle stayed in a current subdomain.

- Particle moved into the current subdomain and must be handled by the current process.
- Particle moved out of the current subdomain and should be deleted from the list of particles handled by the process

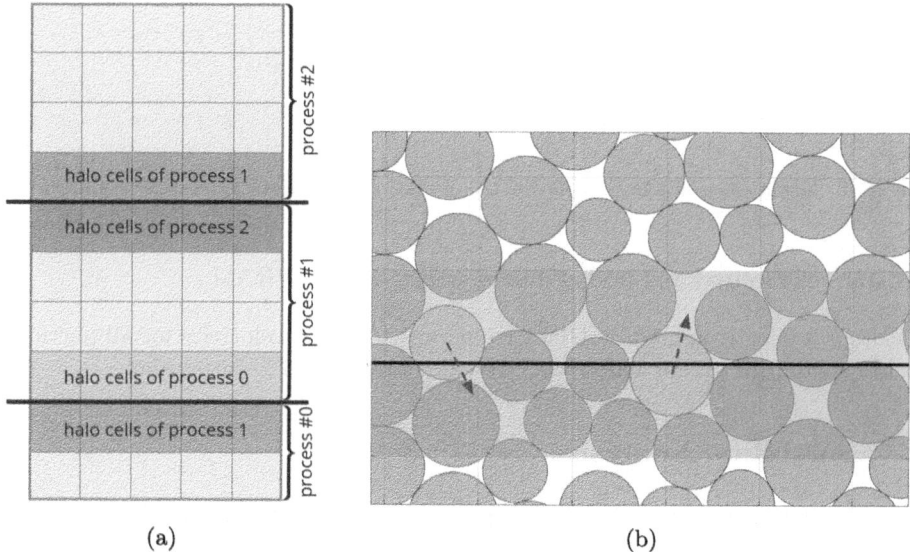

(a)   (b)

Fig. 5. Example of a domain decomposition for each process (a), possible particle movements to be handled separately (b).

To take into account all of the above cases, we implemented the following algorithm (Fig. 6):

1. Calculate positions and velocities for particles in halo cells.
2. For each adjacent process, if particles are moved out of the current subdomain, fill an array with their indices.
3. Transfer them to RAM as well as the first and/or the last row of the subgrid in order to send them as halo cells for adjacent processes
4. Send the first and/or the last rows via MPI to adjacent processes
5. Receive similar arrays from adjacent processes.
6. If there exist particles moved through the boundary: send and/or receive corresponding arrays prepared in step 2.
7. If particles moved into the current subdomain, insert them into the list of particles handled by the current process and delete them from particles in halo cells
8. If particles move out to an adjacent process, delete them from the list of particles handled by the current process.

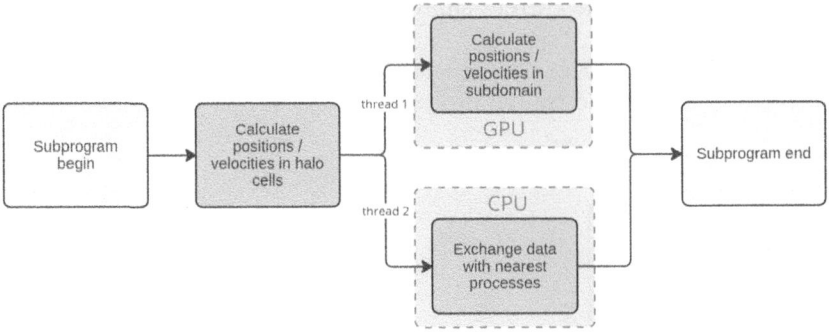

Fig. 6. Subprogram for executing both calculations and data exchange in parallel.

9. Transfer received and updated halo arrays back to VRAM.

Steps 3-9 are executed on CPU, while positions and velocities for all particles inside a subgrid, except halo cells, are calculated on GPU in parallel.

5   Scalability Analysis

Any parallel program using computations on a distributed memory system can be tested for strong and weak scaling. The former shows its capability to gain more efficiency when more resources are added to the system, which can be estimated using the formula

$$E_{strong} = \frac{t_1}{Nt_N},$$

where t_N is the execution time measured for a program on N processes. In a perfect case, every process uses all its resources, and the whole program works strictly in parallel, which gives $E_{strong} = 1$. However, in reality, there is almost no way to avoid at least some parts of serial code being present since processes have to transfer data to each other, which has to be synchronized at some point. Moreover, there exists a bottleneck when adding more processes to the system, leading to a considerable decrease in efficiency. The reason for this is that the amount of data exchanged between processes significantly exceeds the amount of calculations made by each individual process. If this state is reached, it makes no sense to keep adding resources as it will not speed up the execution time.

Figure 7a shows the result of a strong scaling test of the implemented algorithm ran on 1, 2, 4, 8, and 16 MPI processes with CPUs Intel Xeon CPU E5-2697 and GPUs NVIDIA Tesla K40. Each sample contained 112819 particles. It can be seen that efficiency reaches the value of about 0.8 at 8 processes, and after that, it rapidly decreases, meaning that for the given sample size, no speedup would be gained for more than cluster nodes.

Week scaling, in its turn, is measured as

$$E_{weak} = \frac{t_1}{t_N},$$

for a series of problems, their size increased so that the amount of work remains intact for every process. E_{weak} indicates how much the serial part of the code is affected by increasing the total amount of work. In a perfect case, it should be at $E_{weak} = 1$, meaning that data transfers and other serial parts do not take more time concerning the problem size.

Figure 7b illustrates the weak scaling test results for samples with their size increasing, as shown in Table 1. It is evident that the efficiency of the implemented algorithm mostly remains constant for any number of processes and is experiencing negligible changes in value, which is probably related to the fact that, due to the randomized particle generation based on Poisson disk Sampling, it seems impossible to achieve the exact multiple of the number of particles in a scaled domain. However, the overall trend leads to the conclusion that the algorithm has little dependence on the problem size.

Table 1. Domain size and the number of particles for weak scaling.

N processes	1	2	4	8	16
Domain size, mm × mm	6 × 12	6 × 24	6 × 48	6 × 96	6 × 192
Number of particles	112 827	225 699	451 431	902 108	1 804 499

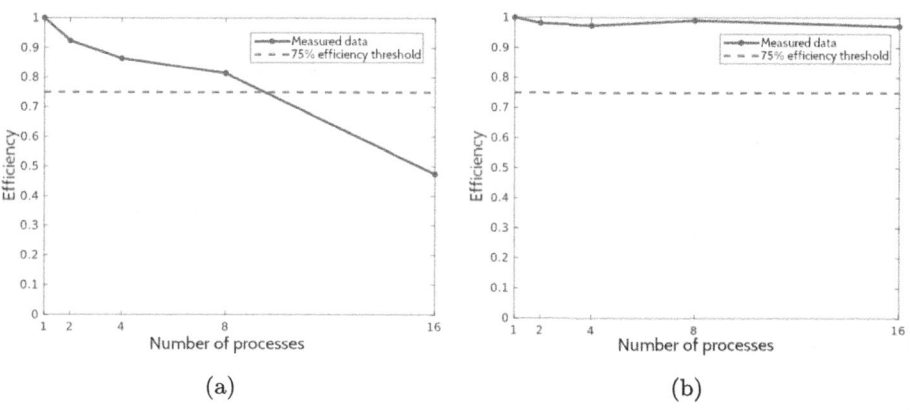

Fig. 7. Results of strong (a) and weak (b) scaling tests.

6   Conclusion

The discrete element method is a preferable approach to model solid media experiencing discontinuities of any sort, e.g., crack forming and propagation or contact problems, than continuum-based methods since it avoids their major drawbacks as the necessity to point out the initial state of a crack and treat adjacent nodes in a specific way to correctly bind discontinuities with governing equations based on continuum mechanics assumptions. However, for DEM simulations, a given sample is discretized as a set of particles, which should be numerous enough to provide correct results, which makes this method rather demanding both in time and memory resources.

In this paper, we proposed an algorithm combining data exchanges between computer cluster nodes in distributed-memory systems with GPU computations. The former allows to overcome both RAM and VRAM limitations of a single node, while the latter is a widely known way to significantly reduce the execution time of a program containing a large number of identical operations, also known as SIMD (Single Instruction, Multiple Data).

The principal peculiarity when performing DEM simulations is not only to transfer via MPI effectively but to keep track of particles moved through a boundary between adjacent processes. The proposed algorithm redistributes particles between processes, deleting them or adding to the list of particles inside a current subdomain, respectively, in parallel with GPU calculations to decrease the time loss of calling transferring functions.

Strong and weak scaling test analyses were conducted for the implemented algorithm, showing its effectiveness in adding more computational resources to the fixed-size problem and increasing the problem size according to the allocated resources. The decrease in strong scaling effectiveness with an increasing number of nodes is a typical behavior interpreted as a certain threshold, beyond which the size problem for each process makes GPU computations take less time to overlap data transfers. This effect is inevitable for any program using MPI and indicates the maximum amount of resources to handle the given problem size effectively.

Acknowledgments. This study was funded by the Russian Science Foundation (grant no. 19-77-20004-П).

Disclosure of Interests. The authors have no competing interests to declare that are relevant to the content of this article.

References

1. Cundall, P.A., Strack, O.: A discrete numerical model for granular assemblies. Geotechnique **29**(1), 47–65 (1979)
2. Gray, G.G., Morgan, J.K., Sanz, P.: Overview of continuum and particle dynamics methods for mechanical modeling of contractional geologic structures. J. Struct. Geol. **59**, 19–36 (2014)

3. Lisjak, A., Grasselli, G.: A review of discrete modeling techniques for fracturing processes in discontinuous rock masses. J. Rock Mech. Geotech. Eng. **6**(4), 301–314 (2014)
4. Chen, F., Xia, Y., Klinger, J.L., Chen, Q.: A set of hysteretic nonlinear contact models for DEM: theory, formulation, and application for lignocellulosic biomass. Powder Technol. **399**, 117100 (2022)
5. Yan, Z., Wilkinson, S.K., Stitt, E.H., Marigo, M.: Discrete element modelling (DEM) input parameters: understanding their impact on model predictions using statistical analysis. Comput. Part. Mech. **2**(3), 283–299 (2015). https://doi.org/10.1007/s40571-015-0056-5
6. Luding, S.: Introduction to discrete element methods: basic of contact force models and how to perform the micro-macro transition to continuum theory. Eur. J. Environ. Civ. Eng. **12**(7–8), 785–826 (2008)
7. Hardy, S., McClay, K., Munoz, J.A.: Deformation and fault activity in space and time in high-resolution numerical models of doubly vergent thrust wedges. Mar. Pet. Geol. **26**(2), 232–248 (2009)
8. Bridson, R.: Fast Poisson disk sampling in arbitrary dimensions. SIGGRAPH Sketches **10**(1), 1–1 (2007)
9. Lubachevsky, B.D., Stillinger, F.H.: Geometric properties of random disk packings. J. Stat. Phys. **60**, 561–583 (1990)

Monitoring CO_2 in Seismic Data Using Neural Network

Elena Gondyul$^{(\boxtimes)}$ ⓘ, Vadim Lisitsa ⓘ, and Dmitry Vishnevsky ⓘ

Sobolev Institute of Mathematics SB RAS, 4 Acad. Koptug Avenue, 630090
Novosibirsk, Russia
gondyulea@ipgg.sbras.ru,gondyulea@gmail.com

Abstract. Accurate monitoring of CO_2 migration in subsurface reservoirs is critical for understanding the behavior of injected greenhouse gases. This study proposes a neural network-based approach to improve the accuracy of seismograms used in time-lapse seismic monitoring. The method consists of two stages: first, a neural network predicts changes in seismograms corresponding to velocity model variations between consecutive monitoring steps, allowing for the approximation of spatio-temporal dependencies and facilitating wavefield extrapolation. The seismograms at this stage are generated using a coarse computational grid to reduce computational costs.

In the second stage, a neural network is employed to mitigate numerical dispersion in the predicted seismogram differences generated via classical modeling under the assumption of an unchanged velocity model. The trained network is then applied to all seismograms obtained in the first stage. This approach enables a more precise estimation of CO_2 migration patterns, providing valuable insights into subsurface dynamics.

The proposed approach significantly accelerates seismic modeling and its application to monitoring greenhouse gases in reservoir rocks.

Keywords: Deep Learning · Monitoring CO_2 · Seismic modeling

1 Introduction

The capture and flooding of carbon dioxide (CO_2) and other greenhouse gases in geological formations is a crucial strategy to mitigate the effects of human impacts on the environment. To ensure contentment of the injection process, it is essential to select the injection point and rate, assess the long-term storage stability, and prevent leakage. This requires the use of numerical methods for simulation of the long-term evolution of CO_2, as well as seismic modeling for monitoring through changed seismograms. Time-lapse seismic surveys and their simulation provide valuable information about the spatio-temporal evolution of the CO_2 plume. However, numerical dispersion, an artifact arising from the discretization of wave equations in computational simulation often degrades the accuracy of synthetic seismograms used for interpretation and forecasting.

O. Gervasi et al. (Eds.): ICCSA 2025 Workshops, LNCS 15888, pp. 330–342, 2026.
https://doi.org/10.1007/978-3-031-97596-7_22

Traditional numerical methods, such as finite-difference and finite-element approaches, attempt to mitigate dispersion errors through refined discretization and higher-order schemes. However, these solutions are computationally expensive, especially when modeling large-scale reservoirs with complex geological structures. As an alternative, deep learning-based methods such as neural network NDM-net (Numerical Dispersion Mitigation neural network) have demonstrated the ability to correct numerical dispersion [4,6]. Furthermore, the neural network NDM-net has demonstrated good performance in correcting errors during velocity model disturbances due to changes in its discretization.

In this study, it is suggested to employ a framework utilizing seismic modeling and the neural network NDM-net based on pix2pix to suppress numerical dispersion in seismograms and to predict seismograms at the next stage of monitoring. The aim is to accelerate monitoring CO_2 emission by the classical calculation of seismograms using a coarse computational grid for the total amount of sources in an unmodified velocity model and part of seismograms using a fine computational grid to form a training dataset. The proposed approach offers a computationally efficient alternative to traditional direct modeling methods, which makes real-time seismic monitoring more feasible.

1.1 Related Works

The most effective method for monitoring the condition of a reservoir during the process of fluid substitution, such as CO2 injection, is through the use of seismic monitoring techniques [17,18,24]. At the same time, numerical modeling is essential to understanding and analyzing the manifestations of variations in the petrophysical properties of reservoirs in seismic areas. Furthermore, seismic modeling allows the testing of algorithms for processing seismic data and assessing their suitability for mapping such changes.

Classical methods, such as finite difference [12,14,16,20,23], finite elements [8], discontinuous Galerkin method [2,15], spectral elements [11,22] and others require a significant amount of computational resources and time, particularly when it comes to calculating multiple sets of sources for different velocity models. But it is the finite difference and their variants that are most commonly used in seismic exploration and seismic monitoring due to their high efficiency, coupled with acceptable accuracy. However, it still remains a cost in the task of monitoring greenhouse gases.

Neural networks have recently begun to be applied in the field of hydrocarbon monitoring, for example, through the use of the Fourier neural operator [25] as a proxy for the fluid-flow simulator [26]. They are also used in the detection of hydrocarbon plumes from seismic images [13,21]. In real conditions, it is suggested to use alternative techniques such as gravitational sensing in combination with classical methods like surface seismic monitoring and neural networks [1].

2   Framework

Changes in seismic data during injection of CO_2 demonstrate how reservoir properties change [10]. In this study, we assume that reservoir properties change relatively slowly over time and do not take into account the physics of multiphase fluid flow, i.e. density ρ and velocities V_p, V_s change on average over the entire layer, as shown in Fig. 1. The velocity model and its properties are denoted as $M^i = \{V_p^i, V_s^i, \rho^i\}$, where $i \in [1, N]$ is the index signifying the stage of the greenhouse injection and N is the final stage of monitoring.

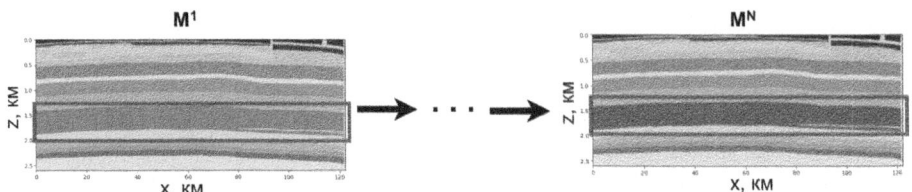

Fig. 1. Changing the properties of one of the layers of the Vanavar velocity model.

The aim of this research is to obtain the evolution of seismograms in the most cost-effective manner possible, therefore, in most cases, it is proposed to use a coarse computational grid to generate a training sample using the finite difference method. As shown in the schematic diagram (Fig. 2), our proposed methodology consists of the two-stage process using a neural network NDM-net (Numerical Dispersion Mitigation neural network) in order to enhance the efficiency of seismic monitoring for CO_2 migration in an oil reservoir.

The first stage involves using a neural network to generate changes in seismograms corresponding to the modified velocity model, that is, the one that was changed at a subsequent monitoring stage and the velocity model at the previous monitoring stage. This allows the network to approximate the spatio-temporal dependence, facilitating the extrapolation of wave field evolution. The seismograms used at this stage are modeled using coarce computational grid to reduce costs.

At the second stage, a neural network is used to reduce the numerical dispersion in the changes in the seismograms generated by the classical method, assuming the use of an unchanged velocity model M^1 in which migration has not yet occurred and velocity model M^2. And then the trained neural network is applied to all generated seismograms in the first stage. This process enables effective estimation of CO_2 migration, providing valuable insights into the behavior of greenhouse gas movement.

The entire proposed algorithm contains the following steps:

1. Classical seismic modeling is carried out for the unmodified velocity model M^1 for the entire set of sources using a coarse computational grid with characteristic step h_1, in order to obtain seismograms $\boldsymbol{u}_{h_1}^1(t, x_o, x_s^k), k \in [1, N_s]$, where N_s is the total number of sources.

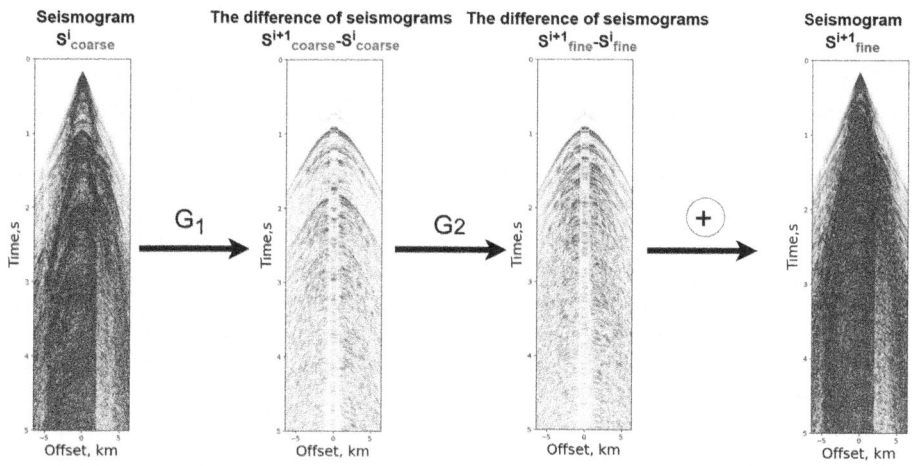

Fig. 2. Framework for monitoring CO_2 during changes in seismograms using neural networks approximating operators G_1 and G_2.

2. A set of indexes of the source positions $D_t \subset \{1, N_s\}$ is generated in order to create a training set.
3. Classical seismic modeling is carried out for the modified models $M^i, i \in [2, N]$ using a coarse computational grid with characteristic step h_1, in order to obtain $\boldsymbol{u}_{h_1}^i(t, x_o, x_s^k), k \in D_t$.
4. The difference in seismograms between current monitoring step and the next step $d\boldsymbol{u}_{h_1}^i(t, x_o, x_s^k) = \boldsymbol{u}_{h_1}^{i+1}(t, x_o, x_s^k) - \boldsymbol{u}_{h_1}^i(t, x_o, x_s^k), k \in D_t$ are calculated to create training set.
5. After that, numerical simulation of wave fields is carried out to generate seismograms $\boldsymbol{u}_{h_2}^1(t, x_o, x_s^k)$ and $\boldsymbol{u}_{h_2}^2(t, x_o, x_s^k), k \in D_t$ using a fine computational grid with characteristic step $h_2 < h_1$ for a limited number of sources using velocity models M^1 and M^2.
6. The difference of the refined seismograms for the first and second step of greenhouse gas injection $d\boldsymbol{u}_{h_2}^i(t, x_o, x_s^k) = \boldsymbol{u}_{h_2}^{i+1}(t, x_o, x_s^k) - \boldsymbol{u}_{h_2}^i(t, x_o, x_s^k), k \in D_t$ are calculated.
7. Training of the NDM-net for operator approximation:

$$G_1 : \boldsymbol{u}_{h_1}^i(t, x_o, x_s^k) \to d\boldsymbol{u}_{h_1}^i(t, x_o, x_s^k).$$

8. Training NDM-net to approximate the following operator:

$$G_2 : \hat{d}\boldsymbol{u}_{h_1}^i(t, x_o, x_s^k) \to d\boldsymbol{u}_{h_2}^i(t, x_o, x_s^k),$$

where $\hat{d}\boldsymbol{u}_{h_1}^i(t, x_o, x_s^k) = G_1(\boldsymbol{u}_{h_1}^i(t, x_o, x_s^k))$.
9. Applying sequentially to all seismograms corresponding to velocity model M^{i+1} to obtain seismograms:

$$\hat{\boldsymbol{u}}_{h_2}^{i+1}(t, x_o, x_s^k) = \hat{\boldsymbol{u}}_{h_2}^i(t, x_o, x_s^k) + \hat{d}\boldsymbol{u}_{h_2}^i(t, x_o, x_s^k).$$

2.1   Neural Network

To correct the numerical solution and reduce the numerical dispersion of the recorded signal as well as predicted seismograms for the next step of the monitoring CO_2 the Numerical Dispersion Mitigation neural network (NDM-net) is used [5]. Initially, a neural network was used for training to convert coarse grid data into a more accurate one. In particular, this neural network reduced the numerical dispersion in the seismograms. Later, the same neural network demonstrated its effectiveness in reducing errors caused by rough velocity model sampling, i.e. when it is perturbed [7]. Thus, under the condition of a small change in the properties of the medium and the corresponding velocity model, the NDM-net neural network can transfer seismograms from the current monitoring step to the next.

We used pix2pix architecture [9] which consists of two sub-neural networks: generator and discriminator. Generator is a slightly modified U-net [19], which contains an encoder-decoder with interconnecting skip connections. The encoder converts the input data into a representation with a smaller dimension in hidden layers using convolution operations. The decoder is structurally identical to the encoder and recovers data back using reverse convolution operators. Downsampling and upsampling layers include the convolutional layer with kernel size $(4 \times 4 \times 4)$, activation function $ReLU(\cdot) = \max(0, \cdot)$ for decoder and $LeakyReLU(\cdot) = \max(0, \cdot) + c\min(0, \cdot)$ with negative slope coefficient $c = 0.2$ for encoder. Discriminator if a simple classifier based in convolution operations.

A mini-batch stochastic gradient descent (SGD) is used to speed up the algorithm. To estimate the number of epochs, the method of early stopping is used, checking the loss function on the validation dataset, which has a size of 10% of the training dataset.

A neural network for the approximation of the operator G_1 was trained by minimizing the loss function in order to select parameters Θ_1:

$$
\begin{aligned}
\mathcal{L}_1(\Theta_1) = arg\min_{G_1} max_{D_1} E_{k \in D_t}[\log D_1(G_1(\boldsymbol{u}_{h_2}(t, x_o, x_s^k), \Theta_1)) \\
+ log(1 - D_1(d\boldsymbol{u}_{h_1}^i(t, x_o, x_s^k))) \\
+ \lambda(\left\| d\boldsymbol{u}_{h_1}^i(t, x_o, x_s^k) - G_1(\boldsymbol{u}_{h_2}(t, x_o, x_s^k), \Theta_1)\right\|_1)],
\end{aligned}
\tag{1}
$$

where $\Theta_1 = \{\mathbf{W_1}, \mathbf{b_1}\}$ is the network parameters for G_1, which includes the weight matrix $\mathbf{W_1}$ and bias $\mathbf{b_1}$, $\mathbb{E}_{k \in D_t}$ is a mean over the training dataset, $||\cdot||_1$ is the L_1- norm.

A neural network for the approximation of the operator G_2 was alse trained by minimizing the loss function in order to select parameters Θ_2:

$$
\begin{aligned}
\mathcal{L}_2(\Theta_2) = arg\min_{G_2} max_{D_2} E_{k \in D_t}[\log D_2(G_2(\hat{d}\boldsymbol{u}_{h_1}^i(t, x_o, x_s^k), \Theta_2)) \\
+ log(1 - D_1(d\boldsymbol{u}_{h_2}^i(t, x_o, x_s^k))) \\
+ \lambda(\left\| d\boldsymbol{u}_{h_2}^i(t, x_o, x_s^k) - G_1(\hat{d}\boldsymbol{u}_{h_1}^i(t, x_o, x_s^k), \Theta_2)\right\|_1)],
\end{aligned}
\tag{2}
$$

where $\Theta_2 = \{\mathbf{W_2}, \mathbf{b_2}\}$ is the network parameters for G_2, which includes the weight matrix $\mathbf{W_2}$ and bias $\mathbf{b_2}$.

3   Numerical Experiments

We used Vanavar velocity model, which corresponds to an Eastern Siberian region to calculate seismograms. It is a multi-layered structure with prominent vertical intrusions. The model spans 220 km in length and 2.6 km in width. At the same time, we only used the first half of the original model prior to the intrusion as shown in Fig. 1. Therefore, the size of the modified model is 110 km by 2.6 km. The acquisition system comprises 1222 sources spaced 100 m apart. The wavefield is recorded by 512 receivers for each shot, with a maximum source-receiver separation of 6.4 km. The receivers are spaced 25 m apart. The source is a Ricker wavelet with a central frequency of 30 Hz. For seismic monitoring the properties of the medium, such as density ρ and velocities V_p and V_s, change gradually. Specifically, they change by 3% at each step in the range $[1, N]$, where $N = 4$.

To create the training set, seismic simulation is performed, which involves solving a system of equations from the dynamic theory of elasticity using the finite difference method on staggered grids. This has been discussed previously in the publications [3,5,6]. We calculated two sets of seismograms using a coarse grid with a characteristic pitch of 5 m and a fine grid with a characteristic pitch of 2.5 m. The recording time of the seismogram was 4 s with a time discreteness of 1 ms.

The sample of seismograms used for training is created so that the size of the sample for approximating the operator G_1 is 30% of the total number of seismograms at each step in the seismic monitoring process, i.e., sources multiplied by the number of monitoring steps, and the size of the sample used for approximating operator G_2 is 30% of the number of source locations. After that, the data is normalized for stable operation of the neural network, i.e. the values of the seismograms are converted to the range $[-1, 1]$. The training parameters are presented in Table 1.

Table 1. Parameters of the neural networks

Number of epochs	100	Batch size	5
Learning rate	1e-4	Momentum parameters	$\beta_1 = 0.5, \beta_2 = 0.999$
Input data dimension	512×4096	Coefficient λ	10000
Output data dimension	512×4096		

3.1   Results and Discussion

One of the key stages of the proposed algorithm is the training of a neural network to approximate operator G_1 and discriminator D_1. Learning and validation curves (Fig. 3A) indicate that the neural network has learned well. Similar learning and validation patterns are observed when training a network that approximates operator G_2 and discriminator D_2 (Fig. 3B). At the same time, training time on an NVIDIA GeForce RTX 3090 with 8 GB memory and Intel Core CPU with 256 GB RAM card was approximately 300 and 100 min for the first and second scenarios, respectively.

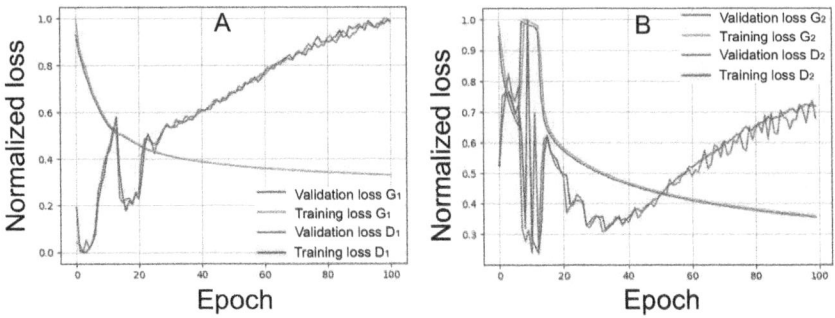

Fig. 3. The normalized training and validation losses for neural networks G_1, D_1 (A) and neural networks G_2, D_2 (B).

Examples of results obtained using two operators, i.e. generated seismograms $\hat{\boldsymbol{u}}_{h_2}^2(t, x_o, x_s^k) = \hat{\boldsymbol{u}}_{h_2}^1(t, x_o, x_s^k) + G_2(G_1(\boldsymbol{u}_{h_1}^1(t, x_o, x_s^k))$ corresponding to the second velocity model M^2 (Figures 4A, 4B, 4C), demonstrate that they visually resemble the numerical solution to the problem of seismic wave propagation on a fine computational grid $\boldsymbol{u}_{h_2}^2(t, x_o, x_s^k)$ (Figures 4D, 4E, 4F).

In order to evaluate the quality of neural networks, we used the error in terms of the L_2-norm:

$$\varepsilon(\hat{\boldsymbol{u}}_{h_2}^{i+1}(t, x_o, x_s^k), \boldsymbol{u}_{h_2}^{i+1}(t, x_o, x_s^k)) = \frac{||\hat{\boldsymbol{u}}_{h_2}^{i+1}(t, x_o, x_s^k) - \boldsymbol{u}_{h_2}^{i+1}(t, x_o, x_s^k)||_2}{||\boldsymbol{u}_{h_2}^{i+1}(t, x_o, x_s^k)||_2} \times 100\%,$$

where $\hat{\boldsymbol{u}}_{h_2}^{i+1}(t, x_o, x_s^k) = \hat{\boldsymbol{u}}_{h_2}^i(t, x_o, x_s^k) + G_2(G_1(\boldsymbol{u}_{h_1}^i(t, x_o, x_s^k))$. Using this formula, we can also calculate the initial discrepancy between the solutions on the fine and coarse computational grids in a similar manner.

The overall trend in the error ε and initial error ε_{init} for each source (Fig. 5) indicates that numerical dispersion is reduced average by a factor of 4 (from 114.6% to 27.6% in terms of L_2-norm with standard deviation 5.6% and 10.6%, respectively). However, some seismograms have recovered relatively poorly after using neural networks. This may be because the training set is equally distributed and does not include a wide variety of seismograms. This problem was discussed in [6].

For the velocity model M^4 after sequential application of neural networks, we also constructed a relative error similar to the velocity model M^2 (Fig. 6.

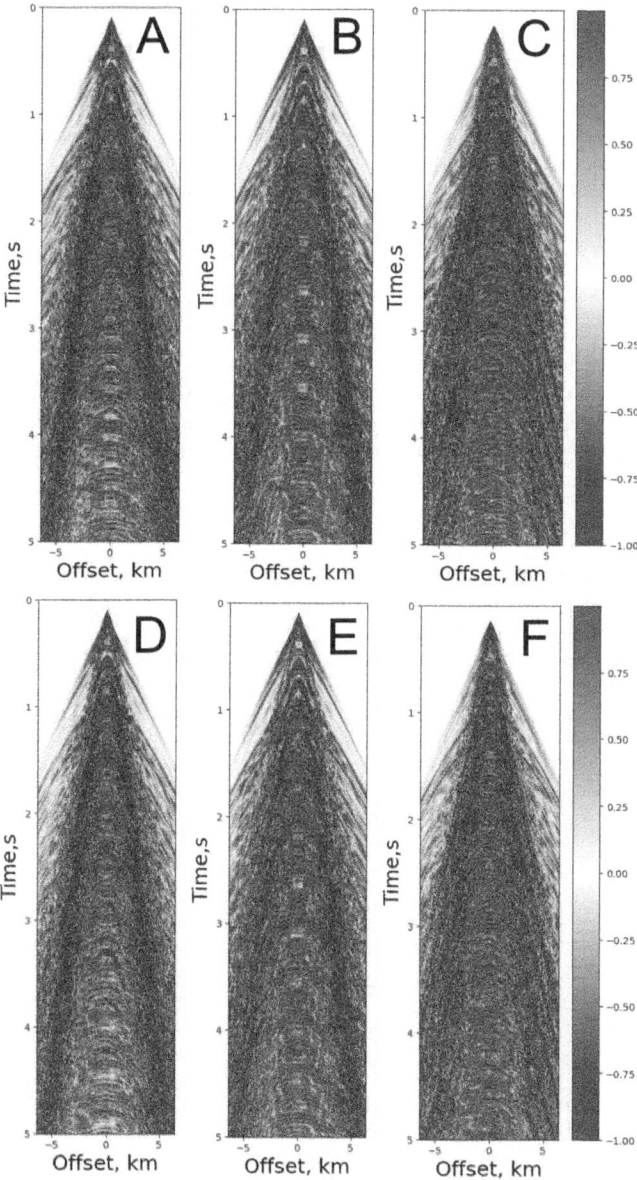

Fig. 4. Generated seismograms $\hat{\boldsymbol{u}}_{h_2}^2(t, x_o, x_s^k)$ (A,B,C) for the random source positions and corresponding seismograms calculated on a fine grid $\boldsymbol{u}_{h_2}^2(t, x_o, x_s^k)$ (D,E,F).

However, in this case, there is a significant drop in the quality of the results of using neural networks. This is due to the fact that when neural networks are consistently applied to the seismograms of each velocity model, an error accumu-

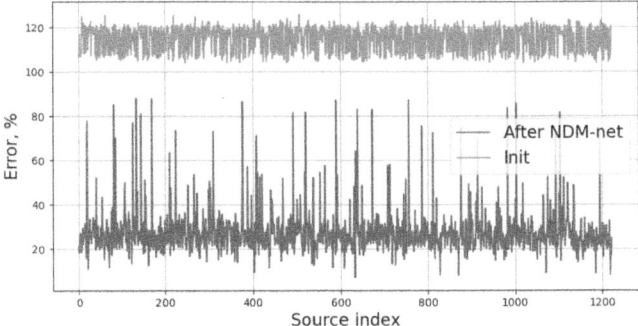

Fig. 5. The relative error between seismogram calculated on a fine grid and coarse grid solution (orange line) and the relative error between neural network post-processed seismogram and fine solution (blue line) for each source position and velocity model M^2. (Color figure online)

lates. At the same time, the numerical dispersion, in this case, is suppressed on average in L_2-norm from 134.8% to 27.4% with a standard deviation of 39.6% and 13.4%, respectively.

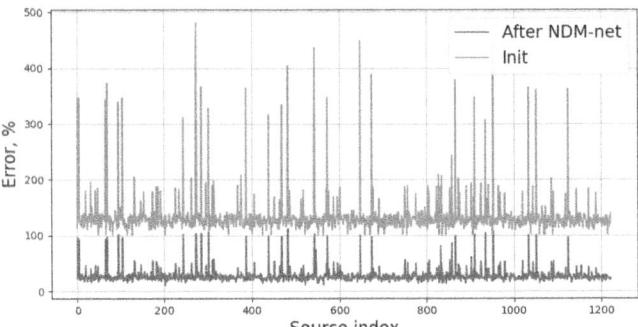

Fig. 6. The relative error between seismogram calculated on a fine grid and coarse grid solution (orange line) and the relative error between neural network post-processed seismogram and fine solution (blue line) for each source position and velocity model M^4. (Color figure online)

Random generated seismograms after sequential application of neural networks for the velocity model M^4 are shown in Fig. 7. Subtle noise appears on the generated seismograms, due to the reusable sequential use of neural networks.

Therefore, the proposed approach allows for a significant reduction in the computational time required for solving the direct seismic problem. Specifically, it will take approximately 29352 min to compute all seismograms for both the

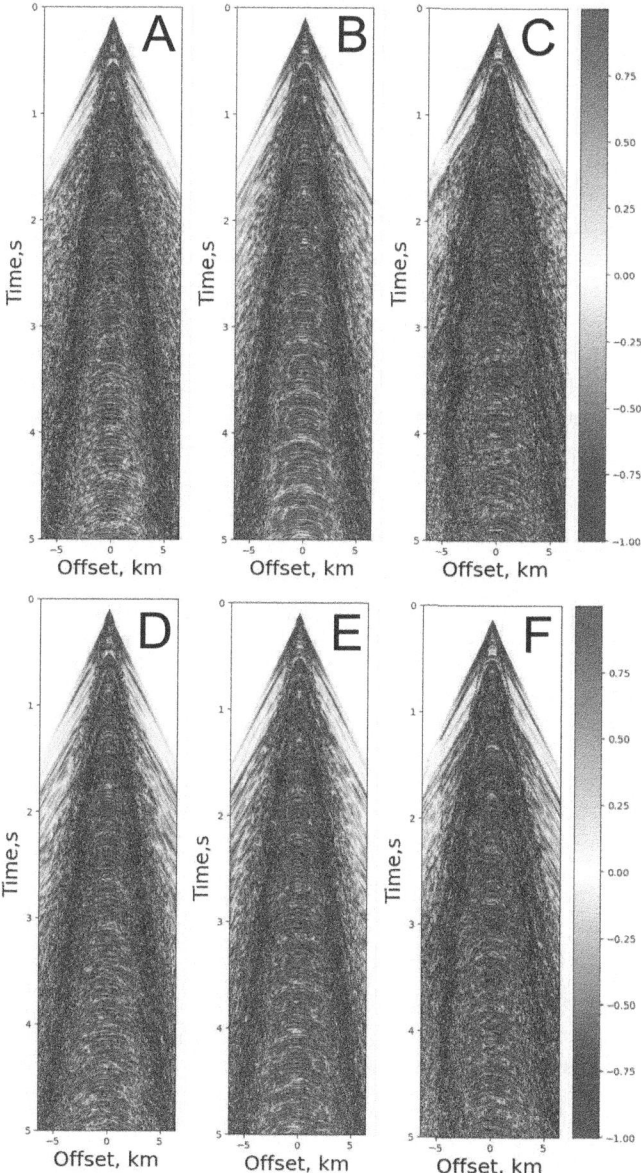

Fig. 7. Generated seismograms $\hat{\boldsymbol{u}}_{h_2}^4(t, x_o, x_s^k)$ (A,B,C) for the random source positions and corresponding seismograms calculated on a fine grid $\boldsymbol{u}_{h_2}^4(t, x_o, x_s^k)$ (D,E,F).

modified and unmodified velocity models. In contrast, the training and implementation of a neural network would take approximately 4926 min, resulting in a 6x acceleration of the overall process.

4   Conclusion

This study presents a neural network-based approach to improve the accuracy of seismograms when monitoring a CO_2 reservoir. The proposed technique includes two-stage neural network training, which makes it possible to predict changes in the seismogram due to changes in the velocity model and refine numerical solutions obtained on a coarse computational grid. The results of numerical experiments confirm that the neural network copes well with the test data, while the training time at the first stage and the second, along with the formation of a training sample, is 6 times less than in the case of seismic modeling of a complete set of seismograms for modified velocity models using a fine computational grid. Quantification using the normal error indicator L_2 demonstrates a significant decrease in numerical variance, while average errors decrease fourfold. These results indicate that the proposed method effectively improves the accuracy of frame-by-frame seismic monitoring while maintaining computational efficiency.

Future work may focus on extending this approach to three-dimensional seismic data, incorporating multiphase flow physics to improve generalization, and exploring alternative neural network architectures to further reduce numerical distortion.

Acknowledgments. This study was funded by Russian Science Foundation grant no. 22-11-00004П.

References

1. Celaya, A., Araya-Polo, M.: Joint inversion of time-lapse surface gravity and seismic data for monitoring of 3d co2 plumes via deep learning (2023). https://arxiv.org/abs/2310.04430
2. Dumbser, M., Kaser, M.: An arbitrary high-order discontinuous Galerkin method for elastic waves on unstructured meshes - ii. the three-dimensional isotropic case. Geophys. J. Int. **167**(1), 319–336 (2006). https://doi.org/10.1111/j.1365-246X.2006.03120.x
3. Gadylshin, K., Lisitsa, V., Gadylshina, K., Vishnevsky, D.: Optimization of the training dataset for numerical dispersion mitigation neural network. In: Gervasi, O., Murgante, B., Misra, S., Rocha, A.M.A.C., Garau, C. (eds.) Computational Science and Its Applications – ICCSA 2022 Workshops, pp. 295–309. Springer International Publishing (2022)
4. Gadylshin, K., Lisitsa, V., Gadylshina, K., Vishnevsky, D.: Frequency domain numerical dispersion mitigation network. In: Gervasi, O., et al. (eds.) Computational Science and Its Applications – ICCSA 2023 Workshops, pp. 31–44. Springer Nature Switzerland, Cham (2023)
5. Gadylshin, K., Vishnevsky, D., Gadylshina, K., Lisitsa, V.: Numerical dispersion mitigation neural network for seismic modeling. Geophysics **87**(3), T237–T249 (2022)
6. Gondyul, E., Lisitsa, V., Gadylshin, K., Vishnevsky, D.: Numerical dispersion mitigation neural network with the model-based training dataset optimization. In: Gervasi, O., et al., (eds.) Computational Science and Its Applications – ICCSA 2023 Workshops, pp. 19–30. Springer Nature Switzerland (2023)

7. Gondyul, E., Lisitsa, V., Gadylshin, K., Vishnevsky, D.: Numerical dispersion mitigation neural network with velocity model correction. Comput. Geosci. **196**, 105806
   (2025). https://doi.org/10.1016/j.cageo.2024.105806, https://www.sciencedirect.
   com/science/article/pii/S0098300424002899
8. Idesman, A., Pham, D.: Finite element modeling of linear elastodynamics problems with explicit time-integration methods and linear elements with the reduced
   dispersion error. Comput. Methods Appl. Mech. Eng. **271**, 86–108 (2014)
9. Isola, P., Zhu, J., Zhou, T., Efros, A.A.: Image-to-image translation with conditional adversarial networks. CoRR **abs/1611.07004** (2016), http://arxiv.org/
   abs/1611.07004
10. Ivandic, M., Bergmann, P., Kummerow, J., Huang, F., Juhlin, C., Lueth, S.:
    Monitoring co2 saturation using time-lapse amplitude versus offset analysis of 3d
    seismic data from the ketzin co2 storage pilot site, Germany. Geophys. Prosp.
    66(8), 1568–1585 (2018). https://doi.org/10.1111/1365-2478.12666, https://www.
    earthdoc.org/content/journals/10.1111/1365-2478.12666
11. Komatitsch, D., Vilotte, J.P.: The spectral element method; an efficient tool to
    simulate the seismic response of 2D and 3D geological structures. Bull. Seismol.
    Society Am. **88**(2), 368–392 (1998)
12. Levander, A.R.: Fourth-order finite-difference P-SV seismograms. Geophysics
    53(11), 1425–1436 (1988)
13. Li, B., Li, Y.E.: Neural network-based co2 interpretation from 4d Sleipner seismic
    images. J. Geophys. Res.: Solid Earth **126**(12), e2021JB022524 (2021)
14. Lisitsa, V., Vishnevskiy, D.: Lebedev scheme for the numerical simulation of wave
    propagation in 3d anisotropic elasticity. Geophys. Prospect. **58**(4), 619–635 (2010).
    https://doi.org/10.1111/j.1365-2478.2009.00862.x
15. Lisitsa, V., Tcheverda, V., Botter, C.: Combination of the discontinuous Galerkin
    method with finite differences for simulation of seismic wave propagation. J. Com-
    put. Phys. **311**, 142–157 (2016)
16. Lisitsa, V., Tcheverda, V., Vishnevsky, D.: Numerical simulation of seismic waves in
    models with anisotropic formations: coupling Virieux and Lebedev finite-difference
    schemes. Comput. Geosci. **16**(4), 1135–1152 (2012)
17. Paffenholz, J.: Introduction to this special section: The role of advanced modeling
    in enhanced carbon storage. Lead. Edge **40**(6), 408–412 (2021)
18. Pevzner, R., et al.: Feasibility of time-lapse seismic methodology for monitoring the
    injection of small quantities of co2 into a saline formation, co2crc otway project.
    Energy Proc. **37**, 4336–4343 (2013). https://doi.org/10.1016/j.egypro.2013.06.336
19. Ronneberger, O., Fischer, P., Brox, T.: U-net: Convolutional networks for biomed-
    ical image segmentation. In: Medical Image Computing and Computer-Assisted
    Intervention (MICCAI). LNCS, vol. 9351, pp. 234–241. Springer (2015). http://
    lmb.informatik.uni-freiburg.de/Publications/2015/RFB15a
20. Saenger, E.H., Gold, N., Shapiro, S.A.: Modeling the propagation of the elastic
    waves using a modified finite-difference grid. Wave Motion **31**, 77–92 (2000)
21. Sheng, H., Wu, X., Sun, X., Wu, L.: Deep learning for characterizing co2 migration
    in time-lapse seismic images. Fuel **336**, 126806 (2023)
22. Tromp, J., Komatitsch, D., Liu, Q.: Spectral-element and adjoint methods in seis-
    mology. Commun. Comput. Phys. **3**(1), 1–32 (2008)
23. Virieux, J.: P-SV wave propagation in heterogeneous media: Velocity-stress finite-
    difference method. Geophysics **51**(4), 889–901 (1986)
24. Wang, Z., Harbert, W.P., Dilmore, R.M., Huang, L.: Modeling of time-lapse seismic
    monitoring using co2 leakage simulations for a model co2 storage site with realis-
    tic geology: Application in assessment of early leak-detection capabilities. Int. J.

Greenhouse Gas Control **76**, 39–52 (2018). https://doi.org/10.1016/j.ijggc.2018.06.011

25. Wen, G., Li, Z., Azizzadenesheli, K., Anandkumar, A., Benson, S.M.: U-FNO–an enhanced Fourier neural operator-based deep-learning model for multiphase flow. Adv. Water Resour. **163**, 104180 (2022)

26. Yin, Z., Siahkoohi, A., Louboutin, M., Herrmann, F.J.: Learned coupled inversion for carbon sequestration monitoring and forecasting with fourier neural operators. In: Second International Meeting for Applied Geoscience; Energy. p. 467–472. Society of Exploration Geophysicists and American Association of Petroleum Geologists (Aug 2022). https://doi.org/10.1190/image2022-3722848.1, http://dx.doi.org/10.1190/image2022-3722848.1

Spectral Decomposition to Solve the Elasticity Problem in Quasi-static Formulation

Sergey Solovyev$^{(\boxtimes)}$ and Vadim Lisitsa

Institute of Mathematics SB RAS, Koptug ave. 4, 630090 Novosibirsk, Russia
511ssa@mail.ru

Abstract. In this paper we consider the problem of numerical solution of the boundary value problem of the theory of elasticity in static formulation in a rectangle with arbitrary boundary conditions. For this purpose, we use the approach of splitting in the direction of the Laplace operator based on its spectral decomposition, which is similar to the discrete Fourier transform but does not require periodicity of the boundary conditions. A fast matrix-to-vector multiplication algorithm is proposed using an efficiently software-implemented matrix multiplication algorithm. Numerical experiments are performed to show the effectiveness of the proposed method with the ability to solve the elasticity problem on a mesh of 10^9 nodes on systems with 128G RAM.

Keywords: Poroelasticity · Biot equation · Elasticity · finite differences · Laplace operator · spectral decomposition · SLAE · iterative methods · HPC · shared memory systems

1 Introduction

While calculating the effective elasticity tensor of a viscoelastic medium described by the differential equations of Biot [3] in the frequency domain, it is necessary to numerically solve the boundary value problem of the theory of elasticity in the static formulation. This leads to the question of solving the direct problem of finding the components of the displacement vector u, the components of the strain tensor ε and the stress tensor σ according to the given boundary conditions and the inhomogeneous stiffness tensor. Despite the method of discretisation of the boundary value problem by finite difference, volume or finite element methods, the problem of solving the resulting System of Linear Algebraic Equations (SLAE) arises. The solution of SLAE is the most resource consuming part and one of the most effective approaches is the use of preconditioned iterative methods. In addition, the boundary conditions for the initial differential formulation significantly affect the properties of SLAEs. For example, the Neumann-type conditions (the derivatives of the solution along the normal to

S. Solovyev developed the algorithm and did the numerical simulations using the supercomputer facilities of Siberian Supercomputer Center (Cluster NKS-30T) under the support of RSCF grant no. 19-77-20004-$\varPi$.

the surface are defined) cause ill-conditioned the SLAE, and it affects the convergence of the iterative process and the construction of the preconditioner. The construction of a preconditioner, and the choice of an iterative algorithm, are independent and important areas of research. The most effective preconditioners are multigrid methods [4,5], both Geometrical Multigrid and Algebraic Multigrid; methods based on incomplete factorisation (IL(0), ILU(p)); and Domain Decomposition methods, which are a set of methods based on the principle of 'divide and conquer' developed mainly for solving differential equations in 2D and 3D domains [8]. The most efficient and most commonly used are the conjugate gradient (CG) methods for SLAEs with self-adjoint matrices and bisadjoint gradients with stabilisation (BCGStab) for square matrices of the general form [8]. These preconditioning methods, as well as the iterative methods, are effectively implemented in software packages such as Intel MKL [1], PETSc [2], J. S. Saad's SPARSKIT [6], Tim Davis's UMFPACK MATLAB [7], and J. S. Sahad's UMFPACK [6]. Saad [6], UMFPACK by Tim Davis (MATLAB [7]). Despite the wide variety of methods implemented, the best approach is often to develop a specialised algorithm for a particular boundary value problem. This paper is devoted to the development of a numerical algorithm for solving the elasticity boundary value problem in a homogeneous medium in the static formulation. This solution can be used as an effective preconditioner both for solving the inhomogeneous elasticity problem and as a stand-alone problem. The main idea of this work is to use the method of spatial decomposition along different axes with the use of the 1D spectral decomposition of the Laplace operator. The method consists in reducing the original problem to a sequence of one-dimensional problems, which leads to a significant reduction in computational resources. The quasi-static formulation of the elasticity problem with constant Lamé coefficients, various boundary conditions such as Dirichlet and Neumann are considered. The equations and boundary conditions are discretised by a second order finite difference approximation on shifted rectangular meshes. This approximation leads to a positive definite SLAE with real coefficients (semidefinite in the case of the Neumann boundary condition). The paper consists of the following sections: The first describes the differential formulation of the elasticity problem, the finite difference approximation, the structure of the obtained SLAE and the solution idea. The second section is devoted to a detailed description of the spectral decomposition of the Laplace operator, as well as the fast multiplication of this operator based on the spatial decomposition method. The third section deals with the mixed derivatives of the elasticity operator, their singular decomposition and the correlation with the spectral decomposition of the Laplace operators, which form the 'diagonal' part of the elasticity operator. The fourth section describes the solution of the elasticity problem itself: based on the results of the previous sections, the splitting of the elasticity operator is presented with a description of the fast multiplication algorithm, and the numerical method for solving the SLAE is described. The last, fifth section is directly dedicated to numerical experiments. The developed algorithm has been tested: the correctness of the solution obtained, the efficiency of memory usage and the high computational speed have been demonstrated. In addition, a comparison is made with direct methods optimised for solving sparse SLAEs.

2 Problem Statement, Proposed Solution

It is needed to numerically solve the elasticity equation. In two dimensions it looks like this:

$$
\frac{\partial}{\partial x}\left[(\lambda + 2\mu)\frac{\partial u_x}{\partial x} + \lambda\frac{\partial u_z}{\partial z}\right] + \frac{\partial}{\partial z}\left[\mu\left(\frac{\partial u_x}{\partial z} + \frac{\partial u_z}{\partial x}\right)\right] = 0,
$$
$$
\frac{\partial}{\partial x}\left[\mu\left(\frac{\partial u_x}{\partial z} + \frac{\partial u_z}{\partial x}\right)\right] + \frac{\partial}{\partial z}\left[\lambda\frac{\partial u_x}{\partial x} + (\lambda + 2\mu)\frac{\partial u_z}{\partial z}\right] = 0
$$

$$(1)$$

In the equations (1) λ and μ are the Lame coefficients.

First, rewrite it in the form (2) and simplify it by considering the operator consisting of 2-dimensional Laplace operators and mixed derivative operators (3).

$$
\left[\frac{\partial}{\partial x}(\lambda + 2\mu)\frac{\partial}{\partial x} + \frac{\partial}{\partial z}\mu\frac{\partial}{\partial z}\right]u_x + \left[\frac{\partial}{\partial x}\lambda\frac{\partial}{\partial z} + \frac{\partial}{\partial z}\mu\frac{\partial}{\partial x}\right]u_z = 0,
$$
$$
+ \left[\frac{\partial}{\partial z}\lambda\frac{\partial}{\partial x} + \frac{\partial}{\partial x}\mu\frac{\partial}{\partial z}\right]u_x + \left[\frac{\partial}{\partial z}(\lambda + 2\mu)\frac{\partial}{\partial z} + \frac{\partial}{\partial x}\mu\frac{\partial}{\partial x}\right]u_z = 0.
$$

$$(2)$$

$$
\left[\frac{\partial}{\partial x}\frac{\partial}{\partial x} + \frac{\partial}{\partial z}\frac{\partial}{\partial z}\right]u_x + \left[\frac{\partial}{\partial z}\frac{\partial}{\partial x}\right]u_z = 0,
$$
$$
\left[\frac{\partial}{\partial x}\frac{\partial}{\partial z}\right]u_x + \left[\frac{\partial}{\partial z}\frac{\partial}{\partial z} + \frac{\partial}{\partial x}\frac{\partial}{\partial x}\right]u_z = 0.
$$

$$(3)$$

The computational domain is rectangular; the boundary conditions are of Dirichlet or Neumann. The discretisation of the differential equation is performed by a second order finite difference on staggered grids with constant steps in each direction. The u_x components are located in the centre of the vertical edges and the u_z components are located in the centre of the horizontal edges. The boundary of the computational domain lies along the centres of the edges. An example of the grid $N_x = 6 \times N_z = 4$ is shown in Fig. 1.

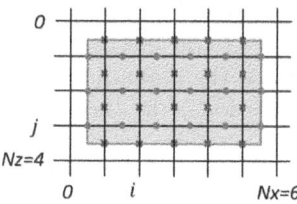

Fig. 1. Example of the computational mesh $N_x = 6 \times N_z = 4$.

As a result of finite-difference approximation, we obtain a system of linear algebraic equations (SLAE) that is positive definite (in the case of Dirichlet and Neumann type boundary conditions) or semi-definite (Neumann conditions only).

This SLAE can be represented as a large-block 2×2 form where diagonal blocks correspond to approximations of Laplace operators and non-diagonal blocks correspond to mixed derivatives (4). In the general case, the number of unknown components u_x is not equal to u_z, and the blocks A_{11} and A_{22} corresponding to the Laplace approximations for these components are square of different sizes, while the blocks A_{12} and A_{21} are rectangular and equal with transpose precision: $A_{21} = A_{12}^t$. For the given example (A_{11} is a matrix of size 20×20 obtained by their two-dimensional Laplace approximation on a mesh of 5×4, A_{22} is a matrix of size 18×18 for a mesh of 6×3, matrices A_{12} and A_{21} are 18×20 and 20×18, respectively.

$$\left[\begin{array}{cc} \frac{\partial}{\partial x}\frac{\partial}{\partial x} + \frac{\partial}{\partial z}\frac{\partial}{\partial z} & \frac{\partial}{\partial z}\frac{\partial}{\partial x} \\ \frac{\partial}{\partial x}\frac{\partial}{\partial z} & \frac{\partial}{\partial z}\frac{\partial}{\partial z} + \frac{\partial}{\partial x}\frac{\partial}{\partial x} \end{array} \right] \Rightarrow A = \left[\begin{array}{cc} A_{11} & A_{12} \\ A_{21} & A_{22} \end{array} \right] \tag{4}$$

The idea of the solution the SLAE, derived from the Eq. 3, is based on the spectral decomposition of the Laplace 1D and on the spatial decomposition along different axes of the 2D (and, in general, 3D) Laplace operator. In the initial formulation of the elasticity problem, direct application of the splitting method to the elasticity operator is not possible because of the mixed derivatives and their off-diagonal blocks A_{21} and A_{12}, Therefore, we assume to use the decomposition of the Laplace operators corresponding to the diagonal blocks A_{11} and A_{22} of the original matrix to transform the matrix A to a large-block 2×2 matrix with diagonal blocks consisting only of the main diagonal. First, we describe the spectral decomposition of the Laplace operator along one direction. Then we apply the splitting scheme to the 2D Laplace operator as well as to the mixed derivative operator.

3   Spectral Decomposition of the Laplace Operator

3.1   Laplace 1D Singular and Spectral Decomposition

As a result of finite-difference approximation of the second derivative $-\frac{\partial^2}{\partial x^2}$ on a uniform mesh (without restriction of generality with grid spacing equal to one), we obtain the well-known symmetric three-diagonal matrix with values equal "2" on the main diagonal and "-1" on the two nearest diagonals. The values of the first and the last elements on the main diagonal will be different (depending on the type of boundary conditions). In the example of the matrix (5, left), $a = b = 1$ corresponds to the Dirichlet condition, and $a = b = 0$ corresponds to the Neumann condition. Also, the matrix A_n can be represented as products of some other operator B_n by its conjugate: $A_n = B_n B_n^*$. It is easy to see that this matrix is a finite-difference approximation of the first-order operator $-\frac{\partial}{\partial x}$ (5, right).

$$A_n = \begin{pmatrix} a^2+1 & -1 & & & 0 \\ -1 & 2 & -1 & & \\ & \ddots & \ddots & \ddots & \\ & & -1 & 2 & -1 \\ 0 & & & -1 & b^2+1 \end{pmatrix}, B_n = \begin{pmatrix} -a & 1 & & & 0 \\ 0 & -1 & 1 & & \\ & \ddots & \ddots & \ddots & \\ & & & -1 & 1 \\ 0 & & & & -1 & b \end{pmatrix} \quad (5)$$

For the matrix A_n we know how to obtain its spectral decomposition: $A_n = V_n D_n^2 V_n^*$ (diagonal matrix D_n^2, dense orthogonal matrix V_n). Based on this decomposition, it is easy to compute the singular decomposition $B_n = V_n D_n W_n^*$ associated with the spectral decomposition of A_n. The matrices B_n and W_n are rectangular, the number of nodes in the mesh n determines the dimensions of the matrices:

$$B_n^{[n\times(n+1)]}, A_n^{[n\times n]}, V_n^{[n\times n]}, D_n^{[n\times n]}, W_n^{[(n+1)\times n]} \quad (6)$$

Further, the orthogonality properties of these matrices are used: $V_n V_n^* = I, V_n^* V_n = I, W_n^* W_n = I$.

3.2   Laplace: 2D-Decomposition

To obtain the 2D spectral decomposition of the Laplace operator approximated on a rectangular mesh of n horizontal and m vertical nodes (Fig. 3, left), let us consider the second derivatives and their matrices. Schematically, the mesh corresponding to the operator $-\frac{\partial^2}{\partial x^2}$ does not contain horizontal connections (Fig. 2, right), and mesh of the operator $-\frac{\partial^2}{\partial y^2}$ does not contain vertical ones (Fig. 2, centre).

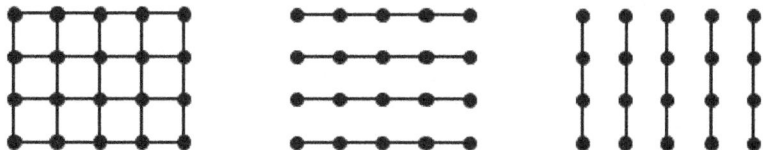

Fig. 2. On the left: rectangular mesh for approximating the Laplace $\frac{\partial^2}{\partial x^2} + \frac{\partial^2}{\partial y^2}$; in the centre—the mesh for approximating the second derivative in the horizontal direction ($\frac{\partial^2}{\partial x^2}$); on the right—in the vertical direction ($\frac{\partial^2}{\partial y^2}$).

Using horizontal node numbering, the operator $\frac{\partial^2}{\partial x^2}$ yields a block-diagonal matrix $\overline{A}_{nm}$ of m identical A_n blocks, while $\frac{\partial^2}{\partial y^2}$ yields a block-tri-diagonal matrix $\overline{\overline{A}}_{nm}$ with blocks – unit matrices multiplied by the elements of the matrix obtained from the 1D Laplace approximation on a grid of m nodes A_m. The result of the sum of these two matrices is the finite-difference 2D Laplace operator $\hat{A}_{nm}$ (7).

$$
\left.
\begin{array}{l}
A_n = \begin{pmatrix} a_{11} & \cdots & a_{1n} \\ \vdots & \ddots & \vdots \\ a_{n1} & \cdots & a_{nn} \end{pmatrix} \Rightarrow \overline{A}_{nm} = \begin{pmatrix} A_n & & & \\ & A_n & & \\ & & A_n & \\ & & & A_n \end{pmatrix} \\
A_m = \begin{pmatrix} a_{11} & \cdots & a_{1\,m} \\ \vdots & \ddots & \vdots \\ a_{m1} & \cdots & a_{mm} \end{pmatrix} \Rightarrow \overline{\overline{A}}_{nm} = \begin{pmatrix} a_{11}I & \cdots & a_{1\,m}I \\ \vdots & \ddots & \vdots \\ a_{m1}I & \cdots & a_{mm}I \end{pmatrix}
\end{array}
\right\} \Rightarrow \hat{A}_{nm} = \overline{A}_{nm} + \overline{\overline{A}}_{nm}
\tag{7}
$$

This representation of a matrix as a direct sum can also be done for the matrices of its spectral decomposition. That is, the matrices $\overline{V}_{nm}$ and $\overline{D}_{nm}$ of the spectral expansion $\overline{A}_{nm} = \overline{V}_{nm}\overline{D}_{nm}\overline{V}^t_{nm}$ (and also $\overline{\overline{A}}_{nm}$ and $\overline{\overline{D}}_{nm}$ for $\overline{\overline{A}}_{nm} = \overline{\overline{V}}_{nm}\overline{\overline{D}}_{nm}\overline{\overline{V}}^t_{nm}$) are obtained by the same way from the matrices V_n, D_n, V_m, V_m of the spectral expansion of the 1D Laplace (matrices A_n and V_m).

It is easy to check that any matrix $\overline{M}_{nm} \in \{\overline{A}_{nm}, \overline{V}_{nm}, \overline{D}_{nm}\}$ is permutable with $\overline{\overline{M}}_{nm} \in \{\overline{\overline{A}}_{nm}, \overline{\overline{V}}_{nm}, \overline{\overline{D}}_{nm}\}$, i.e. $\overline{M}_{nm}\overline{\overline{M}}_{nm} = \overline{\overline{M}}_{nm}\overline{M}_{nm}$. Using this property and the orthogonality property of the matrices $\overline{V}_{nm}$ and $\overline{\overline{V}}_{nm}$, we obtain the spectral decomposition for the 2D Laplace $\hat{A}_{nm} = \hat{V}_{nm}\hat{D}_{nm}\hat{V}^t_{nm}$ (8), where $\hat{V}_{nm} = \overline{V}_{nm}\overline{\overline{V}}_{nm}$, and $\hat{D}_{nm} = \overline{D}_{nm} + \overline{\overline{D}}_{nm}$.

A few remarks about the properties of the above matrices. Despite the fact that $\hat{V}_{nm}$ is a dense matrix and at large sizes of its storage, computational operations with it are extremely inefficient, this can be overcome by implicitly representing it. That is, the operation of multiplication of $\hat{V}_{nm}$ by a vector can be performed by successive multiplications of two matrices $\overline{\overline{V}}_{nm}$ and $\overline{V}_{nm}$. Let us consider this operation in details.

$$
\hat{A}_{nm} = \overline{V}_{nm}\overline{\overline{V}}_{nm}(\overline{D}_{nm} + \overline{\overline{D}}_{nm})\overline{\overline{V}}^t_{nm}\overline{V}^t_{nm})
\tag{8}
$$

A schematic representation of the multiplication of a matrix $\overline{\overline{V}}_{nm}$ by some vector x and the multiplication of $\overline{V}_{nm}$ by a vector y is shown by the formula (9).

$$
\begin{pmatrix} z_1 \\ \vdots \\ z_{nm} \end{pmatrix} = \begin{pmatrix} v_{11}I & \cdots & v_{1\,m}I \\ \vdots & \ddots & \vdots \\ v_{m1}I & \cdots & v_{mm}I \end{pmatrix} \begin{pmatrix} y_1 \\ \vdots \\ y_{nm} \end{pmatrix}, \quad \begin{pmatrix} y_1 \\ \vdots \\ y_{nm} \end{pmatrix} = \begin{pmatrix} V_nI & 0 & 0 \\ 0 & \ddots & 0 \\ 0 & 0 & V_nI \end{pmatrix} \begin{pmatrix} x_1 \\ \vdots \\ x_{nm} \end{pmatrix}
\tag{9}
$$

Let us write vectors x and y as matrices X and Y of n rows and m columns with column-wise storage, i.e., the element at the intersection of the i-th row and j-th column in matrix X has index $k = i + j*n$ in vector x, and the k-th element of the vector is equal to the (i, j)-th element of the corresponding matrix. So, the matrix-vector multiplication operation (9, right) is rewritten as matrix-matrix operation $Y = V_n X$ (Fig. 3, right).

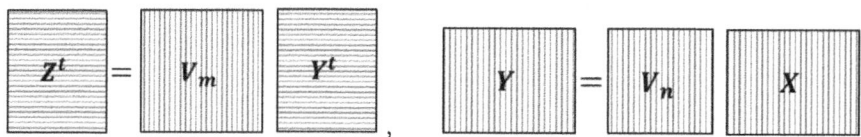

Fig. 3. Schematic representation of fast matrix multiplication with column-wise storage of matrix elements Y, V_n and X in memory. Left: $Y = V_n X$, right: $Z^t = V_m Y^t$.

When multiplying a block matrix $\overline{\overline{V}}_{nm}$ by a vector y (Fig. 9 on the left), with the above order of entry of elements and representing vectors y and z as matrices Y and Z, each element of the first column V_m is multiplied by all the first n-elements of y. Each element of the second column V_m is multiplied by the second group of n-elements of y, and so on. This algorithm is equivalent to multiplying the matrix V_m by the transposed matrix Y^t, with row-wise storage (Fig. 3, left).

Using an additional transpose, the operation of multiplying the matrix $\hat{V}_{nm} = \overline{V}_{nm}\overline{\overline{V}}_{nm}$ by the vector x can be rewritten as $Z = V_n X V_m^t$ (Fig. 4).

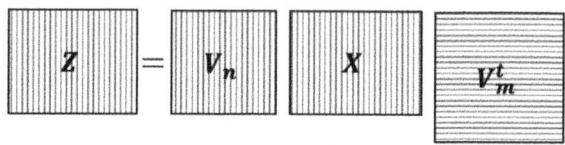

Fig. 4. Schematic representation of the fast multiplication $Z = V_n X V_m^t$.

An important property of this representation is that when changing the numbering direction in matrices (from column-wise to row-wise storage), it is not necessary to physically perform transposition (copying of matrix elements). It is sufficient to use matrix multiplications from already developed and well optimised matrix multiplication implementations that work with different numeration of dense matrices.

4 Elasticity Operator: Mixed Derivatives

4.1 Splitting Scheme

Let us write the matrix A_n (discrete 1D operator of the second derivative) as the product of the matrix obtained from the approximation of the first derivative by its adjoint (the elements of the matrix are real and we will use the "transpose" operator): $A_n = B_n B_n^t$.

In 2D space, the second derivative operators will have the form: $\overline{A}_{nm} = \overline{B}_{nm}\overline{B}_{nm}^t$ and $\overline{\overline{A}}_{nm} = \overline{\overline{B}}_{nm}\overline{\overline{B}}_{nm}^t$. Here $\overline{B}_{nm}$ – a block-diagonal matrix contains of m rectangular bidiagonal blocks B_n, $\overline{\overline{B}}_{nm}$ –a block-diagonal matrix whose blocks are unit matrices of size n multiplied by the elements of matrix B_m (see 10).

$$\overline{B}_{nm} = \begin{pmatrix} B_n & & & \\ & B_n & & \\ & & B_n & \\ & & & B_n \end{pmatrix}, B_n = \begin{pmatrix} b_{11} & b_{12} & 0 & \cdots & 0 \\ 0 & b_{22} & b_{23} & \ddots & \vdots \\ \vdots & \ddots & \ddots & \ddots & 0 \\ 0 & \cdots & 0 & b_{nn} & b_{nn+1} \end{pmatrix};$$

$$\overline{\overline{B}}_{nm} = \begin{pmatrix} b_{11}I & b_{12}I & 0 & \cdots & 0 \\ 0 & b_{22}I & b_{23}I & \ddots & \vdots \\ \vdots & \ddots & \ddots & \ddots & 0 \\ 0 & \cdots & 0 & b_{mm}I & b_{mm+1}I \end{pmatrix}, B_m = \begin{pmatrix} b_{11} & b_{12} & 0 & \cdots & 0 \\ 0 & b_{22} & b_{23} & \ddots & \vdots \\ \vdots & \ddots & \ddots & \ddots & 0 \\ 0 & \cdots & 0 & b_{mm} & b_{mm+1} \end{pmatrix}$$

$$(10)$$

We use such a decomposition for the blocks $A_{11}, A_{22}, A_{12}, A_{21}$ of the matrix A (4). Because of the staggered grids, the Laplace operator for the horizontal component of the solution has the dimension of n along the horizontal axis is $N_x - 1$ and $m = N_z$ along the vertical axis; for the vertical component—$n = N_x$, and $m = N_z - 1$. Thus, the diagonal blocks A_{11}, A_{22} can be represented as (11)):

$$A_{11} = \overline{B}_{Nx-1,Nz}\overline{B}_{Nx-1,Nz}^t + \overline{\overline{B}}_{Nx-1,Nz}\overline{\overline{B}}_{Nx-1,Nz}^t$$
$$A_{22} = \overline{B}_{Nx,Nz-1}\overline{B}_{Nx,Nz-1}^t + \overline{\overline{B}}_{Nx,Nz-1}\overline{\overline{B}}_{Nx,Nz-1}^t. \qquad (11)$$

The off-diagonal blocks A_{12}, A_{21} can be writen are expressed in a same maner. The matrix A_{12} (mixed derivatives $\frac{\partial}{\partial x}\frac{\partial}{\partial z}$) is represented as $A_{12} = \overline{B}_{nm}\overline{\overline{B}}_{nm}^t$. It is important to note that the matrix $\overline{\overline{B}}_{nm}^t$ operates on the vertical components in the space of dimension ($n = N_x$, $m = N_z - 1$), and $\overline{B}_{nm}$ operates on the horizontal components in the space of another dimension ($n = N_x - 1$, $m = N_z$). That is, $A_{12} = \overline{B}_{Nx-1,Nz}\overline{\overline{B}}_{Nx,Nz-1}^t$ (Fig. 5, left). To check the correct use of dimensions: if in the formula (10) we set N_x and N_z in the matrix representation, we obtain in the product the number of rows equal to the dimension of the horizontal component space, and the number of columns – vertical. The same reasoning can be done for the block A_{21} (Fig. 5, right).

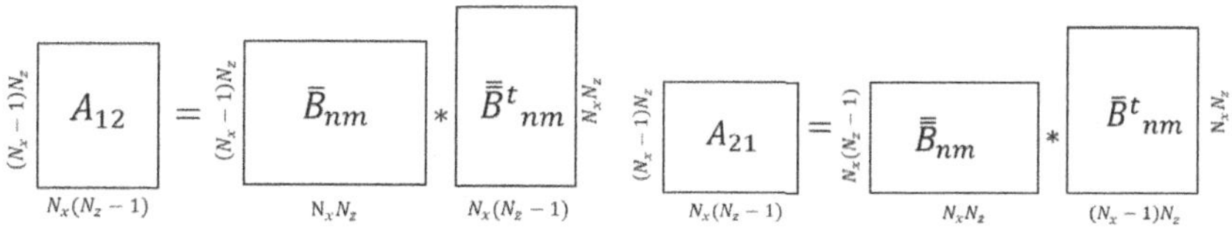

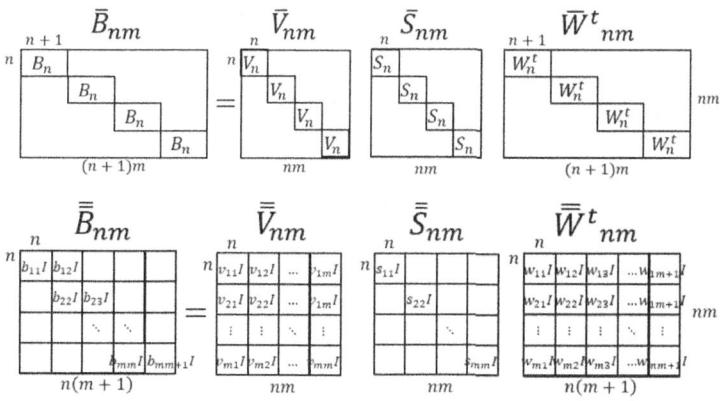

Fig. 5. Schematic illustration of diagonal blocks A_{12} and A_{21}.

4.2 SVD Decomposition

Using one-dimensional singular expansions $B_n = V_n S_n W_n^t$ and $B_m = V_m S_m W_m^t$, we obtain the block representation of the matrices $\overline{B}_{nm} = \overline{V}_{nm}\overline{D}_{nm}\overline{W}_{nm}^t$ and $\overline{\overline{B}}_{nm} = \overline{\overline{V}}_{nm}\overline{\overline{D}}_{nm}\overline{\overline{W}}_{nm}^t$ (Fig. 6).

Fig. 6. Block representation of the singular expansion of the 2D operators $\frac{\partial}{\partial x}$ and $\frac{\partial}{\partial z}$.

The matrices $\overline{V}_{nm}$ and $\overline{\overline{V}}_{nm}$ – consist of the eigenvectors of the matrices $\overline{A}_{nm}$ and $\overline{\overline{A}}_{nm}$, and the matrices $\overline{S}_{nm}$ and $\overline{\overline{S}}_{nm}$ are diagonal, consisting of singular values of these matrices (roots from the diagonal matrices of the eigenvalues of $\overline{D}_{nm}$ and $\overline{\overline{D}}_{nm}$).

5 Inversion of the Elasticity Operator

5.1 Splitting Scheme for Elasticity Operator

Let us summarise the above conclusions with respect to the matrix A:

$$A = \begin{pmatrix} A_{11} & A_{12} \\ A_{21} & A_{22} \end{pmatrix} =$$

$$\begin{pmatrix} \overline{B}_{Nx-1,Nz}\overline{B}_{Nx-1,Nz}^t + \overline{\overline{B}}_{Nx-1,Nz}\overline{\overline{B}}_{Nx-1,Nz}^t & \overline{B}_{Nx-1,Nz}\overline{\overline{B}}_{Nx,Nz-1}^t \\ \overline{B}_{Nx,Nz-1}\overline{B}_{Nx-1,Nz}^t & \overline{B}_{Nx,Nz-1}\overline{B}_{Nx,Nz-1}^t + \overline{\overline{B}}_{Nx,Nz-1}\overline{\overline{B}}_{Nx,Nz-1}^t \end{pmatrix}$$

$$(12)$$

Using the spectral and singular expansions we obtain:

$$
\begin{aligned}
A_{11} &= \overline{V}_{Nx-1Nz}\overline{\overline{V}}_{Nx-1Nz}(\overline{D}_{Nx-1Nz} + \overline{\overline{D}}_{Nx-1Nz})\overline{\overline{V}}^{t}_{Nx-1Nz}\overline{V}^{t}_{Nx-1Nz} \\
A_{12} &= \overline{V}_{Nx-1Nz}\overline{S}_{Nx-1Nz}\overline{W}^{t}_{Nx-1Nz}\overline{\overline{W}}_{NxNz-1}\overline{\overline{S}}_{NxNz-1}\overline{V}^{t}_{NxNz-1} \\
A_{21} &= \overline{\overline{V}}_{NxNz-1}\overline{\overline{S}}_{NxNz-1}\overline{\overline{W}}^{t}_{NxNz-1}\overline{W}_{Nx-1Nz}\overline{S}_{Nx-1Nz}\overline{V}^{t}_{Nx-1Nz} \\
A_{22} &= \overline{V}_{NxNz-1}\overline{\overline{V}}_{NxNz-1}(\overline{D}_{NxNz-1} + \overline{\overline{D}}_{NxNz-1})\overline{\overline{V}}^{t}_{NxNz-1}\overline{V}^{t}_{NxNz-1}
\end{aligned}
\tag{13}
$$

The matrix A is factorised into the product of the orthogonal matrices $\hat{V}$, $\hat{V}^{t}$ and the matrix $\hat{A}$ with diagonal blocks consisting only of diagonal elements:

$$
A = \hat{V}\hat{A}\hat{V}^{t},
$$

$$
\hat{V} = \begin{pmatrix} \overline{V}_{Nx-1Nz}\overline{\overline{V}}_{Nx-1Nz} & 0 \\ 0 & \overline{V}_{NxNz-1}\overline{V}_{NxNz-1} \end{pmatrix}
$$

$$
\hat{A} = \begin{pmatrix} \overline{D}_{Nx-1Nz} + \overline{\overline{D}}_{Nx-1Nz} & \hat{A}_{12} \\ \hat{A}_{21} & \overline{D}_{NxNz-1} + \overline{\overline{D}}_{NxNz-1} \end{pmatrix},
\tag{14}
$$

$$
\hat{A}_{12} = \overline{\overline{V}}^{t}_{Nx-1Nz}\overline{S}_{Nx-1Nz}\overline{W}^{t}_{Nx-1Nz}\overline{\overline{W}}_{NxNz-1}\overline{\overline{S}}_{NxNz-1}\overline{V}_{NxNz-1}
$$

$$
\hat{A}_{21} = \overline{V}^{t}_{NxNz-1}\overline{\overline{S}}_{NxNz-1}\overline{\overline{W}}^{t}_{NxNz-1}\overline{W}_{Nx-1Nz}\overline{S}_{Nx-1Nz}\overline{\overline{V}}^{t}_{Nx-1Nz}
$$

As a result, the solution of the system $Ax - b$ leads to the solution the system(15).

$$
\begin{aligned}
\hat{V}z &= b \\
\hat{A}y &= z \\
\hat{V}^{t}x &= y
\end{aligned}
\tag{15}
$$

Due to the orthogonality of $\hat{V}$, the solution of the first and third equations are trivial, let us focus on the solution of the second equation. The spectral properties of the matrix $\hat{A}$ remain the same as for A, but the off-diagonal blocks $\hat{A}_{12}$ and $\hat{A}_{21}$ are dense. Despite this, the operation of multiplying the matrix $\hat{A}$ by a vector can be performed very efficiently by using an approach similar to the dense matrix multiplication in the method of separation of variables for the 2D Laplace operator (see Fig. 4) to multiply the blocks $\hat{A}_{12}$ and $\hat{A}_{21}$ by vectors. That is, multiplication of the product of the matrices $\overline{\overline{V}}^{t}_{Nx-1Nz}\overline{S}_{Nx-1Nz}\overline{W}^{t}_{Nx-1Nz}\overline{\overline{W}}_{NxNz-1}\overline{\overline{S}}_{NxNz-1}\overline{V}_{NxNz-1}$ by vector u_z is rewritten as a multiplication of matrices $S_{N_x-1}W^{t}_{N_x-1}V_{N_x}U_z S_{N_z-1}W^{t}_{N_z-1}V_{N_z-1}$. This is shown schematically in Fig. 7.

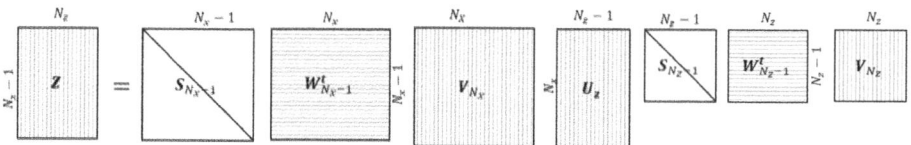

Fig. 7. Schematic representation of the multiplication of the matrix $\hat{A}_{12}$ by the vector u_z.

To simplify the counting of the arithmetic operations, let us consider the square computational domain ($N = N_x = N_z$). Then multiplying of the matrix $\hat{A}_{12}$ by a vector requires $O(8N^3) + O(4N^2)$ matrix of "add" and "multiply" operations, while formally at dense representation $\hat{A}_{12}$ requires $O(2N^4)$ operations.

The total number of operations required to multiply a matrix $\hat{A}$ by a vector is $O(16N^3) + O(12N^2)$. Theoretically, the second term could be ignored, but in practice, from a computational point of view, dense matrix multiplication operations are maximally optimised and parallelized. However, the multiplication of a diagonal matrix by a vector is not optimised. The reason is that the number of memory accesses of these operations is of the same order: $2N^2$ for multiplying two square matrices and N^2 for multiplying a diagonal matrix by a square matrix.

The multiple multiplication of $\hat{A}$ by a vector can be further optimised by pre-multiplying the matrices $F_{N_x-1} = S_{N_x-1}W^t_{N_x-1}V_{N_x}$, and $F_{N_z-1} = S_{N_z-1}W^t_{N_z-1}V_{N_z-1}$. The operation of multiplication of block $\hat{A}_{12}$ by vector u_z is written in the form $F_{N_x-1}U_zF_{N_z-1}$ (see Fig. 8).

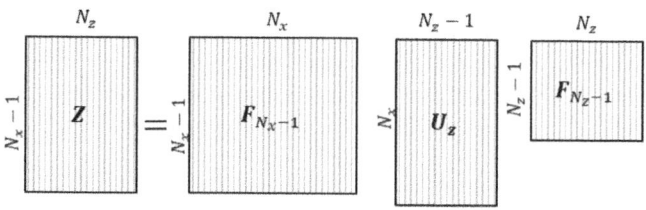

Fig. 8. Schematic representation of the optimised multiplication of matrix $\hat{A}_{12}$ by vector u_z

As a result, the total number of operations when multiplying the matrix $\hat{A}$ by a vector twice smaller is $O(8N^3) + O(4N^2)$ operations.

Note that all of this section is about the simplified elasticity operator (3). For the original one, with constant Lame coefficients (1), the decomposition of the matrix A will have the form (16).

$$\hat{A}_{11} = D_{11} = (\lambda + 2\mu)\overline{D}_{Nx-1Nz} + \mu\overline{\overline{D}}_{Nx-1Nz}$$
$$\hat{A}_{22} = D_{22} = \mu\overline{D}_{NxNz-1} + (\lambda + 2\mu)\overline{\overline{D}}_{NxNz-1}$$
$$\hat{A}_{12} = (\lambda + \mu)\hat{A}_{12}^t = \overline{V}_{Nx-1Nz}^t \overline{S}_{Nx-1Nz} \overline{W}_{Nx-1Nz}^t \overline{\overline{W}}_{NxNz-1} \overline{S}_{NxNz-1} \overline{V}_{NxNz-1}$$

$$(16)$$

5.2 Solution SLAE Algorithm

To solve the system $\hat{A}u = b$, we use the preconditioned conjugate gradient algorithm. The preconditioner $\hat{B}$ is a matrix consisting of diagonal blocks $\hat{A}_{11}$ and $\hat{A}_{22}$. This preconditioning is equivalent to solving by conjugate gradients (17) the system with matrix $\overline{A} = \hat{B}^{-1/2}\hat{A}\hat{B}^{-1/2}$.

$$\overline{A} = \begin{pmatrix} I & \overline{A}_{12} \\ \overline{A}_{21} & I \end{pmatrix}$$

$$\overline{A}_{12} = \overline{A}_{21}^t = D_{11}^{-1/2}\hat{A}_{12}D_{22}^{-1/2}$$

$$r_0 := b - \overline{A}x_0; \quad p_0 = r_0$$
$$Loop \; j = 0, 1, \ldots \; until \; converge$$
$$q_i = \overline{A}p_j$$
$$\alpha := \frac{(r_j, r_j)}{(q_j, p_j)}$$
$$x_{j+1} := x_j + \alpha_j p_j$$
$$r_{j+1} := r_j - \alpha_j q_j$$
$$\beta_j := \frac{(r_{j+1}, r_{j+1})}{(r_j, r_j)}$$
$$p_{j+1} := r_{j+1} + \beta_j p_j$$

$$(17)$$

As a result, the solution of the original SLAE $Ax = b$ consists of the next steps:

1. Compute: 1D singular decompositions;
2. Solve: $\hat{V}z = b$ using the orthogonality property of $\hat{V}$;
3. Product: $\overline{z} := \hat{B}^{-1/2}z$ using the diagonality property of $\hat{B}$;
4. Solve: SLAE $\overline{A}\overline{y} = \overline{z}$ by conjugate gradients;
5. Product: $\overline{y} := \hat{B}^{-1/2}y$ using the diagonality property of $\hat{B}$;
6. Solve: SLAE $\hat{V}^t x = y$ using the orthogonality property of $\hat{V}$.

The most expensive point is #3, which is implemented in software using optimised functions from mathematical libraries. As mentioned above, to simplify FLOP counting, we assume $N = N_x = N_z$. Then the dimensions of the SLAEs and vectors are equal to $2N^2$. Two groups of operations can be considered: 1) multiplication of dense matrices of size $N \times N$ (blocks appearing in the multiplication of $\overline{A}p_j$), 2) addition of vectors with dimensions of order N^2 (recalculation of x_{j+1}, r_{j+1} and p_{j+1}). The number of arithmetic operations in the first case is $O(N^3)$ (estimates are given in the previous section); for vector addition, the number of operations is $O(N^2)$. It is also important to take into account the number of access to RAM, which is approximately the same in both cases: $O(N^2)$. In the context of numerical experiments, we analyse these operations separately. It is also worth estimating the amount of memory needed to store SLAEs and intermediate data (see Table 1).

Table 1. Amount of memory used by different functions or data structures.

Data	Number of memory elements for storage
Right hand side b	$2N^2$
Matrix A (CSR format)	$10N^2$
Spectral decomposition A	$8N^2$
(modification of $\hat{V}, \hat{B}, \hat{A}$)	$5N^2$ (square mesh)
Iterative algorithm (vectors $x_{j+1}, r_{j+1}, p_{j+1}, q_{j+1}$)	$8N^2$

Due to symmetry, the matrix A consists of 10 diagonals of size $n = N^2$. However, it is possible to avoid storing the original matrix by using on-the-fly matrix element generation during the operation of multiplication by a vector.

To store the above decomposition of A into multipliers, we need $8N^2$ elements, i.e. $\hat{V}$ – four dense matrices $V_{N_x-1}, V_{N_z}, V_{N_x}, V_{N_z-1}$ of size $N \times N$, a diagonal $\hat{B}$ of size $2N^2$ and two dense blocks F_{N_x-1}, F_{N_z-1} of size $N \times N$ defining the operation of multiplying the matrix $\overline{A}$ by a vector. Also, the iterative algorithm needs to store four vectors $x_{j+1}, r_{j+1}, p_{j+1}, q_{j+1}$ of size $2N^2$, as well as a pair of temporary arrays of size N^2 needed in the process of multiplying $\overline{A}$ by a vector. To estimate the peak load, it is worth noting that the initial matrix A as well as the right-hand side of b are not used in the iterative process; technically, they can be removed from memory and an estimate of $16N^2$ elements for the peak load can be obtained. Recall that these estimates are true for both square and rectangular meshes. In the case of square meshes ($N_x = N_z$) we can save on memory by using two vectors V_{N_x-1}, V_{N_x-1} instead of four, and one vector F_{N_x-1} and get a peak load of $13N^2$.

Next, we present the results of numerical experiments.

6   Numerical Experiments

There are some statements that should be checked in the experiments. The 1st one is the independence of the convergence rate on the mesh size. The second statement – dependence of convergence rate on coefficients λ and μ and on boundary types (Dirichlet or Neuman). The third investigation should be made – comparison of the iterative algorithm with commercial sparse direct solver from Intel MKL. The criteria of comparison are computation time and memory consumption. The quality of the solution is checked by the relative residual $||b - Ax||/||b||$.

The computations were performed in double precision on **Intel(R) Xeon(R) CPU E5-2680 v3 @ 2.50GHz, 256G RAM**.

Memory usage optimisation makes it possible to solve the problem on a mesh of 10^9 nodes on a server with 128G RAM. The convergence of the iterative process does not critically depend on both the boundary conditions and the ratio of λ and μ. Although, as expected, the number of iterations increases when the

Table 2. Dependence of the number CG iterations on different physical properties for the largest problem. The stopping criteria is relative residual 10^{-10}.

Computational mesh: 10^9 nodes ($N_x = N_z = 32\,000$)	Iteration number	Computational time, s.	Relative residual of initial SLAE
$\lambda = 10\mu$, Neumann	35	13506	$3.5 * 10^{-9}$
$\lambda = \mu$, Neumann	16	6735	$3.7 * 10^{-9}$
$\lambda = \mu$, Dirichlet	8	3905	$1.5 * 10^{-11}$

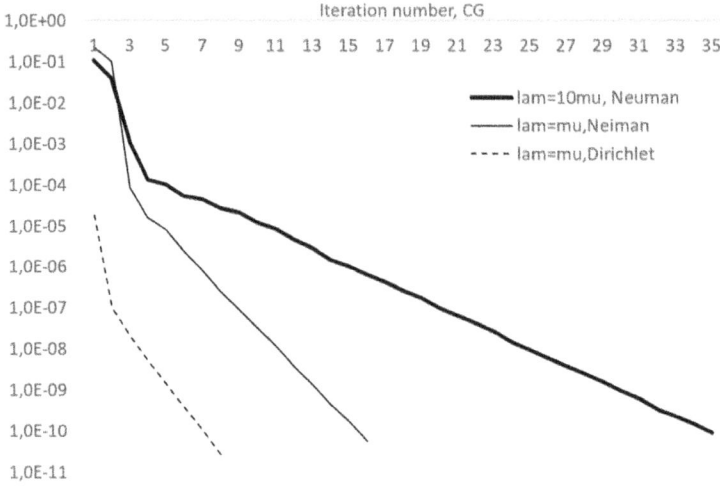

Fig. 9. The relative residual behaviour of the iterative process for the example of three variants of the problem.

Table 3. CG computational process profiling with a stopping criterion on the relative residual 10^{-10}.

$\lambda = 10\mu$, Neumann; computational mesh $N_x = N_z =$	Memory consumption, G	Number of iterations	CG computational time, s.	Time to solve initial SLAE, s.	Initial SLAE relative residual
1 000	0.1	40	1.2	1.3	$0.6 * 10^9$
2 000	0.5	39	6.9	7.4	$0.7 * 10^9$
4 000	1.9	39	37.5	39.9	$0.7 * 10^9$
8 000	7.4	38	238	251	$1.3 * 10^9$
16 000	29.4	36	1671	1767	$2.5 * 10^9$
32 000	117.5	35	12786	13506	$3.5 * 10^9$

ratio λ/μ increases, as well as when the Neumann condition is used (Table 2 and Fig. 9).

The convergence rate does not depend on the mesh size. For significantly different values of the coefficients λ and μ for 8 nested meshes, the characteristics

Table 4. Computational time for operations of different complexity: GEMM (N^3) and vector addition/multiplication (N^2); memory cost as a function of mesh size.

$\lambda = 10\mu$, Neumann; computational mesh $N_x = N_z =$	Memory consumption, G	Number of iterations	GEMM (N^3)	Other functions (N^2 and less)
1 000	0.1	40	0.6	0.6
2 000	0.5	39	4.2	2.7
4 000	1.9	39	27.1	10.4
8 000	7.4	38	198	40
16 000	29.4	36	1504	167
32 000	117.5	35	11818	968

of the computational process are shown in Table 3. The profiling of the counting time for different arithmetic operations is shown in Table 4.

Comparison with direct solver showed the effectiveness of the proposed algorithm, but it should be noted that direct methods are intended mainly for solving problems in inhomogeneous media, as well as in areas with complex geometry.

Table 5. Comparison with direct solver for high contrast λ/μ ratio.

$\lambda = 10\mu$, Neumann; computational mesh $N_x = N_z =$	Memory consumption, G		Time to solve initial SLAE, s.	
	Spectral decomposition	Direct solver	Spectral decomposition	Direct solver
1 000	0.1	5.1	1.3	11.2
2 000	0.5	14.5	7.4	50.4
4 000	1.9	53.9	39.9	254
8 000	7.4	No memory	251	No memory
16 000	29.4	No memory	1767	No memory
32 000	117.5	No memory	13506	No memory

7   Conclusion

For the numerical solution of the elasticity problem in the quasi-static state, an algorithm for the construction of a preconditioner in a rectangular domain with arbitrary boundary conditions has been developed. It uses the approach of splitting scheme in different directions together with the spectral decomposition of the Laplace operator. This approach has allowed the development of an efficient algorithm for solving the elasticity problem in a homogeneous medium. The proposed algorithm is 'memory limited', so its implementation uses the functionality of the high performance dense matrix multiplication (GEMM), giving efficiency close to the peak CPU. Computational experiments confirmed the high performance of the algorithm on various examples. In particular, the elasticity problem was solved on a computational mesh of 10^9 nodes on a server with 128G RAM.

References

1. Intel math kernel library documentation. https://software.intel.com/en-us/intel-mkl/
2. Balay, S., et al.: PETSc users manual. Tech. Rep. ANL-95/11 - Revision 3.5, Argonne National Laboratory (2014)
3. Biot, M.A.: Theory of propagation of elastic waves in fluid-saturated porous solid i. low-frequency range. J. Acoust. Soc. Am. **28**, 168–178 (1956)
4. Briggs, W., Henson, V., McCormick, S.: A Multigrid Tutorial, 2nd Edition (2000)
5. Huckle, T.: Multigrid preconditioning and toeplitz matrices (2000)
6. Saad, Y.: A basic tool-kit for sparse matrix computations. Web cite (2021). https://www-users.cse.umn.edu/~saad/software/SPARSKIT/
7. Trujillo-Ortiz, A.: Roystest. MATLAB Central File Exchange (2020). https://www.mathworks.com/matlabcentral/fileexchange/17811-roystest
8. Saad, Y.: Iterative Methods for Sparse Linear Systems. PWS Publishing, New York (1996)

Numerical Implementation of Boundary Conditions for Finite Difference Method on Staggered Grid for Wave Propagation in Saturated Porous Medium

Galina Reshetova[1]([✉]) ⓘ and Evgeniy Romenski[2] ⓘ

[1] Institute of Computational Mathematics and Mathematical Geophysics SB RAS, Novosibirsk 630090, Russia
kgv@nmsf.sscc.ru
[2] Sobolev Institute of Mathematics SB RAS, Novosibirsk 630090, Russia
evrom@math.nsc.ru

Abstract. This paper presents a numerical implementation of boundary conditions in the finite difference staggered grid method for a Hyperbolic Thermodynamically Compatible (HTC) model of wavefields simulations in a three-phase model of a deformable porous medium saturated with a mixture of two fluids. A number of test problems on the propagation of high-frequency waves have been solved and it has been shown that the developed numerical method is applicable to non-stationary processes in domains of complex structure. The method can also be applied to obtain a steady-state solution of the equilibrium equations of a saturated porous medium by solving a nonstationary system.

Keywords: Wavefield simulation · Fluid saturated porous medium · Boundary conditions · Staggered grid finite difference scheme

1 Introduction

In recent years, in connection with the development of new technologies and the need to intensify the development of natural resources, there is a need to model wave processes in porous media. The most widely accepted model for this is the Biot model [1,2] and its generalizations (see [3] and references therein), which are generally accepted in the geophysical community. However, this model has significant limitations in its applicability, namely, it is unclear how to generalize it to the case when the saturating fluid is multiphase, when the medium is subject to finite deformations, etc.

This paper is based on the use of a Hyperbolic Thermodynamically Compatible (HTC) model for simulations of wavefields in a saturated deformable porous medium, which was proposed and studied in [4–8]. These equations are derived from the general multiphase HTC model, which in turn is obtained on the basis of the theory of HTC equations of continuum mechanics (see [11] and references

O. Gervasi et al. (Eds.): ICCSA 2025 Workshops, LNCS 15888, pp. 359–375, 2026.
https://doi.org/10.1007/978-3-031-97596-7_24

therein). The governing equations of the model form a first-order hyperbolic system and, due to their structure, allow the use of an effective finite difference method on a staggered grid. Our previous studies of wavefields in domains of complex structure were performed for unbounded domains using the Perfectly Matched Layers (PML) method. In fact, to solve many practical problems, it is necessary to study wavefields in bounded domains, that is, to use boundary conditions. The aim of this work is the numerical implementation of boundary conditions for the finite difference method on a staggered grid.

The rest of the paper is organized as follows. In Sect. 2 the governing equations for wave propagation in the porous medium saturated with the mixture of two fluids are formulated and boundary conditions, which are used in the numerical test problems are presented. Section 3 presents solutions to a series of test problems, including a plane wave propagating from a boundary, the interaction of a plane wave with an inclusion, and finding a steady-state solution of a medium in equilibrium by solving non-stationary equations. Finally, the Appendix provides a description of the finite difference scheme used in the calculations on a staggered grid.

2   Governing Equations for Wavefields in a Porous Medium Saturated with a Two-Phase Fluid

2.1   Governing Equations of the Model

To model wavefields in a deformed porous medium saturated with a mixture of two fluids (in our case the gas-liquid mixture), we use the Hyperbolic Thermodynamically Compatible (HTC) model [8]. The system of governing equations presented below can be obtained using a general multiphase model of a mixture of liquids saturating a deformed porous medium. The equations of this general model are hyperbolic, and its solutions satisfy the laws of thermodynamics (conservation of energy and increase in entropy). The simplified linear model that we use in this paper is also hyperbolic and satisfies the thermodynamic law of energy dissipation [8].

Let us assume that the mixture of fluids consists of two liquids with numbers 1 and 2, and that the deformed skeletal phase has number 3. Then the porosity is equal to $\phi = 1 - \alpha_1^0 - \alpha_2^0$. Assume also that the constant phase mass densities are ρ_1^0, ρ_2^0, ρ_3^0, and then the mass density of the mixture is $\rho_0 = \alpha_1^0 \rho_1^0 + \alpha_2^0 \rho_2^0 + \alpha_3^0 \rho_3^0$. Let us formulate a three-dimensional version of governing equations. The complete set of state variables for the description of the medium consists of the velocity vector of the mixture V^i, $i = 1, 2, 3$, the velocities of movement of the first and second phases relative to the third phase (relative velocities) W_1^i, $i = 1, 2, 3$ and W_2^i, $i = 1, 2, 3$, shear stress (deviatoric part of the stress tensor) Σ_{ik}, $i, k = 1, 2, 3$, and pressure P.

Using the above notations, we formulate a closed system for wavefields that includes equations for the mixture velocity and relative velocities, as well as for pressure and shear stress, and has the form

$$\rho_0 \frac{\partial V^i}{\partial t} + \frac{\partial P}{\partial x_i} - \frac{\partial \Sigma_{ik}}{\partial x_k} = \Phi^i, \tag{1a}$$

$$\frac{\partial W_1^i}{\partial t} + \left(\frac{1}{\rho_1^0} - \frac{1}{\rho_3^0} \right) \frac{\partial P}{\partial x_i} = -\Lambda_1^i, \tag{1b}$$

$$\frac{\partial W_2^i}{\partial t} + \left(\frac{1}{\rho_2^0} - \frac{1}{\rho_3^0} \right) \frac{\partial P}{\partial x_i} = -\Lambda_2^i, \tag{1c}$$

$$\frac{\partial P}{\partial t} + K \frac{\partial V^k}{\partial x_k} + K_1' \frac{\partial W_1^k}{\partial x_k} + K_2' \frac{\partial W_2^k}{\partial x_k} = 0, \tag{1d}$$

$$\frac{\partial \Sigma_{ik}}{\partial t} - \mu \left(\left(\frac{\partial V^i}{\partial x_k} + \frac{\partial V^k}{\partial x_i} \right) - \frac{2}{3} \delta_{ik} \left(\frac{\partial V^1}{\partial x_1} + \frac{\partial V^2}{\partial x_2} + \frac{\partial V^3}{\partial x_3} \right) \right) = -\frac{\Sigma_{ik}}{\tau}, \tag{1e}$$

Here, $K = \left(\frac{\alpha_1^0}{K_1} + \frac{\alpha_2^0}{K_2} + \frac{\alpha_3^0}{K_3} \right)^{-1}$ is the bulk modulus of the three-phase mixture, where K_1, K_2, K_3 are the phase bulk moduli. $K_a' = (\alpha_a^0 - c_a^0)K, (a = 1, 2)$, where $c_1^0 = \alpha_1^0 \rho_1^0 / \rho^0$, $c_2^0 = \alpha_2^0 \rho_2^0 / \rho^0$ are the mass fractions of fluids, $\mu = c_1^0 \mu_1 + c_2^0 \mu_2 + c_3^0 \mu_3$ is the shear modulus of the mixture and μ_1, μ_2, μ_3 are the shear moduli of the phases. In addition, we assume that the shear moduli of the liquids are zero, which means that $\mu = c_3^0 \mu_3$.

The equations have right-hand sides that are responsible for external forces or processes related to internal interactions between phases. For example, the term Φ^i in equation (1a) is responsible for the sources of external forces that can generate seismic waves within the porous medium. The terms Λ_1^i, Λ_2^i in the equations (1b), (1c) for relative velocities and Σ_{ij}/τ in the equation (1e) for shear stress describe interfacial friction and shear stress relaxation respectively.

The total stress tensor of the mixture can be computed as $\sigma_{ik} = \Sigma_{ik} - P$ and is connected with the total strain tensor of the mixture ε_{ik} via Hooke's law:

$$\sigma_{ik} = \lambda(\varepsilon_{11} + \varepsilon_{22} + \varepsilon_{33})\delta_{ik} + 2\mu\varepsilon_{ik}. \tag{2}$$

The shear stress and pressure are connected with the strain tensor as

$$\Sigma_{ik} = 2\mu \left(\varepsilon_{ik} - \delta_{ik} \frac{(\varepsilon_{11} + \varepsilon_{22} + \varepsilon_{33})}{3} \right), \quad P = -K(\varepsilon_{11} + \varepsilon_{22} + \varepsilon_{33}). \tag{3}$$

Here the bulk modulus K and shear modulus μ of the mixture are defined above, and Lame constant λ can be computed with the use of the relation $K = \lambda + \frac{2}{3}\mu$.

The system(1) is hyperbolic, and in the one-dimensional case its characteristic velocities, equal to the velocities of two longitudinal waves (fast and slow compression waves), can be calculated by the formula

$$C_1 = \frac{1}{\sqrt{2\rho_0}} \sqrt{\left(\tilde{K} + \frac{\rho_0 Q}{\rho_1^0 \rho_2^0 \rho_3^0}\right) + \sqrt{\left(\tilde{K} + \frac{\rho_0 Q}{\rho_1^0 \rho_2^0 \rho_3^0}\right)^2 + 4(K - \tilde{K})\frac{\rho_0 Q}{\rho_1^0 \rho_2^0 \rho_3^0}}} \quad (4)$$

$$C_2 = \frac{1}{\sqrt{2\rho_0}} \sqrt{\left(\tilde{K} + \frac{\rho_0 Q}{\rho_1^0 \rho_2^0 \rho_3^0}\right) - \sqrt{\left(\tilde{K} + \frac{\rho_0 Q}{\rho_1^0 \rho_2^0 \rho_3^0}\right)^2 + 4(K - \tilde{K})\frac{\rho_0 Q}{\rho_1^0 \rho_2^0 \rho_3^0}}} \quad (5)$$

and the shear wave can be calculated by the formula

$$C_3 = \sqrt{\frac{\mu}{\rho_0}}, \quad (6)$$

where $\tilde{K} = K + \frac{4}{3}\mu$, $Q = \rho_2^0(\rho_3^0 - \rho_1^0)K_1' + \rho_1^0(\rho_3^0 - \rho_2^0)K_2'$.

In [8] it was shown that the solutions of system (1) admit the additional energy dissipation law

$$\frac{\partial \mathcal{E}}{\partial t} + \frac{\partial \Pi_k}{\partial x_k} = -\mathcal{Q}, \quad (7)$$

where the total energy $\mathcal{E}$ of the porous medium is equal to

$$\mathcal{E} = \rho_0 \frac{V^i V^i}{2} + \frac{\rho_0}{2} \sum_{a=1}^{2} c_a^0 \sum_{k=1}^{3} (W_a^k)^2 - \frac{\rho_0}{2} \sum_{k=1}^{3} \left(\sum_{a=1}^{2} c_a^0 W_a^k\right)^2 + \frac{1}{2K}P^2 + \frac{\Sigma_{ij}\Sigma_{ji}}{4\mu},$$

$$(8)$$

and $\Pi_k = PV^k + \sum_{a=1}^{2}(\alpha_a^0 - c_a^0)PW_a^k - \Sigma_{ik}V^i$ is the energy flux and $\mathcal{Q} = \sum_{a=1}^{2} \mathcal{E}_{W_a^i}\Lambda_a^i + \frac{1}{\mu\tau}\Sigma_{ij}\Sigma_{ji}$ is the energy loss. Here, summation over repeating indices i, j is assumed.

Note that when solving the problem in the two-dimensional case in the plane x_1, x_2, the component of the deviator Σ_{33} can be non-zero and is found from the identity $\Sigma_{11} + \Sigma_{22} + \Sigma_{33} = 0$.

Note also that in all test cases below, we do not take into account dissipative source terms (interfacial friction and relaxation of shear stress), setting $\Lambda_1^i = 0$, $\Lambda_2^i = 0$, $\tau = \infty$.

2.2 Boundary Conditions

Let us consider the most common case of boundary conditions, when stresses are defined on the boundary. The system (1) is hyperbolic, so, according to the theory, the number of boundary conditions should coincide with the number of characteristics going from the boundary into the domain. The solutions of the equations(1) are characterised by three velocities, corresponding to two compression waves (fast and slow) and a shear wave. This means that we must define three boundary conditions. We consider two conditions with given normal and shear stresses, as well as the condition of no flow along the normal to the boundary.

If $\mathbf{n}$ is the normal vector to the boundary, and $\sigma = \Sigma - P\mathbf{I}$ is the total stress tensor, then the boundary conditions for the stresses read as

$$(\sigma, \mathbf{n}) = \mathbf{F}(t), \tag{9}$$

where in the two-dimensional case $\mathbf{F}(t) = (F^1(t), F^2(t))^T$ and $F^1(t), F^2(t)$ are given functions. In component form (9) reads as $\sigma_n = F^1(t)$, $\sigma_t = F^2(t)$, where σ_n, σ_t are normal and tangential stresses. To set the no-flow condition, it is sufficient to set one relative velocity to zero, and the equality of the second relative velocity to zero follows from the equations (1b) and (1c). We set the no-flow condition as

$$(\mathbf{W_1}, \mathbf{n}) = 0, \tag{10}$$

which automatically implies $(\mathbf{W_2}, \mathbf{n}) = 0$ and we will add this to the list of boundary conditions in the finite difference scheme.

In the numerical test cases presented below we consider the rectangular domain $(x, y) \in [-a, a] \times [-b, b]$ with the following boundary conditions

$$\sigma_{11}|_{x=-a} = F_1^1(t), \ \sigma_{12}|_{x=-a} = F_1^2(t), \ W_1^1|_{x=-a} = 0, \ W_2^1|_{x=-a} = 0, \tag{11}$$

$$\sigma_{11}|_{x=a} = F_2^1(t), \ \sigma_{12}|_{x=a} = F_2^2(t), \ W_1^1|_{x=a} = 0, \ W_2^1|_{x=a} = 0 \tag{12}$$

$$\sigma_{22}|_{y=-b} = F_3^1(t), \ \sigma_{12}|_{y=-b} = F_3^2(t), \ W_1^2|_{y=-b} = 0, \ W_2^2|_{y=-b} = 0, \tag{13}$$

$$\sigma_{22}|_{y=b} = F_4^1(t), \ \sigma_{12}|_{y=b} = F_4^2(t), \ W_1^2|_{y=b} = 0, \ W_2^1|_{y=b} = 0. \tag{14}$$

3 Numerical Simulations

In this section, we perform a numerical analysis of the key characteristics of small-amplitude wave propagation in a porous medium containing a saturated compressible mixture of two fluids. To numerically solve the system of equations (1), we use finite difference methods on a staggered grid [12–14] with a fourth order accuracy in space and a second order accuracy in time.

3.1 Finite Difference Approximation

The derivation of finite difference scheme for solving system (1) using the staggered grid follows a similar approach to that in [12,13]. The staggered grid finite difference method is based on the finite volume discretization technique discussed in particular in [14] and is often used for systems of equations derived from physical conservation principles. A major advantage of this method is that it avoids the need to approximate the fluxes during the computation, as these values are predetermined, thereby increasing both the efficiency and reliability of the approach. Within this framework, we specify the deviatoric stresses, presure and velocities at distinct grid points in both space and time, achieving a fourth order accuracy approximation with a minimum difference scheme stencil.

First, we construct a grid within the (t, x_1, x_2) time-space framework, with integer nodes at $t^n = n\Delta t$, $x_1^i = i\Delta x_1$, $x_2^j = j\Delta x_2$ and with semi-integer nodes at $t^{n+1/2} = (n + 1/2)\Delta t$, $x_1^{i+1/2} = (i + 1/2)\Delta x_1$, $x_2^{j+1/2} = (j + 1/2)\Delta x_2$. Here Δt and Δx_1, Δx_2 denote the grid spacing in time and space respectively.

We assume that the material parameters remain constant within each grid cell $[x_1^{i-1/2}, x_1^{i+1/2}] \times [x_2^{j-1/2}, x_2^{j+1/2}]$, allowing potential discontinuities at the grid boundaries. The mixture velocity V^1 and the relative velocities W_1^1 and W_2^1 are defined at the nodes $(n, i + 1/2, j)$ and are denoted as $(V^1)_{i+1/2,j}^n$, $(W_1^1)_{i+1/2,j}^n$, and $(W_2^1)_{i+1/2,j}^n$. Similarly, the velocities V^2, W_1^2 and W_2^2 are defined at the nodes $(n, i, j+1/2)$ and are denoted as $(V^2)_{i,j+1/2}^n$, $(W_1^2)_{i,j+1/2}^n$ and $(W_2^2)_{i,j+1/2}^n$.

The pressure and diagonal deviatoric stresses are assigned to the integer nodes in space and semi-integer nodes in time at $(n + 1/2, i, j)$, denoted as $(P)_{i,j}^{n+1/2}$, $(\Sigma_{11})_{i,j}^{n+1/2}$ and $(\Sigma_{22})_{i,j}^{n+1/2}$. The shear stress is assigned to the nodes $(n + 1/2, i + 1/2, j + 1/2)$ and denoted as $(\Sigma_{12})_{i+1/2,j+1/2}^{n+1/2}$. The spatial configuration of the nodes on the staggered grid is shown in Fig. 1.

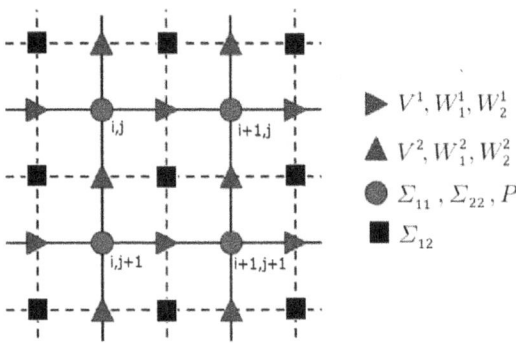

Fig. 1. The relative position of deviatoric stresses, pressure, mixture velocities and relative velocities on the staggered grid.

For compactness, we introduce a few notations for a discrete function $f_{i,j}^n = f(t^n, x_1^i, x_2^j)$:

- Second-order central difference operators

$$D_t[f]_{i,j}^n = \frac{(f)_{i,j}^{n+1/2} - (f)_{i,j}^{n-1/2}}{\Delta t}, \qquad A_t[f]_{i,j}^n = \frac{(f)_{i,j}^{n+1/2} + (f)_{i,j}^{n-1/2}}{2}, \quad (15)$$

- Fourth-order central difference operators (Levander stencil)

$$D_1[f]_{i,j}^n = \frac{1}{\Delta x_1}\left\{ \frac{9}{8}\left((f)_{i+1/2,j}^n - (f)_{i-1/2,j}^n\right) - \frac{1}{24}\left((f)_{i+3/2,j}^n - (f)_{i-3/2,j}^n\right)\right\}, \tag{16}$$

$$D_2[f]_{i,j}^n = \frac{1}{\Delta x_2}\left\{ \frac{9}{8}\left((f)_{i,j+1/2}^n - (f)_{i,j-1/2}^n\right) - \frac{1}{24}\left((f)_{i,j+3/2}^n - (f)_{i,j-3/2}^n\right)\right\}, \tag{17}$$

– Volumetric arithmetic averaging

$$\langle f \rangle_{i+1/2,j}^n = (f_{i,j}^n + f_{i+1,j}^n)/2, \qquad \langle f \rangle_{i,j+1/2}^n = (f_{i,j}^n + f_{i,j+1}^n)/2, \qquad (18)$$

– Harmonic averaging by [15]

$$\{f\}_{i+1/2,j+1/2}^n = \left[\frac{1}{4} \left(\frac{1}{f_{i,j}^n} + \frac{1}{f_{i+1,j}^n} + \frac{1}{f_{i,j+1}^n} + \frac{1}{f_{i+1,j+1}^n} \right) \right]^{-1}. \qquad (19)$$

Using these notation, the finite difference equations can be written as

$$D_t[V^1]_{i+1/2,j}^{n-1/2} = -1/\langle \rho^0 \rangle_{i+1/2,j} D_1[P]_{i+1/2,j}^{n-1/2} +$$
$$+1/\langle \rho^0 \rangle_{i+1/2,j} \left(D_1[\Sigma_{11}]_{i+1/2,j}^{n-1/2} + D_2[\Sigma_{12}]_{i+1/2,j}^{n-1/2} \right) + (\Phi^1)_{i+1/2,j}^{n-1/2},$$

$$D_t[V^2]_{i,j+1/2}^{n-1/2} = -1/\langle \rho^0 \rangle_{i,j+1/2} D_2[P]_{i,j+1/2}^{n-1/2} +$$
$$+1/\langle \rho^0 \rangle_{i,j+1/2} \left(D_1[\Sigma_{12}]_{i,j+1/2}^{n-1/2} + D_2[\Sigma_{22}]_{i,j+1/2}^{n-1/2} \right) + (\Phi^2)_{i,j+1/2}^{n-1/2},$$

$$D_t[W_1^1]_{i+1/2,j}^{n-1/2} = -\langle 1/\rho_1^0 - 1/\rho_3^0 \rangle_{i+1/2,j} D_1[P]_{i+1/2,j}^{n-1/2} - A_t[A_1^1]_{i+1/2,j}^{n-1/2},$$

$$D_t[W_2^1]_{i+1/2,j}^{n-1/2} = -\langle 1/\rho_2^0 - 1/\rho_3^0 \rangle_{i+1/2,j} D_1[P]_{i+1/2,j}^{n-1/2} - A_t[A_2^1]_{i+1/2,j}^{n-1/2},$$

$$D_t[W_1^2]_{i,j+1/2}^{n-1/2} = -\langle 1/\rho_1^0 - 1/\rho_3^0 \rangle_{i,j+1/2} D_2[P]_{i,j+1/2}^{n-1/2} - A_t[A_1^2]_{i,j+1/2}^{n-1/2},$$

$$D_t[W_2^2]_{i,j+1/2}^{n-1/2} = -\langle 1/\rho_2^0 - 1/\rho_3^0 \rangle_{i,j+1/2} D_2[P]_{i,j+1/2}^{n-1/2} - A_t[A_2^2]_{i,j+1/2}^{n-1/2},$$

$$D_t[P]_{i,j}^n = -(K)_{i,j} \left(D_1[V^1]_{i,j}^n + D_2[V^2]_{i,j}^n \right) -$$
$$-(K_1')_{i,j} \left(D_1[W_1^1]_{i,j}^n + D_2[W_1^2]_{i,j}^n \right) - (K_2')_{i,j} \left(D_1[W_2^1]_{i,j}^n + D_2[W_2^2]_{i,j}^n \right),$$

$$D_t[\Sigma_{11}]_{i,j}^n = (\mu)_{i,j} \left(\tfrac{4}{3} D_1[V^1]_{i,j}^n - \tfrac{2}{3} D_2[V^2]_{i,j}^n \right) - (1/\tau)_{i,j} A_t[\Sigma_{11}]_{i,j}^n,$$

$$D_t[\Sigma_{22}]_{i,j}^n = (\mu)_{i,j} \left(\tfrac{4}{3} D_2[V^2]_{i,j}^n - \tfrac{2}{3} D_1[V^1]_{i,j}^n \right) - (1/\tau)_{i,j} A_t[\Sigma_{22}]_{i,j}^n,$$

$$D_t[\Sigma_{12}]_{i+1/2,j+1/2}^n = \{\mu\}_{i+1/2,j+1/2} \left(D_1[V^2]_{i+1/2,j+1/2}^n + D_2[V^1]_{i+1/2,j+1/2}^n \right) -$$
$$- \{1/\tau\}_{i+1/2,j+1/2} A_t[\Sigma_{12}]_{i+1/2,j+1/2}^n.$$

The scheme obtained is an explicit finite difference scheme of fourth-order accuracy in time and space for a homogeneous elastic medium. The stability conditions and dispersion properties can be found in [12].

3.2   Approximation of Boundary Conditions on Staggered Grid

The setting of boundary conditions is often problem-specific and can vary depending on the physical nature of the process being modelled. For example, in geophysical problems when modelling underground aquifers in the context of oil or gas field development, constant wall pressure is required.

When approximating boundary conditions by finite differences on staggered meshes, it is important to note that some variables may be specified at integer nodes and others at semi-integer nodes. It is known that such a shift of nodes and variables significantly affects the accuracy and stability of the numerical solution, and also provides a more accurate representation of the physical processes occurring at the boundaries of the computational domain.

For example, the values of physical parameters such as pressure or temperature are often specified in integer mesh nodes. This approach ensures that conditions at the boundaries are accurately accounted for, contributing to a more accurate representation of values at points where transitions occur. Conversely, components such as velocities or gradients associated with flow may be specified in semi-integer nodes. This is because such nodes facilitate a more accurate approximation of derivatives and interactions between neighboring nodes, which is particularly important for dynamic processes.

Approximation of boundary conditions using both integer and semi-integer nodes allows us to take into account various physical processes occurring on the boundary of the region, while ensuring the required accuracy of calculations by the difference scheme.

The approximation of the boundary conditions (11)–(14) on the staggered grid introduced in Sect. 3.1 is shown in the Fig. 2. The nodes where specific boundary conditions occur are highlighted in red.

Below, three test problems are considered using the developed finite difference method on a staggered grid.

3.3   Test 1

Consider a two-dimensional homogeneous poroelastic medium saturated with a mixture of water and gas in a solid deformable skeleton. The properties of the skeleton and pore fluid are given in Table 1.

The simulations were performed for the square computational domain $(x, y) \in [-a, a] \times [-b, b]$ with $a = b = 0.01\ m$. The nodes of the uniform finite grid $2000 * 2000$ have a spatial discretization of $1 \cdot 10^{-5}\ m$ and time step of $1 \cdot 10^{-9}\ s$.

The wavefield is exited by the forces applied to the domain boundaries as follows:

$$\sigma_{11}|_{x=-a} = F_1^1(t), \ \sigma_{12}|_{x=-a} = 0, \ W_1^1|_{x=-a} = 0, \ W_2^1|_{x=-a} = 0, \qquad (20)$$

$$\sigma_{11}|_{x=a} = 0, \ \sigma_{12}|_{x=a} = 0, \ W_1^1|_{x=a} = 0, \ W_2^1|_{x=a} = 0 \qquad (21)$$

$$\sigma_{22}|_{x=-b} = 0, \ \sigma_{12}|_{x=-b} = 0, \ W_1^2|_{x=-b} = 0, \ W_2^2|_{x=-b} = 0, \qquad (22)$$

$$\sigma_{22}|_{x=b} = 0, \ \sigma_{12}|_{x=b} = 0, \ W_1^2|_{x=b} = 0, \ W_2^1|_{x=b} = 0. \qquad (23)$$

where $F_1^1(t)$ is a Gaussian pulse function with source frequency $f_0 = 10^6$ and time delay $t_0 = 1/f_0\ s$:

$$F_1^1(t) = exp[-(\pi f_0(t - t_0))^2], \qquad (24)$$

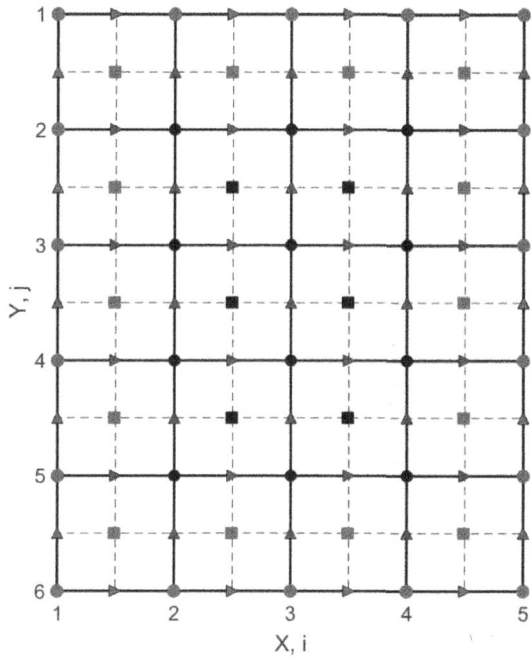

Fig. 2. Nodes involved in approximating the boundary conditions (11)–(14) on the staggered grid. The nodes where specific boundary conditions are defined are highlighted in red colour. (Color figure online)

The boundary conditions are chosen so as to excite a plane wave propagating from left to right along the x-axis.

This simple test allows us to evaluate both the seismic wave propagation velocities in porous media as a function of the composition of volume fractions, and the correctness of the numerical realization of the boundary conditions themselves.

Depending on the chosen phases, the model (1) can describe a purely elastic medium with given seismic velocities, such as pure solid ($\alpha_1^0 = 0$, $\alpha_2^0 = 0$, $\alpha_3^0 = 1$), pure air ($\alpha_1^0 = 1$, $\alpha_2^0 = 0$, $\alpha_3^0 = 0$) or pure water ($\alpha_1^0 = 0$, $\alpha_2^0 = 1$, $\alpha_3^0 = 0$), or a porous medium containing one or two fluid phases in different proportions.

Consider a homogeneous poroelastic medium containing a solid deformable skeleton saturated with 70% water ($\alpha_1^0 = 0$, $\alpha_2^0 = 0.7$, $\alpha_3^0 = 0.3$). The properties of the skeleton (Solid phase) and the water (Fluid2) are given in Table 1.

For the chosen boundary conditions we should obtain two plane waves propagating from left to right along the x-axis. The velocities of these waves should correspond to the velocities calculated by formulae (4), (5).

Figure 3 shows numerical snapshots of the wavefield component V^1 at times $t = 4 * 10^{-6}$ s and $t = 9 * 10^{-6}$ s. The amplitude of the corresponding plain wave is indicated by the red line at the bottom of the snapshots.

As expected, fast and slow (in the Biot regime) plane compression waves are observed in Fig. 3. The numerically estimated velocities 1950 m/s for the fast P-wave and 280 m/s for the slow P-wave agree well with the values obtained from the velocity estimation formulae (4), (5), which are 1954 m/s and 277 m/s respectively.

Table 1. Physical parameters used for simulation in homogeneous test cases.

State	Property	Parameters	Value	Unit
Fluid1: (air)	Fluid density	ρ_1^0	1.225	kg/m^3
	Sound velocity	c_1	330	m/s
	Bulk modulus	$K_1 = \rho_1^0 c_1^2$	0.00013	GPa
Fluid2: (water)	Fluid density	ρ_2^0	1040	kg/m^3
	Sound velocity	c_2	1500	m/s
	Bulk modulus	$K_2 = \rho_2^0 c_2^2$	2.34	GPa
Solid phase:	Solid density	ρ_3^0	2500	kg/m^3
	P-wave velocity	v_p	6155	m/s
	S-wave velocity	v_s	3787	m/s
	Bulk velocity	c_s	4332	m/s
	Bulk modulus	$K_3 = \rho_3^0 c_s^2$	46.91	GPa
	Shear modulus	$\mu = \rho_3^0 v_s^2$	35.85	GPa

3.4   Test 2

Let us consider two numerical test problems in a homogeneous poroelastic medium containing in the center of the domain a homogeneous purely elastic inclusion in the form of a circle of radius 0.1 with material parameters $v_p = 6000$ m/s, $v_s = 4000$ m/s, $\rho = 2500$ kg/m^3. The domain size and finite difference grid are the same as in Test1.

In the first simulation the surrounding homogeneous poroelastic medium is the same as in Test 1, i.e. it consists of a solid skeleton and water ($\alpha_1^0 = 0$, $\alpha_2^0 = 0.7$, $\alpha_3^0 = 0.3$), while in the second simulation we consider a porous medium consisting of a solid skeleton with a mixture of two fluid phases, 10% air and 70% water ($\alpha_1^0 = 0.1$, $\alpha_2^0 = 0.7$, $\alpha_3^0 = 0.2$).

The results of calculations are shown in Figs. 4 and 5. As can be seen from the figures, the presence of an additional air phase in the medium significantly reduces the wave velocity. According to formulas (4), (5), these velocities should

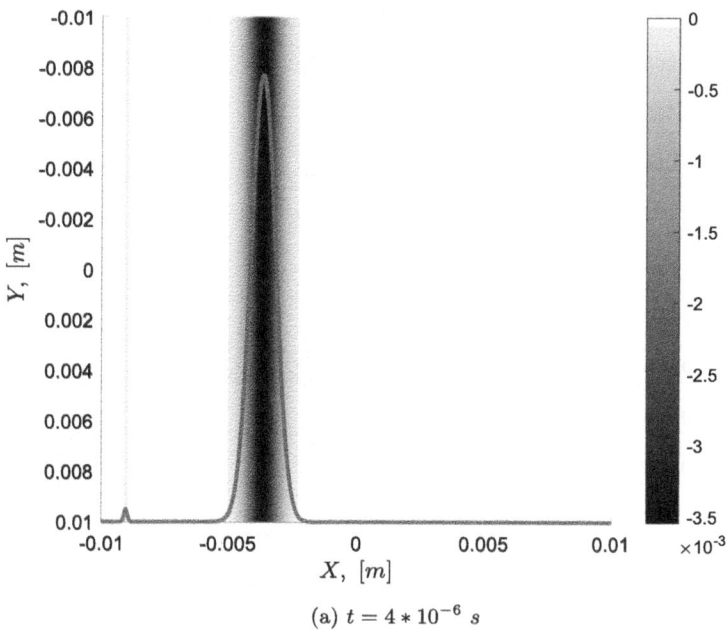

(a) $t = 4 * 10^{-6}\ s$

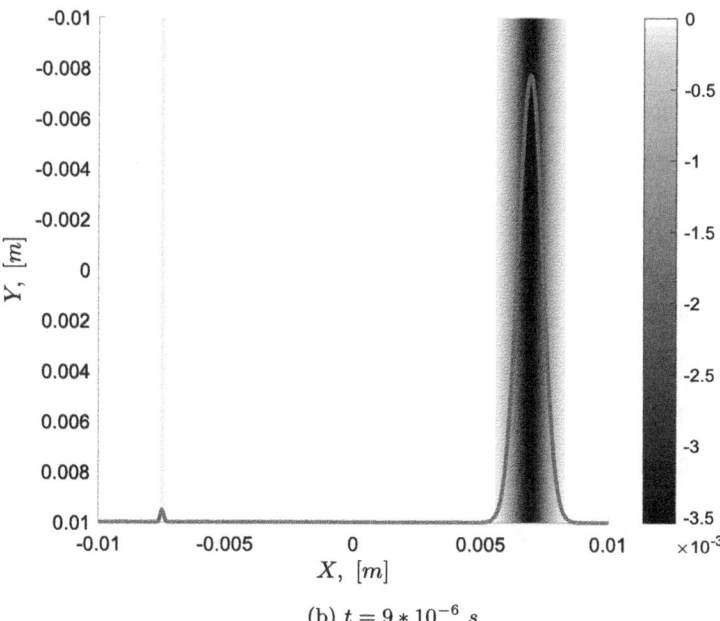

(b) $t = 9 * 10^{-6}\ s$

Fig. 3. Snapshots of the wavefield velocity V^1 at times $t = 4 * 10^{-6}\ s$ and $t = 9 * 10^{-6}$ s. The amplitudes of the corresponding plane waves are indicated by the red line at the bottom of the images. (Color figure online)

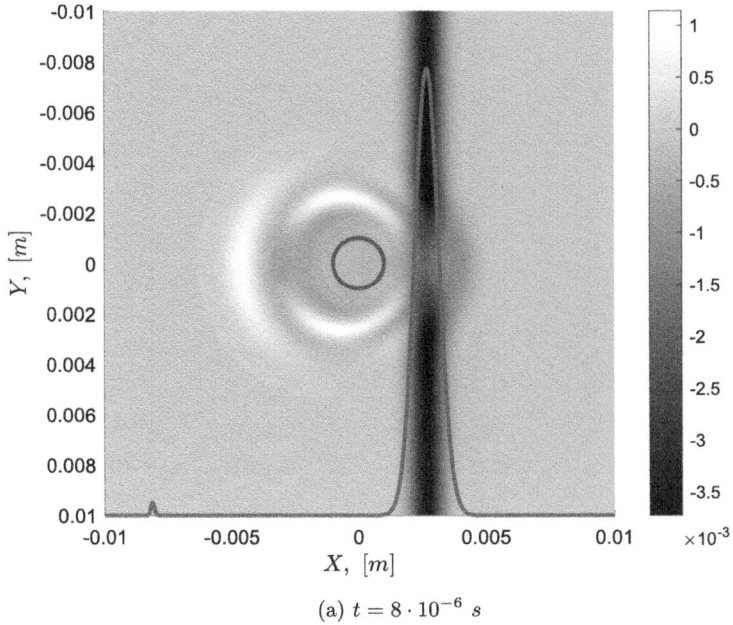

(a) $t = 8 \cdot 10^{-6}$ s

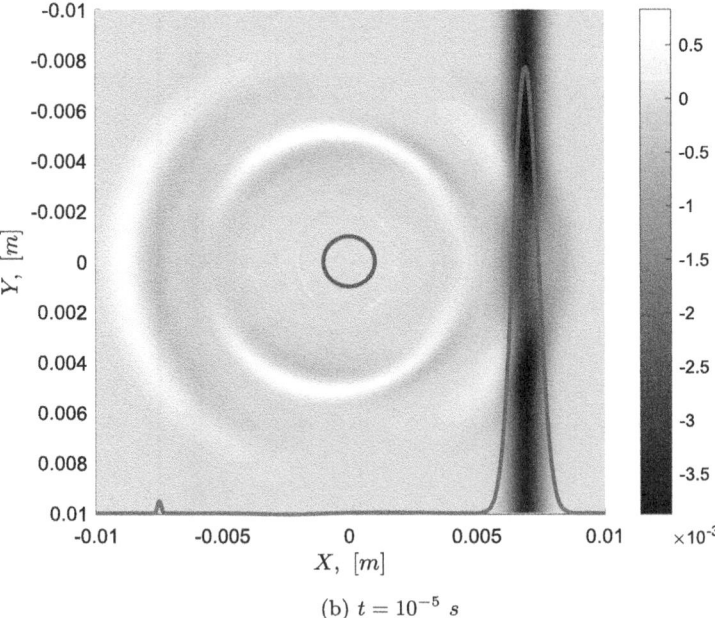

(b) $t = 10^{-5}$ s

Fig. 4. Snapshots of the wavefield velocity V^1 at times $t = 8 \cdot 10^{-6}$ s and $t = 10^{-5}$ s for the surrounding homogeneous poroelastic medium consisting of a solid skeleton saturated with water ($\alpha_1^0 = 0, \alpha_2^0 = 0.7, \alpha_3^0 = 0.3$). The amplitudes of the corresponding plane waves are indicated by the red line at the bottom of the images. (Color figure online)

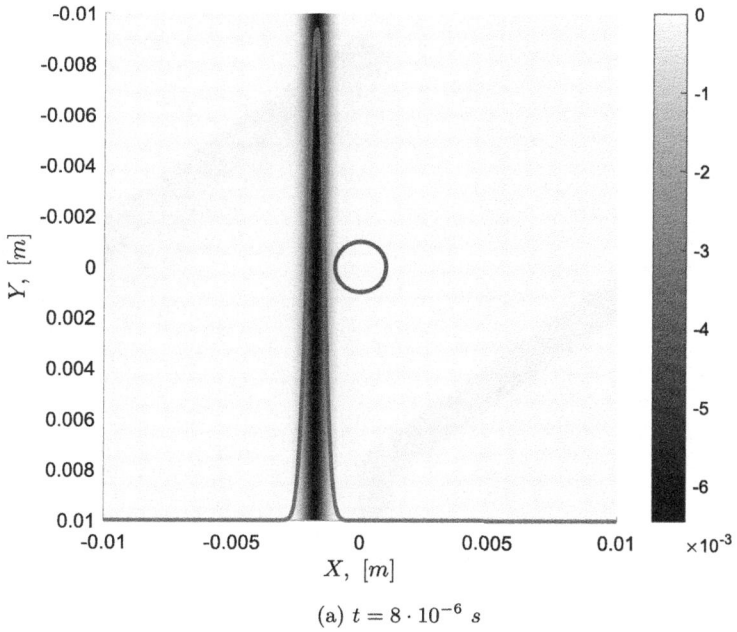

(a) $t = 8 \cdot 10^{-6}$ s

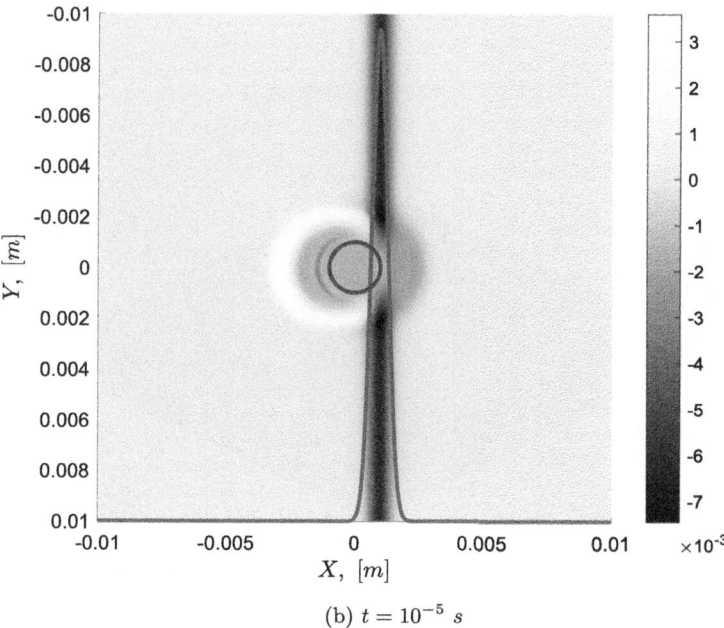

(b) $t = 10^{-5}$ s

Fig. 5. Snapshots of the wavefield velocity V^1 at times $t = 8 \cdot 10^{-6}$ s and $t = 10^{-5}$ s for the surrounding homogeneous poroelastic medium consisting of a solid skeleton saturated with a mixture of air and water ($\alpha_1^0 = 0.1$, $\alpha_2^0 = 0.7$, $\alpha_3^0 = 0.2$). The amplitudes of the corresponding plane waves are indicated by the red line at the bottom of the images. (Color figure online)

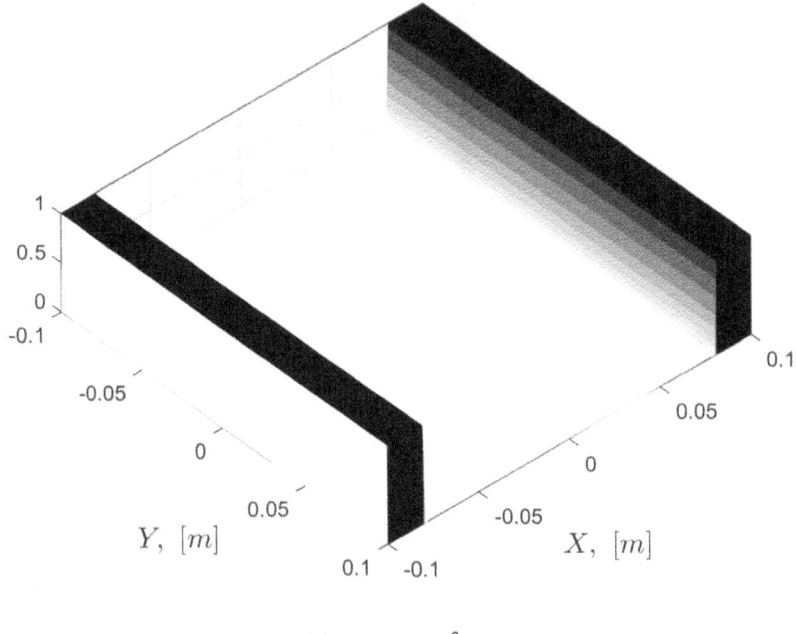

(a) $t = 2 \cdot 10^{-6}$ s

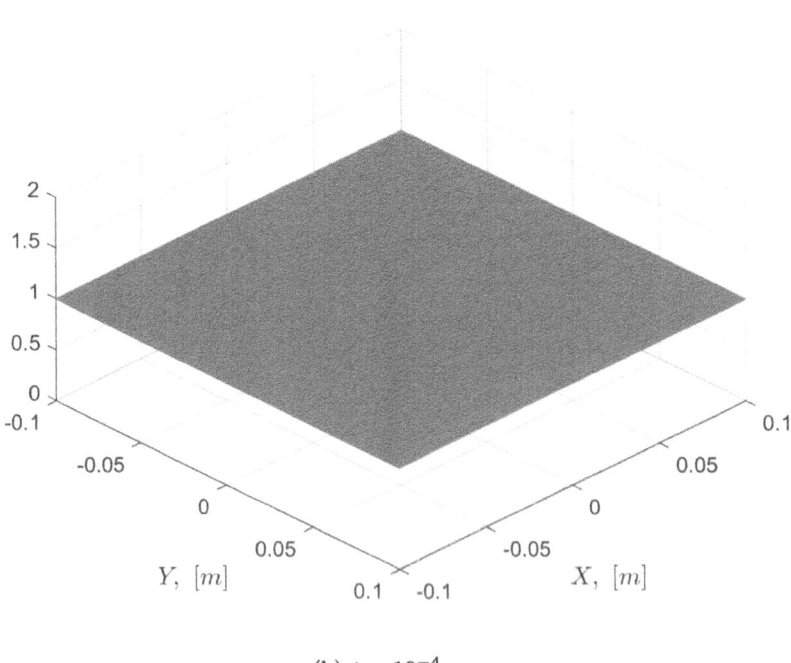

(b) $t = 10^{-4}$ s

Fig. 6. Snapshots of the stress tensor component σ_{11} at times $t = 2 \cdot 10^{-6}$ s and $t = 10^{-4}$ s.

be 1032 m/s for a fast P-wave and 329.5 m/s for a slow P-wave. Numerical estimates of the velocities give values that agree well with the theoretical estimates.

Note that when plane waves are reflected from a circular object placed in a poroelastic medium, not only longitudinal waves but also transverse waves are generated, which can be clearly seen in Fig. 4.

3.5   Test 3

This test shows how a problem of static equilibrium of poroelastic body can be solved using a dynamic poroelasticity system (1) with given boundary conditions using an iterative relaxation method. This approach has been used, for example, to estimate the elastic properties of rock samples from their tomographic images [9].

We propose to find a solution of static poroelastic problem

$$\frac{\partial \sigma_{ik}}{\partial x_k} = 0, \quad i, k = 1, 2, 3, \tag{25}$$

$$\sigma_{ik} = \lambda(\varepsilon_{11} + \varepsilon_{22} + \varepsilon_{33})\delta_{ik} + 2\mu\varepsilon_{ik}. \tag{26}$$

with boundary conditions (11)–(14) by finding the steady-state solution of the system (1) by adding dissipative relaxation terms $\beta V^i, \beta W_1^i, \beta W_2^i$ to the equations of motion:

$$\rho_0 \frac{\partial V^i}{\partial t} + \beta V^i + \frac{\partial P}{\partial x_i} - \frac{\partial \Sigma_{ik}}{\partial x_k} = 0, \tag{27a}$$

$$\frac{\partial W_1^i}{\partial t} + \beta W_1^i + \left(\frac{1}{\rho_1^0} - \frac{1}{\rho_3^0}\right)\frac{\partial P}{\partial x_i} = 0, \tag{27b}$$

$$\frac{\partial W_2^i}{\partial t} + \beta W_2^i + \left(\frac{1}{\rho_2^0} - \frac{1}{\rho_3^0}\right)\frac{\partial P}{\partial x_i} = 0, \tag{27c}$$

where β is a small positive constant chosen empirically. The convergence to the static problem follows from the virial theorem [10], §10.

As an example, consider the problem (25)–(26) with boundary conditions (11)–(14), where we assume the functions $F_1^1(t) = F_2^1(t) = 1$, $F_3^1(t) = F_4^1(t) = 0$, $F_1^2(t) = F_2^2(t) = F_3^2(t) = F_4^2(t) = 0$. In this case, the exact solution of the problem is $\sigma_{11} = 1$.

The simulation was carried out using the computational domain and parameters of the medium presented in Test 1 of this section. The boundary conditions were approximated according to the scheme in Fig. 2 of Sect. 3.2.

Figure 6 shows snapshots of the stress tensor component σ_{11} at two time instants. The upper snapshot in Fig. 6 shows the wavefield at the moment of its excitation by a constant stress set at the lateral boundaries of the domain. After the wavefield has propagated inside the domain, we switch on damping parameter ($\beta = 0.001$) and the process starts to converge to the solution of the stationary problem $\sigma_{11} = 1$.

This iterative approach can be useful in the case of a general three dimensional problem, since direct methods for solving static problems require a large amount of RAM.

4   Conclusion

A numerical method for solving some boundary value problems for a Hyperbolic Thermodynamically Compatible (HTC) model of a deformable porous medium saturated with a mixture of two liquids has been developed. The method is based on a finite difference scheme on a staggered grid, for which the formulated basic equations are perfectly suited. A set of test cases for wave propagation in rectangular domain is solved, including a test problem for obtaining a steady-state solution by solving a non-stationary system. The developed method can be applied to the analysis of wavefields in areas with a complex structure, as well as to the evaluation of the effective elastic moduli of a saturated porous medium - a problem that we plan to investigate.

Acknowledgments. The development of the mathematical model by E. Romenski was financially supported by the Russian Science Foundation (Project No. 19-77-20004), the development of the numerical method and the simulations performed by G. Reshetova was carried out under state contract with ICMMG SB RAS FWNM-2025-0004.

Disclosure of Interests. The authors declare that they have no known competing financial interests or personal relationships that could have appeared to influence the work reported in this article.

References

1. Biot, M. A.: Theory of propagation of elastic waves in fluid-saturated porous solid. I. Low-frequency range. J. Acoust. Soc. Am. **28**(2), 168–178 (1956)
2. Biot, M. A.: Theory of propagation of elastic waves in a fluid-saturated porous solid. II. Higher frequency range. J. Acoust. Soc. Am. **28**(2), 179–191 (1956)
3. Carcione, J.M., Morency, C., Santos, V.: Computational poroelasticity - a review. Geophysics **75**(5), 75A229-75A243 (2010)
4. Romenski, E., Reshetova, G., Peshkov, I., Dumbser, M.: Modeling wavefields in saturated elastic porous media based on thermodynamically compatible system theory for two-phase solid-fluid mixtures. Comput. Fluids **206**, 104587 (2020)
5. Reshetova, G., Romenski, E.: Diffuse interface approach to modeling wavefields in a saturated porous medium. Appl. Math. Comput. **398**, 125978 (2021)
6. Romenski, E., Reshetova, G., Peshkov, I.: Two-phase hyperbolic model for porous media saturated with a viscous fluid and its application to wavefield simulation. Appl. Math. Model. **106**, 567–600 (2022)
7. Reshetova, G., Romenski, E.: Modeling of temperature-dependent wave fields in deformable porous media saturated with fluid. Numer. Anal. Appl. **17**(4), 358–371 (2024)
8. Reshetova, G., Romenski, E.: Modeling the variability of seismic properties of frozen multiphase media depending on temperature. Siberian Electron. Math. Rep. **21**(2), B203–B231 (2024)
9. Reshetova, G., Khachkova, T.: Parallel numerical method to estimate the effective elastic moduli of rock core samples from 3D tomographic images. In: Dimov, I., Farago, I., Vulkov, L. (eds.) FDM 2018. LNCS, vol. 11386, pp. 452–460. Springer, Cham (2019). https://doi.org/10.1007/978-3-030-11539-5_52

10. Landau, L.D., Lifshitz, E.M.: Mechanics. Nauka, Moscow (1988)
11. Peshkov, I., Pavelka, M., Romenski, E., Grmela, M.: Continuum mechanics and thermodynamics in the Hamilton and the Godunov-type formulations. Continuum Mech. Thermodyn. **30**(6), 1343–1378 (2018). https://doi.org/10.1007/s00161-018-0621-2
12. Virieux, J.: P-SV wave propagation in heterogeneous media: velocity-stress finite-difference method. Geophysics **51**(1), 889–901 (1986)
13. Levander, A.R.: Fourth-order finite-difference P-SV seismograms. Geophysics **53**(11), 1425–1436 (1988)
14. Samarskii, A.A.: The Theory of Difference Schemes. CRC Press, Boca Raton (2001)
15. Moczo, P., Kristek, J., Vavrycuk, V., Archuleta, R.J., Halada, L.: 3D heterogeneous staggered-grid finite-difference modeling of seismic motion with volume harmonic and arithmetic averaging of elastic moduli and densities. Bull. Seismol. Soc. Am. **92**(8), 3042–3066 (2002)

Machine Learning-Based Preconditioner to Solve Poisson Equation

Ekaterina Chekmeneva[1], Tatyna Khachova[2], and Vadim Lisitsa[3]([envelope])[iD]

[1] Novosibirsk State University, Pirogova st. 2, 630090 Novosibirsk, Russia
e.chekmeneva@g.nsu.ru
[2] Institute of Petroleum Geology and Geophysics SB RAS, Koptug ave. 3,
630090 Novosibirsk, Russia
[3] Institute of Mathematics SB RAS, Koptug ave. 4, 630090 Novosibirsk, Russia
lisitsavv@ipgg.sbras.ru

Abstract. In this paper, we present an attempt to construct a preconditioner based on the machine learning to solve Poisson equation. We use the Conjugate Gradient method. To precondition the algorithm we suggest approximating the inverse Laplace operator with using the U-Net. We consider the supervised learning where the vector of unknowns and right-hand sides are known; thus, we use the relative L^2 error as the loss function of the network training. We illustrate that U-Net with five convolutional layers provide insufficient accuracy of inverse Laplace operator approximation, so that the constructed conjugate gradient method stabilizes and possesses irreducible residual.

Keywords: Poisson equation · Conjugate gradient · preconditioner · Machine Learning

1 Introduction

The numerical solution of the Poisson equation in heterogeneous media has broad applications, including modeling: electric potential distribution in heterogeneous materials [10,25]; steady-state temperature fields [3]; species distribution governed by diffusion processes. Additionally, solving the Poisson equation is a critical step in fluid flow simulations, particularly in: multi-phase flows in open channels when projection-based methods are employed [11,12], multi-phase flows in porous media [14].

Upon discretization, the Poisson equation yields a system of linear algebraic equations (SLAEs) with a self-adjoint, positive-definite matrix—provided the original differential operator retains these properties. Such systems are efficiently solved using Krylov subspace methods, with the Conjugate Gradient (CG) method being particularly widespread [21]. However, the convergence rate of CG deteriorates with increasing matrix condition number, which grows with problem size and the contrast in material heterogeneity.

The research was supported by the Russian Science Foundation grant no. 22-11-00004-П.

To accelerate convergence, various preconditioning techniques have been developed:

- Algebraic preconditioners, including Jacobi, incomplete LU factorization [9, 13,21], and low-rank approximations of the matrix or its LU factors [24].
- Geometrically inspired methods, such as domain decomposition [18] and multigrid techniques [4,23], later generalized to algebraic formulations.
- Physics-based preconditioners, which approximate the inverse of a simplified Laplace operator. A key challenge is ensuring efficient inversion at each iteration [10].

The development of the machine and deep learning methods gave rise to the new direction of the preconditioners construction [1,15,16]. The general principle of the ML-based preconditioenrs design is the speed-up of the incomplete LU and Cholesky factorization construction or the approximation of the inverse operator directly. Following our previous works on physics-based preconditioners [10] we suggest focusing on the ML-based approximation of the inverse Laplace operator as preconditioner. The remaining of the paper has the following structure. We formulate the mathematical problem in Sect. 2. The principles of the ML-based preconditioner are discussed in Sect. 3. The numerical experiments are presented in Sect. 4.

2   Statement of the Problem

2.1   Mathematical Formulation

Assume the Poisson equation with variable coefficients stated in a rectangular domain $\Omega = [X_1, X_2] \times [Y_1, Y_2]$:

$$\nabla \cdot (\sigma(x,y)\nabla\psi(x,y)) = f(x,y). \tag{1}$$

Coefficient $\sigma(x,y)$ is assumed to be strictly positive and bounded. In this work, we consider the mixed boundary conditions, so that Dirichlet conditions are stated for $x = X_1$ and $x = X_2$, but Neumann conditions are stated for $y = Y_1$ and $y = Y_2$:

$$\begin{aligned} \psi(X_1, y) = \psi^1, \quad \psi(X_2, y) = \psi^2, \\ \nabla\psi \cdot \vec{n}(x, Y_1) = 0, \, \nabla\psi \cdot \vec{n}(x, Y_2) = 0. \end{aligned} \tag{2}$$

In these notations, $f(\vec{x})$ is the right-hand side, ψ^1 and ψ^2 are boundary conditions.

To solve the stated problem we suggest using the conservative finite differences with harmonic averaging of the coefficient σ when used on the cells faces, as described in [10,17,22].

The discretized problem can be represented as a system of linear algebraic equations:

$$A\vec{\psi} = \vec{g}, \tag{3}$$

where matrix A is self-adjoin positive definite of the size $N_x N_y \times N_x N_y$, $\vec{\psi}$ is the vector representation of the unknowns, and $\vec{g}$ is the vector containing the discretized right-hand sides and the boundary conditions, N_x and N_y are the numbers of grid points in each spatial direction.

2.2   Conjugate Gradient Method with Preconditioner

Matrix A of the system (3) is symmetric and positive definite; thus, one may apply the Conjugate Gradient method to solve the system. However, convergence rate of the method strongly depends on the matrix condition number [21]. The condition number of the system may be high; moreover, it increases with the problem size and the contrast of the coefficient σ. To decrease the condition number and to speed up the convergence rate the preconditoning is used; so that modified problem

$$B^{-1/2} A B^{-1/2} B^{1/2} \vec{\psi} = B^{-1/2} \vec{g}$$

is solved. Operator B is called the preconditioner. The new matrix $B^{-1/2} A B^{-1/2}$ is also symmetric and positive definite if B possesses the same properties. It is clear, that construction of $B^{-1/2}$ may be troublesome, so a simple algebraic manipulations allow to rewrite the CG algorithm for preconditionnered system in the following form:

1. $\vec{r}_0 = \vec{g} - A\vec{\psi}_0$, $\vec{p}_0 = B^{-1}\vec{r}_0$, $\vec{q}_0 = \vec{p}_0$;
   do until converge
2. $\alpha_j = \frac{(\vec{q}_j, \vec{r}_j)}{(A\vec{p}_j, \vec{p}_j)}$;
3. $\vec{\psi}_{j+1} = \vec{\psi}_j + \alpha_j \vec{p}_j$
4. $\vec{r}_{j+1} = \vec{r}_j - \alpha_j A\vec{p}_j$, $\vec{q}_{j+1} = B^{-1}\vec{r}_{j+1}$;
5. $\beta_j = \frac{(\vec{q}_{j+1}, \vec{r}_{j+1})}{(\vec{q}_j, \vec{r}_j)}$;
6. $\vec{p}_{j+1} = \vec{q}_{j+1} + \beta_j \vec{p}_j$

In these notations $\vec{\psi}$ is the solution vector, $\vec{g}$ is the original right-hand side, $\vec{r}$ is the residual vector, and $\vec{q}$, $\vec{p}$ are auxiliary vectors.

The most intense part of the algorithm is the computation of the preconditionner action $B^{-1}\vec{r}_{j+1}$. There are several different ways to construct the preconditioner B and compute $B^{-1}\vec{r}_{j+1}$. The most universal approach is based on the algebraic principles. For example, the Jacobi preconditioner requires inversion of the main diagonal of the original matrix. It is a fast but not very efficient approach. Incomplete LU and Cholesky decomposition-based preconditioners improves the convergence but require storage of factors, which leads to high memory consumption. An efficient approach to precondition Poisson solvers is the use of multi-grid methods [21,23]. However, multi-grid efficiency strongly depends on the contrast in the coefficients σ. In fact, the ideal preconditioner is $B = A$. In this case, the process would converge in one iteration. However, the inversion of matrix B is troublesome. So, the set of approaches was suggested, where matrix $B \approx A$ in some sense, but to be relatively easy to invert. In particular, the operator corresponding to a homogeneous model $\sigma = const$ can be considered, after that it is inverted using pseudo-spectral method [2,10,19], or the spectral 1D matrix decomposition may be applied. This approach strongly improves the convergence of the CG for Poisson equation, however its efficiency degenerates with the increase of the coefficient contrast. Moreover, use of the pseudo spectral and spectral approach requires intense computations at each iteration. To speed up the computation of the preconditioner action; i.e., $B^{-1}\vec{r}_{j+1}$ for any matrix B we suggest using the Machine Learning methods.

3 ML-Based Preconditioner

The main assumption of the suggested approach is that one needs to solve Poisson equation for fixed model $\sigma(x, y)$ for numerous different right-hand sides. In this case, it is reasonable to train neural network that approximate $B^{-1}\vec{r}$ and then apply it multiple times as a preconditionner. In this research we suggest constructing the preconditioner to approximate the inverse operator, rather than reducing matrix condition number or matrix norm directly, as suggested in [16]. So, we need to construct a map

$$\mathcal{F}[\vec{r}] = \vec{q}_F \approx B^{-1}\vec{r}.$$

In this research, we use the U-net [20] which is a convolution neural network being widely used for image processing, seismic data processing [5–8]. In particular the U-net with five convolutional layers is constructed as presented in Fig. 1. To train the U-net we considered a series of images $U_1, ..., U_m$ of the size 128×128 pixels. These images can be represented as vectors $\vec{u}_1, ..., \vec{u}_m$ of the length of 128^2. We computed the action of the Laplace operator on the dataset to get the second series of vectors $\vec{v}_1, ..., \vec{v}_m$, so that $\vec{v}_k = A\vec{u}_k$ and represented them as images $V_1, ..., V_m$. We trained the U-net to map the set $V_1, ..., V_m$ to the set $U_1, ..., U_m$, thus we train it to invert matrix A. The loss function was

$$Loss = \sum_{k=1}^{m} \left[\lambda_{rel} \frac{\|\vec{u}_k - \mathcal{F}[\vec{u}_k]\|_2^2}{\|\vec{u}_k\|_2^2} + \lambda_{pos} \max\{0, -(\vec{u}_k, \mathcal{F}[\vec{u}_k])\} \right],$$

where λ_{rel} and λ_{pos} are weights, and $(,)$ denotes standard inner product of vectors. The second term is sued to enforce the mapping $\mathcal{F}[\vec{u}_k]$ being positive definite, because it is crucial property of the preconditioner of the conjugate gradient method.

First, we trained the network using a set of 768 pairs of random pictures as a training dataset and 256 pairs as a validation dataset. We applied the Laplace operator to those pictures and trained the network to recover the images. An example of original picture, the result of Laplace operator action and the recovered image are presented in Fig. 2. Use of such pictures simplify visual interpretation of the U-Net results, however, these plots may not be representative if used in conjugate gradient method, where preconditioner is applied to the residual vector.

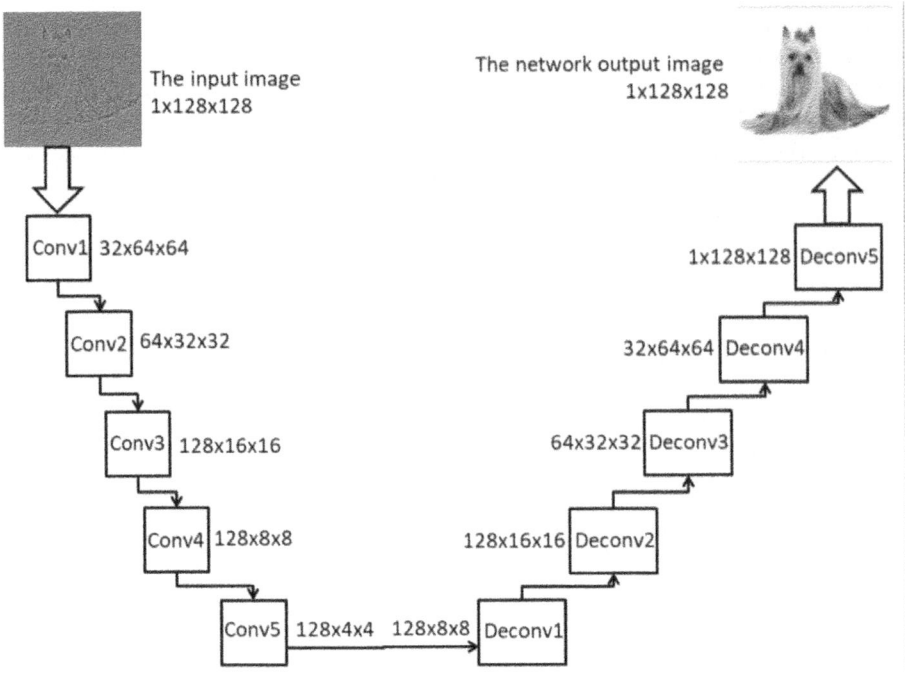

Fig. 1. The architecture of the U-net.

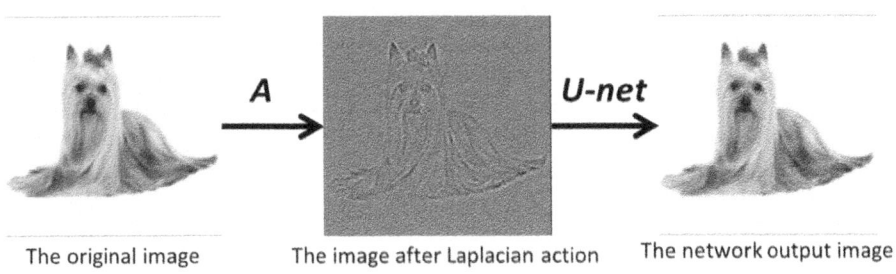

The original image   The image after Laplacian action   The network output image

Fig. 2. An example of U-Net application to recover the image. Original image - left, action of Laplace operator - middle, and recovered image - right.

Second, we trained the U-Net on a series of the residuals appeared in the CG algorithm. We used a picture from the set described above, applied Laplace operator to obtain the right-hand side and then started CG iterations without preconditioning. As the result, we obtained a series of vectors $\vec{p}_j$ and $A\vec{p}_j$ which were used to train the U-Net, an example of original and recovered vectors are provided in Fig. 3.

Fig. 3. An example of U-Net application to recover vector $\vec{p}_j$ from CG iterations. Original image - left, action of Laplace operator - middle, and recovered image - right.

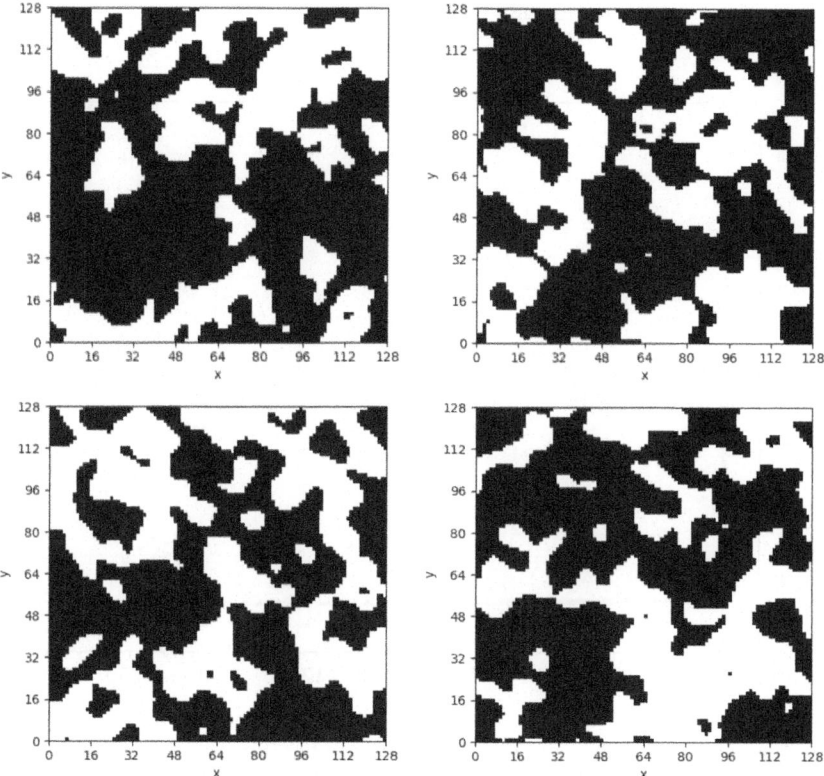

Fig. 4. Examples of models with porosity 35% top left, 40% top right, 45% bottom left, 50% bottom right.

4   Numerical Experiments

For our numerical experiments we considered the inhomogeneous models; i.e., $\sigma = \sigma(x, y)$, is a binary distribution defined as truncated Gaussian distribution with correlation length equal to 10 grid points and total porosity varied in $\{30\%, 35\%, 40\%, 45\%, 50\%\}$. The examples of the models with different total porosity are provided in Fig. 4. We assumed the conductivity of the pore-filling material σ_1 (colored wire in Fig. 4), whereas the conductivity of the matrix σ_2 (black) varied within the set $\{10^{-4}, 10^{-3}, 10^{-2}, 10^{-1}\}$. These models are close to real digital rocks where the conductivity of the pore filled fluid is much higher than that of the insulating matrix. Moreover, the geometry of the pore space of the sandstones is well predicted by the two-point statistics, thus can be approximated by the truncated Gaussian distribution.

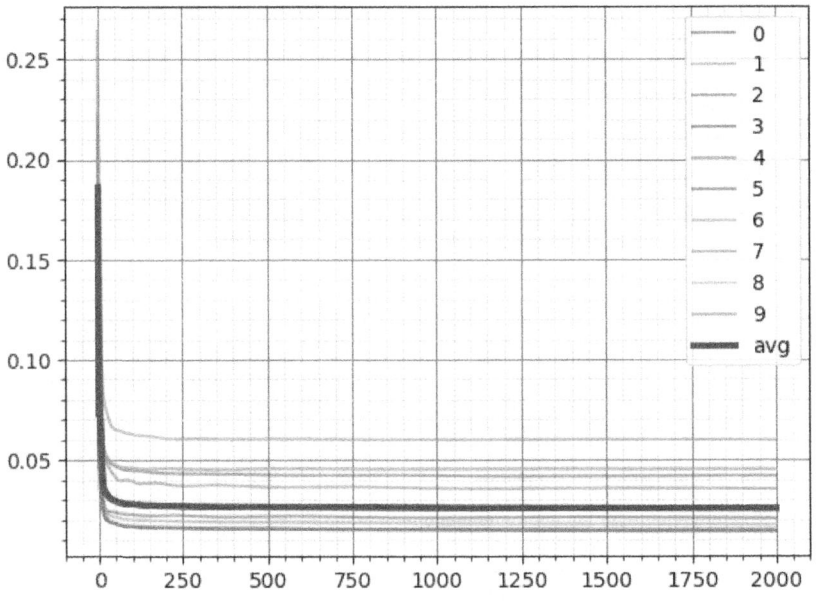

Fig. 5. Residual depending on the iteration number for the model with contrast $\sigma_1/\sigma_2 = 10^1$. Thin lines correspond to experiments for different models, thick line represent averaged values over the model realizations.

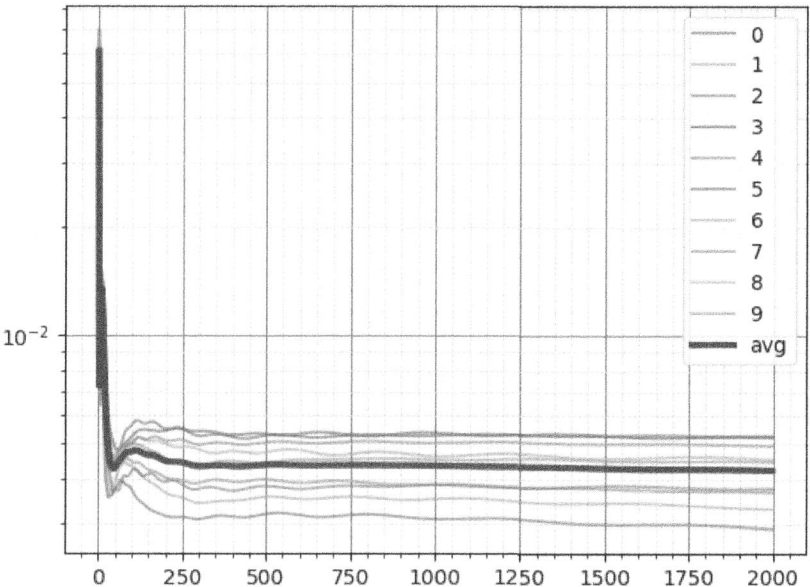

Fig. 6. Residual depending on the iteration number for the model with contrast $\sigma_1/\sigma_2 = 10^2$. Thin lines correspond to experiments for different models, thick line represent averaged values over the model realizations.

To study the effect of the model inhomogeneity on the convergence of the preconditioned conjugate gradient method we considered ten statistical model realizations for each fixed porosity and conductivity contrast. So, in total 200 different models were considered. For each model we trained U-Net which is not a practical way to go, but it is expected to provide the highest possible accuracy. In fact, we trained the net to construct the inverse operator without any additions approximations.

For each of 200 models we applied CG to solve the system of equations for several different right-hand sides. We used pictures from our collection as the true solution, applied the inhomogeneous Laplace operator to obtain the right-hand sides, and then use preconditioned CG to reconstruct the original solution. Unfortunately, the designed algorithm did not converge. So, we considered the residual behavior is ML-based preconditioner was applied to CG for different

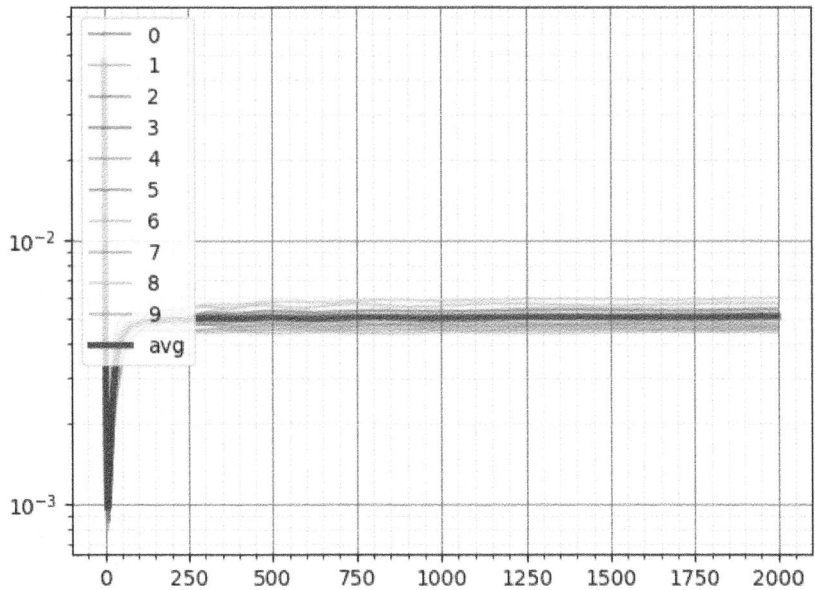

Fig. 7. Residual depending on the iteration number for the model with contrast $\sigma_1/\sigma_2 = 10^3$. Thin lines correspond to experiments for different models, thick line represent averaged values over the model realizations.

models. Figures 5, 6, 7 and 8 provide the residuals over the iteration number for 10 realizations of the model with fixed porosity equal to 45% but with different conductivity contrasts. According to the provided plots, the residual rapidly decreases at the first several iterations, and after that it goes to an asymptotic value far from zero. These value is independent of the model porosity, but sensitive to the conductivity contrast. To estimate these dependence we estimated the irreducible error for all experiments and compute its mean value over all statistical models and realizations, but for fixed conductivity contrast. Moreover, we estimated the mean value of the U-Net loss function over statistical models and realizations. The values of the mean U-Net loss function and the irreducible error are provided in Table 1. Note, that U-Net loss function reaches approximately the same value of about 30% for all conductivity contrasts. However, the irreducible residual decrease with the increase of the contrast.

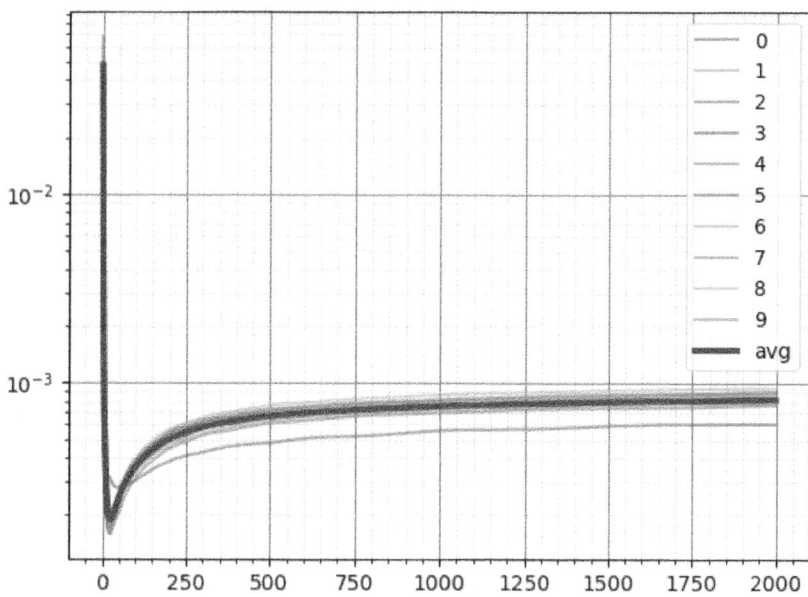

Fig. 8. Residual depending on the iteration number for the model with contrast $\sigma_1/\sigma_2 = 10^4$. Thin lines correspond to experiments for different models, thick line represent averaged values over the model realizations.

Table 1. L^2 error of the ML-recovered images and irreducible residual for different conductivity contrasts.

σ_1/σ_2	L^2 error	Irr. residual
10^4	0.28	$9.48 \cdot 10^{-4}$
10^3	0.24	$5.22 \cdot 10^{-3}$
10^2	0.28	$4.57 \cdot 10^{-3}$
10^1	0.34	$1.76 \cdot 10^{-2}$

5   Conclusions

We presented the approach to construct the machine learning-based preconditioner to solve Poisson equation with conjugate gradient method. We suggested the preconditioner to approximate the inverse Laplace operator for the fixed but spatially varied coefficients. We used the U-Net to approximate the action of the inverse Laplace operator with direct minimization of the relative error (not residual). We managed to achieve the accuracy of the ML-based approximation of only 30%. As the result, this accuracy was not enough to ensure the convergence of the conjugate gradient method. The designed "preconditined" algorithm does not converge to the solution but stabilizes possessing irreducible relative residual of about 10^{-3}. In this research, we also ignored the fact that the preconditioner in CG method should be linear self-adjoin and positive-definite operator. So, possible way to improve the quality of the ML-based preconditioning is to include these conditions to restrict the ML training loss function.

References

1. Azulay, Y., Treister, E.: Multigrid-augmented deep learning preconditioners for the Helmholtz equation. SIAM J. Sci. Comput. **45**(3), S127–S151 (2023). https://doi.org/10.1137/21m1433514
2. Belonosov, M., Kostin, V., Neklyudov, D., Tcheverda, V.: 3d numerical simulation of elastic waves with a frequency-domain iterative solver. Geophysics **83**(6), T333–T344 (2018)
3. Dorn, C., Schneider, M.: Lippmann-Schwinger solvers for the explicit jump discretization for thermal computational homogenization problems. Int. J. Numer. Meth. Eng. **118**(11), 631–653 (2019)
4. Evstigneev, N.M., Ryabkov, O.I., Gerke, K.M.: Stationary stokes solver for single-phase flow in porous media: a blastingly fast solution based on algebraic multigrid method using GPU. Adv. Water Resour. **171**, 104340 (2023)
5. Gadylshin, K., Gondyul, E., Lisitsa, V., Gadylshina, K., Vishnevsky, D.: Mitigation of numerical dispersion in seismic data in spectral domain with neural networks. Soil Dyn. Earthq. Eng. **187**, 109028 (2024). https://doi.org/10.1016/j.soildyn.2024.109028
6. Gadylshin, K., Lisitsa, V., Vishnevsky, D., Gadylshina, K.: Hausdorff-distance-based training dataset construction for numerical dispersion mitigation neural network. Comput. Geosci. **180**, 105438 (2023). https://doi.org/10.1016/j.cageo.2023.105438
7. Gadylshin, K., Vishnevsky, D., Gadylshina, K., Lisitsa, V.: Numerical dispersion mitigation neural network for seismic modeling. Geophysics **87**(3), T237–T249 (2022)
8. Gondyul, E., Lisitsa, V., Gadylshin, K., Vishnevsky, D.: Numerical dispersion mitigation neural network with velocity model correction. Comput. Geosci. **196**, 105806 (2025). https://doi.org/10.1016/j.cageo.2024.105806
9. Haber, E., Ascher, U.M., Aruliah, D.A., Oldenburg, D.W.: Fast simulation of 3D electromagnetic problems using potentials. J. Comput. Phys. **163**(1), 150–171 (2000)
10. Khachkova, T., Lisitsa, V., Reshetova, G., Tcheverda, V.: GPU-based algorithm for evaluating the electrical resistivity of digital rocks. Comput. Math. Appl. **82**, 200–211 (2021)
11. Khachkova, T.S., Lisitsa, V.V., Gondul, E.A., Prokhorov, D.I., Kostin, V.I.: Two-phase flow simulation algorithm for numerical estimation of relative phase permeability curves of porous materials. Russ. J. Numer. Anal. Math. Model. **39**(4), 209–221 (2024). https://doi.org/10.1515/rnam-2024-0020
12. Kim, J.: Phase-field models for multi-component fluid flows. Commun. Comput. Phys. **12**(3), 613–661 (2012)
13. Lee, B., Min, C.: Optimal preconditioners on solving the Poisson equation with Neumann boundary conditions. J. Comput. Phys. **433**, 110189 (2021)
14. Lee, S., Wheeler, M.F.: Enriched Galerkin methods for two-phase flow in porous media with capillary pressure. J. Comput. Phys. **367**, 65–86 (2018). https://doi.org/10.1016/j.jcp.2018.03.031

15. Li, M., Wang, H., Jimack, P.K.: Generative modeling of sparse approximate inverse preconditioners. In: Lecture Notes in Computer Science. Computational Science – ICCS 2024, vol. 14834, pp. 378–392. Springer Nature Switzerland (2024)
16. Li, Y., Chen, P.Y., Du, T., Matusik, W.: Learning preconditioners for conjugate gradient PDE solvers. In: Krause, A., Brunskill, E., Cho, K., Engelhardt, B., Sabato, S., Scarlett, J. (eds.) Proceedings of the 40th International Conference on Machine Learning. Proceedings of Machine Learning Research, vol. 202, pp. 19425–19439. PMLR (2023). https://proceedings.mlr.press/v202/li23e.html
17. Lisitsa, V., Podgornova, O., Tcheverda, V.: On the interface error analysis for finite difference wave simulation. Comput. Geosci. **14**(4), 769–778 (2010)
18. Loisel, S., Szyld, D.: On the geometric convergence of optimized Schwarz methods with applications to elliptic problems. Numer. Math. **114**(4), 697–728 (2010)
19. Pleshkevich, A., Vishnevskiy, D., Lisitsa, V.: Sixth-order accurate pseudo-spectral method for solving one-way wave equation. Appl. Math. Comput. **359**, 34–51 (2019)
20. Ronneberger, O., Fischer, P., Brox, T.: U-Net: convolutional networks for biomedical image segmentation. In: Medical Image Computing and Computer-Assisted Intervention (MICCAI). LNCS, vol. 9351, pp. 234–241. Springer (2015). http://lmb.informatik.uni-freiburg.de/Publications/2015/RFB15a
21. Saad, Y.: Iterative Methods for Sparse Linear Systems. SIAM (2003)
22. Samarskii, A.A.: The theory of difference schemes. Pure Appl. Math. **240**. CRC Press (2001)
23. Stuben, K.: A review of algebraic multigrid. J. Comput. Appl. Math. **128**(1–2), 281–309 (2001)
24. Xia, J.: A robust inner–outer hierarchically semi-separable preconditioner. Numer. Linear Algebra Appl. **19**(6), 992–1016 (2012). https://doi.org/10.1002/nla.1850
25. Zhan, X., Schwartz, L.M., Toksöz, M.N., Smith, W.C., Morgan, F.D.: Pore-scale modeling of electrical and fluid transport in Berea sandstone. Geophysics **75**(5), F135–F142 (2010)

Implementation of the Spectral Preconditioner to Solve Poisson Equation

Vadim Lisitsa$^{(\boxtimes)}$ (ID), Aleksei Manaev, and Sergey Solovyev

Institute of Mathematics SB RAS, Koptug avenue 4, Novosibirsk 630090, Russia
lisitsavv@yandex.ru

Abstract. In this paper, we present an original preconditioner to solve Poisson equation for strongly heterogeneous media. We suggest using the Conjugate Gradient method with the preconditioner based on the solution of the Poisson equation for homogeneous media. Corresponding operator is easy to invert by spectral method, where spectral decomposition is applied in two spatial directions and the Gauss elimination method is applied to solve a series of 1D problems. We illustrate that use of such precondtioner strongly decreases the number of iterations to solve the original Poisson equation, moreover the number of iterations weakly depends on the problem size. Implementation of the suggested approach using modern GPUs allows solving problems of up to the size of 1000^3 voxels.

Keywords: Poisson equation · Conjugate gradient · preconditioner

1 Introduction

Numerical solution of Poisson equation in strongly heterogeneous media has numerous applications. In particular, it describes electric potential distribution in heterogeneous materials [1,9,23], steady state temperature distribution [5], and steady state species distribution due to diffusion. Also, one needs solving Poisson equation as a part of fluid flow simulation either multi-phase flows in open channels if the projection-based methods are applied [10,11] or multi-phase flows in porous media if IMPES schemes are used [13,17].

Then discretized, Poisson equation leads to the system of linear algebraic equations with self-adjoin positive definite matrix (if the original differential operator had the same properties). Such systems of equations can be efficiently solved using Krylov-type iterative methods, and in particular the Conjugate Gradient method is widely used [18]. However, the convergence rate of CG method strongly depends on the matrix condition number, which increases with the problem size and inhomogeneity contrast in Laplace operator. To speed-up the convergence different types of preconditioners were designed. The most universal preconditioners are based on purely algebraic consideration of the problem.

The research was supported by the Russian Science Foundation grant no. 19-77-20004-II.

They include the Jacobi and incomplete LU factorization of the matrix [7,12,18], low-rank approximation of the matrix or its LU factors [22]. The other set of approaches are originated on the geometrical point of view with further evolution to pure algebraic versions, such as domain decomposition methods [15], and multigrid methods [6,20]. The third type of preconditioners are based on the approximation of the physical process; i.e., use the inverse Laplace operator corresponding to a simpler model as a preconditioner. The main issue of this approach is the necessity to invert the operator at each iteration, thus it should be done fast and efficient. In particular, we suggest using the Laplace operator corresponding to a homogeneous media as a repconditioner [9]. It can be easily inverted using pseudo-spectral method as discussed in applications to fluid flow simulations [3,4,8]. In our previous research [9] we suggested using similar technique to solve Poisson equation for strongly hetrerogeneous media. In this paper, we present the improvement of the approach. We applied the Conjugate Gradient method instead of BiCGStab, we use the spectral decomposition of the discretized operator instead of the continuous case, and the cuBLAS functionality was utilized. As the result, the suggested approach allows solving Poisson equation inside the domain of the size of up 1000^3 voxels with a single GPU in 5 to 30 min depending on the model heterogeneity.

2   Mathematical Problem Formulation

Consider Poisson equation

$$\nabla \cdot (\sigma(\vec{x})\nabla\varphi) = f(\vec{x}), \tag{1}$$

stated inside a domain $\Omega = [X_1^L, X_1^R] \times [X_2^L, X_2^R] \times [X_3^L, X_3^R]$. In general, any correct boundary conditions can be stated on $S = \partial\Omega$. However, in this research we focus on the statements typical for the digital rock physics, where Neumann boundary conditions are applied at the sides of the sample, which corresponds to a sample placed inside an insulator. The potential difference is applied at the two sides, that is the Dirichlet conditions. Formally it can be written as

$$\begin{aligned}
\varphi|_{X_2=X_2^L} = \varphi^L, \; \nabla\varphi \cdot \vec{n} = 0|_{X_2=X_2^L}, \; \nabla\varphi \cdot \vec{n} = 0|_{X_3=X_3^L}, \\
\varphi|_{X_2=X_2^R} = \varphi^R, \; \nabla\varphi \cdot \vec{n} = 0|_{X_2=X_2^R}, \; \nabla\varphi \cdot \vec{n} = 0|_{X_3=X_3^R}.
\end{aligned} \tag{2}$$

In these notations, φ is the unknown function, which can be considered as the electric potential, $\sigma(\vec{x})$ is the electric conductivity, which is rapidly varying and strongly heterogeneous, but bounded function, $\vec{x}$ is the vector of spatial variables, $f(\vec{x})$ is the right-hand side, φ^L and φ^R are boundary conditions (applied potentials).

2.1   Finite-Difference Approximation

To approximate the Eq. (1) in the internal points we suggest using the second order finite difference scheme:

$$\frac{1}{h_1}\left(\tilde{\sigma}_{i_1+1/2,i_2,i_3}\frac{\varphi_{i_1+1,i_2,i_3}-\varphi_{i_1,i_2,i_3}}{h_1}-\tilde{\sigma}_{i_1-1/2,i_2,i_3}\frac{\varphi_{i_1,i_2,i_3}-\varphi_{i_1-1,i_2,i_3}}{h_1}\right)$$
$$+\frac{1}{h_2}\left(\tilde{\sigma}_{i_1,i_2+1/2,i_3}\frac{\varphi_{i_1,i_2+1,i_3}-\varphi_{i_1,i_2,i_3}}{h_2}-\tilde{\sigma}_{i_1,i_2-1/2,i_3}\frac{\varphi_{i_1,i_2,i_3}-\varphi_{i_1,i_2-1,i_3}}{h_2}\right)+$$
$$+\frac{1}{h_3}\left(\tilde{\sigma}_{i_1,i_2,i_3+1/2}\frac{\varphi_{i_1,i_2,i_3+1}-\varphi_{i_1,i_2,i_3}}{h_3}-\tilde{\sigma}_{i_1,i_2,i_3-1/2}\frac{\varphi_{i_1,i_2,i_3}-\varphi_{i_1,i_2,i_3-1}}{h_3}\right)=f_{i_1,i_2,i_3},$$
$$i_1=2,...,I_1-1,\ i_2=2,...,I_2-1,\ i_3=2,...,I_3-1.$$

$$(3)$$

In these notations functions φ_{i_1,i_2,i_3} and f_{i_1,i_2,i_3} are the grid functions defined at the integer grid points $\varphi_{i_1,i_2,i_3}\approx\varphi((x_1)_{i_1},(x_2)_{i_2},(x_3)_{i_3})$ and $f_{i_1,i_2,i_3}\approx f((x_1)_{i_1},(x_2)_{i_2},(x_3)_{i_3})$. The conductivity σ is also defined at the integer grid points; i.e., however, it is used in the half-integer points, where is it modified to preserve the second order of convergence at the discontinuous coefficients:

$$\tilde{\sigma}_{i_1+1/2,i_2,i_3}=2\left(\frac{1}{\sigma_{i_1+1,i_2,i_3}}+\frac{1}{\sigma_{i_1,i_2,i_3}}\right)^{-1},$$
$$\tilde{\sigma}_{i_1,i_2+1/2,i_3}=2\left(\frac{1}{\sigma_{i_1,i_2+1,i_3}}+\frac{1}{\sigma_{i_1,i_2,i_3}}\right)^{-1},\qquad(4)$$
$$\tilde{\sigma}_{i_1,i_2,i_3+1/2}=2\left(\frac{1}{\sigma_{i_1,i_2,i_3+1}}+\frac{1}{\sigma_{i_1,i_2,i_3}}\right)^{-1}.$$

The mathematical background of this type of coefficients averaging can be found in [9, 14, 19, 21].

Approximation of the Eq. (1) in the vicinity of the boundaries involve the boundary conditions explicitly to keep the operator self-adjoin. We provide the equations for $i_1=1$, $i_2=1$, and $i_3=1$, the equations at the opposite sides can be derived in the same manner:

$$\frac{1}{h_1}\left(\tilde{\sigma}_{3/2,i_2,i_3}\frac{\varphi_{2,i_2,i_3}-\varphi_{1,i_2,i_3}}{h_1}-\tilde{\sigma}_{1/2,i_2,i_3}\frac{\varphi_{1,i_2,i_3}}{h_1}\right)$$
$$+\frac{1}{h_2}\left(\tilde{\sigma}_{1,i_2+1/2,i_3}\frac{\varphi_{1,i_2+1,i_3}-\varphi_{1,i_2,i_3}}{h_2}-\tilde{\sigma}_{1,i_2-1/2,i_3}\frac{\varphi_{1,i_2,i_3}-\varphi_{1,i_2-1,i_3}}{h_2}\right)$$
$$+\frac{1}{h_3}\left(\tilde{\sigma}_{1,i_2,i_3+1/2}\frac{\varphi_{1,i_2,i_3+1}-\varphi_{1,i_2,i_3}}{h_3}-\tilde{\sigma}_{1,i_2,i_3-1/2}\frac{\varphi_{1,i_2,i_3}-\varphi_{1,i_2,i_3-1}}{h_3}\right)\qquad(5)$$
$$=f_{i_1,i_2,i_3}-\varphi^L_{i_2,i_3},$$
$$i_2=2,...,I_2-1,\ i_3=2,...,I_3-1.$$

$$\frac{1}{h_1}\left(\tilde{\sigma}_{i_1+1/2,1,i_3}\frac{\varphi_{i_1+1,1,i_3}-\varphi_{i_1,1,i_3}}{h_1}-\tilde{\sigma}_{i_1-1/2,1,i_3}\frac{\varphi_{i_1,1,i_3}-\varphi_{i_1-1,1,i_3}}{h_1}\right)$$
$$+\frac{1}{h_2}\left(\tilde{\sigma}_{i_1,3/2,i_3}\frac{\varphi_{i_1,2,i_3}-\varphi_{i_1,1,i_3}}{h_2}\right)+$$
$$+\frac{1}{h_3}\left(\tilde{\sigma}_{i_1,1,i_3+1/2}\frac{\varphi_{i_1,1,i_3+1}-\varphi_{i_1,1,i_3}}{h_3}-\tilde{\sigma}_{i_1,1,i_3-1/2}\frac{\varphi_{i_1,1,i_3}-\varphi_{i_1,1,i_3-1}}{h_3}\right)=f_{i_1,1,i_3},$$
$$i_1=2,...,I_1-1,\ i_3=2,...,I_3-1.$$

$$(6)$$

$$\frac{1}{h_1}\left(\tilde{\sigma}_{i_1+1/2,i_2,1}\frac{\varphi_{i_1+1,i_2,1}-\varphi_{i_1,i_2,1}}{h_1} - \tilde{\sigma}_{i_1-1/2,i_2,1}\frac{\varphi_{i_1,i_2,1}-\varphi_{i_1-1,i_2,1}}{h_1}\right)$$

$$+\frac{1}{h_2}\left(\tilde{\sigma}_{i_1,i_2+1/2,1}\frac{\varphi_{i_1,i_2+1,1}-\varphi_{i_1,i_2,1}}{h_2} - \tilde{\sigma}_{i_1,i_2-1/2,1}\frac{\varphi_{i_1,i_2,1}-\varphi_{i_1,i_2-1,1}}{h_2}\right) + \tag{7}$$

$$+\frac{1}{h_3}\left(\tilde{\sigma}_{i_1,i_2,3/2}\frac{\varphi_{i_1,i_2,2}-\varphi_{i_1,i_2,1}}{h_3}\right) = f_{i_1,i_2,1},$$

$$i_1 = 2, ..., I_1 - 1, \; i_2 = 2, ..., I_2 - 1.$$

The resulting system can be written in a short matrix-vector form as

$$A\vec{\varphi} = \vec{g}, \tag{8}$$

where $\vec{\varphi}$ is the vector representation of the unknown function with the following indexing $j = i_1 + (i_2-1)I_1 + (i_3-1)I_1 I_2$ (the order of the indices can be permuted without the loss of generality). The matrix A is sparse, self-adjoin, and positive definite. Vector $\vec{g}$ is formed from the right-hand sides f_{i_1,i_2,i_3} and the boundary conditions $\varphi^L_{i_2,i_3}$ and $\varphi^R_{i_2,i_3}$.

2.2   Conjugate Gradient Method

To solve system (8) we suggest using the Conjugate Gradient method with preconditioner. The algorithm can be represented as follows [18]:

1. $\vec{r}_0 = \vec{g} - A\vec{\varphi}_0, \; \vec{p}_0 = B^{-1}\vec{r}_0, \; \vec{q}_0 = \vec{p}_0;$
2. $\alpha_j = \frac{(\vec{q}_j, \vec{r}_j)}{(A\vec{p}_j, \vec{p}_j)};$
3. $\vec{\varphi}_{j+1} = \vec{\varphi}_j + \alpha_j \vec{p}_j$
4. $\vec{r}_{j+1} = \vec{r}_j - \alpha_j A\vec{p}_j, \; \vec{q}_{j+1} = B^{-1}\vec{r}_{j+1};$
5. $\beta_j = \frac{(\vec{q}_{j+1}, \vec{r}_{j+1})}{(\vec{q}_j, \vec{r}_j)};$
6. $\vec{p}_{j+1} = \vec{q}_{j+1} + \beta_j \vec{p}_j$

This algorithm requires the storage of four vectors: $\vec{\varphi}_j$, $\vec{r}_j$, $\vec{q}_j$, and $\vec{p}_j$. Also, one more vector is needed which is $A\vec{p}_j$. Two matrix-vector multiplications should be performed at each iteration, they are $A\vec{p}_j$ and $B^{-1}\vec{r}_{j+1}$. Matrix B is the preconditioner which is constructed to reduce the condition number of the matrix $B^{-1}A$. Among the approaches to construct the preconditioners one may mention algebraic approaches such as incomplete LU, algebraic multigrid [18,20], also geometric multigrid preconditioner is efficient for smoothly varying coefficient $\sigma(\vec{x})$. The other way around is to construct the preconditioner based on physical properties of the simulated process. In fact, it is preferred matrix B to be as close to the original matrix A as possible but easy to invert. In [2,9] a spectral preconditionner was suggested, where matrix B corresponds to the Laplace operator with constant coefficient $\sigma = const$. In this case, the inversion of operator can be done using pseudo-spectral method [16]. It means that the Fast Fourier Transform (FFT) is applied along two spatial directions (in the considered case they are x_2 and x_3) and after that the series of 1D problems along

x_1 direction can be solved. A detailed description of this approach is presented in [9], where it was implemented to precondition BiConjugate Gradient method. However, implementation of the FFT assumes the periodic boundary conditions, whereas use of Neumann boundary conditions requires the sine transform [8]. It can be implemented either by the even continuation of the original array or by the proper permutation of the arrays elements [8]. However, use of different combinations of the boundary conditions at the sides of the computational domain leads to different transofrms. To overcome this difficulty, we suggest using explicit eigen-decomposition of 1D operators along x_2 and x_3 directions.

3 Spectral Preconditioner

Consider the Poisson equation with constant coefficient σ and construct its finite-difference approximation (3). Its matrix representation can be written as

$$B\vec{\psi} = \vec{w},$$

where vectors ψ and $\vec{w}$ have the same order of elements as $\vec{\varphi}$ in Eq. 8. Matrix B can be represented as the sum of three simple tri-diagonal matrices:

$$B = B_1 + B_2 + B_3,$$

each of these matrices represent approximation of the derivative with respect to the corresponding direction. They have the following form:

$$B_1 = \frac{\sigma}{h_1^2} \begin{pmatrix} T & & 0 & & 0 & & \\ & \ddots & & & & \ddots & \\ 0 & & T & & & & 0 \\ \hline & & & \ddots & & & \\ 0 & & & & T & & 0 \\ & \ddots & & & & \ddots & \\ & & 0 & & 0 & & T \end{pmatrix},$$

where matrix T is the tridiagonal matrix

$$T = \begin{pmatrix} 2 & -1 & & & \\ -1 & 2 & -1 & & \\ & \ddots & \ddots & \ddots & \\ & & -1 & 2 & -1 \\ & & & -1 & 2 \end{pmatrix},$$

$$B_2 = \frac{\sigma}{h_2^2} \left(\begin{array}{cccc|ccc} I & -I & & & & 0 & \\ -I & 2I & -I & & & & \\ & \ddots & \ddots & \ddots & & & \ddots \\ & & -I & 2I & -I & & \\ & & & -I & I & & & 0 \\ \hline & & & & \ddots & & \\ \hline & 0 & & & & I & -I \\ & & & & & -I & 2I & -I \\ & & & & & & \ddots & \ddots & \ddots \\ & & & & & & & -I & 2I & -I \\ & & 0 & & & & & & -I & I \end{array} \right) ,$$

where I is the identity matrix of the size I_1, and

$$B_3 = \frac{\sigma}{h_3^2} \left(\begin{array}{ccc|ccc|ccc} I & & & -I & & & & & \\ & \ddots & & & \ddots & & & & \\ & & I & & & -I & & & \\ \hline -I & & & 2I & & & -I & & \\ & \ddots & & & \ddots & & & \ddots & \\ & & -I & & & 2I & & & -I \\ \hline & & & \ddots & & & \ddots & & & \ddots \\ \hline & & & -I & & & 2I & & & -I \\ & & & & \ddots & & & \ddots & & & \ddots \\ & & & & & -I & & & 2I & & & -I \\ \hline & & & & & & -I & & & I & \\ & & & & & & & \ddots & & & \ddots \\ & & & & & & & & -I & & & I \end{array} \right) .$$

It is clear that the eigenvalues of the matrices B_2 and B_3 coincide with those of matrices

$$C_2 = \left(\begin{array}{ccccc} 1 & -1 & & & \\ -1 & 2 & -1 & & \\ & \ddots & \ddots & \ddots & \\ & & -1 & 2 & -1 \\ & & & -1 & 1 \end{array} \right), \; C_3 = \left(\begin{array}{ccccc} 1 & -1 & & & \\ -1 & 2 & -1 & & \\ & \ddots & \ddots & \ddots & \\ & & -1 & 2 & -1 \\ & & & -1 & 1 \end{array} \right),$$

but the size of the matrix C_2 is I_2, and size of C_3 is I_3. If we denote by V_2 the matrix of the eigenvectors of C_2 (same for C_3):

$$
V_2 = \begin{pmatrix}
v_{11}^2 & v_{12}^2 & \cdots & v_{1I_2-1}^2 & v_{1I_2}^2 \\
v_{21}^2 & v_{22}^2 & \cdots & v_{2I_2-1}^2 & v_{2I_2}^2 \\
\vdots & \vdots & \ddots & \vdots & \vdots \\
v_{I_2-11}^2 & v_{I_2-12}^2 & \cdots & v_{I_2-1I_2-1}^2 & v_{I_2-1I_2}^2 \\
v_{I_21}^2 & v_{I_22}^2 & \cdots & v_{I_2I_2-1}^2 & v_{I_2I_2}^2
\end{pmatrix}.
$$

then the matrices of the eigenvectors of $B_2 = U_2\Lambda_2U_2^T$ and $B_3 = U_3\Lambda_3U_3^T$ can be represented as:

$$
U_2 = \begin{pmatrix}
\begin{matrix} v_{11}^2 I & \cdots & v_{1I_2}^2 I \\ \vdots & \ddots & \vdots \\ v_{I_21}^2 I & \cdots & v_{I_2I_2}^2 I \end{matrix} & \\
\hline
& \ddots & \\
& & \begin{matrix} v_{11}^2 I & \cdots & v_{1I_2}^2 I \\ \vdots & \ddots & \vdots \\ v_{I_21}^2 I & \cdots & v_{I_2I_2}^2 I \end{matrix}
\end{pmatrix},
$$

$$
U_3 = \begin{pmatrix}
\begin{matrix} v_{11}^3 I & & \\ & \ddots & \\ & & v_{11}^3 I \end{matrix} & \cdots & \begin{matrix} v_{1I_3}^3 I & & \\ & \ddots & \\ & & v_{1I_3}^3 I \end{matrix} \\
\hline
\begin{matrix} \vdots \\ v_{I_31}^3 I \\ & \ddots \\ & & v_{I_31}^3 I \end{matrix} & \cdots & \begin{matrix} \vdots \\ v_{I_3I_3}^3 I \\ & \ddots \\ & & v_{I_3I_3}^3 I \end{matrix}
\end{pmatrix}.
$$

The main point is that application of the eigenvalue decomposition to any of the considered matrices B_2 or B_3 does not change the other two matrices; thus, the following change of variables can applied

$$
\vec{\gamma} = U_2^T U_3^T \vec{\psi},
$$

and the system transforms to

$$
U_2^T U_3^T (B_1 + B_2 + B_3)U_3U_2\vec{\gamma} = (B_1 + \Lambda_2 + \Lambda_3)\vec{\gamma} = U_3^T U_2^T \vec{w} = \vec{s}. \tag{9}
$$

Note, that matrices Λ_2 and Λ_3 are diagonal, thus the problem was reduced to a series of 1D problems which may be soled with direct Gauss elimination process with $O(I_1)$ floating point operations. Eigenvectors and eigenvalues of matrices C_2 and C_3 can be found analytically.

It means, that to invert the preconditioner, one needs to apply two series of matrix-vector multiplications with the matrix size coinciding with 1D size of the computational domain, and after that solve a series of the systems with tridiagonal matrices. Below we discuss the practical aspects of the algorithm implementation.

4   GPU-Based Implementation

Implementation of the described algorithm to GPU-based architecture is closely related to that presented previously in [9]. The main feature of the suggested implementation is that all variables are stored in GPU memory during the simulation, and only the final result $\vec{\varphi}$ is copied to the RAM. Thus, the algorithm is almost free from device-to-host or host-to-device memory copy. The array of the electric conductivity σ_{i_1,i_2,i_3} is read from file and copied to the GPU memory at the beginning. After that, memory is allocated on GPU for the solution $\vec{\varphi}$ and for the auxiliary arrays used in the CG: $\vec{r}$, $\vec{p}$, $\vec{q}$.

The preconditioned CG algorithm requires execution of four main types of the operations: action of the Laplace operator on a vector; i.e. $A\vec{p}_j$; computation of the inner products, computation of the linear combinations of vectors, and action of the preconditioner $B^{-1}\vec{r}_{j+1}$. The action $A\vec{p}_j$ is implemented directly, using formula (3). This is the stencil computation, thus it is free from data dependencies and it is easy to parallelize on the multi-core architecture. To execute the dot product and compute linear combinations we used the cuBLAS "dot" and "axpy" functions respectively.

The most time consuming procedure is the computation of action of the preconditioner $B^{-1}\vec{r}_{j+1}$. To invert the operator, we need to apply the spectral decomposition, as described above. The approach is based on the construction of the eigenvectors and eigenvalues of 1D operators. We assume the model is homogeneous, thus the matrices of the eigenvectors V_2 and V_3 can be computed using analytical formulae, same for the eigenvalues. Note, that apart from the theoretical constructions, we do not need to store matrices U_2 and U_3, but only the compact matrices V_2 and V_3 are required. The size of these matrices is $I_2 \times I_2$ and $I_3 \times I_3$, respectively. It means, that they require only a few Mb of memory to store them. The action of matrices U_2 and U_3 on a vector can be computed using their compact representation V_2 and V_3 using the cuBLAS functionality, in particular, "gemm" functionality is used, which allows to represent series of matrix-vector multiplications as a matrix-matrix multiplication with high optimization. The resulting series of systems (9) is solved then using Gauss elimination. Note, that the resulting 1D problems are independent and their size is relatively small equal to I_1. The matrices of the 1D systems are tridiagonal, thus the systems can be solved independently. Moreover, due to the small size of each problem, a single system can be solved using a single core. Note, that the total number of eigenvalues is $I_2 I_3 \approx 10^6$, thus, all available GPU cores are involved in embarrassingly parallel computations. Then the series of 1D solutions is obtained, the inverse transoms $\gamma = U_3^T U_2^T \vec{w}$ are computed using "gemm" function from cuBLAS. Thus, all computationally intense procedures in the algorithm are executed with the highly optimized cuBLAS functionality.

5   Numerical Experiments

We omit the experiments on the algorithm verification. We reproduced the experiments, presented in [9], estimating the effective electric conductivity of layered media. Moreover, for all experiments described below we performed simulation using the presented algorithm and compared the results with those obtained using the algorithm from [9]. For our experiments we used the CT-scan of the Betheimer sandstone. The resolution of the image was 2 mkm per voxel. The size of the image was 750 voxels in each direction. In our simulations we used either parts of the image; i.e., we cropped the images to get a smaller one. To perform simulations for the sample of the higher size than 750^3 we extended the sample periodically. The images of the considered samples are provided in Figs. 1, 2 and 3. The filled regions in the figures correspond to the mineral grains and the empty space represent the pore space. We assumed the pore space filled with conductive fluid with electric conductivity equal to one; i.e., $\sigma(\vec{x}) = 1$ if $\vec{x}$ belongs to the pore space. We varied the electric conductivity of the grains $\sigma_g \in \{10^{-1}, 10^{-2}, ..., 10^{-5}\}$. Formally, the insulators like calcite, quarts, feldspar and others may have much lower conductivity. However, in this case, one may consider them absolutely insulating and solve the Poisson equation only in the pore space, instead of the whole sample. So, we omit extremely high contrasts. The case, when the conductivities of the fluid and matrix coincide; i.e., $\sigma_g = 1$ is also excluded, because it corresponds to the homogeneous material, and the suggested preconditioner will be the same as the original operator; thus, the algorithm converges in one iteration.

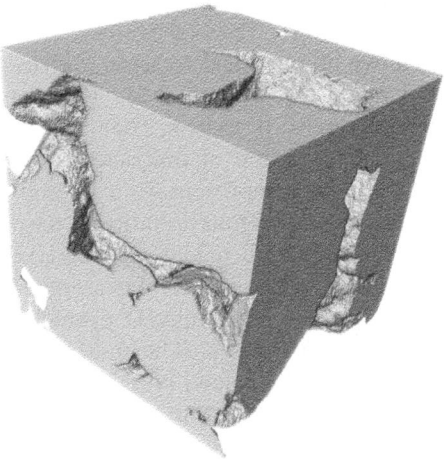

Fig. 1. The example of the model of the size 200^3 voxels

Fig. 2. The example of the model of the size 400^3 voxels

Fig. 3. The example of the model of the size 800^3 voxels

First, we performed simulations for the model of the size of 200^3 voxels. We varied the conductivity of the core matrix. Also, the simulations were done using two GPUs: nVidia A100 GPU with 80 Gb of memory and RTX 2080Ti GPU with 12 Gb of memory. These simulations were done to make the timing measurements consistent with those provided in [9]. The results are presented in Table 1. Note, that A100 GPU allows solving the problem ten times faster

Table 1. Number of iterations and timing of solving Poisson equation inside the domains of 200^3 voxels.

σ_g	no. iterations	time (s) RTX 2080	time (s) A100
10^{-1}	64	3.51	0.34
10^{-2}	157	8.49	0.87
10^{-3}	379	20.54	2.12
10^{-4}	781	42.39	4.06
10^{-5}	887	47.27	4.82

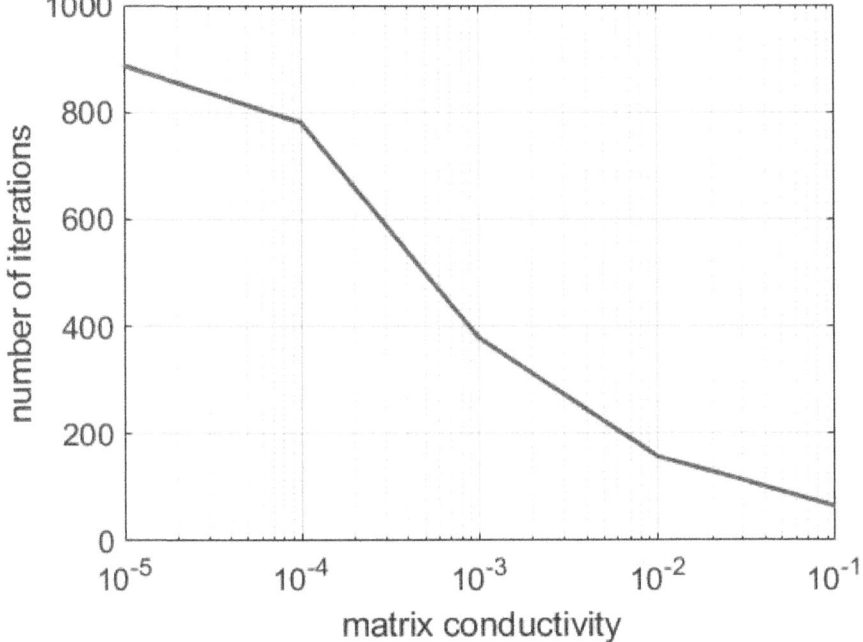

Fig. 4. Number of iteration in dependence on the conductivity contrast

than RTX2080. Number of iterations was, as expected, the same, because it does not suppose to depend on the computing architecture. The number of iterations increases with increase of the conductivity contrast. However, as it may be noted in Fig. 4, the number of iterations depends almost linearly on the $\ln \sigma_g$.

The second series of experiments was performed on the A100 GPUs only and were oriented on the large-scale simulations. We dealt with samples of the size of 200^3, 400^3, 800^3, and 1000^3 voxels, but restricted the considerations with only two values of matrix conductivity $\sigma_g = \{10^{-2}, 10^{-4}\}$. Number of iterations and timings are provided in Tables 2 and 3. Provided numbers of the iterations are

Table 2. Number of iterations and timing of solving Poisson equation in dependence on the problem size for $\sigma_g = 10^{-2}$.

size	no. iterations	time (s) A100	time per it. (s)
200^3	157	0.87	0.0055
400^3	215	9.36	0.0435
800^3	271	121.02	0.4466
1000^3	289	341.00	1.1799

Table 3. Number of iterations and timing of solving Poisson equation in dependence on the problem size for $\sigma_g = 10^{-4}$.

size	no. iterations	time (s) A100	time per it. (s)
200^3	783	4.06	0.0052
400^3	1094	46.68	0.0427
800^3	1387	812.34	0.5857
1000^3	1514	1812.78	1.1973

required to achieve the relative residual norm equal to 10^{-6}. Note, that in both cases the number of iterations are weakly dependent on the size of the computational domain. The number of iterations increases with the domain size, but the growth rate is lower than linear. In particular, increase of the computational domain from 200 to 800 points lead to the increase of the iterations number by the factor of only 1.75. We need to point out that we compare the number of iterations with respect to the size of the computational domain, whereas the actual size of the system of linear equations is 200^3 to 1000^3. It means that the increase of the number of iterations with the growth of the problem size is negligible. We also figured out, that time per a single iteration (which includes matrix-vector multiplication $A\vec{p}_j$ and action of the preconditioner $B^{-1}\vec{r}_{j+1}$) is proportional to the problem size. It means, that the action of the perconditioner does not increase the computational complexity of the algorithm; i.e., it requires the number of flops proportional to the problem size.

6   Conclusion

We presented an original approach to construct preconditioner for numerical solution of Poisson equation for strongly heterogeneous media. The idea of the preconditioner is based on that, presented in [9], where the inverted Laplace operator corresponding to the homogeneous model is used to precondition the problem when solved with Conjugate Gradient method. Apart from the previous approaches we suggested solving Poisson equation for homogeneous media using eigenvalue decomposition of two 1D matrices, approximating Laplace operator with given boundary conditions. After that the change of variables is applied by the action of the eigenvectors matrices and the resulting series of 1D systems with tridiagonal matrices are solved using direct methods. All the matrix-vector and matrix-matrix multiplications are executed with the help of cuBLAS functionality. We applied the approach to compute the electric potential in digital rock samples with different rock matrix conductivity. We illustrated that number of iterations of the preconditioned CG algorithm is almost independent on the problem size, however, iterations linearly depend on the logarithm of the conductivity contrast. Finally, we illustrated that use of modern GPUs (A100 series) allows solving Poisson equation in a domain of the size up to 1000^3 in 5 to 30 min depending on the model heterogeneity with a single GPU.

References

1. Andra, H., et al.: Digital rock physics benchmarks - part ii: Computing effective properties. Comput. Geosci. **50**, 33–43 (2013)
2. Belonosov, M., Kostin, V., Neklyudov, D., Tcheverda, V.: 3D numerical simulation of elastic waves with a frequency-domain iterative solver. Geophysics **83**(6), T333–T344 (2018)
3. Costa, P.: A FFT-based finite-difference solver for massively-parallel direct numerical simulations of turbulent flows. Comput. Math. Appl. **76**(8), 1853–1862 (2018). https://doi.org/10.1016/j.camwa.2018.07.034
4. Crialesi-Esposito, M., et al.: Flutas: a GPU-accelerated finite difference code for multiphase flows. Comput. Phys. Commun. **284**, 108602 (2023). https://doi.org/10.1016/j.cpc.2022.108602
5. Dorn, C., Schneider, M.: Lippmann-schwinger solvers for the explicit jump discretization for thermal computational homogenization problems. Int. J. Numer. Meth. Eng. **118**(11), 631–653 (2019)
6. Evstigneev, N.M., Ryabkov, O.I., Gerke, K.M.: Stationary stokes solver for single-phase flow in porous media: a blastingly fast solution based on algebraic multigrid method using GPU. Adv. Water Resour. **171**, 104340 (2023)
7. Haber, E., Ascher, U.M., Aruliah, D.A., Oldenburg, D.W.: Fast simulation of 3D electromagnetic problems using potentials. J. Comput. Phys. **163**(1), 150–171 (2000)
8. Hasbestan, J.J., Xiao, C.N., Senocak, I.: Pittpack: an open-source poisson's equation solver for extreme-scale computing with accelerators. Comput. Phys. Commun. **254**, 107272 (2020). https://doi.org/10.1016/j.cpc.2020.107272
9. Khachkova, T., Lisitsa, V., Reshetova, G., Tcheverda, V.: GPU-based algorithm for evaluating the electrical resistivity of digital rocks. Comput. Math. Appl. **82**, 200–211 (2021)
10. Khachkova, T.S., Lisitsa, V.V., Gondul, E.A., Prokhorov, D.I., Kostin, V.I.: Two-phase flow simulation algorithm for numerical estimation of relative phase permeability curves of porous materials. Russ. J. Numer. Anal. Math. Model. **39**(4), 209–221 (2024). https://doi.org/10.1515/rnam-2024-0020
11. Kim, J.: Phase-field models for multi-component fluid flows. Commun. Comput. Phys. **12**(3), 613–661 (2012)
12. Lee, B., Min, C.: Optimal preconditioners on solving the poisson equation with neumann boundary conditions. J. Comput. Phys. **433**, 110189 (2021)

13. Lee, S., Wheeler, M.F.: Enriched galerkin methods for two-phase flow in porous media with capillary pressure. J. Comput. Phys. **367**, 65–86 (2018). https://doi.org/10.1016/j.jcp.2018.03.031
14. Lisitsa, V., Podgornova, O., Tcheverda, V.: On the interface error analysis for finite difference wave simulation. Comput. Geosci. **14**(4), 769–778 (2010)
15. Loisel, S., Szyld, D.: On the geometric convergence of optimized schwarz methods with applications to elliptic problems. Numer. Math. **114**(4), 697–728 (2010)
16. Pleshkevich, A., Vishnevskiy, D., Lisitsa, V.: Sixth-order accurate pseudo-spectral method for solving one-way wave equation. Appl. Math. Comput. **359**, 34–51 (2019)
17. Redondo, C., Rubio, G., Valero, E.: On the efficiency of the impes method for two phase flow problems in porous media. J. Petrol. Sci. Eng. **164**, 427–436 (2018). https://doi.org/10.1016/j.petrol.2018.01.066
18. Saad, Y.: Iterative Methods for Sparse Linear Systems. SIAM (2003)
19. Samarskii, A.A.: The Theory of Difference Schemes, Pure and Applied Mathematics, vol. 240. CRC Press (2001)
20. Stuben, K.: A review of algebraic multigrid. J. Comput. Appl. Math. **128**(1–2), 281–309 (2001)
21. Vishnevsky, D., Lisitsa, V., Tcheverda, V., Reshetova, G.: Numerical study of the interface errors of finite-difference simulations of seismic waves. Geophysics **79**(4), T219–T232 (2014)
22. Xia, J.: A robust inner–outer hierarchically semi-separable preconditioner. Numer. Linear Algebra Appl. **19**(6), 992–1016 (2012). https://doi.org/10.1002/nla.1850
23. Zhan, X., Schwartz, L.M., Toksöz, M.N., Smith, W.C., Morgan, F.D.: Pore-scale modeling of electrical and fluid transport in berea sandstone. Geophysics **75**(5), F135–F142 (2010)

Algorithm for Restoring the Electrical Resistivity of a Medium with Plane-Parallel and Coaxial-Cylindrical Interface Boundaries Based on Lateral Logging Sounding Data

Dmitry Prokhorov$^{(\boxtimes)}$ [ID] and Veronika Chepelenkova [ID]

Sobolev Institute of Mathematics SB RAS, 4 Koptug Avenue, Novosibirsk,
Russia 630090
prokhorovdi@ipgg.sbras.ru

Abstract. This paper presents an algorithmic complex designed to restore the properties of a medium with plane-parallel and coaxial-cylindrical interface boundaries based on lateral logging sounding data. The complex includes an algorithm for direct numerical modeling of lateral logging sounding (LLS) and an algorithm for restoring the electrical resistivity of formations with drilling fluid invasion zones according to the LLS curves.

Keywords: Lateral logging sounding · Direct methods for SLAE · Nelder-Mead method

1 Introduction

Electrical resistivity is the most important parameter determining the reservoir properties of rocks. Therefore, lateral logging sounding occupies one of the leading positions in the geophysical studies of oil and gas wells. In LLS, measuring and current electrodes are located on the axis of the borehole, coinciding with the medium symmetry axis. A two-dimensional axisymmetric distribution of the resistivity of the rocks surrounding the borehole must be determined. The uniqueness of the solution in the case of the two-dimensional piecewise constant resistivity has been proven in [5].

In this paper we use alternative approach. The algorithm for solving the inverse problem is based on using the non-gradient Nelder-Mead minimization method [6,12]. This method consists of sequentially moving and deforming the simplex around the extremum point in the parameter space of the inverse problem. The Nelder-Mead method does not use the gradient of the objective function, which makes it possible to significantly simplify both the mathematical justification and the software implementation of the algorithm for solving the inverse problem.

O. Gervasi et al. (Eds.): ICCSA 2025 Workshops, LNCS 15888, pp. 402–418, 2026.
https://doi.org/10.1007/978-3-031-97596-7_27

The solution to the direct problem uses the finite difference method and the direct SLAE solution method with a sparse matrix of coefficients. A finite-difference approximation of the electric field potential distribution equation reduces the problem of numerical simulation of LLS to the solution of an SLAE with a sparse matrix and a set of right-hand sides. As a rule, the direct SLAE solution method consists of three stages:

1. Symbolic factorization.
2. Numerical factorization.
3. Solution.

The first stage is the most time-consuming due to the weak parallelization of [14]. However, the developed algorithm for solving the inverse problem is constructed so that all direct problems (arising within the framework of solving the inverse problem) are approximated on the same computational grid, which leads to the fact that all direct problems have the same sparse coefficient matrix template. It means that symbolic factorization is performed exactly once at the beginning of the algorithm. Then, the matrix coefficients are changed on the fly without violating the sparse matrix template.

Based on the nature of the task (a single execution of a complex and difficult-to-parallelize operation and SLAE solution for many right-hand sides), the optimal choice is to use the NVIDIA cuDSS [1] library for graphics accelerators. Since cuDSS entails storing the matrix in GPU memory, the algorithm is designed to avoid extremely time-consuming exchanges between video and CPU memory. Therefore, the matrix is loaded into VRAM once, and then, when the environment parameters change, the coefficients are changed directly in the graphics accelerator's memory.

Using cuDSS provides a considerable performance boost in solving this problem compared to libraries focused on solving SLAE using the CPU. However, it is worth noting that due to the rapid development of artificial intelligence technologies, graphics accelerators have become an expensive and scarce commodity, which entails significant restrictions on using the developed algorithm (availability of appropriate infrastructure). Nevertheless, it is not difficult to reorient the algorithm to CPU usage. For example, the Intel MKL PARDISO [2] library can be used with Intel Xeon Phi KNL [11] multithreaded processors. Also, SLAE can be solved by iterative methods (for example, the biconjugate gradient stabilized method [15]).

2   Problem Statement

In a cylindrical coordinate system with radial symmetry, the potential distribution of the electric field is described by the equation:

$$\frac{1}{r}\frac{\partial}{\partial r}\left(r\sigma\frac{\partial U}{\partial r}\right) + \frac{\partial}{\partial z}\left(\sigma\frac{\partial U}{\partial z}\right) = -g, \tag{1}$$

where U — electric field potential, about σ — electrical conductivity, g — in case of point source of direct current with intensity I at the middle of the borehole at point z_0 is $\frac{I}{2\pi}\delta(r)\delta(z - z_0)$. For the Eq. 1, a mixed boundary value problem with boundary conditions is posed:

$$\frac{\partial U}{\partial r}\Big|_{r=0} = 0, \ U\Big|_{\sqrt{r^2+z^2}\to\infty} = 0. \tag{2}$$

3   Finite-Difference Scheme

To approximate the Eq. 1, we introduce a uniform rectangular grid with steps h_z, h_r along the directions z and r, respectively. The grid nodes are points with coordinates $z_{m_z} = h_z m_z$ and $r_{m_r} = h_r m_r$, where the indices m_z, m_r take half-integer values. Setting the grid cells:

$$C_{m_z,m_r} = [h_z(m_z - 1/2), h_z(m_z + 1/2)] \times [h_r(m_r - 1/2), h_r(m_r + 1/2)]. \tag{3}$$

The potential and conductivity are considered constant inside the grid cell, while they may have discontinuities at the cell boundary. Then the finite-difference approximation of the Eq. 1 has the following form:

$$
\begin{aligned}
&\frac{\tilde{\sigma}_{m_z+1/2,m_r}}{h_z^2}U_{m_z+1,m_r} + \frac{\tilde{\sigma}_{m_z,m_r+1/2}r_{m_z,m_r+1/2}}{r_{m_z,m_r}h_r^2}U_{m_z,m_r+1}+ \\
&+\frac{\tilde{\sigma}_{m_z-1/2,m_r}}{h_z^2}U_{m_z-1,m_r} + \frac{\tilde{\sigma}_{m_z,m_r-1/2}r_{m_z,m_r-1/2}}{r_{m_z,m_r}h_r^2}U_{m_z,m_r-1}- \\
&-\left(\frac{\tilde{\sigma}_{m_z+1/2,m_r} + \tilde{\sigma}_{m_z-1/2,m_r}}{h_z^2}+ \right.\\
&\left.+\frac{\tilde{\sigma}_{m_z,m_r+1/2}r_{m_z,m_r+1/2} + \tilde{\sigma}_{m_z,m_r-1/2}r_{m_z,m_r-1/2}}{r_{m_z,m_r}h_r^2}\right)U_{m_z,m_r} = \\
&= -g_{m_z,m_r}.
\end{aligned} \tag{4}
$$

Since the boundary value problem for the system of Eqs. 1 is posed in unbounded space, the finite-difference scheme is constructed in the corresponding unbounded space. It is impossible to solve such a problem in practice. Therefore, a limited computational area is allocated from the space $\Omega = [Z_{min}, Z_{max}] \times [0, R_{max}]$. At the boundaries of $z = Z_{min}$, $z = Z_{max}$ and $r = R_{max}$, the Dirichlet condition is set: $U = 0$. Let $Z_{max} = M_z h_z$ and $R_{max} = M_r h_r$. Then, the finite-difference analog of the Dirichlet condition:

$$
\frac{U_{-1/2,m_r} + U_{1/2,m_r}}{2} = \frac{U_{M_z-1/2,m_r} + U_{M_z+1/2,m_r}}{2} = \\
= \frac{U_{m_z,M_r-1/2} + U_{m_z,M_r+1/2}}{2} = 0. \tag{5}
$$

A finite-difference analog of the Neumann condition:

$$\frac{U_{m_z,1/2} - U_{m_z,-1/2}}{h_r} = 0. \tag{6}$$

When creating SLAE, values in nodes outside the Ω domain are excluded from the expression 4. From the Dirichlet condition 5:

$$
\begin{aligned}
U_{-1/2,m_r} &= -U_{1/2,m_r}, \\
U_{M_z+1/2,m_r} &= -U_{M_z-1/2,m_r}, \\
U_{m_z,M_r+1/2} &= -U_{m_z,M_r-1/2}.
\end{aligned}
\tag{7}
$$

From the Neumann condition 6:

$$
U_{m_z,-1/2} = U_{m_z,1/2}.
\tag{8}
$$

However, this approach worsens the quality of the solution since the Dirichlet condition is not set at infinity. It is possible to distance the boundary conditions without significantly increasing computational costs by using the theory of optimal grids [4,9]. Uniform grids are used in this work for ease of implementation, and the boundary condition is set at a given distance from some computational area of interest.

The matrix of SLAE 4 is not symmetric but can be symmetrized by row and column operations. Let the initial SLAE have the form:

$$
\mathcal{A}x = b,
\tag{9}
$$

then, multiplying from the left by the diagonal matrix, we obtain the equivalent system:

$$
D_r\mathcal{A}x = D_rb.
\tag{10}
$$

If we apply to the matrix $\mathcal{A}$ column operation, then the transformed system will no longer be equivalent to the system 9:

$$
D_r\mathcal{A}D_c\bar{x} = D_rb,
\tag{11}
$$

however, the solution x of the original system 9 can be obtained from the solution $\bar{x}$ of the system 11:

$$
x = D_c\bar{x}.
\tag{12}
$$

So, the SLAE matrix 4 can be symmetrized by matrices:

$$
D_r = \begin{pmatrix} \sqrt{r_{1/2,1/2}} & & & 0 \\ & \sqrt{r_{1/2,3/2}} & & \\ & & \ddots & \\ 0 & & & \sqrt{r_{M_z-1/2,M_r-1/2}} \end{pmatrix},
\tag{13}
$$

$$
D_c = \begin{pmatrix} \dfrac{1}{\sqrt{r_{1/2,1/2}}} & & & 0 \\ & \dfrac{1}{\sqrt{r_{1/2,3/2}}} & & \\ & & \ddots & \\ 0 & & & \dfrac{1}{\sqrt{r_{M_z-1/2,M_r-1/2}}} \end{pmatrix}.
\tag{14}
$$

That is, $D_c = D_r^{-1}$. Next, we will denote $D_r = D, D_c = D^{-1}$.

After the transformation, the finite difference scheme will take the form:

$$\frac{\tilde{\sigma}_{m_z+1/2,m_r}}{h_z^2}U_{m_z+1,m_r} + \frac{\tilde{\sigma}_{m_z,m_r+1/2}r_{m_z,m_r+1/2}}{\sqrt{r_{m_z,m_r}r_{m_z,m_r+1}}h_r^2}U_{m_z,m_r+1}+$$

$$+\frac{\tilde{\sigma}_{m_z-1/2,m_r}}{h_z^2}U_{m_z-1,m_r} + \frac{\tilde{\sigma}_{m_z,m_r-1/2}r_{m_z,m_r-1/2}}{\sqrt{r_{m_z,m_r-1}r_{m_z,m_r}}h_r^2}U_{m_z,m_r-1}-$$

$$-\left(\frac{\tilde{\sigma}_{m_z+1/2,m_r} + \tilde{\sigma}_{m_z-1/2,m_r}}{h_z^2}+\right.$$

$$\left.+\frac{\tilde{\sigma}_{m_z,m_r+1/2}r_{m_z,m_r+1/2} + \tilde{\sigma}_{m_z,m_r-1/2}r_{m_z,m_r-1/2}}{r_{m_z,m_r}h_r^2}\right)U_{m_z,m_r}$$

$$= -\sqrt{r_{m_z,m_r}}g_{m_z,m_r}. \tag{15}$$

The electrical conductivities at the cell faces are calculated by the harmonic mean of the conductivities of neighboring cells [10]:

$$\tilde{\sigma}_{m_z+1/2,m_r} = \frac{2\sigma_{m_z+1,m_r}\sigma_{m_z,m_r}}{\sigma_{m_z+1,m_r} + \sigma_{m_z,m_r}},$$

$$\tilde{\sigma}_{m_z,m_r+1/2} = \frac{2\sigma_{m_z,m_r+1}\sigma_{m_z,m_r}}{\sigma_{m_z,m_r} + \sigma_{m_z,m_r+1}}. \tag{16}$$

Since the matrix must be positively defined for the Cholesky decomposition [7], the left and right sides of the system 15 are multiplied by -1.

The function g is considered a point source of direct current, that is, for a given pair of indices s_z, s_r and a given current value I_0 $g_{s_z,s_r} = I_0$, for all other indices $m_z \neq s_z \wedge m_r \neq s_r$ $g_{m_z,m_r} = 0$.

3.1   Numerical Simulation of the Lateral Logging Sounding

Let us consider a model of a medium with plane-parallel and coaxial-cylindrical section boundaries [3]. A vertical cylindrical borehole of radius r_c filled with drilling mud with resistance ρ_{wb} intersects a horizontal pack of layers of limited thickness h^i with resistances ρ_l^i, as well as unlimited (enclosing) formations with resistances $\overline{\rho_{adj}}$ and $\underline{\rho_{adj}}$. Drilling mud invasion zones (media with resistances ρ_{inv}^i) can be formed between the borehole and the layers. The distance from the axis of the borehole to the interface between the invasion zones and the layers is denoted as r_{inv}^i.

Let us describe the lateral logging sounding (LLS) process in an environment with plane-parallel and coaxial-cylindrical interface boundaries. Potential difference measurements are performed using several probes on the axis of the well with a step of Δd. The probe is defined by four points A, O, M, N (Fig. 1). A current source with a current strength of I is located at point A. The potential difference ΔU is measured between the electrodes M and N and conditionally refers to the point O, which is the middle of the segment MN.

Thus, the probe can be set by a pair of distances $L = AO$—the distance from the source to the measuring point ΔU and $l = MN$— the distance between the receiver electrodes. Thus, each of the probes moves along the axis of the borehole in steps of Δd, measuring the potential difference ΔU at a distance of L from the current position of the source. The different positions of the source correspond to the different right sides for the SLAE 15. Thus, the numerical simulation of the LLS is reduced to solving a matrix equation of the form

$$\mathcal{A}X = B, \tag{17}$$

where the matrix $\mathcal{A}$—coincides with the SLAE matrix 15, B—is a matrix of right-hand sides, the columns of which have a form similar to that of the right-hand side of SLAE 15. The columns of the matrix X—specify the distribution of the electrical potential for the corresponding source. ΔU for a given probe position can be found by calculating the difference between the two corresponding elements of the solution column vector from X.

It is worth noting that the number of right-hand sides can be reduced since the exact position of the sources at the same current strength for different probes form the same right-hand sides. Therefore, ΔU can be obtained from a single solution vector. This optimization is implemented by grouping the measurements by the source coordinate after reading the parameters of the probes and measuring points ΔU.

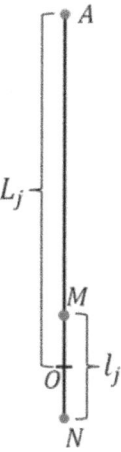

Fig. 1. The scheme of the probe

4   Inverse Problem of the Lateral Logging Sounding

Let us consider the medium with plane-parallel and coaxial-cylindrical interface boundaries, for which $r_c, \rho_{wb}, h^i, \overline{\rho_{adj}}, \underline{\rho_{adj}}$, as well as the number of layers N_l are known. The parameters $\rho_l^i, \rho_{inv}^i, r_{inv}^i, 1 \leq i \leq N_l$ are considered unknown. They form the M data space.

In addition to the medium, N_z probes with known parameters $L_j, l_j, I_j, 1 \leq j \leq N_z$ are specified. For each probe, a set of points $x_{j,k}$ is set, where the potential difference $\Delta U_{j,k}, 1 \leq j \leq N_z, 1 \leq k \leq K_i$ is measured. The $\Delta U_{j,k}$ values are known. Denote $\Delta U_j = (\Delta U_{j,1}, ..., \Delta U_{j,K_j})$ is a vector of known potential differences for the probe j. This vector belongs to the dimension space of the j-th probe $\boldsymbol{\Delta U_j}$. Then we form the vector $\Delta U = (\Delta U_1 \cdot \Delta U_2 \cdot ... \cdot \Delta U_{N_z})$ by concatenating ΔU_k. ΔU belong to the dimension space $\boldsymbol{\Delta U}$.

Let us define the operator of the direct problem $F(m) = (F_1(m) \cdot F_2(m) \cdot ... \cdot F_{N_z}(m)) : M \rightarrow \boldsymbol{\Delta U}$, which maps the model m into $F(m) \in \boldsymbol{\Delta U}$, based on the solution of the 17 with m parameters. Then the inverse problem can be formulated as follows:

$$\text{Find } \tilde{m} \in M \mid E(\tilde{m}) = \min_{m \in M} E(m),$$

$$E(m) = \sum_{j=1}^{N_z} \frac{||F_j(m) - \Delta U_j||_j}{||\Delta U_j||_j}, \tag{18}$$

where $||x||_j$—the 2-norm on the vector space $\boldsymbol{\Delta U_j}$.

It is worth noting that to reduce the number of calculations, especially in the case of an excess of data, the projective operators P_j can be introduced: $\boldsymbol{\Delta U_j} \rightarrow \boldsymbol{\Delta U}$. Examples of such operators include selecting each k-th value from the vector ΔU_j, selecting values of ΔU_j corresponding to a certain range of coordinates $x_{j,k} \in [a, b]$, and not using probe data (i.e., $P_j : \boldsymbol{\Delta U_j} \rightarrow 0$ for some j). The global sensitivity analysis method [8,13] can also be used to build a representative sample of $\Delta U_{j,k}$. In terms of projections, the formulation of the inverse problem is changing:

$$\text{Find } \tilde{m} \in M \mid E(\tilde{m}) = \min_{m \in M} E(m),$$

$$E(m) = \sum_{j=1, P_j \not\equiv 0}^{N_z} \frac{||P_j \circ F_j(m) - P_j(\Delta U_j)||_j}{||P_j(\Delta U_j)||_j}. \tag{19}$$

5   Nelder-Mead Method

The Nelder-Mead simplex algorithm is a complete search method for solving the problem of unconditional optimization of $\min f(\boldsymbol{x})$, where $f : \mathbb{R}^n \rightarrow \mathbb{R}$—objective function [6,12]. A simplex of dimension n is a convex hull of $n + 1$ vertices. Denote the simplex with vertices $\boldsymbol{x}_1, \boldsymbol{x}_2, ..., \boldsymbol{x}_{n+1}$ as Δ. The Nelder-Mead algorithm generates a sequence of simplices approximating the minimum point of the objective function. At each iteration, the vertices of the simplex $\{\boldsymbol{x}_j\}_{j=1}^{n+1}$ are sorted according to the values of the objective function: $f(\boldsymbol{x}_1) \leq f(\boldsymbol{x}_2) \leq ... \leq f(\boldsymbol{x}_{n+1})$. The vertex $\boldsymbol{x}_1$ is considered the best, and $\boldsymbol{x}_{n+1}$ is considered the worst.

The algorithm uses four operations: reflection, expansion, contraction, and shrink. Each of the operations is set by a corresponding parameter: α (reflection), β (expansion), γ (contraction), and δ (shrink). The standard algorithm parameters are the values $\{\alpha, \beta, \gamma, \delta\} = \{1, 2, \frac{1}{2}, \frac{1}{2}\}$. The center of gravity of the n best vertices is denoted as

$$\bar{x} = \frac{1}{n} \sum_{i=1}^{n} x_i. \tag{20}$$

In these terms, one iteration of the Nelder-Mead algorithm has the following form:

1. **Order.** Calculate the value of the function f for each of the $n+1$ vertices Δ and sort the vertices in ascending order by the value of f.
2. **Reflection.** Calculate the reflected point $x_r = \bar{x} + \alpha(\bar{x} - x_{n+1})$. Find $f_r = f(x_r)$. If $f(x_1) \leq f_r < f(x_n)$, replace the point x_{n+1} with the point x_r.
3. **Expansion.** If $f_r < f(x_1)$, calculate the expanded point $x_e = \bar{x} + \beta(x_r - \bar{x})$ and find the value of $f_e = f(x_e)$. If $f_e < f_r$, replace the point x_{n+1} with the point x_e, otherwise replace the point x_{n+1} with the point x_r.
4. **External contraction.** If $f(x_n) \leq f_r < f(x_{n+1})$, calculate the point of external contraction $x_{oc} = \bar{x} + \gamma(x_r - \bar{x})$ and find the value of $f_{oc} = f(x_{oc})$. If $f_{oc} < f_r$, replace the point x_{n+1} with the point x_{oc}, otherwise go to step 6.
5. **Internal contraction.** If $f_r \geq f(x_{n+1})$, calculate the point of internal contraction $x_{ic} = \bar{x} - \gamma(x_r - \bar{x})$ and find the value of $f_{ic} = f(x_{ic})$. If $f_{ic} < f(x_{n+1})$, replace the point x_{n+1} with the point x_{ic}, otherwise go to step 6.
6. **Shrink.** For $2 \leq i \leq n+1$, calculate the new points $x_i = x_1 + \delta(x_i - x_1)$.

Justification of operations:

1. Reflection: if x_{n+1} is the worst point, then the minimum is assumed to be in the opposite direction.
2. Expansion: if the reflected point is a new minimum, then it is assumed that the approximation will improve even more if the point is moved further in the same direction.
3. Contraction: if reflection does not provide a good approximation, then the minimum is assumed to lie inside the simplex.
4. Shrink: if moving away from the worst point did not give a better approximation, all points are approaching the best.

The algorithm can be stopped when one of the following conditions is met:

1. $\max_{1 \leq i,j \leq n+1} |f_i - f_j| < \epsilon$—the change in the values of the objective function has become too small.
2. $\max_{1 \leq i,j \leq n+1} \|x_i - x_j\| < \delta$—the change in the points of the simplex has become too small.
3. The iteration limit has been reached: $num\_it > it\_max$.

4. The limit on the number of function calculations f has been reached: $num\_f\_eval > f\_eval\_max$.

The input data for the Nelder-Mead algorithm is an n-dimensional simplex, that is, $n + 1$ points of an n-dimensional space. This simplex can be chosen based on an approximation based on some a priori knowledge of the objective function. Either the simplex can be chosen randomly. If the constraints on the parameters are known, the Nelder-Mead algorithm can be modified to optimize the limited area. Consider the parameter x lying in the range $[a, b]$, and introduce the equivalent normalized parameter $\tilde{x} \in [0, 1]$. The one-to-one correspondence between them is given as $x = a + (b - a)\tilde{x}$. If during the execution of iterations of the Nelder-Mead algorithm (for example, during reflection or stretching), the parameter $\tilde{x}$ falls outside the range of $[0, 1]$, then its value is assumed to be 0, with $\tilde{x} < 0$ or 1, with $\tilde{x} > 1$.

Generalizing the proposed approach to the n-dimensional case, we assume optimization is performed in the n-dimensional unit cube. If a point goes beyond its limits, it is projected onto the area's boundary.

6   Results

The true data was obtained by simulation with ANSYS. The known parameters of the one-layer medium are presented in Table 1, and the parameters that should be recovered are shown in Table 2. Similarly, the known parameters of the three-layer medium are in the Table 3, and the unknown ones are in the Table 4.

To solve the inverse problem (19), the function $E(m)$ is minimized by the Nelder-Mead algorithm. Solving a series of direct problems that arise at each iteration of the algorithm is carried out using the NVIDIA cuDSS library.

Table 1. Known parameters of the one-layer medium

r_c (m)	ρ_c ($\Omega \cdot m$)	$\overline{\rho_{adj}}$ ($\Omega \cdot m$)	ρ_{adj} ($\Omega \cdot m$)	h (m)
0.1	1.7	5.0	5.0	3.0

Table 2. Unknown parameters of the one-layer medium

r_{inv} (m)	ρ_{inv} ($\Omega \cdot m$)	ρ_l ($\Omega \cdot m$)
0.3	30	10

Table 3. Known parameters of the three-layer medium

r_c (m)	ρ_c ($\Omega \cdot m$)	$\overline{\rho_{adj}}$ ($\Omega \cdot m$)	ρ_{adj} ($\Omega \cdot m$)	h^1 (m)	h^2 (m)	h^3 (m)
0.1	1.7	5.0	5.0	3.0	5.0	3.0

Table 4. Unknown parameters of the three-layer medium

Layer number	$r_{inv}(m)$	$\rho_{inv}(\Omega \cdot m)$	$\rho_l(\Omega \cdot m)$
1	0.2	30	10
2	0.5	40	7
3	0.3	30	15

Test calculations using the single-layer medium have shown that for different pairs of ρ_{inv}, r_{inv}, obtaining a fairly close result to the observed data is possible. This effect is called the U-equivalence of lateral logging sounding curves [3]:

$$\frac{\rho_{inv} - \rho_l}{\rho_c} \ln \frac{r_{inv}}{r_c} = U_{idem}. \tag{21}$$

Thus, a curve C appears in the parameter space, each point c_i of which is a minimum in some neighborhood, except points on the curve $B_\epsilon(c_i) \backslash C$. Using a minimization method based on calculating the gradient would lead to the algorithm hitting this curve and descending along it to a global minimum. However, the Nelder-Mead algorithm does not use the gradient of the objective function; moreover, due to discretization, r_{inv} can only take a finite number of values, and therefore, the curve splits into several unrelated local minima. When the Nelder-Mead algorithm "gets stuck" in one of these minimums, it can no longer find a global one. Nevertheless, the search for a global minimum is possible. The case of a single-layer environment is described in the Subsect. 6.1, and a three-layer environment is described in the Subsect. 6.2.

6.1   One-Layer Medium

The known parameters of the one-layer medium are presented in the Table 1. The list of probes is shown in the Table 5. When solving the inverse problem, only the values of $\Delta U_{j,k}$ corresponding to points from a given interval are used. For each probe, this interval is indicated in the last column of the Table 5. The $z = 0$ level is considered the middle of the layer.

Table 5. Parameters of probes

Probe number	$L(m)$	$l(m)$	Range
1	0.45	0.1	$[-2.5, 3.0]$
2	1.05	0.1	$[-2.5, 3.5]$
3	2.25	0.5	$[-3, 5.5]$
4	4.25	0.5	$[-4.5, 9.0]$
5	8.5	1.0	$[-5, 15.0]$

A priori estimates are known for unknown medium parameters:

$$1.5r_c \leq r_{inv} \leq 12r_c$$
$$0.5\rho_c \leq \rho_{inv} \leq 500\rho_c \quad\quad (22)$$
$$0.03125\rho_{inv} \leq \rho_l \leq 4\rho_{inv},$$

Substituting the known parameters values, we get:

$$0.15 \leq r_{inv} \leq 1.2$$
$$0.85 \leq \rho_{inv} \leq 850 \quad\quad (23)$$
$$0.0265625 \leq \rho_l \leq 3400.$$

The size of the computational domain is $[-45.5, 45.5] \times [0, 31.2]$ with spatial sampling steps $h_z = 0.05$ and $h_r = 0.025$. This size is chosen based on the following considerations. First, the minimum coordinate of the source is determined——13.5, then the maximum coordinate of the receiver—15.5. These values define the initial range of the calculated area along the z axis. The initial range of r is determined by the maximum radius of the invasion zone—$[0, 1.2]$. Then, the area's boundaries are moved by $30\,\mathrm{m}$ in each direction, resulting in the size of the computing area $[-43.5, 45.5] \times [0, 31.2]$. For symmetry concerning the point $z = 0$, the range along the z axis is expanded to $[-45.5, 45.5]$. The computational grid size at a given sampling step is 1820×1248 nodes.

For each of the values of r_c from the range $[0.2, 1.2]$ in increments of 0.1 (Table 6), the Nelder-Meade algorithm restores the remaining two parameters. In the Table 6, the value of the objective function on the found solution is written in column E. The value of Ev_num denotes the number of solved direct problems, and It_num is the number of iterations of the Nelder-Mead algorithm.

Table 6. The results of restoring the parameters of the one-layer model

r_{inv}	ρ_{inv}	ρ_l	E	Ev_num	It_num
0.2	42.06	10.37	0.099	99	52
0.3	30.01	10.30	0.079	141	74
0.4	25.52	10.24	0.077	139	74
0.5	23.54	9.97	0.087	170	90
0.6	22.27	9.70	0.118	144	76
0.7	21.31	9.42	0.151	123	67
0.8	20.63	9.13	0.186	98	52
0.9	20.13	8.87	0.221	119	63
1.0	19.75	8.65	0.255	245	133
1.1	19.46	8.48	0.280	93	49
1.2	19.22	8.31	0.317	102	53

Thus, the minimum is reached for the values $r_c = 0.4(m)$, $\rho_{inv} = 25.52(\Omega \cdot m)$ $\rho_l = 10.24(\Omega \cdot m)$. Found parameter values for $r_c = 0.3$ almost coincides with the

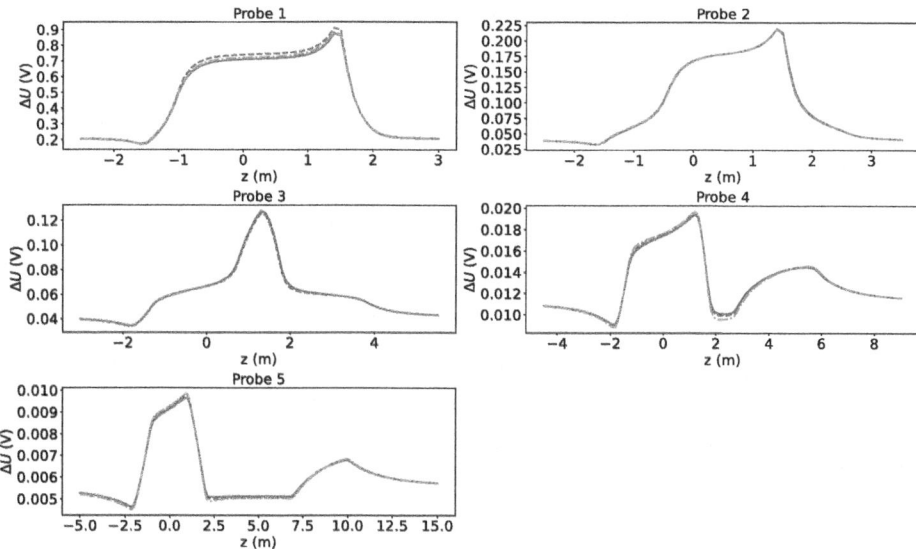

Fig. 2. LLS curves. Blue—true data. Orange—simulation result for optimal parameters. Brown - simulation result for true parameters (Color figure online)

true values. However, the value of the objective function for this set of parameters is higher than for $r_c = 0.4$. This effect is explained by the error in solving the direct problem (Fig. 2).

We also note that the found values of ρ_l are close enough to the actual value of ρ_l for any value of r_c. This observation will be used to restore the parameters of the three-layer environment.

On a device with an NVIDIA RTX 3090 Ti 24 GB graphics accelerator, the calculation took 70 min, of which 10 s was the symbolic factorization of the matrix A from the matrix Eq. 17, and the rest of the time was iterations of the Nelder-Meade algorithm. Thus, the average time to solve one direct problem without considering symbolic factorization is 2.86 s.

6.2 Three-Layer Medium

The known parameters of a single-layer medium are presented in the Table 3. The list of probes is shown in the Table 7. When solving the inverse problem, only the values of $\Delta U_{j,k}$ corresponding to every second point from the specified interval are used. For each probe, this interval is indicated in the last column of the Table 5. The $z = 0$ level is considered the middle of the second layer.

The design area configuration is set for the same reasons as in the 6.1 subsection. The size of the calculated area—$[-45.5, 45.5] \times [0, 31.2]$, spatial sampling steps—$h_z = 0.05$ and $h_r = 0.025$, computational grid size—1820×1248 nodes.

The task is solved in three stages. The first stage is to find the values of the layers resistivities ρ_l^i using an observation from the Sect. 6.1. It is assumed

Table 7. Parameters of probes

Probe number	$L(m)$	$l(m)$	Range
1	0.45	0.1	$[-10.6, 9.2]$
2	1.05	0.1	$[-10.0, 9.8]$
3	2.25	0.5	$[-8.8, 11.0]$
4	4.25	0.5	$[-6.8, 13.0]$
5	8.5	1.0	$[-7.0, 15.0]$

that even for far from true values of ρ_{inv}^i and r_{inv}^i, found by the Nelder-Mead values of ρ_l^i will be close to the true values. Therefore, random values of the parameters $r_{inv}^i, 1 \leq i \leq 3$ are selected from the range $[0.15, 1.2]$. The remaining six parameters are found for the selected values by the Nelder-Mead algorithm. This operation is repeated 128 times.

These calculations were launched on a node with 8 NVIDIA A100 80 GB GPUs. Using MPI technology, 128 runs of the Nelder-Meade algorithm were divided between 8 GPUs (16 runs each). The computation time is 10 h.

As a result of each run, nine parameters and the value of the objective function E were obtained. Parameter sets with a $E > 1$ are filtered out and do not participate in further parameter determination. ρ_l^i are found as a weighted average of the values of ρ_l^i among the remaining parameter sets in the sample. The weight of the set is defined as $\frac{1}{E}$. Thus, the resistivity values of the layers $\rho_l^1 = 10.21, \rho_l^2 = 7.10, \rho_l^3 = 15.18$ are established. These values are used in the second step to restore the remaining parameters.

Restoration of the remaining parameters is similar to the process described in Sect. 6.1. At the second stage, for the given values $\rho_l^1 = 10.21, \rho_l^2 = 7.10, \rho_l^3 = 15.18$, the parameters $r_{inv}^i, 1 \leq i \leq 3$ vary in the range $[0.2, 1.2]$ in 0.2 increments. For each triple r_{inv}^i, the Nelder-Mead algorithm restores the parameters $\rho_{inv}^i, 1 \leq i \leq 3$. $6 \times 6 \times 6 = 216$ runs of the algorithm take 4.5 h when running in parallel on 8 NVIDIA A100 80 GB GPUs. Note that the data from the fifth probe is not used in this case (i.e., $P_5 \equiv 0$); this is because, the measurements of the fifth probe primarily depend on the resistivity of the layers that have already been determined. At the same time, the positions of the source for the fifth probe do not coincide with the positions of the sources for all other probes, therefore, the exclusion of this probe from the calculation reduces the number of columns in the matrices X, B (Eq. 17).

The smallest error values are achieved for the values r_{inv}^i lying at the vertices of the cube $[0.2, 0.4] \times [0.4, 0.6] \times [0.2, 0.4]$. The values of the objective function and the corresponding reconstructed parameters ρ_{inv}^i are presented in the Table 8.

The minimum is reached for the parameter values $r_{inv}^1 = 0.2, r_{inv}^2 = 0.6, r_{inv}^3 = 0.4$. Since the objective function is the sum of the relative errors for each of the four probes, the value $E = 0.0343$ means that, on average, the relative error for each probe does not exceed 1% (Fig. 3).

Table 8. The smallest values of the objective function E and the corresponding medium parameters

$r_{inv}^1(m)$	$r_{inv}^2(m)$	$r_{inv}^2(m)$	E	$\rho_{inv}^1(\Omega \cdot m)$	$\rho_{inv}^2(\Omega \cdot m)$	$\rho_{inv}^3(\Omega \cdot m)$
0.2	0.4	0.2	0.0995	29.59	45.57	39.40
0.2	0.4	0.4	0.0979	29.58	45.57	26.73
0.2	0.6	0.2	0.0531	29.00	36.49	38.14
0.2	0.6	0.4	0.0343	28.95	36.44	26.30
0.4	0.4	0.2	0.1082	19.34	45.61	39.41
0.4	0.4	0.4	0.1053	19.36	45.60	26.75
0.4	0.6	0.2	0.0558	19.28	36.44	38.26
0.4	0.6	0.4	0.0375	19.33	36.39	26.30

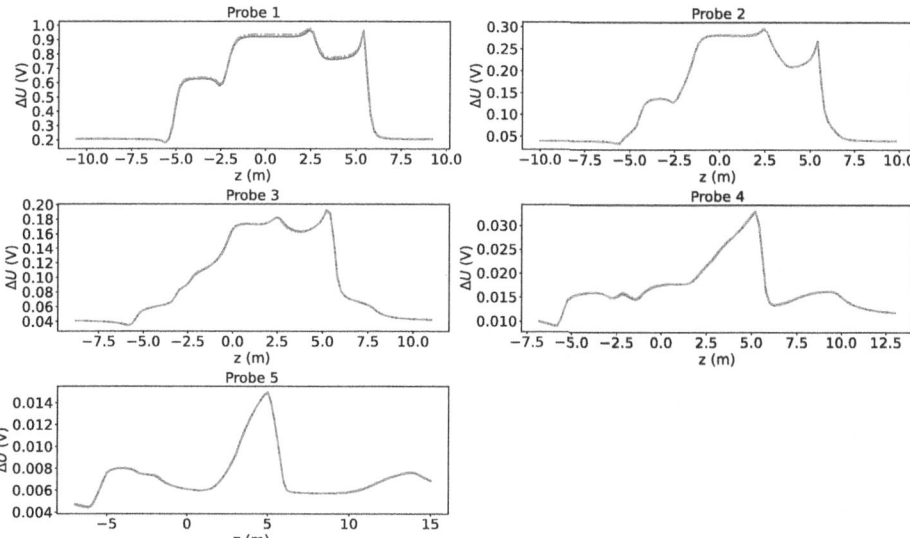

Fig. 3. LLS curves. Blue— (Color figure online)true data. Orange—simulation result for optimal parameters.

In the third stage, the solution is refined on a smaller grid with spatial sampling steps $h_z = 0.025$ and $h_r = 0.025$. Similarly to the previous stage, the parameters $r_{inv}^1, r_{inv}^2, r_{inv}^3$ vary in increments of 0.05 in the ranges $[0.2, 0.4], [0.5, 0.6], [0.2, 0.4]$ respectively. That is, the parameters are refined inside the found cube with the lowest values of the objective function at the vertices (the interval $[0.4, 0.6]$ for the parameter r_{inv}^2 was reduced to $[0.5, 0.6]$ based on the fact that the value of the objective function on the right edge of the interval is significantly lower than on the left). To reduce the calculation time, instead of a priori estimates of the range ρ_{inv}^i, new ranges are used based on the maximum and minimum values of ρ_{inv}^i from the Table 8. Thus, the search interval ρ_{inv}^1 is considered to be the interval $[19, 30]$, for ρ_{inv}^2—$[36, 46]$, for ρ_{inv}^3—$[26, 40]$. Reducing the search interval significantly speeds up the Nelder-Mead algorithm running time (up to 10 min), which allows us to perform the entire calculation using 8 NVIDIA A100 80 GB GPUs in 1.5 h. The minimum error $E = 0.0340$ is reached for the set of parameters in Table 9.

Table 9. The recovered parameters of the three-layer medium

Layer number	$r_{inv}(m)$	$\rho_{inv}(\Omega \cdot m)$	$\rho_l(\Omega \cdot m)$
1	0.2	29.44	10.21
2	0.55	38.24	7.10
3	0.3	29.8	15.18

7   Conclusion

The algorithm has been developed to solve the inverse problem of lateral logging sounding using the Nelder-Mead method (deformable simplex method). Since calculating the objective function during the solution of the inverse problem requires solving a series of direct problems, the core of the complex is the solver of the direct problem of electric field potential distribution in general and the LLS problem in particular. The direct problem solver is constructed using the finite difference method. The resulting SLAE has a symmetric matrix, making it possible to use a Cholesky decomposition. Moreover, due to the constancy of the sparse matrix template, the time-consuming symbolic factorization operation is performed only once. The key advantage in solution speed is the direct SLAE solver from the NVIDIA cuDSS library. Even though cuDSS is inferior to the solvers implemented for the CPU (Intel MKL PARDISO) in terms of the execution time of symbolic factorization, since this operation is difficult to parallelize, cuDSS has a considerable advantage at the stage of calculating the solution based on the decomposed matrix.

The parameters of the medium with plane-parallel and coaxial-cylindrical interfaces were restored for one layer with drilling mud invasion and three layers (also with drilling mud invasion) using the developed algorithm. The calculation for a single-layer environment took 70 min on a personal computer with a modern NVIDIA RTX 3090 Ti 24 GB GPU. Restoring the parameters of a three-layer environment is a much more time-consuming task. The total calculation time using 8 NVIDIA A100 80 GB GPUs is 14 h. This time can be significantly reduced. At the second stage, the variation of the invasion radii over the entire range can be replaced by searching the octants of the cube $[0.15, 1.2] \times [0.15, 1.2] \times [0.15, 1.2]$, which would lead to the final area $[0.2, 0.4] \times [0.4, 0.6] \times [0.2, 0.4]$ not for 216, but for 45 solutions to the inverse problem, moreover, restoring the parameters ρ_{inv}^i for boundary values of r_{inv}^i from the range $[0.15, 1.2] \times [0.15, 1.2] \times [0.15, 1.2]$ would allow us to get a significantly smaller search range for ρ_{inv}^i (since this was done at the third stage of the solution). Solutions to the inverse problem with random parameters of the invasion zones were used to search for layers resistivities. Since the layers resistivities are being restored reasonably well, regardless of the parameters of the penetration zones, the number of launches can be significantly reduced. The proposed optimizations will reduce the total calculation time for a three-layer environment to 3–4 h (when using 8 NVIDIA A100 80 GB GPUs).

Another option to reduce the calculation time is to use gradient minimization methods. Even though the Nelder-Mead algorithm has been successfully applied to solving the inverse problem, the minimum configuration in the parameter space suggests that gradient methods can significantly increase search speed. However, gradient minimization methods significantly complicate the algorithm.

The accuracy of parameters recovery is relatively high (especially for layers electrical resistivity). Nevertheless, the recovered values of drilling mud invasion radii may be overestimated (the error value is up to one borehole radius), which in turn also introduces a small error in the electrical resistivity of the invasion zone. This problem arises due to the use of a coarse grid and the insufficient removal of boundary conditions. Both problems can be solved using optimal grid theory. The construction of an optimal grid will significantly improve the processing of boundary conditions and reduce the overall size of the grid, which in turn will allow using a smaller step of spatial discretization.

Acknowledgments. The research was supported by the Russian Science Foundation grant no. 19-77-20004-П.

Disclosure of Interests. The authors have no competing interests to declare that are relevant to the content of this article.

References

1. NVIDIA cuDSS. https://developer.nvidia.com/cudss. Accessed 03 Mar 2025
2. Belonosov, M.A., Kostov, C., Reshetova, G.V., Soloviev, S.A., Tcheverda, V.A.: Parallel numerical simulation of seismic waves propagation with intel math kernel library. In: Manninen, P., Öster, P. (eds.) Applied Parallel and Scientific Computing, pp. 153–167. Springer Berlin Heidelberg
3. Dahnov, V.: Electric and Magnetic Methods of Borehole Research. Nedra, Moscow (1981). in Russian
4. Druskin, V., Knizhnermann, L.: Gaussian spectral rules for the three-point second differences: I a two-point positive definite problem in a semi-infinite domain. SIAM J. Numer. Anal. **36**, 442–464 (1999)
5. Druskin, V.: On the uniqueness of the solution of the inverse problem of electrical exploration and electrical wiring for piecewise constant conductivities. News of the USSR Academy of Sciences. Phys. Earth **1** (1982), in Russian
6. Gao, F., Han, L.: Implementing the Nelder-mead simplex algorithm with adaptive parameters. Comput. Optim. Appl. **51**(1), 259–277 (2012)

7. Gilbert, J., Schreiber, R.: Highly parallel sparse Cholesky factorization. SIAM J. Sci. Stat. Comput. **13** (1990)
8. Gondyul, E., Gadylshin, K., Lisitsa, V., Vishnevsky, D.: Reducing numerical dispersion in pseudo-3D space and constructing training dataset. In: Gervasi, O., Murgante, B., Garau, C., Taniar, D., C. Rocha, A.M.A., Faginas Lago, M.N. (eds.) Computational Science and Its Applications – ICCSA 2024 Workshops, pp. 352–366. Springer Nature Switzerland
9. Ingerman, D., Druskin, V., Knizhnerman, L.: Optimal finite difference grids and rational approximations of the square root i. elliptic problems. Commun. Pure Appl. Math. **53**, 1039–1066 (2000)
10. Khachkova, T., Lisitsa, V., Reshetova, G., Tcheverda, V.: GPU-based algorithm for evaluating the electrical resistivity of digital rocks. Comput. Math. Appl. **82**, 200–211 (2021)
11. Kulikov, I., et al.: Numerical modeling of hydrodynamic turbulence with self-gravity on intel Xeon Phi KNL. In: Sokolinsky, L., Zymbler, M. (eds.) Parallel Computational Technologies, pp. 309–322. Springer International Publishing
12. Nelder, J.A., Mead, R.: A simplex method for function minimization. Comput. J. **7**(4), 308–313 (1965)
13. Sobol, I.M.: Global sensitivity indices for nonlinear mathematical models and their monte Carlo estimates. Math. Comput. Simul. **55**(1), 271–280 (2001)
14. Solovyev, S.: Application of the low-rank approximation technique in the gauss elimination method for sparse linear systems. Num. Methods Programm. **3**, 441–460 (2014)
15. Solovyev, S., Lisitsa, V.: Field-split iterative solver vs direct one for quasi-static Biot equation. In: Voevodin, V., Sobolev, S., Yakobovskiy, M., Shagaliev, R. (eds.) Supercomputing, pp. 86–99. Springer Nature Switzerland, Cham (2023)

Constructing Dependence of Electrical Parameters on Porosity and Water Saturation for Digital Models of High-Permeability Rock Samples

Tatyana Khachkova[1]([✉]) [ID], Vadim Lisitsa[2] [ID], Vladislav Krutko[3],
and Alexander Avdonin[3]

[1] Institute of Petroleum Geology and Geophysics SB RAS, Koptug ave. 3,
Novosibirsk 630090, Russia
KhachkovaTS@ipgg.sbras.ru
[2] Institute of Mathematics SB RAS, Koptug ave. 2, Novosibirsk 630090, Russia
[3] Gazpromneft NTC, Moika River emb. 75-79 D, Saint-Petersburg 190000, Russia

Abstract. The present study focuses on the numerical evaluation of
Archie's coefficients – specifically, the cementation parameter and saturation exponent – using a digital model of a high-permeability rock
sample. Accurate estimation of these parameters is critical for reservoir
development planning and optimizing hydrocarbon recovery through formation stimulation techniques.

To derive the coefficients, we construct two relationships: the formation factor versus porosity and the resistivity index versus water saturation. The paper presents a methodology and case studies for establishing
these dependencies. The proposed approach involves solving two optimization problems to perform a linear regression in a logarithmic scale,
based on both the generalized and classical forms of Archie's law.

Keywords: Electrical parameters · Formation factor · Porosity ·
Resistivity index · Water saturation · Digital models ·
High-permeability samples · CT-images

1 Introduction

In recent years, there has been a rapid development of numerical methods for
rock characterization. The achievements are driven by three key factors: (1)
improvements in X-ray tomography resolution, enabling the generation of highly
accurate three-dimensional rock models; (2) increased computational power of
modern systems; and (3) progress in numerical algorithms, which together facilitate pore-scale simulation of complex physical and chemical processes.

To date, numerous algorithms have been developed to estimate key petrophysical parameters, including porosity, absolute permeability [2,7,12,13], relative permeabilities [1,3,11], elastic moduli [2,9,14,16], electrical resistivity
[2,10,18], geometric and topological pore-space characteristics [5], etc. These
computational tools enable researchers to investigate relationships between rock

O. Gervasi et al. (Eds.): ICCSA 2025 Workshops, LNCS 15888, pp. 419–432, 2026.
https://doi.org/10.1007/978-3-031-97596-7_28

properties, analyze an influence of various factors on estimates, predict a behavior of the objects under study and so on.

The present work focuses on the electrical properties of reservoir rocks. As hydrocarbon reserves are typically quantified using electrical logging data – interpreted through Archie's empirical laws – accurate determination of Archie's coefficients (the cementation parameter m and saturation exponent n) is critical for reservoir development and enhanced hydrocarbon recovery strategies. However, the conventional Archie's model (m = 2, n = 2) applies only to clean, water-wet rocks, a condition rarely met in natural reservoirs [15].

To extend Archie's framework to other rocks, it's constructed two key relationships: (1) the formation factor versus porosity and (2) the resistivity index versus water saturation. We propose a methodology for deriving these dependencies using digital rock models of high-permeability samples, combining numerical simulations with optimization-based regression analysis.

For a monomineralic rock saturated with a single-phase formation fluid, the formation factor (F) is defined as the ratio of the rock's electrical resistivity ($\hat{\rho}$) to the fluid's electrical resistivity (ρ^{fl}):

$$F = \frac{\hat{\rho}}{\rho^{fl}}.$$

This definition is applied when the resistivity of the rock's mineral matrix ρ^s is significantly higher than that of the fluid. Thus, typical resistivity values for mineralized fluids are below unity ($\rho^{fl} < 1$), while dielectric minerals (quartz, micas, feldspars, etc.) exhibit extremely high resistivities ($\rho^s = 10^{12} - 10^{15}$). Semiconductor minerals (carbonates, sulfates, halides, etc.) also demonstrate relatively high resistivity ($\rho^s = 10^4 - 10^8$). In contrast, clay minerals (hydromicas, montmorillomonite, kaolinite, etc.) are characterized by substantially lower resistivities ($\rho \leq 10^4$). Consequently, for rocks composed primarily of minerals from the first two categories, the formation factor can serve as a quantitative characteristic of the pore space structure, since a rock conductivity is provided exclusively by the fluid phase. However, the contribution of clay minerals cannot be neglected, in which case the formation factor no longer represents pore space characteristics alone.

In this study, it is assumed that only dielectric or semiconductor rocks are considered. In this case, it follows from physical considerations that with a porosity equal to one, the entire volume under study will be occupied by fluid, and the resistivity of the entire "sample" will exactly coincide with that of the fluid. In this case, the formation factor will be equal to one. If there are no pores in the sample, or only isolated pores are present, the formation factor is close to zero. Based on experimental data, Archie's empirical law [4] was established, which relates the formation factor to the rock porosity (φ) through the equation:

$$F(\varphi) = \varphi^{-m}, \tag{1}$$

where m is the cementation parameter characterizing a specific rock. Later, in the work [17], a correction of this equation was proposed:

$$F(\varphi) = \alpha \varphi^{-m}, \tag{2}$$

where parameter α is the tortuosity of the pore space. Both parameters are empirically derived as regression coefficients.

Archie's laws also establish relationships between other key parameters: the resistivity index (RI) and water saturation (S_w). Recall that the resistivity index represents the ratio between the rock (formation) electrical resistivity ρ_t at partial water saturation S_w and the resistivity ρ_0 of the fully water-saturated rock (formation):

$$RI = \frac{\rho_t}{\rho_0}.$$

The classical form of Archie's law for the resistivity index is expressed as:

$$RI(S_w) = S_w^{-n}, \tag{3}$$

where n is the saturation exponent. The generalized Archie's law can be written as:

$$RI(S_w) = \alpha S_w^{-n}, \tag{4}$$

where parameter α is the saturation distribution factor.

The following section details the mathematical framework for constructing such dependencies, using the formation factor and porosity as an example.

2   Theoretical Foundations of Constructing Dependencies

Let the formation factors $F_1, ..., F_N$ be known for a set of N samples with porosity values $\varphi_1, ..., \varphi_N$, then the formula (2) can be conveniently written as:

$$\ln F = \ln \alpha - m \ln \varphi,$$

that is, on a logarithmic scale, Archie's law describes a linear relationship between the logarithms of the formation factor and the porosity. If we assume that the results of numerical simulations must satisfy the formula specified, then for all $j = 1, ..., N$ the following relationships must be satisfied:

$$\ln F_j = \ln \alpha - m \ln \varphi_j,$$

as a result, an overdetermined system of linear equations was obtained for determining the parameters $\ln \alpha$ and m:

$$\begin{pmatrix} 1 & -\ln \varphi_1 \\ 1 & -\ln \varphi_2 \\ \vdots & \vdots \\ 1 & -\ln \varphi_N \end{pmatrix} \begin{pmatrix} \ln \alpha \\ m \end{pmatrix} = \begin{pmatrix} \ln F_1 \\ \ln F_2 \\ \vdots \\ \ln F_N \end{pmatrix}.$$

The solution of such a system can be obtained in a generalized sense [8], that is, one that minimizes the discrepancy. To construct this solution, it is sufficient to consider the problem:

$$
\begin{pmatrix} 1 & \cdots & 1 \\ -\ln\varphi_1 & \cdots & -\ln\varphi_N \end{pmatrix}
\begin{pmatrix} 1-\ln\varphi_1 \\ 1-\ln\varphi_2 \\ \vdots & \vdots \\ 1-\ln\varphi_N \end{pmatrix}
\begin{pmatrix} \ln\alpha \\ m \end{pmatrix}
=
\begin{pmatrix} 1 & \cdots & 1 \\ -\ln\varphi_1 & \cdots & -\ln\varphi_N \end{pmatrix}
\begin{pmatrix} \ln F_1 \\ \ln F_2 \\ \vdots \\ \ln F_N \end{pmatrix}
$$

or

$$
\begin{pmatrix} N & -\sum\ln\varphi_j \\ -\sum\ln\varphi_j & \sum(\ln\varphi_j)^2 \end{pmatrix}
\begin{pmatrix} \ln\alpha \\ m \end{pmatrix}
=
\begin{pmatrix} \sum\ln F_j \\ -\sum\ln\varphi_j \ln F_j \end{pmatrix}.
$$

The resulting system is easily solvable, and its solution exactly coincides with the generalized solution of the original system of equations. Although its condition number can be quite high if the range of porosity variation is small.

This solution minimizes the discrepancy:

$$
r = \sqrt{\sum_{j=1}^{N}(\ln F_j - \ln\alpha + m\ln\varphi_j)^2}.
$$

It should be understood that this solution is not a solution to the minimization problem

$$
\sum_{j=1}^{N}(F_j - \alpha\varphi_j^{-m})^2 \to \min,
$$

however, if we represent the residual vector r in the form

$$
r_j = \ln F_j - \ln\alpha + m\ln\varphi_j,
$$

assuming that $r_j \ll 1$ (otherwise it is possible to perform normalization by considering, for example, $r_j/\|\ln F\|$), then the following representation is true:

$$
\frac{F_j}{\alpha\varphi_j^m} - 1 = e^{r_j} - 1.
$$

Respectively,

$$
\sum_{j=1}^{N}\left(\frac{F_j}{\alpha\varphi_j^m} - 1\right)^2 = \sum_{j=1}^{N}(e^{r_j} - 1)^2 = \sum_{j=1}^{N}r_j^2 + O(|r|^3).
$$

That is, assuming the residual is small on a logarithmic scale, the resulting solution will be a fairly accurate approximation of the solution to the minimization problem.

$$
\sum_{j=1}^{N}\left(\frac{F_j}{\alpha\varphi_j^m} - 1\right)^2 \to \min.
$$

If it is necessary to refine the obtained solution, gradient methods can be used.

Further analysis of the quality of the obtained solution will be carried out on a logarithmic scale. It is convenient to introduce two measures. The first is the relative norm of the discrepancy:

$$R = \frac{r}{\| \ln F_j \|_2} = \frac{\sqrt{\sum_{j=1}^{N}(\ln F_j - \ln \alpha + m \ln \varphi_j)^2}}{\sqrt{\sum_{j=1}^{N}(\ln F_j)^2}},$$

the second is the reliability coefficient, defined as

$$R^2 = 1 - \frac{r^2}{\sigma(F_j)} = 1 - \frac{\sum_{j=1}^{N}(\ln F_j - \ln \alpha + m \ln \varphi_j)^2}{\sum_{j=1}^{N}(\ln F_j - < \ln F_j >)^2},$$

where $<>$ - denotes the average value. That is, R^2 determines the proximity of the residual to the standard deviation of the measurements.

The minimization algorithm described above allows constructing the dependence of the formation factor on porosity according to the modified Archie law, which takes into account the tortuosity parameter α. If Archie's law is considered in the classical formulation, that is, with $\alpha = 1$, then the minimization problem is written as:

$$\sum_{j=1}^{N}(\ln F_j + m \ln \varphi_j)^2 \to \min,$$

or in the form of a problem of finding a generalized solution to a system of linear algebraic equations of the form:

$$\begin{pmatrix} - \ln \varphi_1 \\ - \ln \varphi_2 \\ \vdots \\ - \ln \varphi_N \end{pmatrix} (m) = \begin{pmatrix} \ln F_1 \\ \ln F_2 \\ \vdots \\ \ln F_N \end{pmatrix}$$

or

$$\sum_{j=1}^{N}(\ln \varphi)^2 m = \sum_{j=1}^{N} \ln F_j \ln \varphi_j.$$

Obviously, all the above considerations about the accuracy assessment and the reliability coefficient remain true in the simplified case under consideration. However, due to the fact that optimization is carried out relative to only one parameter, the error value is expected to be higher.

3 Constructing the Dependence of the Formation Factor on the Porosity for Digital Models

3.1 Digital Models of High-Permeability Rock Samples

In this part of study, we consider two digital models of high-permeability sandstone:

1. Berea sandstone model with 'VSG reference segmentation' from the benchmarks study [2].
2. Bentheimer sandstone model obtained from the DigitalRocksPortal repository (project ID 317: '11 Sandstones: raw, filtered and segmented data').

Two-dimensional cross-sections of both samples are presented in the Fig. 1. The Berea sandstone model has dimensions of $724 \times 724 \times 1024$ voxels at 0.74 um/voxel resolution, with a porosity of 18.4%. The Bentheimer model size is $1000 \times 1000 \times 1000$ voxels at 2.25 um/voxel resolution, and a porosity is 26.7%.

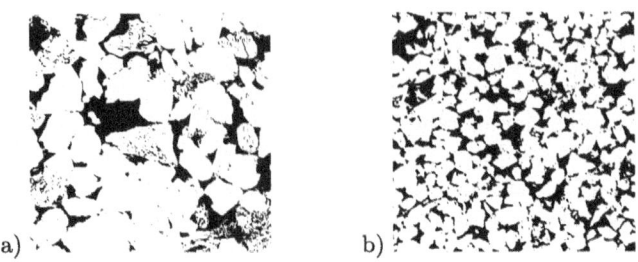

Fig. 1. Two-dimensional cross-sections of high-permeability sandstone models: a) Berea (0.74 um); b) Bentheimer (2.25 um).

To validate our computational results, we employ the digital rock physics benchmarks from [2]. This reference presents calculated by different methods formation factors for digital Berea sandstone samples with varying segmentation approaches and porosity values, as shown in their Fig. 7b. For verification purposes, we reproduce this figure (including legend) below as Fig. 2.

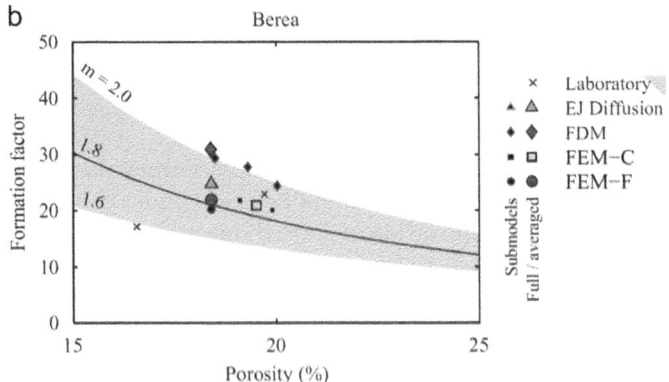

Fig. 2. Figure 7b from [2]. The values of formation factor calculated for a Berea sandstone samples. The gray shaded area and solid line represent Archie's law with different cementation factors.

3.2   Numerical Experiments

To construct the dependence of the formation factor on the porosity of the digital models, each model was divided into cubic subsamples of 400^3 voxels. The 1000^3 Bentheimer sample was partitioned into 3 segments along each axis (resulting in 27 subsamples), while the smaller Berea sample was divided into 2 segments along the X and Y axes and 3 segments along the Z axis (yielding 12 subsamples).

For each full-size digital sample and all subsamples, the porosity values were calculated first, followed by the resistivity and formation factor values for each of the three directions (calculating the values of the electrical resistivity and resistivity index were carried out using a solver belonging to Gazpromneft NTC). After that, the mean values were obtained by arithmetic averaging across the three spatial directions. The calculated formation factor values for all digital samples are presented in Figs. 3 - 4. In addition to the values obtained, the plots include curves representing Archie's law for the formation factor and the porosity: $F = \varphi^{-m}$. For the cementation parameter m, the values of 1.6, 1.8, 2.0 were used from [2].

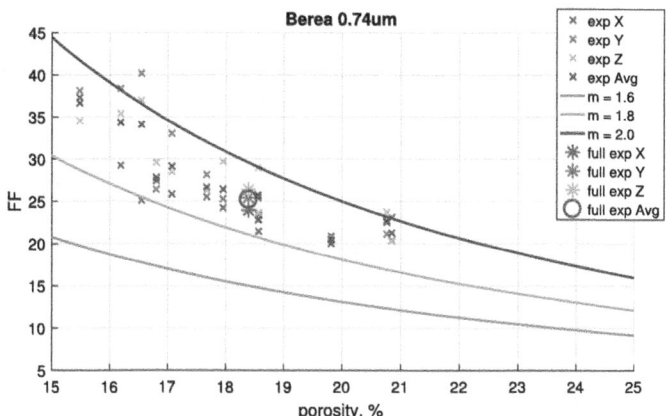

Fig. 3. Calculated formation factor values for the full-size Berea (0.74 um) digital sample and all its 400^3-voxel subsamples.

A comparison of our calculation results for the full-size samples (Fig. 3) with the benchmarks from [2] (Fig. 2) reveals excellent agreement between the values. The closest match is observed with the results obtained by the EJ Diffusion method in the cited study. Furthermore, Fig. 3 demonstrates that both the formation factor of the full-size sample and its subsamples fall well within the range of cementation parameters ($m \in [1.6, 2.0]$) proposed by [2]. This consistency is also evident for the Bentheimer sample (Fig. 4), where all calculated values align perfectly with the same range of cementation parameters.

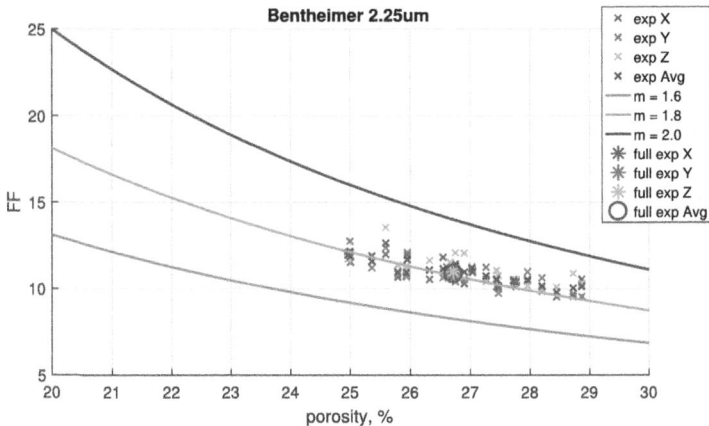

Fig. 4. Calculated formation factor values for full-size Bentheimer (2.25 um) digital sample and all its 400^3-voxel subsamples.

Next, to construct the dependencies of the formation factor on porosity, the methodology outlined in Sect. 2 was applied to our numerical results. Figures 5 and 6 present the numerical experiment results for all rock subsamples, along with estimated formation factor – porosity dependencies obtained by solving two optimization problems. The solid curves represent fits based on the generalized Archie's law, while the dashed curves correspond to the classical Archie's law formulation (where $\alpha = 1$). Tables 1 and 2 provide the calculated values of the parameters α and m, along with the relative residual and the parameter R^2 values for each sample and for two different approximations.

Table 1. Approximation of the dependence of the formation factor on porosity for the Berea (0.74 um) digital model.

	$F = \alpha\varphi^{-m}$				$\tilde{F} = \varphi^{-m}$		
	α	m	res	R^2	m	res	R^2
X	2.58	1.33	0.028	0.64	1.88	0.032	0.53
Y	0.46	2.38	0.03	0.82	1.92	0.033	0.79
Z	1.15	2.85	0.026	0.79	1.93	0.026	0.79
All	1.1	1.85	0.033	0.71	1.91	0.033	0.71

The tables reveal that, when applying the generalized Archie's law, there is a stable difference in the regression coefficient estimates depending on the direction in which the resistivity assessment was carried out. A possible reason for such a discrepancy may be attributed to the anisotropic geometry and topological complexity of the pore space. In contrast, when applying the Archie's law in the

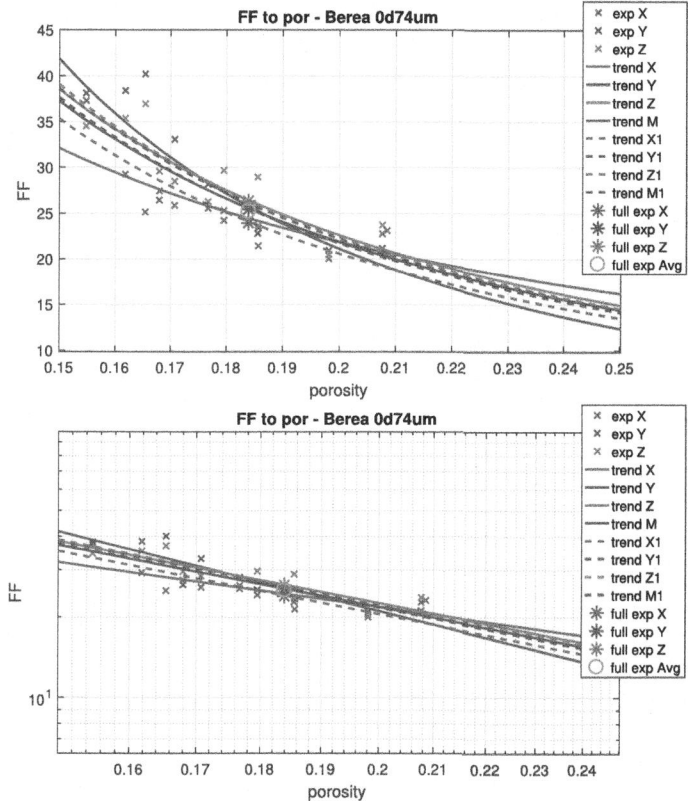

Fig. 5. The dependence of the formation factor on porosity for Berea (0.74 um) sandstone in linear and logarithmic scale.

Table 2. Approximation of the dependence of the formation factor on porosity for the Bentheimer (2.25 um) digital model.

	$F = \alpha\varphi^{-m}$				$\tilde{F} = \varphi^{-m}$		
	α	m	res	R^2	m	res	R^2
X	1.8	1.37	0.017	0.67	1.81	0.018	0.6
Y	1.58	1.47	0.018	0.86	1.81	0.019	0.64
Z	2.36	1.18	0.019	0.53	1.83	0.022	0.37
All	1.88	1.34	0.018	0.61	1.82	0.02	0.53

classical formulation, the estimates of the cementation parameter coefficients are close to each other. In addition, they are in very good agreement with the source [2]. However, applying the generalized Archie's law often demonstrates a significant deviations of the coefficient α from unity, as well as a reduced relative residuals and higher values of the coefficient R^2. Consequently, the usage of such form allows to significantly increase the accuracy of the approximation.

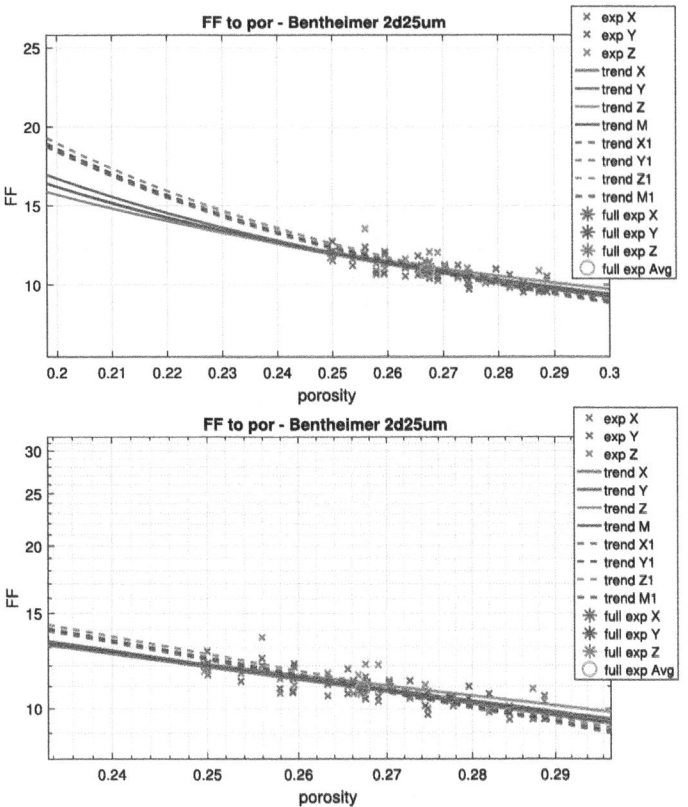

Fig. 6. The dependence of the formation factor on porosity for Bentheimer (2.25 um) sandstone in linear and logarithmic scales.

4 Constructing the Dependence of the Resistivity Index on the Water Saturation for Digital Models

In this part of work, we considered Berea sandstone model obtained from the DigitalRocksPortal repository (project ID 317: '11 Sandstones: raw, filtered and segmented data'). The model size is $1000 \times 1000 \times 1000$ at 2.25 um/voxel resolution and the porosity is 21.7%.

The resistivity index – water saturation $(RI - S_w)$ relationship is constructed using partially water-saturated rock models. These model sets are generated through either:

1. Primary drainage simulation, where the non-wetting phase displaces the wetting phase;
2. Imbibition simulation, where the wetting phase gradually displaces the nonwetting one, as that the wetting phase fraction in the pumped mixture progressively increasing during each imbibition cycle.

In this study, we first simulated primary drainage for the selected rock sample, generating a set of models with varying water saturations. For each model, we calculated both the water saturation and resistivity index.

Subsequently, we performed imbibition simulations using three irreducible water saturation values ($S_{wir} = 0.05, 0.2, 0.3$), conducting three parallel simulation scenarios. This produced distinct sets of partially saturated models for each S_{wir} case. Similar to the drainage case, we computed the key parameters (RI and S_w) for all models.

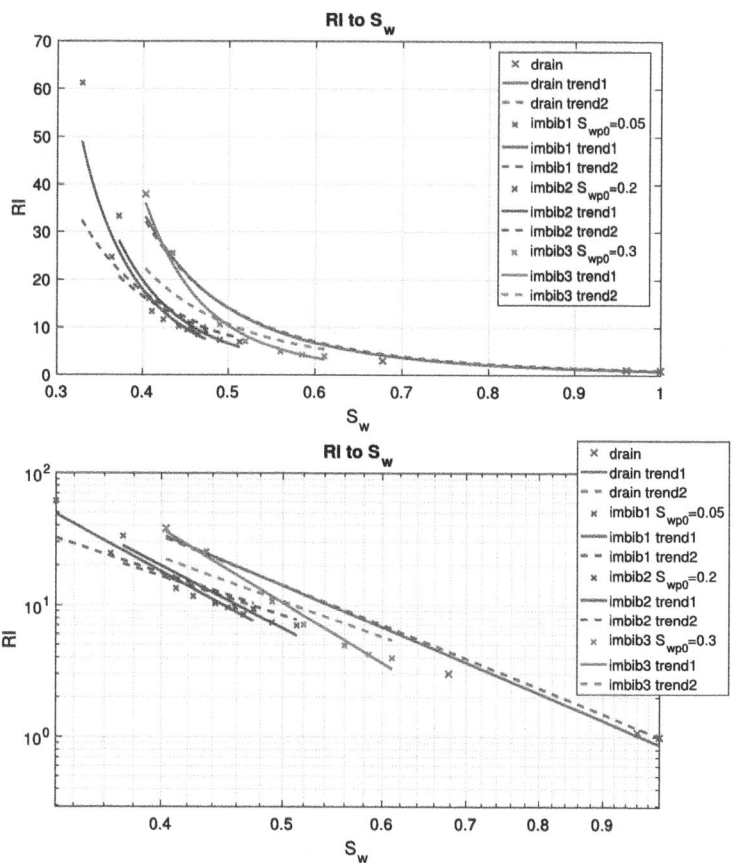

Fig. 7. The dependence of the resistivity index on water saturation for Berea (2.25 um) sandstone in linear and logarithmic scales.

Using these datasets, we solved two optimization problems to construct linear regressions. Figure 7 presents the saturation parameter versus water saturation relationships for both drainage and imbibition cases. The solid curves represent the trends derived from the generalized Archie's law, while the dashed curves correspond to the classical Archie's law formulation with $\alpha = 1$.

Table 3 summarizes the results: $RI - S_w$ dependencies obtained for drainage case and for three distinct imbibition scenarios. The table includes the coefficients α and n, along with the relative residual (res) and coefficient of determination (R^2) values for both approximation methods.

Table 3. Approximation of the dependence of the resistibity index on water saturation for the Berea (2.25 um) model.

	$RI = \alpha S_w^{-n}$				$\tilde{RI} = S_w^{-n}$		
	α	n	res	R^2	n	res	R^2
Drainage	0.88	4.00	0.098	0.98	3.82	0.112	0.98
Imbib, $S_{wir} = 0.05$	0.17	5.11	0.055	0.94	3.13	0.102	0.80
Imbib, $S_{wir} = 0.2$	0.22	4.90	0.052	0.94	3.07	0.096	0.81
Imbib, $S_{wir} = 0.3$	0.19	5.78	0.047	0.98	3.42	0.152	0.81

The results demonstrate that when applying the generalized Archie's law, the regression coefficients for imbibition vary significantly depending on the irreducible water saturation (S_{wir}). At the same time, using the classical Archie's law

TABLE 2—WETTABILITY vs. SATURATION EXPONENT AT 77°F FOR BEREA AND ELGIN SANDSTONES AND A SET OF DIFFERENT CRUDE OILS DESIGNATED BY API GRAVITY (after Siddiqui[14])

Core	I_w	n	γ_o (°API)
	Berea Cores		
101	0.463	2.71	39
102	0.430	1.54	42
103	0.430	2.76	38
104	0.392	2.18	41
105	0.358	2.95	38
106	0.231	3.90	36
107	0.187	3.35	35
108	0.185	3.58	32
109	0.181	3.62	37
110	0.169	3.43	32
111	0.127	4.00	37
112	0.101	3.17	35

Fig. 8. Table 2 from [6] presents laboratory experimental data for Berea sandstone samples.

formulation gives closer saturation exponent values across all imbibition cases. Furthermore, these classical Archie's law estimates show excellent agreement with laboratory measurements reported in [6]. Figure 8 reproduces Table 2 from [6], presenting experimental data for Berea sandstone samples. The measured saturation exponents range from 1.54 to 4.0, with a mean value of 3.1. Notably, our numerically derived saturation exponent for imbibition (3.2) closely matches this laboratory average.

5   Conclusion

The present study focuses on the numerical evaluation of Archie's coefficients – specifically, the cementation parameter and saturation exponent – using a digital model of a high-permeability rock sample. Accurate estimation of these parameters is critical for reservoir development planning and optimizing hydrocarbon recovery through formation stimulation techniques.

To derive the coefficients, we construct two relationships: the formation factor versus porosity and the resistivity index versus water saturation. The paper presents a methodology and case studies for establishing these dependencies. The proposed approach involves solving two optimization problems to perform a linear regression in a logarithmic scale, based on both the generalized and classical forms of Archie's law.

The presented results reveal a significant discrepancy in the regression coefficient estimates when applying the generalized Archie's law, dependent on (1) the direction of resistivity assessment (for $F - \varphi$ dependence); (2) the irreducible water saturation (for $RI - S_w$ dependence). In contrast, the classical form of Archie's law yields cementation parameter (saturation exponent) estimates that are mutually consistent across all direction (imbibition cases) and are in good agreement with the values reported by [2,6].

However, the generalized Archie's law frequently produces a coefficient α significantly deviating from 1, while exhibiting reduced relative residual and higher R^2 values. These results indicate that the generalized form substantially improves approximation accuracy compared to the classical model.

Acknowledgments. T. Khachkova performed numerical simulations under the support of Russian Science Foundation (grant no. 25-21-00352, https://rscf.ru/en/project/25-21-00352/)

References

1. Alpak, F.O., Riviere, B., Frank, F.: A phase-field method for the direct simulation of two-phase flows in pore-scale media using a non-equilibrium wetting boundary condition. Comput. Geosci. **20**(5), 881–908 (2016). https://doi.org/10.1007/s10596-015-9551-2

2. Andra, H., et al.: Digital rock physics benchmarks - Part II: computing effective properties. Comput. Geosci. **50**, 33–43 (2013)

3. Apourvari, S.N., Arns, C.H.: Image-based relative permeability upscaling from the pore scale. In: Advances in Water Resources (2015)
4. Archie, G.E.: Classification of carbonate reservoir rocks and petrophysical considerations. AAPG Bull. **36**(2), 278–298 (1952)
5. Bazaikin, Y.V., Malkovich, E.G., Derevschikov, V.S., Lysikov, A.I., Okunev, A.G.: Evolution of sorptive and textural properties of CaO-based sorbents during repetitive sorption/regeneration cycles. Chem. Eng. Sci. **152**, 709–716 (2016)
6. Donaldson, E.C., Siddiqui, T.K.: Relationship between the archie saturation exponent and wettability. SPE Form. Eval. **4**(03), 359–362 (1989)
7. Gerke, K.M., Karsanina, M.V., Katsman, R.: Calculation of tensorial flow properties on pore level: Exploring the influence of boundary conditions on the permeability of three-dimensional stochastic reconstructions. Phys. Rev. E **100**(5), 053312 (2019)
8. Godunov, S.K., Antonov, A.G., Kirilyuk, O.P., Kostin, V.I.: Guaranteed accuracy of solving systems of linear equations in Euclidean spaces. Nauka, Novosibirsk (1992). (in Russian)
9. Khachkova, T., Lisitsa, V., Reshetova, G.: Effect of interface roughness on the elastic properties of 3D layered media. Probab. Eng. Mech. **75**, 103571 (2024)
10. Khachkova, T., Lisitsa, V., Reshetova, G., Tcheverda, V.: Gpu-based algorithm for evaluating the electrical resistivity of digital rocks. Comput. Math. Appl. **82**, 200–211 (2021)
11. Khachkova, T.S., Lisitsa, V.V., Gondul, E.A., Prokhorov, D.I., Kostin, V.I.: Two-phase flow simulation algorithm for numerical estimation of relative phase permeability curves of porous materials. Russ. J. Numer. Anal. Math. Model. **39**(4), 209–221 (2024). https://doi.org/10.1515/rnam-2024-0020
12. Lisitsa, V., Khachkova, T., Sotnikov, O., Islamov, I., Ganiev, D.: Numerical evaluating the permeability of rocks based on correlation dependence on geometry. Lect. Notes Comput. Sci. **14106**, 91–102 (2023). https://doi.org/10.1007/978-3-031-37111-0_7
13. Mostaghimi, P., Blunt, M., Bijeljic, B.: Computations of absolute permeability on micro-CT images. Math. Geosci. **45**(1), 103–125 (2013)
14. Saenger, E.H., et al.: Analysis of high-resolution x-ray computed tomography images of Bentheim sandstone under elevated confining pressures. Geophys. Prospect. **64**(4), 848–859 (2016)
15. Shamsi, A.T., Talabani, S., Vaziri, H., Islam, M.: In-depth investigation of the validity of the archie equation in carbonate rocks. SPE (2001). https://doi.org/10.2118/67204-MS
16. Shulakova, V., et al.: Computational elastic up-scaling of sandstone on the basis of x-ray micro-tomographic images. Geophys. Prospect. **61**(2), 287–301 (2013)
17. Winsauer, W.O., Shearin, H.M. P. H. Masson, Williams, M.: Resistivity of brine-saturated sands in relation to pore geometry. AAPG Bull. **36**(4), 253–277 (1952)
18. Zhan, X., Schwartz, L.M., Toksöz, M.N., Smith, W.C., Morgan, F.D.: Pore-scale modeling of electrical and fluid transport in Berea sandstone. Geophysics **75**(5), F135–F142 (2010)

Effect of Power-Law Parameters on Time Step Size in CFD-DEM Simulations of Non-newtonian Fluid-Driven Fracture

Daniyar Kazidenov[ID] and Yerlan Amanbek[✉][ID]

Department of Mathematics, School of Sciences and Humanities, Nazarbayev University,
Kabanbay Batyr 53, Astana, Kazakhstan
{daniyar.kazidenov,yerlan.amanbek}@nu.edu.kz

Abstract. Selection of a suitable time step size is essential for accurate CFD-DEM simulations involving non-Newtonian fluids. This study explores the effect of power-law parameters, the consistency index (K) and the flow behavior index (n), on time step sensitivity during fluid-driven fracture initiation in granular media. The results show that the power-law parameters have a strong effect on fracturing behavior. Less viscous fluids create infiltration-dominated linear fractures with lower peak pressures, while more viscous fluids produce wider fractures dominated by grain displacement and higher peak pressures. The analysis of injection pressures at various time step sizes indicates that CFD time step sensitivity is influenced more by the flow behavior index rather than the consistency index. Lower flow behavior indices ($n = 0.1$ and 0.2) demonstrate relatively accurate results at a higher time step ($\Delta t = 10^{-4}$s). In contrast, when n increases to 0.3, the errors become more significant, which in turn requires a reduction in the time step to $\Delta t = 10^{-5}$s.

Keywords: Time step · Fracture initiation · CFD-DEM modeling

1 Introduction

Injection of polymer solutions underground, which is common practice in many subsurface applications, may result in the formation of fractures when the injecting fluid pressure exceeds the mechanical strength of the rock. The behavior and physical characteristics of these fractures are complicated and influenced by various factors, such as solid material properties, rock heterogeneity, in situ stress conditions, fluid rheology, and flow conditions [8, 17, 23]. Understanding the mechanisms of fracture initiation is crucial for predicting further fracture behavior and enhancing engineering design strategies for effective fracture management. Therefore, reliable and high-fidelity simulations are essential to accurately capture fluid flow dynamics and fluid-particle interactions, particularly when accounting for the non-Newtonian behavior of polymer solutions.

Numerical models based on the discrete element method (DEM) are commonly used to study fracture initiation and propagation. In DEM, the reservoir rock is represented as a granular medium consisting of individual particles. The material properties and interactions of particles can be defined according to the rock type. Modeling of

© The Author(s), under exclusive license to Springer Nature Switzerland AG 2026
O. Gervasi et al. (Eds.): ICCSA 2025 Workshops, LNCS 15888, pp. 433–446, 2026.
https://doi.org/10.1007/978-3-031-97596-7_29

fluid flow through porous regions between particles is performed by coupling DEM with other numerical approaches. In DEM-based simulations, fluid-driven fracturing occurs through particle displacements induced by fluid forces. Most studies examine mechanisms of fracture initiation by analyzing how fluid properties and flow conditions influence particle displacements. Particle displacement becomes the primary process instead of infiltration during the injection of more viscous fluids, contributing to fracture creation [25, 26]. Similarly, an increase in injection rates results in larger fracture openings, reducing the fluid velocity and limiting the infiltration into the surrounding medium [10]. Numerous studies indicate that the fracturing process is strongly affected by solid material properties [22, 25] and stress conditions [25].

The coupling of DEM with computational fluid dynamics (CFD) has been widely accepted as a reliable approach for simulating fluid-driven fracture initiation and propagation [20, 21, 24]. CFD-DEM is an Eulerian-Lagrangian approach that couples the fluid phase (Eulerian) with discrete particle interactions (Lagrangian). In CFD-DEM, fluid flow is represented as a continuous phase, and governed by the system of locally averaged Navier-Stokes equations for mass and momentum conservation, whereas particles are tracked individually and their motion is solved using Newton's second law. Particle-particle and particle-wall interactions are handled using contact models. The coupling of CFD and DEM integrates fluid-particle interactions, which are governed by drag force models. The coupling system is typically categorized into three groups based on fluid cell and particle sizes: unresolved, semi-resolved, and resolved. The unresolved setting uses larger fluid cells than the average particle size, whereas in the resolved approach, a particle is resolved by many small fluid cells. In the semi-resolved case, the particle size is approximately the same as the fluid cell size. The accuracy of coupling simulations is determined by the time step size and the coupling interval between CFD and DEM. Small time step sizes and intervals lead to more accurate results but with longer simulation time, while larger ones reduce simulation time with greater errors.

This study extends the findings of earlier research on fracture initiation induced by polymer solutions in granular media [13]. Injected polymer solutions demonstrate non-Newtonian behavior, which is represented by the power-law model. In this model, the fluid viscosity is characterized by two parameters: the consistency index (K) and the flow behavior index (n). These parameters directly influence the fluid's resistance to flow and, consequently, the injection pressure during fracturing. The accuracy of the pressure field is strongly influenced by both the selected time step size and the rheological parameters of the fluid. Therefore, selecting an appropriate time step size based on the specific rheological parameters is essential for maintaining simulation accuracy and stability. In this study, we numerically explore how the power law parameters affect time step size in the fluid phase of the fracture initiation model. Our primary aim is to optimize the time step size based on different combinations of these parameters.

2   Model Formulation

2.1   Governing Equations for the Solid Phase

In the current study, the fracture initiation process is modeled using the CFD-DEM coupling approach. DEM represents the rock as a granular medium consisting of individual particles, whereas CFD describes the fluid flow within the porous region of the medium. The interaction of the fluid phase with the solid phase is described by a fluid-particle interaction force.

The motion of particles is calculated by Newton's second law, which accounts for particle-particle and fluid-particle interactions, and gravity:

$$m_i \frac{dv_i}{dt} = f_{pf,i} + \sum_{j=1}^{k_c} \left(f_{c,ij} + f_{damp,ij} \right) + m_i g \tag{1}$$

$$I_i \frac{d\omega_i}{dt} = \sum_{j=1}^{k_c} T_{ij} \tag{2}$$

where v_i and ω_i represent the particle translational and angular velocities, m_i and I_i are the particle mass and inertia, $f_{pf,i}$ is the sum of all forces acting by fluid on a particle, $f_{c,ij}$, $f_{damp,ij}$ and T_{ij} denote particle-particle contact force, viscous damping force and torque, $m_i g$ is the gravitational force, and k_c is the number of contacting particles.

The particle-particle contact force is calculated using the modified version of the Johnson-Kendall-Roberts (JKR) contact model [11], where the surface energy density describes the cohesion (bonding) of particles. When the applied stress is greater than the adhesive strength, the particles unbond each other and no new bonds form after unbonding [12, 14, 16]. It is expressed in terms of the normal component of contact force:

$$f_{c,ij}^{(n)} = \frac{4E^* a^3}{3R^*} - \sqrt{16\pi\gamma E^* a^3} \tag{3}$$

where $E^* = \left(\frac{1 - v_1^2}{E_1} + \frac{1 - v_2^2}{E_2} \right)^{-1}$ is the effective Young's modulus, where E_1, E_2 and v_1, v_2 represent the Young's modulus and the Poisson's ratio of the particles, γ denotes the surface energy density, a represents the radius of contacting surface, and $R^* = \left(\frac{R_i R_j}{R_i + R_j} \right)$ is the effective radius, where R_i and R_j represent the radius of particles.

In the fluid-particle interaction system, particles experience an additional force due to the surrounding fluid. The fluid-particle interaction force $f_{pf,i}$ represents the sum of all forces exerted by the fluid on a particle:

$$f_{pf,i} = f_{d,i} + f_{\nabla p,i} + f_{\nabla \cdot \tau,i} + f_{Ar,i} \tag{4}$$

where $f_{d,i}$, $f_{\nabla p,i}$, $f_{\nabla \cdot \tau,i}$ and $f_{Ar,i}$ denote the drag, pressure gradient, viscous and Archimedes forces, respectively.

2.2 Coupled CFD-DEM Model

The fluid flow in the porous region (α_f) of a granular medium is modeled by solving the Navier-Stokes equations with local averaging [28], where the pressure gradient, viscous and gravitational forces are merely shared between the fluid and solid phases:

$$\begin{cases} \dfrac{\partial \alpha_f}{\partial t} + \nabla \cdot (\alpha_f \boldsymbol{u}) = 0 \\ \dfrac{\partial (\rho_f \alpha_f \boldsymbol{u})}{\partial t} + \nabla \cdot (\rho_f \alpha_f \boldsymbol{u}\boldsymbol{u}) = -\alpha_f \nabla p + \alpha_f \nabla \cdot \boldsymbol{\tau} + \rho_f \alpha_f \boldsymbol{g} + \boldsymbol{F}_{pf}^A \end{cases} \tag{5}$$

where ρ_f, $\boldsymbol{u}$ and p denote the fluid's density, velocity and pressure, respectively, α_f is the volume fraction occupied by fluid in a granular medium, $\boldsymbol{\tau} = \mu_f \left((\nabla \boldsymbol{u}) + (\nabla \boldsymbol{u})^T \right)$ represents the stress tensor, where μ_f is the fluid dynamic viscosity and $\boldsymbol{F}_{pf}^A = \dfrac{1}{\Delta V} \Sigma_{i=1}^n \left(\boldsymbol{f}_{d,i} + \boldsymbol{f}_i'' \right)$ corresponds to the volumetric fluid-particle interaction force, where $\boldsymbol{f}_i''$ includes all forces except drag, pressure gradient, and viscous forces, ΔV represents the fluid cell's volume.

The injected fluid is characterized as non-Newtonian and its rheology is described by the power-law model, expressing the viscosity as follows:

$$\mu_f(\dot{\gamma}) = K \dot{\gamma}^{(n-1)} \tag{6}$$

where $\dot{\gamma}$ represents the shear rate and K represents the consistency index, which describes the fluid's resistance to flow. Smaller values correspond to lower viscosity, whereas larger values indicate higher viscosity. n is the flow behavior index, which shows whether fluid is shear-thinning ($n < 1$), shear-thickening ($n > 1$), or Newtonian ($n = 1$).

The drag force is the dominant component in the overall fluid-particle interaction force, which directly influences particle motion and has an indirect effect on fluid dynamics. In the current study, the drag force model is derived from the modified Blake-Kozeny equation for the pressure drop [2] and corresponds to power-law fluid flow in multi-particle systems, accounting for the fluid's rheological parameters. This model includes power-law parameters (K and n), allowing a realistic representation of fluid rheology effect on drag force.

The drag force exerted on an individual particle is defined by:

$$\boldsymbol{f}_{d,i} = f \cdot \frac{\rho_f |\boldsymbol{u}_i - \boldsymbol{v}_i| (\boldsymbol{u}_i - \boldsymbol{v}_i)(1 - \alpha_f) V_{p,i}}{d_{p,i} \alpha_f} \tag{7}$$

where $f = \dfrac{\frac{150}{12} \left(9 + \frac{3}{n}\right)^n \alpha_f^{2(1-n)} (1 - \alpha_f)^n}{Re_{p,i}}$ denotes the Fanning friction factor, $\boldsymbol{u}_i - \boldsymbol{v}_i$ is the relative velocity between fluid and particle, $V_{p,i}$ and $d_{p,i}$ represent the particle volume and diameter, respectively and $Re_{p,i} = \dfrac{\rho_f d_{p,i}^n |\boldsymbol{u}_i - \boldsymbol{v}_i|^{2-n}}{K}$ is a particle Reynolds number, which incorporates power-law parameters of the fluid.

2.3   Calculation of Critical Simulation Time Step

The system of Navier-Stokes equations (Eq. 5) is numerically solved using the cfdem-SolverPiso solver [18] based on Pressure-Implicit with Splitting of Operators (PISO) algorithm [9]. This approach uses the finite volume method (FVM) incorporating the momentum transfer between fluid and solid phases. In CFD-DEM coupling, the selection of appropriate time step is critical for achieving convergence in nonlinear calculations. A smaller time step results in more accurate results but increases simulation time, while a larger time step may cause instability and unrealistic behavior. In DEM, the critical time step is commonly calculated using methodologies based on material parameters such as mass and stiffness [1] and the Rayleigh time step [19]. The latter uses particle material parameters such as radius, density, shear modulus and Poisson's ratio. In CFD, the critical time step is typically computed using the Courant-Friedrichs-Lewy (CFL) condition [4] expressed as follows:

$$C = \Delta t \left(\sum_{i=1}^{n} \frac{u_i}{\Delta x_{cfd,i}} \right) \leq C_{max} \tag{8}$$

where C denotes the Courant number, Δt is the CFD time step, $\Delta x_{cfd,i}$ represents the size of a single cell and n indicates the number of spacial coordinates, which is typically $n = 1, 2$ and 3. Depending on the time-integration scheme of the solver, in general, C_{max} should have a value equal to or less than 1. Physically, the CFL condition requires that the flow should not propagate beyond a single cell in one time step.

In fluid flows dominated with diffusion and with lower Reynolds number, where viscous effects are significant, the critical time step is determined by diffusive time step criterion expressed as follows:

$$\Delta t \leq \frac{\Delta x_{cfd,i}^2}{2\nu} \tag{9}$$

where ν is the kinematic viscosity. From a physics standpoint, this criterion indicates that smaller cell sizes and high viscous fluids require smaller time steps. This typically important with explicit solvers where the time step has a greater influence on stability. However, in implicit solvers such as PISO, the time step can be larger, but accuracy and convergence should still be taken into account. In CFD-DEM coupling with PISO-based solvers, the CFD time step is much larger than DEM time step and should be selected carefully to achieve both stability and computational efficiency. In general, the coupling interval, which is the ratio between the CFD time step and the DEM time step, typically ranges between 10 and 100 in CFD-DEM simulations [15]. However, in creeping flows with lower Reynolds numbers, the coupling interval may vary.

3   Simulation Settings

In the current study, the numerical model replicates the Hele-Shaw cell experiment by injecting fluid into a sample confined under stress. In order to reduce computation cost, the half region and one layer of particles are used. The numerical model used in this work has been successfully validated by comparing numerical results with experimental data of fracture initiation induced by power-law polymer solutions [13]. The schematic representation is shown in Fig. 1. The model includes solid phase and fluid phase domains of equal dimensions. The solid phase domain contains a total of 45000 particles of uniform size accommodated in a single layer. The dimensions of the region are 600 mm × 300 mm × 2 mm. A stress σ_3 is applied at the left and right boundaries, while $\sigma_1 = 2 \cdot \sigma_3$ is applied at the top boundary, and the bottom boundary is fixed. The interaction between the particles and walls is treated as frictionless.

The fluid phase domain consists of a total 10000 mesh cell configured as $50 \times 100 \times 2$ in the XYZ directions. The injection of fluid occurs through the inlet patch with size of 50 mm. Outlet patches are placed at the left, right and top boundaries. The boundary conditions are detailed in Table 1.

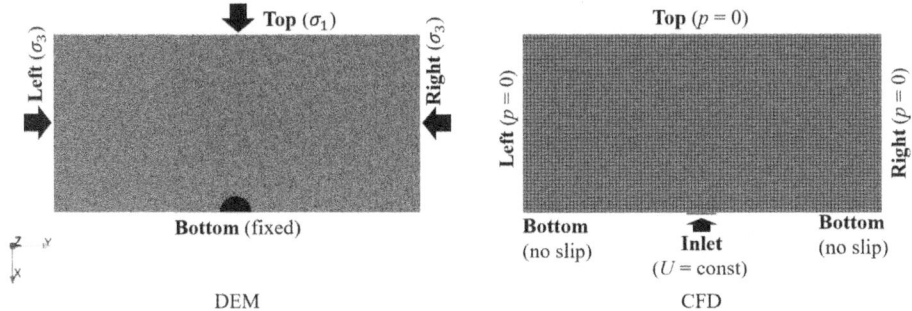

Fig. 1. Simulation setup for the fracture initiation model.

Table 1. Boundary conditions applied in fracture initiation simulations.

Boundary	DEM	CFD
Bottom	fixed	no slip
Inlet	fixed	$U = $ const
Left	$\sigma_3 = $ const	$p = 0$
Right	$\sigma_3 = $ const	$p = 0$
Top	$\sigma_1 = $ const	$p = 0$

Table 2 presents the material properties of the simulated particles. Most parameters including density, Poisson's ratio, Young's modulus and friction coefficient are primarily based on similar studies [21,24]. As the granular medium is assumed weakly cohesive, the surface energy density (γ) is set to a lower value of 1 J/m^2 ensuring weak bonding of particles.

Table 2. Particle material parameters used in the simulation.

Young's modulus, E (Pa)	10^6
Friction coefficient, μ	0.5
Density, ρ_p (kg/m^3)	2650
Poisson's ratio, ν	0.3
Surface energy density, γ (J/m^2)	1

The fluid cell size is chosen to meet the unresolved condition in CFD-DEM coupling, ensuring that each cell contains multiple particles [3]. The DEM time step is set to 10^{-5} s, which is equivalent to 3.48% of the critical time step based on the Rayleigh approach [19]. The CFD time step is defined as 10^{-4} and 10^{-5} s, maintaining a coupling interval of $N = 1$ and $N = 10$ for the current CFD-DEM framework. An open-source software package, CFDEM [6], is used for the simulations, which integrates the commercial DEM software Aspherix [18] and the open-source CFD software OpenFOAM [27]. A PISO-based algorithm is utilized to calculate the system of Navier-Stokes equations [7]. The first-order Euler scheme is used for time discretization, while the second-order Gauss linear scheme is applied for spatial derivatives. The simulation domain is decomposed into a $2 \times 4 \times 1$ grid configuration along the X, Y, and Z axes, respectively, for parallel processing across 8 cores.

The computational domain used in the current study is designed in three dimensions, but consists of only one solid particle layer and two fluid cells in the z-direction, effectively representing a quasi-2D configuration. This approach is selected to balance computational efficiency with the inherent three-dimensional requirements of the solvers used in the CFD-DEM framework. Due to the limited thickness of the domain, particle and fluid motions, as well as their interactions in the z-direction are negligible, thus corresponding to two-dimensional assumptions. Despite its simplicity, the current model is capable of capturing basic mechanisms of fluid-driven fracture initiation in granular media. Future work will focus on the use of fully three-dimensional configurations to investigate more complex fracture dynamics and extend their applicability to real-world applications.

4   Numerical Results

4.1   Effect of the Power-Law Parameters on Fracture Initiation

This study focuses on the injection of shear-thinning fluids ($n < 1$), as it represent the typical rheological properties of polymer solutions widely used in various subsurface applications such as enhanced oil recovery, hydraulic fracturing, and soil remediation. Many polymer-based solutions, such as partially hydrolyzed polyacrylamide (HPAM), xanthan gum, and guar gum, exhibit shear-thinning behavior, in which viscosity decreases with increasing shear rate. Accordingly, this section examines the effect of variations in rheological parameters on fracture initiation induced by different shear-thinning fluids. Table 3 presents the properties of injected fluids, including power-law parameters. As presented in the table, all fluids have the same density and different consistency indices (K) ranging from 1 to 5 Pa·s. Each fluid is characterized by various flow behavior indices of 0.1, 0.2 and 0.3. The injection velocity in all simulation cases is $1.4 \cdot 10^{-3}$ m/s, corresponding to the creeping flow regime. The average particle Reynolds number is approximately $Re_p \approx 10^{-6}$.

Table 3. Injected fluid properties.

Fluid	Consistency index, K (Pa·s^n)	Flow behavior index, n	Density, ρ_f (kg/m³)
Fluid A	1		
Fluid B	2		
Fluid C	3	0.1, 0.2, 0.3	998
Fluid D	4		
Fluid E	5		

Figure 2 demonstrates the snapshots of fracture initiation induced by power-law fluids with different rheological parameters (K and n). At $K = 1$ Pa·s, $n = 0.1$ (Fluid A), the fluid has less viscosity, which does not lead to any fractures. The fluid with $K = 2$ Pa·s, $n = 0.1$ (Fluid B) represents medium viscosity and creates a single linear fracture path perpendicular to the direction of less confining stress. $K = 5$ Pa·s, $n = 0.1$ (Fluid E) has more viscous behavior and creates wider radial fractures dominated by grain displacement. An increase in n from 0.2 to 0.3 enhances the effect of K and leads to a rise in overall viscosity. For example, $K = 1$ Pa·s creates two linear fractures directed primarily perpendicular to the less applied stress, while $K = 2$ Pa·s creates multiple linear fractures propagated in the radial direction. $K = 1$ Pa·s leads to more viscosity, which leads to wider radial fractures. These findings show that power-law parameters play a crucial role in fracture initiation, its shape and propagation behavior.

Figure 3a shows the velocity profile of fluid during fracture initiation induced by $K = 2$ Pa·s and $K = 5$ Pa·s (both at $n = 0.2$). Medium viscous fluid with $K = 2$ Pa·s has a higher velocity concentration on the fracture tip, and creates fractures whose orientation is dictated by the applied maximum stress. Therefore, the particles moves toward the less load. On the other hand, fluids with higher viscosity ($K = 5$ Pa·s) produce fractures with relatively lower velocity. In this case, the velocity affects the particles uniformly and exceeds the stresses exerted from all directions leading to a radial fracture shape. Viscosity profiles indicate that fluids with lower viscosity infiltrate wider into the domain, see Fig. 3b. A significant viscosity change can be observed outside the fracture, particularly near the fracture tip and domain boundaries. In the case of $K = 5$ Pa·s, the viscosity does not significantly alter outside the fracture limiting the infiltration through the domain.

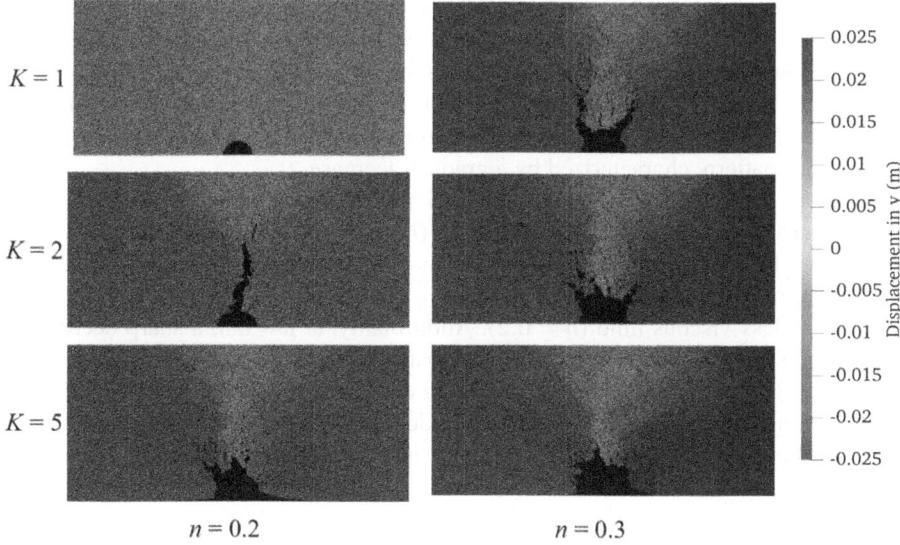

Fig. 2. Fracture initiation of $K = 1$ Pa·s, $K = 2$ Pa·s and $K = 5$ Pa·s at $n = 0.2$ and 0.3.

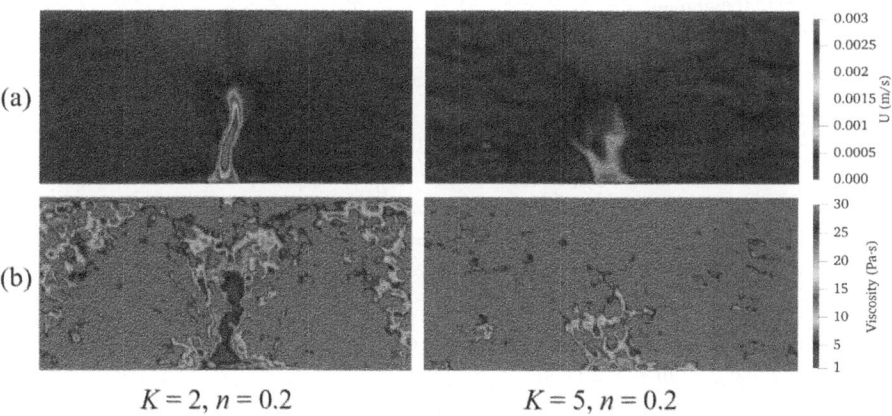

Fig. 3. (a) Velocity and (b) viscosity profile during fracture initiation at $K = 2$ Pa·s and $K = 5$ Pa·s (both $n = 0.2$).

4.2   Injection Pressure During Fracture Initiation

Figure 4a shows the injection pressure over time during fracture initiation at various consistency indices ($K = 1, 2, 3, 4$ and 5 Pa·s) and the same flow behavior index ($n = 0.2$). The behavior of fracture initiation can be evaluated by the evolution of the fluid injection pressure. Initially, the pressure rises and reaches its peak (maximum value of the pressure), indicating the onset of fracturing. Subsequently, the pressure may decrease gradually, drop sharply, or remain stable depending on the rate of fracture formation. In general, an increase in the consistency index leads to higher injection pressures in all cases observed. Cases of medium and higher consistency indices ($K = 2$-5 Pa·s) show clear peak pressures, while the lowest consistency index of $K = 1$ Pa·s demonstrates gradual pressure over time with no fracture initiation. Since the flow behavior index is the same in all cases, the pressure evolution over time follows a relatively similar pattern, characterized by a gradual decrease.

Figure 4b demonstrates the pressure injection history at the same consistency index ($K = 2$ Pa·s) and various flow behavior indices ($n = 0.1, 0.2$ and 0.3). Fluid with $n = 0.1$ does not produce any fracture, as indicated by a stable injection pressure throughout the entire simulation. More viscous fluid ($n = 0.3$) results in a higher peak pressure compared to less viscous fluid ($n = 0.2$). Additionally, at n = 0.3, a sharp decrease in injection pressure is observed, indicating a faster fracture opening rate. On the other hand, at $n = 0.2$, the fractures are created in a constant rate, as reflected by a gradual decrease in injection pressure. These findings demonstrate that the flow behavior index magnifies the effect of the consistency index and significantly influences the overall viscosity and fracturing behavior.

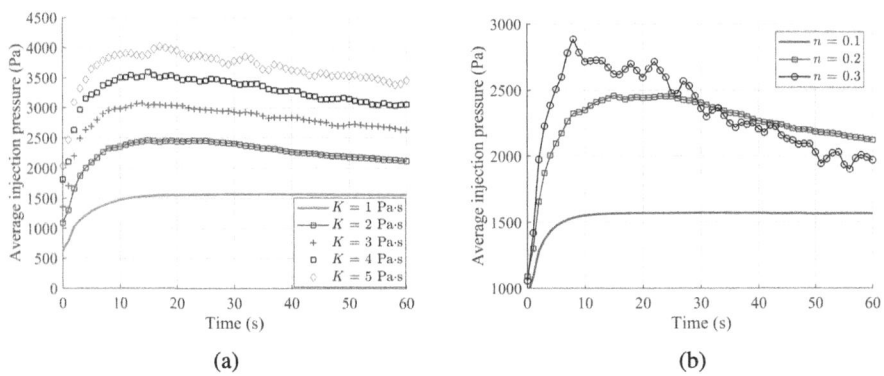

Fig. 4. Comparison of injection pressure over time: (a) $K = 1, 2, 3\ 4$ and 5 Pa·s (all $n = 0.2$) and (b) $n = 0.1, 0.2$ and 0.3 (all $K = 2$ Pa·s).

Figure 5 shows the comparison of pressure evolution over time of injected fluids at different CFD time steps of $\Delta t = 10^{-5}$ s ($N = 1$) and $\Delta t = 10^{-4}$ s ($N = 10$). From the comparison of injection pressures over time it can be stated that the power law parameters significantly affect the pressure evolution and require careful selection of a time step. For example, the pressure data at $n = 0.1$ and 0.2 is relatively similar in both time step cases. On the other hand, $n = 0.3$ shows significant discrepancies, resulting in an overall RMSRE of 11.56 %. Therefore, at $n = 0.3$ the simulation time step of $\Delta t = 10^{-5}$ s is suitable.

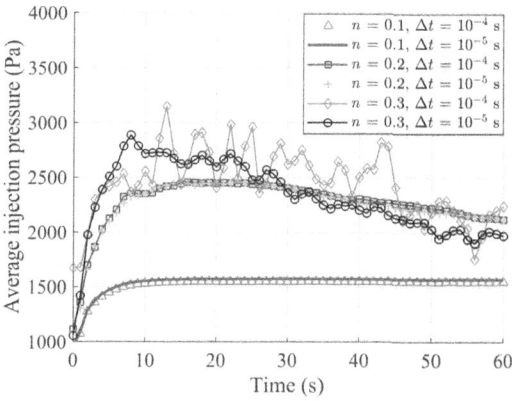

Fig. 5. Injection pressure obtained at CFD time steps of $\Delta t = 10^{-4}$ and $\Delta t = 10^{-5}$ s for cases $K = 2$ Pa·s at $n = 0.1, 0.2$ and 0.3.

Figure 6 represents the Root Mean Squared Relative Error (RMSRE) calculated for various values of the consistency index (K) and the flow behavior index (n). The RMSRE is calculated by comparing simulation results with reference time step of $\Delta t = 10^{-5}$ s against those using increased time step of $\Delta t = 10^{-4}$ s. It is defined as follows:

$$RMSRE = \sqrt{\frac{1}{n} \sum_{i=1}^{n} \left| \frac{p_{N=1}^{i} - p_{N=10}^{i}}{p_{N=1}^{i}} \right|^2} \times 100 \tag{10}$$

where $p_{N=1}^{i}$ represents the i-th injection pressure computed at $\Delta t = 10^{-5}$ s ($N = 1$), $p_{N=10}^{i}$ represents the i-th injection pressure computed at $\Delta t = 10^{-4}$ s ($N = 10$) and n is the total number of data points. As shown in the figure, the RMSRE is relatively lower for small values of n (0.1 and 0.2) even at higher K. As n increases to 0.3, the errors growth significantly, particularly at the range of $K = 2 - 5$ Pa·s. This shows that the flow behavior index (n) has a more pronounced effect on time step sensitivity compared to the consistency index (K), as evidenced by the larger errors observed in simulations with less shear-thinning fluids ($n = 0.3$).

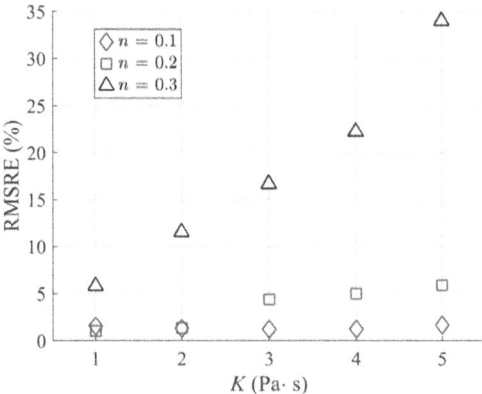

Fig. 6. RMSRE of injection pressure at different power-law parameters.

5   Conclusion

The primary aim of this study is to numerically explore the influence of non-Newtonian rheological parameters on the selection of an appropriate simulation time step size. Particularly, it investigates fracture initiation in weakly cohesive granular media induced by shear-thinning fluids. The flow behavior of non-Newtonian fluids is modeled using the power-law approach, and the drag force acting on particles accounts for their rheological properties. Obtained results show that fracture initiation and propagation behaviors are strongly influenced by power-law parameters. Less viscous fluids tend to create more stress-dependent linear fractures, while more viscous fluids lead to radial fractures with significant grain displacement. Furthermore, in lower-viscosity fluids, the velocity is concentrated at the fracture tip, promoting wider infiltration, while higher-viscosity fluids limit infiltration with a more uniform velocity distribution. An increase in the consistency index at a fixed flow behavior index leads to higher injection pressures during fracture initiation while the overall pressure profile pattern remains similar across all cases. Fluids with a higher flow behavior index result in a higher peak pressure and a more rapid pressure drop, facilitating a faster fracture initiation rate. In contrast, fluids with moderate to lower flow behavior indices lead to lower peak pressures with a more gradual pressure decline, creating fractures at a constant rate. A comparison of injection pressures at different time step sizes shows that the flow behavior index (n) has a stronger influence on CFD time step sensitivity than the consistency index (K). Simulations remain relatively accurate at a higher time step size ($\Delta t = 10^{-4}$ s) for lower flow behavior index values ($n = 0.1$ and 0.2). However, an increasing n to 0.3 results in greater errors, requiring a reduction in the time step size to $\Delta t = 10^{-5}$ s to maintain accuracy. These findings indicate that selecting a suitable time step size is essential for accurately modeling of fracture initiation induced by power-law fluids, particularly for higher flow behavior indices. This study emphasizes the importance of rheological properties in determining fracture propagation patterns, fluid infiltration and simulation stability, providing valuable insights for modeling non-Newtonian fluid-driven fracture initiation in granular media.

Acknowledgments. The authors acknowledge the support of the research grant no. AP19575428, from the Ministry of Science and Higher Education of the Republic of Kazakhstan. The authors appreciate the support of the Nazarbayev University Faculty Development Competitive Research Grant (NUFDCRG), Grant No. 20122022FD4141.

References

1. Belytschko, T.: An overview of semidiscretization and time integration procedures. Computational Methods for Transient Analysis(A 84-29160 12-64). Amsterdam, North-Holland, 1983, pp. 1–65 (1983)
2. Christopher, R.H., Middleman, S.: Power-law flow through a packed tube. Ind. Eng. Chem. Fundam. **4**(4), 422–426 (1965)
3. Clarke, D.A., Sederman, A.J., Gladden, L.F., Holland, D.J.: Investigation of void fraction schemes for use with CFD-DEM simulations of fluidized beds. Ind. Eng. Chem. Res. **57**(8), 3002–3013 (2018)
4. Courant, R., Friedrichs, K., Lewy, H.: Über die partiellen differenzengleichungen der mathematischen physik. Math. Ann. **100**(1), 32–74 (1928)
5. Duan, K., Kwok, C.Y., Wu, W., Jing, L.: Dem modeling of hydraulic fracturing in permeable rock: influence of viscosity, injection rate and in situ states. Acta Geotech. **13**, 1187–1202 (2018)
6. Goniva, C., Kloss, C., Deen, N.G., Kuipers, J.A., Pirker, S.: Influence of rolling friction on single spout fluidized bed simulation. Particuology **10**(5), 582–591 (2012)
7. Goniva, C., Kloss, C., Hager, A., Pirker, S.: An open source CFD-DEM perspective. In: Proceedings of OpenFOAM Workshop, Göteborg, pp. 22–24 (2010)
8. Hurt, R.S., Germanovich, L.N.: Parameters controlling hydraulic fracturing and fracture tip-dominated leakoff in unconsolidated sands. In: SPE Annual Technical Conference and Exhibition. OnePetro (2012)
9. Issa, R.I.: Solution of the implicitly discretised fluid flow equations by operator-splitting. J. Comput. Phys. **62**(1), 40–65 (1986)
10. Jin, L.: Experimental and numerical modeling of fluid injection into unconsolidated formations (2017)
11. Johnson, K.L., Kendall, K., Roberts, A.: Surface energy and the contact of elastic solids. Proc. R. Soc. Lond. A. Math. Phys. Sci. **324**(1558), 301–313 (1971)
12. Kazidenov, D., Amanbek, Y.: Permeability estimation from pore to darcy in cemented granular media using resolved CFD-DEM model. Results Eng. **24**, 103359 (2024)
13. Kazidenov, D., Amanbek, Y.: CFD-DEM modeling of fracture initiation with polymer injection in granular media. Particuology **97**, 58–68 (2025)
14. Kazidenov, D., Khamitov, F., Amanbek, Y.: Coarse-graining of CFD-DEM for simulation of sand production in the modified cohesive contact model. Gas Sci. Eng. 204976 (2023)
15. Kazidenov, D., Omirbekov, S., Amanbek, Y.: Optimal time-step for coupled CFD-DEM model in sand production. In: Computational Science and Its Applications–ICCSA 2023 Workshops: Athens, Greece, July 3–6, 2023, Preprint. Springer (2023)
16. Kazidenov, D., Omirbekov, S., Zhanabayeva, M., Amanbek, Y.: Experimental and numerical study of the effect of polymer flooding on sand production in poorly consolidated porous media. Geoenergy Sci. Eng. **249**, 213746 (2025)

17. Kissinger, A., et al.: Hydraulic fracturing in unconventional gas reservoirs: risks in the geological system, part 2: modelling the transport of fracturing fluids, brine and methane. Environ. Earth Sci. **70**, 3855–3873 (2013)
18. Kloss, C., Goniva, C., Hager, A., Amberger, S., Pirker, S.: Models, algorithms and validation for opensource dem and CFD-DEM. Progress Comput. Fluid Dyn. Int. J. **12**(2–3), 140–152 (2012)
19. Li, Y., Xu, Y., Thornton, C.: A comparison of discrete element simulations and experiments for sandpiles composed of spherical particles. Powder Technol. **160**(3), 219–228 (2005)
20. Li, Z., Espinoza, D.N., Balhoff, M.T.: Fluid-driven fracture mechanisms in granular media: insights from grain-scale numerical modeling. Granular Matter **23**(4), 1–18 (2021). https://doi.org/10.1007/s10035-021-01161-y
21. Li, Z., Espinoza, D.N., Balhoff, M.T.: Simulation of polymer injection in granular media: implications of fluid-driven fractures, water quality, and undissolved polymers on polymer injectivity. SPE J. **28**(01), 289–300 (2023)
22. Li, Z., Sun, Z., Espinoza, D.N., Balhoff, M.T.: Grain-scale modeling of polymer-driven fracture initiation and wellbore injectivity. In: SPE Improved Oil Recovery Conference, p. D021S034R001. SPE (2020)
23. Shovkun, I., Espinoza, D.N.: Propagation of toughness-dominated fluid-driven fractures in reactive porous media. Int. J. Rock Mech. Min. Sci. **118**, 42–51 (2019)
24. Sun, Z., Balhoff, M.T., Espinoza, D.N.: Fluid injection induced fracture initiation based on a resolved CFD-DEM approach. In: 52nd US Rock Mechanics/Geomechanics Symposium. OnePetro (2018)
25. Sun, Z., Li, Z., Espinoza, D.N., Balhoff, M.T.: Fluid-driven fractures in granular media: insights from numerical investigations. Phys. Rev. E **101**(4), 042903 (2020)
26. Tomac, I., Gutierrez, M.: Coupled hydro-thermo-mechanical modeling of hydraulic fracturing in quasi-brittle rocks using BPM-DEM. J. Rock Mech. Geotech. Eng. **9**(1), 92–104 (2017)
27. Weller, H.G., Tabor, G., Jasak, H., Fureby, C.: A tensorial approach to computational continuum mechanics using object-oriented techniques. Comput. Phys. **12**(6), 620–631 (1998)
28. Zhu, H., Zhou, Z., Yang, R., Yu, A.: Discrete particle simulation of particulate systems: theoretical developments. Chem. Eng. Sci. **62**(13), 3378–3396 (2007)

Physics Informed Kolmogorov-Arnold Network for Two-Phase Flow Model with Experimental Data

Daulet Kalesh[1] , Timur Merembayev[1] , Sagyn Omirbekov[2] ,
and Yerlan Amanbek[1(✉)]

[1] Department of Mathematics, School of Sciences and Humanities, Nazarbayev
University, Kabanbay batyr 53, Astana, Kazakhstan
[2] National Laboratory Astana, Nazarbayev University, Kabanbay batyr 53, Astana
010000, Kazakhstan
{daulet.kalesh,timur.merembayev,sagyn.omirbekov,
yerlan.amanbek}@nu.edu.kz

Abstract. The recently introduced neural network structure, known as
the Kolmogorov-Arnold Network (KAN), provides greater interpretability and accuracy compared to ordinary Multi-Layer Perceptrons (MLPs)
due to its use of spline functions. The primary goal of this research is
to propose a novel Physics-Informed Neural Network (PINN) architecture based on KAN for solving the Buckley-Leverett equation, aiming to
study its performance versus a conventional MLP-based PINN.

We conducted a comparative analysis between the KAN and MLP
architectures. We found that they both achieved comparable accuracy.
However, the KAN's training process is approximately twice as time-
consuming as that of the MLP. When validating with experimental data,
the KAN architecture showed enhanced robustness when trained with a
hybrid optimizer approach that combines the Adam and L-BFGS optimizers rather than using L-BFGS alone. Moreover, increasing the number of layers and neurons in the KAN model improved its predictions,
nearly matching the MLP-based PINN results for modeling the laboratory experiment.

The results highlight the promising potential of KAN-based PINNs,
especially when optimized architectures and hybrid training approaches
are used for modeling fluid dynamics in porous media.

Keywords: Physics-Informed Neural Networks · Kolmogorov-Arnold
Network · Hybrid Optimization · Buckley-Leverett equation · Porous
Media Flow

1 Introduction

Kolmogorov-Arnold Networks (KANs) are a class of neural networks inspired
by the Kolmogorov-Arnold representation theorem, which posits that any multivariate continuous function can be expressed as a sum of continuous functions

O. Gervasi et al. (Eds.): ICCSA 2025 Workshops, LNCS 15888, pp. 447–460, 2026.
https://doi.org/10.1007/978-3-031-97596-7_30

of one variable [14]. One of the key advantages of KANs is their ability to place learnable activation functions on the edges of the network graph rather than at the nodes, as is typical in Multi-Layer Perceptrons (MLPs).

KANs are effective in various tasks, including function regression and partial differential equations (PDEs) solving [13,14]. They have also been demonstrated to be more efficient and accurate than traditional MLPs in these tasks (reference). For example, KANs have been used to approximate complex functions with greater interpretability and accuracy, making them valuable for scientific applications [13].

The authors [15,18] used a Fourier-based Kolmogorov-Arnold Network module, complemented by two dropout strategies. Empirical results demonstrate notable gains in performance, underscoring that a carefully chosen nonlinear feature transformation—particularly one that remains tractable to train can yield better recommendations than "light" graph network variants that omit such transformations altogether. FourierKAN is a well-validated approach that enriches user-item representations while preserving training stability, offering a promising new direction.

However, KANs also have some limitations. For instance, they can be computationally expensive to train, especially for large-scale datasets. Additionally, KANs may not be as widely adopted as more conventional models such as CNNs or RNNs [4,19].

A novel approach to solving PDEs through Physics-Informed Neural Networks (PINN) with KAN was introduced by Wang et al. [17] regarded as Physics-Informed Kolmogorov-Arnold Network (PIKAN). MLP-based PINNs were shown to have struggled with heterogeneous and multiscale problems, as well as handling complex boundary conditions [3]. The authors evaluated PIKAN with various PDE forms, such as strong, energy, and inverse, and assessed its performance for multi-scale, heterogeneous, and non-linear problems. PIKAN resulted in higher accuracy and faster convergence for most PDEs, showcasing better alignment with Finite Element Method (FEM). Despite all of this, it struggles with complex geometric PDEs and is sensitive to grid size due to the risk of overfitting.

The authors [1] applied PIKAN to the Buckley-Leverett equation in the context of waterflooding in oil reservoirs. The research paper demonstrates that PIKANs achieve accuracy comparable to PINNs but experience greater fluctuations during training, indicating areas for further optimization. Additionally, they did not consider PIKAN's time efficiency compared with PINN. Nonetheless, their study established the feasibility and potential of PIKANs in simulating fluid dynamics within porous media, highlighting their advantages for simulations and potential for broader applications in reservoir modeling and history matching.

In fluid dynamics, modeling two-phase flow in porous media is essential in various engineering and scientific applications, particularly in the oil and gas industry. Understanding and accurately simulating such processes is critical for optimizing enhanced oil recovery, designing effective CO_2 sequestration, understanding groundwater contamination, and analyzing fluid behavior in subsurface environments. These simulations also support cost-effective field planning through simulations and decision-making. While conventional numerical methods such as Finite Volume or Finite Difference schemes, especially when GPU-accelerated, can be more computationally efficient and stable, they often require fine meshes and strict adherence to the CFL condition for explicit schemes. Recent advances in machine learning, such as PINNs, particularly when integrated with KAN, offer an alternative mesh-free solution that inherently avoids such restrictions. Moreover, PINNs provide the advantage of integrating underlying physics with experimental or simulation data, enhancing flexibility and enabling data-driven modeling where conventional methods may fall short. This supports better decision-making capabilities in oil field operations and reservoir engineering.

In this paper, we investigate the PINN with various architectures, including KAN and MLP, for the two-phase flow problem. Initially, we evaluate the PINN-KAN model by conducting a comparative analysis with MLP predictions and along with the analytical solution of the Buckley-Leverett equation. The verified KAN model is further validated for the laboratory experimental data, where we explore the impact of various optimization techniques and modifications to the depth and complexity of the KAN architecture. The computational performance and accuracy of the models are reported for fluid dynamics phenomena in a porous media.

2   Problem

In this study, we consider a problem that involves two-phase fluid flow in porous media. The problem is regarded as the Buckley-Leverett equation involving two immiscible and incompressible fluid phases (e.g., oil (o) and water(w)) with neglected gravity and capillarity. The governing equation for this case is a hyperbolic conservation law PDE, which is defined as follows:

$$\frac{\partial u(x,t)}{\partial t} + \frac{\partial f(u(x,t))}{\partial x} = 0. \tag{1}$$

where $u(x,t)$ is the displacing phase (water) saturation at position x and time t. The fractional flow function $f(u)$ describes the relationship between saturation and the volumetric flux. For this study, we consider the fractional flow with non-convex case given by:

$$f(u) = \frac{u}{u^2 + \frac{(1-u)^2}{M}}, \tag{2}$$

where $M = \frac{\mu_o}{\mu_w}$ is the mobility ratios of viscosities oil μ_o and water μ_w. The task is to solve for $u(x,t)$ given initial and boundary conditions:

$$u(x,0) = 1 \quad u(0,t) = 0 \tag{3}$$

Additionally, the equation can be analytically solved by a method of characteristics (MOC) [10]. However, solving this problem might be challenging due to the nonconvex nature, which often can result in multiple shock saturations and discontinuities [11]. To address these issues, a vanishing viscosity method can be used for these kinds of hyperbolic PDEs, modulated by a small viscosity coefficient ϵ:

$$\frac{\partial u(x,t)}{\partial t} + \frac{\partial f(u(x,t))}{\partial x} = \epsilon \frac{\partial^2 u(x,t)}{\partial x^2}. \tag{4}$$

By incorporating the diffusion term, the hyperbolic PDE becomes parabolic. This stabilizes the numerical solution by smoothing sharp fronts and discontinuities while maintaining the system's important physical features.

3   Methods

3.1   PINN

Deep neural networks, such as MLP, were used in this paper. which typically apply sequences of linear and nonlinear functions [5,8]. We denote MLP which consists the input layer $\mathbf{X} = [x, t]$ taking space x and time t, L hidden layers N_l and the output layer N_L which all defined as follows:

$$\mathcal{N}_0(\mathbf{X}) = \mathbf{X} \in \mathbb{R}^{d_{in}} \tag{5}$$

$$\mathcal{N}_l(\mathbf{X}) = \sigma(\mathbf{W}_l \mathcal{N}_{l-1}(\mathbf{X}) + \mathbf{b}_l), \quad \text{for} \quad l = 1, \ldots, L-1, \tag{6}$$

$$\mathcal{N}_L(\mathbf{X}) = \mathbf{W}_L \mathcal{N}_{L-1}(\mathbf{X}) + \mathbf{b}_L \in \mathbb{R}^{d_{out}}. \tag{7}$$

where weights $\mathbf{W}_l \in \mathbb{R}^{N_l \times N_{l-1}}$ and biases $\mathbf{b}^l \in \mathbb{R}^{N_l}$ connect the input $\mathbb{R}^{d_{in}}$ and output $\mathbb{R}^{d_{out}}$ spaces with activation function σ.

Based on the above MLP definitions, we aimed to solve $u(x,t)$ of our PDE, which results in PINNs, the modern neural network capable of estimating physics problems. We define the solution as follows:

$$\hat{u}_\theta(x,t) \approx u(x,t). \tag{8}$$

with set of series of weights and biases $\theta = \{W_1, W_2, \ldots, W_L, b_1, b_2, \ldots, b_L\}$,. To ensure that the learned solution satisfies the governing PDE, we define the residual loss of PDE r_θ, incorporating a diffusion term [6] to address challenges with saturation fronts:

$$r_\theta(\mathbf{X}) = (\hat{u}_\theta)_t + f(\hat{u}_\theta)_x - \epsilon(\hat{u}_\theta)_{xx} \tag{9}$$

The goal of PINN is to approximate $\hat{u}_\theta(x,t)$ by minimizing the following loss function with mean squared error (MSE) during the learning process:

$$\mathcal{L}(\theta) = \mathcal{L}_{\mathcal{U}}(\theta) + \mathcal{L}_{\mathcal{R}}(\theta), \tag{10}$$

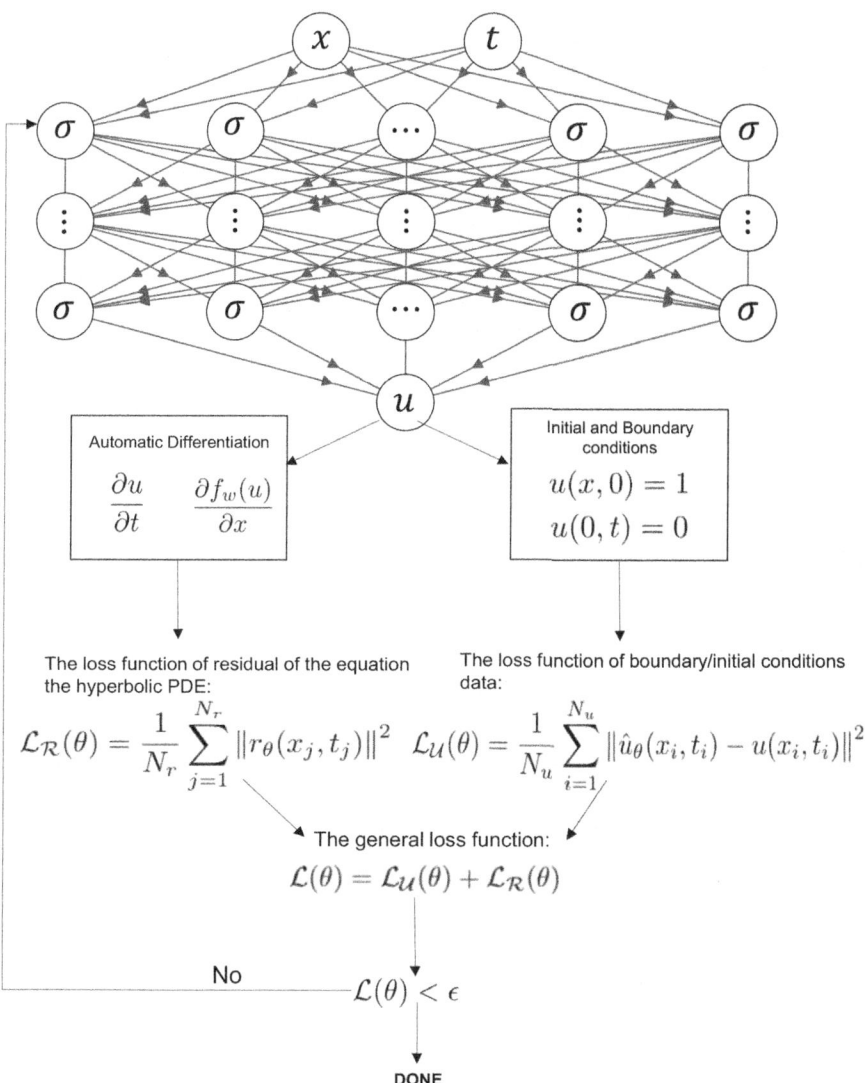

Fig. 1. A schematic representation of the PINN architecture based on the MLP architecture.

where $\mathcal{L}_{\mathcal{U}}(\theta) = \frac{1}{N_u} \sum_{i=1}^{N_u} \|\hat{u}_\theta(x_i, t_i) - u(x_i, t_i)\|^2$ – boundary and initial conditions' loss function, $\mathcal{L}_{\mathcal{R}}(\theta) = \frac{1}{N_r} \sum_{j=1}^{N_r} \|r_\theta(x_j, t_j)\|^2$. – the loss function of the residual of the PDE. Figure 1 demonstrates the full scheme of PINN based on MLP architecture.

PINNs are considered unsupervised machine learning aiming to solve well-posed PDEs and their boundary data. It can be achieved through automatic differentiation (AD) of the *Tensorflow* library which computes the necessary partial derivatives to enforce the residual of the PDE $r_\theta(x, t)$ and updates the network parameters $\theta^* = \arg\min_\theta \mathcal{L}(\theta)$ using the gradient-based limited-memory Broyden-Fletcher-Goldfarb-Shanno (L-BFGS) optimizer.

In implementing PINN under MLP architecture, a fully connected feed-forward neural network was used containing 8 hidden layers with 20 neurons per layer, each with the activation function tanh. The weights were initialized through the Glorot normal initializer [7]. The network uses $N_u = 300$ boundary and initial condition points and $N_f = 10000$ collocation points distributed within the domain generated by Latin Hypercube Sampling.

3.2 KAN

KAN offers a compelling alternative to conventional MLP. While MLPs trace their foundations to the universal approximation theorem, KANs draw on the Kolmogorov-Arnold representation theorem [13,14]. Formally, a KAN can be written as:

$$KAN = f(x) = \sum_{q=1}^{2n+1} \Phi_q(\sum_{p=1}^{n} \phi_{q,p}(x_p)) \tag{11}$$

where each $\phi_{q,p}$ is a univariate function that processes the input variable x_p, and Φ_q is another univariate function that acts on these transformed inputs. According to the Kolmogorov-Arnold theorem, the "inner" set of functions corresponds to a KAN layer with $n_{in} = n$ and $n_{out} = 2n + 1$, while the "outer" set corresponds to a KAN layer with $n_{in} = 2n + 1$ and $n_{out} = n$. Thus, the Kolmogorov-Arnold representation is achieved by composing these two layers. A practical enhancement in KAN involves the introduction of a basis function $b(x)$, making the activation function $\phi(x)$ the sum of $b(x)$ and an additional spline component:

$$\phi(x) = w(b(x) + spline(x)) \tag{12}$$

where $spline(x)$ is typically expressed as a linear combination of B-splines with trainable coefficients. This formulation increases flexibility and expressive power while preserving a manageable framework for function approximation. In Fig. 2, the complete scheme of PINN based on KAN architecture is shown.

Despite its expressive strengths, standard KAN can be challenging to train because of its spline-based formulation, which runs counter to the goal of devising a more straightforward yet effective replacement for the feature transformation component. In a research paper [13], the author introduces FastKAN, an efficient re-implementation of Kolmogorov-Arnold Networks (KANs) that significantly improves computational speed without sacrificing accuracy. The core innovation lies in approximating the traditionally used 3-order B-spline basis with Gaussian radial basis functions (RBFs) [12]. The RBF network is defined as:

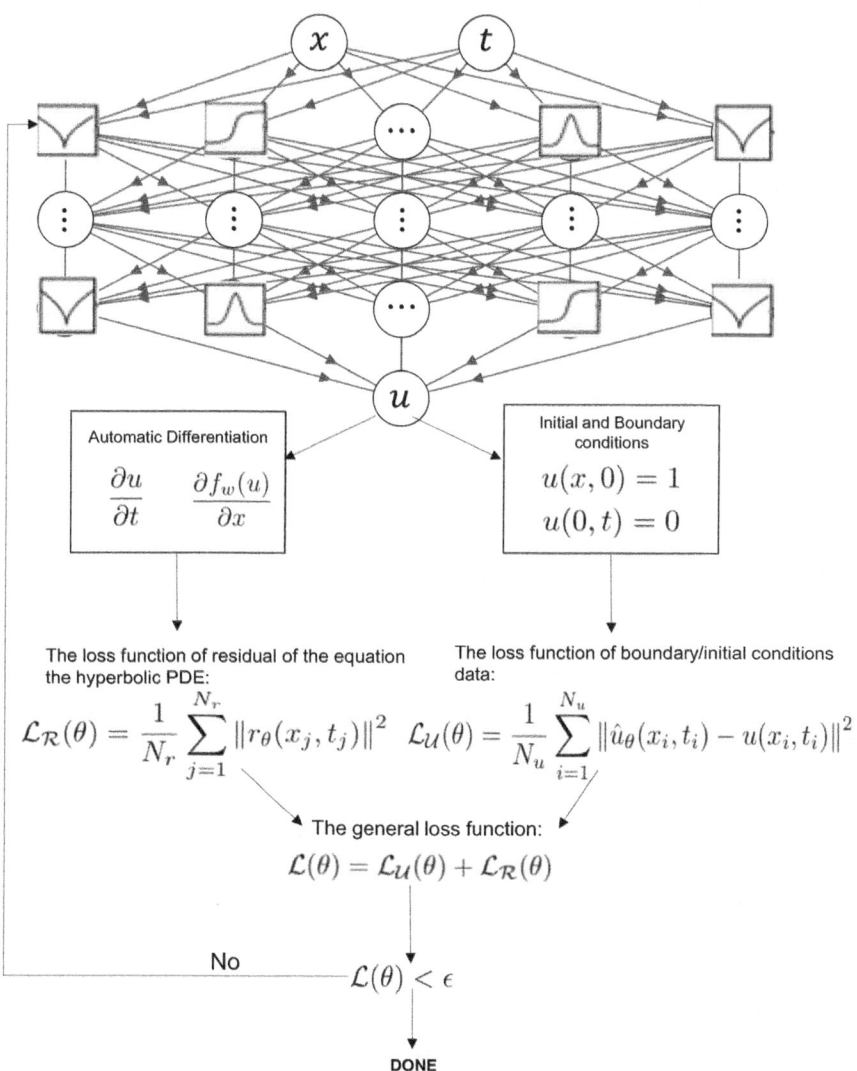

Fig. 2. A schematic representation of the PINN architecture based on the KAN architecture.

$$f(x) = \sum_{i=1}^{N} w_i \phi(||x - c_i||) \tag{13}$$

where w_i are weights and ϕ is a radial basis function. And $\phi(x) = exp(-\frac{r^2}{2h^2})$, where r is the radial distance and h is the spread of a function.

This simplification reduces complexity and computational overhead, achieving over three times the speed of prior KAN implementations. Additionally, the study conclusively shows that KANs can be viewed as a specific type of RBF network with fixed centers.

To implement KAN-PINN, the boundary and collocation points remained consistent with those used in MLP. Instead of employing 8 hidden layers as in the MLP, the KAN-PINN utilized 5 KAN-layers with 5 spline neurons in each, based on observations from [17]. However, instead of Adam optimizer from the observation [17], the KAN-PINN model was trained under L-BFGS optimizer as MLP for comparison purposes.

4   Results

4.1   Assesment of KAN and MLP

This section presents the numerical and graphical results obtained using PINN under MLP and KAN architectures to solve the Buckley-Leverett equation. Includes comparative analyzes of the accuracy and performance of these models.

Figure 3 shows comparisons of the MLP and KAN models for different diffusion coefficients ($\epsilon = 0.01, 0.025, 0.05$) together with the exact solution without diffusion at various time steps. We took the mobility ratio $M = 2$, considering oil to be twice as viscous as water. For all cases, both models closely approximate the exact solution, though some deviation near the saturation front can be observed. As ϵ varies, both architectures show robustness to changes in the diffusion coefficient. However, KAN exhibits slightly better stability as ϵ increases.

In Table 1, we calculated the root mean square error (RMSE) for the PINN MLP and KAN models across all time instances in Fig. 3, quantifying the deviation of models' predictions from the exact solution. The MLP outperforms KAN slightly at $\epsilon = 1 \times 10^{-2}$, but, in general, the KAN achieved comparable accuracy to the MLP. Regarding the training time, KAN models required approximately 2–3 mins, whereas MLP models were trained in about 1–1.5 min. The results in a speedup factor in the range of 2.39–2.56 indicate that MLP learns roughly twice as fast as KAN. The training time difference may be attributed to the simplicity of activation functions in MLP compared to the more complex spline functions in KAN, despite the fact KAN employed fewer parameters and fewer parameters than MLP.

Table 1. RMSE values and training times for MLP and KAN at different ϵ values.

ϵ	1×10^{-2}	2.5×10^{-2}	5×10^{-2}
RMSE_{KAN}	0.092	0.085	0.100
RMSE_{MLP}	0.067	0.084	0.107
Training Time (T_{KAN})	170 s	193 s	149 s
Training Time (T_{MLP})	71 s	80 s	58 s
Speedup ($T_{\text{KAN}}/T_{\text{MLP}}$)	2.39	2.41	2.56

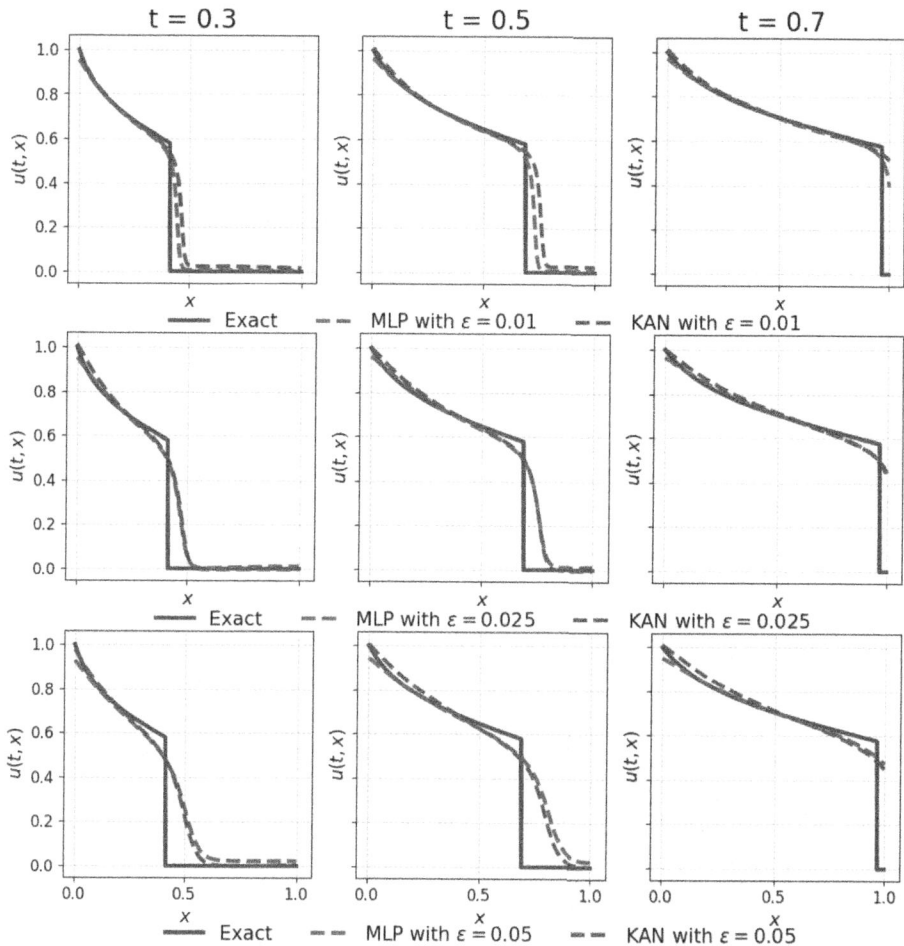

Fig. 3. Predictions of MLP and KAN for different values of diffusion coefficient ϵ with an exact solution without diffusion.

4.2 Optimization Impact on KAN for the Laboratory Experiment

In the following sections, we demonstrate the capabilities of KAN architecture in modeling laboratory experiments. The experimental study was conducted by Omirbekov et al. [16], where displacement of a Dense Non-Aqueous Phase Liquid (DNAPL) by a polymer solution was investigated [21]. We gathered all measured parameters of interacted fluids from the study, including viscosities, boundary conditions to adjust the mobility ratio $M = \frac{\mu_{\text{dnapl}}}{\mu_{\text{polymer}}}$ for PINN models where $\mu_{\text{dnapl}} = 4.47$ and $\mu_{\text{polymer}} = 200$ [20]. This resulted in the mobility ratio $M = 0.0235$, which shows the significant contrast between the viscosities of the DNAPL and polymer phases.

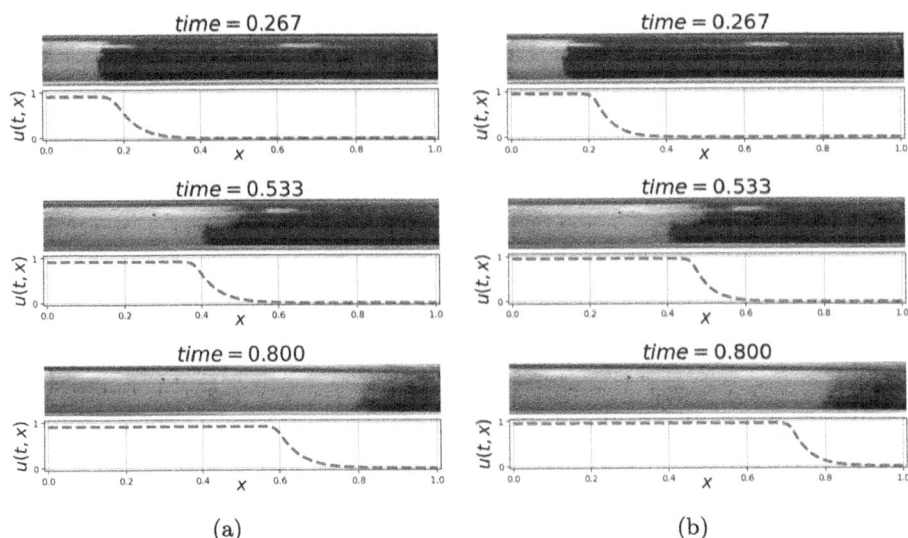

Fig. 4. Comparison of KAN optimization methods at $\epsilon = 3.75 \times 10^{-2}$: (4a) KAN at $\epsilon = 3.75 \times 10^{-2}$ with L-BFGS; (4b) KAN at $\epsilon = 3.75 \times 10^{-2}$ with hybrid optimizers (Adam with L-BFGS).

After several investigations of the diffusion coefficient for the experiment, we determined that $\epsilon = 3.75 \times 10^{-2}$ is optimal. The KAN training parameters, collocation, and boundary points remained the same.

In Fig. 4a, predictions of the KAN model with the laboratory data using L-BFGS optimization were demonstrated at three various time steps. The training loss reached 1.23×10^{-2}. Although the model seemingly captured the saturation front at the first time step ($t = 0.267$), its performance failed at later time steps, indicating that the model may not be fully trained or optimized.

To address the issue, we utilized a hybrid optimization strategy by combining Adam with L-BFGS [2]. Specifically, the KAN model was first trained using Adam for 5000 epochs, then switching to L-BFGS for fine-tuning. Figure 4b shows the results of the hybrid approach. It can be remarked that the hybrid optimizer significantly enhances the performance of the model, especially in capturing the sharp fronts across all time steps. The final training achieved 5.19×10^{-3}, which is notably lower than the one obtained with only L-BFGS.

4.3 Modeling KAN and MLP for the Experimental Data

The section compares the PINN performance of KAN models with MLP models for the laboratory experiment, which is focused on the impact of structural differences in KAN architectures.

The obtained KAN model with a hybrid approach was compared with the MLP model with the same diffusion coefficient ($\epsilon = 3.75 \times 10^{-2}$) and the opti-

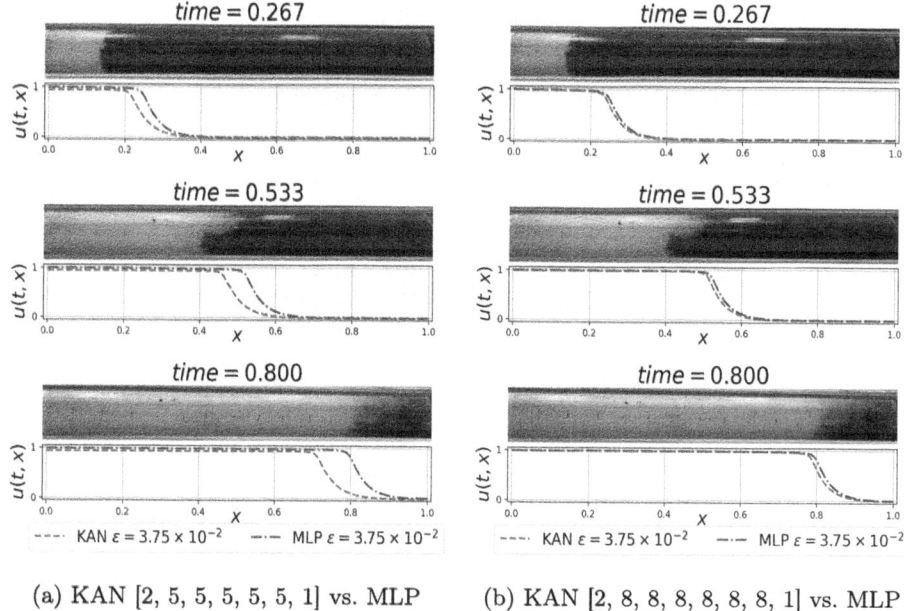

(a) KAN [2, 5, 5, 5, 5, 5, 1] vs. MLP   (b) KAN [2, 8, 8, 8, 8, 8, 8, 1] vs. MLP

Fig. 5. Comparison of KAN architectures with different layer sizes against MLP at $\epsilon = 3.75 \times 10^{-2}$.

mizer. The comparison is shown in Fig. 5a, where the initial KAN architecture was [2, 5, 5, 5, 5, 5, 1], a structure roughly adapted from the architectural explorations in recent work on PI-KANs [17]. Both models demonstrated comparable results at the first and second time steps ($t = 0.267, t = 0.533$), though the approximation of the KAN at the last time step was lagging than the MLP.

To further investigate the influence of architecture depth, we evaluated another KAN model with the structure [2, 8, 8, 8, 8, 8, 8, 1], also trained with a hybrid optimizer. This deeper architecture was chosen empirically to assess the impact of increased representational capacity on the KAN's performance for this problem. As shown in Fig. 5b, increasing the number of layers and neurons in the KAN structure significantly improved KAN performance, resulting in an approximation identical to the MLP across all time steps. The MLP architecture's depth was kept consistent throughout these comparisons to isolate the effect of the KAN's structural variations.

Another observation was made by comparing the KAN model trained under constant diffusion ($\epsilon = 3.75 \times 10^{-2}$) with the MLP model with a spatially dependent diffusion function ($\epsilon(x) = 0.04x^2 + 0.05x + 0.0015$) adopted from our previous work [9] to evaluate the KAN's performance against it. Figure 6 illustrates this comparison along with laboratory experiment images across three time steps where the KAN is structured with [2, 5, 5, 5, 5, 5, 1] layers. As shown in the figure, KAN's saturation shock approximations are smoother due to its fixed dif-

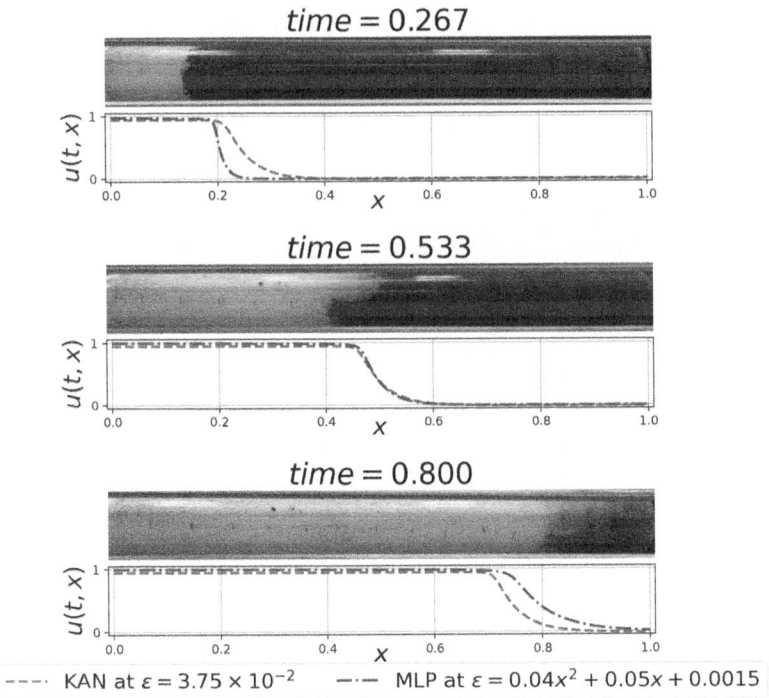

Fig. 6. Comparison of KAN [2, 5, 5, 5, 5, 5, 1] with constant diffusion ($\epsilon = 3.75 \times 10^{-2}$) and MLP with spatially dependent diffusion function ($\epsilon(x) = 0.04x^2 + 0.05x + 0.0015$).

fusion coefficient. Despite this, it closely matches the gradient pattern predicted by MLP. The MLP captures more details, especially with its varying diffusion function. The KAN model, however, performs well even with simpler assumptions, showcasing the trade-off between the MLP's details and the KAN model's efficiency, which makes KAN a practical option for its simplicity and accuracy.

5   Conclusion

This research explored the effectiveness of PINNs with Multi-Layer Perceptron (MLP) and Kolmogorov-Arnold Networks(KAN) architectures in solving the Buckley-Leverett equation for two-phase flow in porous media, validated by the laboratory experimental data.

Comparative analysis revealed that while MLP slightly outperformed KAN regarding training speed, the KAN architecture achieved comparable accuracy and demonstrated improved robustness under varied diffusion conditions. Furthermore, employing a hybrid optimization strategy combining Adam and L-BFGS significantly enhanced KAN's accuracy, especially in capturing sharp saturation fronts observed experimentally rather than using L-BFGS alone.

Additionally, increasing the depth and complexity of the KAN architecture notably improved its predictive accuracy, achieving parity with the MLP results across all tested scenarios. The comparison between the initially architectured KAN model with the constant diffusion coefficient and the MLP model with the spatially dependent diffusion function highlights that while the MLP provides more detailed predictions with varying diffusion, the KAN model demonstrates robust performance and generalization under simpler assumptions, showcasing its effectiveness even without complex spatial variability. These findings underscore the potential of KAN, especially when implemented with optimized network architectures and hybrid training methods, for modeling complex fluid dynamics in porous media.

Acknowledgments. The authors acknowledge the support of the research grants no. AP19575428 and AP22784980, from the Ministry of Science and Higher Education of the Republic of Kazakhstan. The authors appreciate the support of the Nazarbayev University Faculty Development Competitive Research Grant (NUFDCRG), Grant No. 20122022FD4141.

References

1. Rao, X., Liu, Y., He, X., Hoteit, H.: Physics-informed Kolmogorov-Arnold networks (PIKANs) for solving the Buckley-Leverett equation in waterflooding reservoirs. In: SPE Reservoir Simulation Conference, p. D012S001R009. SPE (2025). https://doi.org/10.2118/223891-MS

2. Almajid, M.M., Abu-Al-Saud, M.O.: Prediction of porous media fluid flow using physics informed neural networks. J. Petrol. Sci. Eng. **208**, 109205 (2022)

3. Baydaulet, U., Omarova, P., Merembayev, T., Yedilkhan, A.: Modeling siltation of river channels using the physics-informed neural networks method and numerical simulation. Eng. Sci. **33**, 1296 (2024)

4. Bodner, A.D., Tepsich, A.S., Spolski, J.N., Pourteau, S.: Convolutional Kolmogorov-Arnold networks. arXiv preprint arXiv:2406.13155 (2024)

5. Cybenko, G.: Approximation by superpositions of a sigmoidal function. Math. Control Sig. Syst. **2**(4), 303–314 (1989)

6. Fuks, O., Tchelepi, H.A.: Limitations of physics informed machine learning for nonlinear two-phase transport in porous media. J. Mach. Learn. Model. Comput. **1**(1), 19–37 (2020)

7. Glorot, X., Bengio, Y.: Understanding the difficulty of training deep feedforward neural networks. In: Proceedings of the Thirteenth International Conference on Artificial Intelligence and Statistics, pp. 249–256. JMLR Workshop and Conference Proceedings (2010)

8. Hornik, K., Stinchcombe, M., White, H.: Multilayer feedforward networks are universal approximators. Neural Netw. **2**(5), 359–366 (1989)

9. Kalesh, D., Merembayev, T., Omirbekov, S., Amanbek, Y.: Application of physics-informed neural networks for two-phase flow model with variable diffusion and experimental validation. Results Eng. **26**, 105439 (2025)

10. Lax, P.D.: Hyperbolic systems of conservation laws and the mathematical theory of shock waves. SIAM (1973)

11. LeVeque, R.J.: Finite Volume Methods for Hyperbolic Problems, vol. 31. Cambridge university press (2002)
12. Li, Z.: Kolmogorov-Arnold networks are radial basis function networks. arXiv preprint arXiv:2405.06721 (2024)
13. Liu, Z., Ma, P., Wang, Y., Matusik, W., Tegmark, M.: KAN 2.0: Kolmogorov-Arnold networks meet science. arXiv preprint arXiv:2408.10205 (2024)
14. Liu, Z., et al.: KAN: Kolmogorov-Arnold networks. arXiv preprint arXiv:2404.19756 (2024)
15. Mehrabian, A., Adi, P.M., Heidari, M., Hacihaliloglu, I.: Implicit neural representations with fourier kolmogorov-arnold networks. arXiv preprint arXiv:2409.09323 (2024)
16. Omirbekov, S., et al.: Experimental study of DNAPL displacement by a new densified polymer solution and upscaling problems of aqueous polymer flow in porous media. J. Contam. Hydrol. **252**, 104120 (2023)
17. Wang, Y., et al.: Kolmogorov–Arnold-informed neural network: a physics-informed deep learning framework for solving forward and inverse problems based on kolmogorov–arnold networks. Comput. Methods Appl. Mech. Eng. **433**, 117518 (2025). https://doi.org/10.1016/j.cma.2024.117518
18. Xu, J., et al.: Fourierkan-GCF: fourier kolmogorov-arnold network–an effective and efficient feature transformation for graph collaborative filtering. arXiv preprint arXiv:2406.01034 (2024)
19. Yang, X., Wang, X.: Kolmogorov-arnold transformer. arXiv preprint arXiv:2409.10594 (2024)
20. Omirbekov, S., Zhaidarbek, B., Amanbek, Y.: Effect of fluid rheology on sand production: Comprehensive study. In: ARMA US Rock Mechanics/Geomechanics Symposium, p. D042S062R010. ARMA (2024)
21. Zhumabek, M., et al.: Stability and rheological characterization of colloidal gas aphrons: influence of xanthan gum and sodium dodecyl sulfate. Discover Appl. Sci. **7**(5), 1–18 (2025)

Author Index

O. Gervasi et al. (Eds.): ICCSA 2025 Workshops, LNCS 15888, pp. 461–462, 2026.
https://doi.org/10.1007/978-3-031-97596-7

The manufacturer's authorised representative in the EU is Springer
Nature Customer Service Centre GmbH, Europaplatz 3, 69115 Heidelberg,
Germany. If you have any concerns regarding our products, please
contact ProductSafety@springernature.com

Printed and bound by CPI Group (UK) Ltd, Croydon, CR0 4YY

28/04/2026

02098521-0017